STELLENBOSCH HANDBOOKS IN AFRICAN CONSTITUTIONAL LAW

BOOK TWO

Constitutional Adjudication in Africa

Edited by

CHARLES M FOMBAD

OXFORD
UNIVERSITY PRESS

OXFORD
UNIVERSITY PRESS

Great Clarendon Street, Oxford, OX2 6DP,
United Kingdom

Oxford University Press is a department of the University of Oxford.
It furthers the University's objective of excellence in research, scholarship,
and education by publishing worldwide. Oxford is a registered trade mark of
Oxford University Press in the UK and in certain other countries

First Edition published in 2017

Impression: 1

Published in the United States of America by Oxford University Press
198 Madison Avenue, New York, NY 10016, United States of America

British Library Cataloguing in Publication Data
Data available

Library of Congress Control Number: 2017945367

ISBN 978–0–19–881021–6

Printed and bound by
CPI Group (UK) Ltd, Croydon, CR0 4YY

Stellenbosch Handbooks in African Constitutional Law

The *Stellenbosch Handbooks in African Constitutional Law* is a series of books that engage with contemporary issues of constitutionalism in Africa in a unique and highly original manner. The first experiment in democratic and constitutional governance in Africa that started after independence was soon overtaken by dictatorships, and arbitrary and repressive rule. The pulling down of the Berlin Wall, followed by the collapse of the communist dictatorships in Eastern Europe, unleashed a fresh wind of democratization and new hopes for the establishment and entrenchment of constitutional governance and constitutionalism in Africa. This series is designed to avoid a mere repetition of the now well-rehearsed concerns and doubts about constitutionalism on the continent and instead to identify, analyse, and promote serious discussion on the critical issues that can shape, refine, and deepen the strides being taken towards consolidating constitutionalism in Africa.

Although comparative constitutional law has now emerged strongly in the last two decades as a major field of legal scholarship, most of the extensive research and publications that have been carried out have focused mainly on the well-established democracies. The only African country that has occasionally attracted some research interest from a comparative law perspective is South Africa. The few books that do present some perspectives on African comparative constitutional law focus narrowly and exclusively on developments in either Anglophone, Francophone, or Arabophone Africa but with nothing cutting across these divides. However, since 1990, Africa has been undergoing profound and far-reaching constitutional developments that deserve to attract the attention of comparatists. Very limited comparative law research has been carried out to understand the nature of these constitutional changes, review their impact on the attempts to entrench an ethos of constitutionalism on the continent, and assess the prospects for the future.

The overriding objective of the *Stellenbosch Handbooks in African Constitutional Law* series is as follows. First, the series will stimulate interest in comparative constitutional law research and studies on the different constitutional traditions operating in Africa by presenting a comprehensive analysis of the latest thinking, research, and practice. In this way, the series intends to fill the huge knowledge gap in the existing literature on comparative African constitutional law, as well as point to directions for future research.

Secondly, each volume will, for the first time, bring together high-quality innovative and original material from diverse perspectives written by scholars and legal practitioners drawn from the different constitutional traditions operating on the continent. In this respect, each volume will strive to cover Anglophone, Arabophone, Francophone, Hispanophone, and Lusophone Africa. In many respects, this will ensure that the African voice is heard in the global constitutional debate. Thirdly, because most African countries share many common features, such as the colonial legacy, geographical proximity, and social, economic, political, and cultural conditions, the books in the series adopt a comparative approach that highlight gaps and good practices in a manner that will provide a rich source of authoritative information for promoting an intra-African legal dialogue and the cross-fertilization of ideas across the different constitutional traditions.

Finally, the books in the series are intended to act as a repository for the accumulation of knowledge, experience, and expertise on the continent. Each handbook stands alone and is intended to provide an invaluable source of authoritative reference material for academics, researchers, students at all levels, legal practitioners, and policy-makers.

Stellenbosch Handbooks in African Constitutional Law

Titles Published in the Series

Separation of Powers in African Constitutionalism
Edited by Charles M Fombad

Preface

Like the first book published in this series, this second book is also based on the Third Stellenbosch Annual Seminar on Constitutionalism in Africa. The stated aim of the *Stellenbosch Handbooks in African Constitutional Law Series* being to publish works of high quality and originality dealing with topical issues of constitutional law in Africa, this volume is devoted to the vitally important issue of constitutional review on the continent.

The essays in the volume span a broad array of themes that trace the manner of reception of constitutional review in different African countries, their evolution over time, to the most recent developments following the revival of elements of modern constitutionalism in the post-1990 constitutional reforms in African countries. Although in many respects the rise and expansion of constitutional review in Africa reflect global trends, the developments on the continent show distinctive features that have hardly been fully analysed in any comprehensive and comparative manner. This volume tries to fill this gap in the literature.

It is obvious that one volume cannot adequately capture the rich and diverse practices in Africa. Nevertheless, taken as a whole, the essays collectively offer valuable insights on the state of constitutional adjudication on the continent, an area where there have been both positive and negative developments, and the prospects for the future. In line with one of the fundamental objectives of this series, the issue of an effective system of constitutional adjudication is not only crucial to sustaining the momentum of the transition to genuine constitutionalism and respect for the rule of law, but it provides a fertile and rich source for promoting an intra-African legal dialogue and the cross-fertilization of ideas across the different constitutional traditions. The essays illustrate that the effectiveness of the model of constitutional review now depends on careful craftsmanship of the model more than anything else. The essays also provide food for thought, and it is my hope that they will provoke serious debate and discussions on how to improve constitutional adjudication, especially in those African countries where the systems are defective and an impediment to constitutional justice.

I am profoundly indebted to the Director of the Stellenbosch Institute for Advanced Study (STIAS), Professor Hendrik Geyer, and his team led by Professor Johann Groenewald, as well as the Director of the Institute for International and Comparative Law in Africa (ICLA) of the University of Pretoria, Professor Christof Heyns, through whose collaboration the seminar series is funded. I would also like to express my gratitude to Mr Alex Flach of OUP, who assisted with the finalization of the project for this series, and all his colleagues at OUP who have been very helpful and understanding in moving the project forward. I am equally indebted to several colleagues who took time off from their busy schedules not only to write the chapters and travel to Stellenbosch to present them, but also to cope with the numerous reviewers' comments that were required before the chapters were approved for publication in this volume. I am sure they will agree with me that the outcome was worth the hard work.

On a personal note, I would like to thank my family. My long-suffering wife, Madeleine, and the children have had to endure long periods of my absence while working on this and other books in the series. All this is greatly appreciated. I dedicate this volume to Madeleine and the children, Manga, Njumba, Tosah, Tichanung, and Bi-Ake, who make everything worthwhile.

Charles M Fombad
Pretoria, August 2016

Table of Contents

PART 3 THE IMPACT OF TRANSJUDICIALISM ON CONSTITUTIONAL ADJUDICATION

PART 4 CONSTITUTIONAL ADJUDICATION AND PROMOTION OF CONSTITUTIONALISM

PART 5 DECISION-MAKING AND WORKING PRACTICES

PART 6 CONCLUSION

Table of Cases

ANGOLA

BENIN

BOTSWANA

BURUNDI

CAMEROON

DEMOCRATIC REPUBLIC OF CONGO

ETHIOPIA

GAMBIA

GHANA

INDIA

KENYA

LESOTHO

NIGERIA

SENEGAL

SOUTH AFRICA

UGANDA

UNITED KINGDOM

UNITED STATES OF AMERICA

ZIMBABWE

INTERNATIONAL COURTS

African Commission

Table of Legislation

NATIONAL LEGISLATION

List of Abbreviations

ACHPR	African Charter on Human and Peoples' Rights
African Children's Committee	African Committee on the Rights and Welfare of the Child
African Commission	African Commission on Human and Peoples' Rights
African Court of Justice	African Court of Justice and Human Rights
African Democracy Charter	African Charter on Democracy, Elections and Governance
ANC	African National Congress
ANCL	African Network of Constitutional Lawyers
AU	African Union
CCMA	Commission for Conciliation, Mediation, and Arbitration
CEDAW	Convention on the Elimination of All Forms of Discrimination Against Women
CENA	*Commission Electorale Nationale Autonome*
CJN	Chief Justice of Nigeria
COS	*Conseil d'Orientation et de Supervision*
CPDM	Cameroon Peoples' Democratic Party
CSOs	civil society organizations
CUD	Coalition for Unity and Democracy
DPSPs	Directive Principles of State Policy
DRC	Democratic Republic of the Congo
EACJ	East African Court of Justice
ECHR	European Convention on Human Rights
ECOWAS	Economic Community of West African States
ELECAM	Elections Cameroon
EPRDF	Ethiopian People's Revolutionary Democratic Front
FCT	federal capital territory
FEDECO	Federal Electoral Commission
FJSC	Federal Judicial Service Commission
FPI	Front Populaire Ivoirien
ICCPR	International Covenant on Civil and Political Rights
ICJ	International Court of Justice
ICPC	Act Independent Corrupt Practices and Other Related Offences Act
INEC	Independent National Electoral Commission
JSC	Judicial Services Commission
KPC	Katangese Peoples' Congress
LGBTI	lesbian, gay, bisexual, transsexual, and intersex
LOTC	*Lei Orgânica do Tribunal Constitucional*
LPC	*Lei Orgânica do Processo Constitutional*
LRC	Legal Resources Centre
Maputo Protocol	Rights of Women in Africa
MDGs	Millennium Development Goals
MINATD	Ministry of Territorial Administration and Decentralization
MPLA	Movimento Popular de Libertação de Angola
MPs	members of parliament
NAACP	National Association for the Advancement of Colored People
NBA	Nigerian Bar Association
NEO	National Electoral Observatory
NGOs	non-governmental organizations
NJC	National Judicial Council
NLC	National Liberation Council

OAU	Organisation of African Unity
OHADA	Organisation pour l'Harmonisation en Afrique du Droit des Affaires
PDCI	Parti Démocratique de Côte d'Ivoire
PDP	People's Democratic Party
PIL	Public Interest Litigation
PVC	permanent voter card
QPC	*Question Prioritaire de Constitutionnalité*
RECs	regional economic communities
SADC	Southern African Development Community
SJSC	State Judicial Service Commission
UDHR	Universal Declaration of Human Rights
UN	United Nations
UNDP	Union for Democracy and Progress Party
VIN	voter identification number

List of Contributors

Adem K Abebe, Editor—ConstitutionNet, International IDEA, Constitution Building Programme, The Hague, The Netherlands.

Sègnonna Horace Adjolohoun, Principal Legal Officer at the African Court on Human and People's Rights, Arusha, Tanzania.

Samuel Kofi Date-Bah, former Justice of the Supreme Court of Ghana.

Bonolo Ramadi Dinokopila, Head of Law Department, Faculty of Law and Social Science, University of Botswana.

Charles M Fombad, Head of the Comparative Constitutional Law Unit at the Institute for International and Comparative Law in Africa, University of Pretoria.

James Fowkes, Professor, Department of Public Law, Faculty of Law, University of Munster, Germany.

Richard J Goldstone, former Justice of the Constitutional Court of South Africa.

Ameze Guobadia, Research Professor at the Nigerian Institute for Advanced Legal Studies, University of Ghana.

Theodore Holo, President of the Constitutional Court of Benin.

Magnus Killander, Associate Professor and Head of Research at the Centre for Human Rights, University of Pretoria.

Kofi Quashigah, Dean of the Law Faculty at the University of Ghana.

Christa Rautenbach, Professor at North-West University.

André Thomashausen, Chair of the Department of Public, Constitutional, and International Law at the University of South Africa.

List of Contributors

Introduction

Charles M Fombad

Courts generally, and courts exercising constitutional jurisdiction in particular, have been crucial in Africa's post-1990 transition politics. Although many scholars have commented on the general nature of the post-transition constitutional reforms, not much attention has been paid to the changing role of courts, especially with respect to constitutional disputes. However, a fundamental cause of the undermining of constitutionalism in post-independence Africa was the numerous restrictions that prevented courts from intervening when constitutions were violated in some countries, and the fact that the judiciaries in most countries were reduced to handmaidens of the various dictatorial regimes in place. As a result, they were weak and ineffective and, thus, incapable of operating effectively either as guardians of the constitutions, protectors of human rights, or impartial enforcers of the rule of law. However, since the 1990 wave of constitutional reforms, the role of constitutional courts or courts exercising the power to interpret and apply constitutions have become a critical aspect to the ongoing process of constitutional construction, reconstruction, and maintenance.

The changing role of constitutional courts or courts exercising a constitutional jurisdiction in Africa today to some extent reflects the global expansion of judicial power, which started in many advanced democracies after the Second World War. These developments appear, at least from the texts of the revised or new constitutions, to have resulted in fundamental changes in the nature and role of courts exercising jurisdiction in constitutional matters. This has been particularly significant in Francophone Africa where, before the 1990s, constitutional disputes in most of these countries were reserved to a chamber operating within the Supreme Court, and access to challenge the constitutionality of laws was illogically reserved only for the very politicians who made these laws. Although one may mention the expansion of constitutional justice in Africa mainly because of the developments in Francophone, Lusophone, and Hispanophone Africa, the developments in Anglophone Africa have been equally dramatic and significant.

Be that as it may, no region in the world provides as much diversity in form and practice of constitutional review as Africa. The essays in this second volume of the *Stellenbosch Handbooks in African Constitutional Law* series offer a first attempt to undertake a critical and comparative examination of the interplay of the diverse forms of constitutional review models on the continent. This is of particular importance because, over the last two decades, some of these courts have been asked to decide a litany of hotly contested and often sensitive disputes of a social, political, and economic nature.

As the list of areas in which these courts have intervened has grown, so too have their powers, actual or potential. By identifying and examining the different models of constitutional review adopted, these essays consider the extent to which these courts are contributing to enhancing constitutionalism and respect for the rule of law on the continent. The essays show how the long-standing negative image of African courts is slowly changing. The different ways in which these courts have responded to the variety of constraints, incentives, and opportunities that have been provided by the constitutional reforms of the last two decades to act as the bulwark against authoritarianism is the subject of this volume.

The essays are divided into six parts, indicating some of the broad areas of interest in constitutional adjudication from a comparative perspective. The first part provides an overview of the different models of constitutional review on the continent. Part 2 briefly examines the salient features of constitutional adjudication in selected countries, which illustrate the different models of constitutional review on the continent. In Part 3, the impact of transjudicialism on constitutional adjudication is discussed. This is followed in Part 4 by two chapters that examine the impact of constitutional adjudication on the promotion of constitutionalism. Part 5 examines the contrasting techniques of decision-making and the working practices in the apex constitutional courts in three jurisdictions. The last part of the book, Part 6, contains the concluding remarks in which the prospects for constitutional justice in Africa are considered in light of the emerging realities and contemporary imperatives.

In the opening chapter, Fombad provides an overview of the contemporary models of constitutional review in Africa. Because the present approaches to constitutional adjudication in Africa have been and continue to be influenced by Western models from the colonial period, the chapter begins with a review of the main classical models of constitutional adjudication. He notes that although two main models, the centralized and decentralized models, of constitutional adjudication were adopted in the independence constitutions, these were hardly ever effective for a variety of reasons. As a result, there was a general failure of constitutional review which, in many respects, substantially contributed to the absence of constitutionalism in pre-1990 Africa.

In analysing the present trend, he shows that over two-thirds of modern African constitutions have adopted the centralized model and the rest the decentralized model, the only exception being Ethiopia, with a mixed or hybrid system in which constitutional review is carried out by the legislature. It is only after a careful examination of the scope of jurisdiction, the types of review carried out, and the forms of judicial decisions and remedies provided that the distinctions between the two main models of adjudication emerge very clearly. Although the centralized model is clearly the dominant form of constitutional review on the continent, Fombad shows, after a careful analysis of the relevant constitutional provisions, that there is some evidence of convergence, with clear signs of cross-systemic fertilization of ideas between the different models. For example, unlike before the 1990s, most civilian jurisdictions now provide for concrete review and have modified the access rules to allow individuals to have access to the constitutional courts.

On the other hand, some common law jurisdictions now allow for abstract review and, to mitigate the risk of legal uncertainty caused by a multiplicity of precedents on constitutional issues by lower courts, constitutions, such as that of South Africa and Zimbabwe, provide that any declaration of unconstitutionality of legislation will only take effect after it has been confirmed by the apex constitutional court. There nevertheless remain significant differences in approach, which in many respects is bound to have an impact on the quality of constitutional justice. Fombad shows that, although there has been progress in constitutional justice that is bound to affect the overall landscape of constitutionalism, Francophone Africa continues to lag behind.

Nevertheless, he points out that one lesson that can be drawn from the two most successful and active constitutional courts on the continent, the Constitutional Courts of Benin and South Africa, is that the quality of constitutional justice depends less on the model and more on the powers that have been conferred on the court. There are, thus, still too many countries that have adopted constitutional courts, more for its symbolic value than out of a genuine desire to ensure constitutional justice for their people. He concludes by pointing out that the increasingly popular resort to the centralized model will only enhance the prospects for constitutional justice if the review of constitutionality is carried out by independent courts rather than by quasi-judicial or quasi-administrative bodies such as the constitutional council, which is largely controlled and vulnerable to manipulation by politicians.

Fombad's introductory overview in Chapter 1 provides the necessary background for the discussion in Part 2 of the archetypical examples of the different models of constitutional adjudication on the continent. A number of important factors influenced the choice of countries selected for the case studies in Part 2 of the book. First, there was a need to ensure that all the main models of constitutional adjudication on the continent were covered. In doing so, account was taken of the different variations within the two main models. Thus, three countries were selected to illustrate the operation of the centralized French 1958 Constitutional Council model. From these three, the Benin Constitutional Council represents the most modern and liberal form of this model, while the Cameroon Constitutional Council reflects the original form with all its weaknesses and limitations. The third example, the Angolan Constitutional Court, illustrates the approach adopted in Lusophone Africa.

There are also three case studies on the decentralized model. In this category, the South African Constitutional Court, very similar to the Benin Constitutional Court, illustrates a modified and liberal form of the decentralized model. The Supreme Courts of Ghana and Nigeria illustrate the more conventional forms of the decentralized model. The second part of the book concludes with the unique hybrid or mixed model of constitutional adjudication operating in Ethiopia. It is thus a balanced and representative group reflecting the subtleties of constitutional adjudication within the different models that operate in Africa.

The discussion of the three case studies illustrating the centralized model of constitutional adjudication starts with Adjolohoun in Chapter 2. He starts by pointing out that Benin has moved from a country where political turbulence and the frequency of military *coup d'etats* caused it to be termed 'the sick child of Africa', to one of Africa's most successful transitions from authoritarianism to democracy. This, he suggests, can by and large be attributed to the adoption of Francophone Africa's most liberal constitution in 1990, under which was established one of the most effective examples of a centralized model of constitutional adjudication. Although the manner of appointment of judges effectively results in the president of the republic having the last word on who acts as a judge, the most unusual aspect of the Benin model and which makes it unique and progressive are the unusually wide-ranging powers conferred on the court. This has enabled it to render decisions that affect many aspects of the social, economic, and political life of the country.

Particularly significant are the powers to deal with issues of human rights and the right of direct access to this court granted to ordinary citizens. Adjolohoun points out that in the early years after its establishment, the Benin Constitutional Court adopted a rather cautious and restrictive approach to dealing with issues, especially human rights violations. The court has now become more decisive and has rendered numerous decisions that have not only promoted greater respect for human rights, such as the award of monetary compensation to victims of human rights abuses, but has enhanced the ethos of constitutionalism and respect for the rule of law in many decisions restraining threatened abuses of power by both the executive and the legislature.

In spite of the fact that the Benin model is considered to be the most successful in Francophone Africa, Adjolohoun points out that the newly elected President of Benin has initiated constitutional reforms one objective of which is to limit the role the executive plays in the appointment of judges of the Constitutional Court. It is clear from this that there is a broad recognition of the important role that this court has played in sustaining the country's short transition to democracy and a desire to ensure that this is sustained.

In sharp contrast to Adjolohoun's account, in Chapter 3 Fombad looks at the Cameroon Constitutional Council, which he describes as an 'embodiment of paradoxes and contradictions', and a 'faithful servant of an unaccountable system'. According to Fombad, the paradox of the Cameroonian system arises not only from the fact that, although it was introduced in 1996, it essentially replicates the original and clearly outdated French Constitutional Council approach of 1958, but also that has it has never been established. Its functions are presently being discharged by the Supreme Court, although the legality of this is highly suspect. Furthermore, its powers of review, which are mainly by way of abstract review, the only exception being election disputes, are very limited. Save for election disputes, access to the Council is restricted to the very political elites who have no reason to petition it. For the twenty years of its existence, its primary function, to 'ensure the regularity of presidential, parliamentary elections and referendum operations', has been carried out in an incompetent and manifestly partisan manner.

With no avenue for challenging any violations of the Cameroonian Constitution, Fombad shows that the present system of constitutional review in Cameroon has left the country with no effective means of ensuring that the constitution is respected. As a result, the president and his accomplices only respect and comply with the constitution or respect the rule of law when it is convenient for them, and it is they who ultimately are the supreme judges of constitutionality, not the courts nor even the Constitutional Council. It is, therefore, not surprising that Cameroon, by all contemporary indicators of good governance and respect for the rule of law, is one of the few African countries that, since 1990, has made the least progress in entrenching constitutionalism and respect for the rule of law. Fombad contends that this system under which the president reigns and rules and is unaccountable to anyone but himself is perfectly in line with the original 1958 Constitutional Council as designed by the late French President, Charles de Gaulle. He concludes that the Cameroon Constitutional Council does no more than provide a veneer of constitutionalism and democracy that effectively obfuscates constitutional legality, respect for the rule of law, and electoral justice.

The last case study on the centralized model is the chapter written by Thomashausen, in which he examines the constitutional adjudication in Angola. He points out that, although it is based on the Portuguese centralized model of constitutional adjudication, the 2010 Constitution introduced some elements of the decentralized system. An example of such a decentralized element, according to Thomashausen, are the powers the constitution grants to ordinary courts to hear individual complaints against the unconstitutional encroachment upon fundamental rights and freedoms, including administrative acts. Nevertheless, the Angolan Constitutional Court remains the final arbiter of issues of unconstitutionality of law.

Apart from this, access to the court is limited to certain specified institutions. Although the constitution allows the court when dealing with disputes, especially those concerning the violation of fundamental rights and freedoms, to seek guidance in international human rights instruments, in only one of the more than 347 judgments examined by Thomashausen did the court refer to any of these instruments. In spite of the impressive number of cases the court has dealt with, Thomashausen says that the Angolan Constitutional Court has 'disappointed many who believed it would soften the authoritarian nature of the Dos Santos presidency, in power for the past 35 years'. Nevertheless, he points out that some of the judgments have contributed to the strengthening of the principle of the supremacy of the constitution.

Another visible sign of progress is the abandonment of the practice and tradition of enforcing the so-called 'socialist legality'. In spite of this, Thomashausen does not see any prospect of the court changing its conservative inward-looking approach whereby the court only refers to and relies on the writings of scholars from kindred legal traditions, in particular Portugal, Spain, France, and, occasionally, Germany. He concludes that, because the present government has used a legal loophole which provides that judges whose terms have expired should only vacate their office when they have been replaced to retain the present conservative bench, confidence and interest in placing matters before the court is likely to diminish, and extra-judicial forms of protests and defence of fundamental rights may increase.

In Chapter 5 Quashigah examines the role that the Supreme Court of Ghana has played in promoting constitutionalism and the rule of law in Ghana within the framework of a decentralized system. Although the idea of introducing a centralized system through the establishment of a Council of State to deal with all constitutional matters with some form of abstract jurisdiction was once mooted, the constitution-makers settled on a decentralized system in the 1992 Constitution. The key feature of the model consists of a Supreme Court with wide-ranging original, appellate, reference, and supervisory jurisdiction, as well as jurisdiction to handle election petitions relating to the election of the president. The High Court, however, has exclusive original jurisdiction to deal with all disputes concerning the enforcement of fundamental human rights and freedoms.

Focusing on the role the Supreme Court has played in promoting constitutionalism in the country, Quashigah highlights a number of important principles that have emerged from some of its decisions. One example is the categorical refusal by the Supreme Court to restrain itself by the so-called political question doctrine. It has also taken the view that the formulation of the directive principles of state policy in the Ghanaian constitution, unlike the approach adopted in the constitutions of countries such as Nigeria and India, are such that there is no presumption of their non-justiciability. A lengthy debate concerning the court's reference jurisdiction was settled when the court made it clear that all lower courts were not bound to refer all allegations that a matter raised an issue relating to the interpretation of the constitution to it, unless this was clear and unambiguous. Quashigah also discusses two controversial cases involving judges of the Supreme Court, which in his opinion had the 'potential to undermine and compromise the concept of separation of powers'. He nevertheless concludes that, because the court has made itself relevant in the socio-economic life of the people, the average citizen looks up to it 'as the last bastion for the protection of the values of democracy and constitutionalism'.

In another variant of the decentralized model, this time within a federal system, Guobadia, in Chapter 6, examines the formal structures for constitutional adjudication in Nigeria. In analysing the system of judicial review in Nigeria, Guobadia examines the institutions, processes, and eligibility criteria for judicial appointments, the powers of the courts, the nature and scope of their jurisdiction, and the access of these courts to litigants, as well as the impact of the courts' processes and outcomes on the legal system.

Focusing on the two appellate courts and emphasizing their approach to the determination of disputes, she assesses the contributions of the courts through decided cases, to some key subjects around which good governance, respect for the rule of law, and constitutionalism revolves. Some of the issues include the federal structure, particularly the autonomy and mutual non-interference of the federating units, the legislative competence of the federal and state governments with particular emphasis on concurrent powers, the separation of powers, and the law-making procedure and election disputes. In assessing the impact of the courts, Guobadia examines issues relating to the judges' style of reasoning, as well as the direct and subtle policy and other influences (including transnational influences) that have shaped these decisions. In conclusion, she is less certain as to whether the creation of a constitutional division within the Supreme Court will enhance the court's ability to deal with constitutional disputes expeditiously and efficiently.

In Chapter 7, Fowkes reviews the key features of the evolution of the South African Constitutional Court from a centralized to a decentralized model of constitutional review. Among the anomalies, which in his opinion made the demise of the centralized system almost inevitable, were the problems caused by the distinction between non-constitutional matters reserved for the other courts, and constitutional issues which were the only issues the Constitutional Court had the jurisdiction to deal with. In his opinion, the evolution within its short life from a transitional compromise that combined elements of both centralized and decentralized review to a system of decentralized review, arguably, still with some elements of both systems, should, in spite of some upheavals and problems, 'conduce to a more constitutionally coherent jurisprudence and to the more rapid constitutionalization of the entire body of South African law'.

In reviewing the appointment of judges to the Constitutional Court, he argues that the mechanism put in place has left the executive in effective control of the process and increasingly given rise to a growing perception that the system favoured the appointment of judges with a more modest conception of their judicial role and who are less likely to exercise power against the government. However, he admits that there is hardly any evidence, insofar as the Constitutional Court is concerned, that any of the judges has acted as a 'political puppet of some sort'. Although the main form of review remains concrete review, there are two instances of concrete review that he discusses. The access rules to constitutional justice in his opinion are generous, but he points out that the real obstacles litigants face are more practical. This is because of the considerable cost of litigation, which is compounded by the delays of having to go through several levels of courts before reaching the apex court, all of which is not made easier by the Constitutional Court's conservative approach to direct access.

Fowkes provides an elaborate analysis of what he categorizes as three views on the impact of the Constitutional Court on constitutionalism in South Africa. In his opinion, the first viewpoint consists of those who think the court has a relatively low profile and that many South Africans do not treat the court as particularly significant. It is worth noting that this is in sharp contrast to Quashigah's opinion of the impression of Ghanaians about the role of their Supreme Court, although it should be added that this is a conclusion that seems more impressionistic than factual. The second viewpoint is one that he ascribes to the ruling African National Congress (ANC), which views the 'judiciary and/or constitution' in more hostile terms as an obstacle. A third viewpoint is a radical version of the second, and consists of those who see the courts as reactionary institutions and 'bastions of white power', who are seen as 'counter-revolutionary' forces.

In the face of this polarization, Fowkes makes three important points clear. First, he points out that some of the claims of this viewpoint are not well supported by facts because there is little concrete evidence that the Constitutional Court, in particular, can be seen as a defender of white minority interests or as generally hostile to the ANC. Secondly, in spite of its rhetoric, the ANC policy towards the judiciary has been far more nuanced and, in general, has passed major reforms that are 'often salutary and have at least the potential to strengthen the courts'. Thirdly, there are few signs that judicial independence has actually been compromised. In concluding, Fowkes says that the debate between the different views will continue, but 'good historical judgments, especially of current controversies, must await the luxury of hindsight and greater temporal detachment'.

The unique Ethiopian system of constitutional adjudication, where the power of reviewing the constitutionality of laws and other government decisions is carried out by the House of Federation, the second legislative chamber, rather than the courts, is discussed by Abebe in Chapter 8. He points out that, despite being a second chamber, the House of Federation has an insignificant direct role in the law-making process. The decision to keep the constitution away from the courts, according to him, lies in the historical and ideological leanings of the dominant political groupings that drafted the constitution.

In this respect, the Ethiopian example confirms contemporary theories of constitutional design, noted by Fombad, in Chapter 1, according to which dominant political groups controlling the constitution-drafting processes and who are likely to sustain their power after the adoption of the constitution, do not have any incentives to establish powerful institutional constraints on the political organs, such as constitutional judicial review. Abebe points out that, in practice, the constitutional adjudication system in Ethiopia has largely been inconsequential. The total number of cases brought before this body, while improving, remains insignificant. Despite the adoption of a number of controversial laws and government decisions with significant constitutional implications, the House of Federation, according to Abebe, has only invalidated a single law in more than two decades of its existence. The House has failed to use the few significant cases to establish itself as a prominent constitutional actor. He argues that the House has generally played a legitimizing rather than constraining role in politically sensitive constitutional cases.

In spite of this, Abebe feels that the failure of the constitutional adjudication system in Ethiopia may not be attributed solely to design faults. Even if the regular courts were given the power to review the constitutionality of laws and government decisions, the absolute dominance of the ruling party and the threats of government reprisal would have induced judicial restraint. He concludes by contending that the task of establishing a strong system of government founded on constitutionalism should not focus solely on constituting strong and independent constitutional adjudication organs. Changes to the overall political party and electoral systems are necessary to build a self-sustaining and balanced system capable of correcting constitutional misfortunes. This, he argues, is because constitutionalism is, at its core, a political as much as a legal endeavour.

The issue of transjudicialism on constitutional adjudication in Africa is the theme of the third part of the book. This commences in Chapter 9 with Dinokopila's examination of the impact of regional and sub-regional courts and tribunals on constitutional adjudication. This is a topic not widely covered in the literature and which is often coloured by the increasingly questionable monist/dualist approach to the incorporation of international law. Dinokopila points out that the progressive move towards regional integration has seen the increase, not only in regional and sub-regional institutions whose main objectives include the promotion of constitutionalism, respect for the rule of law, and human rights, but also the proliferation of regional courts and tribunals with a mandate to ensure that member states respect the norms and other commitments contained in their founding treaties.

This has raised the vitally important question of the domestic impact of the decisions and jurisprudence that these institutions generate. A number of complex issues arise. One of these is the question of the impact of the non-binding recommendations made by institutions such as the African Commission on Human and Peoples' Rights (African Commission) and the African Committee on the Rights and Welfare of the Child (African Children's Committee). Dinokopila supports the view of those scholars who argue that, once the findings of these institutions become final, and are contained in the Institution's activity report and is approved by the AU Assembly or Executive Council, they become binding. He discusses and cites numerous cases from Anglophone African jurisdictions where the jurisprudence of the numerous regional and sub-regional courts and tribunals, especially the African Commission on Human and Peoples' Rights (African Commission), have been cited with approval and relied upon in domestic courts.

The reasons for this reliance vary but include the concern for the rule of law, the desire to promote universal values, the desire to uncover values inherent within the domestic regime, the willingness to invoke the logic of judges in other jurisdictions, and the concern to avoid a negative impression created in the minds of the international community. He points out that this does not prove problematic where the state whose courts are citing and relying on the decision is a party to the treaty setting up the regional or sub-regional court or tribunal. However, Dinokopila points out that there are some instances where reliance on the jurisprudence of these regional courts and tribunals raises theoretical concerns. This is the case where it has resulted in what is increasingly referred to as 'creeping monism', that is, instances where the domestic court cites and relies on the jurisprudence of an international court or tribunal established under a treaty which the state has ratified but has not domesticated.

Practices such as these have led to doubts about the continuous relevance of the monist/dualist paradigm. On the one hand, whilst most civilian jurisdictions are monist in the sense that ratified treaties lead to automatic domestic application of the treaty; this is hardly the reality because these states usually require some procedural steps to be followed before this occurs. On the other hand, the practice of some common law domestic courts to cite and use the decisions of courts and tribunals established under treaties which the state has not domesticated results in transposition into national law by judicial rather than legislative *fiat*. This assault on dualism through the judicial incorporation of treaties, regardless of its limited purposes, and raises questions about judicial encroachment onto the legislative domain. Apart from these exceptional cases, Dinokopila concludes that there is clear evidence that the jurisprudence of regional and sub-regional courts is now playing an increasingly important role in constitutional adjudication, although this development is mainly the case in Anglophone Africa.

Continuing the theme of the impact of transjudicialism, Killander in Chapter 9 focuses on the effects of international legal norms on constitutional adjudication in Africa. He sets out by pointing out that African constitution drafters have borrowed liberally from external sources, particularly international and foreign laws. Focusing on the protection of human rights, he points out that almost all African constitutions have in one form or another adopted bills of rights based on international and regional standards. However, the influence of these norms is shown to revert to the pre-colonial period.

The focus of the chapter, however, is on the way in which international and regional human rights standards have influenced and shaped the adjudication of the human rights provisions in African constitutions. Killander examines the diverse approaches used in different African constitutions to incorporate these international and regional human rights standards. Some states explicitly incorporate specific international instruments as part of the constitution or make treaties superior to national law or merely incorporate these norms as ordinary law. It is clear that there is no uniform pattern.

Looking at the role these international norms play in constitutional adjudication, Killander, like Dinokopila in the preceding chapter, points out that the widely assumed view that common law countries follow the dualist approach and civil law countries the monist approach is too simplistic. This is particularly the case in respect of common law countries, where most recent constitutions have raised the status of international norms in such diverse and sometimes obscure terms that judges, in the process of interpreting and applying the human rights provisions in the constitutions, now have considerable scope for invoking and applying treaties that have not been directly incorporated in what is clearly emerging as a process of judicial incorporation of treaties. Perhaps no constitution has gone as far as that of the Seychelles in giving judges the powers to take notice of diverse forms of soft laws emanating from treaty bodies established to monitor the enforcement of these international human rights instruments.

In some cases, Killander suggests that national judges may feel the pressure to consider and apply international norms because of alternative courts applying international law, such as the courts and tribunals established under sub-regional instruments such as the Economic Community of West African States (ECOWAS) Court of Justice. However, Killander adds a number of important caveats. First, civil law constitutional jurisprudence shows that courts in these countries generally only cite the legal provision being applied, be it the constitution, national legislation, or a treaty. Secondly, while most constitutions, unlike in the past, have provided considerable scope for the application of international human rights standards, and the courts, especially in Anglophone Africa, regularly invoke and apply this, in some countries substantial differences between the text and practice remain because of the actual realities.

To prove this point, he gives the example of Mali, which has signed and ratified both the Protocol to the African Charter on Human and Peoples' Rights on the Rights of Women in Africa and the Convention on the Elimination of All Forms of Discrimination Against Women (CEDAW) and reinforced this by a provision in the constitution which gives these treaties precedence over national legislation. However, strong pressure from conservative forces prevented the Malian President from signing into law a piece of legislation abolishing discrimination against women. Killander concludes by suggesting that the use of international human rights norms to enhance the quality of constitutional adjudication will be enhanced by, amongst other things, international networking and knowledge sharing among judges, as well as increased human rights advocacy to amend entrenched patriarchal and outdated customary practices.

The two chapters in Part 4 of the book focus on the role of constitutional adjudication generally, in the promotion of constitutionalism in Africa. In Chapter 11, Adjolohoun uses Hirschl's analytical framework of the three faces of the judicialization of politics or juristocracy to examine the extent to which constitutional courts and other courts exercising jurisdiction in constitutional matters have become involved in adjudicating issues that are either fundamentally or constitutionally within the domain of the other coordinate branches of government in Africa. He starts his analysis by tracing the jurisprudential origins and development of the political question doctrine in the United States and the extent to which it has influenced constitutional adjudication in Africa. His discussion of the political role played by constitutional courts on the continent focuses on four main areas, namely human rights adjudication, electoral processes, the separation of powers, and the prerogatives of the coordinate branches of government and so-called pure politics. He subsequently undertakes a similar analysis of judicialization of politics in African regional fora.

The protection of human rights was one of the core elements of constitutionalism entrenched in post-1990 African constitutions. Adjolohoun undertakes a comparative case study of the role politics has played in human rights adjudication in three jurisdictions, namely in the Constitutional Courts of Benin, South Africa, and Uganda. A similar comparative analysis is carried out in respect of the role of courts in electoral processes. However, this time the focus is on Côte d'Ivoire and Senegal. In dealing with the separation of powers in respect of the prerogatives of the coordinate branches of government,

Adjolohoun using three case studies shows that in the Democratic Republic of the Congo (DRC), the political question doctrine was not raised. By contrast, in both Ghana and Nigeria, the issue has been widely debated, with the American approach always at the fore, although after periods of uncertainty owing to decisions either way, it now seems fairly settled that there is a rejection of the application of the political question doctrine in these two jurisdictions.

Arriving at this conclusion, Adjolohoun's conclusions are similar to those of Quashigah in respect of the situation in Ghana. In discussing what he refers to as 'pure politics', Adjolohoun examines the question as to whether there are instances where democracy is made in the courts. In doing so, he focuses on sensitive political issues such as the amendment of the constitution and the term limit debate. The case studies used (consisting of cases decided in Benin, Burundi, and Senegal) explore the divergent and sometimes very controversial decisions African constitutional court judges have taken, clearly illustrating and in some respects confirming Hirschl's view of juristocracy and the judicialization of politics.

In the last part of his discussion, Adjolohoun examines a number of cases, mostly decided by the African Commission on Human and Peoples' Rights, and some by courts and tribunals set up by some of the regional economic communities (RECs), which are supposed to be enforced at municipal level and thus have impacted on the constitutional order. As he correctly concludes, the perception of judicialization of politics or politicized adjudication is a global rather than a regional phenomenon. Whilst the chapter shows that in many instances the intervention of judges has advanced democracy and constitutionalism as well as protected the constitution against threats from the political branches, it has sometimes also protected and legitimized dictators and brought some societies to the brink of civil strife and conflict. He concludes by suggesting that politicians should take responsibility for their political failures and should avoid dragging courts into political adventures that threaten democracy and constitutionalism.

In Chapter 12, Rautenbach explores the role the indigenous concept of *ubuntu* has played in promoting constitutionalism in the context of constitutional adjudication. She suggests that *ubuntu* 'can be regarded as South Africa's gift to constitutionalism', and she traces its first formal recognition to the text of the interim constitution of 1994. Although this concept does not appear in the final constitution of 1996, her discussion shows that the concept in all its forms and manifestations has continued to manifest itself not only in court decisions, but also in legislation and legal writings. In spite of the lack of general agreement on its exact nature and scope, Rautenbach explains how the concept has slowly emerged and its progressive seepage into the legal landscape through numerous decisions of the Constitutional Court where it has been referred to, and the debates it has provoked in legal circles. She also discusses examples of statutes where the concept has been incorporated either directly or indirectly.

From a cursory examination of foreign jurisprudence, she is able to identify a number of cases in Lesotho and Uganda where the concept has been invoked and applied. Her discussion quite clearly shows that *ubuntu* has ardent supporters, as well as strong critics. While the inherent vagueness and ambiguity of the concept exposes it to criticism, especially by some who view it as nothing more than 'a catchphrase with soap opera soothing qualities', and a mere 'marketing device to put an African imprimatur on a set of civil liberties and freedoms forged out of Western instruments', it will be self-defeating to ignore its potential. It must, as she puts it, be seen as part of the process of 'Africanization' or 'indigenisation' of South African and African law as a whole. It is a concept giving voice to something distinctively African that needs to be carefully nurtured and progressively developed to its full potential.

Part 5 of the book examines the decision-making processes and working practices of selected constitutional courts. For obvious reasons, the two most successful and popular examples of constitutional adjudication in Africa, the Constitutional Court of Benin, depicting a centralized model, and the South African Constitutional Court, as an example of the decentralized model, are used as case studies. A third example examined is the Supreme Court of Ghana. Each of these three chapters approaches the topic from a different perspective but ultimately reveals the distinctive features of each approach.

Theodore Holo, the incumbent president of the Benin Constitutional Court, examines the process of handling petitions before this Court in Chapter 13. He points out that the democratic transition, which started in Benin in February 1990, has had the Constitutional Court as the cornerstone of its institutional architecture and a key instrument for building a culture of respect for the rule of law. He considers that the flexibility the court exhibits in handling petitions and the manner in which these petitions are processed as the two unique features of the Benin Constitutional Court's approach to constitutional adjudication. Access to the court is deliberately made very simple and not constrained by complicated or sophisticated procedural or other technical rules. Thus, the court will rule on a matter even if the applicant made a mistake or failed to comply with certain procedural rules.

The court will even assume jurisdiction on its own initiative in matters dealing with the violation of fundamental human rights. When petitions are received by the court, the president of the court usually assigns this for investigation by a rapporteur who, with the aid of an assistant, investigates the matter. They may, if deemed necessary, hear the parties or rely entirely on the written submissions. At the end of their investigations, a report is prepared. This report is ultimately adopted with or without changes by a full bench of judges as the court's judgment and communicated to the parties. Although dissenting opinions are not allowed, the judges nevertheless often deliberate and try to reach a consensus, but are never allowed to reveal the details of their deliberations publicly. Nevertheless, academics, journalists, and the general public freely comment on the decisions of the court. Holo points out that when the court considers it necessary to clarify a decision not understood by the general public, a press release is issued by the Secretary-General of the court, sent to the media and posted on the court's website. He concludes by reiterating that the approach adopted by the court displays a determination to focus on issues of human rights violations and defence of the constitutional order without overly dwelling on errors of procedure or form committed by the parties.

In Chapter 14 Justice Richard Goldstone, retired judge of the South African Constitutional Court, traces the birth of this court and its distinctive features. While Fowkes in his chapter examined what the court presently looks like, having evolved from an essentially centralized to a decentralized model, Goldstone explains how the court started and developed some of the unique features reflected in the nature and quality of its widely respected judgments. Some of the innovations that Goldstone points to include the use of law clerks to assist the judges in preparing their judgments, a media-friendly policy by which a media summary of each judgment is prepared and circulated after a judgment is delivered, and the freedom of the media to provide a full television broadcast of oral arguments. Another important innovation is the manner of writing judgments which, as Goldstone explains, differs significantly from that of most apex courts. Unlike the situation in the Benin Constitutional Court, the South African Constitutional Court sits in bench to hear all oral arguments. Although the hearings are followed by an elaborate debate among the judges, the Chief Justice decides in advance which member of the Court will write the first draft judgment.

This, as Goldstone puts it, explains the sometimes unusual order in which some of the judgments of the Court are reported. The first draft judgment usually contains the relevant background and history of the case, 'even if this judgment becomes a sole dissent, it will be reported first in order that the judgments that follow are understood'. He concludes that, although some of the court's judgments, especially those relating to socio-economic rights, have been criticized for being deferential to the executive, the court has played, and continues to play, a crucial role in the development of democracy in the country.

In Chapter 15, retired Justice Kofi Date-Bah of the Ghanaian Supreme Court provides a perspective to the decision-making and working practices of another apex court. Unlike the two preceding apex courts, the Ghanaian Supreme Court has original, appellate, supervisory, and review jurisdictions, in addition to jurisdictions over certain other miscellaneous matters such as acting as an election court in relation to presidential elections. Again, unlike the Benin and South African Constitutional Courts, it sits in panels whose numbers depend on the particular jurisdiction being exercised. Date-Bah points out that cases are assigned to the panels by the chief justice and decisions are arrived at by majority vote of the judges on the panel after deliberation during a judgment conference, although there is room for concurrent, separate, and dissenting opinions. He also points out that since the introduction of prior filing of the statement of case, counsel tends to dispense with extended oral arguments, especially in relation to appeals.

Apart from issues such as the enforcement of fundamental rights, which are reserved for the High Court, Date-Bah points out that access rules in constitutional matters in the Supreme Court are very broad. It could not have been otherwise, for since the '1992 constitution imposes an obligation on citizens to defend it, this implies that all citizens have standing to go before the Supreme Court in their quest to defend the constitution'. Date-Bah concludes by pointing out that the court has a collegial approach, while at the same time preserving the autonomy of judges. However, its working practices will need to continue to evolve to adapt to its layered functions.

In the concluding chapter, Fombad looks at what lessons may be learnt from these diverse approaches to promoting constitutional justice in Africa. It is clear that the threefold classification into the centralized, decentralized, and hybrid model oversimplifies a wide diversity of practices, where each country has tried to design a system that best addresses its needs. It will also be misleading to conclude that there is so much convergence that the overall picture appears to be one of hybridization. It is unlikely that the main differences marking the different models will disappear easily, especially since these are deeply embedded in and operate within different legal traditions inherited at independence.

Is there any basis for arguing that one model must be preferred over another? It is significant that the two most active and, arguably, most successful constitutional courts on the continent, those of Benin and South Africa, are typical examples of the two competing models. What these courts nevertheless prove is that there is considerable scope for cross-fertilization, and Fombad argues that this provides the basis and an impetus for an intra-African dialogue and possibly an evolution towards models particularly adapted to addressing Africa's peculiar needs. After considering a number of pointers indicating a mixture of successes and failures, he concludes by examining some of the issues that need to be addressed.

The 16 chapters in this volume go a long way towards providing the reader with a broad overview from which to understand and appreciate the different ways in which modern

African constitutionalism is grappling with the issue of constitutional justice. No credible constitutional system can take root without an effective and efficient system of ensuring that the constitution is respected and that any violations of its provisions are promptly sanctioned. The book shows that there have been successes and failures and that enormous challenges are still foreseen. Nevertheless, by bringing all these different experiences and practices together, important lessons may be learnt, which will assist policy-makers, constitution designers, and researchers to understand and appreciate what is happening and to see what needs to be done to overcome present challenges and failures.

PART 1

GENERAL OVERVIEW

1

An Overview of Contemporary Models of Constitutional Review in Africa

Charles M Fombad

1. Introduction

It is perhaps trite to say that a constitution, however comprehensive, foolproof, well written and well meaning it may purport to be, is only as good as the mechanism provided within it to ensure that its provisions are properly implemented and that any violations thereof are promptly sanctioned. A critical bulwark of constitutionalism is, therefore, the existence of an efficient and effective mechanism for controlling and compelling compliance with the letter and spirit of the constitution.[1] In the absence of this, the constitution may not be worth the piece of paper on which it is written and is probably as good as non-existent.[2] This is perhaps one of the most important lessons that African constitution designers appeared to have learnt as they tried to protect the sanctity of the new or revised post-1990 constitutions.

In fact, one of the most remarkable aspects of Africa's transition from authoritarianism to constitutional democracy, based on the fundamental principles of modern constitutionalism, respect for human rights, and the rule of law, has been the role and prominence given to courts, particularly constitutional courts or the courts exercising constitutional jurisdiction. Prior to the 1990s, the scope for constitutional justice was either fairly limited, as was the case in Anglophone Africa, or almost absent, as was generally the case in the other parts of Africa. African leaders and the ruling elites regularly ignored, violated, or changed constitutions with impunity to suit their whims. Human rights violations were the norm as military and one-party dictatorships flourished. By the end of this dark era, African courts and their judges had in one way or another and to different degrees been compromised to a point of impotence.

One of the most important constitutional reforms undertaken by African constitution designers was, therefore, aimed at transforming the courts into independent and credible bodies able to protect the constitution, good governance, and human rights. Current developments with respect to constitutional review in Africa in many respects reflect the global expansion of judicial power generally, and constitutional adjudication in particular.[3] However, unlike in other parts of the world, a comprehensive and comparative

[1] See further Charles M Fombad, 'Post-1990 Constitutional Reforms in Africa: A Preliminary Assessment of the Prospects for Constitutional Governance and Constitutionalism' in Alfred Nhema and Paul Tiyambe Zeleza, *The Resolution of African Conflicts* (OSSREA 2008) 179–99.

[2] As one US judge put it: '[t]he US constitution would be just a piece of paper today if there were not independent judges to enforce it'. See the Hon Richard Arnold, 'Should More Limits be Placed on the Federal Judiciary? No' (1997) 70 *Spectrum* 29.

[3] On the global expansion of constitutional review see generally Chester Neal Tate and Torbjorn Vallinder (eds), *The Global Expansion of Judicial Review* (New York University Press 1997); Mauro Cappelletti, *Judicial Review in the Contemporary World* (Bobbs-Merrill Co Inc 1971); Mauro Cappelletti, 'The Judicial Process in Comparative Perspective' (1970) 58(5) *California Law Review* 1021; Patricio Navia and Julio Rios-Figueroa, 'The Constitutional Adjudication Mosaic of Latin America' (2005) 38 *Comparative Political Studies* 189; and

analysis of the nature, scope, and potential impact of these changes on constitutional and democratic consolidation in Africa has not been undertaken.

The main focus of this chapter is to provide an introductory overview of the expanding scope of constitutional adjudication in Africa. Since constitutional developments in Africa have been shaped and continue to be shaped by its colonial legacy as well as more recent developments globally, the second section looks at the classic models of constitutional review as they explain the variation in form and substance of the developments in Africa, both prior to and after the 1990s. Some of the reasons why constitutional review was not successful in post-independence Africa are considered in section 3. The nature and scope of contemporary African constitutional review models are discussed in section 4. In analysing their nature, scope, and potential impact, the critical question is whether the changes made are sufficiently robust to counter the omnipresent threat of a relapse to the dictatorships of the pasts.

Section 5 draws tentative conclusions from analysing the divergent and convergent trends and assesses their possible impact on future developments. It is clear that, since the 1990s, almost all African countries have in one form or another introduced bodies mandated to review the constitutionality of laws. The forms of these bodies vary, as do their jurisdiction as well and their level of effectiveness. In the conclusion, it is argued that constitutional review in one form or another has now been widely recognized in Africa. However, the critical issue remains that of determining whether these bodies are able to ensure the proper and effective interpretation and application of constitutions without yielding to political manipulation. Have these changes transformed African constitutions from nominal and semantic instruments into normative ones that can effectively control and constrain Africa's notoriously unruly political elites?

2. Background: Classic Models of Constitution Review

As pointed out above, and this point bears repeating, present-day African constitutional review methods have been and are still influenced by Western models that were imposed during the colonial period. We will start by looking at these classic models. This will be followed by an examination of how they were received after independence and how they evolved up until the dramatic reforms of the 1990s.

A brief review of these classic Western models will explain, although not necessarily justify, why they were adopted in Africa. Before identifying what these classic models are, it is necessary to preface this with two preliminary remarks.

First, in some of the literature, a distinction is sometimes made between constitutional review, in a narrow sense, and judicial review, of which it can be considered a sub-category. In this sense, judicial review refers to the powers given to courts to strike down legislation that is incompatible with the constitution and is essentially an objective law-interpreting role. This is distinguished from the broader view of constitutional review, where a court goes beyond ordinary review and is invited to decide essentially political disputes, such as disputes between the different branches and levels of government.[4] Whatever the merit

Tom Ginsburg, 'The Spread of Constitutional Review' in Keith Whittington, R Daniel Kelemen, and Gregory A Caldeira (eds), *The Oxford Handbook of Law and Politics* (OUP 2008).

[4] See Donald Kommers, 'An Introduction to the Federal Constitutional Court' (2001) 2 *German Law Journal* 30; and Tom Ginsburg, 'The Global Spread of Constitutional Review' in Whittington, Keleman, and Caldeira (n 3); see also Tom Ginsburg and Mila Versteeg, 'Why Do Countries Adopt Constitutional Review?' (2014) 30 *Journal of Law, Economics and Organization* 587.

of this distinction, it needs to be pointed out that this chapter uses constitutional review broadly to cover both situations. As will be shown later, it must be noted that some of these disputes are more politically loaded than others.

Secondly, a distinction is also sometimes made between weak-form and strong-form constitutional review based on the relative powers of the court that exercises constitutional review and parliament.[5] In a weak constitutional review system, a court's declaration of invalidity on grounds of unconstitutionality may be superseded or overridden by a subsequent Act of Parliament. The best form of this may arise under the United Kingdom's Human Rights Act 1998 (which can be considered as one of the important instruments that make up the country's unwritten constitution). This Act only allows United Kingdom courts to declare an Act of Parliament to be inconsistent with the 1998 Act (which is based on the European Convention on Human Rights), but it has no powers to declare it invalid. Parliament has the discretion to decide whether or not to amend the impugned Act to conform to the court's declaration.

Another form of weak judicial review is provided for under section 33 of Canada's Constitution Act 1982. This section provides an 'override' mechanism which enables parliament, by a simple majority, to validate for at most five years, unless extended, a statute that has been declared by the courts to be inconsistent with the Canadian Charter of Rights and Freedoms. Other forms of weak review occur where courts only deliver an advisory opinion which is not binding. By contrast, a strong form judicial review occurs where the court's determination that a particular law is unconstitutional is final and binding on all persons and organs unless the court overrules itself in another case or a constitutional amendment is enacted that alters the law which formed the basis of the court's original decision.

From a comparative law perspective, two main models of constitutional review have dominated the world, namely the decentralized (often referred to as the American, concrete, disperse, or diffuse) model, and the Austrian (often referred to as the European, concentrated or centralized) model. Between and within these two models are numerous variations. These include the hybrid or mixed systems, which combine elements of the centralized and decentralized model, and the system of limited review which operates in certain countries. These models constitute the classic approaches that will be briefly examined below. The focus will be on their nature, their underlying philosophy and the advantages and disadvantages of each model.

2.1 The decentralized model

The decentralized concrete model is usually traced to the famous judgment of Chief Justice Marshall in the 1803 case of *Marbury v Madison*.[6] It is, however, important to note that the idea of judicial review did not spring new and fully developed from the brow of the chief justice.[7] A century of American history and a long line of precedents paved the way for

[5] See generally Mark Tushnet, *Weak Courts, Strong Rights: Judicial Review and Social Welfare Rights in Comparative Constitutional Law* (Princeton University Press 2008); and Mark Tushnet, 'The Rise of Weak-form Judicial Review' in Tom Ginsburg and Rosalind Dixon (eds), *Comparative Constitutional Law* (Edward Elgar Publishing 2011); and Albert Chen, 'The Global Expansion of Constitutional Judicial Review: Some Historical and Comparative Perspectives' in *Festschrift in Honour of Professor Satoru Osanai* (Chuo University 2013) 3–25.

[6] 5 US (I Cranch) 137 (1803).

[7] See in general Mauro Cappelletti, *Judicial Review in the Contemporary World* (Bobbs-Merrill Co Inc 1971) chs 2 and 3; Mauro Cappelletti, *The Judicial Process in Comparative Perspective* (Clarendon Press 1989) ch 3;

Chief Justice Marshall's judgment. The remote antecedent of this system of constitutional adjudication may be traced from classical antiquity and medieval thinkers up until the period just before the American War of Independence.[8]

It is also important to note its English common law roots. English colonies were often founded as commercial enterprises and were managed under crown charters. These charters operated as constitutions in the colonies and the colonies were allowed to make their own laws, provided that any such laws contrary to the sovereign will of the English Parliament were declared invalid. The effect of this was to empower judges to disregard local legislation which was not consistent with English law. It was this approach that laid the foundation for Chief Justice Marshall's declaration that: '[t]he principle, supposed to be essential to all written constitutions, that a law repugnant to the constitution is void, and that courts, as well as other departments, are bound by that instrument'.[9]

It was this model of constitutional adjudication that most of Anglophone Africa adopted after independence. Under this model, constitutional matters are dealt with by ordinary courts during normal proceedings (*incidenter*). The review is of a concrete and repressive nature and the decisions of the court take effect only *inter partes*, although they eventually have some *erga omnes* effect because of the principle of *stare decisis*.

The *Marbury* decision marked the final concretization of what has now become firmly established as the decentralized model. It also marked the first wave in the global spread of constitutional review.[10] As Cappelletti points out, the rationale behind the decentralized system is, on the face of it, both logical and simple. It is the function of the courts to interpret laws and, when two laws conflict, it is the duty of the judge to decide which of them should prevail. The normal rule is that the higher law prevails: *superior derogate legi inferiori*.[11] Any errors can therefore be corrected, as decisions made by lower courts can be appealed all the way to the highest court. Since a court only deals with concrete disputes that are presented in the factual context in which they arose, the court has the benefit of arguments from both sides of the dispute, which will enable it to reach a fair and just decision. Since constitutional courts are decentralized, the cost of litigation will not be too high. Another advantage of the decentralized system is that the lower courts act as a filter of sorts and often decide a majority of cases, thus ensuring that the superior courts only deal with very important cases.

In spite of its advantages, the decentralized model has a number of weaknesses. Although the appellate proceedings provide for the correction of wrong decisions, this process can be lengthy and costly. Appeals—and ultimately constitutional justice—are, therefore, for the most part only available to the rich, who can afford to pay the cost of litigation. If the litigants are too poor to appeal, the law could be left in a state of uncertainty, especially where conflicting decisions from courts of the same level given in different judicial districts are not appealed for a final determination by a superior court. This gives rise to inconsistency in cases where lower courts decide similar cases differently, until a final decision is made at the highest level.

Arne Mavcic, *The Constitutional Review* (BookWorld 2001); and Arne Mavcic, 'Seminar on Constitutional Jurisdiction' (Grand Park Hotel, Ramallah, 25 October 2008) http://www.venice.coe.int/WebForms/documents/?pdf=CDL-JU(2008)026-e (last accessed 13 April 2017).

[8] See Mauro Cappelletti, 'The Judicial Process in Comparative Perspective' (1970) 58 *California Law Review* 1021.

[9] 5 US (I Cranch) 137 (1803).

[10] See Ginsburg (n 4).

[11] See Cappelletti (n 8) 1037.

Before we turn to the centralized model, it is important to point out that the *Marbury* decision was formulated by the Supreme Court because there was no explicit provision in the United States constitution providing for judicial review.

2.2 The centralized model

The centralized model is based on the work of the Austrian scholar, Hans Kelsen, who did much to develop and popularize it as an alternative to the American judicial review method. The main feature of this model is the fact that constitutional adjudication is carried out by a centralized, often specialized, tribunal established independently outside the judicial branch during special proceedings (*principaliter*). The judges are essentially political appointees who need not have any legal qualifications and are appointed by political institutions. Although as a rule such tribunals undertake only abstract (preventive) review, they have in recent years undertaken concrete (repressive) review, especially with respect to electoral matters. The decisions taken have an *erga omnes* effect.

The development of Kelsen's centralized constitutional review model, which was incorporated into the Austrian constitution of 1920, marked the beginning of the second wave of judicial review. This model was widely adopted in Europe, and the French have developed a particular form of the model—the constitutional council system—which has very widely been replicated in Francophone Africa and, to a certain extent, in Arabophone, Lusophone, and Hispanophone Africa. Because of the influence it has had in Africa, we will briefly examine the French form of this model. Before doing so, however, a number of general observations need to be made about the centralized model.

2.2.1 The centralized model generally

The centralized model aptly reflects the deep-seated historical and philosophical approaches to the judiciary and judicial office of the American and other common law countries, on the one hand, and the European civil law countries, on the other. Five main justifications have often been offered to defend the centralized model. First, because of the civil law countries' rather rigid adherence to the constitutional separation of powers, and the fear of a self-seeking and anti-democratic judiciary, Kelsen designed the constitutional court as a special and more explicitly political body that would operate outside the judicial branch. Its political character was underlined by the manner in which its members were appointed and the sort of questions it had to deal with. The centralized approach to constitutional review is seen as the best way to preserve the separation of powers and allow the constitutional court to exercise oversight over all three and not just two branches of government.

Secondly, the risk of uncertainty and inconsistency in the development of constitutional jurisprudence is eliminated because one centralized body makes all the decisions. This would not be possible in a normal civilian court system comprising a plurality of courts specializing in different subject matters and lacking a single supreme court for all matters.[12] Furthermore, the decentralized approach would be unsuitable for civil law systems that do not strictly adhere to the system of *stare decisis*. As a result, if each judge were allowed to decide on the constitutionality of statutes, there would be confusion since some

[12] The traditional structure of civilian court systems consists of separate hierarchies of administrative, labour, fiscal, social, civil, and criminal courts, each with its own apex court at the summit.

judges would enforce statutes that have been declared unconstitutional by others, regardless of the position of the judge in the hierarchy of courts. A judge may also change his or her position on the same facts the very next day. The individualized effect of decisions would mean that each party would have to initiate a separate action in order to escape the effect of a law that had been declared unconstitutional in a case concerning another party.

Thirdly, the centralized model allows for the early high-level consideration of constitutional issues. Fourthly, it avoids delays in getting to the highest court and uncertainty about the state of the law on a particular issue, which would drag on through appeals in a decentralized system. Finally, through the emphasis on abstract a priori review, the courts operating in this system are able to invalidate a bad law before it comes into force and causes any damage or hardship.

However, the centralized system of constitutional review also has a number of weaknesses. First, since there is only one court, located in a capital city that deals with all constitutional matters, there is always a risk of high costs in litigating such disputes and delays caused by the inevitable backlog of having only one court to deal with these cases. Secondly, there is not always a clear distinction between cases that raise constitutional issues and those that do not. As a result, a party may invest considerable time and money in bringing a matter before the constitutional court, only for it to be dismissed on the grounds that it does not raise a constitutional issue and must instead be pursued before one of the other courts. Thirdly, since the constitutional court acts as the court of first and final resort, there is no opportunity for errors to be corrected, unless a similar issue is raised in a subsequent case and the court changes its mind. Fourthly, those who preside in these courts do not have to be legally trained and, even if they are judges, they may lack the experience, maturity, and psychological balance needed to discharge such delicate quasi-political functions. This is because civil law judges are 'career judges' who enter the judiciary at an early age and are usually promoted based on the discretion of politicians. These same politicians are well placed to bring pressure to bear on the judges to decide matters in a way that will favour their positions.

It is difficult to see how political appointees can make decisions on political issues involving those who appointed them without being exposed to undue political influence. As will be seen later in this chapter, it is a system which, because of the extensive involvement of courts in political disputes, is virtually transformed into another level of the legislature.[13]

2.2.2 The French Constitutional Council variant

The French variation of the centralized model, although influenced by Kelsen and the ideology of separation of powers, was substantially shaped by the obsessive Gallic fear of legal dictatorship through a 'government of judges'.[14] In fact, the late President

[13] In fact, Hans Kelsen viewed the constitutional court as a complement to the legislature which, by nullifying unconstitutional laws, plays the role of a negative legislator. See generally Hans Kelsen, 'Judicial Review of Legislation: A Comparative Study of the Austrian and the American Constitution' (1942) 4 *The Journal of Politics* 183.

[14] This approach can be traced to pre-revolutionary France. Because of the bad reputation of royal courts (or *parlements*, as they were called) before the French Revolution, one of the first measures that the revolutionaries took was to break the powers of these courts by subordinating them to the complete control of the executive. See Denis Tallon, 'The Constitution and the Courts in France' (1979) 27 *American Journal of Comparative Law* 567; John Henry Merryman, 'The French Deviation' (1996) 44 *American Journal of Comparative Law* 109; and Michael Henry Davis, 'The Law/Politics Distinction, the French *Conseil Constitutionnnel*, and the US Supreme Court' (1986) 34 *American Journal of Comparative Law* 45.

Charles de Gaulle, author of the 1958 French Fifth Republic Constitution, designed the Constitutional Council as the handmaiden of a strong and dominant executive that would ensure that parliament did not encroach upon the powers of the executive. He did not anticipate that the Council would become an arbiter of fundamental constitutional rights.[15] Several factors rendered the Council ineffective as a means for settling constitutional disputes. First, it was initially allowed to deal only with a priori abstract reviews. Secondly, ordinary citizens had no access to the Council, and those who had *locus standi*, such as the president of the republic and the presidents of the national assembly and senate, had little reason to ask the Council to review legislation which, in most cases, they had initiated. Thirdly, the political nature of the appointments made it more of a political quasi-administrative body than a body suitable for resolving constitutional disputes.

Although the French have resolutely clung to the idea that no judicial organ should be given the power to review the constitutionality of statutes, the underlying philosophy and approach of constitutional adjudication in France have changed in an incremental and indirect manner to allow for some form of constitutional review, more by default and opportunism than by design. First, in the 1970s, the Constitutional Council created for itself the power and duty to control the conformity of non-promulgated legislation beyond what was then stated in the constitution.[16] Secondly, control of the constitutionality of laws was enlarged through the work of the French Council of State and the Court of Cassation.[17] Thirdly, the guarantee of individual rights that France lacked at national level was to a significant degree available at the supranational level, through its membership of the European Union and its various judicial bodies.[18] Finally, the constitutional reforms of 2008 introduced some form of concrete review into the French system and opened the way for individual access to the Council subject to a filtering process involving the two highest courts, the Court of Cassation (highest court for ordinary matters) and the Council of State (highest court for administrative matters).

In many respects, the French Constitutional Council has developed a system of constitutional review that has taken the concept of separating constitutional adjudication from ordinary adjudication much further than Kelsen recommended. However, because of its political composition and the manner in which it operates, similar to a review chamber of parliament, it is more of a political body under the control of self-interested politicians than a judicial body designed to protect and enforce the constitution.[19]

[15] See William Pickles, *The French Constitution* (Stevens 1960) 30, who described the French Constitutional Council as an adjunct of the president of the Republic. The orientation of the French Constitutional Court had more to do with constraining the legislature than the protection of rights.

[16] The role of the Constitutional Council expanded considerably as a result of the Constitutional Council's landmark decision of 1971 in *Liberté d'Association* (décision no 71-44 DC), which Laurent described as France's *Marbury v Madison*. See Pech Laurent, 'Rule of Law in France' in Randall Peerenboom (ed), *Asian Discourses of Rule of Law* (Routledge 2004) 79–112.

[17] See generally Charles M Fombad, 'The New Cameroonian Constitutional Council' (1998) 24 *Journal of African Law* 172.

[18] In fact, Merryman (n 14) points out that the French legal system which, in its pure form, is a deviant from the European *jus commune* is now returning to the European mainstream. See also Doris Marie Provine, 'Courts in the Political Process in France' in Herbert Jacob and others (eds), *Courts, Law, and Politics in Comparative Perspective* (Yale University Press 1996) 197.

[19] The French Republican tradition is firmly anchored on parliamentary sovereignty and is hostile to constitutional adjudication by ordinary courts. A statute is considered to be the manifestation of sovereignty and not subject to any external control, especially by judges. In this regard, the Constitutional Council is considered as part of the legislature and, in playing a quasi-legislative role, helps to preserve the essential idea of the sovereignty of the law.

The centralized and decentralized models of constitutional review discussed above correspond in varying degrees to the strong form of judicial review. We will now consider two models that differ from them in several respects.

2.3 Mixed or hybrid models and jurisdictions with limited constitutional review

Mixed or hybrid models combine different aspects of the centralized and decentralized models. As a result, there are several variations of this, particularly in South America, where this method of constitutional adjudication is fairly common. Their hybrid nature also means that many display features of both a strong and weak form of constitutional review. Typical examples include the hybrid systems, which operate in Venezuela and Colombia. Ordinary courts have the power to decide not to apply an unconstitutional law.[20] However, only a single court has the power to invalidate such a law. In the Portuguese system, a finding of unconstitutionality by an ordinary court will apply only to that specific case. However, three findings of unconstitutionality of a law will trigger a review by the Constitutional Court.

As with the mixed or hybrid model, the approach adopted by countries with a limited system of constitutional review varies considerably. In a general sense, this model includes all countries with a weak form of constitutional review, such as Canada and the United Kingdom mentioned above. The prevalence of this system in a number of common law countries almost gives the impression that a new and distinctive model of constitutional review is emerging in the Commonwealth.[21] As noted earlier, with respect to the United Kingdom and Canada, the same to a certain extent is true of New Zealand and Australia (at least at state level). The courts may make a formal declaration that a piece of legislation is 'incompatible' with a bill of rights norm. Such a declaration does not affect the validity, continuing operation, or enforcement of the impugned provisions. The traditional principle of parliamentary sovereignty remains intact because parliament retains the discretion to comply with or ignore the court's declaration, sometimes by a simple parliamentary majority against changing the law. In Canada, the 'notwithstanding' clause in section 33 of the Charter of Rights and Freedoms gives the federal parliament and provincial legislatures powers to override, for a certain period, legislation that has been determined to be unconstitutional.

Outside the Commonwealth, there are many other examples of systems with such limited constitutional review. The Nordic countries, especially Finland and Sweden, have developed a similar system of weak constitutional review that also limits the role of judicial oversight. Under the so-called 'clear mistake rule', courts may only set aside a statute when its unconstitutionality is beyond all reasonable doubt.[22] In Sweden, courts can set aside a statute in cases of 'manifest' contrast with the constitution.[23] This review coexists with an *ex ante* constitutional review that can be carried out by an *organ* of parliament (called the

[20] See further Vicki Jackson and Mark Tushnet, *Comparative Constitutional Law* (2nd edn, Foundation Press 2006) 466; and Alan Brewer-Carias, *Constitutional Protection of Human Rights in Latin America. A Comparative Study of Amparo Proceedings* (Cambridge University Press 2009); Kelsen (n 13).

[21] See further Stephen Gardbaum, *The New Commonwealth Model of Constitutionalism: Theory and Practice* (Cambridge University Press 2013); and Francesco Duranti, 'New Models of Constitutional Review' (2014) 5 *Comparative Law Review* 1.

[22] See further Jaakko Husa, 'Guarding the Constitutionality of Laws in the Nordic Countries: A Comparative Perspective' (2000) 48 *American Journal of Comparative Law* 345.

[23] See art 14, ch XI of the constitution of Sweden (SFS nr: 1974:152).

Council of Legislation, composed of retired judges and other experts) at the request of either the government or parliament. In practice, if the Council of Legislation has raised no constitutional objections to a statute, the courts, in their *ex post* control, hardly ever set aside the same statute for unconstitutionality. In Finland, courts are empowered to set aside statutes only on grounds of 'manifest contrast' with the constitution.[24] *Ex ante* constitutional control is also carried out by the Parliamentary Constitutional Law Committee. The courts cannot declare the existence of any 'manifest' conflict with the constitution in their *ex post* control if the Committee during its *ex ante* control had not ascertained the existence of any such conflict.

Mention must also be made of the Dutch approach, which is at the other end of the scale. Constitutional review in the Netherlands is done exclusively within the legislature, effectively shutting out any judicial oversight of legislative enactments.

Two points need to be noted here. First, there seems to be a deliberate attempt to limit the role of courts and promote what one analyst has referred to as 'dialogue' between the legislature and the judiciary.[25] Secondly, the evidence from both the Commonwealth and the Nordic countries shows that there is growing mutual respect between the two branches, as witnessed on those rare occasions when the legislatures have complied with determinations made by the courts.[26]

With this background established, we will next look at how these models were received in African countries on gaining their independence, and how these models have influenced present-day approaches in Africa.

3. Failure of Constitutional Review under the Post-independence Constitutions?

At independence, most African countries adopted the constitutional review mechanisms that were being used by the former colonial powers, often with some minor adjustments. For example, the British had formally adjusted the *Marbury* principle to the realities of a written constitution. In light of the rationales for the different models of constitutional review discussed in the previous section, particularly the question of compatibility with the legal system operating within these countries, the adoption of the colonial models was almost inevitable.

The lack of an effective system of constitutional review contributed substantially to the absence of constitutionalism in pre-1990 Africa. The reasons for this will briefly be examined in order to consider whether the weaknesses that made constitutional review either impossible or unworkable have been addressed in the past two decades of constitutional reform. From this perspective, at least five main reasons for the failure of the mechanism of constitutional review to check the abuse of post-independence African constitutions may be identified.

The first is that some constitutions provided no procedure for reviewing and checking against any violations of their provisions. For example, the Liberian constitution of 26 July 1847, the oldest in Africa, had no provision providing for judicial review. Neither did the Ethiopian constitution of 4 November 1955.[27]

24 Constitution of Finland 1999 ch 10.

25 Peter Hogg and Alison Bushell, 'The Charter Dialogue between Court and Legislatures (Or Perhaps the Charter of Rights isn't Such a Bad Thing after All)' (1997) 35 *Osgoode Hall Law Journal* 75.

26 See Duranti (n 21).

27 The Libyan constitution of 1951 makes no reference to constitutional review either.

Secondly, the issue of constitutional review became irrelevant in most countries after the military took over and suspended their constitutions. Between 1956, when the tide of independence rose, and 2001, it has been estimated that there were about 108 attempted *coups d'état*, of which eighty were successful.[28] Military dictatorships being the very antithesis of constitutional governance and constitutionalism, it is, therefore, not surprising that very little constitutional review took place under these regimes. The high number of states that came under military rule, combined with the many other countries that adopted a one-party system, ensured that there was hardly any room for debate or competition, both of which usually generate disagreement and other forms of conflict that require the intervention of a neutral third party. As Ginsburg and Versteeg have rightly pointed out, electoral competition and the uncertainties in the electoral market were among the factors that encouraged the adoption of constitutional review. Without such competition, either for votes or for ideas, there was no reason to have recourse to constitutional courts.[29]

A third point to note is that the institution of private litigation to attack governmental activity on constitutional grounds is not only a sensitive matter but also a potentially costly enterprise, given the cost of hiring competent counsel and the payment of court fees. Where the opponent is the government, the matter could either drag on without end for years, or diverse forms of pressure could be exerted on the petitioner to discourage him or her from pursuing the matter. Generally, however, post-independence African leaders did everything possible to focus their people's minds not on the constitution or rights consciousness, but rather on the developmental priorities of overcoming the challenges of underdevelopment and poverty. Contesting rights and challenging governmental action or omissions was not considered patriotic. It is, therefore, not surprising that there are so few reported cases on constitutional matters because few people had the courage or the means to take on their governments.

Fourthly, and closely related to the previous point, is the problem of judicial timidity and the abdication of responsibility by deferring and pandering to the perceived or actual wishes of the executive. For many years, this had a detrimental effect on constitutional adjudication in many African countries. Confidence in litigating constitutional matters was in some cases dampened by the unpredictable attitude of judges when dealing with such disputes, especially matters that were perceived to be of a sensitive political nature. An example of such judicial deference is the famous Ghanaian case of *Re Akoto*,[30] where the petitioner challenged the constitutionality of the Preventive Detention Act, relying in part on a declaration of principles set out in Article 13 of the constitution. The Supreme Court, in a rather bizarre decision, declared that Article 13 was not part of the constitution.[31]

Some of these courts were deferent for understandable reasons. Many young African governments had little patience with judges whom they perceived as trying to use judicial power to overturn government decisions in a manner that they felt threatened their power to rule. It must also be remembered that in the post-independence euphoria and for

[28] For example, in the space of one year, 1965–1966, nine successful *coups* displaced the existing regimes in Algeria, Benin, Burkina Faso, Burundi, Central African Republic, Chad, Democratic Republic of the Congo (then known as Zaire), Ghana, and Nigeria. See generally Crawford Young, *The Postcolonial State in Africa: Fifty Years of Independence 1960–2010* (University of Wisconsin Press 2012); and Martin Meredith, *The State of Africa: A History of Fifty Years of Independence* (Free Press 2006).

[29] See Ginsburg and Versteeg (n 4). [30] [1961] Ghana Law Reports 523.

[31] ibid 535, where the Chief Justice justified his decision thus: 'It will be observed that Article 13(1) is in the form of a personal declaration by the President and is in no way part of the general law of Ghana. In other parts of the Constitution where a duty is imposed the word "shall" is used but throughout the word used is "should". In our view the declaration merely represents the goal which every President must pledge himself to attempt to achieve. It does not represent a legal requirement which can be enforced by the courts'.

many years thereafter, many African politicians had made it clear that what the continent needed were accelerators and not brakes on governmental activities.[32]

Fifthly, and perhaps most serious, was the fact that many of the mechanisms provided for in post-independence constitutions for controlling constitutional legality were simply doomed to fail because they were inherently defective. This is particularly so in Francophone and other civilian jurisdictions in Africa, where the overwhelming majority of countries merely copied the Fifth French Republic Constitutional Council model of 1958 with few significant changes. Most of these countries provided for the establishment of a constitutional chamber to operate within the Supreme Court, which was given the powers of and expected to operate in the same way as the French Constitutional Council,[33] or created their own Constitutional Councils.[34] It is not surprising that hardly any disputes were ever handled by any of these bodies before the 1990s because the drafters of these constitutions blindly copied the French Constitutional Council model, including what have been referred to as its 'original sin'[35] and 'congenital defects'.[36] As pointed out above, this included the fact that those most vulnerable to a violation of their constitutional rights, the ordinary citizens, had no *locus standi,* except in electoral matters, to take matters before these bodies. The review jurisdiction was also defined very narrowly to cover only a few restricted matters, such as electoral disputes and sometimes disputes between the different institutions. In general, as with their French progenitor, the review was only abstract.

It is now necessary to examine the nature and scope of the changes introduced after the 1990s before assessing the extent to which these changes have remedied many of the defects that had made constitutional adjudication a fading hope rather than a practical reality in post-independence Africa.

4. Nature and Scope of Contemporary Models of Constitutional Review in Africa

Although most contemporary African constitutional review designs are substantially based on inherited colonial models, there are also many signs of creative borrowing from and the imaginative combination of many features of the different classic models. This section will focus on five issues. First, we will identify the main models of constitutional review on the continent. Secondly, we will look at the scope of jurisdiction conferred on these courts; thirdly, the types of review carried out; fourthly, the scope of access to the courts; and fifthly, the nature of the decisions that are rendered.

Some of the terminology that has been used needs to be clarified. First, the use of the term 'constitutional court' should be understood, unless the context indicates otherwise,

[32] See Robert Seidman, 'Judicial Review and Fundamental Freedoms in Anglophonic Independent Africa' (1974) 35 *Ohio State Law Journal* 820.

[33] See eg art 56 of the 1960 constitution of Benin; art 57 of the 1960 constitution of Burkina Faso; art 95 of the 1962 constitution of Burundi; art 58 of the 1961 constitution of the Republic of Congo; art 59 of the 1960 constitution of Gabon; art 42 of the 1960 constitution of Mali; art 102 of the 1962 constitution of Rwanda; art 70 of the 1963 constitution of Togo.

[34] See eg art 64 of the 1963 constitution of Algeria; and art 32 of the 1960 constitution of the Central African Republic.

[35] See Patrick Juillard, 'L'Aménagement de l'Article 61 de la Constitution' (1974) 90 *Revue de Droit Public* 1703, 1767.

[36] See Mauro Cappelletti and William Cohen, *Comparative Constitutional Law: Cases and Materials* (Bobbs-Merrill 1979) 47.

as referring to all courts, whether specifically known by that name or not, which carry out constitutional review or exercise jurisdiction in constitutional matters. In the decentralized systems that operate in many Anglophone African countries, save in a few cases, there is no court called a constitutional court, but rather a series of courts given jurisdiction in constitutional matters, usually starting with the High Court and ending with the highest court in the hierarchy of courts, which may be a Court of Appeal or a Supreme Court.

Secondly, a distinction is made between 'common law jurisdictions' and 'civil law jurisdictions'. The former refers to the Anglophone African countries that were previously British colonies. The latter refers to civilian jurisdictions in not only Francophone but also Hispanophone and Lusophone Africa. Although the other civil law jurisdictions differ from that of Francophone African countries, which were all influenced by the French Fifth Republic Constitution of 1958, their general approach to constitutional adjudication is informed by the same underlying philosophical doctrines and approaches, even though there are some subtle differences between them.

Bearing this in mind, we can now examine what forms of constitutional models operate on the continent.

4.1 Main models of constitutional review in Africa

Of the fifty-four African countries whose post-1990 constitutions were examined, thirty-six (66.6%)[37] of them have adopted the centralized model, fifteen (27.7%)[38] the decentralized model, and only one, Ethiopia, the mixed or hybrid model.[39] Although the general trend appears to suggest that most countries have designed systems of constitutional review very much along the lines of what they inherited at independence, there are a number of exceptions. For example, whilst all African countries with a civilian legal tradition have adopted the centralized model, not all Anglophone African countries have adopted the decentralized model. In fact, four of these countries, Sierra Leone, South Sudan, Tanzania, and Zambia, have adopted the centralized model.[40]

Of the thirty-six countries that have adopted the centralized model, some of the constitutions refer to a constitutional court (seventeen countries), or constitutional council (nine countries) or another name, such as supreme court (ten countries). From a careful analysis of the provisions regulating the constitutional courts in these thirty-six countries, it is possible to distinguish which group of countries is characterized by a very progressive system of constitutional review. The best example of this is Benin which, in its 1990 constitution, in many respects set the pace for the modern approach in Africa. This may even be regarded as being well ahead of France, the country from which this system was copied, which was only able to introduce some limited reforms to its own system eighteen years later, in 2008. At the other extreme are countries which, in spite of the dawn of a

[37] These are Algeria, Angola, Benin, Burkina Faso, Burundi, Cameroon, Central African Republic, Chad, Comoros Islands, Côte d'Ivoire, Democratic Republic of the Congo (DRC), Djibouti, Egypt, Equatorial Guinea, Gabon, Guinea, Madagascar, Mali, Mauritania, Morocco, Mozambique, Niger, Rwanda, Republic of Congo, São Tomé and Principe, Senegal, Sierra Leone, Somalia, South Sudan, Tanzania, Togo, Tunisia, Zambia, Cape Verde, and Sudan.

[38] These are Botswana, the Gambia, Ghana, Kenya, Lesotho, Liberia, Malawi, Mauritius, Namibia, Nigeria, Seychelles, South Africa, Swaziland, Uganda, and Zimbabwe.

[39] Libya's 2011 constitution, very much like the one it replaced, contains no provision dealing with constitutional review. It was not possible to gain access to the English version of the latest constitution of Guinea Bissau.

[40] In the case of Tanzania and Zambia, this is what appears in the present draft constitutions, which are still under discussion.

new era of constitutionalism in Africa, have retained the constitutional council model of the 1958 constitution in its original form. The best example of this conservative approach is Cameroon, which in 1996 provided for the establishment of a Constitutional Council.

The only remarkable departure from what appears to be the trend in Africa is the Ethiopian constitution of 1994, which provides for the only hybrid or mixed model on the continent. Article 84(1) and (2) of its constitution provides for what clearly amounts to a review of constitutionality by the legislature itself—a model which comes close to the Swedish and Finnish models mentioned earlier.

Be that as it may, the form and model of constitutional review on their own are not important; what is of crucial importance is the ability of the body provided for to act as an effective, efficient, and competent protector and defender of constitutional rights and constitutionalism. One important way of assessing the effectiveness of a constitutional court is by examining the scope of its jurisdiction. We will now turn our attention to this.

4.2 Scope of jurisdiction

It is when we examine the scope of the jurisdiction of modern African constitutional courts that the differences between those operating within a centralized and those operating within a decentralized system come into play. For analytical purposes, a distinction could be made between the scope of the grant of primary jurisdiction and that of the grant of ancillary jurisdiction.[41]

4.2.1 Primary jurisdiction

Primary jurisdiction refers to the powers that a constitutional court is typically created to exercise. This usually comprises three main powers. First is the power of constitutional review, which refers to the formal powers that a court has to strike down any piece of legislation or administrative action for violating the constitution. Second is the power to safeguard human rights and, third, the powers to resolve conflicts of competence disputes between central and local government, and between government agencies inter se.

Generally, the primary jurisdiction conferred on constitutional courts in Anglophone Africa is based on a combination of three main factors. First, it can be said that the common law courts have historically asserted the power of judicial review as an inherent incidence of the general process of adjudication. This doctrine may be traced from Lord Coke CJ's pronouncements in the *Dr Bonham*'s case,[42] which was affirmed by Chief Justice Marshall in *Marbury*'s case, when he declared:

> It is emphatically the province and duty of the judicial department to say what the law is. Those who apply the rule to particular cases must of necessity expound and interpret that rule. If two laws conflict with each other, the courts must decide on the operation of each.[43]

A similar reasoning was adopted in *Glenister v President of the Republic of South Africa and Others*,[44] when Langa CJ said:

[41] See generally Tom Ginsburg and Zachary Elkins, 'Ancillary Powers of Constitutional Courts' (2009) 87 *Texas Law Review* 1431; and Wen-Chen Chang and others, *Constitutionalism in Asia: Cases and Materials* (Hart Publishing 2014).

[42] (1610) 8 Co Rep 114 (Court of Common Pleas).

[43] 5 US (1 Cranch) 137, 177 (1803).

[44] 2009 (1) SA 287 (CC); 2009 (2) BCLR 136 (CC) [33]. See also *Doctors for Life v Speaker of the National Assembly and Others* 2006 (6) SA 416 (CC); 2006 (12) BCLR 1399 (CC) [68], where the court pointed out that it had a duty to intervene to prevent any violation of the constitution.

In our constitutional democracy, the courts are the ultimate guardians of the Constitution. They not only have the right to intervene in order to prevent the violation of the Constitution, they also have the duty to do so.

Secondly, a power of constitutional review may be inferred from the general provisions in the constitutions of Anglophone countries, which vest judicial powers in the courts.[45] This general power may be qualified by a provision that vests powers to deal with certain aspects of constitutional review, the most frequent being the enforcement of fundamental rights, on specific courts, such as the High Court,[46] and the powers to interpret the constitution on another court. Thirdly, and perhaps comprising the strongest basis of constitutional review in Anglophone constitutions, is the supremacy provision, which expressly or implicitly states that the constitution is the supreme law of the land and that any law or action inconsistent with it is invalid to the extent of the inconsistency.[47] The existence of this power is even more compelling when the constitution expressly recognizes it by declaring void all laws that are inconsistent with its provisions.

By contrast, although centralized courts are created exclusively to deal with constitutional matters, the exact scope of their jurisdiction depends on the powers expressly or implicitly conferred on them by the constitution. The principle of constitutional supremacy does not carry the same weight and impact under centralized systems as it does within decentralized systems. When the powers of the courts provided for under the thirty-six African constitutions that adopted the centralized model are examined very closely, the differences between not only the centralized and decentralized models but also between the progressive and conservative approaches within the centralized model become very glaring. For example, under the Benin constitution, the Constitutional Court has been given express powers to exercise all three primary jurisdictional functions, namely review of constitutionality,[48] safeguarding of human rights,[49] and dealing with disputes concerning conflicts of competence.[50] At the other end is Cameroon's Constitutional Council, on which is conferred only very limited powers of constitutional review.[51]

4.2.2 Ancillary jurisdiction

Apart from the primary powers, the approach with respect to ancillary powers also differs between the decentralized and centralized systems in Africa. 'Ancillary powers' refers to 'those powers that fall outside the prototypical constitution-review function'.[52] Unless the contrary is expressly or impliedly stated, courts in Anglophone countries are able to

[45] See eg s 103(2) of the 1999 Malawian constitution, which states: 'The judiciary shall have jurisdiction over all issues of judicial nature and shall have exclusive authority to decide whether an issue is within its competence'. See also s 165(1) of the South African constitution of 1996 which states: 'The judicial authority of the Republic is vested in the courts'.

[46] See eg s 18 of the Botswana constitution of 1966 and ss 37 and 132(1)(b) of the 1996 constitution of the Gambia. Under art 33 of the Ghanaian constitution of 1992, issues concerning the enforcement of fundamental rights and freedoms are reserved to the High Court, whilst the Supreme Court under art 130(1)(a) has exclusive jurisdiction over all other issues relating to the enforcement or interpretation of the constitution. It is debatable whether the High Court can limit itself to only enforcing the provisions on fundamental rights and freedoms without indulging in their interpretation, which function is reserved to the Supreme Court.

[47] See eg s 2 of the South African constitution of 1996, which states, inter alia: 'This Constitution is the supreme law of the Republic; law or conduct inconsistent with it is invalid ...'.

[48] See art 121 of the Benin constitution of 1990. [49] ibid art 117. [50] ibid arts 104 and 117.

[51] See arts 46 and 47(1) of the Cameroon constitution of 1996.

[52] See Tom Ginsburg and Zachary Elkins, 'Ancillary Powers of Constitutional Courts' (2009) 87 *Texas Law Review* 1431.

exercise many of the powers that could be assumed to be ancillary powers. Under certain of these countries' constitutions, some of these issues are expressly reserved for special courts.[53]

In civilian jurisdictions where the centralized system has been adopted, a defined list of ancillary functions is usually conferred on the constitutional courts. These range from supervising elections and referenda[54] to the regulation of political parties,[55] the review of treaties,[56] the determination of presidential vacancy,[57] the declaration of a state of emergency,[58] the impeachment of the president (sometimes with other high government officials),[59] acting as a depository for declarations of assets,[60] acting as a *tribunal de conflit* (body to resolve conflicts of jurisdiction),[61] and a host of other issues. These are but a few examples of a long list of quasi- or extra-judicial functions that constitutional courts are increasingly required to perform. These ancillary powers vary considerably, not only in the extent to which they may require the constitutional court to refer to the constitutional text, if at all, but also in the degree to which they place these courts in the thick of potentially serious political controversies. Are these courts equipped to discharge these functions? Before we come back to this point, let us look at the types of review they carry out.

4.3 Types of review

Prior to the 1990s, Anglophone African countries that adopted the decentralized approach to constitutional adjudication did this mainly by way of concrete review; that is, the courts reviewed the constitutionality of a norm only where there was a real case or controversy. There was provision for some form of abstract review; that is, review of the constitutionality that takes place in the absence of a real case or controversy, but such cases rarely arose.[62] The exact opposite was true in the civil law jurisdictions in Africa, where abstract

[53] For example, electoral courts; see art 48(2) of the 1992 constitution of Ghana; arts 105(1) and (2), 140, and 163(3)(a) of the 2010 constitution of Kenya; s 76(3) and (5) of the 1999 constitution of Malawi; s 233(2) of the 1999 constitution of Nigeria; and arts 86, 104, 140, and 167 of the 1995 constitution of Uganda. Another example is art 88(4)(e) of the 2010 Constitution of Kenya, which gives the Independent Electoral and Boundaries Commission powers over the 'settlement of electoral disputes, including disputes relating to or arising from nominations but excluding election petitions and disputes subsequent to the declaration of election results'.

[54] See eg art 163 of the Algerian constitution of 2008; arts 4, 49, 81, and 117 of the Benin constitution of 1990; art 154 of the Burkina Faso constitution of 1991; art 48 of the Cameroonian constitution of 1996; arts 32 and 60 of the Côte d'Ivoire constitution of 2000; and arts 11, 83, and 84 of the constitution of Gabon 1990.

[55] See art 180(2)(c) of the 2010 constitution of Angola; art 156 of the Burkina Faso constitution of 1991; and art 72 of the Madagascar constitution of 2010.

[56] See eg arts 119(d) and 227 of the 2010 constitution of Angola; arts 150 and 155 of the Burkina Faso constitution of 1991; art 296 of the Burundi constitution of 2005; art 47(1) of the Cameroonian constitution of 1996; art 98 of the constitution of Central African Republic of 2013 (provisional constitution); arts 161 and 220 of the 1996 constitution of Chad; and art 216 of the DRC constitution of 2006.

[57] See eg arts 130 and 132(6) of the 2010 constitution of Angola; art 121 of the constitution of Burundi of 2005; art 6(4) of the constitution of Cameroon of 1996; and art 76 of the 1996 constitution of Chad.

[58] See eg art 68 of the Benin constitution of 1990; art 59 of the constitution of Burkina Faso of 1991; art 115 of the 2005 constitution of Burundi; and art 48 of the 2013 constitution of Central African Republic.

[59] See arts 77, 117, and 135 of the Benin constitution of 1990; art 233 of the Burundi constitution of 2005; arts 164–7 of the constitution of DRC of 2006; and art 145 of the 2003 constitution of Rwanda.

[60] See art 99 of the constitution of the DRC of 2006; art 36 of the 2010 constitution of Guinea; art 41 of the Madagascar constitution of 2010; and art 51 of the Niger constitution of 2010.

[61] See art 161 of the constitution of DRC of 2006.

[62] The most prevalent form of this was the provision in most Anglophone countries appearing in the bill of rights or section dealing with fundamental human rights, which usually gave individuals the right to invoke these provisions merely by alleging that '[a]ny of the provisions ... has been, is being or is likely to be contravened in relation to him ...'. In other words, there was no need to prove an actual violation; a potential violation was sufficient. See examples of this in s 18(1) of the Botswana constitution of 1966. It also continues to feature in some recent constitutions. For example, art 33(1) of Ghana's 1992 constitution states that: 'Where a person

Table 1 Comparing the types of review in Benin and South Africa

Country	Abstract review		Concrete review
	A priori	A posteriori	
Benin	Articles 97 and 117: constitutionality of organic laws and of laws in general in advance of their promulgation.	Article 121: ordinary laws after their promulgation into law.	Articles 114 and 118: general powers of concrete review.
	Articles 117 and 123: all the regulations of the internal National Assembly, the Economic and Social Council and the High Authority of Audio-Visuals and of Communications, before their implementation.		
	Article 121: any ordinary legislation before promulgation into law.		
South Africa	Section 79(4)(b): The President may refer a bill to the Constitutional Court for a consideration of its constitutionality.	Section 80(1): Members of the National Assembly may apply to the Constitutional Court for an order declaring that all or part of an Act of Parliament is unconstitutional.	Sections 165 and 167: general powers of concrete review.
	Section 121(2)(b): The premier of a province may refer a bill to the Constitutional Court for a consideration of its constitutionality.	Section 122(1): Members of a provincial legislature may apply to the Constitutional Court for an order declaring that all or part of a provincial Act is unconstitutional.	

review was the norm and concrete review the exception (generally limited to matters such as election disputes). Even though the changes that have taken place since the 1990s reforms still fall within the decentralized/centralized models divide, there have been a number of interesting developments. From these developments, two general observations can be made.

First, the constitutions of only two countries in Africa make provision for the combination of elements of abstract review, both a priori and a posteriori to the promulgation of legislation, and open concrete review. It is not surprising that these are the constitutions of the countries with the most active constitutional courts on the continent, namely the Benin Constitutional Court and the South African Constitutional Court. As Table 1 above shows, Benin has not only retained abstract review, but has also incorporated an open system of concrete review, while South Africa has incorporated elements of abstract review along with the concrete review normally associated with decentralized systems.

alleges that a provision of this Constitution on the fundamental human rights and freedoms has been, is being or is likely to be contravened in relation to him, then, without prejudice to any other action that is lawfully available, that person may apply to the High Court for redress'.

Secondly, all constitutions in civilian jurisdictions provide for prior review of all organic legislation before their promulgation into law (a priori abstract review).[63] With respect to ordinary legislation, pre-promulgation review was the norm but, since the 1990s, post-promulgation review is allowed under many of the progressive constitutions. Concrete constitutional review is also allowed for many constitutional matters in most civilian constitutions. As regards the group of countries that have adopted the conservative approach, constitutional courts are not only limited to abstract review, but concrete review is not allowed except in issues concerning elections.[64] The restrictions of the jurisdiction *rationae materiae* are closely linked with the other equally important issue of who has *locus standi* to bring matters before the courts: it is the jurisdiction *rationae personae* that we will now turn to.

4.4 Types of access

However broad the jurisdiction of a constitutional court may be, it will serve no purpose if there are unreasonable restrictions which prevent litigants from approaching the court. As pointed out earlier, one of the major weaknesses of the constitutional council model that most African civilian jurisdictions copied was the fact that only a restricted group of persons and institutions had *locus standi* to seize it. More importantly, private individuals had no right of access. This virtually ensured that hardly any matter was brought before these courts. By contrast, in Anglophone Africa, one of the major obstacles to constitutional litigation was the high cost of litigation. This made access difficult for the poor and other vulnerable members of society, who were often the principal victims of constitutional violations.

Access restrictions are certainly necessary to filter out frivolous claims and vexatious litigants. This is particularly so where there is only one constitutional court for an entire country, as is the case in civilian jurisdictions. In trying to assess whether the scope for access to constitutional justice today is better than it was before the 1990s, a distinction needs to be made between direct access and indirect access.

4.4.1 Direct access

Direct access refers to those circumstances under which an individual whose constitutional right has been violated can approach the court. While direct access has always been the norm in the common law systems, it has been the exception in the civilian systems. Although there have been serious attempts to broaden the scope of individual access in most civilian systems, there are still a good number of countries where, except in electoral matters, private individuals do not have direct access to the constitutional court.[65]

[63] In civilian systems, organic laws have an intermediate status between the ordinary law and the constitution itself. They have a constitutional scope and force and, therefore, override ordinary statutes. They are more flexible because they can be enacted by parliament without going through the cumbersome process of amending the constitution. See further Francis Haman and Michel Troper, *Droit Constitutionnel* (31st edn, LGDJ 2009) 41.

[64] Examples of these are the Constitutional Courts of Burkina Faso (see constitution of 1991); Cameroon (see arts 46 and 47 of the constitution of 1996); Chad (see art 161 of the constitution of 1996); and Côte d'Ivoire (see arts 94–97 of the constitution of 2000).

[65] See eg Algeria (2008 constitution); Burkina Faso (1991 constitution); Cameroon (1996 constitution); Chad (1996 constitution); Côte d'Ivoire (2000 constitution); Djibouti (1992 constitution); Guinea (2010 constitution); Madagascar (2010 constitution); Malawi (1992 constitution); Mauritania (1991 constitution); Morocco (2011 constitution); Rwanda (2003 constitution); Republic of Congo (2001 constitution); São Tomé and Principe (1990 constitution); Senegal (2010 constitution); Togo (1992 constitution); Tunisia (2011 constitution); and Cape Verde (1992 constitution).

The main form of direct access is by way of a right of direct individual action. Usually, an individual has a right of direct action in all common law jurisdictions where his or her constitutionally or legally protected rights or interests have been infringed. These rights or interests must usually be of a personal nature, especially where a party seeks to use the writ of *amparo*.[66]

The doctrine of *locus standi* only permits individuals whose rights or other legally protected interests have been infringed to petition the constitutional court. This is generally not efficient in dealing with constitutional violations involving state interference with public rights or direct infringement of individual rights, especially if the individual concerned lacks the means to bring the matter before the constitutional court. The concept of public interest litigation developed in India since the Indian Supreme Court decision in *SP Gupta v Union of India*[67] has been used to overcome the constraints of the strict application of the *locus standi* doctrine. Public interest litigation operates as a form of *actio popularis*, which allows an individual or group to bring an action without needing to prove that they have any personal interest in the matter. This has been formally entrenched in some post-1990 constitutions, starting with the South African 1996 constitution, which in section 167(6)(a) states:

> National legislation or the rules of the Constitutional Court must allow a person *when it is in the interests of justice* and with leave of the Constitutional Court: (a) to bring a matter directly to the Constitutional Court (emphasis added).

There are a few other examples of this in both civil and common law jurisdictions.[68] However, the most expanded scope for such public interest action to vindicate an individual right is provided for under the 2010 Kenyan constitution. Article 22 provides:

> (1) Every person has the right to institute court proceedings claiming that a right or fundamental freedom in the Bill of Rights has been denied, violated or infringed, or is threatened.
> (2) In addition to a person acting in their own interest, court proceedings under clause (1) may be instituted by—
> (a) a person acting on behalf of another person who cannot act in their own name;
> (b) a person acting as a member of, or in the interest of, a group or class of persons;
> (c) *a person acting in the public interest*; or
> (d) an association acting in the interest of one or more of its members.[69]

In civilian jurisdictions, the right of personal action is the exception rather than the rule, and it was only after the 1990s that many progressive constitutions expressly allowed for such direct action. Article 122 of the 1990 constitution of Benin makes the following provision for what is referred to as a right of complaint:

[66] So far, only art 95(2)(b) of the 1982 constitution of Equatorial Guinea provides for this. It can be invoked by any person who believes that his constitutional rights have been violated regardless of whether it is by a public or private authority. It is a very inexpensive procedure and is often free because it may not require legal counsel, but several conditions need to be met, including a lack of any other mechanism under which to file the claim.

[67] [1982] AIR SC 149.

[68] See eg art 137(3)(a) of the 1995 constitution of Uganda which states: 'A person who alleges that—(a) an Act of Parliament or any other law or anything in or done under the authority of any law; or (b) any act or omission by any person or authority, is inconsistent with or *in contravention of a provision of this Constitution*, may petition the constitutional court for a declaration to that effect, and for redress where appropriate' (emphasis added). The best example of this appears in art 122 of the Benin constitution of 1990, which states: '*Any citizen* may complain to the Constitutional Court about the constitutionality of laws whether directly …' (emphasis added).

[69] See in very similar terms s 85(1) of the 2013 Zimbabwean constitution (emphasis added).

> Any citizen may complain to the Constitutional Court about the constitutionality of laws whether directly or whether by the procedure of the exception of unconstitutionality invoked in a matter which concerns him before a court of law.

There seems to be no reason to assume that this is anything more than a right of direct action, which must be distinguished from the right of complaint in German constitutional practice, which is contingent on the exhaustion of all other legal remedies.

Article 255(2)(g) of the 2004 constitution of Mozambique allows 2,000 citizens to bring an action before the Constitutional Council. It is not exactly clear whether it strictly requires all 2,000 to be actively involved in the action or whether it is sufficient for them to sign a petition. Article 86(2)(d) of the Somali 2012 provisional constitution contains a similar requirement, for 10,000 or more registered voters, but the language suggests that it is simply a minimum number of persons needed to render a matter receivable.

4.4.2 Indirect access

As noted earlier, until the 1990s indirect access was the only means by which constitutional issues could be ventilated in the civilian jurisdictions in Africa. This effectively restricted the right to seize constitutional courts to certain persons or institutions such as the president, parliament, and ordinary courts. The access rules have changed considerably, but the main forms of indirect access consist of referrals from political or government entities, referral from an ordinary court by way of incidental review or exception to unconstitutionality, and referral through a type of filtering process. It must be noted that these referrals can be for the purpose of an abstract review (a priori or a posteriori) or with reference to a specific case (concrete review).

The French Constitutional Council in its original 1958 design excluded the right of direct access and only allowed indirect access limited to the very politicians who, as the main sponsors of legislation, often had little reason to challenge its constitutionality.[70] In all but a few Francophone constitutions,[71] the scope for indirect access has been considerably enhanced. Thus, it is not merely the presidents of the republic, the senate, and the national assembly that may seize the constitutional courts, but also members of both houses of parliament and others. The significant change has been that the threshold for the members of the national assembly and senate who qualify to bring a matter before the constitutional courts has been reasonably lowered to enable opposition parties today to petition for an abstract (the normal practice) and concrete (in most progressive constitutions) review of constitutionality. The threshold varies widely, the broadest being the rare instances where an individual member of parliament is given the power to seize the court, as is provided for under Article 121 of the Benin 1990 constitution, which states:

> The Constitutional Court, at the request of the President of the Republic or *of any member of the National Assembly*, shall give its opinion on the constitutionality of laws in advance of their promulgation (emphasis added).

[70] In this respect, art 61 of the constitution stated, inter alia: 'To the same end, Acts of Parliament may be referred to the Constitutional Council, before their promulgation, by the President of the Republic, the Prime Minister, the President of the National Assembly, the President of the Senate, sixty Members of the National Assembly or sixty Senators'.

[71] It must be pointed out that there are also some referrals reserved for government officials under some Anglophone constitutions, eg under the Malawian constitution of 1994, s 89(1)(h), to refer disputes of a constitutional nature to the High Court.

Although mostly civilian jurisdictions provide for this,[72] South Africa, which is one of the few common law countries to have adopted elements of abstract review (both a priori and a posteriori), gives members of its legislature the powers to challenge legislation on grounds of its constitutionality.[73]

In addition to these traditional forms of indirect access, in recent years, other governmental and semi-governmental entities have been given powers to seize the constitutional courts. For example, under the 2010 Angolan constitution, Article 230 allows parliamentary groups, the Attorney-General, the Ombudsman, and the Bar Association to seize the courts. Article 85 of the 1990 Gabonese constitution allows petitions to be brought by the presidents of the Court of Cassation,[74] of the Council of State, and of the Court of Accounts. In some cases, such as under Article 96 of the 2010 constitution of Guinea, human rights bodies are expressly given the mandate to petition the Constitutional Court on matters dealing with human rights.[75] The only possible explanation for these provisions is the desire to broaden the category of those who qualify to bring claims before the constitutional courts.

A second form of indirect action, which is particularly common in modern civilian constitutions, occurs by way of incidental review. Unlike the previous forms of action, which may occur in the course of an abstract or concrete review, incidental review only occurs in the course of an actual case being heard in court. It gives one of the parties to the matter the right to raise the issue of unconstitutionality and to request that this issue be resolved by the competent court before the case proceeds. For example, Article 46(7) of the 1993 constitution of Seychelles states the following in this regard:

> Where in the course of any proceedings in any court, other than the Constitutional Court or the Court of Appeal, a question arises with regard to whether there has been or is likely to be a contravention of the Charter, the court shall, if it is satisfied that the question is not frivolous or vexatious or has already been the subject of a decision of the Constitutional Court or the Court of Appeal, immediately adjourn the proceedings and refer the question for determination by the Constitutional Court.[76]

In Mozambique, Article 247 of its 2004 constitution allows the referral of a Supreme Court decision which refuses to apply any law on grounds of its unconstitutionality.

The third form of indirect action may occur through the raising of an exception of unconstitutionality. This is where parties to proceedings before an ordinary court raise doubts about the constitutionality of a statute being applied in the proceedings and suggest

[72] A few examples of ways in which access by politicians in the legislature has been broadened will suffice. See arts 228 and 230 of the 2010 constitution of Angola, which provides for petitions by 10% of members of the National Assembly and 20% when invoking art 232(1); it is one-quarter of members of the National Assembly or the Senate under arts 228 and 230 of the 2005 Burundi constitution; one-third of members of the National Assembly or Senate under arts 47(2) and 48(3) of Cameroon's 1996 constitution; 10 members of parliament under art 35 of the 1992 constitution of Djibouti.

[73] In this respect, s 80(2) of the 1996 constitution allows 1one-third of its members of parliament to refer an Act of Parliament to the Constitutional Court and 20% of the members of the provincial legislative council to refer a provincial Act to the Court under s 122(2)(a).

[74] Article 88 of the 1992 constitution of Mali also authorizes the president of the Supreme Court to petition the Constitutional Court.

[75] See also art 245(2) of the 2004 constitution of Mozambique, which authorizes the Attorney-General and the Ombudsman to seize the Constitutional Council.

[76] Article 130(6) of the same constitution repeats this. For examples in other constitutions see art 180(2)(e) of the Angola constitution of 2010; art 70 of the 2013 constitution of Central African Republic; art 80 of the 1992 constitution of Djibouti; and art 120 of the 2014 constitution of Tunisia.

that the matter be referred to the constitutional court. The judge must then consider and justify any refusal and can only do so on a limited number of grounds. An example of a provision that provides for this is Article 22 of the Benin constitution of 1990, which states:

> Any citizen may complain to the Constitutional Court about the constitutionality of laws whether directly or whether by the procedure of the exception of unconstitutionality invoked in a matter which concerns him before a court of law. This must grant a stay until the decision of the Constitutional Court which must be reached within a period of thirty days.[77]

Finally, a matter may go to the constitutional court indirectly through a filtering process. This may be seen as an attempt to balance the need to allow litigants to have access to the court with the need to prevent these courts from being inundated with frivolous and vexatious claims. This filtering process may take various forms. Under Article 80 of the Djibouti constitution of 1992, if a party raises the exception of unconstitutionality, then the court before which the matter has been raised refers the case to the Supreme Court. It is the Supreme Court that will decide whether or not the challenge is well founded, in which case it then refers the matter to the Constitutional Court for a formal determination.[78] Another form of filtering is provided for under the South African constitution. In this regard, section 167(5) states:

> The Constitutional Court makes the final decision whether an Act of Parliament, a provincial Act or conduct of the President is constitutional, and must confirm any order of invalidity made by the Supreme Court of Appeal, the High Court of South Africa, or a court of similar status, before that order has any force.[79]

Section 172(2)(a) and (b) has a similar effect. This ensures that only serious issues raised before the lower courts eventually reach the Constitutional Court, and also that there is a reasonable degree of legal certainty and predictability. In this way, the South African legislator addresses one of the major weaknesses of the decentralized model of judicial review; that is, the risk of divergent interpretation of the same text by the different decentralized courts.

Another equally important issue—besides matters relating to the scope of powers, the type of review, and the form of access—is the type of decisions that the constitutional court makes, which we will turn to next.

4.5 Forms of judicial decisions and remedies

As we have seen, constitutional courts deal with a broad range of issues that may not necessarily involve the strict interpretation or application of the text of the constitution itself. From the preceding discussion, a number of questions arise. Do the decisions that the constitutional courts make reflect the diversity of issues that they have to deal with?

[77] Other examples include art 230 of the Burundi constitution of 2005; art 77 of the constitution of the Central African Republic of 2013; art 36 of the constitution of the Comoros of 2001; art 96 of the constitution of Côte d'Ivoire of 2000; art 162 of the 2005 constitution of DRC; and art 86 of the constitution of Gabon of 1990.

[78] See art 147 of the 1991 constitution of Burkina Faso, which provides that the decision whether a matter that arises in proceedings before an ordinary court should be referred to the Constitutional Council will be decided upon by either the Court of Cassation for matters before the ordinary courts or the Council of State for matters before the administrative courts.

[79] See ss 167(3) and 175(1) of the 2013 Zimbabwe constitution, which provides that orders of invalidity on constitutional grounds made by lower courts will only take effect after they have been confirmed by the Constitutional Court.

Are they given the powers to provide the remedies that will adequately deal with these issues?

An analysis of the powers given to African constitutional courts to resolve constitutional disputes shows that they are required to make either binding or non-binding decisions. The non-binding decisions take the form of different varieties of advisory opinions. This raises a number of interesting issues.

In respect of binding decisions, common law jurisdictions have often given the courts a broad discretion in terms of what orders they may make when a finding of constitutional violation is ascertained, especially when it concerns a human rights provision. A typical example of such a provision will state that the court may 'make such orders, issue such writs and give such direction as it may consider appropriate for the purpose of enforcing or securing the enforcement of any of the provisions'.[80] The 2010 Kenyan constitution is even more elaborate. In Article 23(3) it states that the court may grant any 'appropriate relief, including …', and it then proceeds to list a number of possible remedies. These include a declaration of rights; an injunction; a conservatory order; a declaration of invalidity of any law that denies, violates, infringes, or threatens a right or fundamental freedom in the bill of rights and is not justified under Article 24(e); an order for compensation; and an order of judicial review. Arguably, such broad powers give the court the authority to exercise some of the powers that section 175(5)(b) of the 2013 Zimbabwean constitution expressly confers to its Constitutional Court, namely, the power to

> [m]ake any order that is just and equitable, including an order limiting the retrospective effect of the declaration of invalidity and an order suspending conditionally or unconditionally the declaration of invalidity for any period to allow the competent authority to correct the defect.[81]

Generally, civilian constitutions do not confer similar flexible powers on their constitutional courts.[82] Be that as it may, two points need to be noted. First, the wording of the constitutional provisions in most Anglophone countries either expressly or implicitly allows room for damages or some form of compensation to be awarded to those whose constitutional rights have been violated. This is obviously not the case in civilian jurisdictions. Secondly, the perennial problem of the non-enforcement of binding decisions by governments is addressed in the most innovative and decisive manner by the 1992 Ghanaian constitution, which states that non-compliance with a court order or decision, especially by the executive, is a 'high crime'.[83]

As regards non-binding decisions, these take diverse forms. There are instances where the scope of matters that are subject to such advisory jurisdiction almost corresponds with that

[80] See eg s 18(2)(b) of the 1966 Botswana constitution.

[81] See also a similar approach in s 172(1) of the 1996 South African constitution.

[82] See eg art 159 of the 1991 Burkina Faso constitution and art 231 of the 2005 constitution of Burundi. There are obviously some exceptions. For example, under art 231(4) of the 2010 Angolan constitution, the Constitutional Court may, when necessary 'for the purposes of legal certainty, reasons of fairness or matters of exceptionally important public interest, which must be duly justified', rule that the scope of the effects of the unconstitutionality or illegality be more restricted than would ordinarily be the case.

[83] In this regard, art 2 states: '2. The Supreme Court shall, for the purposes of a declaration under clause (1) of this article, make such orders and give such directions as it may consider appropriate for giving effect, or enabling effect to be given, to the declaration so made. 3. Any person or group of persons to whom an order or direction is addressed under clause (2) of this article by the Supreme Court, shall duly obey and carry out the terms of the order or direction. 4. Failure to obey or carry out the terms of an order or direction made or given under clause (2) of this article constitutes *a high crime under this Constitution and shall, in the case of the President or the Vice-President, constitute a ground for removal from office under this Constitution.* 5. A person convicted of a high crime under clause (4) of this article shall (a) be liable to imprisonment not exceeding ten years without the option of a fine; and (b) not be eligible for election, or for appointment, to any public office for ten years beginning with the date of the expiration of the term of imprisonment' (emphasis added).

of matters that the court is competent to entertain. An example of this is Article 47(4) of the 1996 Cameroon constitution, which states that: '[t]he Constitutional Council shall advise in matters falling under its jurisdiction'. Of narrower scope is Article 163(6) of the 2010 Kenyan constitution, which states:

> The Supreme Court may give an advisory opinion at the request of the national government, any State organ, or any county government with respect to any matter concerning county government.

Numerous constitutions, particularly in civil law jurisdictions, provide that the constitutional court should be 'consulted' in cases where an emergency is going to be declared,[84] or when parliament is going to be dissolved.[85] There are others which state that the 'opinion' or 'advice' of the court should be sought with respect to the regularity of ordinances[86] or before the holding of a referendum,[87] or in a host of other situations.[88] Consulting and obtaining the opinion or advice of the constitutional court, as contemplated by most of these constitutions, is probably understandable as a way of giving it some leeway to mediate these issues, which may not necessarily entail the niceties of legal interpretation. However, given that the court's views on these matters are not binding, what happens where some of the parties involved ignore the advice given?

Where the court is given a discretion in the matter, such as under Article 163(6) of the Kenyan 2010 constitution, it may decide to make its opinion binding if the same issue is brought before it. This will not necessarily be the case in other circumstances because this is the only manner in which the court is given jurisdiction in such matters. This effectively narrows the scope of the court's jurisdiction in dealing with these matters. If one considers the fact that most of the expansion of civilian jurisdictions in Africa has been in favour of giving them powers to make non-binding opinions, decisions, or suggestions, this raises practical questions as to whether there has really been an extension in the scope of constitutional justice.

5. Some Tentative Conclusions on the Assessment of the Prospects and Challenges of Constitutional Justice

At the beginning of this chapter, a number of reasons were given why constitutional adjudication did not function as it should have done to safeguard, protect, and ensure the sanctity of post-independence African constitutions. A brief overview was given of the reforms that have taken place in the past two decades. The question that must now be asked is whether these reforms have sufficiently equipped African constitutional courts to play the role that constitutional courts should play; that is, to act as defenders, protectors, and promoters not only of constitutional democracy but also as bulwark against authoritarianism in all its forms and manifestations. Does the existence of provisions providing

[84] See eg art 68 of the Benin constitution of 1990; art 59 of the 1991 Burkina Faso constitution; art 39 of the 1992 Djibouti constitution; art 90 of the 2010 constitution of Guinea, arts 61 and 65(10) of the 2010 constitution of Madagascar; art 50 of the 1992 constitution of Mali; and art 59 of the 2011 constitution of Morocco.

[85] See eg art 104 of the 2011 constitution of Morocco; art 133 of the 2003 constitution of Rwanda; and art 92 of the 2001 constitution of the Republic of Congo.

[86] See arts 102 and 104 of the 1990 constitution of Benin; art 107 of the 1991 constitution of Burkina Faso; arts 160 and 161 of the 2005 constitution of Burundi; arts 100 and 103 of the 2010 constitution of Niger; and arts 69 and 86 of the 1992 constitution of Togo.

[87] See eg art 86 of the 1996 constitution of Chad; art 33 of the 1992 constitution of Djibouti; art 36 of the 1992 constitution of Mali; art 60 of the 2010 constitution of Niger; art 86 of the 2001 constitution of the Republic of Congo; and art 51 of the 2010 constitution of Senegal.

[88] See eg arts 15(4), 36(1) and 60(2) of the 1996 constitution of Cameroon; and arts 75 and 97 of the 2010 constitution of Côte d'Ivoire.

for constitutional review guarantee accessible, effective, and credible constitutional justice for all?

For a variety of reasons, the above overview can only provide a basis for some tentative conclusions. There are a number of caveats subject to which the conclusions here must be understood. First, there are some indications that many of these new or revised constitutions have raised people's expectations without changing the fundamental realities on the ground because of the wide divergence between the constitutional text and actual practice on the ground. Many African governments adopted constitutions that provided for constitutional courts with little more than symbolic value, for the sake of appearing to be in tune with international best practice more than anything else. For example, Cameroon's constitution of 1996 provided inter alia for the establishment of a constitutional council to deal with constitutional issues, but such a body has not as yet been created. Similarly, the DRC constitution of 2006 provided for the establishment of a constitutional court, but the members of this court were only sworn in in April 2015. In other words, in spite of the clear terms of the constitution, there are still many African leaders who pick and choose what constitutional provisions they will implement.

Secondly, there are a number of countries where, in spite of the existence of constitutions, they are too unstable to be considered as being under any form of constitutional governance. Such is the case with Eritrea, Libya, and Somalia. Even in most reasonably stable countries, the perennial appetite for changing constitutions has merely been diminished, not eliminated.[89] Thirdly, the focus of the preceding analysis has been on what the various constitutions say. No account has been taken in this study of subsidiary legislation, which may complement and possibly fill in gaps. However, it is unlikely that such legislation can create any new rights or obligations that were not provided for in a constitution itself. Hence, it is doubtful that a weak system of constitutional review can be remedied by subsidiary legislation.

Fourthly, many of the provisions in certain constitutions, especially those from the civil law tradition, that regulate important aspects such as the structure, powers, and organization of the constitutional courts, are subject to regulation by ordinary laws. There is often no guarantee that the laws adopted will facilitate and not place obstacles in the way of constitutional adjudication. The country studies and other chapters will throw further light on what actually happens in practice. Nevertheless, the preceding analysis provides a basis for a number of important tentative conclusions.

In many respects, the nature and scope of the powers given to modern African constitutional courts are consistent with certain theories that have been used to explain the expansion and spread of constitutional courts since 1945, but more particularly since the fall of the Berlin Wall and the constitutional reforms in Eastern Europe. In the African context, the so-called 'federal logic of judicial review'[90] is manifested not as an increase in the number of federal jurisdictions, but rather by way of increased decentralization and the deconcentration of powers. The extensive fragmentation of powers, both horizontally and vertically, while expanding the scope of participation in decision-making, has increased the scope for and levels of conflicts that require the mediating role of a constitutional court. It is, therefore, not surprising that most modern African countries,

[89] See generally Charles M Fombad, 'Constitution-building in Africa: The Never-ending Story of the Making, Unmaking and Remaking of Constitutions' (2014) 13 *African and Asian Studies* 429.

[90] See generally Bruce Ackerman, 'The Rise of World Constitutionalism' (1997) 83 *Virginia Law Review* 771–97; and Martin Shapiro, 'Federalism, the Race to the Bottom and the Regulation-averse Entrepreneur' in Harry Scheiber (ed), *North American and Comparative Federalism* (Institute of Governmental Studies Press 1992).

regardless of their system of governance, whether federal or semi-federal (for example Nigeria and South Africa) and even centralized (with widely decentralized and deconcentrated powers), have given constitutional courts powers to deal with conflicts between the different levels of government.[91]

It is also clear that the spread of democracy and a culture of human rights have been very important factors in the adoption of constitutional review by African governments.[92]

One of the modern theories that appears very aptly to explain the approach adopted by constitution designers is that of constitutional review as a form of political insurance. While almost all the countries maintained the systems they inherited at independence, the political dynamics at the time of the drafting of their constitutions played a very important, and sometimes even decisive, part in the potential effectiveness of the design chosen, regardless of the model. According to the political insurance theory, stronger political parties have less desire for an effective and independent constitutional review system than weaker political parties.[93]

The converse is equally true. In other words, where the political elites see themselves losing power or where there is political uncertainty, all parties make an effort to set up an effective system of constitutional review to preserve the bargains embodied in the constitution. This is exactly what happened in Benin in 1990 and in South Africa in 1994. It is, therefore, not surprising that these two countries do not only have the most progressive constitutions of their genre, but also the most effective constitutional courts. The constitution-making process in both countries was an inclusive one in which all parties participated on more or less equal footing and, therefore, had an interest in preserving the hard-earned bargains they had negotiated.

This is clearly in line with the insurance theory. By contrast, countries such as Burkina Faso and Cameroon manifest clear examples of hegemonic preservation that saw the constitution-making process forced on recalcitrant incumbents, who were nevertheless able to retain control and manipulate the outcome to ensure that they did no more than adopt a symbolic and ineffective form of constitutional review that has perpetuated the *status quo ante*.

Although current developments clearly show that the centralized model is the dominant form of constitutional review in Africa, a closer look at the nature of how this model operates suggests that, in spite of the deep theoretical and historical underpinnings that distinguish this from the decentralized model, there are considerable signs of convergence. This is manifested in several ways. First, almost all civilian jurisdictions which at independence focused almost exclusively on abstract review, with *locus standi* for bringing, apart from election disputes, limited only to certain government officials, now

[91] For dealing with conflicts within a unitary but decentralized framework and between institutions see art 117 of the Benin constitution of 1990; art 47(1) of the 1996 Cameroonian constitution; and art 95(2)(f) of the constitution of Equatorial Guinea of 1982. For examples of a federal or quasi-federal framework see ss 232(1) and 251(1)(9) of the 1999 constitution of Nigeria; s 167(4)(a) of the 1996 constitution of the Republic of South Africa; and arts 128(2)(j) and 168(10) of the 2011 constitution of South Sudan.

[92] See generally Lee Epstein, Jack Knight, and Olga Shvetsova, 'The Role of Constitutional Courts in the Establishment and Maintenance of Democratic Systems of Government' (2001) *Law and Society Review* 35, 117–64; and Tom Ginsburg, *Judicial Review in New Democracies: Constitutional Courts in Asian Cases* (Cambridge University Press 2003).

[93] See generally Rebecca Chavez, *The Rule of Law in Nascent Democracies: Judicial Politics in Argentina* (Stanford University Press 2004); Matthew Stephenson, 'When the Devil Turns: The Political Foundations of Independent Judicial Review' (2004) *Journal of Legal Studies* 32, 59–81; and Ginsburg (n 4) 83–7.

provide for concrete review and have also expanded the rules of standing to allow individual citizens to bring claims.

Of course, there are some countries, such as Burkina Faso, Cameroon, Guinea, Mali, Morocco, Mauritania, Rwanda, and Tunisia, where concrete and a posteriori review is still excluded; but these are the exception rather than the rule. One could also suggest that the use of 'filtering' procedures has to some extent 'decentralised' constitutional adjudication. But there are also movements within the decentralized systems towards a more centralized approach. The best example of this is the requirement under the South African and Zimbabwean constitutions that, while other lower courts can declare a piece of legislation or action as unconstitutional, this will only take effect when confirmed by the constitutional court.[94]

Other features associated with the centralized model, which South Africa has adopted, are the several avenues provided for abstract review of legislation.[95] In many respects, the Benin and the South African Constitutional Courts, which are clearly the most dynamic constitutional courts on the continent, manifest many signs of cross-systemic fertilization of ideas and convergence of the two methods. In the case of Benin, we have the exceptional and unusual instance of a Francophone African country thinking outside the 'French colonial box' in which it had been locked since independence, particularly after its reforms of the constitutional council model in 1990 preceded similar reforms in its mother country (France) by eighteen years. Thus, although the centralized model is increasingly more popular, the practical effect of this, however, points to an evolution which favours the use of the traditional court system rather than the historical suspicion of judicial involvement in constitutional adjudication in civil law jurisdictions.

There nevertheless remain significant differences in approach between the centralized and decentralized systems, which are bound to have an impact on the quality of constitutional justice dispensed. In almost all common law jurisdictions, constitutional courts operate from a presumption of broad jurisdiction to settle all disputes concerning the interpretation and application of the constitution unless expressly or implicitly limited,[96] whereas in the civilian jurisdictions the reverse is true. In the latter, the jurisdiction of constitutional courts is often clearly but narrowly defined. It is, however, in respect of what is classified as the ancillary jurisdiction of these courts that a number of interesting issues are raised. The scope for ancillary powers under the civilian-style constitutions is relatively broad. These range from dealing with disputes such as those concerning elections and referenda and issues related thereto, to those concerning political parties, a state of emergency, the review of treaties, impeachment of the president and other senior state officials, the determination of a vacancy in the presidency, advising on matters concerning ordinances, dealing with declarations of assets, and advising on the dissolution of parliament.

The expanding scope of ancillary powers given to constitutional courts in modern civilian constitutions poses a number of serious challenges for the future. These powers vary considerably in the extent to which they require courts to refer to a constitutional text, if

[94] See, however, the recent South African Constitutional Court decision in *Khohliso v S and Another* [2015] JOL 32616 (CC), where the court held that the section 167(5) confirmation of any declaration of unconstitutionality only applied to an Act of Parliament, a provincial Act or conduct of the president and not a decree that had been issued in 1992 under the apartheid regime.

[95] See eg ss 79(4)(b) and (5), 121(2)(b), and 167(4)(b) of the Constitution of the Republic of South Africa.

[96] For example, in some of these jurisdictions, election disputes are reserved for special courts and may only come to the Constitutional Court on appeal. See eg secs 76(3) and (5) of the Malawian constitution of 1999; and sec 285 of the 1999 constitution of Nigeria.

at all. This so-called 'judicialisation' of 'mega' or 'pure politics', as Hirschl calls it, appears to be a modern trend which has seen 'the ever-accelerating reliance on courts and judicial means for addressing core moral predicaments, public policy questions and political controversies'.[97] According to Hirschl, this 'judicialisation' or 'juristocracy'[98] trend has been one of the most important phenomena of the late twentieth and early twenty-first centuries and has been almost unequivocally endorsed by some scholars.[99]

Even if this were so, it is doubtful whether this is an appropriate approach to adopt in Africa's fragile democracies. African constitutional courts are still struggling to gain the respect and confidence of the public and to assert themselves after decades of being under the domination and subordination of powerful and repressive executives. Their involvement in issues that place them in the thick of the bitter political conflicts that have become commonplace today risks undermining their authority and credibility. This is particularly so where they are required merely to express 'opinions', 'suggestions', and 'advice', or are only 'consulted' on these matters. There is increasingly a risk that constitutional adjudicators will be seen not as defenders of constitutionalism and constitutional justice, but rather as a means by which the affluent and powerful elite are able to restrain and control, if not indeed suppress, the wider democratic yearnings and impulses of the people.

This may result in a judicially mediated democracy, not on terms that promote constitutional democracy, but rather on terms that satisfy the ruling elites. The less a court is required to deal with issues requiring an interpretation and application of the constitution, and the more it is involved in, for example, registering political parties or the names of those who declare their assets (especially in situations such as the latter, where the duty of the court is not to verify its accuracy), the more the court could be seen as complicit in any eventual irregularities. This would compromise its credibility and legitimacy vis-à-vis the public. On the other hand, when dragged into unwinnable zero-sum conflicts, Africa's young constitutional courts lack the experience to negotiate their way out of this and, where they antagonize the powerful political elites, this may generate a backlash from the latter who may feel that these unelected judges are overstepping their mandates and overreaching themselves.[100]

There is no debate that the mandate to deal with electoral disputes is one of the most controversial powers modern African constitutional courts have to deal with. While the constitutional courts in civilian jurisdictions are usually given short and unrealistic timelines to deal with these cases, the constitutional courts in common law jurisdictions often deal with such matters as the last resort. The outcomes are hardly ever satisfactory. Faced with unrealistic time constraints and an increasingly dominant party environment, the court either strategically favours the incumbent or, as in common law countries, hides behind legal technicalities or uses protracted delays to achieve the same purpose.[101]

97 Ran Hirschl, 'The New Constitutionalism and the Judicialization of Pure Politics Wordwide' (2006) 75 *Fordham Law Review* 721.

98 See generally Ran Hirschl, *Toward Juristocracy* (Harvard University Press 2004).

99 See Ginsburg and Versteeg (n 4).

100 This is precisely the point that South African courts, particularly its superior courts, have reached vis-à-vis the ruling African National Congress (ANC) government, which interprets every unfavourable judicial decision as an attempt by the judiciary to undermine its authority. For example, the Secretary-General of the ANC, Gwede Mantashe, has in the past described the judiciary as 'counter-revolutionaries' and accused it of 'attempting to overthrow the government'. Another senior minister has criticized it for 'encroaching on the territory of the executive'. See 'Editorial: A Resounding Slap from SA's Judges' *BusinessDayLive* (9 July 2015) www.bdlive.co.za/opinion/editorials/2015/07/09/editorial-a-resounding-slap-from-sas-judges (last accessed 13 April 2017).

101 For examples of cases where courts hide behind technical rules to defeat the ends of substantive justice see the Kenyan case of *Mwai Kibaki v Daniel Arap Moi* Court of Appeal Civil Application No 172 (Election

The entrenchment of constitutional review in modern African constitutions is an indication of the recognition and acceptance of democracy and multi-partyism as the best form of governance. However, the progressive increase in the all-pervasive control now exercised throughout the continent by dominant parties that have also captured the executive and legislature is now one of the greatest threats, not only to the independence of constitutional courts, but also to their ability to operate and dispense fair, objective, and predictable constitutional justice. This has been compounded not only by their increasing involvement in resolving disputes of a political nature, but also by the manner in which those who sit in these courts are selected. From this perspective, there is a major difference between common law jurisdictions and civil law jurisdictions. Unlike in the former, those appointed to sit in constitutional courts in civil law jurisdictions need not all have any legal training,[102] and they are appointed by the increasingly powerful ruling elites.

Another common feature in civilian jurisdictions is the expanding role of the constitutional court acting as a 'negative legislator'. While the legislature functions as a 'positive legislator' by introducing statutes into the legal system, the constitutional courts of almost all the civilian countries studied have been given a wide-ranging role to expunge in an abstract a priori or a posterior proceedings, provisions in statutes which infringe the constitution (negative legislator). This has many implications for the effectiveness of constitutional justice. First, while the legislature has an electoral mandate and thus democratic legitimacy to perform the law-making function, it can hardly be said that constitutional court judges have such a mandate. This is probably where the counter-majoritarian argument and questions about the legitimacy of constitutional review under a written constitution finds its strongest expression, and where the confusion between the court

Petition No 1 of 1998), where it was held that the petitioner had not effected personal or direct service to the respondent who, as president, had surrounded himself with presidential security which made this impossible. In *Rally for Democracy and Progress and Others v Electoral Commission of Namibia and Others* High Court Case No A01/2010, the court held that a petition that was filed at 16:30 instead of 15:00 was out of time and invalid. In *John Opong Benjamin and Others v National Electoral Commission* SC No 2/2012, Supreme Court of Sierra Leone, Judgment of 14 June 2013, the court rejected a petition on the ground that it was filed out of time because of a delay in the payment of costs and the failure of the contracts of lawyers to be on a separate notice. In *Atiku Abubakar v Umaru Musa Yar'adua* SC 72/2008, Supreme Court of Nigeria, Judgment of 12 December 2008, the court held that the fact that the Electoral Act used the word 'and' meant that the petitioner had to choose between the alternatives and could, therefore, only plead one set of grounds and not all of them. Courts have also regularly misused the substantial effect rule, which provides that elections should not be nullified for minor irregularities or infractions of rules, even where evidence is provided of serious irregularities such as fraud, violence, corruption of officials, and cheating. See the decisions in the Ugandan case of *Kizza Besigye v Yoweri Museveni* Presidential Election Petition No 01 of 2006, the Zambian case of *Anderson Mazoka v Levy Mwanawasa* SCZ/EP/01/02/2002, and the Ghanaian case of *Nana Addo Akufo-Addo v John Dramani Mahama* No JI/6/2013. Perhaps the worst problem is the delay in proceedings. In 2003, Olusegun Obasanjo was sworn in as president despite a court order restraining him and his running mate from presenting themselves for swearing in, pending the determination of the substantive election petition in *Buhari v Obasanjo* Suit No SC 133/2003 17 NWLR 587. In Zambia, the presidential election petition in *Anderson Mazoka v Levy Mwanawasa* SCZ/EP/01/02/2002, which started in 2001, was only decided in 2005, just one year before the next elections.

[102] Unlike the pre-1990 period when legal qualifications were not a requisite, there has been some progress in most, but by no means all, civilian jurisdictions. In the latter, it is usually specified that a certain percentage of those who sit in these courts must be legally trained. See eg art 115 of the Benin constitution of 1990, which states that of the seven members, there should be three judges, two jurists, and two other persons. Article 153 of the Burkina Faso constitution of 1991 requires at least six of the 12 members to be jurists. As for Burundi's 2005 constitution, art 226 requires at least three of the seven members to be career magistrates. By contrast, in most common law jurisdictions the constitutions strive to ensure that these courts are constituted of the most experienced and brilliant legal minds. Although experienced judges and jurists are now being appointed to sit in many constitutional courts in civil law jurisdictions, evidence from the Constitutional Councils in Algeria and Senegal shows that difficulties are experienced when judges and jurists with no expertise in constitutional law are appointed to sit on these benches.

as a judicial, quasi-judicial/quasi-administrative, and quasi-judicial/quasi-legislative body becomes acute.

Secondly, if we add to this the fact that constitutional courts in civilian jurisdictions are given exclusive powers not only to decide on a wide range of constitutional issues but also to advise, make suggestions, and be consulted, then the potential for these courts to be overwhelmed is great. In fully appreciating the risk of overwhelming these courts with cases,[103] one can clearly see the difference between substantive constitutionalism which, as will be seen in a later chapter, has opened the floodgates to constitutional adjudication in Benin; and symbolic constitutionalism, where substantive constitutional justice remains an aspiration and not a reality, as in the case of Cameroon's Constitutional Council, which has yet to deal with a real constitutional matter.

Can constitutional courts realistically review, where they are required to do so, or advise, where this is the mandate, every possible piece of organic law, as some of these constitutions require? The problem is often compounded by the fact that these courts are usually given what Dworkin has classified as 'strong discretion', with little or no guidance to indicate on what basis some of their decisions or advice are based, which makes it difficult to render decisions that could guide future conduct.[104] With no formal system of *stare decisis*, there is no guarantee that, even where the constitutional courts intervene in a decisive manner, this will necessarily guide the future conduct of the government or litigants.

6. Conclusion

Looking back on twenty-five years of slow but steady progress, it is clear that the landscape of constitutionalism and constitutional justice has changed considerably. Although the progress is often not perfect and there is still a long way to go in many countries, the progress is real and substantial and provides a solid foundation on which to build for the future. In contrast to just over two decades ago, substantive constitutional justice in all its facets is the norm rather than the exception today. As the Benin Constitutional Court has shown, the question of constitutional justice today is less about what model is in operation and more about what powers the court has been given and whether it can fully utilize them to provide constitutional justice and protect citizens against arbitrary government.

When one looks closely at the work of the Benin and South African Constitutional Courts in the last two decades,[105] one cannot help but see some form of merging and converging of legal cultures and traditions; not to create new hybrids but rather to enhance pre-existing models in such a manner that African legal experts and constitutionalists, in particular, are beginning to look beyond what they inherited at independence, especially with respect to civil law jurisdictions. The burden of the colonial heritage appears to have

[103] It is important to point out that African judiciaries are noted for the delays and backlog of cases that they have to deal with. It only gets worse rather than better when some courts, such as the Constitutional Courts in South Africa and Zimbabwe, are now required to confirm every declaration of unconstitutionality. In the case of South Africa, this requires formal proceedings before the full bench of the Court and, with the 17th amendment of the constitution having made this court the final court of appeal on all matters, it is not clear how the court will cope with the predictable increase in case load with the same number of judges.

[104] On the concept of 'weak' and 'strong' discretion see Ronald Dworkin, 'Judicial Discretion' (1963) 60 *Journal of Philosophy* 624.

[105] On Benin see eg Horace Adjolohoun, *Droits de l'homme et Justice Constitutionnelle en Afrique: Le Modèle Bèninois: à la Lumière de la Charte Africaine des Droits de L'homme et des Peuples* (L'Harmattan 2011); and on the South African Constitutional Court see Theunis Roux, *The Politics of Principle: The First South African Constitutional Court, 1995–2005* (Cambridge University Press 2013).

been so heavy that it has stifled any thinking and reasoning outside of what was perceived as irreplaceable perfect models. That myth is slowly but certainly being unravelled.

Whereas in the past concerns centred on the independence of judges (in both common law and civil law jurisdictions) and the non-availability of constitutional review (in civilian jurisdictions), today the challenge is for the constitutional courts effectively to assert themselves and gain legitimacy. It is clear that the factors which combined to undermine constitutional justice in Africa have not disappeared. The one-party regimes have been replaced by dominant party regimes, which operate with exactly the same impulses. The threat of military dictatorships is barely receding—there are today often no overtly military regimes because the military *coup* leaders quickly don civilian uniforms and adopt other democratic paraphernalia.

In spite of its almost universal appeal, constitutional review remains an enigmatic institution which, apart from what is happening in the Benin and South African Constitutional Courts, has yet to fulfil its full potential in protecting and defending constitutionalism, good governance, and the rule of law. There are still many countries that have adopted constitutional courts for their symbolic value; these series of countries are firmly stuck in the murky middle ground between constitutional democracy and constitutional authoritarianism. This explains why, in spite of the expansion of constitutional justice and 'juristocracy', the increase in judicial resolution of quasi-constitutional issues such as election disputes has not strengthened electoral justice.

Decentralizing constitutional justice appears to be a new phenomenon that holds much promise. Processing claims, whether formally through the hierarchy of courts or informally through a 'filtering' system, will help to narrow down and clarify issues, shift the evidence, improve the quality and sophistication of arguments, and ensure that the apex constitutional court focuses on the most important issues. Perhaps more importantly, the decentralization of constitutional justice not only makes it more widely available to ordinary citizens throughout the country, but also provides an avenue for the principles and values that permeate the constitution to be spread widely, which will gradually entrench the culture of constitutionalism and the rule of law. This is just one example of the cross-systemic fertilization of ideas. Another important example is the concept of abstract review. If properly employed, it could prove useful not only for preventing constitutional violations, but also for preventing or reducing the avenues for conflict between the judiciary and the political branches.

Kommers rightly points out that social and political stability in a democratic state requires effective constitutional review. He adds:

> [T]he brutal instability of German society over the first half of the 20th century testifies to the shortcomings of earlier manifestations of German constitutionalism and the mechanisms for constitutional review upon which those constitutional systems relied.[106]

The same is true, if not more so, of Africa's shambolic experiment with constitutionalism during the first three decades of independence. Again, Kommers could not have stated it better when he makes the point that the stability and prosperity of Germany today 'bespeaks the integrity and efficacy' of its constitutional review.[107] There is no gainsaying that, if Africa's dream of social, economic, and political stability is to be achieved, there must be a strong system of constitutional review to check, control, sanction, and tame its endemically unruly political elites. In spite of the popularity of the centralized model, the manifestly clear movement towards traditional courts

[106] See Kommers (n 4). [107] ibid.

strongly supports the conclusion that Africa will be better served by conferring constitutional review to constitutional courts that operate as independent traditional courts, rather than one that operates like a quasi-administrative/quasi-legislative and quasi-judicial body.

Bibliography

Ackerman B, 'The Rise of World Constitutionalism' (1997) 83 *Virginia Law Review* 771

Adjolohoun H, *Droits de l'homme et Justice Constitutionnelle en Afrique: Le Modèle Bèninois: à la Lumière de la Charte Africaine des Droits de L'homme et des Peuples* (L'Harmattan 2011)

Arnold R, 'Should More Limits be Placed on the Federal Judiciary? No' (1997) 70 *Spectrum* 29

Brewer-Carias A, *Constitutional Protection of Human Rights in Latin America: A Comparative Study of Amparo Proceedings* (Cambridge University Press 2009)

Cappelletti M, 'The Judicial Process in Comparative Perspective' (1970) 58 *California Law Review* 1021

Cappelletti M, *Judicial Review in the Contemporary World* (Bobbs-Merrill Co Inc 1971)

Cappelletti M and Cohen W, *Comparative Constitutional Law: Cases and Materials* (Bobbs-Merrill 1979)

Cappelletti M, *The Judicial Process in Comparative Perspective* (Clarendon Press 1989)

Chang W-C, Thio L, Tan K Y L, and Yeh J, *Constitutionalism in Asia: Cases and Materials* (Hart Publishing 2014)

Chavez R, *The Rule of Law in Nascent Democracies: Judicial Politics in Argentina* (Stanford University Press 2004)

Chen A, 'The Global Expansion of Constitutional Judicial Review: Some Historical and Comparative Perspectives' in *Festschrift in Honour of Professor Satoru Osanai* (Chuo University 2013) 3–25

Davis M H, 'The Law/Politics Distinction, the French *Conseil Constitutionnnel*, and the US Supreme Court' (1986) 34 *American Journal of Comparative Law* 45

Duranti F, 'New Models of Constitutional Review' (2014) 5 *Comparative Law Review* 1

Dworkin R, 'Judicial Discretion' (1963) 60 *Journal of Philosophy* 624

'Editorial: A Resounding Slap from SA's Judges' *BusinessDayLive* (9 July 2015) www.bdlive.co.za/opinion/editorials/2015/07/09/editorial-a-resounding-slap-from-sas-judges (last accessed 13 April 2017)

Epstein L, Knight J, and Shvetsova O, 'The Role of Constitutional Courts in the Establishment and Maintenance of Democratic Systems of Government' (2001) *Law and Society Review* 35

Fombad C M, 'The New Cameroonian Constitutional Council' (1998) 24 *Journal of African Law* 172

Fombad C M, 'Post-1990 Constitutional Reforms in Africa: A Preliminary Assessment of the Prospects for Constitutional Governance and Constitutionalism' in Nhema A and Zeleza P T, *The Resolution of African Conflicts* (OSSREA 2008) 179–99

Fombad C M, 'Constitution-building in Africa: The Never-ending Story of the Making, Unmaking and Remaking of Constitutions' (2014) 13 *African and Asian Studies* 429

Gardbaum S, *The New Commonwealth Model of Constitutionalism: Theory and Practice* (Cambridge University Press 2013)

Ginsburg T, *Judicial Review in New Democracies: Constitutional Courts in Asian Cases* (Cambridge University Press 2003)

Ginsburg T, 'The Global Spread of Constitutional Review' in Whittington K, Kelemen R D, and Caldeira G A (eds), *The Oxford Handbook of Law and Politics* (OUP 2008)

Ginsburg T, 'The Spread of Constitutional Review' in Whittington K, Kelemen R D, and Caldeira G A (eds), *The Oxford Handbook of Law and Politics* (OUP 2008)

Ginsburg T and Elkins Z, 'Ancillary Powers of Constitutional Courts' (2009) 87 *Texas Law Review* 1431

Ginsburg T and Versteeg M, 'Why Do Countries Adopt Constitutional Review?' (2014) 30 *Journal of Law, Economics and Organization* 587
Haman F and Troper M, *Droit Constitutionnel* (31st edn, LGDJ 2009)
Hirschl R, *Toward Juristocracy* (Harvard University Press 2004)
Hirschl R, 'The New Constitutionalism and the Judicialization of Pure Politics Wordwide' (2006) 75 *Fordham Law Review* 721
Hogg P and Bushell A, 'The Charter Dialogue between Court and Legislatures (Or Perhaps the Charter of Rights Isn't Such a Bad Thing After All)' (1997) 35 *Osgoode Hall Law Journal* 75
Husa J, 'Guarding the Constitutionality of Laws in the Nordic Countries: A Comparative Perspective' (2000) 48 *American Journal of Comparative Law* 345
Jackson V and Tushnet M, *Comparative Constitutional Law* (2nd edn, Foundation Press 2006) 466
Juillard P, 'L'Aménagement de l'Article 61 de la Constitution' (1974) 90 *Revue de Droit Public* 1703
Kelsen H, 'Judicial Review of Legislation: A Comparative Study of the Austrian and the American Constitution' (1942) 4 *The Journal of Politics* 183
Kommers D, 'An Introduction to the Federal Constitutional Court' (2001) 2 *German Law Journal* 30
Laurent P, 'Rule of Law in France' in Peerenboom R (ed), *Asian Discourses of Rule of Law* (Routledge 2004) 79–112
Mavcic A, *The Constitutional Review* (BookWorld 2001)
Mavcic A, 'Seminar on Constitutional Jurisdiction' (Grand Park Hotel, Ramallah, 25 October 2008) http://www.venice.coe.int/WebForms/documents/?pdf=CDL-JU(2008)026-e (last accessed 13 April 2017)
Meredith M, *The State of Africa: A History of Fifty Years of Independence* (Free Press 2006)
Merryman J H, 'The French Deviation' (1996) 44 *American Journal of Comparative Law* 109
Navia P and Rios-Figueroa J, 'The Constitutional Adjudication Mosaic of Latin America' (2005) 38 *Comparative Political Studies* 189
Pickles W, *The French Constitution* (Stevens 1960)
Provine D M, 'Courts in the Political Process in France' in Herbert J and others, *Courts, Law, and Politics in Comparative Perspective* (Yale University Press 1996) 197
Roux T, *The Politics of Principle: The First South African Constitutional Court, 1995–2005* (Cambridge University Press 2013)
Seidman R, 'Judicial Review and Fundamental Freedoms in Anglophonic Independent Africa' (1974) 35 *Ohio State Law Journal* 820
Shapiro M, 'Federalism, the Race to the Bottom and the Regulation-averse Entrepreneur' in Scheiber H (ed), *North American and Comparative Federalism* (Institute of Governmental Studies Press 1992)
Stephenson M, 'When the Devil Turns ...: The Political Foundations of Independent Judicial Review' (2004) *Journal of Legal Studies* 32
Tallon D, 'The Constitution and the Courts in France' (1979) 27 *American Journal of Comparative Law* 567
Tate C N and Vallinder T (eds), *The Global Expansion of Judicial Review* (New York University Press 1997)
Tushnet M, 'The Rise of Weak-form Judicial Review' in Ginsburg T and Dixon R (eds), *Comparative Constitutional Law* (Edward Elgar Publishing 2011)
Tushnet M, *Weak Courts, Strong Rights: Judicial Review and Social Welfare Rights in Comparative Constitutional Law* (Princeton University Press 2008)
Young C, *The Postcolonial State in Africa: Fifty Years of Independence 1960–2010* (University of Wisconsin Press 2012)

PART 2

ARCHETYPAL EXAMPLES OF DIFFERENT MODELS OF AFRICAN CONSTITUTIONAL ADJUDICATION

2

Centralized Model of Constitutional Adjudication

The Constitutional Court of Benin

Sègnonna Horace Adjolohoun

1. Introduction

Since gaining independence on 1 August 1960 as Dahomey, Benin has experienced an eventful political and constitutional history. Between 1963 and 1972, the country experienced eight *coups d'état*, adopted ten constitutions[1] and had ten presidents.[2] Three major periods followed independence. The period from 1960 to 1972 was one of political instability and successive regime changes. Civilian and military regimes alternated. During this period, the country was sometimes described as 'the sick child of Africa',[3] with reference to its political turbulence and frequent *coups*.[4]

The military *coup* of 26 October 1972 marked the beginning of a second era, when long-serving President General Mathieu Kérékou took over power and subsequently established the Benin Revolutionary People's Party. Kérékou installed a Marxist-Leninist dictatorship for seventeen years and imposed a tight ban on freedoms. The regime routinely abused the human rights of its citizens and transformed the country into a police state, sending the opposition underground.[5]

In 1989, the oil crisis in neighbouring Nigeria adversely affected Benin's economy, and the pro-USSR regime could not bear the democratic wind blowing in the aftermath of the collapse of the Berlin Wall. The long ban on civil and political rights fuelled growing discontent among domestic social and political forces, which resorted to indefinite

[1] The constitutions of 28 February 1959; 26 November 1960; 11 January 1964; the Charter of 1 September 1966; the constitution of 11 April 1968; the ordinances of 26 December 1969; 7 May 1970; 18 November 1974; the Fundamental Law of 26 August 1977, amended by the Constitutional Act of 6 March 1984; and the Constitutional Act of 13 August 1990, which served as a constitution for purposes of the transition to democracy.

[2] Six of the *coups* were successful while three failed. For a comprehensive discussion of Benin's political and constitutional history see Pierre Mêtinhoué, *Les gouvernements du Dahomey et du Bénin: 1957–2005* (CNPMS 2005). See also Maurice Ahanhanzo-Glèlè, *Naissance d'un Etat: l'évolution politique et constitutionnelle du Dahomey, de la colonisation à nos jours* (LGDJ 1969); and Léon Bio Bigou, 'La contribution du pouvoir législatif à la vie politique du Bénin de 1965 à 1979' in CAPAN *L'histoire du pouvoir législatif des indépendances à nos jours* (Actes du colloque parlementaire du cinquantenaire Porto-Novo 2011) 81.

[3] See Noel Dossou-Yovo, 'The Experience of Benin' (1999) 16 *Journal on World Peace* 59 and GriooCom, 'Bénin: de l'enfant malade au modèle démocratique' http://www.grioo.com/ar,benindelenfant maladeaumodeledemocratique,19522.html (last accessed 17 April 2017).

[4] See Bruce A Magnusson, 'Testing Democracy in Benin: Experiments in Institutional Reform' in Richard Joseph (ed), *State, Conflict and Democracy in Africa* (Lynne Rienner Publishers 1999) 221.

[5] See Magnusson (n 4) and Anna Rotman, 'Benin's Constitutional Court: An Institutional Model for Guaranteeing Human Rights' (2004) 17 *Harvard Human Rights Journal* 283.

strikes and country-wide protests demanding change.[6] These events led to the demise of the regime, which agreed to the idea of the first national conference as part of the so-called 'third wave' of democratization[7] and new constitutionalism in Africa. The famous *Conférence des forces vives de la nation* was held in February 1990.[8] Constitutional and liberal democracy, the rule of law, separation of powers, and human rights have been at the heart of this third era of democratic revival, which the country is experiencing to this day.

In pursuit of the objectives set by the National Conference,[9] the new constitution of Benin was the result of a popular endeavour through the referendum of 11 December 1990. Although the debates around the adoption of the 1990 constitution focused on democratization and the protection of fundamental rights because of the grave violations of the past, the new constitution also addressed traditional issues that are dealt with in any document of its kind. Importantly, as a democratic era constitution, the document sought to heal Benin's political and constitutional instability syndrome. Therefore, it marked a radical change from its predecessors.

The 1990 constitution opted for a presidential regime, the separation of powers, the rule of law, human rights, and other commons features of modern constitutionalism. In addition to establishing checks and balances institutions, the new fundamental law set up a Constitutional Court.

In the era of 'new constitutionalism', constitutional adjudicatory bodies have been elevated to the apex of the entire political order, and serve as the guardian and protector of constitutionalism. However, the extent to which and the manner in which these bodies have influenced constitutional democracies around the world vary depending on several factors, among which prominently feature the model of constitutional review adopted and the overall constitutional operation of the system.

Compared with their counterparts in the American and Anglo-Saxon traditions, constitutional adjudicatory bodies of the Kelsenian, French-adapted, and European adopted models are known to exhibit peculiar features. In Africa, the Constitutional Court of Benin has been termed as the most Kelsenian model of its kind, arguably the leading concentrated model of constitutional review on the continent. After two decades of practice, the achievements of Benin's 'constitutional revolution' speak for themselves. The country has never missed any of its presidential, legislative, or municipal elections since 1991. Six presidential elections have been held and four presidents have alternated in power in twenty-seven years of democratic renewal.[10] Once known as the most unstable nation in the era preceding the so-called 'third wave of democratisation', the country has not experienced a single *coup d'état* and not a single change was made to its constitution in the last twenty-seven years.

[6] See Frédéric Joël Aivo, *Constitution de la République du Bénin, La Constitution de tous les records en Afrique* (Editions CACI 2010).

[7] See Charles M Fombad and Nathaniel A Inegbedion, 'Presidential Term Limits and Their Impact on Constitutionalism in Africa' in Charles M Fombad and Christina Murray (eds), *Fostering Constitutionalism in Africa* (Pretoria University Law Press 2010) 7–8.

[8] See Kathryn Nwajiaku, 'The National Conferences in Benin and Togo Revisited' (1994) 32 *The Journal of Modern African Studies* 439, 440.

[9] Benin's National Conference was a popular assembly that brought together representatives of teachers, students, the military, government officials, religious authorities, non-governmental organizations, more than 50 political parties, ex-presidents, labours unions, business interests, farmers, and dozens of local development associations. See Magnusson (n 4) 221.

[10] These are Nicéphore Soglo (1991–1996); Mathieu Kérékou I (1996–2001); Mathieu Kérékou II (2001–2006); Boni Yayi I (2006–2011); Boni Yayi II (2011–2016); and Patrice Talon (2016–to date).

This chapter is an introduction to the Constitutional Court of Benin as a concentrated model of constitutional adjudication. The chapter, however, goes beyond a mere introduction to the court to showcase how central the place and role of the Constitutional Court has been in understanding the success of this new dispensation that has positioned Benin as a model in the region. The chapter first discusses the model, composition, and powers of the Constitutional Court. This is followed by an analysis of the reasoning of the court, while section 3 deals with international influences on its decisions. The last section examines the nature of the court's decisions and their effects.

2. Model, Composition, and Powers

2.1 A centralized model of constitutional adjudication

Although the centralized or decentralized nature of constitutional adjudication is mainly characterized by the structure and operation of the competent body, other features that come with various systems are of relevance in understanding the results they yield. For instance, the centralized constitutional adjudication model is not only characterized by the unitary nature of the body, but also by the fact that it acts as a court of first and last instance and operates outside the judicial branch. As discussed below, the model of constitutional adjudication adopted in Benin, which now also largely applies in Francophone Africa, was initially inspired by the Kelsenian model and the French Constitutional Council variation of this model and subsequently influenced, in some respects, by the American model.

As in most of Francophone Africa, at independence Benin inherited the French legal and judicial system.[11] The new constitutional dispensation of 1990 was not an exception, as the constitution exhibits several features of the 1958 French constitution, not only in terms of the wording of some key provisions, but also regarding the institutions created thereby. For instance, the *Haute Cour de Justice*, vested with powers to prosecute the president and members of cabinet for offences listed in the constitution, is borrowed from the French system.[12] This system of special jurisdiction—which still applies in France as the *Cour de Justice de la République,* although with slight changes—favours political trials over the ordinary judicial system.[13] The functioning of the judiciary and the office of the prosecutor fall within the same category of imported institutions.[14] The same historical rationale applies to the adoption of the civil law tradition in most of Francophone Africa, where the criminal, administrative, and civil law received during the colonial period continues to apply.[15]

As far as the structure of the judiciary is concerned, it is, as is true in most of Francophone Africa, a *sui generis* variant of the French legal system. Nevertheless, it must be noted

[11] See Horace S Adjolohoun and Charles M Fombad, 'Separation of Powers and the Role of the Public Prosecutor in Francophone Africa' in Charles M Fombad (ed), *Separation of Powers in African Constitutionalism* (OUP 2016) 359–83.

[12] See Horace S Adjolohoun, *Entre constitutionnalisme et présidentialisme: succès et dilemmes du nouveau constitutionnalisme béninois 1990-2012* (CEDAT 2013) 49.

[13] See Vie Publique, 'Qui est jugé par la Cour de justice de la République?' http://www.vie-publique.fr/decouverte-institutions/justice/fonctionnement/juridictions-particulieres/qui-est-juge-par-cour-justice-republique.html (last accessed 17 April 2017); Le Monde, 'Françoise Hollande assure qu'il va supprimer la Cour de justice de la République' http://www.lemonde.fr/societe/article/2014/06/25/francois-hollande-assure-qu-il-va-supprimer-la-cour-de-justice-de-la-republique_4444862_3224.html (last accessed 17 April 2017).

[14] See Adjolohoun (n 12) 43–52; and Adjolohoun and Fombad (n 11) 359–83.

[15] See Adjolohoun and Fombad (n 11) 361–2, 369–70.

that at independence, most Francophone African countries opted for a unified Supreme Court model as opposed to the French system of four separate apex courts.[16] The unified Supreme Court was made up of four chambers: criminal, administrative, financial, and constitutional chambers, and was still largely based on the French judicial structure. Prior to the 1990s, there were mutations in many Francophone countries, which resulted first in changes from unified Supreme Courts towards the French model of four separate apex courts and then a return to a unified three-chamber Supreme Court but with a separate constitutional court or council based on the Constitutional Council variant of the Kelsenian model adopted by France.[17]

The focus here is on the way the Benin model of centralized constitutional review has developed since 1990 to be one of the most effective constitutional courts in Africa. A brief background is important. At independence on 1 August 1960, Benin had a *Tribunal d'Etat Chargé du Contrôle et de la Sanction des Institutions Publiques* (a state tribunal mandated to monitor and sanction public institutions).[18] On 26 November 1960, the first constitution of the country post-independence transformed the *Tribunal d'Etat* into a Supreme Court.[19] An Act of 7 October 1965 regulating the operation of the Supreme Court subsequently provided that it would be composed of four chambers with constitutional, judicial, administrative and financial jurisdiction.[20] This structure remained in operation until the 1990 constitutional dispensation.

There was never any constitutional review under the pre-1990 unified Supreme Court model, because, as was the case with similar bodies in Francophone Africa, the constitutional chamber was never operational.[21] This was particularly so during the military era that lasted from 1972 to 1989. The main reason was that the legislation dealing with constitutional adjudication either did not cater for the operation of the specialized chamber or deferred its operation to a later date. For instance, the 1965 Supreme Court law provided for the establishment of a constitutional chamber within the court but postponed the provision for its functions and procedure to a subsequent time.[22] This state of affairs was understandable as, under a one-party regime where state organs were merged with those of the revolutionary party, justice was rendered by 'popular courts'.[23] The difficulty

[16] Until it introduced its Constitutional Council in 1958, France had three separate apex courts with administrative, criminal, and financial jurisdiction respectively: the *Conseil d'Etat* created in 1799, the *Cour de cassation* in 1804, and the *Court des comptes* in 1807 as the apex court with competence to control the use of public money, public expenditure, and account to the citizenry. See Jacques Olivier Bourdon, 'Napoléon et la construction des grands corps de l'Etat' https://francearchives.fr/en/commemo/recueil-2004/40102 (last accessed 17 April 2017); Conseil d'Etat, 'Naissance et évolution' http://www.conseil-etat.fr/Conseil-d-Etat/Histoire-Patrimoine/Histoire-d-une-institution/Ses-fonctions/Naissance-et-evolution (last accessed 17 April 2017).

[17] See Sorry Baldé, *La convergence des modèles constitutionnels: étude de cas en Afrique subsaharienne* (Éditions Publibook Université 2011) 388. See also in general Association Africaine des Hautes Juridictions Francophones, *Opportunités de l'éclatement des cours suprêmes en cours distinctes*, Actes du colloque de Cotonou (14–16 May 2002); Stéphane Bolle, 'Projet de révision constitutionnelle au Sénégal: la renaissance de la Cour suprême' in *La Constitution en Afrique* http://la-constitution-en-afrique.org/article-18009013.html (last accessed 17 April 2017).

[18] See Loi n° 60-1 du 14 mai 1960 relative au Tribunal d'Etat.

[19] See Constitution of Dahomey, Loi no 60-63 du 26 novembre 1960.

[20] See Loi n° 65-35 du 7 octobre 1965 portant composition, organisation, attributions et fonctionnement de la Cour suprême.

[21] See Jean-Baptiste Monsi, 'Benin' in Association Africaine des Hautes Juridictions Francophones, *Opportunités de l'éclatement des cours suprêmes en cours distinctes*, Actes du colloque de Cotonou (14–16 May 2002) 120.

[22] See Loi n° 65-35 du 07 octobre 1965 arts 30 and 39.

[23] See Monsi (n 21); Foundation Zinsou, 'Raconte-moi l'indépendance: 1972–1991, les années Kérékou' http://www.racontemoilindependance.org/Raconte_Moi_lIndependance/1972_1991.html (last accessed 17 April 2017).

for established courts to perform judicial review functions under military or one-party dictatorships in Francophone Africa was not peculiar to Benin. A striking example is that of the Administrative Chamber of the Supreme Court of Togo, which, from independence to 2000, handled fewer than forty complaints and delivered only a handful of judgments.[24] As was the case for most pre-1990s constitutional bodies in Francophone Africa, Benin's constitutional adjudication mechanism was, therefore, more symbolic than real. More generally, because most of the constitutional or administrative disputes brought before those bodies were of a political nature, pursuing them amounted to challenging acts of repressive autocratic regimes, which very few citizens would dare to do.[25]

Under the 1990 constitutional dispensation, Benin adopted a peculiar model of judicial organization that borrowed from the Kelsenian model of a separate constitutional body while retaining unity for the three other chambers within a Supreme Court. Comparative trends in Francophone Africa include Senegal, which moved from a unified Supreme Court to the purely French model of four separate courts, namely, the *Cour de cassation* (criminal and civil matters); the *Conseil d'Etat* (administrative matters); the *Conseil constitutionnel* (constitutional matters); and the *Cour des Comptes* (financial matters). Another variant, Mali, moved from a unified Supreme Court to the four-court system before returning to a two-chamber Supreme Court (criminal, civil and administrative chambers) co-existing with two separate constitutional and financial courts.

In respect of the model of constitutional bodies adopted in Francophone Africa, it appears that in spite of the divergent histories of unifying, splitting, or reunifying the Supreme Court, there was a common trend to emulate the French constitutional review model at the time the constitutional chamber operated within the unified Supreme Court. Even with respect to the splitting of the constitutional body from the unified Supreme Court, the French influence persisted after the start of the new constitutional dispensations inaugurated by the third wave of democratization in the 1990s. Having spearheaded this wave of democratization in Africa, Benin was also instrumental in launching a reformed form of the Kelsenian model of constitutional court and adjudication on the continent. This is with the caveat that, as the subsequent discussion shows, the Benin model seems to have copied from other models, and did not merely replicate the French, Constitutional Council.

We propose a twofold perspective to discuss the centralized nature of the model: first, the institutional structure and, secondly, the procedure and principles of adjudication.[26]

In terms of structure, the court is structured as a single body with jurisdiction to adjudicate constitutional matters. As with similar courts in countries that have adopted the Kelsenian model of constitutional review, the court operates outside of the ordinary judicial system. The latter consists of a hierarchy of courts and tribunals at the apex of which is a three-chamber Supreme Court. The Beninese Constitutional Court is, therefore, an entire jurisdictional system in itself as it is not placed on top of a lower courts structure. It is neither divided into chambers or sections, as opposed for instance to the German and Spanish Constitutional Courts, which similarly follow the centralized model.[27]

24 See Monsi (n 21); 'Dieudonné Esso, 'La Justice Administrative a du Plomb dans l'Aile au Togo' *Le Libéral* (19 October 2011) 3; Focus Info, 'Justice Administrative Togolaise: une Juridiction à la Traîne' (27 March 2015) http://www.focusinfos.net/index.php/offre-emploi/item/558-justice-administrative-togolaise-une-juridiction-a-la-traine (last accessed 17 April 2017).

25 See Nada Youssef, *La Transition Démocratique et la Garantie des Droits Fondamentaux* (Editions Publibook Université 2011) 614–15; Esso (n 24).

26 See Guillaume Drago, *Contentieux constitutionnel français* (Thémis droit PUF 2011) 46.

27 See Gilles Badet, *Les Attributions Originelles de la Cour Constitutionnelle du Bénin* (Friedrich Ebert Stiftung 2013) 158–63.

One issue that arises from the unified model in terms of its structure is the relationship it has with the ordinary judicial system. In the case of Benin, the problem appears to have been resolved by Article 124 of the constitution, which states that decisions of the Constitutional Court are binding on all entities, including courts. Although this provision has been generally applied without any controversy, there is indeed potential for conflict between the ordinary courts and the Constitutional Court. This is because Article 131 of the constitution also provides that the decisions of the Supreme Court are 'final and binding on the executive, the legislature and all courts'. What will happen if there are conflicting decisions?

The Constitutional Court had an opportunity to assert its authority as the regulator of the entire judicial system. In a judgment of 20 November 1998, the Administrative Chamber of the Supreme Court heard a case of unfair dismissal of 438 civil servants. The Chamber found in favour of 111 of them and ordered the government to reinstate them.[28] Dissatisfied with this decision, the unsuccessful civil servants filed a petition with the Constitutional Court in which they claimed a violation of their rights to equality. In DCC 03-083, the Constitutional Court found that the principle of equality was breached and ordered that the remaining civil servants should be afforded the same treatment as those who were successful in the Supreme Court case.[29] However, indirectly, the Constitutional Court appeared to have overruled the Supreme Court's judgment or at least affirmed its judicial authority as the supreme harmonizer of the entire legal order. Several decisions of the court with similar implications are discussed later in this chapter.

As pointed out earlier, similar to centralized courts, the Constitutional Court of Benin acts as a court of first and final instance, although it may be asked to review its decisions in cases of material errors.[30] It has done so in a number of decisions, defining a material error as a typographical error in the spelling of a name or a concept, or an omission in the decision. The court usually holds that such correction of material error does not have any effect on the *res judicata* of the decision under review.[31] The court is usually careful to distinguish cases of material errors from those where the petitioners indirectly tried to secure a review of a decision. In such instances, the court has dismissed the requests for seeking to challenge the *res judicata* of the initial decision, in violation of Article 124 of the constitution, which states that decisions of the Constitutional Court are final and binding.[32]

Commentators have argued that the Benin constitutional adjudication system offers the most liberal access rules.[33] This is true with respect to centralized models of constitutional review especially in Africa, where access to the court is usually restricted to certain persons, such as politicians, public authorities, and some state organs and agencies. The Benin model allows wide access to individuals and groups not only to vindicate their rights but also to participate directly in the maintenance of the entire constitutional order. We focus here on the type of petitioners and conditions of access. How these prerogatives

[28] See Arrêt no 33/CA du 20 novembre 1998, Affaire *Collectif des Agents Permanents de l'Etat dégagés de la Fonction Publique représenté par AMOUSSOU Didier et Consorts c. Etat Béninois* http://coursupremebenin.com/index.php/component/k2/item/42-33-ca-20-11-98 (last accessed 17 April 2017).

[29] See DCC 03-083 of 28 May 2003. [30] See Court Rules art 22.

[31] See eg DCC 13-149 of 8 October 2013 and DCC 14-044 of 27 February 2014.

[32] See eg DCC 04-046 of 24 April 2004 and DCC 12-076 of 22 March 2012.

[33] See eg Cyrille Gangnon, 'Les Droits Fondamentaux de la Personne Humaine', Séminaire de formation des journalistes (Cotonou 2 août 2005) 1; Badet (n 27) 167–218, Adjolohoun (n 12) 20–1.

have been used in practice and their contribution to the strengthening of the overall constitutional order is discussed later in greater details.

For political stakeholders and public authorities, the president of the republic and any member of parliament may access the court both a priori and a posteriori. A priori, they may seize the court to verify the conformity of laws with the constitution before the concerned laws are promulgated. A posteriori, they may, in their individual capacity, challenge the constitutionality of any law after it has become operational.

While individual Beninois citizens may access the court directly to vindicate their human rights, the constitution further empowers them to play a checks and balances role by initiating constitutional review of laws once they have been assented. This limb of the individual role in constitutional adjudication is one of the major unique features of the Benin model. As is illustrated later in this chapter, the *Constitutional Amendment* cases[34] and other judgments show how constitutional adjudication by individuals and groups provides an important safeguard for democracy.

In terms of standing, the capacity to petition the court is in function of the type of norm that is brought for review. For instance, only the president has standing to initiate review of organic laws prior to their promulgation.[35] The speaker of parliament, and chairpersons of the Media and Communication Authority and the Economic and Social Council are similarly vested with review initiative concerning the adoption and amendments of the internal rules of these respective bodies.[36] On the other hand, the president, any citizen, as well as any association or human rights non-governmental organization may seek the review of laws and regulations likely to breach human rights and public freedoms.[37]

It is worth noting that 'any citizen' is granted standing to seek the review of laws and regulations thus introducing an *actio popularis* approach to constitutional adjudication. While its predecessor, the High Council of the Republic, construed individual standing in a restrictive sense by rejecting the petition of Senegalese nationals,[38] the Constitutional Court has taken a more liberal and purposive approach. For instance, the court admitted a petition from a citizen of Columbia alleging the violation of her fundamental rights.[39] In another case, the court initiated on its own motion, the review of the Revenue Act following the petition of a Danish national challenging the constitutionality of the withdrawal of his passport.[40] The court declared the impugned provisions of the Act unconstitutional thus annulling the administrative decision of withdrawal of the passport. It would seem that the court widened the scope of individual access by espousing a holistic reading of the constitution whose Article 39 provides that 'foreigners on the territory of the Republic of Benin enjoy the same rights and freedoms as Benin citizens ...'.

The court has, however, applied stricter rules when it comes to groups. Thus, it has dismissed petitions from associations for lack of registration. It has considered this as raising the issue of legal capacity,[41] the onus of which lies with the petitioning association.[42]

In spite of the centralized nature of the Benin model of constitutional adjudication, the liberal procedural rules have brought about a very conducive environment for the scrutiny of the operation of state organs, which is so critical in a constitutional democracy. This liberalization of constitutional adjudication from the exclusive precinct of political

[34] See Decisions of the Constitutional Court of Benin DCC 05-139 of 17 November 2005, DCC 05-145 of 1 December 2005 and DCC 11-067 of 20 October 2011.

[35] See Organic Law on the Constitutional Court art 19.

[36] ibid art 21.

[37] ibid art 22.

[38] See Decision DC of 13 August 1992 of the Haut Conseil de la République.

[39] See DCC 96-060 of 26 September 1996.

[40] See DCC 97-045 of 13 August 1997.

[41] See eg DCC 25-94 of 19 July 1994.

[42] See DCC 95-032 of 1 September 1995.

and public authorities to the wider citizenry has proved to be very effective in promoting unity, stability, harmony, and effectiveness of the legal and constitutional order. The composition of the court, to which we will now turn, has also played a role.

2.2 Composition

The Constitutional Court is comprised of seven members: four appointed by the Bureau of the National Assembly and three by the president of the republic for a five-year term renewable only once.[43] The criteria for nomination include professional competence, moral character and integrity. The constitution attempts to ensure a balanced composition of the court between legal experts and non-lawyers. Any bench of the court must, therefore, include at least three professional judges with fifteen years' experience, two being appointed by the Bureau of the National Assembly and one by the president. Nominations must include two legal experts, who must be 'professors of law or legal practitioners', with fifteen years' experience, one appointed by the National Assembly and the other by the president of the republic. The same rules apply to the appointment of the two remaining members of the court, who must be chosen from a list of top civil servants, who are 'personalities of established professional renown'.[44] Members of the court elect its president from among the members who are professional judges and legal experts. One of the early petitions to reach the court raised the issue of who exactly was referred to in the description 'legal expert' or *juriste de haut niveau*. In Decision No 8 DC, the court held that the *juriste de haut niveau* inevitably referred to a professor or legal practitioner.[45]

An issue traditionally arising in relation to the appointment of adjudicators is their independence and that of the body they represent. Article 115 of the constitution of Benin provides several important safeguards to guarantee the independence of Constitutional Court judges. They may not be removed from office during their term and may not be investigated or arrested without the authorization of the Constitutional Court and the Bureau of the Supreme Court sitting in a joint session, except in cases of *flagrante delicto*.[46] In such cases, the presidents of the Constitutional Court and Supreme Court must be seized within forty-eight hours of the arrest. Constitutional Court judges also enjoy immunity of jurisdiction similar to that of ordinary court judges.

In spite of these provisions, it appears that the issue of independence hinges on other factors, such as the very nature of the political regime adopted under the 1990 constitution of Benin and the increased tendency of politicization of constitutional adjudication in Africa. The 1990 constitution established a presidential regime, which combines elements of the French and American models without, however, providing the necessary check and balance mechanisms that guarantee the rule of law and separation of powers. A peculiarity of Benin's presidential regime is the enormous powers vested in the president. For example, he or she is the one who appoints the president of the Supreme Court, almost all members of the Constitutional Court, and other judicial officers. He also has the powers

[43] Constitution art 115.

[44] In practice, those personalities have always been chosen among top civil servants with more than 10 years' experience in the public administration.

[45] See Decision 8 DC of 16 June 1992 which was confirmed by Decision 15 DC of 16 March 1993. In Francophone Africa, the title of professor is conferred upon successful participation in the professional oral examination known as *Agrégation* organized by the *Conseil Africain et Malgache de l'Enseignement Supérieur* (CAMES). Formal requirements to apply to do the examination include the possession of a doctoral degree and the publication of a few articles in accredited journals.

[46] See s 3(3) on the enforcement of Constitutional Court decisions.

to make law under certain specified circumstances, and to influence parliament to adopt legislation rejected by the Constitutional Court. The president is the chairperson of the Judicial Service Commission, and controls the directorate of public prosecution through the ministry of justice.[47]

The appointment procedure of Constitutional Court judges raises doubts as to their ability to act independently. In situations where the incumbent president has a majority in parliament, he virtually has a free hand to appoint all seven members of the Constitutional Court. The absence of a clear gender policy in the appointment system is also worth noting. Although Benin is party to a number of international treaties and other instruments dealing with women's rights and particularly their representation on policy and decision-making bodies,[48] there is not much evidence that these treaty commitments have guided the policy of gender representation in the appointment of judges of the Constitutional Court since its inception in 1991. Successive appointments to the bench reveal that female judges have enjoyed fair representation, including holding the position of chief justice. From the first appointments in 1993, the representation of female judges on the successive seven-judge benches has been as follows: the first bench (1993 to 1998) had one female judge, who was also the president of the court); the second bench (1999 to 2004) had two female judges, one of whom was the president; the third bench (2005 to 2010) was similarly composed as the second bench; the fourth bench (2010 to 2015) had two female judges; and the fifth bench (2015 to date) has two female judges.

The judges may sit for a total of two five-year terms and are vested with powers to adjudicate disputes between the executive, the legislature and the ordinary judicial system. In addition, the court adjudicates disputes arising from the election of the president of the republic and members of parliament. It may also invalidate legislation made by parliament or restore executive-made law that has been disapproved of by an opposition-led parliament.[49]

In light of Benin's strong presidential regime, providing for these mechanisms to govern the appointment of judges with such politically-charged powers leaves wide scope for executive interference and control as well as judicial deference to the appointing authority.[50] Having said that, one needs to contextualize the political appointment of constitutional court judges as a distinctive feature of the Kelsenian or centralized models of constitutional adjudication in its French variance, which inspired most Francophone African countries in the 1990s. In this regard, it is worth recalling that the very creation of the Constitutional Council in France had two contradictory aims. It was meant to 'curb the arbitrariness and hegemony of parliament' and at the same time 'avoid the establishment of a real constitutional tribunal, which is antithetical to the French political

[47] See Horace S Adjolohoun, 'Benin' in *Constitutions of the Countries of the World Online* (Oxford University Press 2012); Horace S Adjolohoun, 'Between Presidentialism and a Human Rights Approach to Constitutionalism: Twenty Years of Practice and the Dilemmas of Amending the 1990 Constitution of Benin' in Morris Mbondenyi and Tom Ojienga (eds), *Constitutionalism and Democratic Governance in Africa: Contemporary Perspectives from Sub-Saharan Africa* (Pretoria University Law Press 2013).

[48] These include the United Nations Convention on the Elimination of All Forms of Discrimination Against Women (CEDAW) (1979); the Dakar Platform for Action (1994); the Beijing Plan of Action (1995); the ECOWAS Gender Policy (2002); the Protocol to the African Charter on Human and Peoples' Rights on the Rights of Women in Africa (2003); the African Union Solemn Declaration on Gender Equality in Africa (2004); the African Union Gender Policy (2008); UN Security Council Resolution 1325 on Women, Peace and Security (2000) and Joint Resolutions 1820 (2008), 1888 and 1889 (2009).

[49] See Charles M Fombad, 'Appointment of Constitutional Adjudicators in Africa: Some Perspectives on How Different Systems Yield Similar Outcomes' (2014) 46(2) *Journal of Legal Pluralism and Unofficial Law* 249–75; see also Adjolohoun in ch 11 of this volume.

[50] See in general Adjolohoun in ch 11 of this volume.

tradition'.[51] In the course of its operation, the French Council progressively overcame these original jurisdictional constraints, thus becoming the more assertive *pouvoir constitutionnel* that it is nowadays.[52]

From a comparative approach, it seems that, while taking inspiration from the French model of constitutional adjudication, African constitutional democracies opted for a format that suited the imperial presidencies imported along with the Kelsenian courts established in the post 1990s constitutions. However, with respect to the specific issue of the political appointment of constitutional judges, the history of each country has surely influenced the option it took. In the case of Benin, the era that preceded the 1972 revolution was marked by political turmoil and constitutional instability illustrated among others by the political curiosity of the *triumvira*, a civilian three-member presidential council.[53] While the main culprit was without a shadow of doubt the military, parliament was equally seen as sharing some responsibility for eight military or civilian coups that occurred between 1963 and 1972.[54] Bearing this in mind, the need to allow a peaceful and undisturbed operation of the presidential regime certainly led the designers of the 1990 political framework to vest powers in the president to appoint members of the Constitutional Court, which is, in many respects, a body with a very political nature.

The success of constitutionalism requires wise political actors who are able to strike a reasonable balance between the demands of presidentialism and those of a constitutional democracy. The Benin model has succeeded in making the independence of appointed members of the Constitutional Court work under a hyper-presidential regime. The court has through its decisions guaranteed the independence of the entire judiciary against any abuse of the appointment and management powers of the president. Having successfully struck the balance for over twenty-seven years, Benin is on the verge of reviewing the applicable norms., the report of the Constitutional Reform Commission set up under the new regime led by President Patrice Talon, elected in 2016, calls for an overhaul of the system of appointment of judges of the court.[55]

2.3 Powers

The Constitutional Court of Benin has been vested with wide-ranging powers with respect to political and social governance. First, the court controls the constitutionality of laws; all acts, decisions, and actions of the executive and its agencies, parliament and the judiciary. Secondly, it adjudicates all matters relating to the functioning of state organs, including organization, operation, appointment, or designation and dismissal of members of those institutions. Thirdly, all disputes between branches of the state and relationships between these are within the jurisdiction of the Constitutional Court. Fourthly, it has jurisdiction over cases involving human rights violations. Finally, the Constitutional Court adjudicates disputes arising from presidential and parliamentary elections. In some of these instances, the court has the power to hear a matter on its own motion or *suo motu*. The following discussion begins by elaborating on the normative framework before showing how the court has used these powers in practice.

[51] Dominique Rousseau, *Droit du Contentieux Constitutionnel* (Montchretien 2010) 23–30.

[52] ibid 30–45.

[53] See Dossou-Yovo (n 3); Adjolohoun 'Benin' (n 47) 1–5.

[54] See in general Mêtinhoué (n 2).

[55] See Frédéric Joël Aivo, 'Présentation du rapport général' Commission nationale technique chargée des réformes politiques et institutionnelles (28 June 2016) Report of the Constitutional Reform Commission (on file with author).

Constitutional review is the exclusive function of the Beninese Constitutional Court. Article 114 of the constitution provides that: '[t]he Constitutional Court shall be the highest court of the state in constitutional matters. It shall be the judge of the constitutionality of the law'. Constitutional review is compulsory for organic and general laws before they are promulgated; for rules of procedure of parliament, the Media and Communication Authority and the Social and Economic Council before their application; for laws and regulations that are likely to breach fundamental human rights and freedoms; and for conflicts arising from the distribution of powers between state organs.[56] Constitutional review may be initiated both a priori, before the impugned bill or regulation is enacted, and a posteriori, when an existing law is brought to constitutional scrutiny.

Competence to initiate constitutional review is shared between the president of the republic, members of parliament and ordinary citizens. Article 121(1) allows the president of the republic and any member of parliament to seek the constitutional review of any laws before their promulgation. In case any such laws are likely to infringe human rights, the court has the power under Article 121(2) automatically to initiate review. Finally, individuals are empowered under Article 122 to challenge directly the constitutionality of any bill or enacted law before the Constitutional Court when they believe such law is not consistent with the constitution.

In addition, the review powers of the court extend to the procedure of *exception d'inconstitutionnalité* (exception to unconstitutionality) known in France as the *Question Prioritaire de Constitutionnalité* (QPC) (preliminary ruling on constitutionality). Under such a procedure, the Constitutional Court of Benin may be requested to undertake the constitutional review of laws in proceedings that are taking place before ordinary courts, including the Supreme Court. In such cases, the proceedings must be suspended until a decision on the constitutional issue is given and such decision is binding on all courts and institutions. It is worth noting that the procedure of *exception d'inconstitutionnalité*, which Benin adopted in its 1990 constitution was only adopted as the *QPC* in France during its 2008 constitutional reforms.

The organic law on the Constitutional Court also extends the power to request the constitutional review of laws likely to infringe human rights to the president of the republic and, most importantly, to any association or non-governmental human rights organizations.[57] These provisions have assisted the court in developing considerably liberal and generous practices in relation to constitutional review and human rights litigation.[58]

As pointed out earlier, individuals have direct access to the Constitutional Court. Individuals are empowered not only to secure the enforcement of their personal rights, but also to challenge the constitutionality of laws and acts of the state, its organs and agents. The court is, therefore, well positioned to playing a leading role in upholding the rule of law. In fact, in the early years of its operation, the court termed itself as 'the cornerstone of the liberal rule of law' and the 'keystone of the entire politico-legal system'.[59]

A novelty in Benin's 1990 constitution, in comparison with other Francophone African constitutions, is certainly the human rights mandate of the Constitutional Court. In fact, the court has specific jurisdiction to entertain suits involving human rights brought by

[56] See art 117. [57] *Loi Organique sur la Cour constitutionnelle* art 22.

[58] See in general Nicaise Médé, *Les grandes décisions de la Cour constitutionnelle du Bénin* (Editions Universitaires Européennes 2012).

[59] See DCC 33-94 of 24 November 1994.

individuals and groups.[60] Direct individual access is provided for in cases of human rights violations by private persons, the state, its agencies or any other entities. In addition, indirect access is provided for through the 'exception of unconstitutionality', whereby proceedings before ordinary courts are suspended pending the decision of the Constitutional Court.[61] Individuals may further initiate a constitutional case or review when they believe a bill, legislation or any act of a state organ is not in accordance with the provisions of the constitution or may violate human rights. The court has developed liberal rules for individual access,[62] and has enjoyed a popular confidence among Beninese.

The court has used its powers to promote legal certainty, clarify the law, and guarantee stability through an effective regulation of the entire social and political order. This has been particularly so when dealing with cases involving the Bill of Rights and its protection of fundamental rights in the course of which, it has set aside many laws and regulations.

An example of the court's contribution to the development of the law has been with respect to the principle of equality in the constitution. Reading the principle of equality together with the right of freedom of association, the court set aside a ministerial *arrêté* (regulation) which imposed a duty on companies importing agricultural inputs to provide evidence of their registration as members of a national cooperative. The court agreed with the petitioners that, owing to the existence of several other similar associations, the impugned ministerial regulation no 081/MICPE/MFE/DC/SG/DCCI/DGID of 29 July 2005 amounted to a breach of the right of equality and the right to freedom of association as recognized and protected under both Article 26(1) of the constitution and Article 3(1) of the African Charter.[63] The court has applied this precedent to declare several executive regulations unconstitutional. These instances include a regulation by the minister of finance to limit access to the revenue office to civil servants from the ministry of finance,[64] and that of the minister of education to deny a civil servant the right to sit for an exam while a colleague of the same professional category is allowed to do so.[65]

On the other hand, the court has rejected petitions where it found that 'specific and identifiable' criteria differentiated the petitioners such as instances where the civil servants involved belonged to two different fields in the academia[66] or when such differentiation is provided for by the law or has a legitimate aim as it promotes public interest and the continuity of the public service and meets the requirement of proportionality. In this latter case, a communiqué by the minister of public service setting 'a good physical condition ... being free from any poliomyelitis and tuberculosis affections ... or being totally cured thereof' as a requirement to apply for a certain position in the public service was deemed legitimate to ensure an effective functioning of the public service.[67]

One decision that is clearly controversial is where the court rejected an attempt to read parity into the equality provisions of the constitution. In this case, parliament enacted legislation prescribing that the list of candidates of a political party or a coalition of parties will be valid only if it included at least of quota of 20 per cent female candidates. Prior to the promulgation of the president as well as several members of parliament sought a review of the law and a declaration that it was unconstitutional. In finding in favour of the petitioners, the court held: that 'the role of the legislator, in its area of competence, is

[60] Constitution art 114. [61] ibid art 122.

[62] See Cyrille Gangnon, 'Les Droits Fondamentaux de la Personne Humaine' Séminaire de formation des journalistes (Cotonou 2 August 2005) (unpublished conference paper on file with author) 1.

[63] See DCC 06-037 of 4 April 2006. [64] See DCC 18-94 of 3 June 1994.

[65] See DCC 01-058 of 27 June 2001. [66] See DCC 06-099 of 11 August 2006.

[67] See DCC 01-005 of 11 January 2001.

to guarantee an equal access to elective positions for men and women; ... by providing a quota for women, the legislator establishes a differentiation based on sex; ...—whereas—such quota provision is in line with neither the letter nor the spirit of the above cited provisions; ... thus, the impugned provisions are contrary to Article 2 of the constitution and Article 3 of the African Charter'.[68]

The rationale behind the position of the court is that only an express clause of the constitution should provide for such specific quota rule least judicially-made positive measures would diminish the enjoyment by one group of citizens to the advantage of another group while members of the two groups are entitled to an objective equality.[69]

The court takes a significantly different approach when it comes to ensuring consistency between domestic law and international law based on treaties and conventions ratified by the state, whether under the *contrôle de constitutionnalité* or the *contrôle de conventionnalité*.[70] A few landmark decisions of the court in that regard are worth mentioning. In the first case, the newly enacted Family Code is referred to the court for review. In an historic ruling, the court held that the provisions of the Code providing for men to take several wives where the same did not apply to women was contrary to Article 26 of the constitution on equality before the law, particularly between men and women. The court also quoted Article 18 of the African Charter, which provides that: 'the State shall ensure the elimination of every discrimination against women and also ensure the protection of the rights of the woman and the child as stipulated in international declarations and conventions'.[71]

Here, in comparison to the political quota case discussed earlier, the court endeavoured to ensure that no new legislation is allowed to enter the domestic legal order if it does not comply with both the constitution and ratified international treaties and conventions, which in monist states such as Benin, take precedence over legislation.

The court made another important pronouncement when it struck down provisions of the Criminal Code relating to adultery. In the case itself, the court held that by providing that the adultery of the man is punishable only when it occurred in the marital home, whereas that of the woman attracts a sanction regardless of the place where it is committed Articles 336 to 339 of the Criminal Code violate the right to equality as provided in Article 26 of the constitution and Articles 2 and 3 of the African Charter.[72] It is worth noting that, in this case, the matter was brought through the procedure of *exception d'inconstitutionnalité*, which allows a party to a case pending before an ordinary court to challenge the constitutionality of any law invoked therein. The ordinary court hearing the matter must suspend the proceedings pending the decision of the Constitutional Court, which then binds the trial court in its judgment.

Another set of decisions by the Court has clarified the law on many issues such as the right of association, demonstration, and assembly. In the first of these series of cases, the court has held that ministerial regulations may not deal with issues reserved for the legislature. In the case, a citizen petitioned the court to declare unconstitutional a regulation of the minister of the interior, which set out conditions limiting the enjoyment of the right of freedom of association. The court declared the regulation unconstitutional on the grounds that the minister had trespassed into the constitutionally delineated province of parliament, which holds exclusive power to restrict freedoms.[73]

[68] See DCC 10-117 of 8 September 2010.

[69] See Badet (n 27) 62–4.

[70] These could be translated as review of the constitutionality of the law, and that of the conformity of the law with international conventions ratified by the state.

[71] See DCC 02-144 of 23 December 2002.

[72] See DCC 09-081 of 30 July 2009.

[73] See DCC 16-94 of 27 May 1994.

The court relied on this precedent when it was called to hear a petition from a student association challenging a decision of the minister of the interior to cancel the registration of the *Union Nationale des Scolaires et Etudiants du Bénin* 'on security grounds'. The court held that the decision to cancel the registration was made on the basis of the same regulation that it had already struck down in its decision DCC 16-94 on limitation of freedom of association referred to above. In a subsequent case concerned with a presidential decree prohibiting judges of the Constitutional Court from joining political parties or movements or requiring them to resign therefrom before they are sworn in, the court acknowledged the fact that the legislature could restrict the enjoyment of freedoms. However, it took the position that such limitation 'may not amount to suppressing the right altogether; consequently, considering the hierarchy of norms, a decree may not supress the exercise of a freedom or a right provided and guaranteed by the constitution'.[74]

On a number of occasions, the court has upheld the separation of powers by restraining executive interferences with the operation of the judiciary. It made a leading pronouncement in this respect when it held that a presidential decree suspending the execution of court orders was in violation of the constitution as it interfered with the independence of the judiciary and breached the principle of separation of powers. The case arose when the *Union Nationale des Magistrats du Bénin* (Benin Magistrates' Association) challenged the government's decision to suspend all court proceedings as well as the execution of court orders pertaining to the enforcement of evictions in 2007.[75] A regulation by the minister of finance opposing the execution of an Appeal Court judgment was similarly found to be in violation of the constitution.[76]

The court had previously taken a relatively strong position regarding the separation of powers and the independence of the judiciary. In 2001, it held that an order by the minister of justice to release a detainee constituted an interference with the operation of the judiciary and a violation of the constitution.[77] In a similar case decided in 2005, the court declared that a letter from a public prosecutor relating to a civil matter pending in court was a violation of the constitution.[78] The court took the same approach by giving a strict interpretation to the principle that judges may not be removed or moved to a new position without the observance of a minimum procedure, including prior consultation and consent. In that respect, the court made it clear that the litigants and ordinary citizens are the final beneficiaries of the independence of judges. In a case decided in 1997, a letter and decrees from the Minister of Justice which omitted to mention the proposed post were therefore declared in violation of the independence of the judiciary and of the constitution.[79] The court also declared unconstitutional the posting of a judge without his or her prior consent.[80]

The Constitutional Court has applied a similar approach in adjudicating cases relating to the appointment of judges, which Article 129 of the constitution says is to be done by the president based on a proposal made by the minister of justice acting upon the opinion of the High Council of Magistracy. The main issues raised in the case were the legal nature of the Council's opinion and the stage in the process at which it must be requested. The court held that the silence of the president had to be interpreted as a refusal to respect the

[74] DCC 33-94 of 24 November 1994.
[75] DCC 07-175 of 27 December 2007.
[76] DCC 08-158 of 30 October 2008.
[77] See DCC 01-018 of 9 May 2001.
[78] See DCC 00-005 of 26 January 2000.
[79] See DCC 97-033 of 10 June 1997.
[80] See DCC 06-063 of 20 June 2006.

opinion of the Council and that such opposition to appointing the complainant, a judge, on the Supreme Court, was a violation of the constitution.[81]

To appreciate the significance of these decisions of the Benin Constitutional Court fully it is important to understand the limited scope of separation of powers and independence of the judiciary in Francophone Africa in general and Benin in particular.[82] In the latter case, while Article 126 of the constitution provides that judges must obey only the law, Article 127(1) makes the president the 'guarantor' of the 'independence of the Judiciary'. Article 127(2) seems to suggest that the president also sees to the independence of judges, as the provision states that 'he [the president] is assisted by the *Conseil Supérieur de la Magistrature*' (High Council of Magistracy), which is the equivalent of the Judicial Service Commission in Anglophone Africa. It must be added that the president is also the president of the *Conseil Supérieur de la Magistrature*. In such a context, there is therefore no surprise that the risks of executive interference with the judiciary are so high.

While protecting the judiciary from executive assaults, the court has not been shy to bring ordinary courts, including the Supreme Court, within the scrutiny of the constitution. For example, when the court has declared a piece of legislation to be contrary to the constitution, ordinary court decisions that are based on it are automatically invalid.[83] In this case, the trial courts, the Tribunal of First Instance of Ouidah and Appeal Court of Cotonou, had decided that the applicants are the owners of a disputed plot of land because the other parties to the case could not own land because they have always been the slaves of the applicants. The Constitutional Court had held this finding to be in violation of fundamental rights as it referred to the 'status of slaves' of the petitioners.[84] Hearing the case on appeal, the Criminal Chamber of the Supreme Court ignored a notification by the Constitutional Court of its initial decision and an order either to postpone the delivery of judgment or reopen hearings. In dealing with a petition from the Supreme Court's decision on the matter,[85] the Constitutional Court declared the decision of the Supreme Court as null and void for violating the constitution.

The Constitutional Court has also often intervened where the behaviour of state organs or public officials has interfered with or threatened the smooth operation of the state. In the process of electing the new bureau of Parliament, the dean (that is, the oldest sitting member of parliament) chairing the session used his power to order the suspension of several members and demanded a proportional political representation in the new bureau. In considering a petition from some members of parliament, the court found that, since no provision of the constitution or rules of parliament imposed such criteria, the suspensions were in breach of the constitution.[86]

Following the resistance of the dean to implement this decision, a group of members of parliament filed a new petition. After ascertaining that there had been non-compliance, the court ordered that 'the "dean" [call] a meeting of the Parliament and [proceed] to have the bureau elected during the same session; failing which, the dean should be replaced by the next oldest [member of the parliament] until the process was completed within 48 hours of the decision'.[87] The decision was complied with in the stipulated time.[88] The following year, the court made a similar order when eight members of the Economic and Social Council decided to block the election of their bureau by boycotting the session. The court ordered that the session be called and elections be completed within seventy-two

[81] See DCC 00-054 of 2 October 2000.
[82] See in general Adjolohoun and Fombad (n 11).
[83] See DCC 09-087 of 13 August 2009.
[84] See DCC 06-076 of 27 July 2006.
[85] See Arrêt no 13/CJ-CT of 24 November 2006.
[86] See DCC 03-077 of 7 May 2003.
[87] See DCC 03-078 of 12 May 2003.
[88] See Badet (n 27) 251.

hours of its decision.[89] In 2008, the Constitutional Court also found the decision of parliament to postpone *sine die* the adoption of a bill authorizing the government to make loans for coastal erosion projects to be in violation of the constitution.[90] After protesting that the decision breached the separation of powers, parliament eventually adopted the bill as ordered by the court.

The court also acted in some instances in a way that appeared to 'discipline' parliament and the executive, not only with respect to their compliance with the constitution or constitutional rules, but also with the court's decisions. For example, the court found parliament in violation of the constitution for not following the proper procedure for electing representatives of political parties on the Electoral Commission. In the same case, the court held that the principle of equality was also violated as political groups with the same number of members sitting in parliament obtained numbers of representatives that were fewer compared to other political parties with the same number of members of parliament.[91] After parliament held fresh elections in implementation of the court's decision, a number of disgruntled members filed a new petition challenging the outcome. The court then found that the parliament had not fully complied with the decision and compelled it to do so. Because the elections interfered with upcoming presidential elections, the court adjusted the schedule.[92]

Similarly, the court stopped attempts to paralyse critical electoral processes. It did so for instance when the *Commission Electorale Nationale Autonome* (CENA) requested the postponement of the second round of the 2001 presidential election as it needed more time to print new ballot papers after the runner-up withdrew from the process. The court, referring to its powers as the regulator of the efficient functioning of public organs, authorized the postponement and set the new date.[93] The court made similar findings when the CENA argued it could not hold the 2006 and 2011 presidential elections on time as the process of distributing voters' cards and finalizing the voters' register had been delayed.[94]

Turning now to its role in upholding the constitutional order as a whole, the court has regulated major political moments in Benin. Here, we discuss the role of the court as the gatekeeper of the constitution and acting in defence of democracy. After it was adopted in 1990, the constitution did not face any social or political test until the issue of its amendment became a public debate in 2004. At an initial stage, the issue was whether the constitution should be amended at all, especially when there was a perception that the purpose was merely to serve personal political purposes and the ambitions of certain persons. Against the backdrop of strong civil society opposition, the Constitutional Court initially opposed these so-called opportunistic amendments in 2006 and 2007.[95]

The 'Do Not Touch My Constitution' social movement, launched as early as 2004, led to a country-wide rejection of any revision in 2006, the final year of former President Mathieu Kérékou's second term in the democratic era. In an environment of social uprisings against any amendment, the Constitutional Court decided in DCC 05-139 and DCC 05-145 that the economic arguments made to justify the amendments to the constitution and the extension of presidential terms were not constitutionally sound.[96] Subsequent

[89] See DCC 04-065 of 29 July 2004.
[90] See DCC 08-072 of 25 July 2008.
[91] See DCC 01-11 of 12 January 2001.
[92] See DCC 01-12 of 22 January 2001.
[93] See EL-P 01-053 of 17 March 2001.
[94] See EL-P 06-019 of 16 March 2006 and EL 11-024 of 4 March 2011, respectively.
[95] For a detailed analysis of constitutionalism and the debate on the revision of the constitution of Benin see in general Adjolohoun, 'Between Presidentialism and a Human Rights Approach to Constitutionalism' (n 47).
[96] See Constitutional Court decisions DCC 05-139 of 17 November 2005 and DCC 05-145 of 1 December 2005.

developments concerning the constitutional revision project 'officially' launched in 2008 attest to the importance of the position of the Constitutional Court regarding opportunistic amendments to the supreme law of the land.

Acting in defence of democracy, the court has made many significant judgments, although there have been issues of jurisprudential consistency. One such instance is when the court had to deal with the political 'majority–minority' issue. The question arose in a dispute between government and parliament on the representation of political parties in the bureau of parliament and its commissions. In 2009, the court decided that the political minority had been entrusted with rights in Parliament since the principle of 'the winner takes all' was not acceptable in a democratic society and were therefore entitled to be represented in the bureau and parliamentary commissions in proportion to their numbers in parliament. In DCC 09-002, the court thus raised the rights of the political minority, which it defined as the party or coalition of parties with the least number of members in parliament, as a *principe à valeur constitutionnelle* (constitutional principle).[97] At the time of the decision, members of the court were believed to be favourably disposed towards the presidential coalition, which had recently lost the majority of seats in parliament.

Surprisingly, the Constitutional Court, with the same composition, in similar circumstances overturned its precedent two years later, after fresh elections in which the presidential coalition emerged with a majority of seats in parliament. In 2011, the court held that proportionality had to be determined *in casu*, and that the 'majority-minority' notion had to be 'enlightened' by the *summa divisio* 'presidential coalition versus opposition'.[98] This jurisprudential move led opposition groups in parliament—the minority of the day—to blame the constitutional tribunal for devaluing the 'minority principle' to the rank of a *principe à géométrie variable*.[99] Critics went as far as suggesting that the court had positioned itself as a *de facto* second chamber of parliament.[100] In spite of the dubious and unconvincing reasoning given by the court, the reversal of its earlier position could simply be seen as a deliberate policy intervention by the court to avoid political tensions with possible dire consequences for Benin's nascent democracy.

An overview of earlier pronouncements with respect to political representation in the appointment of members of some constitutional bodies reveals that the court had observed judicial virtues at some point. In 2001 and 2003, it rejected political representation while reviewing the designation by parliament of its representatives to sit in the *Haute Cour de Justice*.

In a first instance, the court held that political representation was not a criterion set out in the constitution whose Article 135 only prescribes that representatives of parliament on the *Haute Cour de Justice* must be members of parliament.[101] In a subsequent case where parliament used political representation in electing members of the same body, the court held that the criterion is immaterial as the only procedural condition is for the election to be held by secret ballot.[102] In light of this judicial law-making process, it is arguable that erecting the 'majority–minority' rule as a *principe à valeur constitutionnelle* was not a sudden move of the court.

[97] See DCC 09-002 of 8 January 2009.

[98] See DCC 11-047 of 21 July 2011.

[99] The term is used to mean 'a principle that moves according to the minority or the majority of the day'. On a critical analysis of DCC 09-002 of 8 January 2009 and the *principes à valeur constitutionnelle* see Stephane Bolle, 'Décision DCC 09-002: le bon grain et l'ivraie' in La Constitution en Afrique http://www.la-constitution-en-afrique.org/article-26613703.html (last accessed 17 April 2017).

[100] See Aivo (n 6) 14.

[101] See DCC 01-013 of 29 January 2001.

[102] See DCC 03-168 of 26 November 2003.

When one considers the human rights mandate of the Constitutional Court of Benin, it can be argued that individuals have been placed at the heart of the development of constitutionalism. The role played by individual petitioners as discussed earlier is emphasized with respect to human rights adjudication. In terms of the law, Benin may be said to have one of the most advanced human rights normative framework in Francophone Africa. While the constitution, in the same way as many others in Africa, includes references to the Universal Declaration of Human Rights (UDHR) and other human rights norms in the preamble, it goes further to state in the first provision of the Bill of Rights that 'all the rights and duties of the African Charter on Human and Peoples' Rights form part and parcel of the Constitution and of Beninese law'.

It is known that the African Charter is the only international human rights law instrument, which not only provides both for individual and groups' rights but also the justiciability of all generations of rights, that is civil and political, socio-economic and cultural, as well as so-called solidarity rights. It has been argued that the peculiar channel of domestication adopted in Benin amplifies the level of human rights protection.[103]

Another novelty of Benin's centralized model of constitutional adjudication is certainly the human rights mandate of the Constitutional Court. As mentioned earlier, the court has specific jurisdiction to entertain human rights suits brought by individuals and groups.[104] Direct individual access is provided in cases of human rights violation by private persons, the state, its agencies, or any other entities. It should be noted that constitutional human rights provisions bind all categories of both public and private subjects. Private persons, the state, its agencies and social organizations, and corporate entities are bound by these rights as there is no special derogation provided under the constitution for the breach of human rights. The Constitutional Court of Benin has made a huge number of judgments on human rights issues and the obligations that the constitution imposes on public institutions and officials or privates entities such as the police and armed forces,[105] judges,[106] ministers,[107] court presidents and registrars,[108] public education bodies, the secretary general of the government, and private companies.[109]

[103] On the place and role of the African Charter in the constitutional protection of human rights in Benin see in general Latif Sidi, 'La protection des droits humains par la Cour constitutionnelle du Bénin de 1993 à 2005' Mémoire de DEA Chaire UNESCO Université d'Abomey-Calavi (2006) and Horace Adjolohoun, *Droits de l'homme et justice constitutionnelle en Afrique: le modèle béninois à la lumière de la Charte africaine des droits de l'homme et des peuples* (L'Harmattan 2011).

[104] Constitution art 114.

[105] Police officers, including the Director General of Police, have personally been found to be in violation of human rights in DCC 06-057, DCC 06-059, and DCC 06-060 (violation of art 5 of the African Charter; degrading treatment; reparatory order), DCC 06-062 (violation of art 6 of the African Charter; illegal arrest; reparatory order).

[106] See eg Constitutional Court Decisions DCC 03-084 of 28 May 2003 (15 years investigation without judgment, undue delay, violation by the Tribunal of First Instance of Lokossa of art 7-d of the African Charter) and DCC 03-125 of 20 August 2003 (violation of art 7-c of the African Charter, right to defence, violation of art 35 of the Constitution by the investigating judge).

[107] Both ministers and their offices were found to be in violation of human rights. See eg Constitutional Court Decision DCC 01-058 of 27 June 2001, where the Ministry of Education was found in violation of art 26 of the Constitution (equality before the law) for having allowed a teacher access to compete for a professional exam but refused access to a colleague of the same category, specialization and criteria; in DCC 05-067, DCC 06-016 (involving the Minister of Justice for violation of the right to equality and refusal to execute the decision of the Constitutional Court) and DCC 06-052 (involving the Minister of Education).

[108] See DCC 05-114, DCC 05-127 (involving the Chief Registrar of the Supreme Court), DCC 06-046, and DCC 06-113.

[109] For an overview of the human rights case law of the Constitutional court of Benin see Cour constitutionnelle du Bénin, 'Garantie des droits fondamentaux de la personne et des libertés publiques' http://www.cour-constitutionnelle-benin.org/?pg=decisions_gdf (last accessed 17 April 2017).

Perhaps owing to the fact that violations of fundamental rights were frequent in the era preceding the operation of the 1990 Constitution but were seldom litigated, the expanded scope for human rights litigation has resulted in such disputes stealing the limelight in constitutional litigation. Some of the main decisions of the court with respect to human rights protection are worth mentioning, albeit briefly. For example, called upon in DCC 99-051 to determine whether provision for the death sentence in Article 381 of the Benin Criminal Code was a violation of Article 8 of the constitution, which provides that the 'human person is sacred and inviolable' and Article 15, which states that 'everyone has the right to life', the Constitutional Court answered in the negative.[110] The court took the position that there is no express or implicit abolition of the death penalty and concluded that the unqualified right to life cannot in itself mean the inconsistency of the death penalty provision in the criminal law. Considering its express human rights mandate and related powers, the Constitutional Court ought to have advanced the constitutional right to life by setting a more progressive precedent for other courts,[111] namely the Supreme Court.[112]

The ongoing process to amend the 1990 Constitution includes the abolition of the death penalty,[113] although parliament has made this almost inevitable by authorizing the ratification of Optional Protocol 2 to the International Covenant on Civil and Political Rights.[114] Despite this express political will to effect a legislative shift with respect to the issue, the court appeared to have remained seised with the matter as though it understood its role as one of ensuring that law-making changes reflect the spirit of the constitution.

This position of the court is well demonstrated in at least two main jurisprudential moments subsequent to the above-mentioned ratification. In DCC 12-153, while reviewing the new Criminal Procedure Code, the court held that Articles 685(2) and 793—which still provided for the death sentence—were in conflict with Article 147 of the constitution, which states that ratified international conventions take precedence over conflicting domestic legislation. The court thus held that since the country ratified the Protocol, 'no piece of legislation may mention the death penalty anymore'.[115] On 17 December 2012, parliament removed the impugned provisions from the Code in compliance with the court's decisions.[116]

A second jurisprudential moment occurred owing to the concern among civil society and legal practitioners that these legislative and judicial law-making moments did not effectively remove the death penalty from Benin law as the substance of the sentence

[110] In DCC 99-051 of 13 October 1999.

[111] For instance by referring to the more encompassing and progressive wordings of art 4 of the African Charter and the findings of the African Commission in *Interights and Others (on behalf of Bosch) v Botswana* (2003) AHRLR 55 (ACHPR 2003).

[112] For instance, in the *Azonhito* (death penalty) case, the Supreme Court took the view that the constitutional provision for the right to life did not amount to abolition of the death penalty. See *Azonhito and Others v Public Prosecutor*, Cassation decision, 034/CJ-P; ILDC 1028 BJ 2000 (29 September 2000). For the full judgment and analysis of the case see H Adjolohoun, 'Analysis of the case of Azonhito and ors v Public Prosecutor, Cassation decision, 034/CJ-P; ILDC 1028 (BJ 2000)' in International Law in Domestic Courts (subscription service only) http://www.oxfordlawreports.com/subscriber_article?script=yes&id=/oril/Cases/law-ildc-1028bj00&recno=4&module=ildc&category=Benin (last accessed 28 February 2012).

[113] See Decree No 2009-548 of 3 November 2009 of the President of the Republic transmitting the amendment bill to the Parliament.

[114] See Loi n° 2011-11 du 25 août 2011 portant autorisation d'adhésion du Bénin au deuxième Protocole facultatif au PIDCP.

[115] See DCC 12-153 of 4 August 2012.

[116] See Amnesty International, 'Bénin, des vies en suspens: le sort incertain des derniers condamnés à mort' 11–12 http://amnistiepdm.org/3/post/2017/01/benin-des-vies-en-suspens-le-sort-incertain-des-derniers-condamnes-a-mort.html (last accessed 17 April 2017).

survived in the Criminal Code itself.[117] Called upon by two death row inmates to make a determination on the constitutionality of the Criminal Code in proceedings before the Appeal Court of Cotonou, the court affirmed its previous findings. It further held that no person may be subjected to the capital sentence in Benin any more.[118] This judgment prompted parliament to initiate an amendment of the Criminal Code to remove all provisions providing for the death penalty.

The contribution of the Constitutional Court to the improvement of police practices and judicial proceedings is also worth noting. In several cases, starting from DCC 98-065, the court has consistently held that in deciding whether violations have occurred, the focus should be on the intention, effects, and duration of the treatment of accused persons.[119] With regard to the constitutional obligation for courts to complete proceedings within a reasonable time, the Constitutional Court has, from the decision handed down in DCC 03-119, set the factors of reasonable time as depending on the 'circumstances of the case, complexity and multiplicity of procedures, the applicant's behaviour and the behaviour of jurisdictional authorities'.[120] In other instances, the court found undue delay in processes where a 'flagrant case' lasted fourteen months;[121] where no decision was reached in fourteen-year first instance proceedings;[122] or where criminal proceedings had been ongoing for twenty years without an outcome.[123]

A serious weakness with the human rights mandate of the Constitutional Court is that no provision in the constitution expressly grants power to the court to provide remedies, let alone to evaluate the quantum of compensation when it finds that a violation has occurred. However, the right to remedy and reparation is self-evident by reference to the African Charter and the jurisprudence of the African Commission on Human and Peoples' Rights.[124] Moreover, the Constitutional Court has an express human rights mandate and its decisions are final and binding on state and non-state parties.[125]

In its early years (1993–2001), the court adopted a restrictive approach to its human rights jurisdiction. It limited its decisions to declaratory orders and findings of violations. However, from 2002, it inaugurated an 'era of reparation',[126] although awards of reparation still applied on an inconsistent and unprincipled basis. Clear reparation orders with specific quantum for monetary compensation and injunctions to public authorities have been made in a few cases, some of which the government still refuses to comply with.[127] The victims collected monetary compensation in very few instances following new proceedings

[117] See eg African Commission on Human and Peoples' Rights, Annual Report of the Working Group on the Death Penalty (2012) http://www.achpr.org/files/sessions/52nd/inter-act-reps/184/activty_report_workingroup_deathpenalty_eng.pdf (last accessed 17 April 2017).

[118] See DCC 16-020 of 21 January 2016.

[119] See eg DCC 98-065 of 5 August 1998, DCC 99-011 of 4 February 1999, DCC 03-088 of 28 May 2003, DCC 96-084 of 13 November 1996, and DCC 98-100 of 23 December 1998.

[120] DCC 03-119 of 28 August 2003 and DCC 03-167 of 11 November 2003.

[121] DCC 97-006 of 18 February 1997. According to the relevant provisions of the criminal code of procedure, 'flagrant case' or those in which the offender is 'caught in the act' are dealt with under a more expedited procedure than other cases. See arts 19, 20, 27, 40, 48–75 of Benin's new Code of Criminal Procedure, Loi n° 2012-15 portant code de procédure pénale en République du Bénin of 30 March 2012.

[122] DCC 97-011 of 6 March 1997.

[123] DCC 03-144 of 16 October 2003.

[124] See G Musila, 'The Right to an Effective Remedy under the African Charter on Human and Peoples' Rights' (2006) 6 *African Human Rights Law Journal* 442 and N Enonchong, 'The African Charter on Human and Peoples' Rights: Effective Remedies in Domestic Law?' (2002) 46 *Journal of African Law* 197.

[125] Constitution art 124(2).

[126] From DCC 02-052 of 31 May 2002, the court decided that human rights violations must 'open up a right to reparation' based on the African Charter and international jurisprudence including from the European Human Rights Court.

[127] The best illustration of the government's non-compliance is certainly in DCC 06-016 of 31 January 2006, where the Constitutional Court declared that the government had violated the *res judicata* of its decision DCC

in ordinary courts to have the Constitutional Court orders enforced.[128] The government-led process that began in 2008 to amend the constitution includes an express provision for the right to remedy and reparation for human rights violations.[129]

3. Judicial Reasoning

As a starting point, it must be indicated that the Beninese Constitutional Court has seldom reverted to precedential reasoning, except by referring to its own precedents, as discussed in greater detail in the section of this chapter dealing with the influence of foreign precedents on its decisions. The court has, however, on occasion used textual reasoning as a matter of course, as well as analogical and historical reasoning. A few illustrations of decisions by the court falling within each of these reasoning methods are provided.

An overview of the Constitutional Court's case law over the years reveals that its main method of reasoning is textual. Often the court would prefer to limit its reasoning to the text of the constitution. Even where the court referred to, for instance, international instruments, it would nevertheless apply textual standards rather than sources of relevant doctrinal or international jurisprudence. For instance, in DCC 95-024,[130] brought to control the constitutionality of administrative acts taken in the application of Benin's Labour Code, the court merely recalled that: '[a]rticle 6 of the African Charter on Human and Peoples' Rights and Articles 16 and 18(4) of the constitution establish the principle of individual right to liberty'. Ultimately, the court found that the impugned acts were a violation of the constitution.[131]

In some pronouncements, the court would find a violation of key rights in the African Charter by referring only to provisions of the constitution. It would thus hold, for example, that: '[t]he treatment inflicted upon citizens by the Gendarmerie is cruel, inhuman and degrading treatment, which is in violation of the constitution'.[132] Other instances resulted in laconic recitation, typically in the following style: 'In terms of Article 7 of the African Charter, no one shall be inflicted a sanction without having prior access to his case file and presenting his [her] arguments',[133] or '[t]he freedom of movement[134] is a fundamental right guaranteed by Article 25 of the constitution, which may only be restricted subject to law'.[135]

Despite the wide powers bestowed on the Constitutional Court to decide issues with respect to which there were often a considerable number of international precedents, the

05-067 of 12 July 2005 that the complainants 'must be included' in the training of magistrates as their other colleagues; and thus decided that the Minister for Justice had violated the constitution and other that the complainants be reinstated.

[128] Accurate research account for one isolated Constitutional Court Decision DCC 02-058 of 4 July 2002, which was given effect to by the Tribunal of First Instance of Cotonou Judgment No 07/04/Fourth Civil Chamber of 9 February 2004. The complainant collected a monetary award of about US$10,000 for having suffered severe beatings at the hands of the bodyguards of the president of the republic. See Horace S Adjolohoun, 'The "Right to Reparation" as Applied under the African Charter by Benin's Constitutional Court' LLM dissertation (University of Pretoria 2007) 29 (on file with author).

[129] See proposed art 125(4), Decree No 2009-548 of 3 November 2009 by which the government transmitted an amendment bill to the parliament.

[130] 6 July 1995.

[131] See eg DCC 03–071 of 16 April 2003 (violation of the right to equal treatment in access to public service) and DCC 03-083 of 28 May 2003 (cruel treatment personally inflicted on the victim by the General Director of the National Police).

[132] DCC 98-101 of 23 December 1998.

[133] DCC 95-026 of 11 July 1995.

[134] Expressly guaranteed in art 12(1) of the African Charter.

[135] DCC 95-034 of 1 September 1995.

court has hardly used such precedents. For example, for a long time the court has made remedial orders when dealing with human rights petitions.

There have been instances where the court has used both analogical and historical methods of reasoning, although the conclusions arrived at were sometimes suspect. An example of the use of the historical method is the court's decision in the *National Consensus* case.[136] As in the case of any other constitution, Benin's constitution of 1990 may under certain conditions be amended. In turn, what the fundamental law does not mention is whether 'non-consensual' revision is a violation of the spirit of the constitution. The Constitutional Court has responded by carving consensual revision in stone.

In 2006 and 2007, the court dismissed unilateral attempts at amending the constitution on the grounds that the fundamental law had been adopted by the people through a national consensus reached at the 1990 National Conference. The landmark decision of the Constitutional Court on this matter is DCC 06-074, where the court held that such national consensus had become a *principe à valeur constitutionnelle* or 'constitutional principle', which should determine the legal validity of any amendment to the constitution. This case was concerned with an amendment effected behind closed doors by members of parliament to extend their term of office from four to five years.[137] In the view of the court, the principle of 'national consensus' had been adopted by the February 1990 National Conference, which also initiated the December 1990 constitution; and any amendment of the constitution should follow the public and open process adopted by the Conference. The court thus declared the extension of the term contrary to the constitution.[138]

This case, cynically referred to by some as the 'thirty-nine equals forty' case, provides an instance of analogical reasoning by the Constitutional Court. Although the petition itself was concerned with equality before the law, the actual issue involved the age required to stand for election for presidency. Article 44 of the constitution prescribes that candidates should be '*at least* 40 years at the time of application'.[139] Born on 19 November 1976, the petitioner complained that the dismissal of his application in the primaries of his political party to participate in the 2016 presidential election violated his right to equality in the constitution. His claim was brought against the decision of the party to select another candidate born in the same year but on an unspecified date. The petitioner argued that a year should be calculated as from its commencement and not from one date to another date or month in a given year to the same month the next year.

In coming to its decision, the court first reasoned that 'the time of application for the considered election is in the year of the election', and as such it followed that 'the 40-year requirement is to be assessed by the standard of the year of the election' and not by any specific date in that year. The court then took the view that: '[t]he age of a person at any point of a year is equivalent to that at the last day of the year *in application of the French legal adage "a year that is commenced is acquired*" '.[140] On these grounds, the court found for the petitioner without giving any further reasons.[141]

The political element in the case is to be found in the announcement of candidature of the then finance minister in the outgoing president's cabinet. Considered the unofficially-appointed candidate to succeed the president, the minister was perceived to be in a

136 DCC 06-074 of 8 July 2006.
137 See Adjolohoun 'Benin' (n 47) 28.
138 See DCC 06-074 of 8 July 2006. See Adjolohoun in ch 11 of this book.
139 My emphasis.
140 My emphasis.
141 See Decision DCC 15-156 of 16 July 2015.

position similar to that of the petitioner. Many have suggested that the petition was a test case to prepare public opinion for the endorsement by the court of the unqualified minister's candidature.[142] Whatever the argument, the point to note is that, in two decades of constitutional adjudication, the court has found no other authority to determine such an important issue.

4. Transnational Influence on Decisions

It is worth noting from the outset that the Constitutional Court of Benin seldom refers expressly to foreign or international norms and precedents. Other than relying on its own precedents, the court prefers to adjudicate on the basis of the principles and rules rather than making specific or express reference to foreign decisions. Some of the decisions discussed earlier illustrate this general tendency.

The absence of reference to international instruments ratified by the country and the lack of elaborate reasoning has been persistent in the judicial practice of the Beninese Constitutional Court. An interesting illustration is the reluctance of the court to apply a ratified convention for lack of publication in the national gazette.[143] As a general rule, it appears that civil law adjudicators rely on French case law rather than other foreign or international precedents.[144] Although it has in recent years abandoned laconic reasoning, the French Constitutional Council, according to a commentator, had until 2013 never referred to a foreign precedent.[145]

It is true that recent positive developments in French courts have been explained by the influence of the European Court of Human Rights.[146] In light of such a trend, pronouncements by African courts of civil law tradition are rather curious. A few decisions are worth citing. For instance, a decision by the Supreme Court of Rwanda is revolutionary among African civil law jurisdictions.[147] In addition to referring to the Convention on the Elimination of All Forms of Discrimination Against Women (CEDAW), the court referred to case law from South Africa, the United States, and Canada. The jurisprudence of the military courts of the Democratic Republic of the Congo (DRC) are also interesting, both because of their direct application of the Rome Statute on the International Criminal Court and their citing of international case law.[148]

[142] See Marcel Zoumènou, 'Décision DCC 15-156: la Cour constitutionnelle veut rééditer ses turpides de 2011' *La Nouvelle Tribune* http://www.lanouvelletribune.info/benin/24994-decision-dcc-15-156-la-cour-constitutionnelle-veut-reediter-ses-turpitudes-de-2011 (last accessed 17 April 2017); Athanase Dèwanou, 'Le mythe "Cour constitutionnelle" tombe' *Jolome News* http://bj.jolome.com/news/article/dcc-15-156-de-la-cour-constitutionnelle-levee-de-bouclier-contre-la-cour-holo-le-mythe-cour-constitu (last accessed 17 April 2017); Bernado Mariano Houenoussi, 'Komi Koutché: un dauphin providentiel?' *Jolome News* http://bj.jolome.com/news/article/komi-koutche-un-dauphin-providentiel (last accessed 17 April 2017).

[143] See Decision DCC 03-009 of 19 February 2003. For a discussion of related issues see Magnus Killander and Horace Adjolohoun, 'International Law and Domestic Human Rights Litigation in Africa: An Introduction' in Magnus Killander (ed), *International Law and Domestic Human Rights Litigation in Africa* (Pretoria University Press 2010) 6–8.

[144] ibid 9.

[145] See Marie-Claire Ponthoreau, 'Le recours aux précédents étrangers par le juge constitutionnel' Rapport du Congrès de Viennes, Association internationale de droit constitutionnel (2004) 7.

[146] See Elisabeth Lambert Abdelgawad and Anne Weber, 'The Reception Process in France and Germany' in Hellen Keller and Alec Stone Sweet (eds), *A Europe of Rights: The Impact of the ECHR on National Legal Systems* (OUP 2008) 116.

[147] See RS/Inconst/Pén.0001/08/CS, Supreme Court (26 September 2008).

[148] For a summary and analysis of two of these cases in English see Ituri District, *Military Prosecutor v Kahwa Panga Mandro*, First instance decision, RMP No 227/PEN/2006; ILDC 524 (CD 2006); *Military Prosecutor v Bongi Massaba*, Criminal trial judgment and accompanying civil action for damages, RP No 018/2006; RMP

As far as the Constitutional Court of Benin is concerned, it may be said to have been eager to import foreign precedents only through principles but never through express reference. An important illustration in this respect is that of the introduction of the right to reparation for human rights violations. According to sources consulted from within the court, '[a]nalysis and research undertaken on the subject, namely drawing from the constitution's preamble, the African Charter, international doctrine and the European Court's jurisprudence convinced the Court to cross the Rubicon'.[149] However, the court did not expressly cite any of the many international law instruments or case law relating to the right to reparation, including decisions of the African Commission on Human and Peoples' Rights.

On both judicial reasoning and reliance on foreign precedents, it is important to assess the practice of the Benin Constitutional Court in light of the most observed trends. It stems from an overview of such practices that the more an adjudicatory body makes determinations over time, it is meant to establish its authority and notoriety, and tends to rely naturally on its own precedent. It would thus move from an outward case law borrowing trend to a more self-centred approach to judicial determination. In addition, a number of other factors may justify particular methods of reasoning and reliance on foreign case law, such as the legal tradition, the personal and professional background of the adjudicator, and the judicial environment.[150]

5. Nature and Effect of Decisions

In typical civil law tradition, judges of the Constitutional Court of Benin arrive at decisions by consensus rather than by taking a vote. The dissenting, concurring, and separate opinions traditionally utilized in common law courts are equally unknown in the Benin constitutional adjudication model, and in the judiciary in general.

There is no doubt that decisions of the Constitutional Court are final and binding on all state organs, individuals, and non-state entities. Whether the parties in a particular case comply with such decisions is altogether another issue. So far, no particular issue has arisen in respect of individuals or private parties complying with the decisions of the court. The same cannot be said of state organs.

As noted earlier, one problem regarding the powers of the Beninese Constitutional Court, especially in its early years, was whether the court had the power to issue orders or injunctions when it found that state organs had acted in violation of the constitution or had failed to comply with its decisions. The court took a progressive approach

No 242/PEN/06; ILDC 387 (CD 2006). See also Avocats sans Frontières, *Etude de Jurisprudence: L'application du Statut de Rome de la Cour Pénale Internationale par les Juridictions de la République Démocratique du Congo* (March 2009).

[149] See Horace S Adjolohoun, 'The "Right to Reparation" as Appliedunder the African Charter by Benin's Constitutional Court' (n 128) 29.

[150] See Horace Adjolohoun, 'Le Recours aux Précédents Étrangers par la Cour Africaine des Droits de l'Homme et des Peuples' Research Paper on file with author (2016). See also Marie-Claire Ponthoreau, 'Le recours aux précédents étrangers par le juge constitutionnel' Congrès de Viennes, Association internationale de droit constitutionnel (2004) http://www.iacl2014congress.com/fileadmin/user_upload/k_iacl2014congress/General_reports/Ponthoreau-RapportFR.pdf (last accessed 17 April 2017); Guy Canivet, 'Les influences croisées entre les juridictions nationales et internationales. Éloge de la "bénévolance" des juges' *Revue des sciences criminelles et de droit comparé* (2005) http://www.ahjucaf.org/Les-influences-croisees-entre,7177.html (last accessed 17 April 2017); Ludovic Hennebel and Arnaud van Waeyenberge, 'Réflexions sur le commerce transnational entre juges' in I Hachez and others (eds), *Les sources du droit revisitées* (Anthemis 2013) http://papers.ssrn.com/sol3/papers.cfm?abstract_id=2211183 (last accessed 17 April 2017).

to the issue of reparation for human rights violations. Generally, the executive's record regarding compliance with the decisions of the Constitutional Court is mixed. Starting with the decision in DCC 95-024, decided in 1995, the court made it clear that it could not make orders against the executive without breaching the principle of separation of powers, and that there were several cases decided on this premise.[151] However, this position has evolved in subsequent decisions, where the court has made pronouncements in the form of clear injunctions, for instance that the 'complainants [must] be reinstated',[152] thus making orders for the performance of specific actions, as was the case in DCC 05-067, even without expressly indicating the addressee of such order.[153]

The Constitutional Court seems to have received better compliance with respect to decisions concerning parliament. In DCC 03-077, DCC 04-065, and DCC 08-072 referred to earlier involving the internal operation of the National Assembly, the legislative body eventually complied with the court's decisions, albeit after resisting.

As the discussion on the powers of the court has shown, the Benin Constitutional Court has played a tremendous role in the progressive entrenchment of constitutionalism, constitutional democracy, and respect for the rule of law in the country. In doing so, it has interpreted and applied many well-established principles, as well as come up with new principles to deal with some of the peculiar challenges confronting the country. One such move of the court is the introduction of the *principe à valeur constitutionnelle* (constitutional principle), which became one of the key principles in its adjudicatory policy. For instance, the court reverted to that principle to hold that the national consensus is decisive in determining the legality of any amendments to the constitution.[154] At another juncture, the court used the same principle in deciding that the 'majority takes all' is undemocratic and raised the rights of the political minority to the rank of a *principe à valeur constitutionnelle*.[155]

These pronouncements have undoubtedly helped in some situations to prevent political crisis and spared Benin's young democracy the heartache that has led many of the countries in the region to civil strife, street revolutions, or military *coups* from the 2000s onwards. In playing the role of guardian of the constitutional order and political stability, the court prevented several attempts to amend the constitution for purposes that were termed as 'opportunistic' among both political and civil society settings. In defence of democracy, the court stopped political groups holding a majority in parliament or ruling coalitions from using their dominant position or channels such as the referendum to change constitutional provisions that are central to the delicate compromises carefully negotiated in 1990.

Generally, the rate of compliance with and implementation of its decisions has been good. This is an indication of the respect that the court has gained from all stakeholders. It is only in a few instances that there were attempts to ignore its rulings. However, each time this happened, the court successfully asserted itself and its orders were eventually obeyed.[156]

[151] See eg DCC 95-024 of 6 July 1995; DCC 95-029 of 17 August 1995; DCC 03-003; and DCC 03-004 of 18 February 2003; DCC 03-052 of 14 March 2003; and DCC 03-083 of 28 May 2003.

[152] My emphasis.

[153] See eg DCC 05-067 of 12 January 2005 and DCC 06-016 of 31 January 2006.

[154] See in DCC 06-074 of 8 July 2006.

[155] See DCC 09-002 of 8 January 2009.

[156] See DCC 06-052 of 19 April 2006.

6. Conclusion

Although it is a system in motion and despite its shortcomings, the Benin model of centralized constitutional adjudication has earned unmatched credentials in Francophone Africa and the rest of the continent at large. To begin with, the model has succeeded in maintaining the supremacy of the constitution by creating a court with sufficient powers to regulate political interactions and limit the arbitrary use of the powers granted to other branches of state. Even though some of the Constitutional Court's decisions have attracted criticism, one famous phrase has clearly emerged as the citizens' rallying point; that 'judgments of the Constitutional Court are final and binding on all'. Even considering the inherent risks, such an important achievement certainly is the result of a well-tailored, unitary, and concentrated model of constitutional adjudication with the benefit of having one judge to handle disputes and opening its findings to no legal uncertainty.

This is indeed the very rationale behind the concentrated model, which has the purpose of preventing the inconsistent development of constitutional law and altogether strengthening the enforcement of the constitution. The constitution made decisions of the Constitutional Court binding on all courts, including the Supreme Court, which operates at the apex of the ordinary judicial system. The same applies to the *Haute cour de justice*, which is also a specialized court of first and final instance, with jurisdiction over offences committed by the president and members of cabinet. It is clear that, with the power carried by its decisions, the Constitutional Court of Benin is in a position to secure constitutional supremacy and political stability, as it has done in the nearly three decades of its operation.

After more than two decades of constitutional adjudication in Benin, its unitary model has succeeded in protecting its fairly liberal constitutional order. On a continent where the constitutional order in many countries has been seriously compromised by opportunistic presidential term extensions, the fact cannot be overlooked that the Beninese Constitutional Court has been sufficiently confident to reject several attempts at amendments to presidential term limits between 2004 and 2016. While a number of other factors have obviously contributed to this outcome, the design of the Beninese concentrated model has played an important role. The role of the main stakeholders, political actors, members of the judiciary and legal profession, academics, the Constitutional Court judges themselves, and ordinary citizens at large cannot be overstated when it comes to appreciating how effective the normative and institutional framework has proved in practice.

An express mandate to entertain human rights complaints equally is a special feature of the Beninese constitutional adjudication system, which is lacking in Francophone Africa. In view of the problematic operation of the ordinary judicial system, much criticized for its vulnerability to manipulation and abuse by the executive and for inordinate delays in delivering justice, the human rights mandate of the Beninese Constitutional Court has assisted in considerably enhancing not only the protection of human rights but also constitutionalism and the rule of law.

Despite the high reputation of the Beninese constitutional adjudication model, it is not perfect. The ongoing constitutional reforms initiated by Benin's newly-elected leader, President Patrice Talon, is not surprising. The overall goal of the reforms launched in early 2016 is to strengthen some key features of the system. These include the process of appointment of judges and the composition of the court, in order to limit the influence of the executive and to involve the bar, the magistracy and the academia in the appointment process. The removal of the president and minister of justice from the operation of the Judicial Service Commission and appointment of the Chief Justice by her peers is one more change advocated in the proposed amendment. The composition, operation, and very existence of the *Haute cour de justice* mandated to try the president and members of the cabinet is also to be overhauled in order to put an end to the constant culture of impunity allowed by the current involvement of parliament in both their indictment and prosecution. In all, the outcome of the process is expected to increase the efficiency of this model of constitutional adjudication and more generally deepen Benin's considerable progress in entrenching a culture of constitutionalism, democracy, and respect for the rule of law.

Bibliography

Adjolohoun H S, 'The "Right to Reparation" as Applied under the African Charter by Benin's Constitutional Court' LLM dissertation (University of Pretoria 2007) 29 (on file with author)

Adjolohoun H S, 'Benin' *Constitutions of the Countries of the World Online* (Oxford University Press 2012)

Adjolohoun H S, Droits de l'homme et justice constitutionnelle en Afrique: le modèle béninois à la lumière de la Charte africaine des droits de l'homme et des peuples (L'Harmattan 2011)

Adjolohoun H S, *Entre constitutionnalisme et présidentialisme: succès et dilemmes du nouveau constitutionnalisme béninois 1990–2012* (CEDAT Cotonou 2013) 49

Adjolohoun H S, 'Between Presidentialism and a Human Rights Approach to Constitutionalism: Twenty Years of Practice and the Dilemmas of Amending the 1990 Constitution of Benin' in Mbondenyi M and Ojienga T (eds), *Constitutionalism and Democratic Governance in Africa: Contemporary Perspectives from Sub-Saharan Africa* (Pretoria University Law Press 2013)

Adjolohoun H S, 'Le Recours aux Précédents Étrangers par la Cour Africaine des Droits de l'Homme et des Peuples' Unpublished (2016)

Abdelgawad E L and Weber A, 'The Reception Process in France and Germany' in Keller H and Stone Sweet A (eds), *A Europe of Rights: The Impact of the ECHR on National Legal Systems* (OUP 2008) 116

Adjolohoun H S and Fombad C M, 'Separation of Powers and the Role of the Public Prosecutor in Francophone Africa' in Fombad C M (ed), *Separation of Powers in African Constitutionalism* (OUP 2016) 359–83

Ahanhanzo-Glèlè M, *Naissance d'un Etat: l'évolution politique et constitutionnelle du Dahomey, de la colonisation à nos jours* (LGDJ 1969)

Aivo F J, *Constitution de la République du Bénin, La Constitution de tous les records en Afrique* (Editions CACI 2010)

Aivo F J, 'Présentation du rapport général' Commission nationale technique chargée des réformes politiques et institutionnelles (28 June 2016) Report of the Constitutional Reform Commission (on file with author)

Association Africaine des Hautes Juridictions Francophones, *Opportunités de l'éclatement des cours suprêmes en cours distinctes*, Actes du colloque de Cotonou (14–16 May 2002)

Badet G, *Les Attributions Originelles de la Cour Constitutionnelle du Bénin* (Friedrich Ebert Stiftung 2013)

Baldé S, *La convergence des modèles constitutionnels: étude de cas en Afrique subsaharienne* (Éditions Publibook Université 2011) 388

Bio Bigou L B, 'La contribution du pouvoir législatif à la vie politique du Bénin de 1965 à 1979' in CAPAN *L'histoire du pouvoir législatif des indépendances à nos jours* (Actes du colloque parlementaire du cinquantenaire Porto-Novo 2011) 81

Bolle S, 'Projet de révision constitutionnelle au Sénégal: la renaissance de la Cour suprême' in La Constitution en Afrique http://la-constitution-en-afrique.org/article-18009013.html (last accessed 17 April 2017)

Bolle S, 'Décision DCC 09-002: le bon grain et l'ivraie' in La Constitution en Afrique http://www.la-constitution-en-afrique.org/article-26613703.html (last accessed 17 April 2017).

Bourdon J O, 'Napoléon et la construction des grands corps de l'Etat' https://francearchives.fr/en/commemo/recueil-2004/40102 (last accessed 17 April 2017)

Canivet G, 'Les influences croisées entre les juridictions nationales et internationales. Éloge de la "bénévolance" des juges' *Revue des sciences criminelles et de droit comparé* (2005) http://www.ahjucaf.org/Les-influences-croisees-entre,7177.html (last accessed 17 April 2017)

Dèwanou A, 'Le mythe "Cour Constitutionnelle" tombe' *Jolome News* http://bj.jolome.com/news/article/dcc-15-156-de-la-cour-constitutionnelle-levee-de-bouclier-contre-la-cour-holo-le-mythe-cour-constitu (last accessed 17 April 2017)

Dossou-Yovo N, 'The Experience of Benin' (1999) 16 *Journal on World Peace* 59

Esso D, 'La Justice Administrative a du Plomb dans l'Aile au Togo' *Le Libéral* (19 October 2011) 3

Drago G, *Contentieux constitutionnel français* (Thémis droit PUF 2011) 46

Enonchong N, 'The African Charter on Human and Peoples' Rights: Effective Remedies in Domestic Law?' (2002) 46 *Journal of African Law* 197

GriooCom 'Bénin: de l'enfant malade au modèle démocratique' http://www.grioo.com/ar,benindelenfantmaladeaumodeledemocratique,19522.html (last accessed 17 April 2017)

Focus Info, 'Justice Administrative Togolaise: une Juridiction à la Traîne' (27 March 2015) http://www.focusinfos.net/index.php/offre-emploi/item/558-justice-administrative-togolaise-une-juridiction-a-la-traine (last accessed 17 April 2017)

Fombad C M, 'Appointment of Constitutional Adjudicators in Africa: Some Perspectives on How Different Systems Yield Similar Outcomes' (2014) 46(2) *Journal of Legal Pluralism and Unofficial Law* 249

Fombad C M and Inegbedion N A, 'Presidential Term Limits and Their Impact on Constitutionalism in Africa' in Fombad CM and Murray C (eds), *Fostering Constitutionalism in Africa* (Pretoria University Law Press 2010) 7–8

Fondation Zinsou, 'Raconte-moi l'indépendance: 1972–1991, les années Kérékou' http://www.racontemoilindependance.org/Raconte_Moi_lIndependance/1972_1991.html (last accessed 17 April 2017)

Fougère L, 'Les Cours des suprêmes d'Afrique, un témoignage' in Gérard Conac (dir), *Les Cours suprêmes en Afrique* Tome 1 (Economica 1998) 79–81

Gangnon C, *'Les Droits Fondamentaux de la Personne Humaine' Séminaire de formation des journalistes* (Cotonou 2 August 2005) (unpublished conference paper on file with author) 1

Hennebel L and Van Waeyenberge A, 'Réflexions sur le commerce transnational entre juges' in I Hachez and others (eds), *Les sources du droit revisitées* (Anthemis 2013) http://papers.ssrn.com/sol3/papers.cfm?abstract_id=2211183 (last accessed 17 April 2017)

Houenoussi B M, 'Komi Koutché: un dauphin providentiel?' *Jolome News* http://bj.jolome.com/news/article/komi-koutche-un-dauphin-providentiel (last accessed 17 April 2017)

Killander M and Adjolohoun H S, 'International Law and Domestic Human Rights Litigation in Africa: An Introduction' in Killander M (ed), *International Law and Domestic Human Rights Litigation in Africa* (Pretoria University Law Press 2010) 6–8

Le Monde, 'Françoise Hollande assure qu'il va supprimer la Cour de justice de la République' http://www.lemonde.fr/societe/article/2014/06/25/francois-hollande-assure-qu-il-va-supprimer-la-cour-de-justice-de-la-republique_4444862_3224.html (last accessed 17 April 2017)

Magnusson B A, 'Testing Democracy in Benin: Experiments in Institutional Reform' in Richard Joseph (ed), *State, Conflict and Democracy in Africa* (Lynne Rienner Publishers 1999) 221

Médé N, *Les grandes décisions de la Cour constitutionnelle du Bénin* (Editions Universitaires Européennes 2012)

Mêtinhoué P, *Les gouvernements du Dahomey et du Bénin: 1957–2005* (CNPMS 2005).

Monsi J B, 'Benin' in Association Africaine des Hautes Juridictions Francophones, *Opportunités de l'éclatement des cours suprêmes en cours distinctes*, Actes du colloque de Cotonou (14–16 May 2002) 120

Musila G, 'The Right to an Effective Remedy under the African Charter on Human and Peoples' Rights' (2006) 6 *African Human Rights Law Journal* 442

Nwajiaku K, 'The National Conferences in Benin and Togo Revisited' (1994) 32 *The Journal of Modern African Studies* 439, 440

Pellet R, *La Cour des comptes* (Edition La Découverte Paris 1998) 64

Ponthoreau M-C, 'Le recours aux précédents étrangers par le juge constitutionnel' Rapport du Congrès de Viennes, Association internationale de droit constitutionnel (2004) 7

Rotman A, 'Benin's Constitutional Court: An Institutional Model for Guaranteeing Human Rights' (2004) 17 *Harvard Human Rights Journal* 283

Rousseau D, *Droit du Contentieux Constitutionnel* (Montchretien 2010) 23–30

Sidi A L, 'La protection des droits humains par la Cour constitutionnelle du Bénin de 1993 à 2005' Mémoire de DEA Chaire UNESCO Université d'Abomey-Calavi (2006)

Vie publique, 'Qui est jugé par la Cour de justice de la République?' http://www.vie-publique.fr/decouverte-institutions/justice/fonctionnement/juridictions-particulieres/qui-est-juge-par-cour-justice-republique.html (last accessed 17 April 2017)

Youssef N, *La Transition Démocratique et la Garantie des Droits Fondamentaux* (Editions Publibook Université 2011) 614–15

Zoumènou M, 'Décision DCC 15-156: la Cour constitutionnelle veut rééditer ses turpides de 2011' *La Nouvelle Tribune* http://www.lanouvelletribune.info/benin/24994-decision-dcc-15-156-la-cour-constitutionnelle-veut-reediter-ses-turpitudes-de-2011 (last accessed 17 April 2017)

3

The Cameroonian Constitutional Council

Faithful Servant of an Unaccountable System

Charles M Fombad

1. Introduction

The introduction of a new system of constitutional review in Cameroon, particularly after the post-1990 wave of liberal constitutional reforms in Africa, could have been seen as a signal of the country's firm commitment to constitutionalism and respect for the rule of law. On the contrary, the 1996 constitution and the constitutional review system which it provides for is the embodiment of paradoxes and contradictions. While in the 1990s most of Francophone Africa followed the lead of Benin to modify, adjust, and adapt the inherited French Constitutional Council model, Cameroon in 1996 preferred to return to and adopt the original 1958 version in its pure and most ineffective form. This is compounded by the fact that what the constitution provides for and what happens in practice differ completely.

Writing in 1998, two years after this Constitution came into force, the author, after analysing the provisions on the Constitutional Council, concluded as follows:

> In sealing the only viable outlet for challenging unconstitutional acts and electoral fraud by injudiciously opting for the obsolete and discredited mechanism of a politically and manipulable Constitutional Council, the authors of the 1996 constitutional amendment have left Cameroon moving dangerously into an uncertain 21st century.[1]

Was this pessimistic view justified? It is now twenty years since the 1996 Constitution came into force, and yet the functions of the Cameroonian Constitutional Council (Council) are still being 'temporarily' performed by the Supreme Court. This chapter will highlight some of the numerous anomalies and contradictions that such an obsolete system of constitutional review has had in impeding the institutionalization of a culture of constitutionalism and respect for the rule of law, and will suggest that it appears to have been designed to evade rather than promote constitutional accountability.

The rest of the discussion will start with a brief background of how the Council came to be provided for under the Constitution. Subsequently, it will look at its composition. Some of the legal imponderables posed by empowering the Supreme Court to exercise the functions of the Council will be considered. This will be followed by an examination of the powers exercised, the issue of access to constitutional justice, the nature and effect of the decisions rendered, and the impact of the decisions on the promotion of constitutionalism in Cameroon. In conclusion, it will be shown that the existence of a Council whose functions are performed by the Supreme Court is an illusion deliberately designed

[1] See Charles M Fombad, 'The New Cameroonian Constitutional Council in a Comparative Perspective: Progress or Retrogression?' (1998) 42(2) *Journal of African Law* 186.

to disguise the fact that there is no system in place to prevent the political elites from disregarding or violating the constitution.

2. Brief Background

The historical origin of the Cameroonian legal system is a useful starting point to understanding the intricacies of its constitutional review system. The country has gone through two main colonial experiences, namely the German period from 1884, which ended in 1916 after their defeat by combined British and French expeditionary forces in Cameroon. The victorious allies took over and administered different parts of the territory from 1916 to 1961.[2] What is now known as the Anglophone regions (former British zone) and Francophone regions (former French zone) formally reunited under a 1961 federal constitution which established a two-state federation. This was subsequently replaced by a unitary constitution in 1972.[3] It is the latter constitution that was subsequently substantially revised to be what is referred to as the 1996 Constitution.

Having existed under two different colonial masters since 1916, the 1962 reunification of the Anglophone and Francophone regions of Cameroon effectively brought together two divergent and potentially antagonistic legal traditions, each of which came with strong colonial cultural, identity, and loyalty baggage. Today, with a population estimated at 23.5 million people, there also exists a wide diversity of ethnic groups, cultures and languages in the country.[4] In fact, Cameroon boasts an extraordinary multiplicity of about 250 tribes, who speak over 280 different indigenous languages.[5] Superimposed upon this complex mix of ethnic groups and diverse languages is the divide between Anglophones and Francophones. The Anglophones live in two of the ten political regions of the country and are estimated to make up 20 per cent of the population, while the Francophone, who live in eight regions, make up 80 per cent of the population.

Although the country is officially bi-jural in the sense that the inherited English common law and French civil law are supposed to coexist and apply in the Anglophone and Francophone regions respectively,[6] the official policy since 1962 has been one of legal harmonization which in practice has been used as the pretext steadily to displace and replace the English common law in the Anglophone regions with French civil law. Since the demise of the two-state federation, the process of what has effectively become the 'Frenchification' of the legal system has gathered such momentum that the country can at best be said to be bi-jural in French civil law.[7]

More generally, in the public law area, the English law influence in the reunified Cameroon was almost non-existent after reunification. For example, the so-called federal

[2] It has never been clear why, on the defeat of the German forces in Cameroon by a combined British and French force, the two victors decided to share the territory in such an irrational manner with the British taking two small pieces of disjointed territory in the western part of the country and leaving the lion's share to the French. This is not surprising, as the 1884 partition of Africa was equally arbitrary, irrational, and illogical.

[3] The 1961 eternity clause, which provided in art 47 that: '[a]ny proposals for the revision of the present Constitution which impairs the unity and integrity of the Federation shall be inadmissible'.

[4] Estimates of November 2015. See http://countrymeters.info/en/Cameroon (last accessed 17 April 2017).

[5] In fact, the languages listed in some studies for Cameroon are 286; of these, 279 are classified as living languages, 3 as second languages without mother tongue speakers, and 4 as extinct. See 'Languages of the World: Cameroon' http://www.ethnologue.com/country/CM/languages (last accessed 17 April 2017).

[6] The recognition of bi-juralism may be inferred from the preamble as well as art 68 of the constitution.

[7] See further Charles M Fombad, 'Managing Legal Diversity: Cameroonian Bijuralism at a Critical Crossroads' in Vernon Palmer, Mohamed Mattar, and Anna Koppel (eds), *Mixed Legal Systems, East and West* (Ashgate Publishing 2014) 187–217.

constitution, adopted after reunification in 1961, was nothing more than a token amendment to the 1960 constitution of the then independent French Cameroon by an annexure called 'transitional and special dispositions'. What then became the federal constitution of the Federal Republic of Cameroon was nothing more than a law revising the former French Cameroon's independence constitution of 4 March 1960,[8] which was essentially based on the Gaullist French Fifth Republic constitution of 1958.

Insofar as constitutional review was concerned, a limited form of review was provided for by Article 14 of the 1961 constitution. It gave the president alone the absolute discretion to refer federal or federated state laws that violated the constitution to the Federal Court of Justice.[9] The same approach was adopted when a new constitution was adopted in 1972. The only provision providing for some form of constitutional review was Article 10, which stated as follows:

> The President of the Republic shall refer to the Supreme Court under the conditions prescribed by the law provided for in Article 32 any law which he considers to be contrary to his Constitution.

Hence, as under the 1961 constitution, the president alone had the absolute discretion to determine whether or not a law that violates the constitution should be referred for review by the Supreme Court. This is essentially the extent to which there was constitutional review under all of Cameroon's pre-1996 constitutions. It is, therefore, not surprising that hardly a case was ever brought before the Supreme Court for a violation of the constitution.

At this stage it is appropriate to make a few comments about the underlying nature and philosophy of the 1996 constitution, which in many ways explains why the constitutional review system was designed in the way it was and has been operating in the way it does. The constitution was ostensibly adopted in response to popular protests for political and constitutional reforms that started in the early 1990s. However, after the government, with the complicity of the French, managed to weather the storm, by 1996 it felt sufficiently strong to write a new constitution on its own terms.[10] As a result, the constitution is one of the few post-1990 African constitutions that barely reflects any of the critical elements of modern constitutionalism that have been incorporated in most contemporary constitutions. In many respects, it is regressive in that it exhibits all the features of the original Gaullist constitution with all its weaknesses and limitations.

Perhaps its greatest weakness is that it merely reinforced the pre-existing highly centralized autocratic state system in which the president was given extensive powers at the expense of a considerably weak and ineffective legislature and judiciary. For example, the president can, without consulting anybody, appoint and dismiss the prime minister,

[8] Besides, arts 59 stated, inter alia, that: '[t]he revised Constitution shall be published in French and in English, *the French text being authentic*' (emphasis added). See further HNA Enonchong, *Cameroon Constitutional Law: Federalism in a Mixed Common Law and Civil Law System* (Centre d'edition et de Production de Manuels et d'Auxiliaires et de l'Enseignement 1967) 82.

[9] However, Enonchong (n 8) 232–3 suggests that both the West Cameroon Court of Appeal (for the then State of West Cameroon) and the East Cameroon Supreme Court (for the then State of East Cameroon) had the power to interpret the constitution and federal laws. It is difficult to see how this could have been so in light of what art 14 expressly states.

[10] For an analysis of the political crisis of the early 1990s and the manner in which it was violently suppressed, as well as the role of the French see Charles M Fombad and Jonie B Fonyam, 'The Social Democratic Front, the Opposition and the Transition' in John Mukum Mbaku and Joseph Takougang (eds), *The Leadership Challenge in Africa: Cameroon under Paul Biya* (Africa World Press 2004) 453–88.

cabinet members, judges, generals, regional governors, prefects, and the heads of the numerous parastatals. The president can approve or veto newly enacted laws, declare a state of emergency, and authorize public expenditure. He also has extensive powers to legislate and can rule by decree. The constitution professes to introduce, for the first time, what it terms 'judicial power' and judicial independence, but this is effectively neutralized by the unlimited powers given to the president to appoint and dismiss judges. It is, therefore, not surprising that the system of constitutional review introduced is based on the original and largely outdated and discredited French 1958 Constitutional Council model, which had been abandoned, albeit reluctantly, by the French themselves only in 2008, but much earlier by most progressive Francophone countries, instead taking their cue from the Benin Constitution of 1990. The challenge such an archaic system poses to constitutionalism is that, by putting the president at the centre of everything, makes it doubtful whether the constitution really has the force of a supreme overriding law that guarantees the rule of law.

However, nothing exposes the ruse behind the design of the Cameroonian system of constitutional review better than the fact that the Council that was supposed to exercise these functions has for the past twenty years never been established and its functions continue to be exercised by the Supreme Court. A discussion of constitutional justice under these circumstances becomes an analysis of the implications of a carefully crafted illusionary text and the reality behind it. The question generally becomes one of how the special function of constitutional review, supposed to be discharged by a specially created body outside the judiciary, can be discharged by another body within the judiciary.

To what extent is this in conformity with the letter and spirit of the constitution and the rule of law? A good starting point for this and many more of the paradoxes that arise between what the constitution says and how it is distorted in practice is to look at the composition of the Council. It is important, however, at this stage to point out that unless the context clearly indicates otherwise, all references to the Council means the Supreme Court, which is actually performing the functions assigned to the Council.

3. Composition of the Council

The process of appointing constitutional court judges generally is probably one of the most powerful and effective means that could be used by the other two branches of government to interfere with and influence the court. These judges have the difficult task of ensuring that the other branches of government, especially the executive, operate within their constitutional powers and do not abuse their powers. Many of their decisions have far-reaching social and political implications, thus necessitating that great care is taken in appointing them to ensure that they can act independently and impartially. The judges, therefore, need to be insulated from any threats or risk of manipulation that may force them to act unjustly in favour of the state or powerful politicians.

The question, therefore, is whether the procedures provided in the Cameroonian constitution ensure the appointment of persons based on their technical and professional merit as well as their ability to decide matters independently, objectively, and fairly. The fact that the functions of constitutional review are being discharged by the Supreme Court instead of the Council, as provided for by the constitution, has serious implications for the ability of judges to act independently and impartially.

The relevant provision regulating the manner of appointment is worth citing in its entirety. This provision is contained in Article 51of the constitution, which states:

(1) The Constitutional Council shall comprise 11 (eleven) members designated for an eventually renewable term of office of 6 (six) years. These members shall be chosen from among personalities of established professional renown. They must be of high moral integrity and proven competence.
(2) Members of the Constitutional Council shall be appointed by the President of the Republic.
They shall be designated as follows:
- three, including the President of the Council, by the President of the Republic;
- three by the President of the National Assembly after consultation with the Bureau;
- three by the President of the Senate after consultation with the Bureau;
- two by the Higher Judicial Council.
Besides the eleven members provided for above, former presidents of the Republic shall be *ex officio* members of the Constitutional Council for life. In case of a tie, the President of the Constitutional Council shall have the casting vote.

Three comments may be made about these provisions with respect to who makes the appointments and who can be appointed and on what basis such an appointment is made. First, unlike in most other countries, the eleven members of the Council are appointed by the president of the republic. Although the provision actually states that the president directly appoints only three members and the rest are people 'designated' by other political bodies, the reality is that, since the advent of multipartyism in 1992, the complete dominance of the ruling Cameroon Peoples' Democratic Party (CPDM), presided over and controlled by the president, has been unassailable. Similarly, the president and his minister of justice are chair and deputy chair, respectively, of the Higher Judicial Council. It is they who determine when it meets as well as its agenda. The net effect, therefore, is that the president virtually determines who becomes a member of the Council.

Secondly, the independence, competence and effectiveness of a constitutional court judge depends on an appointment process with clearly laid-down objectives and transparent criteria that rely on factors such as qualifications, competence and integrity. True to the original 1958 design, Article 51 of the Cameroon constitution merely states that the 'members shall be chosen from among personalities of established professional renown' and 'must be of high moral integrity and proven competence'. Therefore, they need not be jurists. Thirdly, the original 1996 formulation of Article 51(1) provided that members of the Council were to be appointed for a 'non-renewal term of office of 9 (nine) years'. In 2008, when President Paul Biya decided to remove the two-term presidential term limit from the constitution, this provision was also revised in favour of an open term.

This is a departure from the 1958 French design which, at first sight, gives the impression that this reflects the general desire to remove term limits from the constitution. As will become evident, a better explanation for this is that it reflects the real intentions of making permanent *de facto* what is supposed to be *de jure* temporary and transitional. In spite of the apparent open term, section 18 of Law No 2004/004 of 21 April 2004, which lays down the rules and regulations concerning the membership of the Constitutional Council (hereinafter referred to as the 2004 Law on membership of the Council), provides that the Council 'by a majority vote of two-thirds of its members may, of its own motion or at the request of the designating authority and following an adversarial procedure, terminate the appointment of a member'. Far from being a body with members whose tenure is subject to no term limit, the members remain beholden to the authority who designated or appointed them and who can remove them at any time or—and this is the strangest part—the Council could on its own decide to terminate the membership of any of its own members!

The legality of having the Supreme Court play the role of the Council, supposedly as a temporal measure, but what is now turning out to be a permanent temporary measure, is highly suspect. For one thing, it is difficult to see how twenty years after the constitution came into force, the exercise by the Supreme Court of the functions of the Council can still be considered as a temporal or transitional measure. Perhaps worse still is the fact that Article 51(5) expressly states that '[t]he duties of members of the Constitutional Council shall be incompatible with those of members … of the Supreme Court'.[11] However, for twenty years, judges of the Supreme Court have acted as the Council without any regard to this express prohibition. More difficulties arise from the different manner in which the judges of the Supreme Court are appointed.

Generally, the Supreme Court, when acting as the Council, sits in a panel of joint benches which in principle is composed of at least nineteen judges.[12] The manner in which the judges are appointed is not based on any objective and transparent criteria that rely on factors such as qualifications, competence and integrity. The appointments are made by the president of the republic, supposedly based on the 'opinion' of the Higher Judicial Council which, as pointed out above, is chaired by the president himself, with his minister of justice as deputy chair. The judges are usually appointed from amongst those who have reached the highest rank in the judiciary (usually the fourth grade and beyond it to the exceptional grade). Reaching the grade which qualifies a judge to be appointed to the Supreme Court, however, does not depend on competence and proven record or even integrity, but rather on loyalty to the regime and the willingness displayed in doing its bidding. Similarly, although there is a fixed retirement age of sixty-five for these senior judges, the president can expressly or implicitly waive it for any individual judge as it suits his pleasure. The discretionary powers of the president extend to determining judicial salaries and allowances. As elsewhere in Francophone Africa, judicial salaries have been opportunistically increased to influence the actions of judges when dealing with electoral disputes.[13]

The constitution provides for a Council with a predetermined number of persons who are to be appointed in a specified manner. In practice, it is the judges of the Supreme Court who virtually serve at the pleasure of the president of the republic and who double as members of the Council. It can hardly be predicted who, amongst the numerous judges, will sit in the panel of joint benches which discharges the duty of the Council because the president of the Supreme Court has a free hand to appoint whomsoever he wants to head or be a member of any of the benches and divisions. For a country that professes to be bi-jural, beyond the implicit recognition of the continuous application of both English common law and French civil law in Article 68, there is no explicit requirement that appointments to either the Supreme Court or even the Council should reflect the two

[11] See also a similar prohibition in s 8(1) of the 2004 regulations on membership.

[12] See s 15(1) of Law No 2006/016 of 29 December 2006, regulating the organization and functioning of the Supreme Court, states that the panel of joint benches comprises of the first president, bench presidents and division presidents. Generally, the Supreme Court consists of the judicial bench (consisting of five divisions), the administrative bench (consisting of five divisions) and an audit bench (also consisting of five divisions).

[13] The most notorious instance of this occurred during the 1992 elections. For details of this, see Charles M Fombad, 'The Dynamics of Record-breaking Endemic Corruption and Political Opportunism in Cameroon' in Mbaku and Takougang (n 10) 361–7. In Senegal, former President Abdoulaye Wade, by Decree No 2011-1044 of 26 July 2011, gave judges a substantial salary increase in what most commentators saw as an attempt by him to influence them to allow him to run for a third term, which the Constitutional Court eventually did.

legal cultures. The most that has been done is to appoint a few Anglophone judges to some of the benches, but the potential for any common law influence in any matter that comes before the Supreme Court, whether as an apex court or playing the role of the Council, is almost nil.[14] More generally, there is no requirement that the composition of these bodies should reflect the gender, religious and ethnic diversity of the country.

In the final analysis, those who serve in Cameroon's apex court and, by default, the Council, supposed to ensure the respect for its constitution, are mainly people appointed more as a reward for royalty and commitment to the regime than proven competence in expounding and applying the law. It is, therefore, not surprising that those judges who occupy strategic positions are often forgotten in their positions. For example, the last Chief Justice of the Supreme Court, Alexis Dipanda Mouelle, held this office from 1990 until his retirement in 2014.

Be that as it may, the critical issue is the power exercised by the Council, to which we will now turn.

4. Scope of Review Powers

One of the critical factors to an effective system of constitutional review are the powers given to the review body. The range of issues that the Council is empowered to deal with are regulated by Articles 46 to 48 of the constitution and Law No 2004/004 of 21 April 2004 on the organization and functioning of the Constitutional Council (2004 Law on the functioning of the Council). An analysis of these laws shows that the Council has been vested with both contentious and advisory jurisdiction. The provisions on the former are more elaborate and provide that the Council may undertake constitutional review in three main areas: first, a general power of review of the constitutionality of laws, treaties and agreements; secondly, intervention in the case of conflicts of competence between certain state institutions; and thirdly, ensuring the regularity of elections.

The power to review the constitutionality of laws, treaties, and international agreements is provided for in Articles 47(1) and (3) of the constitution. Although a strict reading of Articles 46 and 47(1) suggests that concrete review is contemplated, Article 47(3) appears to preclude such a conclusion. The latter provides that the review only relates to laws, treaties and international agreements 'prior to their enactment'. Considering the historical provenance of this model of review, it must be assumed that only abstract review is contemplated here. The use of the permissive verb 'may', with respect to requesting the review of laws, treaties, and international agreements, indicates that there is no obligation on anyone to request such a review.

By contrast, the Standing Orders of the National Assembly and the Senate and any subsequent amendments thereof must, prior to their implementation, be reviewed by the Council. What poses the greatest risk to constitutionalism and the rule of law? The standing orders of the National Assembly or the legislation which the National Assembly makes? It is, therefore, paradoxical that the Cameroonian legislature considered the standing orders of the National Assembly and the Senate so important that they must be reviewed for conformity to the constitution, but does not make it mandatory for laws, treaties, and international agreements, which may violate the constitution to be reviewed.

[14] This is partly owing to the fact that the general constitutional framework is essentially borrowed from the French system. In fact, the entire public law in the country is based on the civil law, with probably very little of the common law system left in place, even in Anglophone regions. The other reason is the pervasiveness of Anglophobia—a deep suspicion of Anglophones and a desire to eliminate traces of the Anglophone culture.

The anomalies do not end here. Article 68 of the Constitution provides for the continuous application of 'legislation applicable in the Federal State of Cameroon and in the Federated States on the date of entry into force of this constitution', insofar as they are not repugnant to the constitution. Given that the present model of review gives no institution the powers of concrete review of the constitutionality of existing or promulgated law, who can authoritatively say whether or not any of the old legislation is inconsistent with the constitution?

The second area of intervention by the Council, according to Article 37(1) of the constitution, is with respect to 'conflict of powers between state institutions, between the state and the regions, and between the regions'. Apart from other institutional issues,[15] it is also provided that the presidents of regional executives may refer matters to the Council whenever the interests of their regions are at stake, whatever this means.[16] The vague distribution of legislative powers between the legislature and the executive under Articles 26 to 28 of the constitution provides a potential source of conflict if one branch feels that the other has encroached on its own law-making domain. The Council also has the powers to deal with disputes concerning the admissibility of bills.[17]

Generally, while this limited system of preventive control of constitutionality may in theory prevent unconstitutional legislation from becoming law, the reality is that the extensive executive rules and regulations which the constitution authorizes the executive to enact completely escape any review to ensure that they do not violate the constitution. However, this is the major source of laws that regulate most aspects of daily life and which, in practice, regularly put in jeopardy most of the rights apparently guaranteed in the constitution.

The third main area of competence concerns elections. In this regard, Article 48(1) of the constitution states that the Council shall 'ensure the regularity of presidential elections, parliamentary elections and referendum questions', and adds that 'it shall proclaim the results thereof'. The 2004 Law on the functioning of the Council contains detailed provisions regulating these matters.[18] A careful reading of both the constitution and the 2004 Law clearly indicates that the Council has been given wide-ranging powers in dealing with presidential elections, parliamentary elections, and referendum questions from the preparation and conduct of balloting, through the proclamation of the results to resolving any challenges filed by candidates against the regularity of the elections or referendum. Nevertheless, Law No 2006/011 of 29 December 2006, regulating the organization and functioning of Elections Cameroon (ELECAM), creates a so-called 'independent body responsible for the organization, management and supervision of all election operations and referendums' in Cameroon.

It is difficult to see how the extensive powers given by this 2006 Law to ELECAM can be reconciled with the broad and arguably exclusive powers given to the Council by the

[15] For example, it is provided in art 6(4) that the Council will determine when the presidency is vacant whether as a result of death, resignation or permanent incapacity. For reasons that are not obvious at all, s 38 of the 2004 law on the functioning of the Council states that it must rule on this matter by a two-thirds majority of its members. It is a rule bordering on the bizarre: why should the certification of a presidential vacancy caused by, for example, death, only become valid when the decision is approved by a two-thirds majority of the members of the Council?

[16] See art 47(2) of the constitution. This is a very vague provision. Issues that may affect the interests of a region may well have nothing to do with the interpretation or application of the constitution. Why should these be referred to the Council?

[17] See arts 18(3)(b) and 23(3)(b) of the constitution.

[18] See ss 40–42 and 51–54 on the regularity of elections and referendums; ss 43–46 on presidential elections; and ss 47–50 on parliamentary elections.

constitution. In fact, the net effect has been to reduce the role of the Council to proclaiming the results prepared for it by ELECAM, as well as dealing with electoral disputes. In spite of the questionable constitutional legality of ELECAM, election disputes have been almost the only issues that have come before the Council.

Finally, the advisory jurisdiction of the Council is provided for in Article 47(4) of the constitution, which states that the Council 'shall advice [stet] in matters falling under its jurisdiction'. The wording of this provision, like many other provisions dealing with the Council, is problematic. Formulated in this manner, it appears to suggest that the Council, when seised with any matter, has the right to do no more than merely to issue an advisory opinion. This conclusion is reinforced by section 34 of the 2004, Law which spells this out in more detail.[19]

This, certainly, could not have been the intention of the drafters of the constitution. On the other hand, in those instances provided for in Articles 15 and 36 of the constitution, when the president of the Council is supposed to be consulted, section 37 of the 2004 Law states that he must give a reasoned opinion. Whether reasoned or not, the fact is that the requester of the opinion is not bound by the advice given.[20] This raises the important question of who has the right to approach the Council, to which we now turn.

5. Access to the Council

The problem of access to constitutional justice is one of the main flaws of the French 1958 constitutional council model that Cameroon has blindly adopted in all its constitutions.[21] The general rule is that matters may only be referred to the Council by the president of the republic, the president of the national assembly, the president of the senate, one-third of the members of the national assembly, or one-third of senators. The main exception here relates to electoral disputes. In this regard, Article 48(2) of the constitution states that any challenges in respect of the regularity of presidential or parliamentary elections may be brought before the Council by 'any candidate, political party that participated in the election in the constituency concerned or any person acting as government agent at the election'.

The ordinary citizen in Cameroon, unless he was a candidate to a disputed presidential or parliamentary election, has no right to bring any matter before the Council or, more generally, to challenge any legislation, whether promulgated as law or not, which violates his constitutional rights. In other words, the ordinary citizen has no access to constitutional justice.[22] Those who have the *locus standi* to challenge the constitutionality of any

[19] Section 34 states that this jurisdiction includes 'the interpretation of the Constitution; any point of constitutional, electoral or parliamentary law; and matters expressly mentioned under article 47 of the Constitution and under this law'.

[20] This is equally true, even when the Council itself is consulted, as provided for under arts 59(2) and 60(2) of the constitution.

[21] By the time Cameroon copied the Constitutional Council model, its weaknesses had already become so manifest in France itself that several strategies had been adopted to remedy some of its glaring deficiencies. See generally Charles M Fombad, 'The New Cameroonian Constitutional Council in a Comparative Perspective: Progress or Retrogression?' (1998) 42(2) *Journal of African Law* 186. It was only marginally improved upon during the revision of the French constitution in 2008. However, the French Constitutional Council today is less effective than the Benin Constitutional Court, which although based on the centralized model has borrowed many features of the decentralized model. See the discussion of this by Sègnonna Horace Adjolohoun in ch 2 of this volume.

[22] For example, in *Assigana Tsimi v ELECAM and Republic of Cameroon* (unreported), Tsimi's application for registration as a presidential candidate had been rejected by the electoral commission. He, however, approached the Council to declare the nomination of President Biya as candidate invalid on the grounds that

legislation, such as the president of the republic, the president of the national assembly, and the president of the senate, are the very persons who have no reason to do so; more often than not, the legislation must have been initiated or approved by them. Moreover, the weak system of separation of powers caused by the extensive powers conferred on the president of the republic not only enables him to control and dictate the agenda of parliament, but he also decides who can be nominated for election as the president of both houses of parliament. It is unlikely that any of the presidents of the two houses of parliament will want to disregard the wishes of the president because he can, under the pretext of a 'serious crisis', shorten the term of office of both houses[23] or decline to put them forward to election (their election to their position takes place annually).[24]

At first blush, the idea of allowing one-third of the members of the National Assembly or one-third of the senators the right to petition the Council provides an opening for opposition voices to be heard. Even this avenue has progressively been closed with each election that has taken place since 1990, as the control and dominance of the ruling CPDM party has increased to the extent that the combined opposition can barely make up 20 per cent of either house of parliament.[25] The Council has no powers of *auto-saisine* even if, once it is properly seised of an issue concerning a piece of legislation, sections 19(5) and (6) of the 2004 Law allows it to rule on any issue concerning the entire legislation, provided that the petitioner is duly informed about this.

As pointed out earlier, the only instance when a private citizen can approach the Council is with respect to election petitions. In fact, electoral disputes have practically remained almost the only matters that have been brought before the Council. According to section 42(1) of the 2004 Law on the functioning of the Council, all disputes concerning contested elections must be submitted within seventy-two hours from the date of the close of the poll. This, it is submitted, is an unrealistic time limit. It fails to factor in the time it may take to tabulate the results, which is usually the basis for determining whether or not there were irregularities and their extent. In other words, this time is too short for a party to collect the evidence needed to determine whether or not it is necessary to challenge the results.

Perhaps the main problem is that the seat of the Council is in Yaoundé, the capital city, and all petitions must be filed here. There is no reason, in light of the poor state of roads in the country, to assume that every potential litigant will be able within this short time limit to find his way to Yaoundé. Although in two cases decided in 1997 the Council declared that in determining the seventy-two hours, weekends and public holidays were excluded,[26] this may only provide limited help depending on the day of the week on which the elections were held. Litigation costs will still be high, especially legal fees for lawyers who have to travel and defend petitions in Yaoundé, notwithstanding the fact that election petitions are exempt from stamp duty and registration fees.

Biya had not formally been approved by his party, the CPDM, as their presidential candidate. The Council, after noting that the candidature of Tsimi had been rejected, declared that he lacked the *locus standi* to bring a petition before the Council.

23 Constitution art 15(4).

24 ibid arts 16(2)(a) and 21(2).

25 For example, in the first senate elections held on 14 April 2013, the ruling CPDM party won 56 seats out of 70 and the President appointed 30 members, giving the ruling party 86% control of the 100-member senate. In parliamentary elections held on 17 October 2013, the ruling party won 148 of the 180 available seats, constituting 82% of seats. This basically means that the opposition parties cannot by virtue of their numbers qualify to bring a matter before the Council.

26 Unreported cases involving the constituency of Nde and the constituency of Mayo-Rey in 1997.

Although political parties can also file petitions before the Council, it is not always straightforward. In *Gaga Haman Adji v MINAT and Republic of Cameroon*,[27] the applicant's party had joined forces and campaigned under the banner of another party. The Council held that only a party that had contested the elections under its own party banners and not one that had done so by supporting another party has the right to bring a petition. In other words, ordinary citizens cannot initiate an action before the Council to invalidate any elections or referendum on the general grounds that they were not free and fair.

6. Nature of Opinions and Decisions

The Council's rulings may take the form of an advisory opinion or a binding decision. However, the wording of the relevant legal provisions on this leaves a lot to be desired. For example, Article 50(1) of the constitution states that the decisions of the Council are not subject to appeal and are binding on all public, administrative, military, and judicial authorities, as well as on all natural persons and corporate bodies. This is followed by Article 50(2) of the constitution, which appears to qualify this by stating that 'a provision declared unconstitutional *may* not be enacted or implemented'. The use of the permissive 'may' appears to suggest that compliance is not mandatory, yet the tenor of the whole section is to ensure that legislation inconsistent with the constitution should not be adopted. The uncertainty is compounded by several similar but equally loosely worded provisions in the 2004 Law on the functioning of the Council.[28]

Nothing is explicitly said about the effect of the advice given by the Council under Article 47(4) of the constitution. As noted earlier, there is no reason to assume that an advisory opinion means anything more than what it says, even on matters involving the interpretation of the constitution. What is rather confusing is the fact that there is no absolute clarity as to whether the Council has an unfettered discretion, when seised of a matter, to decide whether to give its ruling by way of a final and binding decision or just to express an advisory opinion.

With regard to elections, section 45 of the 2004 Law allows the Council to cancel, partially or in its entirety, the electoral operations. In the case of referenda, section 53 of the same law requires the Council to establish the existence of any irregularities and then to decide, considering the nature and seriousness of the irregularities, either wholly or partially to uphold the referendum.

One of the first and very rare instances in Cameroon when a law was declared unconstitutional was in 2002, when the Supreme Court declared the Standing Orders of the National Assembly unconstitutional, which provided for a procedure for the National Assembly to certify and confirm the validity of the election of each member of parliament before they take their seat after parliamentary elections. The Court held that the standing orders violated the constitution under which the Council had been given the powers to ensure the regularity of these elections and to proclaim the final results.[29] This was one of

[27] Unreported case of 1997.

[28] For example, s 26 of this law states that, where the Council rules that a provision in a law is unconstitutional and fails to establish whether or not it is severable from the law, the president of the republic may either enact the law excluding the impugned provision or refer the law to parliament for a second reading. What is the situation if parliament votes in favour of maintaining the law as it is with the impugned provisions? Will this override the decision of the Council? The law, it is submitted, complicates rather than clarifies the situation.

[29] See Decision No 001/CC/02-03 of 28 November 2002.

those inconvenient rules that the ruling party was happy to get rid of and the Council was happy to oblige.

As noted earlier, and this point bears repeating, what is so important about standing orders and their constitutionality that they need to be mandatorily reviewed, whereas the laws enacted by parliament and other subsidiary legislation made by the executive escape from such review? It is equally difficult to justify the fact that the standing orders operating today have hardly been adjusted to reflect the multiparty orientation of the 1996 constitution, but this cannot be challenged because the Council only has the powers of abstract review.

Since 1996, hundreds of electoral petitions have come before the Council.[30] A critical review of some of the decisions made by the Council indicates that there is no consistency. This is not only attributable to the fact that many of the relevant laws, especially those regulating elections, often conflict with one another, but also the form of the decisions. In fact, it may be argued that the quality of the decisions is a reflection of the manner in which they are arrived at. According to sections 60 to 64 of the 2004 law on the functioning of the Council, on receiving a petition, the president of the Council assigns it to a particular member, who is referred to as a rapporteur. It is the rapporteur who carries out an investigation and prepares a report and presents it to the Council. The latter may adopt it as it is or with amendments, and this eventually becomes the decision of the Council. Generally, the decisions are written in typical cryptic civilian style: deductive but often shallow; bland, and unclear in their legal reasoning. The terse and often questionable logical legal reasoning in some cases clearly suggests some attempt to rationalize the conclusions arrived at from predetermined positions.[31]

The unrealistic time limits within which decisions concerning electoral petitions must be announced, combined with the fact that the Council is supposed to ensure that all the elections throughout the country were free and fair before proclaiming the results, make it almost impossible for the Council to investigate any electoral dispute seriously. In fact, in 2011, one of the presidential candidates abandoned two petitions that he was arguing before the Council when he received an invitation to attend the ceremony of the official proclamation of the results. He asked how the Council could be sending out invitations for the official proclamation of the results when they had not yet heard his petition asking for a nullification of the results! Declaring this a theatrical farce to which he was not going to be party, he abandoned the petition.[32]

[30] Unfortunately, owing to poor record keeping, the exact number cannot be ascertained.

[31] For example, in a 2004 petition, *Agbor Ashu Emmanuel Omar v Republic of Cameroon* (unreported), the petitioner challenged the acceptance of the presidential applications of some of the candidates, including that of Paul Biya of the ruling CPDM party. The Council ruled that, since Agbor was not a member of the CPDM, he had no standing to challenge Paul Biya's candidature. In the decision, the Council pointed out that the nomination of Paul Biya as presidential candidate for the CPDM could be inferred from the fact that he had been elected as president of the party in 2001 and, under the statute of the party, the president of the party automatically becomes the presidential candidate. This was a correct reading of the constitution of the CPDM, but the electoral code stated that one of the documents to be submitted by a presidential candidate must be a letter confirming the formal nomination of the candidate as a presidential candidate for the party—a matter that required a formal document and not an inference from the CPDM's constitution, as the Council had conveniently done.

[32] See 'Cameroun/Contentieux electoral: Un candidat abandonne les débats' http://journalducameroun.com/camerouncontentieux-electoral-un-candidat-abandonne-les-debats/ (last accessed 17 April 2017). In the words of the petitioner: 'Nous ne pouvons pas, alors que nous demandons une annulation totale de l'élection, tout au moins une reconsidération par le Conseil Constitutionnel du déroulement du scrutin, recevoir une invitation à venir assister à la proclamation des résultats. A mes yeux c'est la preuve suffisante que la position de ce conseil est déjà arrêtée, et moi je me refuse à animer ce théâtre'.

With sentiments such as these, which are by no means isolated,[33] it is not surprising that the quality of elections in Cameroon has been seriously questioned during the last two decades. This raises the question as to what role the Council has played in promoting respect for the constitution.

7. Impact of the Review System on Constitutionalism

There is no gainsaying that an effective constitutional review system can significantly contribute to entrenching democracy, constitutionalism, and respect for the rule of law in any country. As we have seen, the Council has in essence only been involved in adjudicating electoral disputes. Although it has been argued that some of the wide-ranging powers have unlawfully been conferred on the ELECAM, an electoral management body controlled by the government, the Council continues to play an important role. How effective has this been and what impact has it had on electoral justice?

An examination of some of the decisions made by the Council strongly suggests that the Council, when confronted with electoral petitions, has been more interested in looking for procedural flaws and sanctioning non-compliance with filing requirements than with objectively examining and sanctioning violations of electoral laws and other abuses of the electoral process.[34] A number of controversial decisions may be cited to support this conclusion. In the *Lontouo Marcus* case, decided on 1 October 2004,[35] the petitioner challenged the decision of the Ministry of Territorial Administration and Decentralization (MINATD) that had rejected his documents, to stand as a presidential candidate on the grounds that he had made an error with regard to the declaration to respect the constitution. He had in the declaration committed himself to respecting the constitution 'if he was elected'.[36] MINATD, in rejecting his application, said that by subjecting his respect for the constitution to the case where he is elected, he had implicitly indicated that he was ready to violate the constitution before, during, and after the election if he was not elected. When the matter came before the Council, it declared that the erroneous formulation of the declaration to respect the constitution was equivalent to no declaration at all. However, there was no provision in any law that prescribed any particular manner for formulating such declarations.

Another example of blind adherence to formalities is with respect to section 49 of the 2004 Law on the organization and functioning of the Constitutional Council, which provides that a petition 'under pain of inadmissibility' must bear the 'full name, status and address of the petitioner as well as the name of the member(s) of parliament whose election is contested'. The Council has often rejected petitions which do not contain all this information. This ignores the fact that some petitions may have nothing to do with any

[33] Seeeg Asonganyi Tazoacha, 'Cameroon Elections: Supreme Court Misses the Mark Again!' http://recorderline.blogspot.co.za/2013/08/cameroon-elections-supreme-court-misses.html (last accessed 17 April 2017).

[34] See Alain Didier Olinga, 'Justice Constitutionnelle et Contentieux Electoral: Quelle Contribution à la sérénité de la Démocratie Elective et à l'Enracinement de l'Etat de Droit? Le Cas du Cameroun' http://unpan1.un.org/intradoc/groups/public/documents/cafrad/unpan050903.pdf (last accessed 17 April 2017).

[35] Unreported.

[36] The full declaration read as follows: 'Je soussigné, Monsieur Lontouo Marcus, candidat à l'élection présidentielle du 11 octobre 2004, investi par le parti politique Congrès National Camerounais, m'engage sur l'honneur à respecter la Constitution camerounaise au cas où je serais élu'. (I, Mr Lontouo Marcus, candidate for the 11 October 2004 elections, nominated by the Cameroon National Congress party, undertake, if elected, to respect the Cameroon constitution.)

particular individual, but which rather concern the general manner in which the elections were conducted, which were not conducive to ensuring a free and fair outcome.

In 2002 the Union for Democracy and Progress Party (UNDP) petitioned the Council about the elections in the Mayo Banyo constituency. They alleged that many ballot boxes had been installed in the private homes of certain individuals. The Council rejected the petition on the grounds that the matters raised concerned the establishment and organization of voting booths, which was not within its competence. It is difficult to see how the Council could refuse to investigate such flagrant irregularities, but still comply with the constitutional mandate that it should 'ensure that voting is free and fair' and thereafter proclaim the results.

To meet the strict and tight time limits within which it must investigate and decide matters, the Council often has to rely on government officials for evidence. The main officials are the district and divisional officers, as well as the local security chiefs. All these are officials appointed by the president and serve at his pleasure. It is no coincidence that, before each election, government officials are promoted, others demoted, and many more moved all over the country to strategic positions, especially in the stronghold of opposition parties. Perhaps the jewel in the Cameroonian electoral crown is ELECAM. It was established, seemingly, to replace the discredited and oddly named National Electoral Observatory (NEO) as the independent electoral management body.[37] ELECAM is still controlled and managed by well-known CPDM sympathizers and can hardly be expected to play an *amicus curiae* role in matters before the Council. The electoral playing field has never been level because all the electoral laws have been enacted by a parliament dominated by the ruling party. This has made the role of the Council in electoral adjudication very important. However, as noted above, the Council has usually played safe.

The primary function of the Council has been to 'ensure the regularity of presidential elections, parliamentary elections and referendum operations'. An overview of most of the modern indicators of good governance, constitutionalism, and respect for the rule of law strongly confirms what the preceding analysis suggests, that is, that the Council has failed to ensure the regularity of presidential and parliamentary elections. There are several indications of this.

Hardly any of the observer mission reports of the last two presidential and parliamentary elections held in 2004 and 2011 for the former and 2007 and 2013 for the latter have declared the elections free and fair. More often than not, while avoiding outright criticism, the reports usually point to numerous irregularities, most of which focus on the lack of independence of ELECAM. In the 2011 presidential elections, the Commonwealth Experts Team in their post-election press release stated that:

> A peaceful election: Some benchmarks for democratic elections have been met, although the playing field needs to be levelled to increase confidence in the electoral process.[38]

Even more obscure language was used by the Commonwealth in the report on the 2013 legislative elections.[39] The high hopes raised by the reintroduction of multipartyism in

[37] See Charles M Fombad, 'Election Management Bodies in Africa: Cameroon's 'National Electoral Observatory' in Perspective' (2003) 3 *African Human Rights Law Journal* 25.

[38] See Post-election press release, Commonwealth Expert Team, Cameroon Presidential elections http://www.keepeek.com/Digital-Asset-Management/oecd/commonwealth/governance/cameroon-presidential-election-9-october-2011_9781848591332-en#page37 (last accessed 17 April 2017). The subsequent report used more or less similar diplomatic language, but clearly could not declare the elections free and fair.

[39] See Report of the Commonwealth Expert Team, Cameroon Legislative and Municipal Elections (30 September 2013) http://fakoamerica.typepad.com/files/cameroon-2013-cet-report---final.pdf (last accessed 17

1992 have been progressively diminished by the ease and frequency with which elections are regularly rigged in favour of the incumbent and the ruling CPDM. Despite having almost 300 political parties, Cameroon remains essentially a one-party state. The numerous opposition parties often have an ageing leadership and are weak, highly fragmented, and often organized along ethnic lines, thus preventing any one party from becoming a credible threat to the ruling CPDM or forming effective coalitions.

There are other indicators that strongly suggest that the absence of constitutional accountability, largely attributable to an ineffective system of constitutional review, has more or less stalled Cameroon's transition to democracy and the growth of a culture of constitutionalism and respect for the rule of law. One of the most respected international indicators, the Freedom House survey on the state of freedom in the world, which started it surveys in 1972, shows that Cameroon is only one of eight other African countries that have consistently been rated as 'not free'.[40]

The 1990 wave of democratic and constitutional reforms, therefore, appears to have made no change to Cameroon's status. This is not surprising since the leadership, instead of opening up as most other countries were doing, chose that moment to impose an illiberal constitution which did nothing more than to enable the president of the republic to consolidate his powers whilst giving an appearance of permitting multiparty democracy. Even countries with a notoriously poor record of governance have since the 1990s had some spells of relaxation and freedom for their people. Hence, countries such as Swaziland (1990–1992), Eritrea (1995–1998), Central African Republic (1993–2000) and Ethiopia (1992–1998), have at certain periods enjoyed some freedom.[41]

The conclusion that there has been little progress with respect to civil and political rights in Cameroon since the onset of the democratic transition in Africa is borne out by the standard of its elections and the fact that the ruling CPDM is as entrenched as it was before the 1990s. With regard to the rule of law, Cameroon, with a score of 0.40 out of 1.00 is ranked 97th out of 102 countries in the World Justice Project rule of law index 2015.[42] In the Ibrahim Index of African Governance 2015 reports, Cameroon is ranked as 37th out of the fifty-four countries in Africa, and the report concludes that the country's weakest area of performance is in the area of accountability.[43]

This is again not surprising because in a recent survey, public service users were asked how many of them had paid a bribe in the last 12 months, and Cameroon came second on the list with 48 per cent admitting that they had done so.[44] Most of the good governance

April 2017); see also Report of the Centre for Democracy and Electoral Studies Cameroon Citizen Election Observation Mission to the 30 September 2013 Legislative and Municipal Elections in the Republic of Cameroon http://www.gndem.org/CDES_Cameroon_Final_Report_2013 (last accessed 17 April 2017); and Rapport de la Mission d'Observation de l'Union Africaine aux Elections Legislatives et Municipales du 30 Septembre 2013 en Republique du Cameroun http://pa.au.int/en/sites/default/files/Rapport%20Final%20 MOEAU% 20Cameroun%202013.pdf (last accessed 1 June 2016).

40 There was a brief spell from 1972 to 1976 when it was rated as partly free. Other countries with such a poor record are Algeria, Angola, Chad, Democratic Republic of the Congo, Equatorial Guinea, Rwanda, and South Sudan. For details of this survey see Individual Country Rating and Status FIW 1973–2015 https://freedomhouse.org/sites/default/files/Individual%20Country%20Ratings%20and%20Status%2C%201973-2015%20 %28FINAL%29.xls (last accessed 17 April 2017).

41 See Individual Country Rating and Status (n 39).

42 See World Justice Project, Rule of Law Index 2015 http://worldjusticeproject.org/sites/default/files/roli_ 2015_0.pdf (last accessed 17 April 2017).

43 See '2015 Ibrahim Index of African Governance, Country Insights—Cameroon' http://static.moibrahimfoundation.org/u/2015/10/02201321/08_Cameroon.pdf (last accessed 17 April 2017).

44 The first country in this survey of 29 African countries was Liberia. See 'People and Corruption: Africa Survey 2015. Global Corruption Barometer' http://www.transparency.org/whatwedo/publication/people_ and_corruption_africa_survey_2015 (last accessed 17 April 2017).

indicators, therefore, show that there is a problem regarding constitutional governance in Cameroon that has not been helped by the Council, which is supposed to ensure respect for the constitution and the rule of law.

8. Conclusion

In an era that has seen the rapid expansion of constitutional review, even in Francophone Africa, Cameroon has decided to return to a system that is not only completely out of step with modern developments but which shields the organs of state from constitutional accountability for their actions and inaction. Although the approach adopted is not only consistent with earlier constitutions as well as the inherited French legal heritage, it is probably not enough to assume that, unlike the rest of Francophone Africa, Cameroonian politicians and their legal advisers are unable to disentangle themselves from the spell of French stereotypes. A better explanation is that this seemed the most convenient approach to adopt for a regime that has never shown any sign of giving up power. There was no better way to achieve this than to craft a constitution in the way that it did and crown it with a constitutional council. The architect of this model of constitutional review, the late President De Gaulle, designed it to disguise a system in which the president reigns and rules and is unaccountable to anyone but himself. It did not work perfectly for him, but for Cameroon it is working perfectly.

The Cameroonian constitutional review mechanism clearly proves one thing: that the design and operation of the review system can have a negative or positive impact on constitutional developments within a country. The present system, which dates back to the independence and reunification of the country, has had serious consequences for the country's constitutional development. First, it has left in place presidents who only respect and comply with the constitution when it suits them. Of the numerous flagrant constitutional violations committed by Cameroonian presidents, none was as serious and has provided the potential for future conflict as the decision to abolish the federal system.[45]

Secondly, the denial of ordinary citizens of the right to access the Council when their constitutional rights have been violated constitutes a denial of constitutional justice. It is not surprising, therefore, that most indicators on political rights and good governance show that Cameroon is one of the few African countries that has made the least progress in democracy, constitutionalism, and respect for the rule of law since the 1990s. Thirdly, constitutionalism and respect for the rule of law have practically been an illusion in Cameroon since independence without an independent judiciary. This is compounded by the absence of a credible, effective, and efficient system of constitutional review, which could protect citizens from the overbearing and repressive authoritarian regimes that have held power. This, again, is at odds with modern developments.

[45] The federal system was protected by two provisos in art 47 of the 1961 constitution. One proviso stated: 'Any proposal for the revision of the present Constitution which impairs the unity and integrity of the Federation shall be inadmissible'. The other proviso stated: 'Proposals for the revision shall be adopted by simple majority vote of the Members of the Federal Assembly provided that such majority includes a majority of the representatives in the Federal Assembly of each of the Federated States'. These provisions were ignored by the late President Ahmadou Ahidjou when he declared the country a unitary state after a sham referendum in 1972 (with the name United Republic of Cameroon) and his illegality. His successor has continued with the illegality, particularly when by decree he changed the name of the country to 'Republic of Cameroon' in 1984.

One can therefore conclude that the Cameroonian legislature deliberately opted for this outdated system of constitutional review in order hide behind the veneer of constitutionalism and democracy effectively to obfuscate constitutional legality and electoral injustice. In allowing the president to have full control over the mechanisms of constitutional review, constitutional legality depends entirely on the goodwill of the president rather that the dictates of the constitution. The president, and not the Council, has effectively become the ultimate and supreme judge of constitutionality. It leaves the country blindly limping into an uncertain future dependent on the benevolence or otherwise of whoever is president.

Bibliography

Enonchong H N A, *Cameroon Constitutional Law. Federalism in a Mixed Common Law and Civil Law System* (Centre d'edition et de Production de Manuels et d'Auxiliaires et de l'Enseignement 1967)

Fombad C M, 'Election Management Bodies in Africa: Cameroon's 'National Electoral Observatory' in Perspective' (2003) 3 *African Human Rights Law Journal* 25

Fombad C M, 'Managing Legal Diversity: Cameroonian Bi-juralism at a Critical Crossroads' in Vernon Palmer, Mohamed Mattar, and Anna Koppel (eds), *Mixed Legal Systems, East and West* (Ashgate Publishing 2014)

Fombad C M, 'The Dynamics of Record-breaking Endemic Corruption and Political Opportunism in Cameroon' in John Mukum Mbaku and Joseph Takougang (eds), *The Leadership Challenge in Africa: Cameroon under Paul Biya* (Africa World Press 2004)

Fombad C M, 'The New Cameroonian Constitutional Council in a Comparative Perspective: Progress or Retrogression?' (1998) 42(2) *Journal of African Law* 186

Fombad C M and Jonie B Fonyam, 'The Social Democratic Front, the Opposition and the Transition' in John Mukum Mbaku and Joseph Takougang (eds), *The Leadership Challenge in Africa: Cameroon under Paul Biya* (Africa World Press 2004)

Olinga A D, 'Justice Constitutionnelle et Contentieux Electoral: Quelle Contribution à la sérénité de la Démocratie Elective et à l'Enracinement de l'Etat de Droit? Le Cas du Cameroun' http://unpan1.un.org/intradoc/groups/public/documents/cafrad/unpan050903.pdf (last accessed 17 April 2017)

Tazoacha A, 'Cameroon Elections: Supreme Court Misses the Mark Again!' http://recorderline.blogspot.co.za/2013/08/cameroon-elections-supreme-court-misses.html (last accessed 17 April 2017)

4

The Constitutional Court of Angola

Judicial Restraint in a Dominant Party State

André Thomashausen

1. Genesis of the Angolan Constitutional Court

The Constitutional Court of Angola was established in 2008 in terms of Acts 2/08 and 3/08, both of 17 June 2008,[1] thus preceding and anticipating the new constitution of 5 February 2010.[2] Act 2/08 provides for the establishment of the Constitutional Court (*Lei Orgânica do Tribunal Constitucional*—LOTC) and Act 3/08 (also known as the *Lei Orgânica do Processo Constitutional*—LPC) for the procedure before the Constitutional Court. Following the coming into force of the new constitution of 2010, the original enabling legislation for the Constitutional Court had to be amended, by Acts 24/10 and 25/10, both of 3 December 2010.[3]

A specialized constitutional jurisdiction had already existed prior to 2008. Articles 134 and 135 of the previous constitution (Act 92 of 16 September 1992)[4] had provided for the establishment of a constitutional court. However, the Supreme Court exercised constitutional jurisdiction until Acts 2 and 3 of 2008 established a separate constitutional court.[5]

The decision in favour of a separate constitutional court jurisdiction and procedure was taken in the course of the decision of Angola to abandon the one-party state model that had attributed supreme authority to the will of the liberation party, Movimento Popular de Libertação de Angola (MPLA), rather than to the supremacy of the constitution and the rule of law.[6]

Despite the constitutional reforms imposed in 1992 by the settlement terms of the decades long civil war in that country, Angola's President since 1979 and the majority party MPLA continued to exercise unrestrained control over the pace and scope of liberalization, as the civil war resumed from 1994 until 2002. Angolans continue to live under one of the most authoritarian and rigid rules known in post-colonial Africa and

[1] See all relevant legislation as well as all case law on the web pages of the Angolan Constitutional Court at http://www.tribunalconstitucional.ao (last accessed 30 August 2015).

[2] The official text appears in the Government Gazette, Diário da República, Ia Série No 23 of 5 February 2010, 141–87. An English translation provided by the Angolan Parliament is available at http://www.comissaoconstitucional.ao/pdfs/constituicao-da-republica-de-angola-versao-ingles.pdf (last accessed 20 March 2017). French, German, and Spanish translations can be accessed at http://www.comissaoconstitucional.ao/constituicao-da-republica-de-angola.php (last accessed 20 March 2017).

[3] See n 1.

[4] See André Thomashausen, 'Constitutional Law in Extreme Emergencies' in Jürgen Bröhmer (ed), *Internationale Gemeinschaft und Menschenrechte—Festschrift für Georg Ress* (Heymanns 2005) 1295–304.

[5] In terms of art 6 of Lei 23/92 of 16 September 1992.

[6] See reference in n 4 above. See also André Thomashausen, 'The Constitutions of Angola' in Rudiger Wolfrum and Rainer Grote (eds), *Constitutions of the Countries of the World* (Oxford Constitutions Online) http://oxcon.ouplaw.com (last accessed 20 March 2017) (text at nn 4 to 9).

the Constitutional Court, originally envisaged in the 1992 constitution, only came into being in 2008, six years after the summary execution of the opposition leader Jonas Savimbi.

The Angolan political identity since independence was nationalistic and anti-liberal. Until most recently, the country's law schools avoided teaching more than the bare minimum of international or comparative law subjects.[7] Referring to international law, or even international human rights law, was for the duration of the first three decades of independent Angola, viewed as an identification with 'US American imperialism', and regularly triggered accusations of espionage and even treason.

Against this background, it is remarkable that the Constitutional Court was given full administrative, financial, and institutional independence and is annually granted its own budget by Parliament.[8] Its decisions are binding on all public entities or private persons, including all other courts.[9] Its rulings on constitutionality are published in the *Official Gazette*.[10] However, as the *Official Gazette* is not easily accessible, the publication of the judgments on the website of the Constitutional Court are generally referred to. Unfortunately, the chronological listing and publication of the sequentially numbered judgments, called *Acórdãos*, is not searchable and the names of the individual pdf files are purely computer generated and do not follow any intelligible naming convention. Access to the case law of the Constitutional Court thus falls short of normal minimal international standards, as for instance adhered to by the Organisation pour l'Harmonisation en Afrique du Droit des Affaires (OHADA).[11]

The Angolan constitution of 1992 followed the continental European and, in particular, Portuguese models by choosing to introduce a primarily 'concentrated' (as opposed to US-style diffuse) judicial review for constitutional matters.[12] The distinction between 'concentrated' and 'diffuse' models of judicial review of constitutionality is difficult in 'mixed' jurisdictions that follow the Portuguese and French legal tradition. Many European legal systems will provide for a determination of constitutionality of laws in the course of ordinary proceedings before ordinary courts, whilst laws enacted under their new constitutions (often post-dictatorial or totalitarian times, eg Germany, Italy, Spain, and Portugal) can only be contested as unconstitutional in a special Constitutional Court (or Constitutional Council). Hence, constitutional reviews are diffuse (however, with rights of ultimate appeal to the 'concentrated' constitutional courts) in matters of application of 'old' laws, and 'concentrated' in respect of post-constitutional or 'new' laws. In reality, modern constitutional review proceedings are too complex to be easily fitted into the very basic 'diffuse' and 'concentrated' templates. Bearing this in mind, the Angolan system can be characterized as a hybrid diffuse-concentrated model.

[7] The only commentary on the constitution that has thus far been written avoids any reference to writings other than those authored by scholars from Portugal; not even scholars from Brazil are acknowledged, let alone any case law, whether Angolan or other. See Raul Carlos Vasquez Araújo and Elisa Rangel Nunes, *Constituição da República de Angola Anotada*, Tomo 1 (Luanda 2014).

[8] Act 2/2008 (LOTC) art 10. [9] ibid art 6. [10] ibid art 7.

[11] See http://www.ohada.com/jurisprudence.html (last accessed 17 April 2017).

[12] 'Concentrated review' is still defended as a relevant concept by the so-called Venice Commission of the Council of Europe; see eg AM Mavčič, 'Some Comparative Comments to the Introduction of Constitutional Review in the State of Palestine' http://www.venice.coe.int/WebForms/documents/?pdf=CDL-JU(2008)026-e (last accessed 17 April 2017). For a useful listing of links to all constitutional courts' powers see http://www.const-court.be/fr/site_internet/cc.html (last accessed 20 March 2017). For an alternative categorization method see http://www.concourts.net/tab/tab1.php?lng=en&stat=1&prt=0&srt=0 (last accessed 17 April 2017).

2. Composition

The initial (2008) Constitutional Court was composed of seven judges, appointed for a seven-year non-renewable term of office. Article 180 of the new constitution of 2010 increased the number to eleven, and the additional judges were appointed in May 2012.

The Constitutional Court is thus composed of eleven judges: four—including the judge president—who are appointed by the state president; four who are appointed by the national assembly (including the deputy judge president) with a two-thirds majority; two who are appointed by the National Council of the Judiciary; and one judge based on a national and open tender and selection process, conducted by the Constitutional Court itself.

There are no gender or race or minority quotas or considerations imposed by law. However, several national policy documents commit the government to the attainment of balanced gender representation at all national decision-making levels.[13] In the current composition of the court, out of the eleven judges four are women.

According to Article 12 of Act 2/2008 (LOTC), the judges must be Angolan nationals older than 35; must have admission to the legal professions (full legal qualification known as *licenciatura*) of at least fifteen years' standing; must have a 'moral standing without blemish' (*idoneidade moral*); must have their civil and political rights (ie the right to vote and to be elected and hold office); and may not have been convicted of a culpable crime (as opposed to involuntary or negligent offence), punishable with a minimal term of imprisonment of two years.

In terms of Article 12 of the (internal) Rules of the Constitutional Court (*Regulamento Geral do Tribunal Constitucional*),[14] judges are obliged to declare any interest in a matter and either recuse themselves on their own initiative, or accept a ruling by their peers on the effect of such interest. Any prior involvement with a matter (for instance, as a judge or attorney prior to being appointed judge of the Constitutional Court) is deemed to constitute an interest.[15] Judges are also barred from defending any matters other than in their own defence or in defence of their spouses, children, or parents.[16] They must further ensure an irreproachable personal conduct and must act towards their peers and parties intervening in any matter in a considerate manner and discharge all their duties promptly and uphold the good name and dignity of the court.[17]

The judges are guaranteed independence and personal immunity and may not be removed, on the same terms that are applicable to judges of the Supreme Court.[18] In terms of Article 179 of the constitution, judges may not be members of political parties or political associations and may not carry out any 'party-political activities'. They are also barred from holding any other private or public office, except for teaching or legal research commitments. They are specifically forbidden to strike, but may be members of a professional association.

[13] See item 1.2.3 of *Programa de Governo do MPLA para 2012–2017*, http://www.mpla.ao/imagem/ProGovMPLA.pdf (last accessed 17 April 2017); *Programa de Apoio aos Actores Não Estatais* (Fundo Europeu de Desenvolvimento), *Diagnóstico de Género de Angola* (Março 2015) http://eeas.europa.eu/delegations/angola/documents/press_corner/2015/diagnostico_genero_angola_pt_final_digital_pt.pdf (last accessed 17 April 2017).

[14] *Resolução* nº 21/14—Tribunal Constitucional, Diário da República Ia Série no 138 de 28 de Julho de 2014 (Pág 3295). Unfortunately, the Rules are not publicized on the web pages of the court, but on the web pages of the Secretariat of the Council of Ministers http://scm.gov.ao/ (last accessed 17 April 2017).

[15] Rules of the Constitutional Court art 13. [16] ibid art 13(3). [17] ibid arts 14 and 15.

[18] LOTC arts 33–35.

In 2015, the non-renewable seven-year term of the seven judges originally appointed in June 2008 expired. Article 243 of the constitution of 2010 established an important provision that the appointment of judges shall be made in such a way as to prevent the occurrence of vacancies. The rule is understood and applied to prevent judges from vacating their office before a succeeding judge is appointed. The state organs designated to appoint judges are at liberty not to do so and can thus tacitly prolong the terms of office of the judges that they had originally designated. Thus, the three judges appointed in 2008 by the state president, namely Rui Ferreira, Efigénia Lima, and Onofre dos Santos, including the judge president (Rui Ferreira), could remain in office for as long as the state president chooses not to appoint their successors. The same is true for the three judges appointed in 2008 by parliament (Agostinho dos Santos, Luzia Sebastião, and Maria Imaculada Melo) and the single judge designated by the Supreme Court (Miguel Correia).

The state president has thus far shown no interest in replacing his trusted Judge President Rui Ferreira, as he failed to identify an equally competent, prudent, and loyal successor. In 2016 he made a non-controversial replacement for Judge Efigénia Lima with Judge Carlos Magalhães. Parliament (the National Assembly) appointed two new judges, Maria Terezinha da Silva Lopes and Guilhermina Contreiras da Costa Prata, as nominees of the majority party MPLA.

The stalemate regarding the remaining overdue appointments will continue to keep the court insulated from renewal and reinforce the omnipresent power of the state president, summarized by one of Angola's most eminent constitutional law scholars and since 2012 also a judge of the Constitutional Court, Raúl Araújo, as 'the Angolan constitutional reality of a republican monarchy'.[19]

The moving of the court in 2014 from its previous location in a picturesque old colonial palace building to the monumental new building of the Ministry of Justice is symbolic of the permeation of all state institutions, including the judiciary and the Constitutional Court, by the Angolan *raison d'état* ideology. Although many of the judges would have preferred to remain in their original building and thus demarcate independence from the state administration of justice, none decided to risk voicing his or her sentiments.

3. Powers and jurisdiction

As provided for in Article 180 of the constitution and Articles 16 and 32 of the LOTC, the Constitutional Court decides on—

(a) requests for the determination of the unconstitutionality of any law or legal norm (abstract review);
(b) the pre-emptive examination of the constitutionality of any proposed legislation (abstract pre-emptive review);
(c) possible infringements of the Constitution by omission; on appeals against the refusal of an ordinary court to apply a law on the grounds of unconstitutionality;
(d) appeals against the application of an unconstitutional law by a court;
(e) all appeals relating to national elections and disputes arising from a referendum;
(f) mandates of members of the national assembly;
(g) the establishment, legality, and prohibition of political parties;

[19] Raul Carlos Vasques Araújo, *O Presidente da República no Sistema Político de Angola* (Estudos de Direito da Bioética Almedina 2009) 325.

(h) matters of constitutional interpretation submitted to the Court by the State President and or the national assembly; and
(i) conflicts of competency between organs of the state.

The abstract review of constitutionality (also referred to as 'successive review') in terms of Article 16 of the LOTC and Articles 16 and 35 of the LPC is the most generic competence of the court. In terms of Article 18 of the LOTC, it can be requested by the state president, one-tenth of the members of the national assembly (parliament), any parliamentary group, the Attorney-General, the Ombudsman, and the Bar Council. However, no laws adopted pursuant to a referendum may be subjected to a successive review of constitutionality.[20] Until September 2015, the court ruled on a total of six requests for an abstract but successive constitutional review.[21]

The abstract pre-emptive review of constitutionality is carried out at the request of the state president or one-tenth of the members of the national assembly (parliament), provided the request is made within twenty days from the date of receipt of the intended or prospective enactment.[22] A milder variant of this review function is the request for the furnishing of an opinion on the constitutionality of any specific constitutional issue or interpretation, which may be made by the state president, the national assembly as such, or the Council of Ministers.[23] Two important matters were decided in the exercise of the pre-emptive review of constitutionality: on the constitutionality of the mode of appointment for the vice president of the state in the (draft) new constitution of 2010 (*Acórdão* 111), and regarding a sweeping new law to curb money laundering and curtail attorney client privileges (*Acórdão* 330).

The review of a possible violation of the constitution by omission may be requested by the state president, one-fifth of the members of the national assembly, or the Attorney-General, and may result in the Constitutional Court ordering the competent state organ to produce legislation to rectify the omission.[24]

Appeals against the application of an unconstitutional law by a court may be made by any of the parties to a matter after the exhaustion of any ordinary recourses, but are obligatory for the prosecution in matters in which the state may be a party.[25]

A general concrete review jurisdiction has been accepted by the court based on the wording of Article 180(2)(a) of the constitution and the corresponding provision in Article 16(m) of the LOCT. Accordingly, the court enjoys a generic jurisdiction to 'examine the constitutionality of any norm or other acts of the state'. This widely cast provision was, and continues to be, interpreted by the court to grant it the power to hear individual complaints against unconstitutional encroachments of fundamental rights and freedoms, including by administrative acts. The legislature acknowledged this 'inherent' competency of the court in Article 49 of the Constitutional Procedural Law (LPC), naming it the 'extraordinary appeal on grounds of unconstitutionality'. The subsequent amendment of Article 49 of Act 3/08 (LPC) by Act 25/10 confirmed the wide scope of the 'extraordinary appeal' by clarifying and confirming the already existing case law of the Constitutional Court that individual complaints of an unconstitutional encroachment upon fundamental rights and freedoms shall only be heard once all ordinary legal remedies have been exhausted.

[20] LPC art 26(2). [21] Acórdãos 130, 136, 233, 314, 319, and 330. [22] LOTC art 17.
[23] ibid art 20. [24] ibid art 19. [25] ibid art 21.

The revised text of Article 49 states:

> The extraordinary appeal of unconstitutionality in this present provision shall be allowed only following the prior exhaustion of all legally permissible appeals before the ordinary and other courts.

No particular substantive concern is discernible in the choice of naming it the 'extraordinary appeal', other than the sense that this appeal may be characterized as exceptional because it is limited to the cases where the ordinary courts did not see fit to respond positively to a claim of unconstitutionality.

The requirement of the exhaustion of prior legal defences and remedies implies that the courts, in the process of resolving any ordinary appeals, must also rule on the issue of constitutionality, as on any issues of law. In some countries the competency of the ordinary courts to rule on issues of constitutionality have been constrained or excluded, forcing ordinary courts to refer a claim of unconstitutionality to the Constitutional Court for a trial on constitutionality 'within' the ordinary trial, thus leaning in favour of a 'concentrated' model. However, in Germany, this was done only in respect of laws enacted after the coming into force of the new constitution, the Grundgesetz of 1949, so as to prevent possibly conflicting rulings on constitutionality by different ordinary courts, in a number of states within the German federation.[26]

Hence, Germany applies a 'diffuse' system in respect of laws predating the constitution, and a 'concentrated' system in respect of laws passed post the constitution. The Angolan Parliament, sitting as a constituent assembly in 2010, did not opt to make that choice. Consequently, ordinary Angolan courts are not directed to refer any issues of unconstitutionality to the Constitutional Court, providing for a greater leaning in direction of a 'diffuse' model.

Angola considered that the absolute binding force on any authority, judicial and other, of the fundamental rights guarantees, as stipulated in Article 28(1) of the constitution, made it compelling that all courts at all times should apply themselves to any issues of unconstitutionality. By this choice, the Angolan constitutional review model embraces an important element of a 'diffuse' review model, but because a special jurisdiction in a special court is entrusted with the last instance jurisdiction over all issues of unconstitutionality, and because that court will hear an 'extraordinary' constitutionality appeal whenever the ordinary courts have refused to entertain an unconstitutionality appeal, the Angolan constitutional review process is still a concentrated one, albeit of a hybrid kind.[27]

In addition to the above 'classic' review functions, the court also acts as a special electoral court, with the exclusive jurisdiction to hear complaints relating to national elections and disputes arising from a referendum.[28] The reason for this is that the Angolan Electoral Commission does not have judicial powers or functions. As the political parties

[26] In Germany this rule applies in respect of laws passed after the entry into force of the new constitution, the Grundgesetz of 1949; see art 100(1)(1) of the German *Grundgesetz* and art 80(1) BVerfGG; see Martin Borowski, 'The Beginnings of Germany's Federal Constitutional Court' (2003) 16(2) *Ratio Juris* 155–86 at 160, 161 http://www.direitocontemporaneo.com/wp-content/uploads/2014/02/The-Beginnings-of-Germany-s-Federal-Constitutional-Court.pdf (last accessed 17 April 2017); Kai Hamdorf, 'Die Zulässigkeitsvoraus-setzungen der Richtervorlage zum Bundesverfassungsgericht und zu den Verfassungsgerichten der Länder' (2011) *Zeitschrift für Öffentliches Recht in Norddeutschland (NordÖR)* 301–9; further, for a brief overview in English see Donald P Kommers, 'An Introduction to the Federal Constitutional Court' (2001) 2 *German Law Journal* https://static1.squarespace.com/static/56330ad3e4b0733dcc0c8495/t/56bc3a5d2fe1311b083ef8e4/1455176285666/GLJ_Vol_02_No_09_Kommers.pdf (last accessed 17 April 2017).

[27] Jorge Bacelar Gouveia, *Direito Constitucional de Angola* (Lisboa 2014) 609–14 at 612 acknowledges that in respect of the 'concrete' jurisdiction of the Court, it combines both 'diffuse' and 'concentrated' elements of procedure. See also n 12.

[28] LOTC arts 22–26 and 32.

represented in the Angolan Parliament are represented proportionally in the electoral commission, it is an organ that will always be controlled by the majority party. Thus, it was a fundamental decision to strengthen the rule of law and the credibility of all electoral acts by attributing to the Constitutional Court the competency to rule with finality on any electoral matters. This will include matters that may appear technical or unimportant, such as voter registration, candidature disputes, the attribution of mandates of members of the national assembly, and generally any matters regarding the validity of elections. The court is, therefore, always the final authority in declaring an electoral act and electoral results as valid and legally binding.

Another special jurisdiction attributed to the Angolan Constitutional Court regards all matters pertaining to the status, legality, prohibition, dissolution, conduct, and decisions of political parties.[29]

Finally, the court has jurisdiction over conflicts of competency between organs of state, on the application of any one of them.[30]

4. Access to Constitutional Justice

Access to constitutional justice is restricted by the rules of the constitutional review procedure, as codified in the Constitutional Procedural Law (LPC) Act 3/08 as amended by Act 25/10. Several types of constitutional appeals may be invoked only by certain organs of state, or a certain number of members of the national assembly, or the Attorney-General, or the Bar Council. Appeals against the application of an unconstitutional law and individual appeals against any specific act committed by an authority that would offend the constitution are permissible only once all ordinary remedies have been exhausted.[31] This requirement has been strictly applied by the court, but it is not an unusual requirement and only very few jurisdictions will allow for direct constitutionality complaints outside the normal review and appeal procedures.

A further constraint in the case of all appeals in concrete cases of unconstitutionality (appeals against judicial decisions and/or acts of public authority) is the requirement that the application must be made by a duly admitted and practising Angolan attorney, who must be a member in good standing at the Angolan Bar Council.[32]

All constitutional review applications are subject to a preliminary admission procedure. The judge president of the Constitutional Court alone rules on the admissibility of any applications, but his ruling is subject to an appeal to the full bench (the Plenum) of the court.[33] The pre-admissibility review is intended to prevent an overburdening of the court and its two chambers with evidently spurious or vexatious constitutionality appeals. Because the preliminary admissibility ruling is entrusted to one judge only, the procedure provides for a special appeal to the full bench, against non-admission, in terms of Article 8(2) of the LPC. The procedure before the German Constitutional Court provides for an admissibility decision taken by three judges sitting as the pre-admission committee, but their decision is final and cannot be appealed. As a result, the rejection rate of the German court is the highest in the world, at more or less a constant 98 per cent of all human rights appeals being finally rejected.[34] By

[29] ibid arts 27–31. [30] ibid art 16(o). [31] LPC art 49.
[32] ibid art 40. [33] ibid arts 5(3) and 8(2).
[34] Bundesverfassungsgerichtsgesetz (BVerfGG) art 93(d)(1); see in English http://www.bundesverfassungsgericht.de/EN/Verfahren/Wichtige-Verfahrensarten/Verfassungsbeschwerde/verfassungsbeschwerde_node.html

comparison, the Angolan admissibility procedure offers a far better measure of fairness and due process.

From the review of the 347 judgments made by the Angolan Constitutional Court to date, fifteen ruled on appeals against the preliminary rejection of admissibility[35] and, of these, only one was granted admissibility on appeal.[36]

In the event of incomplete or otherwise deficient applications, the judge president in his discretion may grant a grace period of five days for the application to be corrected or completed.[37]

There are no costs except those of individual constitutional review applications in concrete cases, which are subject to costs as generally applicable to all judicial proceedings.

An interesting procedural point is that all matters are conducted by written procedure only, and the court does not conduct any trials or hearings. Article 36(2) of the LPC specifically stipulates that constitutional review appeals against judicial decisions are limited to the issue of constitutionality, to the exclusion of any issues of fact.

There are, therefore, no particular rules for any appearances in court, as there are none. However, the court has the power to request any additional information it may deem expedient and, as confirmed to the author by the current judge president in an interview in April 2011, this could include requesting a party or witness to testify before the court. However, no such personal appearance has thus far occurred.

The constitutional review procedure will also not allow for any class or group actions, a traditional limitation bemoaned by Gomes Canotilho.[38]

5. Remedies

The Angolan Constitutional Court will not provide any remedies other than declaring that a particular legal norm, judicial decision, or administrative act is unconstitutional and, therefore, null and void, or that a particular omission exists and that the resulting *lacuna* in law should be corrected. If issues of other remedies arise, such as the awarding of damages, the Constitutional Court will refer the matter back to the court *a quo*. The reason for this is that the Constitutional Court is strictly an appeal court that will never review or take into consideration issues of fact or evidence, in the sense of the French tradition of the 'cassation' jurisdiction.

6. Style of Reasoning

The current review of 347 judgments shows that 262 judgments are mostly of a technical and procedural nature, pertaining to the court's jurisdiction over all matters concerning political parties, in terms of Article 63 of the LPC. These include disputes between members of parties and their party organs or, for instance, applications by disgruntled individual members

(last accessed 20 March 2017). For detail see Renate Jaeger and Siegfried Broß, 'The Relations between the Constitutional Courts and the Other National Courts, Including the Interference in this Area of the Action of the European Courts' Report of the Constitutional Court of the Federal Republic of Germany http://www.confeuconstco.org/reports/rep-xii/Duitsland-EN.pdf (last accessed 17 April 2017).

[35] *Acórdãos* 108, 115, 120, 125, 127, 133, 134, 150, 167, 223, 228, 232, 239, 331, and 334.

[36] *Acórdão* 232. [37] LPC art 7.

[38] José Joaquim Gomes Canotilho, 'Direito de Acesso à Justiça Constitucional' Estados da Conferência das Jurisdições Constitucionais dos Países de Língua Portuguesa (Luanda Junho de 2011) http://www.tribunal-constitucional.ao/uploads/%7Bc27dfa5e-9628-420e-b7b8-0925368a2afe%7D.pdf (last accessed 17 April 2017).

to declare party congresses null and void,[39] and the dissolution of political parties,[40] and even disputes about the inadmissibility of similar political party symbols or colours.[41]

The textual reasoning of the court follows the Portuguese constitutional law tradition closely, reflecting that most of the court's judges studied or obtained postgraduate qualifications at Portuguese universities, in particular at the University of Coimbra, where the law school prides itself on its 'classic' approach to law and legal hermeneutics. As a result, the reasoning of the court will prefer to seek to interpret a legal provision by reference to its context, objective, and presumed legislative purpose and intention.

An example is the legal opinion that the court was requested to deliver on the issue of whether coalitions of political parties should as such be represented in the state council, considering that Article 76(f) of the constitution only refers to a representation of political parties holding mandates in the national assembly. The legal opinion (*Acórdão* 105) relied on the principle that constitutional norms should always be given the interpretation that secures their most effective and widest application, within their contextual meaning. The court thus ruled that political parties should not be disadvantaged with regard to their representation in the state council on account of having become associated in a coalition of political parties.

References to own precedents continue to be rare in Angolan constitutional judgments. Rather, the courts tend frequently to cite and rely on the writings of Portuguese, French, and Spanish scholars. This must be considered against the background that continental European courts (with the exception of Germany, to some extent) are continuously reluctant to attribute general or 'law-making' authority to judicial decisions.

In a recent judgment (*Acórdão* 314), the court declared as unconstitutional several provisions of a new law of Public Law Professional Associations (Law 3/12), for an encroachment upon the fundamental right of freedom of association, with extensive reference to Spanish scholars, but without citing a single judicial precedent. However, in the court's judgment on the constitutionality of an overreaching provision found in the draconian Law on Crimes against the Security of State of 1978, the court cited several judgments of the Portuguese Constitutional Court.[42] The provision examined on the application of the Angolan Attorneys' Association, namely Article 26 of Act 7/78, provided that 'any act not covered by any other law which endangers or could endanger the Security of the State shall be punishable as stipulated in art. 55 par 5 of the Penal Code', by imprisonment of between two and eight years. The Constitutional Court avoided striking down the provision on the grounds of its vagueness, because shortly before the passing of its judgment an Act amending the old State Security Law (Act 23/2010) had finally been promulgated by the state president and entered into force. The case illustrates the 'soft power' of a Constitutional Court, where the risk of a censuring judgment alone can trigger an appropriate action by another constitutional organ.

The Angolan Constitutional Court will employ all generally acknowledged rules of interpretation, but prefer the more rigorous hermeneutical principles. Deductions made on the basis of analogy are rare. One of the few examples is found in the judgment on the requirement of legal representation in individual applications for the declaration of the unconstitutionality of an administrative (as opposed to judicial) decision.[43] As the wording of Article 40 of the LPC on the requirement of legal representation only applies

[39] LPC art 63(1)(d). [40] ibid art 63(1)(e). [41] ibid art 63(1)(b).

[42] *Acórdão* 130, 6. The court relied on technical arguments to avoid striking down the Crimes against the Security of the State Law.

[43] *Acórdão* 117.

to appeals against judicial decisions, the Constitutional Court extended the application of the provision to individual appeals against administrative acts invoking an analogous application.

> Apart from the example in the legal representation case, the Court has avoided any 'pragmatic' or 'interest-driven' deduction methods.

Historical arguments are sometimes used to distinguish an earlier meaning of a legal concept from a more modern one, in view of a conceptual change over time. For instance, in its Judgment No 319, the court declared unconstitutional several key provisions of the Procedural Rules of Parliament (*Regimento*, Act No 113/12), governing the parliamentary right of putting questions to the executive. The court argued that such a right to put questions existed under the previous (1992) constitution's 'parliamentary foundation' of government, while the new (2010) constitution had established a 'presidential base'.[44]

The court's rulings declaring both the 2008 and, subsequently, the 2012 election results valid (in the exercise of its special jurisdiction as an electoral court of the last instance) are marked by a strictly legalistic and even positivist type of reasoning, discarding as 'irrelevant' the results of vastly different parallel vote counts by the opposition, simply because the electoral law did not provide for any provisions regarding parallel counts.[45]

The case law dealing with *habeas corpus* and other fundamental rights complaints in individual cases tends to favour a broader approach and reasoning beyond a narrow textual meaning of legal provisions. The cautious *pro libertatem* approach in general criminal law and procedure does not extend to the six cases dealing with questions of unconstitutionality in the military courts, or in the context of court martial cases.[46]

In the famous political trial of former Intelligence Chief General Miala (*Acórdão* 106), the court simply refused to engage with the core of the constitutionality complaints by reasoning that it could not review or consider questions of fact. Miala, a three-star general in charge of the Angolan External Intelligence Services had been convicted on 1 October 2008 by the Supreme Military Court to four years' imprisonment for insubordination, for allegedly not having taken part in a military awards ceremony in which he had allegedly been ordered to take part. Publicly, however, he had been accused of and detained for having masterminded a treasonous conspiracy to assassinate President Dos Santos during a public carnival celebration in February 2006, allegedly with assistance of mercenaries recruited in South Africa with the help of South African politicians, who at the time opposed the rise to power of Jacob Zuma.

In accordance with a highly controversial 'Browse Mole Report' leaked at the time by South African intelligence personnel to the media, the presidential ambitions of Zuma had enjoyed the support of President Dos Santos, something Miala had allegedly opposed and cautioned against.[47] The lengthy detention without trial and subsequent conviction of Miala was widely considered a farcical and unconstitutional victimization on instructions of President Dos Santos. In his appeal, Miala argued that he had never committed the

[44] See on this judgment in detail André Thomashausen, 'Super-presidentialism in Angola and the Angolan Judiciary' in Charles M Fombad (ed), *Separation of Powers in African Constitutionalism* (OUP 2016) 182–204.

[45] *Acórdãos* Nos 74, 75, 76, 78, 225, 226, 295, and 310.

[46] *Acórdãos* 106, 146, 336, 337, 339, and 342. For example, in *Acórdão* 106, a case involving a former intelligence chief, General Miala, the Court simply refused to engage with the core issue of the challenge of unconstitutionality.

[47] See http://macua.blogs.com/ (last accessed 17 April 2017).

crime for which he had been convicted, nor would the alleged act of insubordination have justified years of detention and a subsequent term of four years' imprisonment.

The Constitutional Court simply reasoned that it could not and would not review findings of fact, that the term of four years' imprisonment could not be considered disproportionate in view of the fact that the provision in Article 17 of the Military Penal Code, Act 4/94, determined a prison term of between two and eight years, and that the judgment could also not be considered arbitrary because it had cited and applied the relevant laws.

The formalistic reasoning and blanket refusal to consider the findings of facts made by the inferior courts, as in the *Miala* case, can be found in the other human rights cases that could arguably have resulted in a miscarriage of justice.

However, one important exception has been established in the Human Rights case law of the Constitutional Court, namely in respect of the maximum length of detention pending indictment and detention pending trial, in cases of severe crimes for which the Angolan Criminal Procedure Code provides for mandatory pretrial detention, without the option of conditional release, for instance on bail. The important Acórdão 139 ruled in 2011 that the relevant laws and the constitution, limit the period of pretrial detention to a maximum total of 135 days that may not be exceeded under any circumstances. The court specifically referred to its earlier judgments (*Acórdãos* 122 and 124) and stated that, with these, a firm jurisprudence had been established. This jurisprudence was repeatedly confirmed (*Acórdãos* 227, 236, 238, 240, 309, 312, 316, 326, and 335). *Acórdão* 338 in October 2014 again declared the pretrial detention of an accused, in that case in excess of nineteen months, unconstitutional.

Similarly, in other human rights cases without political implications, the court has shown a determination to impose the rule of the law of the constitution rigorously. An example is the case in *Acórdão* 328 in which a driver who had been found driving without a valid driver's licence appealed against a prison sentence of four months' imprisonment on the grounds that a law had been applied in the ordinary courts, which had been repealed by a new Road Traffic Code of 2008. The Constitutional Court ruled that the prison sentence was unconstitutional as it had violated the principle of *nullum crimen nulla poena sine lege*.

7. Transnational Influences on Decisions

References to international law, international conventions, or obligations of Angola under the international legal order are rare in the case law of the Constitutional Court. The judgment refusing to declare unconstitutional a feared Law on Crimes against the Security of the State of 1978 avoided considering the Universal Declaration of Human Rights and the African Charter on Human and Peoples' Rights, even though they had been invoked by the applicant, none other than the Angolan Bar Council.[48] The total of thirty-five judgments (up to 2015) dealing with pretrial detentions, denial of *habeas corpus* petitions, and discriminatory or excessive terms of imprisonment did not make reference to international human rights instruments.[49] The relatively small number of human rights cases naturally arose from individual human rights (unconstitutionality) appeals by the victims

[48] See n 16.

[49] *Acórdãos* 121, 122, 123, 144, 147, 148, 229, 230, 237, 317, 320, 321, 327, 328, 332, 341, and 342 and, on *habeas corpus* specifically, 139, 227, 236, 238, 240, 309, 312, 316, 326, 335, 338, and 340.

of such human rights violations, under Article 49 of Act 3/08 (LPC) and/or Article 21 LOTC (see above section 6).

An important example is the Constitutional Court judgment dealing with a number of criminal convictions in a treason case dealing with secessionist acts in the northern-most province of Cabinda. In this instance, the court referred to the Universal Declaration of Human Rights, the European Convention on Human Rights, the UN Human Rights Conventions and the African Charter, as authorities, but not for moderating the excessive prison sentences that were based on flimsy evidence, but rather to invoke universal authorities in support of 'the paramount importance of the principle of legality', as a bar against 'unconstitutional attempts to change the constitutional order of the state'.[50]

The reluctance of the court to seek guidance in international human rights law cases is inconsistent with the explicit provision in Article 26 of the Angolan constitution, which states:

> (1) The fundamental rights established in this Constitution shall not exclude others contained in the laws and applicable rules of international law.
> (2) Constitutional and legal precepts relating to fundamental rights must be interpreted and incorporated in accordance with the Universal Declaration of the Rights of Man, the African Charter on the Rights of Man and Peoples and international treaties on the subject ratified by the Republic of Angola; and
> (3) In any consideration by the Angolan courts of disputes concerning fundamental rights, the international instruments referred to in the previous point shall be applied, even if not invoked by the parties concerned.

The court is, nevertheless, not willing to embrace international human rights law and case law. One reason may be that the Angolan Constitution contains extensive and state of the art human rights guarantees. Another reason may be that, with the exception of only one judge, the court cannot access and work with English texts and materials other than through Portuguese translations. Arguably, the court should and maybe cannot have avoided taking notice of the abundant references to international human rights law in judgments of the Portuguese Constitutional Court. But the fact is that Angolan Constitutional Court has steadfastly avoided acknowledging and referring to international human rights law, international standards of due process of law, and international human rights case law, as for instance developed by the European Court of Human Rights.

The Angolan Constitutional Court has never ceased to impose on itself careful political self-restraint. The court is all too aware of the fate of the SADC Tribunal in 2010, when its jurisdiction was curtailed by the SADC Summit, after the tribunal had ruled against Zimbabwe in the land seizures case of *Mike Campbell (Pvt) Ltd and Others v Zimbabwe*.[51] The Angolan judges have good reason to fear that their Constitutional Court could suffer a similar fate as the SADC Tribunal, by simple legislative act of the president's overwhelming majority in Parliament. Psychologically, the impact of the curtailment of the jurisdiction of the SADC Tribunal is all the more devastating, as it occurred with the complete acquiescence of all SADC member states, with not even South Africa standing to defend the independence of the highest judicial organ in the region.

[50] *Acórdão* 123.

[51] (2008) AHRLR 199 (SADC 2008). See Laurie Nathan, 'The Disbanding of the SADC Tribunal: A Cautionary Tale' (2013) 35(4) *Human Rights Quarterly* 870, http://repository.up.ac.za/bitstream/handle/2263/42461/Nathan_Disbanding_2013.pdf?sequence=1 (last accessed 17 April 2017).

Regarding the influence of comparative and foreign law generally, the court often finds persuasive authority in the writings of scholars from kindred legal traditions, in particular from Portugal, Spain, France, and, in a few cases, Germany. In seeking legal authority from scholarly writings universally, the Angolan Court follows the tradition of continental European constitutional courts that will refer to the writings of renowned scholars and reasoning in judgments rendered by other European constitutional courts in support of their own reasoning, deductions, and findings.

The Angolan court finds it natural to acknowledge that the Angolan legal system never ceased to pertain to the family of Lusophone nations and, more generally, the Franco-Roman legal family, which also includes Spain. As no *stare decisis* rules apply in this legal tradition, generally other 'judicial decisions and the writings of the most highly-qualified publicists' are considered subsidiary sources of law, as incidentally also stipulated for the World Court in Article 38(1)(d) of the Statute of the International Court of Justice (ICJ). An interesting detail is that the court has never once referred to the writings of Marx and Engels, or Marxist-Leninist philosophy. This marks a conscious and clear departure from the practice and tradition of 'socialist legality' that the judiciary carefully nurtured until 1992.

8. Nature of Decisions

The Angolan Court will decide by majority, and Article 29 of the Rules of the Court makes provision for dissenting and concurring (but distinguishing) opinions, which are published together with the majority ruling. The eleven judges of the court will compose two chambers with identical jurisdiction, whenever required in view of the case load. Each chamber, when constituted, will count five judges. The judge president or his alternate always has a casting vote.[52] The majority of the judges constitutes a quorum.

9. Effect of Decisions

All decisions of the Constitutional Court are final and binding. However, the ruling by the judge president on admission is subject to an appeal to the Plenum of the Constitutional Court.[53]

The decision on constitutionality in the context of a successive (as opposed to pre-emptive) review declares the unconstitutional legal norm null and void *ab initio*, meaning as from the moment on which the unconstitutional legal norm had become effective and applicable. However, such nullity shall not invalidate any judicial decisions taken before the declaration of unconstitutionality.[54] If a criminal law is affected, the Constitutional Court shall rule on the effects of the declaration of unconstitutionality on a case-by-case basis.[55]

In applications for pre-emptive review of constitutionality, a ruling of unconstitutionality will have as its effect that the state president shall be prevented from signing the affected norm into law.[56]

Applications for the review of constitutionality in concrete or individual cases (against judicial decisions or acts of authority) have a suspensive effect[57] and, if successful, produce the effect that the lower court is instructed to retry the matter. The decision on

[52] Rules of the Court art 29(1). [53] LPC art 8(2). [54] ibid art 30(3). [55] ibid art 30(4).
[56] ibid art 25. [57] ibid art 44.

unconstitutionality in this case will only have effect between the parties of the matter reviewed, and will not have general application.[58]

10. Impact of the Court on Constitutionalism

The Angolan Constitutional Court has disappointed many who believed it would soften the authoritarian rule of the Dos Santos presidency, in power for the past thirty-five years, since 20 September 1979. However, and undeniably, the 339 judgments of the Constitutional Court since 2008 and until the end of 2014 have contributed significantly to the strengthening of the principle of the supremacy of the law of the constitution and, thereby, the rule of law generally. The supremacy of the law of the constitution has established a new 'normality' or 'standard' in the political life of Angolans, contrasting the political instrumentalization of the judiciary from 1974 to 1992, as dictated by the constitutional principle of 'socialist legality'.[59]

Thus far, all political parties, and even the government, accept to refer unresolved differences and disputes to the Constitutional Court for decision. The broad jurisdiction of the court ensures that political disputes may be placed before it. All political disputes in one way or another will necessarily involve issues of constitutionality. The authority of the court has been sufficiently strong to command acceptance of its rulings, even where the losing party is convinced that the ruling is wrong, as has happened in the case of the confirmation of the election results as valid, in 2008 and again in 2012.

The court has not been able to break out of its relative isolation in the purely domestic Angolan political landscape and legal fraternity, and has made no particular efforts to establish relations with other courts outside the community of Portuguese-speaking countries. As the study of English is not encouraged in Angola, the language barriers in Angola are far more severe than they are, for instance, in Brazil, Portugal, or even in Mozambique. The Angolan Court is simply not able to accompany or follow the developments of constitutionalism in Anglophone countries.

The isolation of the Angolan Court is, at least to some degree, deliberate. The Angolan Court will sense a natural reluctance, for instance, to present in an international forum its decision in the *Cabinda* case.[60] This is the only decision that referred to the main international human rights instruments, but only in order to lend credibility to the invoking of the 'principle of legality', in support of a ruling that condemned human rights activists as 'separatists' in the province of Cabinda.

The court is understandably shy to propagate its political conservativism. The court will also be painfully aware that no other constitutional court in the world has thus far found it appropriate or useful to refer to a judgment of the Angolan Court. Hence, the impact of the Angolan Constitutional Court on constitutionalism in Southern Africa and beyond is at best generic, in the sense that it constitutes a positive experience that a country such as Angola should have and be capable of sustaining and respecting a constitutional court.

With the postponement of the renewal of the court since 2015, and its prominence in supporting the government and the state generally, disagreement with the court's rulings

[58] ibid art 47.

[59] Article 73 of the 1975 constitution stipulated for the principle of 'socialist legality' so as explicitly to remove and deny the independence of the judiciary, subjecting the courts to the primacy of the MPLA party leadership. See generally George Ginsburgs, 'Socialist Legality in the USSR Since the XXth Party Congress' (1957) 6 *American Journal of Comparative Law* 546.

[60] *Acórdão* 123 of 2010.

will grow. If the court again upholds clearly compromised and fraudulent election results in the next general elections (in 2017), it will probably lose the non-partisan authority that it managed to establish since its inception in 2008. The court will remain significant as a court of last instance in fundamental rights appeals, but as it will produce fewer and fewer judgments in defence of fundamental rights, the confidence and interest of injured parties in placing their matters before the court will diminish and extra-judicial forms of protest and defence of fundamental rights will grow.

Further constitutional reforms that may affect the Constitutional Court are unlikely for as long as the majority party, the MPLA, continues to rule. However, a broad consensus on the benefits of having a constitutional court is firmly in place and it is most unlikely that any political force would want to abolish the constitutional review jurisdiction of a dedicated constitutional court.

Bibliography

Araújo R C V, *O Presidente da República no Sistema Político de Angola* (Luanda 2009)

Araújo R C V and Nunes E R, *Constituição da República de Angola Anotada*, Tomo 1 (Luanda 2014)

Borowski M, 'The Beginnings of Germany's Federal Constitutional Court' (2003) 16(2) *Ratio Juris* 160, 161 http://www.direitocontemporaneo.com/wp-content/uploads/2014/02/The-Beginnings-of-Germany-s-Federal-Constitutional-Court.pdf (last accessed 17 April 2017)

Canotilho J J G, 'Direito de Acesso à Justiça Constitucional' Estados da Conferência das Jurisdições Constitucionais dos Países de Língua Portuguesa (Luanda, Junho de 2011) http://www.tribunalconstitucional.ao/uploads/%7Bc27dfa5e-9628-420e-b7b8-0925368a2afe%7D.pdf (last accessed 17 April 2017)

Fundo Europeu de Desenvolvimento, Programa de Apoio aos Actores Não Estatais, *Diagnóstico de Género de Angola* (Março 2015), http://eeas.europa.eu/delegations/angola/documents/press_corner/2015/diagnostico_genero_angola_pt_final_digital_pt.pdf (last accessed 17 April 2017)

Ginsburgs G, 'Socialist Legality in the USSR Since the XXth Party Congress' (1957) 6(4) *American Journal of Comparative Law* 546

Gouveia J B, *Direito Constitucional de Angola* (Coimbra Editora 2014)

Hamdorf K, 'Die Zulässigkeitsvoraussetzungen der Richtervorlage zum Bundesverfassungsgericht und zu den Verfassungsgerichten der Länder' (2011) *Zeitschrift für Öffentliches Recht in Norddeutschland (NordÖR)* 301–309

Jaeger R and Broß S, 'The Relations between the Constitutional Courts and the Other National Courts, including the Interference in this Area of the Action of the European Courts', Report of the Constitutional Court of the Federal Republic of Germany http://www.confeuconstco.org/reports/rep-xii/Duitsland-EN.pdf (last accessed 17 April 2017)

Kommers D P, 'An Introduction to the Federal Constitutional Court' (2001) 2 *German Law Journal* https://static1.squarespace.com/static/56330ad3e4b0733dcc0c8495/t/56bc3a5d-2fe1311b083ef8e4/1455176285666/GLJ_Vol_02_No_09_Kommers.pdf (last accessed 17 April 2017)

Mavčič A M, 'Some Comparative Comments to the Introduction of Constitutional Review in the State of Palestine' http://www.venice.coe.int/WebForms/documents/?pdf=CDL-JU(2008)026-e (last 17 April 2017)

MPLA, *Programa de Governo do MPLA para 2012–2017* http://www.mpla.ao/imagem/ProGovMPLA.pdf (last accessed 30 August 2015)

Nathan L, The Disbanding of the SADC Tribunal: A Cautionary Tale' (2013) 35(4) *Human Rights Quarterly* 870 http://repository.up.ac.za/bitstream/handle/2263/42461/Nathan_Disbanding_2013.pdf?sequence=1 (last accessed 17 April 2017)

Thomashausen A, 'Constitutional Law in Extreme Emergencies' in Bröhmer J (ed), *Internationale Gemeinschaft und Menschenrechte—Festschrift für Georg Ress* (Heymanns-Köln 2005) 1295–304

Thomashausen A, 'The Constitutions of Angola' in Wolfrum R and Grote R (eds), *Constitutions of the Countries of the World* (Oxford Constitutions Online) http://oxcon.ouplaw.com (last accessed 30 August 2015)

Thomashausen A, 'Super-presidentialism in Angola and the Angolan Judiciary' in Fombad C M (ed), *Second Stellenbosch Constitutionalism Seminar* (2014)

5

The Supreme Court of Ghana under the 1992 Constitution

Nature of Jurisdiction as the Apex Court and Contribution to the Promotion of Constitutionalism

Kofi Quashigah

1. Introduction

This chapter examines the nature and operation of the Supreme Court of Ghana as an apex court especially in constitutional matters and the impact of its role in upholding the principles of constitutionalism and the rule of law under the 1992 Constitution of Ghana. The 1992 Constitution is the basis of the current fourth republic and many of its provisions are better appreciated if its historical antecedents are understood. The current nature of the Supreme Court is a product of the history of Ghana and therefore a brief constitutional history is provided for a better understanding of its nature, functions, and performance under the 1992 Constitution.

The various jurisdictions of the Supreme Court and its own understanding and application of these are considered. This is done with the aim of assessing the extent of its impact on the promotion of constitutional and democratic values under the 1992 Constitution. The approach to the interpretation of the constitution by the Supreme Court, its use of the decisions of the courts of other jurisdictions, and international standards are discussed. This helps in assessing the influence of these international standards on the development of the 1992 Constitution. The fact of the Supreme Court's influence on national development is also considered. Finally, the impact of the personal attitudes of some judges on the Supreme Court and its influence on national affairs is examined.

2. Historical Antecedents

The nature of the judiciary under the 1957 Independence Constitution of Ghana, particularly the appointment and removal process of judges, was carried over from the pre-independence 1954 Constitution. The removal process under the 1957 Constitution was also similar to the pre-independence 1954 Constitution according to which a judge of the Supreme Court could only be removed by the governor after an address to the Assembly (ie legislature) to that effect approved by not less than two-thirds of the members.[1] These provisions were obviously not too protective of the position of the justices of the Supreme Court but the 1960 provisions were even less protective. Under the 1960 Republican

[1] The Gold Coast (Constitution) Order in Council 1954 art 60(2).

Constitution, justices of the superior courts were appointed by the president.[2] Again, it was the president who appointed the chief justice.[3]

With respect to the nature of judicial powers the 1960 Constitution established the Supreme Court and the High Court as the superior courts of Ghana.[4] It further described the judicial power of the state conferred on these two courts as being subject to the provisions of the Constitution and as may be provided for by law. In this regard Article 41(2) of the 1960 Constitution provided that:

> Subject to the provisions of the Constitution the judicial power of the State is conferred on the Supreme Court and the High Court and on such inferior courts as may be provided for by law.

This provision came up for consideration in the case of *Re Akoto*[5] in the Supreme Court, where the applicants challenged the constitutionality of the Preventive Detention Act 1958, which permitted the executive to arrest and detain any individual without trial. It was the case of the applicants that the law was an infringement on the human rights of individuals, as well as derogation from the principle of separation of powers. The Supreme Court held that Parliament was sovereign as provided in Article 20 of the 1960 Constitution, subject only to the following:

> (a) Parliament cannot alter any of the entrenched articles in the Constitution unless there has be a referendum in which the will of the people is expressed;
> (b) Parliament can however of its own volition increase, but not diminish the entrenched articles, and;
> (c) The articles which are not entrenched can only be altered by an Act which specifically amends the Constitution.[6]

With this interpretation of the extent of the power of judicial review the Supreme Court came to the conclusion that the Preventive Detention Act 1958 was not contrary to the constitution and that Parliament was competent to pass such an Act, even in peace time.

In the view of Bennion[7] on this provision, possibly following from his reading of the *Re Akoto* case,[8] the provisions of Article 41(2) meant that the courts were to exercise judicial power 'in accordance with provisions laid down by the authorities on whom legislative power is conferred by the constitution'.[9] Of great significance was his insight on that provision, which he expressed as being that, 'since, as explained above, the legislative power is predominant in the Constitution, it must follow that the judicial power is subject to its exercise'.[10]

Bennion further explained the said Article 41(2) as conferring powers on the legislature 'to divert some part of the judicial power to bodies other than the courts'.[11]

Unfortunately, therefore, the Supreme Court by its decision in the *Akoto* case impliedly held that it was bereft of the power of judicial review.

[2] 1960 Constitution art 45(1).

[3] ibid art 44(1). For the removal of the justices, the 1960 constitutional provision was similar to the 1954 and 1957 provisions—see 1960 Constitution art 45(3).

[4] 1960 Constitution art 41(1).

[5] *Re Akoto and 7 Others* (1961) 2 G&G 1(2d) 579.

[6] ibid 593–4.

[7] Bennion was the technical adviser to the Government of Ghana on preparation of legislation during the period 1959–1961. That period covered the time of the preparation of the 1960 Constitution.

[8] See *Re Akoto and 7 Others* (n 5) 579.

[9] F A R Bennion, *The Constitutional Law of Ghana* (Butterworths 1962) 168.

[10] ibid.

[11] ibid 169.

In order to avoid a possible replay of the above situation, the 1968 Constitution Drafting Commission designed a judicial system that would guarantee the independence of the judiciary. To achieve this objective, the Drafting Commission stated that:

> [w]e propose that in the exercise of the Judicial Power of Ghana the Judiciary, in both its judicial and administrative functions, shall be subject only to this Constitution and shall not be subject to the control and direction of any other person or authority.[12]

This became the standard according to which the judiciary in Ghana came to be structured. In the subsequent 1969, 1979, and 1992 Constitutions, therefore, the Supreme Court was conferred with clearly spelt out powers of judicial review.[13]

Further, in order to provide protection for the judiciary against intrusion from the executive and the legislative, the 1969 Constitution made provision for a Judicial Council. It was intended as an institution to serve as a buffer particularly between the executive and the judiciary. Its functions have, under the current 1992 Constitution, been enhanced to include roles in the appointment, discipline, and removal of judges. For these reasons, the composition of the Judicial Council has been enhanced. It is a much larger and representative body compared with the Judicial Committees established under the 1969 and 1979 Constitutions. Under the 1992 Constitution the Judicial Council is composed of eighteen members, including the chief justice, the attorney-general, four persons who are not lawyers appointed by the president in addition to other institutional representatives such as members of the bench, the Bar Association, the military, the police, the National House of Chiefs, and others. One of its principal functions is to advise the chief justice on the appointment of persons to hold or to act in a judicial office, subject to the approval of the president.[14]

The president is obliged to select from the list submitted by the Judicial Council.[15] In the removal of a judicial officer, the Judicial Council decides by a resolution supported by the votes of not less than two-thirds of all of its members. This is very significant compared with the past. For example, the 1964 constitutional amendment to the 1960 Constitution gave the president the power to appoint and remove judges at his pleasure.

In fact, during the first republic under President Nkrumah, the judiciary was totally emasculated and the country was completely unsafe for anyone in opposition to him. Political discontent rose and eventually led to the overthrow of the 1960 Constitution and, with it, the Nkrumah administration in a military and police *coup d'état* on 24 February 1966. The *coup* leaders formed a new government named the National Liberation Council (NLC), which eventually handed over power to a civilian government under the 1969 Constitution.

In preparation for the return of the country to constitutional rule, the NLC established a Constitution Drafting Commission[16] to ascertain the wishes of the people of Ghana. The Commission consulted the population to find out the type of constitution that would be most suitable for adoption so as to 'ensure that never again would the political sovereignty

[12] ibid. [13] See 1969 Constitution art 106; 1979 Constitution art 118; 1992 Constitution art 130.

[14] 1992 Constitution art 148.

[15] This, however, is not as straightforward as it looks. For instance, in 2015, a suit was filed by the Ghana Bar Association against the most recent appointments to the Supreme Court by President Mahama from a list of nominees from the Judicial Council. The argument of the Ghana Bar Association is that President Mahama should have selected according to the order of merit on the list of nominees. The matter is still pending at the Supreme Court.

[16] Popularly known as the Akufo-Addo Commission, named after its Chairperson, Edward Akufo-Addo.

of our country be allowed to reside so precariously in one man'.[17] The Commission understood its mandate to include the preparation of a proposal for a constitution that would guarantee that: 'so far as is consistent with good government, the executive, legislative and judicial powers of the State shall be exercised by three separate and independent organs'.[18] Further, in order to achieve this objective, the Commission opted for 'clear provisions for maintaining the independence of the judiciary; clear authority for the courts to interpret the provisions of the constitution according to principles of interpretation laid down by the constitution with the correlative power to nullify Acts of the executive'.[19] The Commission proposed that the judicial power of the country should be vested in the judiciary and that no organ or agency of the executive should be endowed with any final judicial power.[20]

Since the 1969 Constitution, there has been consistent effort in the various constitutions to guarantee the independence of the judiciary. It is to realize this objective that the 1992 Constitution provided in Article 127(1) that:

> In the exercise of the judicial power of Ghana the Judiciary, in both its judicial and administrative functions, including financial administration is subject only to this Constitution and shall not be subject to the control or direction of any person or authority.

3. Scope of the Original Jurisdiction of the Supreme Court

3.1 Functions of the Supreme Court

Unlike the Supreme Court under the 1960 Constitution, those courts created under the 1969, 1979, and 1992 Constitutions have been provided with clearly spelt-out powers of judicial review.[21] A general overview of the structure, jurisdiction, and functions of the judiciary under the 1992 Constitution illustrates that it was designed to provide for the following:

(i) to act as an independent entity, free from executive and legislative control in both its judicial and administrative functions so as to shore up the democratic system intended under the constitution

(ii) to police the constitution and ensure conformance to the provisions of the constitution, thereby guaranteeing constitutionalism generally

(iii) to determine and hold the balance, whenever necessary, between the executive and the legislature by upholding the concepts of separation of powers and the rule of law

(iv) to guarantee the liberties of individuals and protect them from invasion by the executive and the legislature and

(v) to serve as the buffer when the democratic system and its institutions are under strain or threatened by crisis.

To enable it to achieve the above objectives, the 1992 Constitution confers a number of jurisdictions on the Supreme Court. These include original jurisdiction, appellate

[17] This was in reference to the dictatorship suffered under President Nkrumah, whose overthrow and replacement by the National Liberation Council paved the way for the adoption of a new constitution.

[18] Memorandum on Proposals for a Constitution for Ghana (1968) para 2.

[19] ibid para 73.

[20] ibid para 607.

[21] See *Re Akoto and 7 Others* (n 5). The Supreme Court held in this case that it lacked the power to declare a law unconstitutional under the 1960 Constitution.

jurisdiction, reference jurisdiction, supervisory jurisdiction, and jurisdiction in election petitions relating to the election of the President.[22]

3.2. The Supreme Court's interpretation of the scope of its original jurisdiction

The closest that Ghana came to the creation of a purely constitutional court was in a proposal by the Committee that prepared the draft of the 1992 Constitution. The Committee proposed the establishment of the Council of State[23] with the function of exercising a special jurisdiction through its Judicial Committee. The proposed jurisdiction of the Judicial Committee was intended to be essentially preventive in character and to be largely confined to bills, proposed regulations and proposed executive measures.[24]

This proposed institution was not comparable in the degree of its authority with, for example, the South African Constitutional Court. It was not intended to derogate from or reduce to any extent the power of the courts. If anything at all, it was intended to complement the functions of the courts by exercising the powers of judicial preview as against the power of judicial review which courts normally exercise.

The full expectations from the exercise of this power of preview were captured as follows:

> ...the purpose of this special jurisdiction is to address situations that have the potential to develop into major confrontations between the organs of state that might threaten the stability of the political order. This special jurisdiction is meant to forestall, diffuse and resolve disputes before they mature into major constitutional disputes. It is not meant to encroach upon the territory of the Judiciary, but to enhance that political stability which is a precondition for the orderly and systematic exercise of normal judicial power.[25]

In spite of these idealistic-sounding objectives, the idea of the Judicial Committee of the Council of State was rejected and did not find its way into the 1992 Constitution. With the benefit of hindsight, and taking into account the now contentious politically charged environment in Ghana, it was perhaps good that the idea was dropped. However, the exercise of some of the functions prescribed for the Judicial Committee could have generated into a turf war between the Judicial Committee and the legislature, which has the power to deliberate on and accept or reject bills.

Earlier, the Commission that had drafted the 1969 Constitution had also proposed that the judiciary be conferred with the power 'to offer, in very limited circumstances, advisory opinions in matters concerning certain aspects of the operation of the constitution'.[26] This was not accepted and, therefore, did not find a place in the 1969 Constitution; neither was it introduced into the 1992 Constitution, as was the case with the constitution of India.[27] As was decided in the case of *JH Mensah v Attorney-General*,[28] the Supreme Court of Ghana will not entertain matters that are moot.[29]

[22] This chapter will focus on the three major jurisdictions: original jurisdiction, reference jurisdiction, and jurisdiction in election petitions.

[23] The Council of State is analogous to the Council of elders in the traditional political systems of Ghana. Its principal function in the traditional system is to advise the chief. See Proposals for a Draft Constitution of Ghana (1991).

[24] ibid para 255. [25] ibid.

[26] Memorandum on the proposals for a Constitution for Ghana (1968) para 511.

[27] See Constitution of India art 143. [28] [1996–97] SCGLR 320.

[29] Except where it is established that subsequent events make it clear that the question could occur again. See *Mensah* (n 28).

Date-Bah, in comparing the Supreme Court of Ghana with the constitutional courts existing in Europe, has pointed out that:'[t]he Supreme Court of Ghana is not a constitutional court in the continental European meaning of the term';[30] nevertheless, upon a liberal examination of the scope of the jurisdiction of the Court, he came to the conclusion, and rightly so, that '[t]he original jurisdiction of the Supreme Court conferred by Article 130 of the 1992 Constitution is what makes the Supreme Court a "constitutional court" in the European or civil law sense of the term'.[31] The 1992 Constitution in Article 130 assigns to the Supreme Court exclusive original jurisdiction in matters relating to the enforcement or interpretation of the constitution, with the exception of the enforcement of the fundamental human rights and freedoms, as provided for in Article 33 of the constitution.

Article 130 provides as follows:

> (1) Subject to the jurisdiction of the High Court in the enforcement of the fundamental human rights and freedoms as provided in article 33 of the constitution, the Supreme Court shall have exclusive original jurisdiction in –
> (a) all matters relating to the enforcement or interpretation of this constitution; and
> (b) all matters arising as to whether an enactment was made in excess of the powers conferred on Parliament or any other authority or person by law or under this constitution.
>
> (2) Where an issue that relates to a matter or question referred to in clause (1) of this article arises in any proceedings in a court other than the Supreme Court, that court shall stay the proceedings and refer the question of law involved to the Supreme Court for determination; and the court in which the question arose shall dispose of the case in accordance with the decision of the Supreme Court.

Article 130(1) came up for interpretation in *Edusei v Attorney-General*,[32] in which the plaintiff applied to the Supreme Court for the enforcement of his fundamental rights. The attorney-general objected to the jurisdiction of the Supreme Court on the basis that, if Article 33(1) is taken together with Articles 130(1) and 140(2), the High Court would be the appropriate forum for the proceedings for the enforcement of the fundamental human rights and freedoms at first instance. Article 33(1) provides:

> Where a person alleges that a provision of this constitution on the fundamental human rights and freedoms has been, or is being or is likely to be contravened in relation to him; then, without prejudice to any other action that is lawfully available, that person may apply to the High Court for redress.

Article 140(2) also provides:

> The High Court shall have jurisdiction to enforce the fundamental human rights and freedoms guaranteed by this Constitution.

The Supreme Court, by majority, came to the conclusion that the effect of Articles 33(1), 130(1), and 140(2) of the 1992 Constitution is that the Supreme Court has no concurrent jurisdiction with the High Court in the enforcement of the fundamental human rights and freedoms contained in Chapter 5 of the 1992 Constitution. The Court further held

[30] Samuel Kofi Date-Bah, *Reflections on the Supreme Court of Ghana* (Wildy, Simmonds & Hill Publishing 2015) 23. For a comparison of the judicial approaches to interpretation by the Supreme Courts of Ghana and Nigeria see generally Atudiwe P Atupare, *Constitutional Justice in Africa* (LexisNexis 2013). See also Seth Yeboa Bimpong-Buta, *The Role of the Supreme Court in the Development of Constitutional Law in Ghana* (Advance Legal Publication 2007).

[31] ibid 28.

[32] [1996–97] SCGLR 1.

that the High Court is the court of first instance and, therefore, has exclusive jurisdiction in the enforcement of the fundamental human rights and freedoms of the individual.

This matter having been settled, there is now no contention that as far as the fundamental human rights and freedoms under Chapter 5 of the constitution are concerned, the Supreme Court lacks original jurisdiction in the enforcement and interpretation of those provisions. This position has been viewed by Date-Bah as the most prudent, because to hold otherwise would have laid the foundation for a chaotic situation in the Supreme Court, where individuals would be at liberty to decide to submit even trivial human rights concerns to the Supreme Court and thereby impair its efficiency.[33]

Another opportunity to expatiate further on the scope of its original jurisdiction and, therefore, its power of judicial review relates to the question of the application of the political question doctrine. This doctrine was allegedly developed for the first time in the United States Supreme Court decision in *Marbury v Madison*.[34] The doctrine has been described as based on the understanding that: '[t]he principle of the separation of powers makes certain questions non-justiciable because adjudicating those questions would intrude on the powers of the political branches of government'.[35]

The Supreme Court in *JH Mensah v Attorney-General*[36] took time to review a number of its previous decisions, including *New Patriotic Party v Attorney-General (31st December* case)[37] and *Tuffuor v Attorney-General*,[38] and came to the definite conclusion that the Supreme Court had the power to determine political questions because the cumulative effect of Articles 2(1)(3)–(5) and 130(1) of the constitution was to 'invest the Supreme Court with an original jurisdiction to entertain all cases relating to the enforcement and interpretation of any provision of the Constitution and all questions relating to the constitutionality of an enactment or any act or omission by any person'.[39]

What is clear to any observer of the Supreme Court of Ghana is that the Court considers its jurisdiction as very wide and would, therefore, not shirk its responsibility through any self-imposed constraint. Justice Acquah, for instance, expressed his position as follows:

> Accordingly, if by the political question doctrine it is meant that where the Constitution allocates power or function to an authority, and that authority exercises that power or function within the parameters of that provision and the Constitution as a whole, a court has no jurisdiction to interfere with the exercise of that function, then I entirely agree that the doctrine applies in our constitutional jurisprudence. For this is what is implied in the concept of the separation of powers. But if by the doctrine it is meant that even where the authority exercises that power in violation of that constitutional provision, a court has no jurisdiction to interfere because it is the Constitution which allocates that power to that authority, then I emphatically disagree.[40]

A critical reading of this view leads to the simple understanding that, so long as the legislature operates within the full ambit of the constitution, the judiciary will not interfere with that exercise of authority for, after all, it is the constitution that is supreme.

Justice Acquah further explained that: '[a]rticles 2(1) and 130(1) of the 1992 Constitution empower the Supreme Court to declare as null and void not only any enactment but also any act or omission of any person which is inconsistent or in contravention of the

[33] See Date-Bah (n 30) 156. [34] 5 US (1 Cranch) 137 (1803).

[35] Mtendeweka O Mhango, 'Separation of Powers in Ghana; The Evolution of the Political Question Doctrine' (2014) 17(6) *PER* 2705, 2706 http://dx.doi.org/10.4314/pelj.V17i6.13 (last accessed 2 April 2017).

[36] See *Mensah* (n 28). [37] [1993–94] 2 GLR 35. [38] [1980] GLR 637.

[39] [1996–97] SCGLR 320, 367 (Acquah JSC). [40] ibid 368.

Constitution'.[41] Reading between the lines, one gets the impression that what Justice Acquah was labouring to convey was that the constitution of Ghana is supreme and the Supreme Court has the final authority to determine what is in accord with the constitution, even where the organ exercising the power is conferred with some degree of discretion. According to him:

> … if even the power or function is entrusted exclusively to an authority … and in the exercise of that function the authority is subject to no direction or control of anybody, article 295(8) of the 1992 Constitution still empowers the Ghanaian courts to enquire into whether that authority is exercising that function in accordance with the Constitution.[42]

At least, in the opinion of Justice Acquah, there is a very strong and clear indication that the Supreme Court was determined not to entertain any principle of self-restraint. Again, in his words:

> Indeed no judicial self-restraint doctrine can sufficiently assist the Ghana Supreme Court to refrain from deciding cases involving the constitutionality or otherwise of a law or action or omission of any authority.[43]

This approach was reflected in *Ghana Lotto Operators Association v National Lottery Authority*,[44] in which the Supreme Court endeavoured to settle the debate, even among its own members,[45] relating to the justiciability or otherwise of the Directive Principles of State Policy. Justice Date-Bah, in expressing the opinion of the Court, explained that:

> [t]here may be particular provisions in chapter 6 which do not lend themselves to enforcement by a court. The very nature of such a particular provision would rebut the presumption of justiciability in relation to it. In the absence of a demonstration that a particular provision does not lend itself to enforcement by courts, however, the enforcement by this court of the obligations imposed in chapter 6 should be insisted upon and would be a way of deepening our democracy and the liberty under law that it entails.[46]

In his most recent publication, Justice Date-Bah expressed his non-judicial opinion on the implications of the decision in *JH Mensah v Attorney-General*[47] which, for the sake of its importance and clarity, may be quoted *in extenso*:

> By this authoritative statement, the Supreme Court laid to rest an idea which had been around in Ghana constitutional discourse since the 1993 case of *New Patriotic Party v Attorney-General (31st December Case)*. The argument was that matters committed by the text of the Constitution to another branch of government, such as the legislature or the executive, are political and therefore the courts should not assume jurisdiction over them. In rejecting the argument, the Supreme Court in the *Mensah* case made it clear that original jurisdiction of the Supreme Court included judging whether any act or omission of any branch of government is in contravention of the Constitution. If it is, irrespective of whether the power over that act or omission has been committed to a particular branch of government and is thus

[41] ibid.

[42] [1996–97] SCGLR 320, 368. The said art 295(8) of the 1992 Constitution provides: 'No provision of this Constitution or of any other law to the effect that a person or authority shall not be subject to the direction or control of any other person or authority in the performance of any function under this Constitution or that law, shall preclude a court from exercising jurisdiction in relation to any question whether that person or authority has performed these functions in accordance with this Constitution or the law'.

[43] ibid.

[44] [2007–2008] SCGLR 1088.

[45] See earlier decisions in *New Patriotic Party v Attorney-General (31st December* case) (n 37) and *New Patriotic Party v Attorney-General (CIBA* case) [1996–97] SCGLR 729.

[46] [2007–2008] SCGLR 1088, 1106.

[47] See *Mensah* (n 28).

considered 'political', the Supreme Court would have jurisdiction over it. *This was a very important clarification.*[48]

The Supreme Court of Ghana, therefore, considers itself not constrained by any self-imposed doctrine in the interpretation of the constitutional provisions. This is as it should be, for the Supreme Court exists for the very purpose of providing a final determination to any question of whether the provisions of the constitution are being respected or not.

4. Nature of the Reference Jurisdiction

Article 130(2) confers the jurisdiction that has been described as reference jurisdiction.[49] This jurisdiction requires that, where a matter relating to the enforcement of the constitution arises in any proceedings in a court other than the Supreme Court, that court should stay the proceedings and refer the question of law to the Supreme Court.[50] This provision, however, leaves open the issue of when exactly there is a question of law. Is there a question of law anytime a lawyer in a case before a lower court alleges that there is a need for constitutional interpretation? Is a judge bound always to refer a matter to the Supreme Court once a claim for interpretation of the constitution is made?

This question came up for determination in the 1971 case of *Republic v Maikankan nd Others*,[51] in which Article 106(2) of the 1969 Constitution, which was the same as Article 130(2) of the 1992 Constitution, came under consideration. The Supreme Court (Bannerman CJ) provided a detailed guide on how to avoid a situation where merely every submission alleging that there is an issue for determination would compel a lower court to refer the matter to the Supreme Court. According to him:

> We wish to comment that a lower court is not bound to refer to the Supreme Court every submission alleging as an issue the determination of a question of interpretation of the Constitution or of any other matter contained in article 106(1)(a) or (b). If in the opinion of the lower court the answer to a submission is clear and unambiguous on the face of the provisions of the Constitution or laws of Ghana, no reference need to be made since no question of interpretation arises and a person who disagrees with or is aggrieved by the ruling of the lower court has his remedy by the normal way of appeal, if he so chooses.[52]

This approach throws the matter back to the lower court before which the allegation of a question for determination is raised. A paradox is thereby created, because the logical implication is that such lower court, while attempting to determine the clarity or non-ambiguity of the law or issue, would in effect in a way be attempting an interpretation of the constitution. In the words of Bannerman CJ:

> To interpret the provisions of article 106(2) of the Constitution in any other way may entail and encourage references to the Supreme Court of frivolous submissions, some of which may be intended to stultify proceedings or the due process of law and may lead to delays such as may in fact amount to denial of justice.[53]

If this were not the case, the Supreme Court could find itself swamped with cases to the extent of reducing its efficiency and importance. It would have lost the capacity to devote

[48] Date-Bah (n 30) 148–9 (emphasis added). [49] ibid 46.
[50] Note that, as already stated, art 130(1) exempts matters relating to fundamental human rights.
[51] (1971) 2 G&G 1476 (2d). [52] ibid 1479. [53] ibid.

itself to cases that really demand serious and deep consideration because of their constitutional implications.

5. Jurisdiction in Election Petitions

The 1992 Constitution is also rooted on the fundamental principle of political pluralism. Together with other fundamental principles, it is intended to guarantee accountability in governance. In the words of Justice Bamford-Addo:

> The people of this country in 1992 promulgated for themselves a constitution, which vested sovereign power in the people and provided a democratic system of government based on *certain fundamental principles*, namely, political pluralism, a majority parliamentary representative rule, under which form of government, all citizens of full age and of sound mind had the right to vote during an election to choose their representative.[54]

The principle of political pluralism protects the other democratic principles under the constitution and any derogation from its practice would destroy all the virtues that go with it. The Supreme Court has in a number of decisions endeavoured to promote this very fundamental principle of democratic pluralism.

The constitution confers on the Supreme Court the power to hear and determine petitions relating to the election of the president. The landmark case of *Nana Addo Dankwa Akufo-Addo and Others v John Dramani Mahama*[55] presented the most dramatic case in which the Supreme Court was faced with a very delicate and tense situation when it had to determine the fate of the 2012 presidential elections. The respondent was declared the winner in the December 2012 presidential elections whereupon the petitioner, one of the presidential candidates who contested the election, filed a petition in the Supreme Court claiming that he, rather than the respondent, was validly elected as President of the Republic of Ghana. The petitioners claimed that the respondent was a beneficiary of a number of malpractices, irregularities, and violations that took place during the elections. The grounds of the petitioners' case were:

- (i) over-voting
- (ii) voting without biometric verification
- (iii) absence of the signature of a presiding officer
- (iv) duplicate serial numbers: occurrence of the same serial number on pink sheet for two different polling stations
- (v) duplicate polling station codes ie occurrence of different result sheets for polling stations with the same polling station codes and
- (vi) unknown polling stations.

The main arguments were that the presiding officers at a number of polling stations did not sign the declaration relating to the results, and that there was over-voting and voting without biometric verification in some polling stations.

Article 49(3) of the constitution requires presiding officers and candidates' representatives at polling stations to sign a declaration stating, among others, the number of votes cast in favour of each candidate. It was a fact that, in some instances, the declared results

54 *Apaloo v Electoral Commission of Ghana* [2001–2002] SCGLR 1, 9–10.
55 Writ No J1/6/2013 of 29 August 2013.

were not signed by the presiding officer, although the petitioners' polling agents in fact signed. The question then was whether those results should be annulled. The Court by majority decision took the view, as expressed by Justice Atuguba, that:'[i]t is globally established that where a constitutional infraction causes no injustice by way of injurious prejudice to a person, such infraction should not have an invalidating effect'.[56]

On the issue of over-voting and voting without biometric verification the Court, by a majority, held that the petitioners had failed to establish these allegations, except to the limited extent admitted by the chairman of the Electoral Commission. The Court further held that the irregularities were not of such a degree as could impact very much on the declared results.

In the end, although the Supreme Court upheld the election of the winner, it went on to propose certain electoral reforms that it hoped would avoid situations of tension similar to what the country had experienced.

Some of the suggested reforms are:

- The voters' register must be compiled and made available to the parties as early as possible.
- A supplementary register may cater for late exigencies.
- The calibre of presiding officers must be greatly improved.
- The pink sheet[57] is too elaborate; a much simpler one is required to meet the pressures of the public, weariness, and lateness of the day at the close of a poll, etc.
- The carbon copying system has to be improved upon.
- The biometric device system must be streamlined to avoid breakdowns and the stress on the electorate involved in an adjournment of the poll.[58]

By its decision, the Supreme Court doused the intense fear that gripped the country over the possibility of the eruption of political violence. The fact that the parties resorted to the Supreme Court rather than to violence on the streets, as had been the case is some other African countries, could be regarded as a show of some degree of confidence or regard for the Court.

6. Promotion of Constitutionalism

The constitution is founded on the fundamental concepts of the sovereignty of the people, the supremacy of the constitution, rule of law, separation of powers, independence of the Judiciary, independence of the media, protection of fundamental human rights, and other basic principles that all go to support the concept of constitutionalism. The Supreme Court has endeavoured, through the exercise of its power of judicial review, to uphold the supremacy of the constitution, particularly through its support for the basic principles underlying the constitution.

A few decisions of the Supreme Court highlight its significant contribution to the gradual strengthening of constitutionalism. In *New Patriotic Party v Attorney-General (31st December Case)*,[59] the Supreme Court held that, although parliament had the right to

[56] ibid. [57] This is a record form on which election results are entered.

[58] See judgment of Justice Atuguba in *Nana Addo Dankwa Akufo-Addo and Others v John Dramani Mahama* (n 55).

[59] See n 45.

legislate, all such legislation had to be within the parameters of the powers conferred on the legislature by the 1992 Constitution. This is because, under Article 1(2) of the constitution, any law found to be inconsistent with any provision of the constitution should, to the extent of the inconsistency, be void.[60] The Court, therefore, held as unconstitutional the Public Holidays Law 1989 (PNDCL 220), which sought to establish 31 December as a public holiday in commemoration of the *coup d'état* of 31 December 1981, which overthrew the 1979 Constitution. The Court refused to give its stamp of approval to an event that was palpably undemocratic and unconstitutional. The Court further held that as long as the Public Holidays Law was found to be unconstitutional, the president or the executive could be restrained by injunction from enforcing it. This was a strong message from the Supreme Court to the executive, particularly in view of the fact that the executive at the time was the transformed military administration that was responsible for the 1981 *coup d'état* which was to be celebrated.

The Supreme Court reflected liberal and democratic spirit of the 1990s in holding that the glorification of a military *coup d'etat* could not be reconciled with the tenets of modern constitutionalism. The majority decision in the *31st December* case could be said to have provided a strong basis for entrenchment of the democratic values inherent in the 1992 Constitution at a very critical stage in the life of the constitution.

Again, in the case of *New Patriotic Party v Inspector General of Police*,[61] the Supreme Court confirmed the supremacy of the constitution over ordinary legislation and executive actions based thereon. It also underpinned the importance of the protection of the right of individuals as guaranteed under the constitution against the invading tendency of the executive. In this case, the Supreme Court declared unconstitutional a Public Order Decree 1972 (NRCD 68), which required a permit from the police before citizens could exercise their right to assembly and demonstration. The facts of the case were that this Decree, which was in force prior to the entry into force of the 1992 Constitution, required in its section 8 that the holding of all public processions and meetings and the public celebration of any traditional custom should be subject to obtaining the prior permission of the police. The plaintiff, which was an opposition political party, applied for and obtained police permits to organize public functions on two occasions but in each case the permit was withdrawn at the last minute. Hence the action in the Supreme Court challenging the constitutionality of the Public Order Decree in the face of Article 2(1)(d) of the 1992 Constitution. The said Article 2(1)(d) provides that:

> All persons shall have the right to—
> (d) freedom of assembly including freedom to take part in processions and demonstrations …

The Supreme Court in its decision held that the right to assembly is fundamental to the democratic system of government guaranteed under the constitution. This decision of the Supreme Court given as early as 1993 set the right tone for the protection of constitutional values.

It is, therefore, clear that the 1992 Constitution is rooted in the principle of the rule of law, separation of powers, and the protection of human rights, among others, and the Supreme Court has reinforced these principles through the exercise of its power of judicial review. The Supreme Court had also sought to redirect the executive onto the democratic path. The tendency of the executive to dominate the most essential institutions of state

[60] ibid headnote 4, following from the pronouncement of Justice Aikins.
[61] [1993–94] 2 GLR 459.

was brought to the fore in the facts giving rise to the case of *National Media Commission v Attorney-General*.[62] Taking into account the experience of dictatorial controls under the Nkrumah regime and the various military regimes the independence of the media was guaranteed under Chapter12 of the 1992 Constitution. One of the provisions intended to secure this independence is Article 168, which provides that the National Media Commission 'shall appoint the chairmen and other members of the governing bodies of public corporations managing the state-owned media in consultation with the President'. In spite of this, the president was appointed the chairman, chief executives and other members of governing bodies of public corporations managing state-owned media. The president argued that he had a right to do so under Article 195(1) of the constitution, which provides as follows:

> Subject to the provisions of this Constitution, the power to appoint persons to hold or to act in an office in the public services shall rest in the President …

The National Media Commission therefore sought a declaration in the Supreme Court that, on a true and proper construction of Articles 168 and 195(1) of the constitution, the powers to appoint the chairmen and other members of the governing bodies of public corporations managing the state-owned media is vested exclusively in the National Media Commission acting in consultation with the president. The Supreme Court considered the two provisions and also took into account the democratic values inherent in the constitution and lent its support to the constitutional protection of the independence of the media by upholding the declaration sought by the National Media Commission. In the words of Justice Acquah, who delivered the lead opinion of the Court:

> The language of article 168 is so plain and unambiguous that it means nothing more than what it says. And it accords with the overall objective of securing the independence and freedom of those public corporations from governmental control.[63]

The position is in line with the democratic principles underlying the 1992 Constitution, because an independent media is key to the guarantee of an accountable government.

Another instance in which the Supreme Court supported the democratic value was the case of *New Patriotic Party v Ghana Broadcasting Corporation*.[64] The facts were that the NPP, which was then an opposition political party, contended that it was also entitled to equal opportunity in terms of air time from the defendant, a state-owned media, to express its view on the 1993 budget, just as the Minister for Finance was granted an almost two-hour period of air time to respond to criticisms levelled against the budget. The plaintiff brought its claim under Article 55(11) of the constitution, which provides that:

> The State shall provide fair opportunity to all political parties to present their programmes to the public by ensuring equal access to the state-owned media.

This provision was interpreted by the Supreme Court as one of the essential provisions designed to support the democratic nature of the constitution. In the words of Francois JSC:

> A denial of opportunity for the expression of opposing views, inherent in a democracy, would amount to moves which may culminate in the creation of a monolithic government which is only one step removed from a one-party government.[65]

[62] (2008) 2 G&G 1825 (ed) 2269. [63] ibid 2271. [64] [1993–94] 2 GLR 354. [65] ibid 368.

This was in reference to the period of the autocratic period under the 1960 Constitution (as amended in 1964), when the country was officially declared a single party state and constitutionalism was jettisoned.

7. The Interpretative Approach

Article 130 of the constitution confers original jurisdiction (subject to the jurisdiction of the High Court in the enforcement of fundamental human rights and freedoms) on the Supreme Court in the enforcement or interpretation of the constitution. In the performance of its mandate as the custodian of the constitutional principles, the Supreme Court has in a number of cases adopted an interpretative approach, through which it has sought to make the constitution relevant to the aspirations of the people.

Over the years the Supreme Court has consistently used the purposive approach as the main mode of its interpretation of the constitution. The constitution is envisaged as a living entity with the expectation that it meets with the aspirations of the people that would evolve from time to time. His Lordship Justice Date-Bah in the case *Agyei-Twum v Attorney-General*[66] explained that a constitutional provision would be understood to have two purposes; that is, its subjective purpose and an objective purpose. According to him:

> The subjective purpose is what the framers of the Constitution actually intended. The objective purpose, on the other hand, is what the provision should be seeking to achieve, given the general purposes of the Constitution and the core values of the legal system and of the Constitution.[67]

In the earlier case of *Asare v Attorney-General*[68] the Supreme Court took the position that, in the determination of the purpose of a provision of the constitution, there should by a balance between the subjective and the objective.

Justice Date-Bah in the *Asare v Attorney-General* case[69] opined that, in the Ghanaian context, 'the core values from which could be distilled the objective purpose of constitutional provisions would include the provisions of chapters five and six of the Constitution and core doctrines such as the doctrine of the separation of powers'.[70]

The now generally accepted purposive approach to interpretation was captured in the oft-quoted words of Sowah JSC in the 1980 case of *Tuffuor v Attorney-General*,[71] as follows:

> The Constitution has its letter of the law. Equally, the Constitution has its spirit ... Its language, therefore, must be considered as if it were a living organism capable of growth and development. A broad and liberal spirit is required for its interpretation. It does not admit of a narrow interpretation. A doctrinaire approach to interpretation would not do. We must take account of its principles and bring that consideration to bear, in bringing it into conformity with the needs of the time.[72]

This principle of interpretation has become the standard according to which the various provisions of the constitution are interpreted. This is an approach that is essential if the constitution is to remain responsive to the fast changing political, economic, and social needs of a very expectant society.

[66] [2005–2006] SCGLR 732. [67] ibid 758. [68] [2003–2004] 2 SCGLR 823. [69] ibid.
[70] ibid 835. [71] [1980] GLR 637. [72] ibid 647.

8. Application of International Standards

Article 33(5) of the constitution seeks to leave the door open for the invocation and application of generally accepted fundamental human rights and freedoms that, although not specifically listed in the constitution, could be considered to be inherent in a democracy. This provision appears to give a free hand to the High Court and the Supreme Court to expand the scope of fundamental human rights and freedoms in keeping with international developments. This principle, and the readiness of the Supreme Court to uphold internationally accepted standards in this respect was upheld by the Supreme Court in the case of *Adjei-Ampofo v Attorney-General*.[73] In this case the plaintiff challenged his prosecution under section 179A(3)(a) of the Criminal Code (Amendment)Act 1993 (Act 458), which provides that:

> (3) Any person through whose wilful, malicious or fraudulent action or omission the State incurs a financial loss commits an offence.

The plaintiff's contention was that the provisions in the said section contravened the well-known international and constitutional law principles against vagueness and overbreadth. According to the plaintiff, although these 'doctrines have not been expressly provided for in the 1992 Constitution they were inherent in all democratic constitutions such as the Ghana Constitution'.[74] The Supreme Court declined to accept the contention of the plaintiff for the reason that he failed to specify any particular provision of the constitution that he wished to be interpreted or enforced against section 179A(3)(a) of the Criminal Code. The court made reference to the earlier case of *NPP v Attorney-General (31st December)*[75] in which it upheld the letter and spirit of Articles 3(3), (4)(7). According to Justice Akuffo, the court declared that:

> Clause (5) of article 33 is certainly not intended to elevate to the status of rights, duties, declarations or guarantees, doctrines such as those relied upon by the plaintiff, which are merely, but admittedly widely accepted, tools for the construction of deeds and statutes.[76]

As stated above, and rightly so, the court expressed the opinion that it would have been ready to apply Article 33(5) if the plaintiff had specified any particular right, duty, declaration, or guarantee which the said section 179A(3)(a) allegedly contravened.

9. Transnational Influences

The Supreme Court is the final court of appeal in Ghana[77] and is not 'bound to follow the decisions of any other court'.[78] In the performance of its interpretative function however, the Supreme Court does not close its eyes to opinions from other jurisdictions, particularly those that have a similar legal and constitutional tradition. In his decision in the *NPP v GBC*,[79] Justice Francois acknowledged that 'some random views expressed on this theme elsewhere, would not be out of place here'.[80] He then proceeded to examine the opinion in a number of US cases including the case of *New York Times Co. v United States (The Pentagon Papers Case)*[81] from which he picked the following quote that—'Any system of prior restraints of expression comes to this Court bearing a heavy presumption against its

[73] [2003–2004] SCGLR 411. [74] ibid 412. [75] [1993–94] SCGLR 35. [76] ibid 419.
[77] 1992 Constitution art 129(1). [78] ibid art 129(2). [79] [1993–94] 2 GLR 354.
[80] ibid 364. [81] 403 US 713 (1971).

constitutional validity'. Justice Francois expressed his approval of this view and suggested that: 'Those words should be observed by the state media as a constant guide, and constitute their creed and testament'.[82]

The importance of these opinions from other jurisdictions is further emphasized when Justice Francois bemoaned the fact that he was compelled to pick the various excerpts of the decisions of the US Supreme Court from *Jerusalem Post Law Reports, 1993*, because of the 'lack of adequate library facilities in this country'.[83] Generally, it is normal practice to see reference made by Justices of the Supreme Court to foreign cases particularly of the US. That is not to say that they consider the decisions of the Courts of other jurisdiction binding; they would approve the scholarship in any foreign jurisdiction where they consider it worthy of consideration but would not consider themselves bound.

In the case of *NPP v IGP*,[84] the court examined the issue of freedom of assembly in various other jurisdictions and also considered with approval the decisions of other courts relating to that issue. In the *JH Mensah* case,[85] the Supreme Court studied the political question doctrine as was developed and practised in the US but came to the conclusion that the doctrine did not apply in Ghana.

In this contemporary world situation, there is much to be said for the practice of examination of the case law from other jurisdictions, particularly so if the expectations behind Article 33(5) of the 1992 Constitution are to be achieved.

10. Supreme Court and National Development

The Supreme Court has come to appreciate its role in shaping the laws in accordance with changing socio-economic circumstances. In the *CIBA* case,[86] the New Patriotic Party, a registered body corporate, brought an action under Article 2(1) of the 1992 Constitution for, among others, a declaration that the Council of Indigenous Business Associations Law, 1993 (PNDCL 312) was inconsistent with the constitution. The defendant, the attorney-general, raised a preliminary objection to the capacity of the plaintiff to bring the action under Article 2(1) because, in the view of the defendant, only natural persons had the capacity to institute an action under that provision.

In its interpretation of that provision, the Supreme Court dismissed the objection, and Justice Akuffo expressed her opinion as follows:

> In these present times, when there is, increasingly, the tendency for natural individuals to join together to form corporate bodies for the advancement and pursuit of their common interests and causes, be they social, economic or political, the artificial legal person has become, and is increasingly becoming, a very important factor in the advancement of human endeavour and a potent vehicle for the individual's effective participation in national development processes of varying nature. Furthermore, in our aspiration towards national economic development, wherein our economy and indeed the global economy, is increasingly driven by corporate enterprise, rather than the enterprise of the natural individual, it is inescapable and even essential that the role of the artificial person is given its due weight.[87]

In its application of the constitution, the Supreme Court has come to appreciate the importance of its relevance in the socio-economic and political circumstances within which Ghana is situated. The Supreme Court would have failed in its constitutional role

[82] [1993–94] 2 GLR 365.
[83] ibid 365. [84] [1993–94] 2 GLR 459. [85] [1996–97] SCGLR 320.
[86] [1996–97] SCGLR 729. [87] ibid 793–4.

if it were not to recognize its role as an important agent for the support, strengthening, and growth of the emergent democratic society. That was the aspiration under the 1992 Constitution and for which purpose the Directive Principles of State Policy prescribe the general directions, according to which all organs of government and individuals must conduct their affairs in the interests of the state.

Article 34(1) mandates that the Directive Principles of State Policy

> ... shall guide all citizens, Parliament, the President, the Judiciary, the Council of State, the political parties and other bodies and persons in applying and interpreting this Constitution or any other law and in taking and implementing any policy decisions, for the establishment of a just and free society.

The judiciary, like all others, is expected to take the principles[88] into account in its application of the provisions of the constitution. However, the true implications of these Directive Principles of State Policy had for some time been the subject of uncertainty in the Supreme Court, calling into question the exact scope of the Court's power of judicial review. This uncertainty was settled in the most recent decision of the Supreme Court in the matter in *Ghana Lotto Operators Association v National Lottery Authority*.[89] Unlike the constitutions of India and Nigeria, which specifically exclude the Directive Principles of State Policy from the adjudicatory powers of the courts, the constitution of Ghana is silent in this respect. In the above-mentioned case, Justice Date-Bah confirmed the authority of the Supreme Court to adjudicate on all aspects of the constitution, including the provisions of the Directive Principles of State Policy.

Expectations from the Supreme Court are, therefore, high, judging from the scope of its various jurisdictions and the injunctions in the Directive Principles of State Policy.

11. Appointment and Removal of Judicial Officers under the 1992 Constitution

To provide for a secure judiciary, the judicial structure is supported by the Judicial Council, which is intended to provide further protection against intrusion by the executive and the legislative. The Judicial Council as an institution is expected to serve as a buffer, particularly between the executive and the judiciary.

During the drafting stage of the 1969 Constitution, the idea of a Judicial Council was discussed and it was intended 'to aid and counsel the chief justice in the discharge of his administrative function'.[90] The functions of the Council have under the current 1992 Constitution been enhanced to include a role in the appointment, discipline, and removal of judges. For these reasons, the composition of the Judicial Council has been enhanced into a much larger body. It is composed of eighteen members, including the chief justice, the attorney-general, and four persons who are not lawyers, appointed by

88 The relevant principles are captured under general headings, including political objectives, which proclaim the virtues of a democratic state dedicated to the realization of a free and just society; economic objectives, which expect the state to take all necessary action to ensure that the national economy is managed to maximize the rate of economic development; social objectives, according to which the state must endeavour to secure and protect a social order founded on the ideals and principles of freedom, equality, justice, probity, and accountability; educational objectives, which expect the implementation of a free compulsory and universal basic education as well as equal and balanced access to tertiary education; cultural objectives, directed towards the encouragement and integration of appropriate customary values into national life.

89 [2007–2008] 2 SCGLR 1088.

90 Memorandum on Proposals for a Constitution for Ghana (1968) para 559.

the president. In addition, there are other institutional representatives such as members of the bench, the Bar Association, the military, the police and the National House of Chiefs. One of its principal functions is to advise the chief justice on the appointment of persons to hold office or to act in a judicial office, but subject to the approval of the president.[91] The president may not appoint without prior recommendation by the Judicial Council.[92]

In the removal of a judicial officer, the Judicial Council decides by a resolution supported by the votes of not less than two-thirds of all its members. The determination of the 1968 Constitution Drafting Committee to protect the judiciary from interference was re-echoed by the Committee of Experts that drafted the 1979 Constitution, as follows:

> The judiciary should be assured full financial and administrative autonomy. This means that the governmental structure should not subordinate the judiciary to any government department or Ministry for the purposes of presenting or realizing its administrative or financial requirements.[93]

This influenced the present approach, as the 1992 Constitution provides in Article 127(1):

> In the exercise of the judicial power of Ghana, the judiciary, in both its judicial and administrative functions, including financial administration, is subject only to this Constitution and shall not be subject to the control or direction of any person or authority.

It was on this basis that, when the Supreme Court came to interpret Article 151 of the constitution, it considered the purported removal of a judicial officer by the president, even though acting on the advice of the Judicial Council, as unacceptable and an unnecessary intrusion into the administration of the judiciary and, therefore, an infringement of Article 127(1) of the 1992 Constitution.[94]

Prior to the entry into force of the 1992 Constitution, the president could, upon receipt of a recommendation by the Judicial Council given in accordance with the Judicial Service Regulations 1963 (LI 319), discipline a judicial officer. With the entry into force of the 1992 Constitution, its Article 151 vests the powers of disciplining judicial officers in the chief justice.

In *Agbevor v Attorney-General*,[95] President Rawlings wrote a letter to Mr Agbevor, a deputy Judicial Secretary, an office that qualified as a judicial office, stating that he 'has accepted the recommendation of the Judicial Council'. Acting on that recommendation, President Rawlings accordingly directed the immediate redeployment of Mr Agbevor out of judicial service for displaying a high degree of incompetence in the discharge of his duties. The Supreme Court castigated the Judicial Council for the recommendation because it had based this on pre-1992 legislation. In doing so, the Supreme Court stated that the president's action was unlawful, even though it was carried out on the advice of the Judicial Council.[96]

91 1992 Constitution art 148.

92 Attention may be drawn to the 2015 suit filed by the Ghana Bar Association against the most recent appointments to the Supreme Court by the president from a list of nominees from the Judicial Council. The argument of the Ghana Bar Association is that the president should have selected according to the order of merit on the list of nominees.

93 Committee of Experts Report on Proposals for a Draft Constitution of Ghana (1991) para 252.

94 *Agbevor v Attorney-General* [2000] SCGLR 403 (Kpegah JSC) 413–14.

95 ibid.

96 ibid 410. In the words of Justice Akufo: 'It is our view that the ultimate responsibility for the unconstitutional act of the President, in purporting to remove the plaintiff as a judicial officer, must be placed squarely at the door of the Judicial Council, which in this instance dismally failed in the performance of its functions'.

In the case of the removal of a justice of the Supreme Court, the constitution requires the determination of a prima facie case by the chief justice. This is required to be followed by the setting up of a committee to investigate the complaint and to make recommendations to the chief justice, who must then forward the recommendations to the president for necessary action.[97] However, where the petition is for the removal of the chief justice, the constitution simply provides that the president shall, acting in consultation with the Council of State, appoint a committee which shall inquire into the petition and recommend to the president, who shall act in accordance with the recommendations of the Committee.[98]

The importance accorded to the manner of removal of judges and the chief justice, in particular, as far as it contributes to the protection of the independence of the judiciary, was highlighted in *Agyei Twum v Attorney-General and Akwetey*.[99] In this case, the Supreme Court rejected a literal interpretation of Article 146(6), which was obviously less protective of the tenure of the chief justice. While Article 146(3) requires the establishment of a prima facie case against the judge of a superior court as one of the initial steps in the removal process, Article 146(6) is silent on the need for the establishment of a prima facie case in respect of the chief justice.

In the *Agyei Twum* case, the Supreme Court was of the view that the literal interpretation of Article 146(6) would mean that: '[o]nce any petition, no matter how frivolous its contents are, is presented to the president, then he has a duty to establish a committee to consider it'.[100] Moreover, since Article 146(10) permits the president, acting on the advice of the Council of State, to suspend the chief justice, an absurd situation could emerge whereby the chief justice could have several petitions hanging over his head and he could remain permanently suspended. In addition, so long as such petitions are entered, the president would have to appoint a committee and that would have tied down the two judges of the Supreme Court who would be serving on the committee. According to Justice Date-Bah:

> This is a scenario that is deeply subversive of the balance of power underlying the 1992 Constitution and the separation of powers that it entrenches. It is, of course, also inimical to the independence of the judiciary.[101]

The Court, therefore, held that, upon a proper purposive construction of the entire Article 146 in the context of the 1992 Constitution, the chief justice must be given the benefit of a prior determination of whether a prima facie case has been established against him before the president may lawfully establish a committee to consider a petition for his removal.[102] The Court was of the view that the prima facie determination should be made by the president in consultation with the Council of State.

The constitution's protection of the position of the chief justice was, therefore, clarified.

12. Behaviour of Some Judges and Consequences for the Integrity of the Institution

The widespread nature of the jurisdiction of the Supreme Court entails that it has become a common venue for causes both paltry and significant. This situation is bound to provide a basis for the old adage that 'familiarity breeds contempt'.

[97] See 1992 Constitution arts 146(1), (2), (3), (4), and (5).
[98] ibid arts 146(6), (7), (8), and (9).
[99] [2005–2006] SCGLR 732.
[100] ibid 756.
[101] ibid.
[102] ibid 786.

The early stages of the Supreme Court under the 1992 Constitution evidenced a number of events that almost derogated from its sanctity as the bastion of democracy. One such episode was what came to be known as the 'Missing page 28'. This matter came before the Supreme Court and was reported as *Republic v Mensa-Bonsu*.[103]

The facts were as follows. After the Supreme Court had delivered its judgment in *New Patriotic Party v Attorney General*,[104] Mr Mensa-Bonsu, a legal practitioner and columnist of the *Free Press* newspaper, secured from the deputy Judicial Secretary a copy of the judgment delivered by Justice Abban. Mr Mensa-Bonsu wrote to Justice Abban, drawing his attention to a comment on page 28 of the judgment, which ascribed to a Dr K A Busia a statement praising the *coup d'état* of 24 February 1966. Mr Mensa-Bonsu pointed out in the letter that the said view was indeed an editorial opinion of the *Graphic* newspaper. He copied the letter to the chief justice and also published it in his column in the *Free Press* of 13 May 1994. He followed this up with an Article in this paper entitled 'Justice Abban is a liar'. In the article, he accused the justice of having engaged in 'judicial chicanery', 'plain falsehood', and further that he had used the bench for 'politics of undisguised partisan nature', and 'done violence to the truth'.

In order to appreciate the political undertones, it is necessary here to point out that Dr Busia was the prime minister who came to office after the military *coup* that toppled President Nkrumah's government. The New Patriotic Party, the applicant in the case before the Court, was the offshoot of the political party to which Dr Busia had belonged. The New Patriotic Party was now in opposition, and the insinuation of Mensa-Bonsu was, therefore, that Justice Abban was using politics against the New Patriotic Party from the bench.

Justice Abban, not satisfied with this attack on his judgment, lodged a complaint with the police who investigated the matter, after which the attorney-general brought a motion for an order to attach the first respondent (Mr Mensa-Bonsu), the second respondent (editor of the *Free Press*), and the third respondent (the *Free Press*) for contempt of court.

Although the Supreme Court found that Justice Abban had indeed changed the offending portion of his judgment, as alleged by Mr Mensa-Bonsu, the majority nevertheless found the latter in contempt of court. For present purposes, there was obviously a danger posed by this case in undermining the integrity of the Supreme Court, particularly when even its own members were divided on the consequences of the publication by the respondents. The words of Justice Aikins, one of the minority justices, were palpably uncomplimentary. According to him:

> I have carefully examined the publications and I fail to see anything scurrilous and abusive against Justice Abban and the administration of justice. The word 'chicanery' simply means 'legal trickery or false argument'. If Justice Abban read page 28 of exhibit MB1, as I have found as a fact, can this action not aptly be described as legal or judicial trickery or false argument? I think the first respondent has not committed any crime. The use of the word 'chicanery' to describe the situation cannot, in my view, be said to be an intemperate or abusive language. Furthermore, any person who tells a lie can be charged with perjury, and perjury is a crime. *Therefore to call such a person, if he is a judge, a liar or a criminal cannot, in my view, amount to contempt of court. After all, a liar is a person who tells an untruth.*[105]

This cannot be said to be a compliment for a member of the Supreme Court, and the consequences for the image of the whole Court cannot be ignored.

[103] [1995–96] 1 GLR 377. [104] [1993–94] 2 GLR 35.
[105] [1995–96] 1 GLR 377, 454–5 (emphasis added).

The embarrassment caused by the issue of 'page 28' to Justice Abban and, therefore, the Supreme Court was not laid to rest in the *Mensa-Bonsu* case. It arose again in *Ghana Bar Association v Attorney-General and Another* (*Abban* case).[106] The facts were that, on 15 February 1995, the president, acting according to Articles 9(1) and 144(1) of the 1992 Constitution and in consultation with the Council of State, nominated Justice Abban for consideration as chief justice. Upon his approval by parliament, as is required by the constitution, he was duly appointed as such on 22 February 1995. The Ghana Bar Association subsequently brought an action in the Supreme Court against the attorney-general as first defendant and Justice Abban as second defendant, seeking inter alia:

> [a] declaration that on a true and proper interpretation of articles 2(1)(a) and (b), 91(1) and (2), 128(4) and 144(1) of the Constitution, the President of the Republic should not have nominated and appointed the second defendant, Mr Justice Isaac Kobina Abban, to the office of Chief Justice since he *is not a person of high moral character and proven integrity.*

We are here faced with a chief justice whose appointment, rather than drawing applause from the bar, instead incited the latter to take up arms against the chief justice of the nation on the ground that 'he is not a person of high moral character and proven integrity'.

The Supreme Court took the view that the relief claimed would, if successful, not only result in the removal of the second defendant as chief justice but also lead to removing him completely from the bench, which would amount to impeaching him. According to the Court, Article 146 of the 1992 Constitution sets out a special procedure for the removal of a judge, and the Supreme Court was, therefore, not ready to 'open the floodgates so wide as to circumvent what is not properly cognizable in the Courts under the Constitution'.[107]

> Justice Abban was saved, yet the dent on the image of the Supreme Court, the apex court of the land, was indelible.

If Justice Abban was accused of surreptitiously using his position on the bench for 'politics of undisguised partisan nature', Justice Kpegah, another justice of the Court, did not in any way hide his political colour. Justice Kpegah (now retired), while still serving as a Supreme Court justice, filed a writ in the same court asking that the government should appear before the Court to answer questions relating to a number of issues that were essentially political in nature, issues that included that the sale of the government's 7 per cent shares in Ghana Telecom to Vodafone and the redenomination of the local currency, the cedi, were fraudulent transactions. The statement of claim further alleged that the government's economic policy based on a 'property-owning democracy' was reflected in the lives of officials and accomplices of the administration.

Justice Kpegah was a known sympathizer of the National Democratic Congress as against the New Patriotic Party which was in power at the time of the suit.

This action did not come to conclusion. Nevertheless, its potential to undermine and compromise the concept of separation of powers was obvious. That would not be conducive to a harmonious collaboration between the various organs of government necessary for the creation of a smooth administration of the country.

Justice Abban remained Chief Justice until his death, and Justice Kpegah continued to serve as justice of the Supreme Court until he retired.[108] Although their continued service

[106] [2003–2004] SCGLR 250. [107] ibid 264–5.

[108] Perhaps it was politically prudent that no attempts were made to impeach either of them because of the possible political tensions that these would have raked up between the two major opposing political parties.

on the bench was tolerated, their decisions undoubtedly lost the air of sanctity that was requisite of the status of a judge of the Supreme Court.

The constitution of Ghana endeavours to guarantee the tenure of judges, thus making it possible for them to hand down judgments without political pressure. It is, however, a different matter if an individual judge decides to pander to the whims of politicians. This behaviour cannot be prevented by constitutional amendments; it is a human attitude that must be addressed, not through legislation but through commitment of individuals to principles.

Another controversial episode was the seemingly 'packing' of the Supreme Court by President Kuffour. During his administration, Mr Tsikata successfully challenged the jurisdiction of the Fast Track High Court in which he was being tried for the offence of causing financial loss to the state for his role in a debt incurred by the Ghana National Petroleum Corporation when he, Mr Tsikata, was its chief executive. The Supreme Court, by a majority decision, declared the creation of the Fast Track High Court unconstitutional.[109] In a bid to reverse this decision, the attorney-general applied to the Supreme Court for a review decision, as is permitted under Article 133 of the constitution. Article 133(2) requires the Supreme Court to be constituted by not less than seven justices of the Supreme Court for this purpose. Notwithstanding the fact that the Supreme Court already consisted of more than seven justices, the president managed to have Justice Afreh appointed to the Supreme Court to join the review panel. As expected, the review panel reversed the earlier decision of the Supreme Court.[110] This event was heavily criticized by many as executive interference in the affairs of the judiciary. It was because of this controversy that the Constitution Review Commission[111] recommended that the constitution be amended 'to ensure that the original panel that decided the case at first instance should, as far as practicable, be the same panel to constitute the review panel'.[112] The Constitution Review Commission further recommended that the constitution be amended to set an upper limit for membership of the Supreme Court as a means of pre-empting a tendency to pack the bench.

13. Conclusion

The Supreme Court of Ghana is not strictly a constitutional court; nevertheless, it possesses powers that enable it to perform functions not dissimilar to those of constitutional courts. The 1992 Constitution, like its predecessors since 1969, is intended to create an institution that would support the principle of supremacy of the constitution. The Supreme Court, therefore, possesses a host of jurisdictions, including its original jurisdiction in the interpretation and enforcement of the constitution. This jurisdiction is subject only to the limited jurisdiction of the High Court in the enforcement of fundamental human rights and freedoms. The consequence of the multifaceted nature of its jurisdiction is that the Supreme Court has become flooded with cases both of constitutional weight and those not as significant. This notwithstanding, the Supreme Court has categorically refused to tie itself down by the doctrine of the political question and the principle of mootness. It has

[109] *Tsatsu Tsikata (No 1) v Attorney-General (No 1)* [2001–2002] SCGLR 189.

[110] *Attorney-General (No 2) v Tsatsu Tsikata (No 2)* [2001–2002] SCGLR 620.

[111] The Constitution Review Commission was established in 2010 by the late President Mills with the mandate to collate the views of Ghanaians on aspects of the 1992 Constitution that should be considered for amendment. Further action on the proposals is still awaited.

[112] Report of the Constitution Review Commission (2011) p. 236, para 150.

repeatedly proclaimed itself as vested with power to determine what exactly the constitution proclaims. In the exercise of its power, it sees itself as the guarantor of the principle of constitutionalism and the rule of law which, together with other principles, constitute the foundation of the 1992 Constitution.

Another significant recognition of the Supreme Court itself is its importance to the life of the people of Ghana. It appreciates that, in the performance of its functions, particularly in the interpretation and enforcement of the constitution, it must make itself relevant in the socio-political life of the people, and it would appear from the general perception that the average citizen looks up to the Supreme Court as the last bastion for the protection of the values of democracy and constitutionalism which they hope to continue to live with.

Bibliography

Atupare A P, *Constitutional Justice in Africa* (LexisNexis 2013)

Bennion F A R, *The Constitutional Law of Ghana* (Butterworths 1962)

Bimpong-Buta S Y, *The Role of the Supreme Court in the Development of Constitutional Law in Ghana* (Advance Legal Publication 2007)

Date-Bah S K, *Reflections on the Supreme Court of Ghana* (Wildy, Simmonds & Hill Publishing 2015) 23

Mhango M O, 'Separation of Powers in Ghana: The Evolution of the Political Question Doctrine' (2014) 17(6) *PER* 2705, 2706 http://dx.doi.org/10.4314/pelj.V17i6.13 (last accessed 2 April 2017)

6

Constitutional Adjudication in Nigeria

Formal Structures and Substantive Impact

Ameze Guobadia

1. Introduction

The adoption by Nigeria of the presidential system under a written constitution between 1979 and 1983[1] and, from 1999 to date, has resulted in an upsurge in constitutional litigation. Two fundamental features of the ensuing system of governance that have given stimulus to this development are: (a) the division of the powers of governance between the three branches of government under a system of separation of powers; and (b) the division of legislative powers between a central government and constituent states under a federal system. The relationships attendant on these arrangements set the stage for horizontal and vertical power contestations between the branches and levels of government, requiring the intervention of an independent arbiter, the judiciary.

The envisaged powers of the judiciary (express and inherent) encapsulate the interpretative and review dimensions of the role of the judiciary under the constitution. The clear mandate given to the judiciary underscores the expanding role of the courts in a democracy that has coincided with its third wave in post-colonial Africa. The constitution of the Federal Republic of Nigeria 1999, as with that of 1979 before it (1979 Constitution), establishes the courts that make up the judiciary and sets out their respective powers and jurisdiction. This is the formal setting in which constitutional adjudication takes place.

The origins of constitutional adjudication in Nigeria, its formal structures, and processes lie in her colonial heritage. At independence in 1960, the British bequeathed a system of governance premised on a geographic division of the country into regions that started with the constitution of 1946. This arrangement evolved into a federal system introduced by the constitution of 1954. Although three regions (the Northern, Eastern, and Western regions) were created by the British colonial administration, a fourth region, the Mid-West region, was added after independence in 1963.

The history and development of the country's judiciary is directly linked to this constitutional history. The systems of governance in operation over time have determined what the structure and workings of the judiciary would be. Under the earliest arrangements, the judicial system was more unified. Within the structure of superior courts of record, there were regional courts. Matters went on appeal from the High Court to the Federal Supreme Court (since restyled the Supreme Court). The In 1967 the Western region created an intermediate court, the Western Region Court of Appeal (since abolished) between the High Court and the Federal Supreme Court, to serve the needs of the region.[2]

[1] This was truncated by military rule, which ended in May 1999.

[2] It should be noted that, in addition to the constitution at the centre, each of the first three regions had its own constitution. By virtue of the Mid-Western Region (Transitional Provisions) Act 1963 (No 19 of 1963) and

The character and operation of the different courts are reflected in the nature, quality, and impact of the decisions issuing from these courts. These are, in turn, a product of the jurisdiction, the different influences, styles, and approaches to reasoning and decision-making, as well as the composition of the different courts. They are also a throw-back to earlier developments preceding the current dispensation and bear eloquent testimony to the process through which they have evolved. Several aspects of the constitutions have come up for consideration by the courts. From the broad array of issues, the impact of the decisions of the courts has depended on different variables, including the subject matter of disputes and the character and status of the courts from which these were delivered.

This chapter examines the formal structures for constitutional adjudication in Nigeria, as well as the substantive impact of their processes and outcomes on the system. It also assesses the contributions of the courts to some key areas and issues around which governance and its systems revolve. These include (a) the federal structure, particularly the autonomy and mutual non-interference of the federating units; (b) the legislative competence of the federal and state governments with particular emphasis on concurrent powers; (c) separation of powers and the law-making procedure; and (d) election disputes.

2. Formal Structures: Courts and 'Access to Court' in Constitutional Disputes

2.1 Structure and composition of the courts

The formal arrangements for constitutional adjudication in Nigeria are decentralized and reflect the federal nature of the state. Judicial functions are vested in the courts established for each of the two tiers of government by sections 6(1) and (2) of the constitution. Although the court system comprises different categories of courts, constitutional adjudication is the preserve of only some of the superior courts of record.[3] These are the High Courts (federal and state); the Court of Appeal; and the Supreme Court. The election tribunals established by the constitution also perform these functions in relation to election disputes.[4]

At the apex of the court system is the Supreme Court, which comprises the Chief Justice of Nigeria (CJN) and such number of justices of the Supreme Court not exceeding twenty-one, as may be prescribed by an Act of the National Assembly.[5] Five justices constitute the court for the purpose of exercising any jurisdiction conferred on it by the constitution,[6] except where it sits to consider constitutional issues, when the panel is increased to seven.[7] The Court of Appeal comprises of a president and not more than 49 justices of the Court of Appeal, out of which there must be at least three learned in Islamic personal law, and three learned in customary law.[8] The High Courts (federal, state, and the federal capital territory (FCT)) are comprised of the chief judge and such number of judges of the high courts as may be prescribed by an Act of the National Assembly or the State House of Assembly, as the case may be.[9] The High Courts are constituted by a judge sitting alone.

At the lowest rung are the High Courts from which appeals go to the Court of Appeal and the Supreme Court. In addition to its appellate jurisdiction, the Supreme

the Constitution (Transitional Provisions) Act 1963 (No 21 of 1963), the laws of the western region in force at the time of the creation of the mid-west applied in the new region until expressly repealed or modified.

[3] The superior courts of record are listed in ss 6(5)(a) to (i) of the constitution and are ten in number.
[4] Constitution s 285. [5] ibid s 230(2). [6] ibid s 234. [7] ibid; see the proviso to s 234.
[8] Constitution s 237(2). [9] ibid ss 249(2), 270, and 255.

Court has original jurisdiction in: (a) any dispute between the federal government and a state government; and (b) disputes between state governments. Appeals also lie from the Court of Appeal to the Supreme Court on questions as to: (a) the interpretation or application of the constitution;[10] (b) the actual or threatened infringement of fundamental rights guaranteed in Chapter IV of the constitution (with the exception of appeals from the National Industrial Court on fundamental rights issues relating to matters within the jurisdiction of the National Industrial Court);[11] (c) the validity of elections to the office of president or vice-president and their tenure of office; as well as (d) whether the office of president or vice-president has become vacant.[12] A High Court may also refer a question involving a substantial question of law that arises in any proceedings for the interpretation or application of the constitution to the Court of Appeal to decide. The decision of the Court of Appeal on the question is binding on the High Court.[13] The Court of Appeal deals with all other matters of interpretation or application of the constitution and fundamental rights in an appellate capacity from the High Court.

The foregoing legal picture underscores the pivotal position of the Supreme Court as the ultimate repository of the judiciary's power of constitutional adjudication except for the very limited exception in the case of fundamental rights issues arising in matters before the National Industrial Court referred to earlier.

2.2 Appointments

In the appointment of judicial officers in Nigeria, the executive, and judicial branches of government play crucial roles. The legislature also participates by confirming the appointment of the heads of the various courts and the justices of the Supreme Court. Under an arrangement which deviates from strict adherence to federalism, a federal body, the National Judicial Council (NJC) plays an active role in the appointment of judicial officers to both federal and state courts. The constitution sets out provisions guiding the eligibility of persons for appointment to the different cadres of judicial office,[14] the institutions, procedures, and persons responsible for making these appointments.[15] Apart from the president, in the case of federal courts, the governor, in the case of state courts, three special bodies, the Federal Judicial Service Commission (FJSC), the State Judicial Service Commission (SJSC), and the NJC are vital to the process.

[10] ibid s 233(2)(b).

[11] ibid s 243(2)–(4). In particular, s 243(4) provides that decisions of the Court of Appeal in respect of civil appeals from the National Industrial Court shall be final. This exception was introduced by an amendment to the constitution. See s 5 of the Constitution of the Federal Republic of Nigeria (Third Alteration) Act 2010. The need to avoid undue delays in the delicate matter of labour disputes is a reasonable explanation for this development.

[12] Constitution s 233(2)(e). Section 239 of the constitution vests original jurisdiction in these matters in the Court of Appeal.

[13] Constitution s 295(2).

[14] Under the constitution, the definition of judicial officer does not include persons who preside over lower courts, such as magistrates or area court judges. See the constitution s 318 Part IV Interpretation, Citation and Commencement.

[15] The constitution gives broad outlines which, in practice, the special judicial bodies, the NJC and the Judicial Service Commissions (federal and state) augment with their own guidelines to facilitate the process of short listing, selection and final appointment.

2.3 The Judicial Service Commissions: the SJSC and the FJSC

The SJSC is created by the constitution.[16] It is chaired by the state chief judge and comprises of eight members, including the attorney-general and the heads of the superior courts in the state. Apart from these statutory members, the other members are the same as in the composition of the FJSC (discussed below). The SJSC is empowered to advise the NJC on suitable persons for nomination as heads and members of the superior courts in the state.

The FJSC, also created by the constitution,[17] comprises the Chief Justice of Nigeria, who is the Chairman; the President of the Court of Appeal; the Attorney -General of the Federation; the Chief Judge of the Federal High Court; the President of the National Industrial Court; two persons, each of whom has been qualified to practise as a legal practitioner in Nigeria for a period of not less than fifteen years, drawn from a list of not less than four persons so qualified, recommended by the Nigerian Bar Association; and two other persons, not being legal practitioners, who, in the opinion of the president, are of unquestionable integrity.[18]

Although the presence of non-lawyers varies their composition somewhat, these judicial bodies could be made more representative with specific provision for female membership. Without necessarily increasing the size of these bodies, such female representation may be prescribed in the quota for both the nominees of the bar and non-lawyers. The deliberations of the bodies will also be enriched by the addition to the membership of law academics and, possibly, representatives of civil society. Overall, a broader composition by the inclusion of these distinct blocks should serve to bolster public confidence in the activities of the bodies. The requirement of a geographic spread in the composition of government and its agencies at all levels under the 'federal character' principle in the constitution[19] makes for some balance in the representation on both bodies of states or local governments, as the case may be.

The composition of these bodies has a direct effect on the credibility of their proceedings. Apart from the statutory members who are there by virtue of their office, all other members are appointed directly or ultimately by the president or the governor, as the case may be. Although the membership of nominees of the Nigerian Bar Association (NBA) in the FJSC is initiated by the NBA, such nominees still have to be 'appointed' by the president from a list submitted by the NBA. By implication, the final choice must be acceptable to the president.[20]

In the case of the SJSC, the legal practitioners who are members are not even nominated by the NBA. They are simply persons who 'in the opinion of the governor are of unquestionable integrity'.[21] It is significant also that Attorney-Generals who are *ex officio* members are appointed to their offices by the governor or the president. Going simply by the numbers, the executive is thus responsible for appointing five out of nine members of the FJSC and five out of eight in the SJSC. It is, therefore, possible for the wish of the governor

[16] Constitution s 197 and Schedule 3, Part 11 para 5.

[17] ibid s 153.

[18] ibid, Schedule 3, Part 1 para E 12 as amended.

[19] ibid s 14. This principle broadly requires that positions and other opportunities in government are adequately distributed across the country or the states, as the case may be, to reflect the diversity of the peoples that make up these units.

[20] This conclusion is reinforced by the constitution s 154(1), which provides that except for *ex officio* members or where other provisions are made in the constitution, the chairman and members of the FJSC shall be appointed by the president.

[21] Constitution, Schedule 3, Part 11 para C5(f).

or president, as the case may be, and their political considerations to influence the deliberations of the bodies and, ultimately, the appointment of judges.

The FJSC is empowered to 'advise the NJC in nominating persons for appointment as heads and members of the federal courts listed in the constitution'.[22] The FJSC has, in furtherance of this power, devised guidelines for the appointment or removal from office of judicial officers. Its most recent guidelines were adopted in October 2014 and they provide detailed provisions for the process. The role of the FJSC is better understood against the backdrop of the more fundamental role of the NJC.

2.4 National Judicial Council: composition

The NJC is also created by the constitution.[23] It is chaired by the CJN. It comprises of twenty-four members. Among them are retired justices of the Supreme Court or Court of Appeal; a number of chief judges of states (serving in rotation); one president of the Customary Court of Appeal (serving in rotation); members of the NBA (who only sit on the Council to consider the nominees for appointment to superior courts of record); and two other persons of unquestionable integrity. There are, in addition, the following *ex officio* members: the next most senior justice of the Supreme Court after the CJN who is the deputy Chairman of the Council; the President of the Court of Appeal; the Chief Judge of the Federal High Court; and the President of the National Industrial Court.[24] Although the same suggestions regarding the composition of the FJSC and SJSC are relevant here, it should be noted that the size and spread of its membership gives ample room for wider representation than the other two bodies. As most of the appointments to the NJC are made by the CJN and not the executive or legislative branches, there is less likelihood of political interference in its activities except where the CJN is individually partisan. The high turnover of chief justices vis-à-vis the tenure of members[25] of the NJC generally, in recent years, has also meant that a serving CJN may not necessarily appoint members during his or her tenure. This has also helped to reduce the likelihood of 'packing' the NJC.

2.4.1 Powers/functions in judicial appointments

The NJC operates at two tiers of government, that is, at federal and state levels. At federal level, the constitution empowers the NJC to recommend to the president from the list of persons submitted to it by the FJSC, persons for appointment to the following judicial offices:

- the CJN
- the justices of the Supreme Court
- the president and justices of the Court of Appeal
- the chief judge and judges of the Federal High Court and
- the president and judges of the National Industrial Court.[26]

22 ibid Schedule 3, Part 1 para 13. 23 ibid s 153. 24 ibid, Schedule 3 para 20.

25 Except for a few members (the heads of state courts) who serve for two years in rotation, on average the non-statutory members serve for renewable terms of five years. From 2006 to 2014, there were six chief justices of Nigeria, each of whom left office on reaching the mandatory retirement age.

26 Constitution as amended, Third Schedule para 21(a)ii.

The NJC is also empowered to recommend to the president from the list of persons submitted to it by the Judicial Service Committee of the Federal Capital Territory, Abuja, persons for appointment to the following judicial offices:

- the chief judge and judges of the High Court of the FCT Abuja
- the Grand Kadi and Kadis of the Shari'a Court of Appeal of the FCT and
- the president and judges of the Customary Court of Appeal, FCT.[27]

With regard to the states, the NJC is empowered to recommend to the governors from the list of persons submitted to it by the State Judicial Service Commissions (SJSC) persons for appointments to the following offices:

- the chief judges of the states and judges of the high courts of the states
- the Grand Kadi and Kadis of the Shari'a Courts of Appeal of the states and
- the presidents and judges of the Customary Courts of Appeal of the states.[28]

Two important factors to note here are the vital role of the legislature in the confirmation of the heads of the various courts and the members of the Supreme Court as well as the nature of the involvement of the NJC in the appointment process. The precise terminology used to describe the input of the NJC in the appointment of the different categories of judicial officers is important as there are variations in the language of the main body of the constitution, as distinct from the schedule. Appointment to the office of chief justice of Nigeria is made by the president *on the recommendation*[29] of the National Judicial Council subject to confirmation of such appointment by the senate. Appointments of other justices of the Supreme Court are made by the president *on the advice*[30] of the National Judicial Council subject to confirmation by the senate. For the states, the appointment of the chief judge is made by the governor of the state *on the recommendation*[31] of the National Judicial Council, subject to confirmation of such appointment by the House of Assembly of the state. Other judges of the High Court of a state are appointed by the governor acting *on the recommendation* of the National Judicial Council.[32]

While in some appointments the role of the NJC is to *advise* the chief executive, in others it is to *recommend* to the chief executive. Although in common parlance both terms 'mean to tell somebody what you think they should do in a particular situation', the *Oxford Advanced Learner's Dictionary*[33] states that: '[a]dvise is a stronger word than "recommend" and is often used when the person giving the advice is in a position of authority. It "can suggest" that the person giving the advice knows better than the one being advised. "Recommend" merely suggests that the one recommending is only "trying to be helpful" '. In all, the dictionary concludes that 'recommend' is often used with more positive advice to tell somebody about possible benefits, and 'advise' with more negative advice to warn about possible dangers. As Nwabueze points out, commenting on the procedure under the 1979 Constitution:

[27] ibid. [28] ibid para 21(c).

[29] Constitution s 231(1) (emphasis added). This provision is in marked contrast to and an improvement on s 211(1) of the 1979 Constitution which vested the power of appointment of the CJN in the President at his discretion, subject to confirmation by a simple majority of the senate.

[30] Constitution s 231(2) (emphasis added). [31] ibid. [32] ibid s 271(2).

[33] Albert Sydney Hornby, *Oxford Advanced Learner's Dictionary* (8th edn, OUP 2010).

> Legally, when a power is made exercisable by someone on the advice of another, no discretion is imported; the power has to be exercised only as advised, the role of the repository of the power being the purely formal and nominal one of merely executing the advice.[34]

This conclusion is, however, debatable in light of the definitions given above.

This rather detailed consideration of both terms is spawned by the controversy that arose in the effort to appoint a substantive chief judge for Rivers State in 2013. The SJSC had sent a list of two judges to the NJC for consideration. The state governor did not appoint the candidate ultimately recommended to him by the NJC, who was also the most senior judge in the state High Court. Instead, the governor sent the name of another judge in the state judiciary, namely, the president of the state's Customary Court of Appeal, to the House of Assembly for confirmation. The House of Assembly confirmed this nominee and he was promptly sworn into office. The appointment of the new chief judge was subsequently queried by the NJC and he was suspended from judicial office. As a result of upheavals arising from the controversy, the Rivers State judiciary was lethargic for several months until the next governorship elections in April 2015 ushered in a new governor, who then appointed the candidate preferred by the NJC.

Fundamental questions arise as to whether a state governor is bound to accept the recommendation of the NJC and whether the NJC is bound to give reasons for its recommendations. The governor of Rivers State had earlier gone to court in the case of *Governor Rivers State and Another v National Judicial Council and Another*,[35] seeking a resolution of certain questions bordering on the role of a state governor and the NJC in the appointment of the chief judge of a state. Among these questions was whether the NJC was constitutionally bound to recommend only the most senior judge in the state judiciary for appointment. Justice Lambo, in the Federal High Court, held that the NJC was not so bound.[36] As so clearly put by one writer: '[a] binding recommendation is a contradiction in terms'.[37]

The constitutional provision neither leaves the appointment of the chief judge entirely in the hands of the governor; nor does it altogether rule out the governor's discretion. Procedurally, the governor may not appoint without the recommendation of the NJC. However, after the NJC has recommended, it has no further role in the matter. What becomes clear is that there is the potential for a stalemate between the governor and the NJC in the appointment process, seeing that neither may act alone. This underscores the need for better management of relations between the NJC and a governor under the extant provisions of the constitution.

As a more effective panacea, the legislature may consider amending the constitution to place a limit on the number of times a governor may reject the recommendation of the NJC, after which he or she must appoint a chief judge. As a further safeguard to the discretion allowed to the governor, the NJC may be constitutionally compelled to send at least three names in each recommendation it makes to the governor, from which a choice must be made.[38] Some thought should also be given to the possibility of requiring the NJC

[34] Benjamin Obi Nwabueze, *The Presidential Constitution of Nigeria* (C Hurst & Co 1981) 303. He concludes that: '[t]he real maker of the appointment under this method is thus the federal or state Judicial Service Commission'. These were the bodies charged with the responsibility under the 1979 Constitution before the establishment of the NJC by the 1999 Constitution now in force.

[35] Suit No FHC/PH/CS/421/2013 (unreported).

[36] Consideration of the details of the matters in issue in that case are outside the scope of this contribution.

[37] See Nwabueze (n 34) 303.

[38] Section 174 of South Africa's 1996 constitution, as amended, forestalls this dilemma by limiting to two the number of times the president may reject the recommendation of the JSC in the appointment of other judges

to accompany its recommendations with reasons and of the governor giving reasons for rejecting such recommendations.

2.4.2 *Eligibility for appointment to judicial office: Constitutional and other criteria*

The constitution sets out criteria for eligibility to the different judicial offices. For the CJN and justices of the Supreme Court, the requirement is fifteen years' post-qualification experience as a lawyer[39] and twelve years' post-call experience[40] for the Court of Appeal. In similar terms, the constitution provides for eligibility to the other courts with variations only on the length of the post-qualification experience required.[41] There is also the added requirement of acceptable expertise in customary law and Islamic law for the states' customary Courts of Appeal and Shari'a Courts of Appeal, respectively.[42] The constitution does not specify the way in which such expertise is to be determined. In the case of appointments to the Shari'a Court of Appeal, the NJC Guidelines specify 'knowledge of Arabic language and grammar'.[43]

The NJC Guidelines make no prescriptions in this regard for customary law. Perhaps previous service presiding over lower customary courts could be considered sufficient expertise. The constitutional criteria are straightforward and do not pose challenges to the appointing authority. It is, of course, expected that within these criteria, those who qualify for appointment would be hard-working persons of unimpeachable integrity[44] who have a sound knowledge of the law.

Under the criteria spelt out in the constitution, the special judicial bodies formulate their own guidelines for deciding on nominations for appointment. This analysis emphasizes the NJC and the FJSC (both federal bodies). As the NJC is mandated to also have an input into judicial appointments in the states, the choice of these two bodies serves to give a feel of these appointments nationwide. The qualities expected of nominees, the eligibility criteria as well as the procedure for nominations by these bodies, are spelt out in their published guidelines. The need for transparency and credibility in the proceedings of the NJC and, in particular, the appointment of judges, cannot be overemphasized. As in the JSCs, the views of all members, including dissents, are heard and recorded at meetings of the NJC. The majority view carries the day. The recent introduction of interviews for candidates by the NJC is a step in the right direction. Perhaps a practice of publishing the names of nominees in the media should also be considered to obtain the comments and input of the wider public in the process. The drawback in this suggestion, however, lies in its potential for unjust vilification of candidates, which often can never be fully redressed.

Appointments to superior courts are to two categories of courts, namely, the High Courts (federal and state) and two appellate courts (the Court of Appeal and the Supreme Court). A tradition has developed of 'inbreeding', in which appointments to

of the Constitutional Court apart from the chief justice and deputy chief justice. It further requires the JSC to send a list of three names over the number of appointments to be made to the president.

[39] Constitution s 231(3). [40] ibid s 238(3).

[41] Ten years in the case of the Federal High Court and state High Courts, the States Customary Court of Appeal and Shari'a Court of Appeal (Constitution ss 250(3), 271(3), 285(3), and 276(3) respectively), among other courts.

[42] Constitution ss 285(3)(a) and (b) and 276(3)(a) and (b) respectively.

[43] NJC Guidelines (2014) rule 4(4)(1)(e).

[44] The requirement of integrity may be inferred from the judicial oath in the Fifth Schedule to the constitution to which judicial officers subscribe.

the Supreme Court are made exclusively from the Court of Appeal. It is doubtful if this 'inbreeding' has in any way given the impression that a distinct culture of professionalism that protects its independence exists in the highest court. The independence of the judiciary at that level is based largely on the integrity of individual justices and the constitutional provisions for their appointment, discipline, and removal that can limit pressure and interference from the political branches. In this regard, the raiding of the residences of judges including some from the apex court by security agents in October 2015 on suspicion of corruption and their subsequent arraignment on criminal charges have debunked any image of professionalism in the courts. While it is still too soon to determine what effect this will have on judicial independence, there is no gainsaying the fact that these activities of the security agencies also fuel accusations of executive pressure on the judiciary.

In their guidelines for appointments to these appellate courts, the FJSC and NJC set much store on seniority and the number of judgments a candidate has delivered in the lower court. Potentially, there is the possibility of reducing the exercise to a game of numbers because it is doubtful if the quality of judgments delivered and the nature of the cases dealt with are actually taken into account.[45] Too much adherence to seniority and geographic spread can also be at the expense of merit. Seniority as a criterion for elevation to the appellate courts will work well where the initial appointment process to the High Courts produces the right calibre of judges, who then move on to become appellate judges. This, of course, takes it for granted that appropriate checks and disciplinary processes are in place and utilized to ensure high ethical standards and professional competence from judges from the beginning right through their judicial careers, with the bad eggs being weeded out over time.

While it cannot be doubted that competent serving judges have been elevated to both appellate courts, the reluctance over time to appoint directly from the bar or academia has, in large measure, deprived these courts, particularly the apex court, of the positive qualities of independence and analytical thinking that a successful practitioner or academic can bring to adjudication, especially in matters of substantive law and, in particular, concept-filled areas such as constitutional law.[46] In what may be termed an improvement, the latest guidelines issued by the NJC now list academia as a source from which appointments to the appellate courts may be drawn.[47] It should be pointed out, however, that before the latest guidelines were introduced, academics were technically not specifically excluded from appointment as many of them were also legal practitioners and fell within that group. Academics in these ranks were simply not the preferred choice of the persons making recommendations and appointments. It is hoped that the latest NJC Guidelines will bring about actual changes in this regard.

Although the recommending and appointing authorities endeavour to ensure an adequate balance of seniority and other eligibility criteria with representation across different divides[48] in judicial appointments, there is no specific requirement of gender representation. It must be noted, however, that the sheer visibility (by number and status) of female judicial officers is illustrative of adequate female representation devoid of tokenism. The immediate past CJN (2012 to 2014) was a woman. There are serving female Supreme Court justices. The current president of the Court of Appeal is

[45] In a different context, the NJC requires all judges to file periodic returns on the number of cases they have conducted and judgments delivered. Since it is virtually impossible for the NJC to verify the claims of every individual judge, the possibility of individual judges being able to inflate their returns cannot be ruled out.

[46] At the appellate level, issues of procedure have been sorted out and the emphasis on substantive law is well within the academic's domain.

[47] NJC Guidelines (2014) rule 3(6).

[48] Including ethnicity and religion.

a woman. There are several female justices of the Court of Appeal. At state level, a number of chief judges are women, alongside a large number of female judges in the different courts. From another perspective, it must be observed that, given the male-oriented society that Nigeria is, the principle of seniority, which was not side-stepped in the choice of candidates, has in fact aided the emergence of female judges at the highest levels.

3. Powers of the Courts in Constitutional Adjudication: Nature and Scope of their Jurisdiction

Section 6 of the constitution describes the nature and extent of the judicial powers vested in the superior courts of record and, thereby, circumscribes their jurisdiction, that is, the right of the individual court to exercise judicial power in a particular case. Section 6(a) provides that the judicial powers vested in the courts 'shall extend notwithstanding anything to the contrary in this Constitution, to all inherent powers and sanctions of a court of law'.

These inherent powers are not defined in the constitution and must be taken to refer to judicial power in its widest sense, covering every determination that a court may make. Section 6(6)(b) states as follows:

> The judicial powers ... shall extend to all matters between persons, or between government or authority and to any person in Nigeria, and to all actions and proceedings relating thereto, for the determination of any question as to the civil rights and obligations of that person.

With regard to the fundamental rights guaranteed in Chapter IV of the constitution, for example, section 46(1) provides:

> Any person who alleges that any of the provisions of this Chapter has been, is being or is likely to be contravened in any State in relation to him may apply to a High Court for redress.

The extent of the wide jurisdiction vested in the courts in constitutional matters is, however, limited by the specific ouster of the courts' jurisdiction with regard to:

(a) any issue or question as to whether any act or omission by any authority or person or as to whether any law or any judicial decision is in conformity with the Fundamental Objectives and Directive Principles of State Policy ... and

(b) any action or proceedings relating to any existing law made on or after 15th January, 1966 for determining any issue or question as to the competence of any authority or person to make any such law.[49]

There is a similar ouster of jurisdiction in relation to the proceedings or determination relating to the impeachment or removal of the president, vice-president, governor, and deputy governor.[50]

3.1 Access to court in constitutional disputes

The courts cannot on their own initiate the process for the exercise of their powers.[51] This must be set in motion by litigants. Apart from the need for a real controversy or question

[49] See s 6(6)(c) and (d). The latter provision is intended to protect the actions taken by the military during the long period of military rule that began on 15 January 1966.

[50] Constitution s 143(10) and (11).

[51] This discussion draws on an earlier article; see Ameze Guobadia, 'Constitutional Adjudication: *Locus Standi*! Recent Trends in Nigerian Courts' (1978–1988) 3 *Nigerian Juridical Review* 37.

to exist, a potential litigant in a constitutional dispute must have the requisite interest or link with the subject matter of the dispute to enable him or her to invoke the court's jurisdiction. This is the *locus standi* rule, which literally means 'standing to sue'. An undue restriction on standing to sue hinders access to court in constitutional cases and limits the scope for expounding the law of the constitution. The *locus classicus* here in Nigeria is the case of *Adesanya v President of the Republic of Nigeria and Another*,[52] in which the Supreme Court gave a rather narrow construction to the concept. The facts of the case are important, and bear setting out in some detail.

The first defendant had appointed the second defendant as chairman of the Federal Electoral Commission under section 141 of the 1979 Constitution at a time when the latter was still the incumbent chief judge of Bendel State. The appointment was confirmed by a majority in the senate. The plaintiff, a senator, did not agree with the confirmation and went to court to challenge the constitutionality of the appointment. The High Court declared the appointment unconstitutional, null, and void. The High Court did not, however, grant the injunctions to restrain the swearing in of the second defendant into office or his acting as chairman of the Electoral Commission. On appeal, the Court of Appeal found that having been a member of the senate that confirmed the appointment, the plaintiff had no right to bring proceedings outside the senate in respect of a matter over which his views had been rejected in the senate. The Court of Appeal reiterated the observation of the lower court, that the plaintiff had no personal interest in the subject matter and no *locus standi* to institute the action. It held that the court could only adjudicate on an alleged breach of the constitution where there is a dispute before it which has been brought by the proper litigants.

The issue was referred to the Supreme Court for interpretation under section 259(3) of the 1979 Constitution. In its analysis of the issues, the Supreme Court gave a very liberal interpretation to the concept, as follows:

> To deny any member of such a society [referring to Nigeria with its complexities] who is aware or believes, or is led to believe, that there has been an infraction of any of the provisions of our Constitution ... access to a court of law to air his grievance on the flimsy excuse of lack of sufficient interest is to provide a ready recipe for organised disenchantment with the judicial process.[53]

The Court was of the opinion that section 1 of the 1979 Constitution[54] not only entitled any person to challenge any breach of the constitution in court, but obliged them to do so. In spite of this, however, the Court denied the plaintiff standing to sue in the case. It drew a distinction between its analysis of the concept and Adesanya's position as plaintiff in the case. In the view of the Court, the subject matter was not a controversy touching on the plaintiff's civil rights and obligations as an individual but as a senator. The Court noted that the plaintiff had not complained about the procedure adopted in the confirmation exercise in the senate. He came to court because his minority position was not accepted by the majority in the senate. It noted further that the plaintiff's participation in the said confirmation proceedings barred him from challenging the action in court.

[52] (1981) SC 112. [53] ibid 131.

[54] The supremacy clause, which was exactly the same as s 1 of the 1999 Constitution.

In the later case of *Attorney-General of Bendel State v Attorney-General of the Federation and 22 Others*,[55] the issue was the proper procedure for exercising federal legislative power. Although the issue of *locus standi* was not seriously canvassed, the Supreme Court did point out that the requisite standing of Bendel State to challenge the constitutionality of the legislation (a money bill) arose from its interest in a share of the public revenue. It held that the plaintiff only had to 'indicate a justiciable dispute to give it *locus standi*'. Bendel State thus successfully challenged the Appropriation Act 1981 as not having been passed in accordance with the procedure set out in the 1979 Constitution.

Subsequent cases in which standing was an issue in the higher courts were not, strictly speaking, constitutional cases. In *Fawehinmi v Akilu*,[56] for example, the Supreme Court recognized the standing of a citizen to apply for an order of *mandamus* to compel the Director of Public Prosecutions to prosecute murder suspects. On a suggestion in *Thomas v Olufosoye*,[57] the Supreme Court refused to consider the latest developments in other jurisdictions on the ground that those developments 'found support in the statute law'[58] of those places.

These later cases have, therefore, not changed or even relaxed the rules on *locus standi* in constitutional litigation. The approach of the Supreme Court remains conservative, as expressed in *Adesanya*. The fear of a floodgate of litigation lies at the root of the approach to standing of the Supreme Court. This stance may be a dampener for public interest litigation in the protection of the constitution. There is something to be learnt from the Ghanaian approach, in which any citizen may challenge a breach of the constitution there being no restrictions on standing to sue. The improved access to court intended by the Fundamental Rights (Enforcement Procedure) Rules 2009, made by the CJN for the practice and procedure of high courts in relation to the protection of the fundamental rights of the individual in Chapter IV of the constitution, is limited in its scope to breaches of the rights guaranteed by the chapter. As a consequence, public interest suits in protection of the constitution in its entirety have not really been a prominent feature of Nigeria's constitutional law. The discussion of actual decisions on the different themes indicated in the introduction to this chapter revolves around cases in which standing has not really been in issue.

Apart from the restrictions imposed by the *locus standi* principle, the courts do not assume jurisdiction over abstract or hypothetical issues. The jurisdiction and powers of the court in constitutional matters are invoked only where a concrete issue is ripe for hearing.

4. Remedies

The remedy of declaration is introduced by the express provision of section 1(3) of the constitution, which renders void any law that is inconsistent with it. Hence, if a law is found to be inconsistent with the constitution, the courts are under a duty to make a declaration of unconstitutionality. According to Nwabueze,[59] the court has no discretion in the matter. In *National Assembly v President Federal Republic of Nigeria*,[60] the Independent National Electoral Commission (INEC) challenged the Electoral Act of 2002 as not having been passed in accordance with the procedure prescribed in the constitution. The Court of Appeal adopted an unusual stance. It found that the Act had not been properly passed,

[55] (1982) 3 NCLR 424. [56] (1987) 4 NWLR (Pt 67) 797. [57] (1986) 2 SC 325.
[58] ibid (Justice Obaseki) 353.
[59] Benjamin Obi Nwabueze, *Constitutional Democracy in Africa* (Spectrum Books Ltd 2003) 232.
[60] (2003) 41 WRN 94 (CA).

as alleged by the INEC, as a mere motion to override the president's veto of the proposed legislation was not the procedure to be followed in subsequently passing it.

The Court refused, nevertheless, to declare the Act unconstitutional. In the lead judgment, Justice Oguntade opined that since the Electoral Act 2002 was, at the time, being used for the conduct of the 2003 elections, striking it down would create problems in the land. It was enough, in his view, that the INEC 'had obtained a vindication for its rights and in the process enabled this court to express its view as to the procedure to be followed when overriding a presidential veto in the law-making process'.[61]

Can the position taken by the Court of Appeal in this case be reconciled with the responsibility thrust on the court under the power of judicial review that flows from section 1(3) of the constitution? The Supreme Court has held that inconsistency with the procedure prescribed for making law in the constitution is as fatal to a law as substantive inconsistency of a law with the constitution itself.[62] As Nwabueze observed, what the constitution prescribes is the nullification of a law that is inconsistent with it. Was the possibility of ensuing chaos referred to in the lead judgment of Justice Oguntade enough to justify the decision? Unfortunately, the appeal filed against the decision of the Court of Appeal was subsequently withdrawn, leaving no room for further consideration of such fundamental issues by the apex court.

In *Attorney-General Lagos State v Attorney-General Federation*,[63] the Supreme Court had to pronounce on the constitutionality of the creation of new local government areas by the Lagos State government and the withholding of funds allocated to local government councils in Lagos State from the federation account by the president. The president's position was that the local government creation exercise remained incomplete until the national assembly made consequential provisions in respect of the names and headquarters of such local government areas by means of an Act. The Supreme Court did affirm the power of Lagos State to create new local government areas pursuant to sections 7(1) and 8(3) of the constitution. However, it held that the new local government areas could not become functional until the national assembly had passed an Act to amend the constitution to reflect the new creations.[64] The Court did not, however, make any order compelling the national assembly to pass the required Act. In similar manner, with regard to the withholding of the state's funds, the Court held that the powers of execution and maintenance of the constitution, vested in the president,[65] did not entitle him to commit an illegality. The Court did not go further to direct the president to release the withheld funds.

The constitution does not generally set out the remedies for most constitutional disputes. However, there is a range of other remedies (apart from declaration) available. These include the injunctive relief as well as the common law remedies of *habeas corpus*, *mandamus*, *certiorari*, and prohibition. In the case of challenges to fundamental rights, in particular, the constitution empowers the High Court to

> make such orders, issue such writs and give such directions as it may consider appropriate for the purpose of enforcing or securing the enforcement within that state of any right to which the person who makes the application may be entitled under this chapter.[66]

A remedy which appears to be a half-way house in judicial review of the constitutionality of legislation is the recourse to the 'blue pencil rule', namely, striking down the

[61] ibid 110.
[62] See *Attorney-General of Bendel State v Attorney-General of the Federation* (1982) 10 SC 1.
[63] (2004) 18 NWLR (Pt 904) 1.
[64] See s 3(6) and Part 1 of the First Schedule to the constitution.
[65] ibid s 5(1).
[66] ibid s 46(2).

unconstitutional provisions in a statute and retaining the valid ones. This has been described as a 'minimalist interpretative approach'.[67] It was used by Justice Niki Tobi in *Attorney-General Lagos State v Attorney-General Federation and 35 Others.*[68]

5. Style of Reasoning

The Nigerian legal system is deeply rooted in the common law tradition. There is strict adherence to judicial precedent. Accordingly, lower courts are bound by the decisions of higher courts, except that such decisions may be properly distinguished from the case before the lower court. In this setting, constitutional adjudication proceeds on the basis of an analogy with previous cases. In the case of the Supreme Court, the doctrine of precedent means that that Court is bound by its own previous decisions. The system is also adversarial, and litigants take charge of presenting their cases in court. The judge operates as an uninvolved umpire and is not expected to descend into the arena of the conflict.

Closely allied to the style of reasoning in constitutional adjudication is the approach to the interpretation or construction of the constitution. In the lead judgment delivered by Justice Udo-Udoma in the Supreme Court in the murder case of *Nafiu Rabiu v the State*,[69] an approach to the construction of the constitution based on the aims it is meant to achieve was prescribed. These aims, according to the judge, were to 'establish a broad framework for governance within which the varying conditions brought about by the dynamics of society can be accommodated. Accordingly, emphasis should not be placed on technical rules of interpretation'.[70] He was of the opinion that, in the interpretation of a written constitution, the court should as far as possible lean towards a broader interpretation except where something in the text or the rest of the constitution would justify a narrow view.[71] A holistic approach to interpretation is implicit in this method.

According to Smith,[72] the first step in constitutional interpretation should be 'a simple reading of the text'. In this approach, there is no recourse to extraneous factors. Such factors become useful only where, in a simple reading of the text, 'the formal language and structure of the Constitution have failed to convey a definitive answer'. Tracing the arguments for the 'injection' of values into constitutional interpretation, he notes that progressively, the debate has raged between the different extremes of value or no value to what values should be injected.

Other Nigerian cases have shown that, far from sticking rigidly to one method, the approach and reasoning of the Supreme Court and the Court of Appeal has been varied, oscillating between several known methods of constitutional interpretation. These range from the strict literal constructionist (textual) approach to a liberal one, including a purposeful interpretation that takes into account the historical, social, and other factors that can throw some light on the intention of the framers.[73] Using this purposeful approach, the Supreme Court, in the lead judgment delivered by Justice Ogundare in *Attorney-General*

[67] See Hakeem O Yusuf, 'The Judiciary and Political Change in Africa: Developing Transitional Jurisprudence in Nigeria' (2009) 7(4) *International Journal of Constitutional Law* 654–82.

[68] (2003) 12 NWLR (Pt 833) 1. [69] (1980) 2 NCR 117. [70] ibid 133. [71] ibid.

[72] Bradley A Smith, 'Constitutional Values and Constitutional Interpretation' (2001) Robert E Henderson Constitution Day Lecture http://www.fec.gov/members/former_members/smith/smithspeecho2.html (last accessed 17 April 2017).

[73] See Oyelowo Oyewo, 'Constitutional Interpretation: Any New Approach?' (2008) 2 *Nigerian Journal of Legislation* 1; see also Jon Roland, *Principles of Constitutional Construction* http:/www.constitution.org/cons/prin_cons.txt (last accessed 17 April 2017).

Federation v Attorney-General Abia State,[74] referred to Nigeria's history, the antecedents of her devolution into regions, and the delimitation of the country's coastal boundaries, as well as international legal instruments to determine the aims of the framers of the constitution. The potential consequences of its interpretation and reasoning have been no less important to the court in arriving at its decisions. This latter factor certainly played a major role in the Supreme Court decision in *Awolowo v Shagari*,[75] a case which, in a sense, marked the beginning of the modern era of constitutional adjudication in post-colonial Nigeria.[76]

In the *Awolowo* case, the first respondent had been returned elected by the electoral umpire as President of Nigeria following the presidential election of 1979. The Presidential Electoral Tribunal was called upon by the plaintiff to nullify the declaration of the returning officer of the Federal Electoral Commission (FEDECO) on a proper interpretation of section 34A of the Electoral Decree No 73 of 1979. The evidence showed that the respondent had received the highest number of votes cast in the elections. The issues, however, boiled down to the correct interpretation of the provision in the Electoral Decree, which specified that to be declared winner, a candidate must score not less than one-quarter of the votes cast at the election in at least two-thirds of all the states in the federation. The states at the time numbered nineteen.

The case turned on what amounted to two-thirds of nineteen states. This was held by the majority of the Court to be 12.66 states. The Court held that the election had been conducted in compliance with the Electoral Decree of 1977 or, as Justice Obaseki stated, 'in substantial compliance'[77] with the Decree. The meaning ascribed by the majority in the Supreme Court to two-thirds of nineteen clearly followed a literal interpretation of the Decree. Justice Kayode Eso delivered a powerful dissenting opinion, about which more follows later.

In *Attorney-General Bendel and Others v Attorney-General Federation*,[78] Justice Eso was of the opinion that technicalities 'serve to destroy the entire constitutional purpose of the court', therefore the Court should not be unduly 'inhibited' by technicalities. In his view, the Supreme Court, more than any other court, 'should be seen to be substantially just', not 'merely appearing to be so'.

In the later case of *Buhari and Another v Obasanjo and Others*,[79] the conduct of the 2005 presidential elections was challenged. The Court's rejection of crucial evidence on which the plaintiff built its case on the technical ground that it was not specifically pleaded as well as the non-joinder of some persons as parties, undermined the scope for proper consideration of the substantial issues that were up for determination.[80]

In *Amaechi and Another v Independent National Electoral Commission (INEC)*,[81] the Supreme Court declared someone who was neither a contestant nor a candidate at the election as having been duly elected governor of Rivers State. This decision will have serious consequences for the development of democracy in Nigeria, particularly with

[74] (2002) 4 SC (Pt 1) 1. [75] (1979) 6–9 SC 51.

[76] For a full discussion of this case in the context of constitutional interpretation see N Graham Douglas, 'Judicial Process Today: Constitutional Interpretation' (1980) *Proceedings and Papers of the Sixth Commonwealth Conference* 20–63.

[77] As in the Electoral Decree 1977 Pt 111. [78] (1981) 10 SC 1.

[79] (2005) 13 NWLR (Pt 941–3) 1.

[80] See also *Atiku Abubakar and Ohers v Umaru Musa Yar' Adua and Others* (2008) 12 SC (Pt 11). For a fuller discussion see Benjamin Nwabueze, *Current Issues and Problems in the Working of Constitutional Democracy in Nigeria* (Gold Press Ltd in association with Giovanni Books (Export) Inc 2011) ch 10.

[81] (2007) 18 NWLR (Pt 1065) 105.

regard to the role of political parties and individual candidates in the electoral process. This is because, in that case, the Court established the questionable precedent that it is the political party and not the individual candidate that is voted for at an election. The decision creates a problem for Nigeria's presidential system, because under that system individual candidates that emerge from the parties are vital to elections. This is different from the British parliamentary system, where elections revolve largely around the political party. Even there, the candidates still matter somewhat. Furthermore, if democracy is also about the people electing their governors and other office holders, deeming someone the winner who was not a candidate in the election clearly undermines the people's right to choose.

It may be argued that the Court was reacting to the improper substitution of the plaintiff's name by the political party after he had actually won the party's primaries for the election. The party had then proceeded to name another person to be its flag bearer in the elections. Improper as the action of the political party was, the expedient thing would have been for the Court to order fresh elections at which the person who actually won the primaries would be the candidate. This is also underscored by the fact that it is difficult to distinguish Nigeria's extant political parties on ideological or other conceptual lines.

Whatever differences there may be often lie in the individuals or groups (ethnic, religious, or regional) that are seriously identified with the parties. Therefore, a vote for or against a party is likely to be hinged also on who its candidate is in a given election. These facts raise questions about the decision of the Supreme Court in the *Amaechi* case, which effectively took away from the political parties and the electorate, respectively, their right to determine who contests and wins an election and placed it in the courts. The Supreme Court could have mitigated the damage done to the electoral process by indicating in its judgment that the decision should not be taken as establishing a precedent, just as the United States Supreme Court did in the case of *George Bush and Others v Albert Gore, Jr and Others*.[82] Here the risk lies in the doubt it would have cast on the judgment and the consequences for the integrity of the judicial system.

The recent case of *Alhassan and All Progressive Congress v Ishaku and Others*,[83] in which the Electoral Tribunal held that the candidate, who had been sworn in as governor of Taraba State, was not nominated at the party's primaries, illustrates the contradictions in the *Amaechi* case. The Electoral Tribunal held that no party primaries had taken place in Taraba State, having found that the exercise undertaken by the party did not amount to primaries. Instead of ordering fresh elections, the tribunal invalidated the election of the governor and proceeded to declare the candidate with the next highest number of votes in the election governor.

Was the tribunal emphasizing the role of the individual candidate in an election? If that were so, it should have ordered the party to hold proper primaries and the INEC to conduct a fresh governorship election in Taraba State to be contested by the proper candidates. The Taraba Electoral Tribunal jumped this vital step in the electoral process, just as the Supreme Court did in the *Amaechi* case. In another recent case, *Peterside v INEC and Wike*,[84] the Election Petition Tribunal ordered fresh elections after coming to the conclusion that the governorship elections had been marred by malpractices. Interestingly, the

[82] http://laws.findlaw.com/us/000/00-949.html (last accessed 17 April 2017).

[83] EPT/TRS/GOV/23/15 (unreported) judgment delivered 7 November 2015.

[84] EPT/RV/GOV/04/2015(unreported) judgment delivered 24 October 2015.

judgments of the Court of Appeal in both the Taraba governorship and *Peterside* cases were overturned by the Supreme Court.[85]

Apart from issues of procedure that were canvassed and adjudicated upon by the Supreme Court in both cases, the court's style of reasoning was firmly displayed in its pronouncements regarding the use of card readers in the electoral process. The INEC introduced card reader machines in its *Guidelines and Regulations for the Conduct of 2015 General Elections* made pursuant to the Electoral Act 2010, as amended.[86] The card readers were a device meant to check the authenticity of voters' cards presented by voters at voting centres by means of the biometric verification of intending voters. They were also meant to forestall and perhaps counter the manipulation of the voters' register. The INEC introduced the card reader with a view to conducting credible elections by checking the propensity for using fake voters' cards that had been known to mar elections in Nigeria.

It is important to note that the Electoral Act 2010, which governed the conduct of the 2015 general elections, did not specifically provide for the use of card readers. The Supreme Court followed its earlier decision in *Okereke v Umahi and Others*,[87] in which it held that the INEC Guidelines and Manual, which authorised the use of card readers, were drawn up in the exercise of powers conferred by the Electoral Act. Consequently:

> [t]he said card reader cannot logically depose or dethrone the voters' register whose juridical roots are firmly embedded or entrenched in the self-same Electoral Act from which it [voters' register] directly derives its sustenance and currency.[88]

The Supreme Court held in the *Wike* case[89] that the introduction of card readers had not done away with the manual accreditation of voters by the voters' register and that the Electoral Act would have to be amended to 'bring the usage of the card reader within the ambit of the substantive Electoral Act'.[90] It should be observed that the INEC did not substitute the card reader for the voters' register. In fact, the Guidelines specifically provided for a two-stage process for voter accreditation, as follows:

> No person shall be allowed to vote at any polling unit/voting point other than the one to which his/her name appears on the register of voters, and he/she presents his/her permanent voter's card, and has been verified by the card reader, or as otherwise determined by the Commission.[91]

The procedure for verification only strengthens the voters' register as it requires that the electoral official shall, on the voter presenting himself for accreditation at the voting point,

(i) request for the permanent voter card (PVC) from the voter

(ii) read the PVC using the card reader to ascertain that the photograph on the PVC is that of the voter and that the polling unit details correspond with those of the polling unit.[92]

Thereafter, the verified voter shall present himself to the designated electoral officer, who then requests the PVC and checks the register of voters to confirm that the voter's name, details, and voter identification number (VIN) are as contained in the register of

85 The Supreme Court decisions will be discussed later.

86 Electoral Act 2010 s 153.

87 SC 1004/2015 delivered on 5 February 2016 (unreported).

88 ibid (Justice Nweze).

89 *Wike Ezenwo Nyesom v Hon (Dr) Dakuku Adol Peterside and Others* SC 1002/2015 delivered 12 February 2016.

90 See the judgment of Justice Kekere-Ekun, who read the lead judgment.

91 Guidelines clause 7.

92 ibid cl 10.

voters. Barring any problems (some of which are identified in the Guidelines), the idea is that the total number of accredited voters cleared by the card readers and voters' register should tally. The Electoral Act 2010 creates the offences of impersonation and voting when not qualified, as follows:

> [a]ny person who votes or attempts to vote at an election knowing that he is not qualified to vote at the election;[93]

and

> any person who transmits or is involved in transmitting to any person as genuine a declaration relating to registration which is false in any material particular, knowing it to be false ...[94]

Can the objective and modalities of the INEC, as set out in its Guidelines, be seriously dismissed as not being in conformity with the Electoral Act 2010? Should they not rather have been seen by the Supreme Court as conducing to the attainment of the objectives of the Electoral Act? This point is made in view of the fact that the strict letters of the law often provide the broad framework within which subsidiary legislation and other regulations are made for effectively implementing the statute.

In this sense, the Supreme Court, as a final court, missed the opportunity of developing a jurisprudence relating to elections and electoral laws by means of the purposeful interpretation of a law and instruments made under it, aimed at curbing the mischief of manipulation of the voters' register and flawed elections. As a court of policy, the Court's rejection of the card reader and passing it back to the legislature has not advanced the democratic project. Sufficient leeway has, therefore, been given for creating bloated voter registers and embarking on other kinds of manipulation of voter details and numbers. There is no guarantee that the legislature, comprising politicians who themselves will seek to be voted for subsequently, will take on the gauntlet. This becomes even more disturbing against the background of the weaknesses of other demographic sources, such as census figures and registers of births and deaths in the country.

A positive outcome of the Supreme Court decisions in the *Wike* and the *Taraba* state governorship case, among others, is that Nigeria has not become a one-party state.[95] The successful parties in each of these cases do not represent the majority party in power at the federal level and in many of the states. As a matter of conjecture, perhaps the Court was, as a matter of policy, conscious of its role as an arm of government with the responsibility to maintain an adequate balance in the system to avoid overheating the polity.

The Court of Appeal decision in *National Assembly v President Federal Republic*[96] shows that the reasoning of a court goes beyond merely interpreting the constitution. The Court of Appeal may have been pragmatic in refraining from making a declaration. To all intents, however, its judgment was a policy decision. This view is underscored by the fact that the appeal against the decision was actually withdrawn. In view of the fact that the Court of Appeal is bound by its own previous decisions, except when a decision can be said to fall within the acceptable exceptions to the rule,[97] that judgment will be a pitfall for the future unless a similar issue finds its way to the Supreme Court and is overruled.

[93] Electoral Act 2010 s 122(1)(e). [94] ibid s 24(1)(d).

[95] See also the Akwa-Ibom state governorship case, *Udom Gabriel Emmanuel v Umana Okon Umana and Others* SC/1/16 delivered on 15 February 2016.

[96] Discussed earlier.

[97] See the Supreme Court decision in *Usman v Umaru* (1992) 7 NWLR (Pt 254) 377/398. For a fuller discussion of *stare decisis* and other issues see Akinlolu Olujinmi, 'State of the Legal Profession in Nigeria' (2011), a lecture delivered at the Nigerian Institute of Advanced Legal Studies (unpublished and on file with author)

6. Transnational Influences on Decisions

External legal sources have sometimes influenced the decisions of Nigerian courts. An example of such a transnational influence is the decision in *Attorney-General Federation v Attorney-General Abia State.*[98] In determining the seaward boundaries of the littoral states in Nigeria for the purpose of the allocation of revenue derived from oil found offshore, the Supreme Court had recourse to international instruments, including the 1982 UN Convention on the Law of the Sea, to determine the seaward boundaries.

In *Attorney-General of Ondo State and Others v Attorney-General of the Federation and Others* (*ICPC* case),[99] the Supreme Court took cognizance of the OECD Convention on Combating Bribery of Foreign Public Officials in International Business Transactions. It also alluded to the UN Economic and Social Council support for a 'centrally-co-ordinated' approach to the anti-corruption effort.

The operation of a system of government based on the allocation of functions to three arms of government under a system of separation of powers since 1999 has, not surprisingly, caused the American system to be a reference point in constitutional adjudication in Nigeria. Decisions of foreign courts are not binding on Nigerian courts. However, where the facts in issue and the circumstances are comparable, a decision of a United States court regarding their constitutional system could be persuasive authority. The Nigerian Supreme Court has on occasion made reference to such decisions, as well as to those of other jurisdictions which could be useful in its judgments, as it did in the *Resource Control* case. Similarly, in the *ICPC* case,[100] Indian, American, and Australian case law was used, in the view of Hakeem Yusuf,[101] 'to seek judicial support for validating legislation that, even by the admission of the Chief Justice, impinged upon the autonomy of the states'.

7. Nature of Decisions: Dissenting Opinions

The decisions of the Supreme Court are made by the majority.[102,103] Each of the justices is also obliged by the constitution to write his or her individual opinion and to give reasons for this opinion or 'state in writing that he or she adopts the opinion of any other justice, who delivers a written opinion'.[104] Dissenting opinions are also a feature of the adjudicatory process in the appellate courts. This is logical in a system that allows individual justices to write their own opinions. Although there is nothing to suggest that there is institutional resistance in the appellate courts to dissenting opinions, dissents do have the potential of weakening the credibility or legitimacy of the 'judgment of the court'. They tend to aid public scrutiny and criticism of such judgments in the consideration of the relative strengths and weaknesses of a contrary view.

There have been notable dissents in constitutional cases, the impact of which cannot be underestimated. In his dissenting opinion in the case of *Awolowo v Shagari*,[105] Justice Kayode Eso was emphatic that the word 'state', as used in the Electoral Decree of 1977, referred to a physical, territorial area. In his words, '[t]he Decree requires that the extent

[98] (2002) 4 SC (Pt 1) 1. [99] (2002) 9 NWLR (Pt 772) 222, discussed later.
[100] ibid. [101] Yusuf (n 67).
[102] This section of the chapter draws heavily on an earlier piece, Ameze Guobadia, 'Dissenting Opinions in the Judicial Process' in Epiphany Azinge (ed), *New Frontiers in Law* (Oliz Publishers 1993) 85.
[103] The constitution s 294(3) prescribes this for all plural member courts. [104] ibid s 294(2).
[105] (1979) 6–9 SC 51 at 137 (emphasis added).

of the geographical spread of the votes received by the candidate should be measured only by the quantum of physical states'. Applying the words of the Electoral Decree to the facts of the case, Justice Eso concluded that the words 'in each of at least two-thirds of nineteen states' meant 'each of at least 13'.

Justice Eso went further to hold that there should be no 'discriminatory interpretation' as regards the computation of votes in the first twelve states vis-à-vis the thirteenth state. As it had been accepted that a candidate must have scored votes in the whole area of the first twelve states, Justice Eso refused to limit the requirement in the thirteenth state to the votes cast in two-thirds of that state. It is important to note that two days after judgment was delivered in *Awolowo v Shagari*, the military government hurriedly amended sections 126 and 164 of the 1979 Constitution, the two provisions corresponding to the provisions of the Electoral Decree of 1977 that had been in issue in the case.[106] It is a plausible inference that subsequent state creation exercises were also influenced by this dissent. The present number of states (36) is easily divisible by three.

In a more recent dissent in the *Urban Planning* case,[107] Justice Ayoola (one of three dissents in a four-to-three majority), advocated an approach of cooperative federalism, which allows the autonomy of states to operate alongside the power of the federal government to promote the goals in Chapter 2 of the constitution. Similarly, Justice Musdapher, in his dissent in the *Monitoring of Local Government Revenue* case, was of the view that on a liberal interpretation of the constitution, the national assembly was not in breach of the principle of state autonomy in passing the 2005 Revenue Monitoring Act. This reasoning is in line with the unanimous decision of the court in the *ICPC* case.[108] In a sense, both dissents suggest that the position of the apex court on mutual non-interference and, by the same token, the application of the federal principle, is yet to be fully settled. The peculiar facts of future cases may swing the court either way. After all, as has been pointed out:

> [A] dissent ... is an appeal to the brooding spirit of the law, to the intelligence of a future day, when a later decision may possibly correct the error into which the dissenting judge believes the court to have been betrayed.[109]

8. Effect of Decisions and Impact on Constitutionalism

Decisions of the Supreme Court are final.[110] Arising from the doctrine of judicial precedent, the decisions are binding on all other courts in the land. The operation of the constitution has generated several controversies that have necessitated the intervention of the judicial function. The response of the Supreme Court to these substantive issues of constitutional law has, to varying degrees, had an impact on constitutionalism. The different issues the Court has dealt with in the last five to ten years include elections to different political offices; the system or process of governance; and corresponding relations within the state, such as the dimensions of the challenge of federalism reflected in matters such as the allocation and division of revenue and power sharing in the creation of new

[106] The explanatory note to the new legislation noted that: '[c]ertain doubts have arisen as to the meaning or purpose of some of the provisions of the Constitution'.

[107] (2003) 12 NWLR (Pt 833) 1 (discussed below).

[108] Discussed below.

[109] Credited to Charles Evan Hughes, Chief Justice of the United States, quoted with approval by Lawrence Baum, *The Supreme Court* (2nd edn, Congressional Quarterly Inc 1980) 117.

[110] See the constitution s 235, which further states that this is without prejudice to the powers of the president or governor to exercise the prerogative of mercy regarding convictions for criminal offences.

local government areas.[111] The latter was the crux of *Attorney-General of Lagos State v Attorney-General of the Federation*,[112] in which Lagos State, standing on its right to create additional local government areas, challenged the withholding by the federal government of the statutory allocations allowable to the local government councils in Lagos State, and demanded their release.

Other issues include the alteration of the constitution;[113] and the scope of the power of the executive of adaptive legislation,[114] which was considered by the Court in the case of *Attorney-General of Abia State and Others v Attorney-General of the Federation*.[115] This case was a fall-out of its earlier decision in *Attorney-General of the Federation v Attorney-General of Abia State and Others*,[116] nullifying the allocation of 7.5 per cent of revenue in the federation account to 'special funds' by the Allocation of Revenue (Federation Account etc) Act Cap 16 Laws of the Federation, 1990 edition, as amended. The said allocation was found to be contrary to the revenue allocation formula under section 162 of the constitution. The exercise of concurrent powers within the underlying notion of the coordinate status of both tiers of government has also been in issue, as has the principle of mutual non-interference of the constituent units under the federal arrangement.

The latter was the subject of *Attorney-General of Ondo State and Others v Attorney-General of the Federation and Others*[117] (*ICPC* case), in which the Supreme Court had to determine whether the Independent Corrupt Practices and Other Related Offences Act (ICPC Act), passed by the National Assembly pursuant to section 4(2) of the constitution, offended the principle of mutual non-interference. The provision states:

> The National Assembly shall have power to make laws for the peace, order and good government of the federation or any part thereof with respect to any matter included in the exclusive legislative list.

The abolition of corrupt practices is a fundamental objective in Chapter 2 of the constitution[118] and, like the rest of the chapter, the provision is non-justiciable.[119] It is not an item on the exclusive or concurrent legislative list and, therefore, should fall within the residual authority of the states. Item 60(a) of the exclusive legislative list is the power of the federal government to establish and regulate authorities for the federation or any part of it to promote and enforce the fundamental objectives and directive principles of state policy.

The case turned on whether this federal Act could be enforced in Ondo State by the federal Attorney-General. Although it did admit that autonomy was a feature of federalism under the constitution, in a unanimous judgment, the Supreme Court nevertheless went ahead to decide that the ICPC Act could create offences as incidental to item 60 of the exclusive list and be implemented in Ondo State. It also held that it did not offend the principle of autonomy of the states and mutual non-interference.[120] This stance was at variance with its earlier decision in *Attorney-General Ogun State and Others v Attorney-General Federation and Others*[121] on the constitutionality of the Adaptation of the Public Order Act. The Court justified its later decision on the basis of the national interest in the policy aims of the ICPC Act.

[111] Constitution s 8. [112] (2004) 18 NWLR (Pt 904) 1. [113] Constitution s 9.
[114] ibid s 315. [115] (2003) 1 SC (Pt 11) 1. [116] (2002) 6 NWLR (Pt 764) 542.
[117] (2002) 9 NWLR (Pt 772) 222. [118] Constitution s 15(5). [119] ibid s 6(6)(c).
[120] For a fuller discussion of this case see Kehinde M Mowoe, *Constitutional Law in Nigeria* (Malthouse Press Ltd 2008) 58–60.
[121] (1982) 3 NCLR 583.

In the view of one commentator, '[t]he Court consciously promoted policy over law displaying an active engagement with the society in transition'. He went further to say that: '[t]he judicial approach constitutes identification with the social realities of its environment'.[122]

The Supreme Court decision in *Attorney-General Abia State and Others v Attorney-General Federation and Others*[123] shows a definite shift in the thinking of the Court. It nullified the Monitoring of Revenue Allocation to Local Governments Act 2005, according to which the federal government encroached upon the power of the states over local governments. Among other infractions of the federal principle, the Monitoring Act directed states to create a State Joint Local Government Account Allocation Committee, with membership that would include the Accountant-General of the federation.

The functions of the Committee were to include rendering returns to the Federation Account Allocation Committee and, ultimately, to the national assembly, as to how funds allocated to the states for the local governments are spent. These matters are all the absolute preserve of the state governments under the constitution, which makes local governments a state concern.[124] The same arrangement places the mode of distribution of money in the state joint local government account among local government councils in the state within the absolute authority of the state government.

The Monitoring Act also criminalized the alteration, deduction, or reallocation of funds standing to the credit of the state joint local government account, into which funds owed to states and local governments from the federation account are paid. The Act further provided that where there has been a default in the allocation or distribution of these monies, the amount in respect of which there has been such a default shall be a first charge on a state's next allocation. In its original jurisdiction the Supreme Court denounced the Monitoring Act as an infraction of the federal principle and its underlying concept of the autonomy of states. In nullifying the Act, the Court opined that the fight against corruption in relation to funds allocated to local governments must not run counter to the constitution. This was indeed a radical departure from its earlier stance in the *ICPC* case. In similar manner, in *Attorney-General Lagos v Attorney-General Federation and Others*,[125] the Court nullified the Nigerian Urban and Regional Planning Act 1992 (formerly a decree of the Military Government), which encroached upon the residual legislative competence of the state government.

A rich array of decided cases has made a significant impact on constitutional development. Much of the impact has occurred at the interface of the adjudicatory function with the electoral process, sometimes with rather dramatic results. This has occurred in disputes arising from election into political offices and the tenure of elected office holders, as illustrated by the *Amaechi, Wike*, and Taraba governorship cases. Another dimension of the impact proceeds from the time frames that have since been set by the constitution for the conclusion of electoral cases[126] as a result of the unnecessary delays in the prosecution of these cases. In the past, such cases were often concluded long after some disputants had assumed office and served a good part of their tenure, thereby diminishing the utility of a subsequent nullification of their election to such offices.

The relative novelty of the presidential system in Nigeria implies that this engagement with the courts will continue into the future. One factor that distinguishes the Supreme Court from other courts is that, as a court of last resort, it is conveniently placed to drive

[122] See Yusuf (n 67).
[123] (2006) 16 NWLR (Pt 1005) 265 (SC).
[124] Constitution s 7(1).
[125] (2003) 6 SC (Pt 1) 24.
[126] See the constitution as amended, s 285.

policy. Other courts are bound by precedent and have little or no room to manoeuvre. Has the Supreme Court played a policy-making or policy-driving role? What policy, if any, is evident in the performance of its adjudicatory functions? As this analysis has shown, the decisions in some of the cases have been driven more by policy than by law. In *Awolowo v Shagari*, for example, the Court was intent on the principle that substantial compliance with the requirements of the law was enough basis for an electoral victory.

There is increasing willingness by the courts to look into matters otherwise termed political questions by inquiring into compliance by the political branches with constitutionally laid-down procedure,[127] a further illustration of a policy direction. Does the Court's role as the ultimate guardian of the constitution contradict a policy-making role? Undue emphasis on technicality by the Court in some cases has limited its scope for dealing with substantial constitutional issues. Given the charge to the judiciary in the constitution, it is a fair comment to say that the system could be better served.

In commenting on the impact of the judiciary in general, and the Supreme Court in particular, it is reasonable to situate these developments in the proper historical context. Over three decades of military rule took its toll on the judiciary, as it did on the other branches of government. Unlike the legislature and executive, which were altogether suspended, the judiciary continued to exist, although under rather severe limitations. Restrictions on its jurisdiction by means of decrees and edicts as well as the power of the military to flout its orders with impunity[128] served to whittle down the seeming gains in its not being suspended. Consequently, the challenges to the apex court and, indeed, the entire judiciary, in this 'third wave of democracy' include claiming lost ground and asserting itself and its powers effectively, as an arm of government with the final say on the activities of the constituent units in the federation and the other branches in disputes about the exercise of power. This it has certainly started to do, as the cases discussed have shown.

A major part of the task before the judiciary is the deepening of democracy. A number of electoral disputes have demonstrated the varying dimensions of this project and what is required of the judiciary. By undertaking their constitutional role unhindered, the courts have begun to reinforce the place of the judiciary in the scheme of things as guardians of the constitution. In addition, there is a consciousness that is developing in the polity that the constitution places limits and obligations on the exercise of power. There is also the increasing tendency of the populace to have recourse to the courts as a matter of course. This really is the rule of law. The corresponding principles that flow from this and the constitutional arrangements in general include the supremacy of the constitution and the separation of powers. While the process has begun, it is clear that the deepening of democracy is yet to be firmly accomplished. *Amaechi* and some of the other election cases discussed attest to this.

The response of the other branches to the pronouncements of the courts and tribunals gives an indication of the impact of the judgments. As some of the cases show, this has not always been positive. An example can be found in the Lagos State local government creation case, and the controversy over the withholding of their funds by the president. The legislature did not take the cue to make the consequential changes to the names and headquarters of the local councils listed in the constitution to complete the exercise undertaken by Lagos State. Both the executive and legislature can respond to judgments by changes in policy, legislation, and procedure, respectively, designed to implement court decisions.

[127] *Ugwu v Ararume* (2007) 12 NWLR (Pt 1048) 367; see also *Inakoju v Adeleke* (2007) ALL FWLR (Pt 353) 3.

[128] See eg the Supreme Military Council Supremacy and Enforcement of Powers Decree No 28 of 1970. These issues came up for consideration in *Lakanmi v Attorney-General, Western Region* [1971] 1 UILR 201.

In *Bendel State v the Federation*,[129] the legislature was compelled to follow the procedure set out in the 1979 Constitution to pass a money bill. At another level, constitutional adjudication can in fact trigger the difficult process of constitutional amendment. In this regard, as has already been noted, new timelines for the conclusion of election cases have been introduced by the constitution[130] as a result of delays previously experienced in the prosecution of electoral cases. Perhaps more fundamental, however, are those amendments that may be triggered by the legal issues in the *ratio decidendi* of decided cases. There is, therefore, more that the legislature can do, as the Lagos State local government creation case illustrates.

The impact of the courts in constitutional adjudication can also be assessed from the extent to which their judgments promote the welfare of the populace. There is a Hobbesian quality to this. The effort to save society from the state of insecurity abhorred by Hobbes leads to a social contract between the people and the state in which the people surrender their rights[131] to the state in return for security. The constitution is the manifestation of this contract, which itself is limited by the terms of the 'surrender' by the people.

In modern times, this security for which the people surrender their rights has taken on a wider meaning. Beyond the guarantee of law and order and the regulation of relations in the state, it embraces such issues as 'food security'; the provision of adequate shelter; the protection of the environment; and other elements that are conducive to the welfare of the populace and captured in some constitutions[132] as socio-economic rights.[133] The terms of the contract between the state and the people should address these issues. The response of the state to these demands and the ever-changing notion of security and its challenges can similarly be assessed thereby.

One might ask in what context the judgments of the courts really address issues of the security of the individual in this broad sense. Examining these issues from the standpoint of constitutional adjudication ultimately leads to the question of how well the courts have promoted the enjoyment of all categories of rights set out in the constitution. In truth, here there is a deficit as the Nigerian judiciary is yet to develop a jurisprudence that consciously interprets the non-justiciable socio-economic rights in Chapter 2 of the constitution to ensure their actual enjoyment by the populace (as has been done by Indian courts). Progressively, the impact of the Nigerian judiciary will come to be measured by this yardstick in light of the growing expectations of the populace of their elected office holders.

9. Conclusion

The cases discussed illustrate that the Supreme Court has been busy and cannot be dismissed as irrelevant. In light of some of its decisions, questions may indeed arise as to how well the Court has fostered democracy and continued to support the rule of law. There is no doubt that the apex court would be more effective as the constitutional court if it were to shed the rather unwieldy load it currently carries as the final court in every kind

[129] (1982) 10 SC 1 (n 62).

[130] 180 days and 60 days for the determination of election petitions and appeals, respectively. Amendments introduced by s 9(6) and (7) of the Constitution of the Federal Republic of Nigeria (Second Alteration Act) 2010.

[131] Some of which is embedded in the notion of sovereignty.

[132] The Fundamental Objectives and Directive Principles of State Policy in the Indian and Irish Constitutions and, specifically, ch 11 of Nigeria's 1999 Constitution.

[133] These are categorized as the second generation of rights following after the first generation of rights (the civil and political rights). There is also third generation of rights broadly classified as the right to development, which addresses such concerns as the need to protect the environment.

of dispute emanating from the lower courts.[134] Some of these other matters can then be brought to an end at the Court of Appeal. This would require an amendment of the constitution from which the superior courts of record derive their jurisdiction, as was done with regard to fundamental rights issues arising in disputes before the National Industrial Court, which end at the Court of Appeal.[135]

In spite of this exception, there is still a valid argument for limiting the load of the Supreme Court. This must, however, be considered within the context of recent events supporting the opposite view. Before section 246(3) of the constitution was amended[136] to allow governorship, national and state assembly election disputes to reach the Supreme Court, these disputes ended at the Court of Appeal. Recent decisions of the Court of Appeal in different governorship election appeals, in which different divisions of the Court of Appeal gave conflicting judgments on substantially the same legal issues, that is, the validity of the use of card readers in the voting process,[137] provide ample justification for such matters going on further appeal to the apex court.

In addition, Nigerian law does not contain anything of the practice in some other jurisdictions of a system of court registrars administratively sorting out cases filed in the apex court to determine what should be taken to court and what can be disposed of in chambers. Given the level of the country's development, it is not certain whether such a process will work in Nigeria. As lofty as it sounds, it carries with it the possibility of having cases deserving a proper hearing being rejected for less than altruistic reasons.

The suggestion by Nwabueze that a constitutional division be created within the Court to which only constitutional matters are referred may be a viable compromise. This way, other categories of cases may still be heard in the Supreme Court. A full court of seven justices must sit to hear a constitutional case, which means that a constitutional division will deplete the number of justices available to sit in any matter. For the suggestion to work, therefore, the number of justices in the Court has to be increased from the current limit of twenty-one set by the constitution.[138]

There is no legal impediment to the Supreme Court overruling itself. The Court should, however, be more open to doing so in circumstances where the interests of justice would be better served. Justification for this view also lies in the fact that there being no opportunity for further appeal from the apex court, overruling itself, where necessary, could be a way out of a quagmire. This is something that should not be done on impulse, as the judicial process itself is sufficiently structured to reduce the occurrences of serious errors that would justify the Supreme Court overruling itself.

The House of Lords in the United Kingdom in recent times did this in the *Pinochet* case.[139] As Lord Browne-Wilkinson opined in the case, the power to do so derives from the inherent jurisdiction of the court. It is significant that it was in the same *Pinochet*

[134] A point alluded to by Justice Kayode Eso in his foreword to D A Guobadia and A O Adekunle, *The Uwais Court: The Supreme Court and the Challenge of National Development,(1995–2006)* (Nigerian Institute of Advanced Legal Studies 2007) xv.

[135] Constitution s 243(4) and n 11 above. It should be observed that the peculiar nature of industrial disputes made this concession inevitable as the practical effect of further appeal in such matters may, rather, unduly delay the resolution of the substantive industrial dispute from which the fundamental rights issue arose.

[136] By the Constitution of the Federal Republic of Nigeria (Second Alteration) Act 2010 s 8.

[137] See eg *APC v JOK Agbaje and Others* (2015) LPELR-25668 (CA) in the Lagos Division; the *Taraba* case in the Abuja Division; the *Rivers Governorship* appeal; and the *Akwa Ibom Governorship* disputes, respectively (the last three already discussed).

[138] The actual number of justices in that court is 15.

[139] *In Re Pinochet* decided August 2015 < https://www.publications.parliament.uk/pa/ld199899/ldjudgmt/jd990115/pino01.htm > accessed 17 April 2017.

case that the court overruled its earlier decision that Pinochet had no immunity from extradition and prosecution for crimes against humanity. The action of the apex court was based on the fact that there was some perception that there was good reason to disqualify Lord Hoffmann, one of the justices who sat on the case, from participating in the case. A differently-constituted House of Lords had to sit to reconsider the case. In this regard, the *Adesanya* judgment on *locus standi*, the stance of the Court on the use of card readers in the electoral process, as demonstrated in the recent Rivers State governorship appeal (*Wike* case), among others, should be reconsidered. This will not detract from the implied infallibility of that court because, as one jurist put it, referring to the United States Supreme Court, '[w]e are final not because we are infallible; rather we are infallible because we are final'.[140]

Bibliography

Azinge E, *New Frontiers in Law* (Oliz Publishers 1993)

Baum L, *The Supreme Court* (2nd edn Congressional Quarterly Inc 1980)

Graham-Douglas N, 'Judicial Process Today: Constitutional Interpretation' in Proceedings of the Sixth Common Wealth Law Conference (1980)

Guobadia D A and Adekunle A O, *The Uwais Court: The Supreme Court and the Challenge of Legal Development 1995-2006* (Nigerian Institute of Advanced Legal Studies 2007)

Guobadia A, 'Constitutional Adjudication: *Locus Standi*—Recent Trends in Nigerian Courts' (1978–1998) 3 *Nigerian Juridical Review* 37

Guobadia A, 'Dissenting Opinions in the Judicial Process' in Azinge E (ed), *New Frontiers in Law* (Oliz Publishers 1993) 85

Henderson R F, 'Constitutional Values and Constitutional Interpretation' http//www.fec.gov/member/former_members/smithspeecho2.html (last accessed 17 April 2017)

Hornby A S, *Oxford Advanced Learner's Dictionary* (8th edn, OUP 2010)

Kousoulas D G, *On Government: A Comparative Introduction* (Wadsworth Publishing Co 1968)

Mowoe K M, *Constitutional Law in Nigeria* (Malthouse Press Ltd 2008)

Nwabueze B, *Constitutional Democracy in Africa*, Vol 1 (Spectrum Books Ltd 2008)

Nwabueze B, *Current Issues and Problems in the Working of Constitutional Democracy in Nigeria* (Gold Press Ltd 2011)

Olujinmi A, 'State of the Legal Profession in Nigeria' Nigerian Institute of Advanced Legal Studies 2011)

Oyewo O, 'Constitutional Interpretation: Any New Approach?' (2008) 2 *Nigerian Journal of Legislation* 1

Roland J, 'Principles of Constitutional Construction' http://www.Constitution.org|cons\prin_cons.txt (last accessed 17 April 2017)

Yusuf H O, 'The Judiciary and Political Change in Africa: Developing Transitional Jurisprudence in Nigeria' (2009) 7(4) *International Journal of Constitutional Law* 654–82

140 Justice Robert Jackson in *Brown v Allen*, 344 US 443(1953). Quoted by Justice Oputa in *Adegoke Titus v Adesanya* (1989) 3 NWLR (Pt 109) 250, and with approval by Justice Kayode Eso (n 134) xiii.

7

Constitutional Review in South Africa

Features, Changes, and Controversies

James Fowkes

1. Introduction

Twenty years on, the South African Constitution and Constitutional Court have attained considerable status in global comparative debates and within Africa, especially Anglophone Africa. The aim of this chapter is to outline key features of the South African system of judicial review as it has emerged. Given both the limited scope of the chapter and the fact that South Africa is a relatively well-known case, the particular aim is to draw attention to areas where change has been considerable but not always noted—jurisdiction, the declining use of comparative law—and, as important, to identify features that have proved enduring over the system's twenty years of life. The chapter will conclude with an overview of differing viewpoints on the status and impact of the judiciary, and the Constitutional Court in particular, in South African society and politics.

2. Jurisdiction: The Evolution from Compromise, to Divided, to Diffuse Review

Perhaps the most dramatic changes have occurred in the division of jurisdiction within the judicial system. Today, following the passage of the Constitution Seventeenth Amendment Act of 2012, the Constitutional Court is, despite its name, an apex court of general jurisdiction.[1] Constitutional review is decentralized, and the Supreme Court of Appeal and High Courts below the Constitutional Court have general constitutional jurisdiction (subject to some exceptions and provisos, as will be seen). But this structure, broadly like that of the United States, is very different from what was initially established.

In its first instantiation, in the 1993 interim constitution, constitutional jurisdiction was divided up between the courts. The Constitutional Court had general highest constitutional jurisdiction, and the default position was that this jurisdiction was exclusive. However, substantial exceptions were carved out of this centralized review model.[2] The High Courts had rather broad constitutional jurisdiction, including in respect of constitutional disputes at local government level (but not higher) and local and provincial legislation (but not national legislation). They also had jurisdiction over executive and administrative conduct, and any 'alleged violation or threatened violation of any fundamental right'.[3] This added up to a substantial constitutional jurisdiction, and the parties, moreover, could consent to a High Court hearing a constitutional matter not otherwise

[1] Constitution Seventeenth Amendment Act of 2012.

[2] Constitution of the Republic of South Africa Act 200 of 1993 s 98(2) and (3).

[3] ibid s 101(3).

within its jurisdiction.[4] If these courts encountered a constitutional matter falling outside their jurisdiction, they were to refer it to the Constitutional Court after making any findings of fact necessary for its proper adjudication. The referral mechanisms were not especially clear in the 1993 text, involving a number of complexities over whether lower courts should suspend proceedings or instead resolve what issues they could before referring the matter to the Constitutional Court, and this led to some confusion in practice.[5]

These jurisdictional exceptions did not, however, apply to the Appellate Division, the old highest court under the apartheid system. It had 'no jurisdiction to adjudicate any matter within the jurisdiction of the Constitutional Court', and could become involved in the referral process only in 'mixed' cases raising both constitutional and non-constitutional matters, where an appeal would lie from a High Court decision to the Appellate Division.[6]

This structure reflected the situation present during the transition. During the negotiations and debates over drafting, there was reluctance to accept that the apartheid era apex court, stocked with apartheid era appointees, would oversee the new constitution.[7] A new Constitutional Court was, therefore, created, and the 1993 interim constitution balanced a desire to ensure that a wider array of judges would have the power to enforce the new rights with the concern that only the new court should rule on certain sensitive issues (the matters on which even the High Courts lacked constitutional jurisdiction), and should have the final say on all constitutional issues (as the court of ultimate constitutional appeal). This structure, however, was a compromise, and was apparently always intended to be temporary.[8] This makes sense, given that the main reason for it—that the judges sitting in 1993 had all been appointed by the apartheid regime—was of course something that would change with time. The passage of the 17th Amendment thus represents the foreseen end of a transitional arrangement.

An important question prompted by the creation of the new Constitutional Court, however, was what to do with the existing Appellate Division, a court of high status and seniority possessed of considerable legal expertise, at least in certain areas. The 1993 Constitution's provision that the Constitutional Court's jurisdiction would be separate from that of the Appellate Division was based on a distinction between constitutional and non-constitutional matters. Constitutional matters would usually be heard in the first instance by the High Courts, thereafter taking one appeal route to the new Constitutional Court. Non-constitutional matters (and possibly also the 'mixed' matters raising both constitutional and non-constitutional matters) would be heard in the same courts of first instance, but would take a second route to the Appellate Division. These arrangements, therefore, implicitly left the Appellate Division to carry on with what it had been doing before, a nod to continuity the interim constitution did nothing to reconcile with the radical anti-continuity of its other provisions.

This troubled interim pattern was substantially preserved in the 1996 Constitution, which retained the two apex courts. The Constitutional Court was the highest court in

[4] ibid s 101(6). [5] ibid s 102; see eg *S v Mhlungu* 1995 (3) SA 867 (CC).

[6] 1993 Constitution ss 101(5), 102(3)–(6), 102(12).

[7] See eg Heinz Klug, *The Constitution of South Africa: A Contextual Analysis* (Hart Publishing 2010) 230–2.

[8] As far as I know, this was never formally stated at the time, but the late Chief Justice Chaskalson, a key adviser to the ANC on constitutional matters during the constitutional negotiations and naturally deeply involved in many high-level discussions thereafter while in office, indicated at a public meeting in 2006 that there was a general sense that a single apex court system was superior, when the time was right for it. See 'Remarks for former Chief Justice Chaskalson' (General Council of the Bar of South Africa Human Rights Committee Conference on the Justice Bills, Judicial Independence and the Restructuring of the Courts, Johannesburg, 17 February 2006) http://www.sabar.co.za/conference_transcript.pdf (last accessed 20 April 2017).

constitutional matters; the former Appellate Division, now renamed the Supreme Court of Appeal, was the highest court in non-constitutional matters. The main change was that the Supreme Court of Appeal gained constitutional jurisdiction: It would now be able to hear appeals 'in all matters', but would only be the court of final authority in non-constitutional cases.[9]

The system of constitutional review was, therefore, decentralized further. The persistence of the constitutional/non-constitutional distinction, however, created a number of problems. It is a conceptually troubled distinction in a system of constitutional supremacy, where all law is supposed to be subject to the constitution and so, strictly speaking, there is no such thing as a non-constitutional matter. If the constitution in question had been of quite limited scope, the distinction may have made sense. It might also have made sense if some legal questions were considered settled and could uncontroversially be answered without reference to constitutional issues. However, in a system introducing a very expansive constitution that was not only supreme but foreshadowed considerable change throughout the legal system, the idea that any body of law could be easily put to one side as uncontroversially constitutional was utterly implausible. Everything, potentially, was meant to be the subject of serious constitutional scrutiny. The 1996 Constitution underlined this by providing for both direct and indirect horizontal application of rights and explicitly conferring on courts the mandate to develop the common and customary law in line with constitutional values.[10]

However, the distinction nevertheless was in the text. Sense, therefore, had to be made of it, and the incentives of the judges and other parties involved naturally influenced how this was done. The interim constitution had explicitly called on the Appellate Division to decide 'mixed' questions without reaching constitutional issues if possible (and otherwise refer them to the Constitutional Court, given that it was precluded in that text from considering constitutional questions).[11] The 1996 text's extension of constitutional jurisdiction did not change this pattern much, since it gave the renamed Supreme Court of Appeal a strong incentive to preserve as large as possible a sphere of 'non-constitutional law' in respect of which it would still be the court of final appeal and authority.

This had two rather predictable results. First, the two apex courts fought a polite jurisdictional battle, in which the Appellate Division/Supreme Court of Appeal sought to define as much law as 'non-constitutional' as possible. The Constitutional Court, with final interpretive authority over the constitution's provisions on jurisdiction, inevitably won that battle, and correctly asserted that there were not two bodies of law, but one, under the constitution.[12] The court, however, still had to make sense of the constitution's concept of 'non-constitutional jurisdiction'.[13] Considerations of collegiality also favoured finding a meaningful role for the Supreme Court of Appeal. The Constitutional Court's

[9] Constitution of the Republic of South Africa 1996 s 168(3) (as the text stood prior to the 17th Amendment).

[10] ibid ss 8, 39. See further eg Dennis Davis, 'Transformation and the Democratic Case for Judicial Review: The South African Experience' (2007-2008) 5 *Loyola University Chicago International Law Review* 45; Dennis M Davis and Karl Klare, 'Transformative Constitutionalism and the Common and Customary Law' (2010) 26 *South African Journal on Human Rights* 403.

[11] 1993 Constitution (n 2) s 102(5) and (6).

[12] See especially *Commissioner for Customs and Excise v Container Logistics (Pty) Ltd, Commissioner for Customs and Excise v Rennies Group Limited t/a Renfreight* 1999 (3) SA 771 (SCA) and *Pharmaceutical Manufacturers Association of South Africa: In re Ex Parte President of the Republic of South Africa* 2000 (2) SA 674 (CC).

[13] See eg *S v Boesak* 2001 (1) SA 912 (CC) and *Fraser v ABSA Bank Limited* 2007 (3) SA 484 (CC) paras 35-47. In practice, the distinction was effectively rendered 'illusory'; Sebastian Seedorf, 'Jurisdiction' in Stuart Woolman and Michael Bishop (eds), *Constitutional Law of South Africa* (2nd edn, Juta & Co 2005) 4-125.

solution was to hold that certain areas of law were especially within the Supreme Court of Appeal's areas of expertise, and that it would be important for litigants to take such issues to that court before approaching the Constitutional Court.[14] This applied, above all, to private law areas such as delict (tort) and contract.

This had a number of undesirable consequences. It meant that the appellate chain came to contain both 'apex' courts on many matters, adding to the time and expense of litigation (in combination with the rarity of grants of direct access by the Constitutional Court, discussed below). This not only increased the ability of rich litigants to simply outspend their opponents. It also meant that, to seek to avoid the expensive final step of the Constitutional Court, litigants had an incentive *not* to frame issues in constitutional terms in the court of first instance, in the hope of making the Supreme Court of Appeal decision's dispositive of the case. Conversely, once that court had ruled, a dissatisfied party would then have an incentive to try and reframe the case—at the last moment, in appellate terms—to introduce a constitutional element in order to obtain a further appeal to the Constitutional Court. The Constitutional Court would then be faced with an invidious choice between hearing an argument not properly foreshadowed on the record and argument of previous courts, contrary to a normal appellate process, or—if it responded to that concern by rejecting the last minute attempt to reframe the issue as a constitutional one—risking stunting its own jurisdiction and potentially neglecting important constitutional questions.

Finally, this bifurcated jurisdiction encouraged the view that certain areas of private law should be left more or less as they were, notwithstanding the new constitution. Lawyers (especially private lawyers) not used to arguing in constitutional terms stood before judges not used to judging in constitutional terms, and so no one was likely to object to a neglect of constitutional issues in the way a case was framed or decided. The Supreme Court of Appeal, in a continuation of the polite jurisdictional battle, had no particular reason to welcome constitutional framing, since that would make its decision subject to appeal.

Jurisdictional rules, therefore, served to exacerbate the deeper gravitational pull of the old, established system. The Constitutional Court sought to respond, ruling in 2001 that all judges were obliged to consider constitutional questions and develop the common law in line with constitutional values, whether or not the parties sought this outcome or framed their pleadings that way. It also emphasized the importance of raising constitutional arguments in the court of first instance.[15] Both rules were regularly ignored. The result has been a substantial neglect of the constitutional development of parts of the legal system, especially in private law (although, again, this is not the only cause).[16]

For all these reasons, the decision to establish the Constitutional Court as a general apex court is to be welcomed.[17] The distinction between constitutional and non-constitutional matters need not now trouble South African law further. The place of the Supreme Court of Appeal in the system, however, is still rather an unanswered question. Earlier suggestions to establish it as a true circuit court, rather than an appeal court with a fixed seat, were resisted within the legal community, partly on the grounds that this would

[14] See Kate Hofmeyr, 'Rules and Procedure in Constitutional Matters' in Woolman and Bishop (n 13) 5.1–5.49 and cases cited therein.

[15] *Carmichele v Minister of Safety and Security* 2001 (4) SA 938 (CC); for the same principle in the customary law context see *Shilubana v Nwamitwa* 2009 (2) SA 66 (CC).

[16] The Court has also been cautious (not always unreasonably so) of entering too rapidly into large-scale reform of complicated law in the context of single cases.

[17] See further Carole Lewis, 'Reaching the Pinnacle: Principles, Policies and People for a Single Apex Court in South Africa' (2005) 21 *South African Journal on Human Rights* 509.

make positions on the court less desirable and would thus reduce the quality of available appointees.[18] This is a concern, although true circuit courts exist in other countries and so this may represent a temporary transitional difficulty rather than an enduring objection. Quality candidates may also be encouraged to apply if appointment to the Supreme Court of Appeal is a regular route to appointment to the more prestigious Constitutional Court, as is increasingly becoming the case.

During the short life of the Constitutional Court, therefore, South Africa has completed a transition from a transitional compromise combining elements of centralized and decentralized review, to a system of a generally-decentralized constitutional jurisdiction for all judges above magistrate's court level, with a single apex court of final, general jurisdiction. The development was not without its upheavals and problems remain, but the moves to date should at least be conducive to a more constitutionally-coherent jurisprudence and to the more rapid constitutionalization of the entire body of South African law.

2.1 Appointment of judges

South Africa's approach to judicial appointments reflects both its lamentable apartheid history and the nature of what has succeeded it. For the same reason that a new Constitutional Court was created, the new text avoided requiring judges to have long formal experience within the system in order not to exclude virtually all candidates other than the white males favoured under the apartheid system. Thus, the constitution does not even require that judicial appointees must hold a law degree; they must simply be 'appropriately qualified' and 'a fit and proper person' (and, in the case of candidates for the Constitutional Court, a South African citizen).[19]

In practice, all persons appointed as judges have held a law degree; the effect of the transition was mainly that a number of early appointments, including to the Constitutional Court, were of persons with relatively little experience as judges (although often with extensive experience as practising lawyers). Over time, this has changed as candidates of all races and genders acquire significant judicial experience, and appointments now tend to be made from within the judicial hierarchy. Some early appointments were made from the ranks of the academy, again reflecting the relative flexibility of the transition, but in contrast to a system such as Germany, there are no signs that law professors will come to dominate the ranks of judges in the Constitutional Court.

This reversion to the traditions of common law judicial hierarchy is one of several areas where the post-apartheid legal system, in a context where issues of legitimacy are particularly complex, places continued reliance on the traditional foundations of judicial legitimacy in pre-apartheid legal culture.[20]

Judges are appointed by the Judicial Services Commission (JSC), a body consisting of senior judges, representatives from the profession, legislators from both houses, and the cabinet minister responsible for the administration of justice.[21] In theory, this diverse body was supposed to reduce executive control over appointments (although the departing apartheid government originally overestimated the degree to which they might exert

[18] See eg Submissions to the Portfolio Committee on Justice and Constitutional Development on behalf of the General Bar Council of South Africa, 37–8 www.sabar.co.za (last accessed 14 April 2017).

[19] 1996 Constitution (n 9) s 174(1).

[20] See further on these broader debates the sources cited in James Fowkes, *Building the Constitution: The Practice of Constitutional Interpretation in Post-Apartheid South Africa* (Cambridge University Press 2016) 103.

[21] 1996 Constitution (n 9) ss 174, 178.

influence from within the executive as a result of power-sharing agreements, and had initially supported executive appointments).[22] In practice, the African National Congress (ANC) government has wielded considerable power within the JSC, and exercises something close to effective control over appointments.[23] A number of high-quality appointments have nonetheless been made, although there is a growing perception (discussed below) that recent appointments have favoured judges with a more modest conception of the judicial role who are thought less likely to exercise power against the government.

A detailed examination of the JSC exceeds the scope of this chapter. It suffices here to note that different procedures apply for Constitutional Court judges and others. For the Constitutional Court, the JSC must submit to the president three names more than there are appointments to be made. (Thus, if there is one vacancy, the JSC must supply four names; if there are three vacancies, seven.) If the president declines to appoint anyone on that list, there is the possibility of the JSC supplementing it once, but thereafter the president must make appointments from the names given.[24] The balance is, therefore, struck against exclusive executive control, in favour of a body where a party with a strong majority exercises considerable power but is subject, at the very least, to extensive duties of consultation. Appointment of the chief justice and deputy chief justice, in addition, requires consultation with the leaders of the parties represented in the National Assembly.[25] Other judges are appointed on the advice of the JSC.[26]

Diversity, as might be expected, is a central component of the South African judicial appointment process. Section 174(2) of the 1996 Constitution provides that: '[t]he need for the judiciary to reflect broadly the racial and gender composition of South Africa must be considered when judicial officers are appointed'. These considerations are, therefore, openly supposed to inform the selection of candidates for the bench. In practice, efforts to promote racial diversity have been rather more successful than those to promote gender diversity. Although their share of positions still falls short of their demographic numbers, the number of black African judges had increased from three of 165 judges in 1994 to 106 of 243 in mid-2014, or a little less than 44 per cent. Indian and coloured judges made up just over 9 per cent and just over 10 per cent of the 2014 bench respectively, with white judges making up the remainder, slightly more than a third of judges. Black African judges also dominate the heads of courts, including the positions of chief justice and deputy chief justice.

Although the process is not yet completed, the change from the all-white ranks of the judiciary twenty years ago has been dramatic. The position of women has changed less. Except in the case of judges of Indian descent, where women are only slightly less represented than men (4.94 per cent of the overall total versus 5.35 per cent for men in 2014), women make up significantly less than half of the other groups, with white women being the least proportionally represented (9.88 per cent of the overall total versus 26.75 per cent for white men).[27] Less than a third of judges are women; no more than three of the eleven Constitutional Court justices have yet been women at any one time. In the recent

[22] See further Richard Spitz with Michael Chaskalson, *The Politics of Transition: A Hidden History of South Africa's Negotiated Settlement* (Witwatersrand University Press 2000) 204; Theunis Roux, *The Politics of Principle: The First South African Constitutional Court 1995–2005* (Cambridge University Press 2013) 166–68; Fowkes (n 20).

[23] See further Richard Calland, *The Zuma Years: South Africa's Changing Face of Power* (Zebra Press 2013) ch 11.

[24] 1996 Constitution (n 9) s 174(4). [25] ibid s 174(3). [26] ibid s 174(6).

[27] Figures are official National Department of Justice and Constitutional Development statistics, obtained and reproduced by Nomthandazo Ntlama, 'The Transformation of the South African Judiciary: A Measure to Weaken its Capacity?' http://www.nylslawreview.com/wp-content/uploads/sites/16/2014/10/Ntlama.pdf (last accessed 14 April 2017).

appointment process to fill the seat left vacant by the retirement of Justice Skweyiya, the imperative to change this was evident in the fact that only women candidates were nominated. However, considerable work remains to be done in this regard.

2.2 Judicial powers

The most common form of constitutional review in South Africa has been and remains concrete review. As discussed under the next heading, the constitution provides for a number of mechanisms for individuals to trigger concrete review.

The text does, however, also provide for abstract review in two instances, and this has occurred occasionally. First, a Bill becomes an Act only when signed by the president, and the constitution provides that the president may refer a Bill back to parliament if he has doubts about its constitutionality. Should the Bill, after parliament's reconsideration, still not accommodate the president's concerns, he may refer it to the Constitutional Court. The court's ruling is then decisive: if the court upholds the constitutionality of the Bill, the president must sign it; if not, it lapses and, by implication, may not be passed as law in the same form.[28] Review at this stage—that is, after passage but before signature—may only occur in terms of this mechanism and not otherwise, something explicitly provided for in section 167(4)(b) of the constitution and confirmed by the Constitutional Court.[29]

Secondly, after the president signs a Bill, members of parliament (MPs) have thirty days to appeal its constitutionality to the Constitutional Court. Such a bid only succeeds if more than one-third of MPs support the referral. The Act's force may be suspended by the court pending its final decision in the matter.[30] The textual provision for such review does not, as in the case of presidential referral, stipulate that these are the only circumstances in which the court could hear a constitutional challenge to the legislation at that stage of the legislative process.[31]

The court has duly held that it has the power to review the constitutionality of legislation after the president's signature—that is, after a statute becomes an Act but before it comes into force.[32] It has also held that it has jurisdiction to consider constitutional challenges to legislation while it is still being considered by parliament, that is, before being passed or referred to the president for signature.

The court has, however, indicated that it will only exercise this power in the most extraordinary of circumstances and only where no other way to remedy the constitutional harm exists, and, therefore, it is doubtful that such review would ever really be abstract. It would, seemingly, have to raise specific and serious concrete consequences for the court to exercise jurisdiction at all.[33] Similar mechanisms exist at the provincial level, providing for referral by the provincial premier, or by members of the provincial legislature, although in contrast to the national level, the threshold in the latter case is only one-fifth of the members of the relevant provincial legislature and not one-third.[34]

[28] 1996 Constitution (n 9) s 79.

[29] *Doctors for Life International v Speaker of the National Assembly* 2006 (6) SA 416 (CC) paras 42–56.

[30] 1996 Constitution (n 9) s 80.

[31] ibid s 167(4)(b) stipulates that the Constitutional Court may only consider the constitutionality of Bills in the context of such a referral, a proviso not repeated in the following s 167(4)(c) on application by MPs.

[32] *Doctors for Life* (n 29) paras 60–5.

[33] *Glenister v President of the Republic of South Africa* 2009 (1) SA 287 (CC); see also *Van Straaten v President of the Republic of South Africa* 2009 (3) SA 457 (CC); *Doctors for Life* (n 29) paras 67–71.

[34] 1996 Constitution (n 9) ss 121, 122.

The Constitutional Court's powers of review are generally unrestricted now that it is a general court of appeal and, even before it was the general apex court, it had the power to consider and make an order in any constitutional matter. Explicit constraints on what the court can potentially do—such as the rule just noted that it may only consider the constitutionality of a Bill being considered by the president if the president refers the Bill to it—are rare in the 1996 text. Indeed, that may be the only real example. Technically, a restriction is inherent in the section 172(1)(a) provision that a court '*must* declare that any law or conduct that is inconsistent with the constitution is invalid to the extent of its inconsistency' (emphasis added). However, the court has declined to make such an order in circumstances where it deemed inaction to be in the public interest, and thus seems to have arrogated to itself discretion in this regard, despite the text.[35]

The constitutional review power of other courts is subject to some restrictions. No order invalidating provincial or national legislation or conduct of the president is final unless it has been confirmed by the Constitutional Court. Such orders made by other courts are, therefore, deemed to be suspended unless the court confirms them.[36] The procedure for referral is set out in the Constitutional Court Rules: the registrar of the court that made the order must refer the matter to the registrar of the Constitutional Court within fifteen days. Involved parties and organs of state then have an opportunity to join the proceedings, which are thereafter resolved in accordance with directions by the chief justice.[37] Both the Rules and the constitutional text are, however, silent on whether the Court must decide a matter referred to it by another court in these circumstances. The court itself has ruled that it is not obliged to rule on a matter referred to it for confirmation, but must act in the public interest. It has accordingly, for example, declined to decide on a confirmation case where subsequent legislative reform had rendered the matter moot.[38] However, since the public interest is seldom served by categories of government action as important as statutes and presidential conduct being of uncertain validity, cases where the court does not settle confirmation referrals one way or the other will remain rare.

In addition, certain legal questions are reserved to the Constitutional Court and may not be considered by other courts. These matters of exclusive jurisdiction consist of the abstract referrals by legislators, presidents, and premiers during the legislative process noted above, as well as the constitutionality of constitutional amendments, the failure by parliament or the president to fulfil a constitutional obligation, and decisions on disputes between national or provincial organs of government 'concerning the constitutional status, powers or functions' of those organs.[39] The court has tended to interpret these areas of exceptional jurisdiction narrowly. Its approach, in one sentence, is to interpret its own *ultimate* jurisdiction broadly, in the service of the broadest possible constitutional control of issues, while preferring to interpret its own *exclusive* jurisdiction narrowly and hear from other courts first as often as possible. This logic, as will now be seen, also affects its approach to the issue of direct access.

[35] See eg *Richter v Minister of Home Affairs* 2009 (3) SA 615 (CC), especially paras 90–1. I discuss this aspect of the case in Fowkes (n 20) ch 4, and the general issues of the text and the Court's discretion in ch 5.

[36] 1996 Constitution (n 9) ss 167(5), 172(2).

[37] Constitutional Court Rules GG No 25726 31 October 2003, Rule 16 http://www.justice.gov.za/legislation/regulations/r2003/2003_r7827_gg25726-concourt-rules.pdf (last accessed 20 April 2017).

[38] *President of the Ordinary Court Martial v Freedom of Expression Institute* 1999 (4) SA 682 (CC).

[39] 1996 Constitution (n 9) s 167(4).

2.3 Access to constitutional justice and remedies

As a legal matter, the constitution poses few obstacles to access to justice. Standing provisions to enforce fundamental rights are generous, and are further interpreted generously; they have also been extended to apply to other parts of the constitutional text. The legal way is, therefore, very open for individuals to raise constitutional complaints, or to raise them on behalf of others or a class of others, on behalf of organizations, or in the public interest.[40]

The real obstacles faced by litigants are more practical. One set arises from the court structure—as noted, the presence of two higher courts means that litigants will often need to act in three different courts before achieving a final ruling. In labour matters, the chain is even longer still, since decisions of the first and more informal mechanism, the Commission for Conciliation, Mediation, and Arbitration (CCMA), may be appealed to the Labour Court, then to the Labour Appeal Court, and then to the Supreme Court of Appeal and the Constitutional Court, a process that may take and has taken many years and millions of rand to complete.[41] The constitution provides for the possibility of direct access—hearing a matter for the first time in the Constitutional Court—and direct appeal—hearing a matter directly on appeal from the High Court, thus skipping the Supreme Court of Appeal.[42] Litigants regularly ask for these quicker routes, but the court does not often accede. It has maintained that it is usually preferable that important constitutional matters are first thoroughly ventilated in other courts. The court's direct access jurisprudence has been the subject of considerable criticism by scholars seeking to broaden access to justice, but it remains a fixture.[43]

A second set of obstacles arises from the challenges of litigation, and the general lack of steps taken by courts to date to compensate. Generous standing rules, and even a much less restrictive direct access procedure, can remove only the first hurdle between litigants who lack considerable resources and meaningful access to justice: There remains the need to obtain lawyers, to gather evidence, and often to conduct a public campaign surrounding litigation to increase its efficacy. Some South African litigants can do this, but not many. Other systems have taken far more extensive steps to reduce the burdens on litigants. The Indian public interest litigation (PIL) model has seen judges often take these burdens off litigants; the Benin Constitutional Court is pioneering a strikingly similar model in Africa; and more formal models including the Colombian *tutela*, although arising in a rather different legal context, nevertheless provide far cheaper access to an order of court.[44] Social justice litigation in South Africa usually remains the preserve of the rich and of a few organizations; the doors of the courts are functionally closed to many.

[40] ibid s 38; see eg *Lawyers for Human Rights v Minister of Home Affairs* 2004 (4) SA 125 (CC).

[41] The dispute in *CUSA v Tao Ying Metal Industries* 2009 (2) SA 204 (CC), for example, took nearly ten years until finally resolved by the Constitutional Court, and cases lasting six or seven years are not uncommon.

[42] 1996 Constitution (n 9) s 167(6); Constitutional Court Rules (n 37) Rules 18 and 19.

[43] The most prominent critic has been Jackie Dugard; see most recently Jackie Dugard, 'Courts and Structural Poverty in South Africa: To what Extent has the Constitutional Court Expanded Access and Remedies to the Poor?' in Daniel Bonilla Maldonado (ed), *Constitutionalism of the Global South: The Activist Tribunals of India, South Africa, and Colombia* (Cambridge University Press 2013) 293–329 and Jackie Dugard, 'Closing the Doors of Justice: An Examination of the Constitutional Court's Approach to Direct Access, 1995–2013' (2015) 31 *South African Journal on Human Rights* 112.

[44] I discuss some of these developments in James Fowkes, 'Civil Procedure in Public Interest Litigation: Tradition, Collaboration and the Managerial Judge' (2012) 1 *Cambridge Journal of International and Comparative Law* 235; James Fowkes, 'How to Open the Doors of the Court: Lessons on Access to Justice from Indian PIL' (2011) 27 *South African Journal on Human Rights* 434. See further on India's model Arun K Thiruvengadam, 'Swallowing a Bitter PIL? Reflections on Progressive Strategies for Public Interest Litigation in

Next, there is the question of the reaction by those against whom orders are made, especially the government. The ANC government, since 1994, has generally been respectful of judicial authority and of court orders.[45] Problems of non-compliance have, however, arisen. These often arise from incompetence and institutional weakness rather than more cynical motives, with papers not filed in time or acted upon promptly, but that is no less serious for the people whose judicial orders are not enforced. A major decision on non-compliance arose from a case where a man died after the government, despite repeated legal steps having been taken, persistently failed to make even an interim payment arising from a judgment in a medical negligence case arising in a state hospital. The case produced a large-scale supervisory interdict, requiring the government to report on all outstanding judicial orders and the steps it was taking to comply with these. The government complied, but problems of enforcement remain.[46] The ability of an organisation to combine litigation with ongoing monitoring and advocacy often remains important to getting an order fully enforced.[47]

Finally, access to courts is not access to justice without an effective remedy. South African courts have a very wide discretion to 'make any order that is just and equitable' in order to remedy a constitutional inconsistency.[48] In practice, this represents the power to make any order that will be effective, including money damages, retrospective and suspended orders, supervisory and structural interdicts, and temporary orders pending further steps.[49] Judges initially were slow to exercise some aspects of this broad remedial power—the Constitutional Court only issued its first structural interdict in 2005, for example, ten years after the court's creation.[50] While the use of expansive and creative remedies is steadily increasing, the complaint that judges should use bolder and more elaborate remedies is very common in scholarly writing on South African courts.[51]

2.4 Decision-making process and style of reasoning

By far the most dominant form of reasoning in South African courts, especially in the Constitutional Court, starts with a textual argument and proceeds to make a purposive one. Since the purpose concerned frequently has to do with establishing a new state that repudiates the sins of the past, such purposive arguments frequently include an historical component. This approach, therefore, frequently takes the apartheid past as a point of defining contrast, but there is also a more specific link. A dominant interpretation of

India' in Oscar Vilhena, Upendra Baxi, and Frans Viljoen (eds), *Transformative Constitutionalism: Comparing the Apex Courts of Brazil, India and South Africa* (Pretoria University Law Press 2013); on Benin's, which I noted in the previous volume of this series see Anna Rotman, 'Benin's Constitutional Court: An Institutional Model for Guaranteeing Human Rights' (2004) 17 *Harvard Human Rights Journal* 281; and on Colombia's see Manuel Iturralde, 'Access to Constitutional Justice in Colombia: Opportunities and Challenges for Social and Political Change' in Bonilla Maldonado (n 43) 361–403.

[45] See eg Klug (n 7) 7, 241, 248–9, 295; Roux (n 22) ch 4; and see generally Fowkes (n 20).

[46] *Nyati v Member of the Executive Council for the Department of Health Gauteng* 2008 (5) SA 94 (CC); see for subsequent steps and reports the *Nyati* case file www.constitutionalcourt.org.za (last accessed 20 April 2017). On continued reports of non-compliance by the state see eg Steven Budlender, Gilbert Marcus, and Nicholas Ferreira, *Public Interest Litigation and Social Change in South Africa: Strategies, Tactics and Lessons* (The Atlantic Philanthropies 2014) 13.

[47] ibid 101–6, 122–6.

[48] 1996 Constitution (n 9) s 172(1).

[49] See further Michael Bishop, 'Remedies' in Woolman and Bishop (n 13).

[50] *Sibiya v Director of Public Prosecutions, Johannesburg* 2005 (5) SA 315 (CC); *Sibiya v Director of Public Prosecutions, Johannesburg* 2006 (2) BCLR 293 (CC). For a partial earlier exception see the order in *August v Electoral Commission* 1999 (3) SA 1 (CC).

[51] I critique this scholarship in Fowkes (n 20).

the mistakes made by the apartheid judiciary is that they arose from a formal approach to law that focused quite narrowly on text and the will of parliament, and side-lined broader moral or contextual factors.[52]

This parsimonious approach is symbolized by a book, *Die Uitleg van Wette* (*The Interpretation of Statutes*), published by C J Steyn in 1946, the first legal textbook published in Afrikaans. Steyn first worked as a key government lawyer and then as a senior judge, serving as chief justice for twelve years from 1959.[53] This diagnosis of what happened in apartheid courts may be questioned, but it remains an important influence on lawyerly thinking and drives calls for reasoning to be ever more purposive and contextual.[54]

Initially, the South African Constitutional Court was famous for the extensive reliance it placed on comparative sources. Sources from Canada, the United Kingdom, the United States, and Germany, in particular, were commonly cited.[55] A part of the explanation for this relatively extensive reliance on comparative law was that the court was confronting a new constitutional text and needed to fill in many doctrines, and references to foreign law gave its rulings a grounding and a sense of legal credibility they may otherwise have lacked.

On its own, however, this explanation is not completely adequate. In a strongly nationalist setting, references to foreign case law would have weakened rather than strengthened a court's credibility. It is, therefore, important that the South African constitution marked the country's return to the ranks of respectable global citizens, after being one of the world's arch-pariahs during the later apartheid years. The frequent references to foreign law reflected this move, as well as the desire by the first judges to establish a court whose judgments would be internationally respected—a bid in which they were very successful.[56]

As the distance to the founding judgments has increased, the pattern has changed somewhat. As South African authority now frequently exists to be cited for basic doctrines, the number of foreign sources used for such purposes has declined, as the court, understandably, instead cites its own precedents. At least some judges are, however, apparently making an effort to pay greater attention to the domestic jurisprudence of other African countries (which has to date seldom been cited by the court), so a new comparative law approach may be underway. This nascent effort seems to be motivated by a desire to produce a more 'African' jurisprudence, both as a good in itself and as a potential source of local legitimacy.[57]

If comparative law seems to be experiencing a relative decline, however, recent bold decisions imply that the same may not be true for international law. International law

[52] Most famously by John Dugard, 'The Judicial Process, Positivism and Civil Liberty' (1971) 88 *South African Law Journal* 181.

[53] On Steyn and his textbook see Edwin Cameron, 'Legal Chauvinism, Executive-mindedness and Justice—LC Steyn's Impact on South African Law' (1982) 99 *South African Law Journal* 38.

[54] I assess the diagnosis in James Fowkes, 'Apartheid Judging and Dugard's Question: Re-examining the Legend' (forthcoming).

[55] Christa Rautenbach, 'South Africa: Teaching an "Old Dog" New Tricks? An Empirical Study of the Use of Foreign Precedents by the South African Constitutional Court (1995-2010)' in Tania Groppi and Marie-Claire Ponthoreau (eds), *The Use of Foreign Precedents by Constitutional Court Judges* (Hart Publishing 2013).

[56] See eg the analysis along these lines of the Court's first major intervention invalidating the death penalty in *S v Makwanyane* 1995 (3) SA 391 (CC) by Heinz Klug, *Constituting Democracy: Law, Globalism and South Africa's Political Reconstruction* (Cambridge University Press 2000) 145-8; Roux (n 22) 46; and Fowkes (n 20) ch 1.

[57] This comment is made on the basis of informal conversations with judges.

has a more affirmative place in the constitutional framework than foreign law. Courts are bound to prefer reasonable interpretations that are consistent with international law over others that are not, and 'must' consider international law when interpreting the Bill of Rights where they only 'may' consider foreign law.[58] The recent trend, however, goes further still. South Africa is, in theory at least, a dualist system, meaning that obligations entered into at the international level are not automatically enforceable on the domestic plane. Recently, the Constitutional Court apparently overturned this classical position by holding that instruments the government has signed and ratified at the international law are relevant to assessing the domestic constitutionality of steps it takes to give effect to rights, even if those instruments have not been incorporated into domestic law.[59] International commitments are, therefore, effectively converted into justiciable domestic obligations, whether or not they have been incorporated, which is a potentially expansive doctrine given the increasing richness of international legal sources.

The same history that affects the approach to judicial appointments also affects the way judgments are written in the Constitutional Court. It is understood that judges of different backgrounds will have different valuable perspectives to express and that the law will be better if these inform it.[60] This has shaped the mechanics of judgment writing since the court's founding. As appears in more detail from the contribution of former Justice Goldstone in this volume, the process of judgment writing is highly deliberative in comparative terms. Judgments are extensively debated; judges' positions sometimes change as a result of the deliberation; and collegial input is common and encouraged. The value placed on diversity has also, over time, come to affect the attitude to dissents and separate concurrences.

During the court's early years, particularly under Chief Justice Chaskalson, unanimity was usual, probably as a result of conscious efforts to obtain it in order to strengthen the court's nascent interpretative authority and to establish coherent foundations for its jurisprudence. Dissents and separate judgments were not precluded, and were more commonly written than tends to be true, for instance, in continental systems where the suspicion of dissents is a deeper matter of legal culture, rather than merely prudential calculation. A firm effort was, nevertheless, apparently made to write unanimous opinions. By contrast, Chaskalson's successor, Chief Justice Langa, placed a greater emphasis on hearing from multiple voices, and the frequency of dissents increased.[61] An exception remains particularly contentious on such politically-charged matters. The court's judgments are usually issued in the name of the justice who wrote them, but in these exceptional cases the court makes an unusual effort to achieve unanimity and prefers to present a judgment simply in the name of 'the Court'.

[58] 1996 Constitution (n 9) ss 233, 39(1).

[59] *Glenister v President of the Republic of South Africa* 2011 (3) SA 347 (CC), especially 179–202. For commentary see eg Bonita Meyersfeld, 'Domesticating International Standards: The Direction of International Human Rights Law in South Africa' (2013) 5 *Constitutional Court Review* 398; Franziska Sucker, 'Approval of an International Treaty in Parliament: How Does Section 231(2) 'Bind the Republic'' (2013) 5 *Constitutional Court Review* 416; Juha Tuovinen, 'What to Do with International Law? Three Flaws in *Glenister*' (2013) 5 *Constitutional Court Review* 434.

[60] See eg Albie Sachs, *The Strange Alchemy of Life and Law* (Oxford University Press 2011) 142–5.

[61] See Michael Bishop, Lisa Chamberlain, and Sha'ista Kazee, 'Twelve-year Review of the Work of the Constitutional Court: A Statistical Analysis' (2008) 24 *South African Journal on Human Rights* 354, 359–61; Theunis Roux, 'The Langa Court: Its Distinctive Character and Legacy' (2015) *Acta Juridica* 33, especially 37, 48–9.

3. The Court and its Impact on South African Constitutionalism: An Ongoing Debate

Uncontroversial answers to questions about what the South African Constitutional Court has achieved or failed to achieve, about its status or position, and about what lies in its future, are not easy to come by. Opinions about these matters differ quite considerably; a very broad array of events and subjects, of course, is also potentially relevant to the enquiry, and many of these issues are the subject of currently unfolding developments. In the limited context of this chapter, therefore, this final section merely seeks to set out the main different current viewpoints on the issue, to give a sense of the issues, and what is at stake.

A first viewpoint on the position and significance of the Constitutional Court, if it can be called that, should be acknowledged at the outset: inattention. The court has a relatively low public profile and many South Africans do not treat it as particularly significant.[62] This is not necessarily surprising. The court issues a small number of judgments: until recently, the figure was roughly twenty to thirty-five decisions a year, tiny by most global standards. (This has begun to rise since the court's conversion into a general apex court. It issued thirty-nine judgments in 2014, forty in 2015, and fifty-five in 2016.) Its decisions in areas of particular public interest, such as socio-economic welfare programmes, are less common still. Objectively speaking, however, this first viewpoint does underestimate the importance of the court, although the fact that many South Africans pay little attention to the court naturally affects its power and status. Arguments are accordingly heard that the court should be more populist, and more active in socio-economic areas, in order to increase its profile and build a wider basis of public support.[63]

A second viewpoint sees the judiciary and/or the constitution in more hostile terms, as an obstacle. Combative attitudes have become more common in the years since 2008, when political battles within the ANC began to enter the courts in a substantial way and Jacob Zuma, who would become president in 2009, appeared before the Constitutional Court and several other courts in connection with corruption charges, after earlier facing rape charges in a lower court. (The rape charges were dismissed; the corruption charges were ultimately dropped by the prosecutor, a political appointee, on the grounds that former President Mbeki had earlier tainted the prosecution by politically interfering in it.[64]) A perception among prominent politicians that the courts in general and the Constitutional Court in particular are overstepping the proper bounds of their authority in relation to other branches also contributes to these tensions. Apart from a number of public objections to particular judgments, this has prompted a controversial review process, first announced in 2011, in which the cabinet has initiated an assessment of the powers of the Constitutional Court, conducted under government tender by a team of academics.[65]

In their strongest form, those who espouse such views see the court as a reactionary institution, as politically hostile to the ANC or to factions of it, or as a bastion of white

[62] See eg Roux (n 22) 4: '[T]he Court has never built much institutional legitimacy (in the sense of 'diffuse public support')' and the survey work principally by James L Gibson cited therein.

[63] See eg Dugard (n 43) 297.

[64] See eg Mark S Kende, 'Enforcing the South African Constitution: The Fight for Judicial Independence and the Separation of Powers' (2014) 23 *Transnational Law and Contemporary Problems* 35, 38–40.

[65] For further detail see Jonathan Klaaren, 'Transformation of the Judicial System in South Africa, 2012–2013' (2015) 47 *George Washington International Law Review* 481.

power.[66] The academic assessment of scholars such as Ran Hirschl and Michael Mandel, who see the South African constitution as an elite pact betraying the interests of ordinary South Africans, also shares a family resemblance with this view (with the key difference that on these versions the ANC leadership is complicit in the betrayal).[67] More moderate positions see the rather more standard tensions between different branches of government. These tensions arise especially in the context of a relatively new constitution, whose expansiveness potentially gives courts jurisdiction over many issues, and where new lines of authority are accordingly still being settled. Some scholars view these tensions with alarm when they take the form of resistance on the part of senior government and ANC officials, seeing them as signs of a dominant party seeking to subordinate the courts.[68]

It is certainly true that, as a result of these developments, the ANC's long and almost unbroken record of scrupulous public respect for the judiciary began to fray around 2008, and the court was the subject of political attacks and charges of being 'counter-revolutionary', ANC-speak for something constituting an obstacle to the just transformation of South Africa. Insofar as observers are concerned that constitutional damage might result from ANC attempts to concentrate power in itself or to resist the loss of power, their worries are hardly unreasonable from an historical or comparative perspective. However, some of the claims associated with this viewpoint are not very well supported by the facts to date, something any useful assessment of the claims must also take into account.[69]

First, the judiciary in general and the Constitutional Court in particular cannot accurately be understood as defenders of white minority interests or as generally hostile to the ANC. The court usually upholds government policy on redistributive matters and, if it disagrees with the government, it is usually because it believes the constitution requires more redistribution, not less (although it does not rule against the government on this basis nearly as often as its progressive critics believe it should).[70] Cases about things such as state corruption may be a source of significant political tension, but they are hard to describe as instances of courts opposing pro-poor policies.

Secondly, ANC government policy towards the judiciary is far more nuanced than descriptions of attacks and fears of power grabs would reflect. There may be increased friction, but there is also continuing formal respect and, it seems, an ongoing back-room dialogue and large areas of consensus. Witness the fact that, alongside the trends of increased dissent and the controversial assessment process, the government has also passed major reforms that are often salutary and have at least the potential to strengthen the courts.[71] It is significant that, despite the ANC's dominant power, the government has not pushed through policies stripping judicial powers or passed constitutional amendments to this

[66] The most commonly-cited exponent of this view is current Minister of Mineral Resources Ngoako Ramathlodi. His most detailed statement of these views that I am aware of is Ngoako Ramathlodi, 'Viewpoint: What Constitutes the Strategic Political Centre?' (22–28 January 2010) 10(2) *ANC Today*.

[67] Michael Mandel, 'A Brief History of the New Constitutionalism, or "How we Changed Everything so that Everything would Remain the Same"' (1998) 32 *Israel Law Review* 250; Ran Hirschl, *Towards Juristocracy: The Origins and Consequences of the New Constitutionalism* (Harvard University Press 2007).

[68] The most prominent statement is Sujit Choudhry, '"He Had a Mandate': The South African Constitutional Court and the African National Congress in a Dominant Party Democracy' (2010) 2 *Constitutional Court Review* 2; see also eg Kende (n 64).

[69] I offer a more detailed critique of some argument of this sort on democracy-protection in Fowkes (n 20) ch 7.

[70] Kate O'Regan, 'Helen Suzman Memorial Lecture: A Forum for Reason: Reflections on the Role and Work of the Constitutional Court' (2012) 28 *South African Journal on Human Rights* 116; Fowkes (n 20) 4; James Fowkes, 'More Power than Pact: The Over-emphasis on the Negotiated Origins of South Africa's Constitution' (forthcoming).

[71] See Klaaren (n 65).

effect. Some aspects of its reform proposals over the years have certainly been controversial.[72] However, the controversial elements have instead tended to be withdrawn after protest and representations from the legal community.

Thirdly, and finally, there are few signs that judicial independence has actually been compromised. As noted earlier, the government's main strategy to pursue its interests appears to be to appoint judges whom it perceives as taking a more restrained view of the judicial role and, thus, as being less likely to rule against it.[73] As a result, at least partly, it has been much more meaningful to speak of a 'conservative wing' of the court in the last few years than at any other point in its history to date. That said, however, such appointment strategies are a familiar feature in other countries and are not in themselves necessarily sinister, nor even necessarily inappropriate political responses to a world of increased judicial power.[74] Furthermore, in a familiar story, the expectations the government may have of a particular judge do not necessarily play out in practice. Certainly, it would be hard to make the case that any Constitutional Court justice to date has been a political puppet of some sort.

None of this, in the absence of a fortune-telling ability, rebuts the concern that ANC power *could* pose a threat to the courts or the constitution (a concern that in any event is close to a truism in an emerging system with a very powerful, entrenched political party, provided we remember that it is only one possibility, among others). What these arguments do represent, instead, is evidence that the picture, while uncertain and containing concerns and threats, must also at least be acknowledged as a mixed one: the stance of the ANC government towards the judiciary demands, and merits, nuanced and measured assessment.

Where the second school of thought adopts a negative or suspicious attitude to the courts, a third general view, chiefly held by legal scholars, is (not surprisingly) more positive. Its proponents support constitutionalism and the courts and are optimistic about what judicial intervention can achieve. They, therefore, tend to worry that political threats will damage this endeavour. However, especially if they are South African, they are also likely to be critical of the courts for not taking bolder approaches to law reform and the fight against poverty and social injustice. The court's most globally-celebrated decisions are seen as symbols of what rich, bold expressions of justice could achieve; some of its more restrained cases, on the other hand, are seen as abdications.[75] These scholars seek to assist the court or to challenge it in scholarship in the hope of spurring it to greater action.[76] They also increasingly look to other jurisdictions with more expansive courts,

[72] See, on an earlier series of contentious proposals, Catherine Albertyn, 'Judicial Independence and the Constitution Fourteenth Amendment Bill' (2006) 22 *South African Journal on Human Rights* 126. Those proposals were subsequently withdrawn, and the aspects that have subsequently been enacted following the Constitution Seventeenth Amendment Act of 2012 are generally welcomed. Similarly, the current proposals, controversial on their face, have also in several respects turned out to display positive features and are in any event an incomplete process; see Klaaren (n 65).

[73] For a discussion of some of the politics surrounding appointments see eg Calland (n 23) ch 11.

[74] See further James Fowkes, 'Transformative Constitutionalism and the Global South: The View from South Africa' in Armin von Bogdandy and others (eds), *Transformative Constitutionalism in Latin America: A New Latin American* Ius Commune (Oxford University Press 2016) and sources cited therein.

[75] I discuss and challenge these general features of the South African canon in detail in Fowkes (n 20); for shorter statements of aspects of the argument relevant here see James Fowkes, 'Right After All: Reconsidering *New National Party* in the South African Canon' (2015) 31 *South African Journal on Human Rights* 151; James Fowkes, 'Beyond the Bold Standard: Re-interpreting the South African Constitutional Canon' (forthcoming).

[76] See the discussion of scholarly approaches in David Bilchitz, 'Avoidance Remains Avoidance: Is it Desirable in Socio-economic Rights Cases?' (2013) 5 *Constitutional Court Review* 296.

such as Colombia and India, as examples that they argue South African courts would do well to follow.[77]

Proponents of this view often place the court at the centre of the constitutional project, sometimes to the extent of paying implausibly little attention to other constitutional actors. An important strand of writing does emphasise dialogic approaches that involve members of the public, social movements and other state actors. The court's engagement device in the eviction context resonates particularly strongly with these views.[78] But even in this context, the courts, rather than other actors, are usually given pride of place as an initiator or shaper of the constitutional discussion. The most common scholarly response to the engagement cases, moreover, is to criticize them for articulating too little content: As this shows, approaches short of bold rights defences are still most often viewed with concern by legal scholars.[79]

Two revisionary responses to this mainstream view have recently been offered. One argues that the court has been wise to be more restrained than its progressive critics would prefer, in light of the political environment. This argument sees the court as a rather vulnerable body, operating in a dominant party democracy, whose relative restraint, therefore, reflects sensible, politically-aware judging. This contention, made above all in the work of Roux, thus takes a more modest view of the possibilities of judicial action.[80] It sees the court as a potentially vital guardian of the rule of law against political actors and the ANC in particular, and therefore thinks it crucial that the court act so as to preserve its fragile authority—accepting occasional legally-indefensible retreats and regular restraint as the inevitable price of ensuring this. On this view, the court has made a huge contribution to the success of the South African constitutional project to date and probably could not, in context, have made a larger one.

A second revisionary view, advanced principally by myself, gives more constitutional credit to the ANC. Like Roux, it seeks to be more realistic and take more account of politics, but it calls attention to the more positive dimensions of South African constitutional politics since 1994.[81] On this view, the primary reason for South Africa's relative constitutional success, and for the most admired decisions the court has been able to announce, has to do with facts about the ANC and the stances it has adopted on these issues. It sees the South African political environment as having sometimes been conducive to the rule of law, and at least sometimes as highly conducive to the bold and admirable defences of rights, for which the Constitutional Court is globally famous (and for which the court, and sometimes social movements, but not the ANC government, receives the scholarly credit). The court's contribution is, therefore, certainly important and praise is often deserved, but it is frequently better understood as having been a partner to the ANC government in

[77] See eg Dugard (n 43); David Bilchitz, 'Constitutionalism, the Global South and Economic Justice' in Bonilla Maldonado (n 43) 41–95.

[78] An important early example, drawing on Habermas, is Dennis Davis, *Democracy and Deliberation: Transformation and the South African Legal Order* (Juta & Co 1999); an important recent example, drawing on experimentalist approaches, is Stu Woolman, *The Selfless Constitution: Experimentalism and Flourishing as Foundations of South Africa's Basic Law* (Juta & Co 2013). The first book length study of the engagement device will shortly appear as Brian Ray, *Engaging with Social Rights: Procedure, Participation and Democracy in South Africa's Second Wave* (Cambridge University Press 2016).

[79] See both the arguments of fairly strong critics: Bilchitz (n 76); Jackie Dugard, 'Beyond *Blue Moonlight*: The Implications of Judicial Avoidance in Relation to the Provision of Alternative Housing' (2013) 5 *Constitutional Court Review* 264—and more sympathetic ones such as Brian Ray, 'Evictions, Aspirations and Avoidance' (2013) 5 *Constitutional Court Review* 172.

[80] See especially Roux, *The Politics of Principle* (n 22).

[81] See especially Fowkes (n 20).

pursuing the constitutional project, than as having charted a brave lone course in hostile political waters.

The debate between these views continues; good historical judgments, especially of current controversies, must await the luxury of hindsight and greater temporal detachment. Whether bolder judicial action would have had good consequences for the constitution and the judiciary is perhaps the great unanswerable counterfactual of this period. Proponents point out the advantages of popular support for courts, while sceptics note the fates of other courts that chose to be expansive and which have taken on political actors, and consequently suffered a decisive backlash. Exactly what scholarly verdict one should pass on the ANC-in-government is likely to remain a contentious issue. These debates, however, matter a great deal to the future of the Constitutional Court, for it is only if we understand what has to date underpinned its work that we can understand what is entailed by that job going forward, especially as political conditions in South Africa change.

Bibliography

Albertyn C, 'Judicial Independence and the Constitution Fourteenth Amendment Bill' (2006) 22 *South African Journal on Human Rights* 126

Bilchitz D, 'Constitutionalism, the Global South and Economic Justice' in Maldonado B D (ed), *Constitutionalism of the Global South: The Activist Tribunals of India, South Africa, and Colombia* (Cambridge University Press 2013) 41–95

Bilchitz D, 'Avoidance Remains Avoidance: Is it Desirable in Socio-economic Rights Cases?' (2013) 5 *Constitutional Court Review* 296

Bishop M, 'Remedies' in Woolman S and Bishop M (eds), *Constitutional Law of South Africa* (2nd edn, Juta & Co 2005)

Bishop M, Chamberlain L, and Kazee S, 'Twelve-year Review of the Work of the Constitutional Court: A Statistical Analysis' (2008) 24 *South African Journal on Human Rights* 354

Budlender S, Marcus G, and Ferreira N, *Public Interest Litigation and Social Change in South Africa: Strategies, Tactics and Lessons* (The Atlantic Philanthropies 2014) 13

Calland R, *The Zuma Years: South Africa's Changing Face of Power* (Zebra Press 2013)

Cameron E, 'Legal Chauvinism, Executive-mindedness and Justice—LC Steyn's Impact on South African Law' (1982) 99 *South African Law Journal* 38

Choudhry S, ''He Had a Mandate': The South African Constitutional Court and the African National Congress in a Dominant Party Democracy' (2010) 2 *Constitutional Court Review* 2

Constitutional Court Rules GG No 25726 31 October 2003 http://www.justice.gov.za/legislation/regulations/r2003/2003_r7827_gg25726-concourt-rules.pdf (last accessed 20 April 2017)

Davis D, *Democracy and Deliberation: Transformation and the South African Legal Order* (Juta & Co 1999)

Davis D, 'Transformation and the Democratic Case for Judicial Review: The South African Experience' (2007-2008) 5 *Loyola University Chicago International Law Review* 45

Davis D M and Klare K, 'Transformative Constitutionalism and the Common and Customary Law' (2010) 26 *South African Journal on Human Rights* 403

Dugard J, 'Courts and Structural Poverty in South Africa: To What Extent has the Constitutional Court Expanded Access and Remedies to the Poor?' in Maldonado B D (ed), *Constitutionalism of the Global South: The Activist Tribunals of India, South Africa, and Colombia* (Cambridge University Press 2013) 293–329

Dugard J, 'Beyond *Blue Moonlight*: The Implications of Judicial Avoidance in Relation to the Provision of Alternative Housing' (2013) 5 *Constitutional Court Review* 264

Dugard J, 'Closing the Doors of Justice: An Examination of the Constitutional Court's Approach to Direct Access, 1995–2013' (2015) 31 *South African Journal on Human Rights* 112

Dugard J, 'The Judicial Process, Positivism and Civil Liberty' (1971) 88 *South African Law Journal* 181

Fowkes J, 'Transformative Constitutionalism and the Global South: The View from South Africa' in Von Bogdandy A and others (eds), *Transformative Constitutionalism in Latin America: A New Latin American* Ius Commune (Oxford University Press 2016)

Fowkes J, *Building the Constitution: The Practice of Constitutional Interpretation in Post-Apartheid South Africa* (Cambridge University Press, forthcoming 2016)

Fowkes J, 'Apartheid Judging and Dugard's Question: Re-examining the Legend' (forthcoming)

Fowkes J, 'Beyond the Bold Standard: Re-interpreting the South African Constitutional Canon' (forthcoming)

Fowkes J, 'Civil Procedure in Public Interest Litigation: Tradition, Collaboration and the Managerial Judge' (2012) 1 *Cambridge Journal of International and Comparative Law* 235

Fowkes J, 'How to Open the Doors of the Court: Lessons on Access to Justice from Indian PIL' (2011) 27 *South African Journal on Human Rights* 434

Fowkes J, 'More Power than Pact: The Over-emphasis on the Negotiated Origins of South Africa's Constitution' (forthcoming)

Fowkes J, 'Right After All: Reconsidering *New National Party* in the South African Canon' (2015) 31 *South African Journal on Human Rights* 151

Hirschl R, *Towards Juristocracy: The Origins and Consequences of the New Constitutionalism* (Harvard University Press 2007)

Hofmeyr K, 'Rules and Procedure in Constitutional Matters' in Woolman S and Bishop M (eds), *Constitutional Law of South Africa* (2nd edn, Juta & Co 2005) 5.1–5.49

Iturralde M, 'Access to Constitutional Justice in Colombia: Opportunities and Challenges for Social and Political Change' in Maldonado B D (ed), *Constitutionalism of the Global South: The Activist Tribunals of India, South Africa, and Colombia* (Cambridge University Press 2013) 361–403

Kende M S, 'Enforcing the South African Constitution: The Fight for Judicial Independence and the Separation of Powers' (2014) 23 *Transnational Law and Contemporary Problems* 35

Klaaren J, 'Transformation of the Judicial System in South Africa, 2012–2013' (2015) 47 *George Washington International Law Review* 481

Klug H, *Constituting Democracy: Law, Globalism and South Africa's Political Reconstruction* (Cambridge University Press 2000)

Klug H, *The Constitution of South Africa: A Contextual Analysis* (Hart Publishing 2010)

Lewis C, 'Reaching the Pinnacle: Principles, Policies and People for a Single Apex Court in South Africa' (2005) 21 *South African Journal on Human Rights* 509

Mandel M, 'A Brief History of the New Constitutionalism, or "How we Changed Everything so that Everything would Remain the Same"' (1998) 32 *Israel Law Review* 250

Meyersfeld B, 'Domesticating International Standards: The Direction of International Human Rights Law in South Africa' (2013) 5 *Constitutional Court Review* 398

Ntlama N, 'The Transformation of the South African Judiciary: A Measure to Weaken its Capacity?' (*New York Law School Law Review* http://www.nylslawreview.com/wp-content/uploads/sites/16/2014/10/Ntlama.pdf (last accessed 14 April 2017).

O'Regan K, 'Helen Suzman Memorial Lecture: A Forum for Reason: Reflections on the Role and Work of the Constitutional Court' (2012) 28 *South African Journal on Human Rights* 116

Ramathlodi N, 'Viewpoint: What Constitutes the Strategic Political Centre?' (22–28 January 2010) 10(2) *ANC Today*

Rautenbach C, 'South Africa: Teaching an "Old Dog" New Tricks? An Empirical Study of the Use of Foreign Precedents by the South African Constitutional Court (1995-2010)' in Groppi T and Ponthoreau M C (eds), *The Use of Foreign Precedents by Constitutional Court Judges* (Hart Publishing 2013)

Ray B, *Engaging with Social Rights: Procedure, Participation and Democracy in South Africa's Second Wave* (Cambridge University Press 2016)

Ray B, 'Evictions, Aspirations and Avoidance' (2013) 5 *Constitutional Court Review* 172

'Remarks for Former Chief Justice Chaskalson' (General Council of the Bar of South Africa Human Rights Committee Conference on the Justice Bills, Judicial Independence and the Restructuring of the Courts, Johannesburg, 17 February 2006) 23 http://www.sabar.co.za/conference_transcript.pdf (last accessed 20 April 2017)

Rotman A, 'Benin's Constitutional Court: An Institutional Model for Guaranteeing Human Rights' (2004) 17 *Harvard Human Rights Journal* 281
Roux T, *The Politics of Principle: The First South African Constitutional Court 1995–2005* (Cambridge University Press 2013)
Roux T, 'The Langa Court: Its Distinctive Character and Legacy' (2015) *Acta Juridica* 33
Sachs A, *The Strange Alchemy of Life and Law* (Oxford University Press 2011)
Seedorf S, 'Jurisdiction' in Woolman S and Bishop M (eds), *Constitutional Law of South Africa* (2nd edn, Juta & Co 2005) 4-125
Spitz R and Chaskalson M, *The Politics of Transition: A Hidden History of South Africa's Negotiated Settlement* (Witwatersrand University Press 2000)
Sucker F, 'Approval of an International Treaty in Parliament: How Does Section 231(2) 'Bind the Republic'' (2013) 5 *Constitutional Court Review* 416
Thiruvengadam A K, 'Swallowing a Bitter PIL? Reflections on Progressive Strategies for Public Interest Litigation in India' in Vilhena O, Baxi U, and Viljoen F (eds), *Transformative Constitutionalism: Comparing the Apex Courts of Brazil, India and South Africa* (Pretoria University Law Press 2013)
Tuovinen J, 'What to Do with International Law? Three Flaws in *Glenister*' (2013) 5 *Constitutional Court Review* 434
Woolman S, *The Selfless Constitution: Experimentalism and Flourishing as Foundations of South Africa's Basic Law* (Juta & Co 2013)
Submissions to the Portfolio Committee on Justice and Constitutional Development on behalf of the General Bar Council of South Africa, 37–8 www.sabar.co.za (last accessed 20 April 2017)
The *Nyati* case file www.constitutionalcourt.org.za (last accessed 20 April 2017)

8

Unique but Ineffective

Assessing the Constitutional Adjudication System in Ethiopia

Adem K Abebe

1. Introduction

The introduction of constitutional review mechanisms is one of the most common aspects of the post-1990 wave of democratic and constitutional reforms. Only a handful of constitutional drafters in Africa and beyond have resisted the tide of judicial empowerment that has characterized the constitutional and democratic reforms of the last few decades. Ethiopia is one of these.

The 1995 Constitution of Ethiopia is novel not only in underscoring ethnicity as the prominent basis of political and social organization and in recognizing the right to secession;[1] but it also excludes courts from reviewing the constitutionality of laws. Despite the declaration of the supremacy of the constitution, the establishment of a federal form of state, and the dedication of more than a third of the constitution to a robust bill of rights, a combination of features associated with strong constitutional review mechanisms, the Ethiopian constitution has stopped short of recognizing the power of independent courts to review the constitutionality of laws and other government decisions. Instead, it grants exclusive jurisdiction to the House of Federation (House), the second legislative house composed of representatives of ethnic groups, to interpret the constitution and to resolve all constitutional disputes.[2]

In recognition of the technical traits of constitutional interpretation, and since members of the House may not be legal experts, the constitution establishes the Council of Constitutional Inquiry (Council), composed predominantly of legal experts,[3] to make a preliminary determination on constitutional issues. The decisions of the Council are subject to reconsideration, approval, modification, or rejection by the House. The express granting of the power of constitutional interpretation to the House and the Council has largely confined the role of regular courts in the constitutional adjudication process to identifying and referring constitutional issues to the Council.

This chapter describes the unique institutional and procedural aspects of constitutional review in Ethiopia. It also briefly discusses the place of constitutional review in previous Ethiopian constitutions. The chapter locates the unique institutional and procedural choices in relation to constitutional adjudication within the political and ideological background of the dominant actors who drafted and adopted the constitution and continue to dominate the current political space. It explains the continued dearth, despite improvements, of constitutional cases from the perspective of bottlenecks to access to

[1] Constitution of the Federal Democratic Republic of Ethiopia (FDRE) Proclamation No 1/1995 s 39.
[2] FDRE Constitution ss 62(2) and 83(1).
[3] ibid ss 82–84.

constitutional justice. The chapter also explores the reluctance of potential litigators to submit constitutional cases owing to the lack of institutional credibility of constitutional adjudicators. The main cases that the Council and the House have decided on merits are discussed. The chapter concludes with some observations on the prospects of constitutional adjudication in Ethiopia.

2. Constitutional Review in Previous Ethiopian Constitutions

Constitutional review in Ethiopia has historically been of little or no significance. The first written Ethiopian constitution, the 1931 Constitution, did not even declare its supremacy. It rather reaffirmed the supreme authority of the emperor (section 6). Although it recognized a few rights,[4] it was not clear whether courts or other judicial institutions had the authority to enforce such rights, particularly against administrative agencies. The sole responsibility of ensuring that the exercise of power was in accordance with the law, presumably including the constitution, belonged to the emperor. Given the supremacy of the emperor, the validity of laws adopted by him could not be challenged. There was, therefore, no constitutional review of laws.

Similarly, the 1955 Constitution of Ethiopia conferred supreme authority on the emperor.[5] Nevertheless, it also declared the constitution, alongside international treaties ratified by Ethiopia, the supreme law of the land. As such, all laws, decrees, orders, judgments, decisions, and acts inconsistent with the constitution were null and void).[6] Nevertheless, it was not clear how effect was to be given to the supremacy of the constitution. Given the supremacy of the emperor, courts could not be expected to review and to invalidate laws adopted under his command. Nevertheless, since judicial power was vested in the courts,[7] they had the power to give effect to the fundamental rights provisions of the constitution, particularly against administrative agencies. In practice, courts reviewed and, at times, invalidated, among others, ministerial regulations based on the constitutional due process guarantee.[8]

Under the 1987 Constitution of the Peoples' Democratic Republic of Ethiopia, the constitution was the supreme law of the land and any law or decision contrary to it did not have effect.[9] The power to ensure the supremacy of and to interpret the constitution belonged to the Council of State composed of the president of the republic, the vice-president and other members as determined by the National Assembly.[10] The Council also served as the standing body for the National Assembly. Nevertheless, the constitution empowered regular courts to safeguard legally guaranteed rights, freedoms, and interests.[11] As such, even though courts did not have the power of constitutional review over primary legislation,

[4] 1931 Ethiopian Constitution ss 22–28. [5] 1955 Ethiopian Constitution s 26. [6] ibid s 122.

[7] ibid s 108.

[8] Minasse Haile, 'Comparing Human Rights in Two Ethiopian Constitutions: The Emperor's and the "Republic's"—*Cucullus Non Facit Monachum*' (2005) 13 *Cardozo Journal of International and Comparative Law* 1, 46. Haile similarly notes that the Federal Act of Eritrea and Ethiopia Proclamation recognized the power of courts to review the compatibility of laws with the 1955 Constitution and the Federal Act. According to the Act, '[a] final determination by a Federal Court that any legislation or administrative, executive, or judicial order ... is invalid in terms of conformity with Our [the Ethiopian] Constitution or the Federal Act [of Ethiopia and Eritrea], shall have as a consequence that such legislation, order, decree, judgment ... shall be held throughout Our Empire as null and void and unenforceable and inapplicable by any official or courts of Our Empire'. See the 1952 Federation (between Ethiopia and Eritrea) Proclamation. Similarly, s 90 of the 1952 Constitution of Eritrea empowered the Supreme Court of Eritrea to review the constitutionality of laws and other orders.

[9] 1987 Ethiopian Constitution s 118. [10] ibid ss 63(3) and (4), 81 and 82. [11] ibid s 100.

they had the authority to evaluate the compatibility of administrative decisions with fundamental rights. The constitution was overthrown before it could reach the courts.

The 1991 Transitional Period Charter of Ethiopia, which served as a provisional constitution, declared its supremacy. All laws or decisions contrary to it were null and void.[12] However, it was not clear as to which institution had the power of constitutional review. The Council of Representatives, composed of eighty-seven individuals representing national liberation movements, political parties, and other prominent individuals, was given the authority to settle disputes concerning the meanings of the Amharic and English versions of the charter.[13] In addition, the Charter empowered courts to ensure the protection of the fundamental rights recognized in the Universal Declaration of Human Rights (UDHR).[14] It, therefore, recognized judicial review at a minimum of administrative decisions based on human rights standards.

Overall, constitutional review was largely unknown in Ethiopian constitutional history. Whenever the procedure was legally recognized, the power belonged to political organs. Under all constitutions, courts did not have the power to review the constitutionality of primary statutes. Nevertheless, under the 1955 and 1987 Constitutions, as well as the transitional period charter, courts had the mandate to ensure observance of fundamental rights, particularly against administrative agencies.

The current 1995 Constitution has continued the tradition of maintaining the power of interpreting the constitution and of reviewing the constitutionality of primary statutes in the political organs, more specifically the House. The constitution also appears to preclude courts from enforcing constitutional rights against administrative agencies. As noted below, the power to safeguard constitutional rights against administrative decisions belongs to the Council, not the regular courts. Nevertheless, regular courts have on occasion and, in the context of cases pending before them, invoked constitutional rights to support their interpretation of statutes.[15]

3. Constitutional Review under the 1995 Constitution of Ethiopia

This section discusses various procedural and institutional aspects of the constitutional review system in Ethiopia as established in the 1995 Constitution and in other relevant laws. These features demonstrate the uniqueness of the review system.

3.1 Centralized constitutional review

As briefly noted above, the power to interpret the constitution and to resolve constitutional disputes belongs to the House. Under normal circumstances, constitutional disputes reach the House only after the Council has made an initial determination. Where a constitutional question is directly submitted to the House, it refers the matter to the Council.[16] Constitutional disputes may reach the Council through two mechanisms. The first route is judicial referral. Under the constitution and the law establishing the Council,

12 Transitional Period Charter of Ethiopia s 18. 13 ibid s 19. 14 UDHR ss 1 and 9(f).

15 For instance, the Cassation Division of the Federal Supreme Court invoked the principle of the best interests of the child to deviate from a literal interpretation of a provision of the 2000 Federal Family Code; *Miss Tsedale Demissie v Mr Kifle Demissie*, Federal Supreme Court Cassation Division, file 23632 (6 November 2007) (on file with author).

16 Consolidation of the House of the Federation and Definition of its Powers and Responsibilities Proclamation No 251/2001 s 6.

whenever a court is convinced that the resolution of a constitutional issue is necessary for the resolution of a pending legal dispute, the court must stay the proceedings before it and refer the constitutional issue to the Council.[17] Courts may refer constitutional issues either on their own motion or at the request of any of the parties.

The second mechanism is through the submission of direct individual complaints. The constitution does not expressly anticipate processes through which individuals may directly challenge the constitutionality of laws and government decisions. Nevertheless, the law establishing the Council recognizes two possibilities for direct individual access. First, when a court rejects a request from the parties to refer a constitutional matter to the Council, any of the parties may, upon finalization of the court procedure, submit the constitutional issue to the Council.[18] The second possibility relates to the right of individuals to submit constitutional issues concerning the bill of rights against decisions of administrative agencies once the party has exhausted all available remedies.[19] A good example is where a law excludes courts from reviewing the legality of decisions of administrative agencies (laws with ouster clauses). A party may challenge the constitutionality of the ouster clause itself, as well as a specific decision or decisions of the relevant agency.

It is possible to infer from these mechanisms that the Ethiopian constitution establishes a variation of the centralized constitutional review system where the power to decide on the constitutionality of laws and administrative decisions exclusively belongs to a single entity, which has the first and final say on constitutional disputes. The House has the final but not the first say on constitutional issues. While the Council has the first say on constitutional issues, its views are only recommendatory.

The choice of a centralized and politicized constitutional review system may be attributed to three main factors. The first is the establishment of ethnicity as the predominant basis of political organization. The Ethiopian constitution is perhaps the only constitution in the world that starts off with the phrase '[w]e the nations, nationalities and peoples of Ethiopia'.[20] It is also the only African constitution that expressly recognizes the right of ethnic groups to secede from the federation.[21] The constitution also vests sovereignty not in the 'people' as such, but in the nations, nationalities, and peoples.[22]

The granting of the power of interpreting the constitution to the House is intended to reinforce the conferring of sovereignty on ethnic groups.[23] Since the constitution is seen as a compact or an accord between the various warring factions organized along ethnic lines, it was decided that the ethnic groups themselves should have the final say in interpreting their accord.[24] Considering that the House is composed of representatives of ethnic groups, it was a natural choice. The Council was added to complement the interpretative functions of the House. This partly explains why the Council was established as an *ad hoc* entity, which is a common characteristic of advisory organs.

The second reason relates to the ideology of the dominant political forces that drafted the constitution. The constitution was drafted under the tutelage of a left-leaning coalition of ethnic-based political parties, the Ethiopian People's Revolutionary Democratic

[17] FDRE Constitution s 84(2); Council of Constitutional Inquiry Proclamation No 798/2013 s 4.

[18] Council of Constitutional Inquiry Proclamation s 4(5).

[19] ibid s 5.

[20] 1995 Ethiopian Constitution preamble.

[21] ibid s 39.

[22] ibid s 9(1).

[23] Fasil Nahom, *A Constitution for a Nation of Nations* (Red Sea Press 1997) 59, observing that the Ethiopian system of constitutional adjudication emanated from and is consistent with the 'overriding supremacy' of ethnic groups.

[24] Ibrahim Idris, 'Constitutional Adjudication under the 1994 FDRE (Federal Democratic Republic of Ethiopia) Constitution' (2002) 1 *Ethiopian Law Review* 62, 68; Assefa Fiseha, 'Federalism and the Adjudication of Constitutional Issues: The Ethiopian Experience' (2005) 52 *Netherlands International Law Review* 1, 16.

Front (EPRDF). Paul notes that: '[n]one of the political and ethnic forces which make the opposition to [the EPRDF] had participated in the constitution making'.[25] Young similarly observes:[26]

> [C]onstitution-making under the EPRDF has little in common with the bargaining, trade-offs, and compromises that usually typify such processes; rather it reflects the weakness of the country's democratic institutions, the political objectives of the governing party, and its position of dominance within a state where serious opposition had been crushed or marginalised.

As a left-leaning party, the EPRDF was ideologically opposed to empowering courts, composed of unelected judges, to thwart the will of the people. The observations of the Secretary of the Constitutional Commission, the body that drafted the constitution, demonstrate the dilemma and the final resolve to keep the constitution away from the courts:[27]

> How can a constitution that has been ratified by the people's assembly be allowed to be changed by professionals who have not been elected by the people? To allow the courts to do the interpretation is to invite subversion of the democratization process. Since the constitution is eventually a political contract of peoples, nations and nationalities, it would be inappropriate to subject it to the interpretation of judges. It is the direct representatives of the contracting parties that should do the work of interpreting the constitution.

These observations are restatements of the counter-majoritarian problem that has gripped the theoretical debate on constitutional judicial review, particularly in the United States of America.[28] The ideological opposition to constitutional judicial review combined with the centrality of ethnic sovereignty in the newly established political and constitutional dispensation informed the decision to grant the final power of constitutional review to the House.

The lack of trust by the people, especially the political elites, in the judiciary further encouraged the decision to keep the constitution away from the courts. Historically, courts were seen as extensions of the administrative apparatus of the state. They were associated with the massive atrocities committed by the communist military junta that ruled the country from 1974 to 1991. Indeed, the EPRDF government dismissed most of the judges and prosecutors following its ascension to power in 1991. The official mistrust of the judiciary was exacerbated when, during the transitional period (1991–1995), some judges ordered the release of former officials of the Derg regime on constitutional grounds. The newly appointed officials found this judicial 'interference' disconcerting.[29]

This fleeting exasperation reinforced the resolve to limit the power of courts to apply laws adopted by the political organs, without questioning their value, legitimacy, or constitutionality. This may partly explain the decision to take even the power to assess the

[25] James Paul, 'Ethnicity and the New Constitutional Orders of Ethiopia and Eritrea' in Yash Ghai (ed), *Autonomy and Ethnicity: Negotiating Competing Claims in Multi-ethnic States* (Cambridge University Press 2000) 189.

[26] John Young, 'Regionalism and Democracy in Ethiopia' (1998) 19 *Third World Quarterly* 191, 195. See also Theodore M Vestal, 'An Analysis of the New Constitution of Ethiopia and the Process of Adoption' (1996) 3 *Northeast African Studies* 21; and Tsegaye Regassa, 'Making Legal Sense of Human Rights: The Judicial Role in Protecting Human Rights in Ethiopia' (2009) 3 *Mizan Law Review* 287.

[27] Transitional Government of Ethiopia, Constitutional Commission Newsletter No 3 (1994). Newsletters were used to inform the public about the constitutional drafting process.

[28] Barry Friedman, 'The Birth of an Academic Obsession: The History of the Counter-majoritarian Difficulty, Part Five' (2002) 112 *Yale Law Journal* 153.

[29] Informal discussion between the author and Tsegaye Regassa, then lecturer at the University of Addis Ababa, citing his conversations with a former member of the Council of Constitutional Inquiry (16 September 2011).

constitutionality of administrative rules and decisions away from regular courts. As noted above, the 1955 and 1987 Constitutions and the 1991 transitional period charter empowered regular courts to review administrative decisions for compatibility with constitutional rights. Paradoxically, the new constitutional arrangement reinforced the political control of the courts while exacerbating the popular lack of trust in the courts.

3.2 Composition of the House of Federation and the Council of Constitutional Inquiry

The House is composed of representatives of ethnic groups.[30] Each ethnic group has at least one representative and one additional representative for each one million people, living anywhere in the country, belonging to the ethnic group. While all recognized ethnic groups are represented in the House, the bigger ethnic groups have a higher number of representatives.[31] The constitution anticipates two optional mechanisms for the selection of the representatives, as determined by regional law. The representatives may be selected either by regional legislative councils or through direct elections.[32] So far, the legislative councils have appointed all the representatives, and the possibility of directly electing the representatives has not prompted any political or popular interest or debate. Given the fact that the current process allows the dominant forces in regional politics the choice, it is unlikely that these forces will voluntarily decide to transfer the power of selecting the representatives from themselves to the people. It should also be noted that the constitution does not include political diversity requirements in the composition of the House. For instance, the 1996 constitution of South Africa[33] provides that political parties represented in a provincial legislature are entitled to proportional representation in the delegation representing the province in the second house (the Council of Provinces).

The Council is composed of eleven members, including the president and vice-president of the Federal Supreme Court, six legal experts with 'proven professional competence and high moral standing' appointed by the President of Ethiopia upon the recommendation of the House of Peoples' Representatives, and three others nominated by the House of Federation from among its members.[34] The term of office of members appointed by the president is six years, while the term of the members selected by the House of Federation depends on the term of the House itself, which is five years.

In addition to the condition that the members should have competence and integrity, there are no requirements to ensure the diversity of the composition of the Council in terms of gender, religion, or ethnicity. Currently, two out of the eleven members are women. Perhaps most notably, there is no requirement that the six members appointed by

[30] FDRE Constitution s 61.

[31] Currently, the House has 135 members representing 76 recognized ethnic groups. Note that some of the regional states have many ethnic groups with few members. As a result, such states may have a larger representation as a region. Indeed, almost half of the representatives in the House are from the Southern Nations, Nationalities and Peoples Regional State. The Regional State has more than double the number of representatives than any other region.

[32] Ethiopia is unique in that the House of Federation is composed of representatives of ethnic groups. In other federations, members of second houses represent either the people or government of the regions. There are various ways of selecting members of the second house. In some federations, such as Nigeria and the United States, after the 17th amendment, members are directly elected; in India and Ethiopia, members are selected by regional legislatures; in Germany, regional governments (executives) appoint the members; in South Africa, some of the members are appointed by provincial legislatures and the rest by regional governments. Canada is unique in that the federal executive appoints members of the second house.

[33] South African Constitution s 61(1).

[34] FDRE Constitution s 82.

the president must be independent and neutral. As a consequence, a number of members appointed to the Council have been members of or associated with the ruling party, as well as the House of Peoples' Representatives. For instance, a special legal adviser of the prime minister and a member of the ruling party and the House of Peoples' Representatives are currently members of the Council. In addition, the three members appointed from the House of Federation are politicians belonging to the ruling party or its affiliates.

The members of the Council, other than the judges of the Supreme Court, may be removed by the same organs that appointed them on grounds of misconduct, incompetence, or inefficiency.[35] It appears that the power to ascertain whether grounds for removal exist lies with the appointing organs themselves, and not with regular courts or another independent organ. So far, no member of the Council has been removed. In fact, a number of members have served for more than one term, including the legal adviser to the office of the prime minster, who has been a member since the establishment of the Council.

3.3 Jurisdiction of the House of Federation with regard to constitutional review

As indicated above, the power of interpreting the constitution and of resolving 'all constitutional disputes' lies with the House.[36] Despite the apparently clear constitutional provisions empowering the House and the Council to interpret the constitution and to adjudicate all constitutional disputes, there has been substantial scholarly divergence on whether ordinary courts have the power to interpret the constitution and to invalidate unconstitutional laws or other measures.

Fiseha argues that the exclusive powers of the House only relate to the determination of the constitutionality of primary statutes.[37] He bases his argument on section 84(2) of the constitution which, in providing for the process to be followed in resolving constitutional issues that arise in court proceedings, refers to issues involving the constitutionality of 'any federal or state *law*'. The authoritative Amharic version of this provision refers to laws made by federal and regional 'legislative' organs. Similarly, Donovan argues that the drafters of the constitution only had the intention to take away from ordinary courts the power to invalidate primary legislation—federal and state primary statutes—as unconstitutional.[38]

[35] Council of Constitutional Inquiry Proclamation s 19.

[36] FDRE Constitution ss 62(1) and 82–84. This section discusses the powers of the House in relation to constitutional review. Nevertheless, the powers of the House are not limited to constitutional review. The House, in addition, resolves disputes among regional states, and between regional states and the federal government; resolves disputes concerning the right to self-determination, including secession and the creation of new regional states; determines matters necessary for the creation of a single common market over which the House of Peoples' Representatives may enact laws; and decides on the formula to determine federal subsidies to the regional states. Although the House of Federation is considered as a parliamentary organ, it is not largely involved in the ordinary legislative-making process, which is exercised by the House of Peoples' Representatives. The limited legislative functions of the House of Federation include its role in constitutional amendment and its power to determine which civil matters should be under the legislative jurisdiction of the federal or the regional states. See FDRE Constitution ss 62(5) and (8), 105(1)(c), and 105(2)(a).

[37] Assefa Fiseha, 'Constitutional Interpretation: The Respective Role of the Courts and the House of Federation' in Assefa Fiseha and Tsegaye Regassa (eds), *Courts and the Constitution: Proceedings of the Symposium on the Role of Courts in the Enforcement of the Constitution, June 2000* (2001) 6–26; see Fiseha (n 24).

[38] Dolores A Donovan, 'Levelling the Playing Field: The Judicial Duty to Protect and Enforce the Constitutional Rights of Accused Persons Unrepresented by Counsel' (2002) 1 *Ethiopian Law Review* 31.

Both Fiseha and Donovan reinforce their arguments for a residual power of judicial review with the constitutional duty of courts to obey and enforce the constitution, as every measure of enforcement unavoidably involves some kind of interpretation.[39] Idris similarly concludes that: '[a]ny petition on the unconstitutionality of an administrative act or a decision or a custom is within the judicial jurisdiction of an ordinary court'.[40] According to Tadesse, ordinary courts may entertain constitutional challenges against a government decision or directive, but not challenges to constitutionality of statutes.[41] Regassa also argues that judicial review of administrative decisions is an inherent function of courts as is implied, in the case of Ethiopia, in the vesting of all judicial power in the courts.[42]

These authors conclude that Ethiopian courts have the residual power to consider the constitutionality of measures other than primary statutes—both federal and regional—such as cases that involve the alleged violation of constitutional rights by administrative agencies.[43] Bulto, furthermore, argues that the judicial referral of constitutional issues to the Council is 'discretionary as opposed to mandatory'.[44] He argues that courts have the power to declare primary statutes unconstitutional with *inter partes* effect, but without nullifying such laws. Besselink similarly concludes that the House and the Council only have the final and authoritative, but not the exclusive, power of determining the constitutionality of laws.[45]

However, 'law', the constitutionality of which may only be considered by the Council and the House, has been officially defined very broadly to include not only proclamations issued by the federal or state legislative organs (primary statutes), but also government regulations and directives and international agreements.[46] Some scholars consider this definition as an unconstitutional encroachment upon the implied residual jurisdiction of ordinary courts to consider the constitutionality, for instance, of directives, regulations and other executive decisions.[47] In addition, the law establishing the Council provides for procedures through which individuals may challenge the constitutionality of final decisions of any government organ or official after they have exhausted available remedies within the institutional hierarchy.[48] These laws have essentially excluded the regular courts from inquiring into the constitutionality of final administrative decisions.

Arguments in favour of the power of regular courts to decide on the constitutionality of all acts and omissions, except that of primary statutes, rely almost exclusively on section 84(2) of the constitution, which appears to refer only to legislative enactments. They disregard section 83(1), which simply provides that the House shall decide 'all constitutional disputes'. Similarly, section 62(1) clearly provides that the House has 'the power to interpret the Constitution'.[49]

[39] FDRE Constitution ss 9(2) and 13(1). [40] See Idris (n 24) 71.

[41] Memberetsehai Tadesse, *Ye'Ethiopia Hig'ena Fitih Getsitawoch [Features of Law and Justice in Ethiopia]* (2006) 144.

[42] FDRE Constitution s 9(1). See Tsegaye Regassa, 'Courts and the Human Rights Norms in Ethiopia' in Fiseha and Regassa (n 37) 116.

[43] See Fiseha (n 24) 21.

[44] Takele S Bulto, 'Judicial Referral of Constitutional Disputes in Ethiopia: From Practice to Theory' (2011) 19 *African Journal of International and Comparative Law* 99, 101. Bulto argues that: '[t]he interpretation of the constitution has been apportioned between the regular judiciary as a principal organ to adjudicate constitutional issues, and the CCI/HoF [Council /House] which have been given the residual powers to interpret the constitution without rendering a final decision on questions of fact', 105–6.

[45] Leonard Besselink, 'The Protection of Human Rights in Federal Systems—the Case of Ethiopia' in Bayaa Yimam and others (eds), *Proceedings of the 14th International Conference of Ethiopian Studies* Vol 3 (Institute of Ethiopian Studies 2002) 1372–9.

[46] House of the Federation Proclamation s 2(2). [47] See eg Fiseha (n 37) 20; Fiseha (n 24).

[48] Council of Constitutional Inquiry Proclamation s 5.

[49] Some authors make a distinction between 'constitutional interpretation' and 'constitutional disputes' to understand the exact role of courts, and the Council and the House. However, it is only when there is a constitutional dispute of some sort that constitutional interpretation becomes necessary. The two phrases should,

'All constitutional disputes' include any constitutional issue, whether legislative, executive, or judicial, as long as the final determination of the meaning of a constitutional provision is necessary. The consideration of the constitutionality of primary legislation is only part of the broader spectrum of constitutional issues or disputes.[50]

Most importantly, it is sections 62 and 83 of the constitution that determine the substantive issue relating to the organ that has the power to interpret the constitution. Section 84 is intended to outline the power relationships between the Council and the House and the procedure that should be followed to address constitutional disputes arising in judicial proceedings. Hence, whenever there is a case that can only be resolved after determining a constitutional issue, courts have no choice but to refer the constitutional issue to the Council.[51] Granting exclusive power of constitutional review to the House was clearly the intention of the members of the Constitutional Commission who drafted and the Constituent Assembly that adopted the constitution.[52] In an article analysing not only the intention of the drafters but also all the major publications on constitutional adjudication in Ethiopia, Assefa concludes that the 'House of Federation commands all the powers to interpret the Constitution or decide on all constitutional disputes' and that there was no endeavour to divide these powers between the courts and the House.[53]

In sum, in Ethiopia, the power to adjudicate all constitutional disputes including, but not limited to, the constitutionality of primary statutes lies with the House and the Council. The House and the Council have exclusive jurisdiction in invalidating unconstitutional laws and executive decisions. The role of regular courts is limited to referring cases to the Council whenever a pending case cannot be resolved without first determining the constitutionality of the law based on which it is to be decided.[54] Hence, the House, and not independent courts, is the guardian of the Ethiopian constitution. This arrangement

therefore, be understood to refer to issues that require the determination of the meaning of a constitutional provision or provisions. Assefa espoused similar views after considering the minutes of the Constituent Assembly; Getachew Assefa, 'All about Words: Discovering the Intention of the Makers of the Ethiopian Constitution on the Scope and Meaning of Constitutional Interpretation' (2010) 24 *Journal of Ethiopian Law* 139, 166. See also Assefa Fiseha, 'Some Reflections on the Role of the Judiciary in Ethiopia' (2011) 14 *Recht in Afrika* 1, 5, observing that such a distinction is of no practical significance as both powers belong to the same entity, the House.

[50] Assefa (n 49) 165 similarly observes that: '[s]o long as there is a constitutional dispute or a question of constitutionality that needs resolution, it has to be submitted to the Council/House of Federation whether the question is clear or simple or complicated'.

[51] See also Haile (n 8) 55, concluding that: '[r]egular courts have no power to decide constitutional issues'. Courts do not have the discretion to refer a constitutional issue to the Council, as Bulto submitted; Bulto (n 44) 101. If courts are convinced that resolving a constitutional issue is necessary to resolve a non-constitutional case before them, they have no choice but to refer the constitutional issue to the Council. Courts have a discretion only in determining whether (1) there is a constitutional issue; and (2) resolving such issue is necessary to resolve the dispute before them. Even in cases where a court decides that there is no constitutional issue, the parties are allowed to refer the case to the Council within 90 days after the court has rendered the decision. Nevertheless, Bulto is correct in observing that: '[t]here must be a strong justification for direct invocation of constitutional provisions' (112). Not every mundane and peripheral constitutional issue has to be resolved by the Council and the House. The power to decide whether or not there is a constitutional issue allows courts to filter cases to ensure that only unavoidable constitutional issues reach the Council.

[52] For a thorough analysis of all the major publications relating to constitutional adjudication in Ethiopia and a discussion of the debates surrounding constitutional adjudication see Assefa (n 35).

[53] Assefa (n 49) 166.

[54] However, this does not mean that courts have absolutely no role in ensuring the realization of constitutional rights or even in the interpretation of the constitution. Indeed, there are several ways in which courts can discharge their constitutional duty to obey and ensure the observance of the constitution. For instance, courts may only refer cases when they are convinced that there is a need for constitutional interpretation. This requires some sort of preliminary constitutional interpretation. In addition, higher courts interpret constitutional provisions to support their interpretation of ordinary laws, although this is not always specifically stated. This chapter only argues that if and when a constitutional issue which is necessary to resolve a pending case arises in the course of ordinary litigation, courts have to refer the constitutional issue to the Council. See generally Adem Abebe, 'A Constitution without a Guardian: Is the Ethiopian Constitution Really Supreme?' (2013) 5 *Ethiopian Human Rights Law Series* 9.

has created a judiciary with a trifling role in the interpretation and implementation of the constitution and state policies.[55]

Apart from individual cases arising in court proceedings and direct constitutional challenges against administrative decisions in the Council, the proclamation establishing the Council provides that cases that may not be handled by regular courts and which require constitutional interpretation may be submitted to the Council by at least one-third of the members of the federal parliament or state legislative councils, or the federal or regional executive bodies.[56] This provision, as well as anticipating the existence of disputes that may not be handled by courts, opens up vistas of opportunities for the Council to engage in abstract or advisory review.[57] This is so because there is no clear requirement that the dispute be based on a law or regulation that is in force, or be a concrete dispute. Hence, the entities listed in this provision may possibly even take a draft bill to the Council for constitutional determination. This provision also allows the submission of cases on the constitutional implications of measures, such as policies and practices, which have not been expressly catered for in other provisions.[58] For instance, upon a request by the office of the prime minister, the House delivered an advisory opinion on whether the federal government could enact a framework legislation on family law, including basic minimum standards that regional family laws should be compatible with.[59]

Moreover, although the Ethiopian constitution does not establish procedures for seeking advisory or consultative opinions on constitutional issues, the proclamation for the consolidation of the House provides that: '[t]he House shall not be obliged to render a consultancy service on constitutional interpretation'.[60] The *a contrario* reading of this provision may imply that the House may, when it so wishes, provide advisory or consultative or guiding opinions on constitutional issues. For instance, the House provided an interpretation of the constitution upon a request by the *Silte* people to assist regional states in their effort to address demands for internal self-determination within existing regional states—an issue that has not been expressly addressed in the constitution.[61]

3.4 Access to the constitutional review process

The Ethiopian constitution only explicitly addresses instances where constitutional issues arise in judicial proceedings.[62] The proclamation establishing the Council, in addition, recognizes constitutional complaint procedures where individual victims of constitutional rights violations may refer constitutional cases directly to the Council.[63]

[55] Tadesse, former Vice-President of the Federal Supreme Court, similarly observes that the role of Ethiopian courts in the constitutional adjudication procedure is peripheral and negligible; see Tadesse (n 41) 162.

[56] Council of Constitutional Inquiry Proclamation s 3(2).

[57] However, there is no indication as to what kind of cases may not be handled by courts. This provision may as well be creating its own version of the political question doctrine. Cases concerning, for instance, the horizontal separation of powers, disputes between the federal government and the regional states, and policies or foreign relations may fall in this category.

[58] The House has, for instance, developed guidelines on who may raise a claim regarding identity and who may decide on questions related to the right to self-determination based upon the recommendations of the Council; Constitutional issue regarding resolution of claims of identity, House of Federation (April 2001) (on file with author).

[59] Constitutional issue regarding the promulgation of a family code, House of Federation (April 2000) (on file with author). According to the constitution, the power to enact family laws falls within the jurisdiction of regional states. The federal government enacted a family code applicable to residents of the autonomous cities of Addis Ababa and Dire Dawa.

[60] House of Federation Proclamation s 4(2). However, it is not clear whether the House issues an advisory opinion in its capacity as the second legislative chamber or as a constitutional adjudicator.

[61] Resolution of claims of identity case (n 58).

[62] FDRE Constitution ss 84(2) and (3).

[63] House of Federation Proclamation ss 21–23.

If a constitutional issue arises in judicial proceedings, and if the court is convinced that there is a need for constitutional interpretation in deciding the case, it must refer the issue to the Council.[64] The court may refer the case to the Council, either on its own motion or at the behest of any party to the proceeding. In cases where a court rejects the request of a party to refer the matter to the Council, the party may refer the matter to the Council within ninety days of the decision of the court.[65] It is only a constitutional issue that must be referred to the Council. As a result, constitutional interpretation is incidental to the determination of cases pending before courts.[66] The constitutional review system in Ethiopia is, therefore, centralized and largely abstract. Nevertheless, the requirement that a court may only refer a constitutional issue as long as it is necessary to resolve a pending dispute concretizes the incidental and largely abstract nature of constitutional review. It is likely that any constitutional determination will particularly consider the facts of the case pending before the courts.[67]

Individuals may submit constitutional cases arising outside court cases only if the case relates to the fundamental rights provisions of the constitution.[68] In such cases, a person aggrieved by a final decision of a government institution or official may submit his or her case to the Council. Before submitting a case to the Council, the person must exhaust all available administrative remedies. This provision is particularly important in cases where laws preclude the judicial review of administrative decisions (laws that include ouster clauses). In such cases, even though the decision of administrative organs may not be challenged in regular courts as ultra vires, it can be challenged in the Council as unconstitutional.

The proclamations defining the powers and competences of the House and the Council anticipate procedures through which these institutions may invite experts and institutions and gather professional opinions.[69] Although the provisions specifically mention 'invitation', they also open possibilities for *amici curiae* to request to join constitutional cases as professionals. Nevertheless, while the Council and the House have on occasion invited experts, there have not been any instances where a party has requested to join a constitutional case as *amicus curiae*.

Once a constitutional issue has been presented to the Council, it considers whether there is a need for constitutional interpretation. If constitutional interpretation is necessary, the Council provides recommendations to the House for final decision.[70] The House has to decide the case within 30 days from the date it receives the recommendations of the Council.[71] The House is not bound by the recommendations of the Council. If, for any reason, the Council is convinced that there is no need to

64 Council of Constitutional Inquiry Proclamation s 4.

65 Council of Constitutional Inquiry Proclamation s 4(5).

66 Abebe Mulatu, 'Who is "the Interested Party" to Initiate a Challenge to the Constitutionality of Laws in Ethiopia (Under the 1994 FDRE Constitution) (1999) *The Law Student Bulletin* 2, 3, and 4.

67 Pasquino, similarly, observes in the Italian context that: '[i]t is evident, reading the sentences of the Italian Court, that the judgment about the constitutionality of the statute is made, very often, considering the problems that appear in the concrete application of the legislative norm, also considering the specific case the ordinary judge had in front of her when she sent the preliminary question'; see Pasquale Pasquino, 'The New Constitutional Adjudication in France: The Reform of the Referral to the French Constitutional Council in Light of the Italian Model' 18 https://www.pravo.unizg.hr/_download/repository/Pasquino_New-Constitutional-adjudication-France.pdf (last accessed 18 April 2017).

68 Council of Constitutional Inquiry Proclamation s 5.

69 ibid s 9; and House of Federation Proclamation s 10.

70 FDRE Constitution s 84(3)(a).

71 House of Federation Proclamation s 13.

interpret the constitution, it rejects the case.[72] If the constitutional issue was referred to the Council by a court, the Council remands the case to the court that referred the constitutional issue. In cases where the Council rejects a constitutional complaint, a complainant may appeal to the House.[73] If the House accepts the appeal, there is no specific guideline. As such, the House has the discretion either to return the case to the Council for recommendation or to proceed with it.

3.5 Remedies

The Ethiopian constitution does not canvass the nature of remedies the House may issue in cases where it finds a violation of the constitution. The proclamation addressing the power and functions of the House indicates that laws should be presumed constitutional.[74] It also provides that decisions of the House are valid from the date of the decision, unless the House decides otherwise.[75] As such, unless otherwise indicated, decisions invalidating laws do not affect measures undertaken under the law. Before making a final decision on the constitutionality of a law, the House may invite the relevant legislative body to amend, repeal, or modify the law within six months.[76] The proclamation also outlines the principle of partial invalidation in cases where only a part of a law is incompatible with the constitution.[77] Nevertheless, the law may be invalidated in whole if the provision declared invalid is a central element of the law.

There are no constitutional or legal standards concerning the possibility of issuing damages or compensation, particularly in cases of a finding of a violation of human rights. There is also no general constitutional or legal recognition of a right to compensation for losses arising from the violations of human rights or other constitutional provisions owing to state actions or omissions. The Council and the House have thus far not in any case awarded compensation.

Decisions of the House are final, have a general binding effect on all state organs and are applicable in all similar future cases.[78] However, it is not clear whether regular courts may declare unconstitutional a law that contradicts a clear constitutional interpretation established by the decisions of the House. This is particularly so in relation to existing laws or provisions that contain measures more or less similar to laws or provisions that have been declared unconstitutional by the House. It also applies to new laws that contradict existing binding decisions of the House.

It is contended that courts should have the power to refuse to apply laws that are incompatible with the interpretations of the House. For instance, if parliament enacts a law that requires the ability to speak a local language to be able to stand for elections, courts should refuse to apply such legislation as it contradicts the binding decision of the House in the *Election rights* case.[79] A party aggrieved by a decision of the courts to refuse to apply a law may take their case to the Council and, finally, to the House for final determination. If courts do not have the power to declare laws or other acts unconstitutional based on a precedent set by the House, and if they, therefore, have to refer such cases to the Council, the binding nature of the decisions of the House will have limited practical relevance.

[72] FDRE Constitution s 84(3)(b). [73] Council of Constitutional Inquiry Proclamation s 5.
[74] House of Federation Proclamation s 9(1). [75] ibid s 16(1). [76] ibid s 16(2).
[77] ibid s 12. [78] ibid s 11(1).
[79] *Benishangule Gumuz* case, House of Federation (March 2003), House of Federation of the Federal Democratic Republic of Ethiopia (July 2008) 1 *Journal of Constitutional Decisions* 14.

In France, for instance, courts may not refer a constitutional case to the Constitutional Council if the constitutionality of such law has been considered in the *ex ante* procedure and has been declared constitutional, except in cases where new circumstances justify the reconsideration of the constitutionality of the law.[80]

Decisions of the House must be published.[81] However, there is no similar requirement in relation to decisions of the Council. In practice, however, the Council also does not publish its decisions. The Council is only required to provide a written decision rejecting an application to a party who wishes to appeal against its decisions.[82] Since most of the cases before the Council are rejected on the ground that there is no need for constitutional interpretation, only a handful of cases, where the Council had found a violation and were referred to the House, have been published. It must be noted that decisions of the Council finding a violation must always be referred to the House for final review and confirmation.

In contrast, when the Council finds that there is no constitutional violation, it generally rules that there is no need for constitutional interpretation and, therefore, does not refer its decision to the House for confirmation or modification. Nevertheless, a dissatisfied party may appeal to the House against a decision of the Council. The practice of the Council not to refer findings of constitutionality to the House is an arrogation of the final powers of the House.[83]

In cases where the Council finds a violation of the constitution, it automatically refers its recommendations to the House. Although there is no specified time period, the Council is required to decide cases speedily and may not postpone a decision unless there are sufficient reasons.[84]

3.6 Principles of constitutional interpretation

Both the House and the Council have the power to identify and to develop principles of constitutional interpretation.[85] In relation to cases involving fundamental constitutional rights, the interpretation must be made in a manner conforming to the principles of the UDHR, international covenants on human rights, and international instruments adopted by Ethiopia.[86]

The decisions of the Council and the House have so far been very vague, unsystematic, and brief. As a consequence, it is hard to identify a single coherent style of reasoning. Nevertheless, owing to the civil law judicial culture, the decisions largely consist of the analysis of the text of the constitution vis-à-vis the relevant law or decision being challenged. In particular, the two institutions have not systematically considered the limitation of rights and the justification for such limitations.[87] Overall, the Council and the House seem to defer significantly to the limitation of rights by recognizing the wide discretion of the legislative and the executive organs to limit

[80] See Pasquino (n 67) 12. It should be noted that in France courts are prohibited from referring the same law that has been declared constitutional in the *ex ante* procedure. This section is suggesting that Ethiopian courts should not refer laws that are similar to a law that has been previously considered by the Council or the House.

[81] House of Federation Proclamation s 11(2).

[82] Council of Constitutional Inquiry Proclamation s 13.

[83] See eg Bulto (n 44) 119–20.

[84] Council of Constitutional Inquiry Proclamation s 10(4).

[85] House of Federation Proclamation s 7(1).

[86] FDRE Constitution s 13(2); House of Federation Proclamation s 7.

[87] For a detailed discussion of the limitation of rights in Ethiopia see Adem Abebe, 'Limiting Limitations of Human Rights under the Ethiopian Constitution' (2011) 4 *Ethiopian Constitutional Law Series* 60.

rights.[88] Even when the two institutions have found a violation of rights and other constitutional provisions, they have never really seriously considered whether there were grounds for the legitimate limitation of these rights.[89]

The House appears to have endorsed the principle of constitutional avoidance.[90] In the *Election rights* case,[91] the House rejected the findings of the Council that the election law violated the right to stand for election. Nevertheless, the House provided an interpretation of the election law compatible with the constitutional right to stand for election. This case implies that the House will only invalidate laws as unconstitutional if they cannot be interpreted in a manner compatible with the constitution. The case raised questions as to whether the power to interpret the constitution included the power of authoritatively interpreting legislation in the context of constitutional cases.[92]

The Ethiopian constitution does not expressly preclude the Council and the House from authoritatively interpreting domestic legislation in line with the constitution. Nevertheless, the powers of the Council and the House only relate to matters involving constitutional interpretation. Under normal circumstances, the power to provide the final authoritative interpretation of laws belongs to the Cassation Division of the Federal Supreme Court.[93]

The Council and the House do not generally refer to foreign and international law. The only instance where the Council referred to foreign law was in relation to the right to bail case,[94] where the Council, in justifying its finding that parliament had the power to preclude bail to persons charged with certain offences, indicated that, even in the United States, legislation may exclude bail based on the nature of the crime or the severity of the sentence. Similarly, reference to international treaties is inadequate.[95] In all cases, the reference does not go beyond mentioning the name and provision of the relevant treaty. There is, therefore, no analysis.

3.7 Other procedural issues

Decisions of the Council are made by majority vote.[96] Two-thirds of the members of the Council constitute a quorum, that is, at least eight of the eleven members of the Council. In the case of a tie, the chairperson has a casting vote. Individual members of the Council

[88] Constitutional case on the validity of ouster clauses, Council of Constitutional Inquiry (10 February 2009) (on file with author), where the Council held that judicial ouster clauses do not violate the constitutional right of access to justice.

[89] See generally Abebe (n 87).

[90] This principle essentially requires courts to avoid deciding a constitutional question unless it is necessary for purposes of resolving a case. For a discussion of the applicability of the principle in South Africa see Iain Currie, 'Judicious Avoidance' (1999) 15 *South African Journal on Human Rights* 138.

[91] *Benishangule Gumuz* case (n 79).

[92] See Bulto (n 44).

[93] Federal Courts Proclamation No 25/1996 s 10.

[94] Case concerning the constitutionality of the law that excluded bail in corruption offences, Council of Constitutional Inquiry (2004) (on file with author).

[95] *Melaku Fanta* case on the constitutionality of the original criminal jurisdiction of the federal Supreme Court (2014) (on file with author). The Council referred to the International Covenant on Civil and Political Rights. The case involved the compatibility of a legal provision, which granted first instance jurisdiction over criminal cases involving high-level government officials (ministers and above) to the Federal Supreme Court, with constitutional rights to appeal and to equality before the law. The Council and the House found the provision unconstitutional. Interestingly, the Council had rejected a similar challenge to the same laws in a case involving a former minister of defence—Siye Abreha—who was tried in the Supreme Court, despite his objections—see Fasika Tadesse, 'One Case, Contrary Decisions' *Addis Fortune* (Addis Ababa 5 January 2015) http://addisfortune.net/articles/one-case-contrary-decisions/ (last accessed 18 April 2017).

[96] Council of Constitutional Inquiry Proclamation s 11.

may write their dissenting, concurring, or separate opinions. The permission to submit dissenting, concurring, and separate opinions is in line with the practice of regular courts. In fact, in the only case where the House rejected the findings of the Council, it endorsed the interpretation of the minority.[97] The House is empowered to establish a committee drawn from its members to investigate draft proposals submitted to it by the Council, as well as appeals against decisions of the Council that there is no need for constitutional interpretation.[98]

Accordingly, the House has established a Standing Committee on Constitutional and Regional Affairs, which is among others responsible for reviewing the recommendations of the Council and reporting to the full House for a final decision. The Committee decides by majority and is often composed of the highest echelons of state legislative and executive bodies (speakers and deputy presidents of regional states/provinces) who are also members of the House of Federation. The House discusses the recommendations of the Council based on the views of the Standing Committee and takes decisions by consensus and, in the case of a lack of consensus, by majority vote.[99] A decision is considered unanimous if there is no objection to it, as abstention is considered approval. There is no arrangement to write dissenting, concurring, or separate opinions in the House. This is in line with the workings of political organs where the views of the minority are considered defeated.

The Council does not have a duty to hold oral hearings. Moreover, even if the Council decides to hold oral proceedings, the hearings need not be public.[100] The Council determines whether or not proceedings will be public. Government organs also have a duty to explain controversial constitutional issues, if called upon to do so by the Council or the House.[101]

4. Constitutional Review in Practice

The Council does not publish its decisions on applications for constitutional interpretation. Only the House is legally required to publish its decisions. As indicated above, the Council only refers cases to the House when it finds a violation. If the Council finds that there is no violation, it generally rejects the case on the grounds that there is no need for constitutional interpretation. So far, the Council has only referred a handful of cases to the House where it found constitutional violations. In addition, the Council has submitted its views on some constitutional issues referred to it by the House itself.[102] One of the cases involved the subjection of a woman to the jurisdiction of the Shari'a court without her consent.[103] The Council, as was subsequently confirmed by the House, ruled that the compulsory subjection of the woman to the jurisdiction of the Shari'a court without her consent violated section 34(5) of the constitution, which subjects the jurisdiction of religious and customary courts to the consent of all parties to the case.

[97] *Benishangul Gumuz* case (n 79). [98] House of Federation Proclamation s 18.

[99] House of Federation Proclamation ss 14 and 46.

[100] Council of Constitutional Inquiry Proclamation s 10(4).

[101] House of Federation Proclamation s 9(3).

[102] For instance, the case involving the Silte people was referred to the Council by the House—Resolution of claims of identity case (n 58).

[103] *Kedija Beshir* case, House of Federation (May 2004), the House of Federation of the Federal Democratic Republic of Ethiopia (July 2008) 1 *Journal of Constitutional Decisions* 35–41.

In the second case,[104] the electoral board refused to accept applications for candidacy from individuals, most of whom were members of the biggest ethnic groups, who did not speak the local language of the electoral districts habituated by smaller ethnic groups in which they were to stand for election. The Council held that the law, based on which the board had made its decision, had discriminated on the basis of language in violation of section 38 of the constitution. The House interpreted the law as only requiring the ability to speak the official language of the regional legislative council, and not any local language. Accordingly, the House rejected the decision of the Council to the effect that the law was unconstitutional, but found the decision of the board in violation of the law and the constitution.

The third case involved the original jurisdiction of the Federal Supreme Court to try criminal cases involving eminent government officials.[105] During a referral by the court entertaining a corruption case against an important government official with ministerial status, the Council, as confirmed by the House, found the original jurisdiction of the Supreme Court incompatible with the right to appeal of the defendants. This was the first case where the Council and the House invalidated a provision of a law on the basis that it was unconstitutional.

Apart from these three cases, many controversial cases submitted to the Council have been rejected on the ground that they did not raise a constitutional issue. A close look at these decisions reveals an apologetic and justificatory pattern in the Council's reasoning. In one case,[106] the Council ruled that a law completely excluding bail in all corruption cases did not violate the constitutional right to bail. The case resulted from a split within the central committee of the ruling EPRDF party over the handling of the 1998–2000 Ethio–Eritrean War. The winning faction, which included the prime minister, enacted anti-corruption laws.[107] The laws provided the basis for the arrest and prosecution of individuals in the opposing faction, which included the former Defence Minister, Seeye Abraha. When the federal court of first instance ruled that the accused should be released on bail, as was later confirmed by the federal high court, security forces prevented the release of Abraha. In less than two working days, after the order of the court to release the accused on bail, parliament rushed to enact a law that denied bail to all persons accused of corruption offences, regardless of the possible sentence.[108]

A subsequent constitutional challenge against the law was rejected by the Council, which ruled that parliament had the power to determine not only the conditions under which bail may be refused, but also to preclude bail completely in relation to certain offences. The Council failed to consider whether the application of the law to the accused persons violated the constitutional prohibition of the retroactive application of criminal law.

[104] *Benishangul Gumuz* case (n 79). [105] *Melaku Fenta* case (n 95).

[106] *Bail right* case (n 94). The case was submitted directly to the Council by the victim.

[107] Federal Ethics and Anti-corruption Commission Establishment Proclamation No 235/2001, and Anti-corruption Special Procedure and Rules of Evidence Proclamation No 236/2001.

[108] Many refer to the law that denied the right to bail to persons accused of corruption offences as '*Seeye*'s Law'. The provision which denied bail to persons accused of corruption was enacted by an amendment to a law adopted two weeks earlier. The amendment was clearly intended to reverse the court decision freeing Seeye Abraha. For a detailed discussion of the drama that unfolded following the end of the Ethio–Eritrean war, including the dubious process of law making see Elizabeth Belai, 'Disabling a Political Rival in the Name of Fighting Corruption in Ethiopia: The Case of Prime Minster vs Ex-defence Minister Seeye Abraha' (August 2004) http://www.aigaforum.com/TheCaseofSiye.pdf (last accessed 15 April 2017). The law was subsequently revised. Under the current law, persons accused of corruption offences punishable with not more than 10 years have the right to be released on bail, except when the person is likely to abscond or tamper with evidence.

In another case,[109] the Coalition for Unity and Democracy (CUD) in a federal court challenged the decision of the prime minster to suspend the right to assembly and demonstration in and around Addis Ababa for one month following the 2005 elections. The CUD argued that the suspension was contrary to a proclamation governing peaceful demonstrations. The applicants did not base their case on the constitution, as they did not want the case to be referred to the Council (the invocation of a constitutional issue triggers referral to the Council). However, despite objection by the CUD, the court ruled that a constitutional issue was involved and referred the matter to the Council to determine whether the declaration of emergency by the prime minister suspending the right to assembly and demonstration was in line with the constitution. The constitution authorizes the council of ministers, not the prime minister, to declare a state of emergency, subject to subsequent approval by the House of Peoples' Representatives.[110]

Rather than merely applying the procedure governing the declaration of an emergency provided for in section 93 of the constitution, the Council was searching for other provisions from which it could imply the 'power' of the prime minster to declare a state of emergency and to suspend rights without parliamentary approval.[111] The Council should simply have declared that the council of ministers, and not the prime minster alone, could proclaim a state of emergency and declared the proclamation of a state of emergency unconstitutional.[112]

In a case concerning the constitutionality of a regulation of the council of ministers allowing for the dismissal of employees at the discretion of the director of the customs and revenue authority without judicial review,[113] the Council was again evidently searching for justification. The petition challenged the judicial ouster clause in the regulation preventing employees of the authority from applying for judicial review in cases of dismissal without justification or explanation. Section 37 of the constitution guarantees the right of everyone to bring justiciable matters to a court or another tribunal exercising judicial power. The Council ruled that, in a parliamentary form of government, the legislature has the discretion to limit the jurisdiction of courts and, hence, jurisdictional ouster clauses did not violate the constitutional right of access to justice. According to the Council, laws enacted by parliament determine whether or not a matter is justiciable. The inclusion of ouster clauses makes an issue non-justiciable.

Nevertheless, the ouster clauses were adopted in an executive regulation, rather than by the legislature itself. By focusing on the authority of the legislature, the Council failed to address the actual issue. More fundamentally, despite its constitutional status, according to the ruling in this case, the constitutional right of access to courts may be abridged by a

[109] *Emergency declaration* case, Council of Constitutional Inquiry (14 June 2005) (on file with author). Interestingly, the legal adviser to the Prime Minster was one of the members of the Council when the constitutionality of a decision of the Prime Minster was deliberated upon.

[110] FDRE Constitution s 93.

[111] It should also be noted that, despite the fact that the case was a clear instance of derogation from rights, the Council was discussing the requirements applicable to a limitation of rights.

[112] Referring to the failure of the Council to enforce the constitutional procedure of declaring a state of emergency in the *Emergency declaration* case (n 109), Legesse notes that the Council has failed to tackle even 'the most flagrant constitutional violations'; interview with Dr Yared Legesse, Legal Practitioner and Lecturer at the Addis Ababa University, Addis Ababa, Ethiopia (23 September 2011).

[113] *Ouster clauses* case (n 88). The Civil Service Administrative Tribunal referred the constitutional issue to the Council.

piece of legislation.[114] Interestingly, the Council did not investigate the issue as to whether the dismissal of the employees constituted a violation of any of their rights.

These cases, some of the most significant cases regarding constitutional rights the Council has had to decide so far, provided it with the opportunity to enhance its popular standing and legitimacy. Nevertheless, the decisions of the Council merely endeavour to justify or explain the discretionary authority of political actors. This is partly a reflection of the lack of experience with and understanding of genuine limits on political power and their judicial enforcement, ie lack of a culture of constitutionalism. The pervasive political as well as judicial attitude still perceives the role of courts as mere enforcers of laws as adopted.

As indicated in the introductory part, the history of Ethiopia is characterized by the supremacy of politics and political institutions over law and institutions of justice. Given the fact that these cases set binding precedents, any future challenge against ouster clauses or parliamentary discretion is likely to fail. Although the reasoning and approach of the Council in constitutional interpretation has been shallow, simplistic and unsystematic, it is clear that the Council engages in outlining justifications for government action rather than reviewing it critically. Although outcomes may not provide conclusive or sufficient evidence of a lack of judicial independence, the decisions in all these controversial cases, especially when seen in the institutional context of the Council and the sensitivity of the facts of the cases, reflect the absence of institutional checks on political power.[115] Similarly, it is unlikely that the House, a purely political organ, may constrain the exercise of government power, particularly in politically sensitive cases.

Furthermore, several controversial constitutional issues have not reached the Council. For instance, opposition political parties, civil society organizations, the media, and commentators have raised concerns over the constitutionality of some controversial aspects of the media law,[116] anti-terrorism law,[117] and the proclamation of civil societies.[118] The enactment of these laws has legalized the authoritarian tendency of the government in what may be characterized as rule *by* law.[119] Nevertheless, beyond academic and political discourse, no one has challenged the constitutionality of any of these laws.

[114] Interestingly, the chief legal adviser to the director of the Customs and Revenue Authority, whose powers the petitioners challenged, was one of the members of the Council when the case was decided. The relevant laws do not regulate a potential conflict of interest of members of the Council or the House.

[115] John Ferejohn, Frances Rosenbluth, and Charles Shipan, 'Comparative Judicial Politics' (October 2004), observing that: '[c]ourt actions overturning the government can serve as a useful measure of judicial independence' 19 http://leitner.yale.edu/sites/default/files/files/resources/docs/comparativejudicialpolitics.pdf (last accessed 15 April 2017).

[116] Freedom of the Mass Media and Access to Information Proclamation No 590/2008. The law criminalizes, among others, criticism of public officials as an aggravated form of defamation.

[117] Anti-terrorism Proclamation No 652/2009. This law criminalizes, among others, any form of publication that is 'likely' to directly or indirectly 'encourage' terrorism. The law also allows gathering information through surveillance and the interception of all forms of communication. Information obtained through surveillance and interception must be kept in secret. It is, therefore, inaccessible to suspected terrorists. The law furthermore authorizes arrest without a court warrant and the remanding of suspects of acts of terrorism for up to four months without charge. Once charged with terrorism, suspects cannot be released on bail.

[118] Charities and Societies Proclamation No 621/2009. The most restrictive aspect of this law relates to the prohibition to engage in activities related to human rights and democratization issues if a CSO receives more than 10% of its funds from 'foreign' sources.

[119] For a discussion of rule *by* law in Ethiopia see Adem Abebe, 'Rule *by* Law in Ethiopia: Rendering Constitutional Limits on Government Power Nonsensical' (April 2012) *CGHR Working Paper 1* University of Cambridge Centre of Governance and Human Rights. Rule *by* law is a situation where governments use the law to govern, whether or not the law complies with constitutional rights or other higher law requirements. In rule *by* law, 'law is amoral and an instrument of power'—an instrument of maintaining and strengthening power; power controls law and not the other way round. Rule by law is procedural in the sense that any law that is made

The reluctance by these organizations and individuals to approach the Council is partly attributable to the lack of trust in the constitutional review system, emanating from its political character. In fact, the popular faith, even in regular courts, whose independence at least is officially protected, is very low. In an interview, the leader of one of the main opposition political parties indicated that, despite repeated refusals and harassment, they do not resort to courts to enforce their constitutional right to peaceful demonstration as they do not trust the courts. He indicated that: '[u]nder normal circumstances, resorting to court is the way to go about it. But we have doubts on the independence of the courts. The courts have been tested and have failed several times'.[120]

Similarly, in the *CUD* case referred to above, the CUD requested the court to resolve the matter based on existing laws and not to refer the matter to the Council. The Human Rights Council, a prominent Ethiopian human rights non-governmental organization (NGO), is now challenging some aspects of the 2009 Civil Societies Law and decisions of the agency administering the law at the African Commission on Human and Peoples' Rights. The Human Rights Council contested the legality of the decisions of the agency before the regular courts. Nevertheless, it did not challenge the constitutionality of the law and decisions of the agency at the Council.[121] This reluctance to refer cases to the Council reflects the lack of trust in the constitutional adjudication system.

5. Understanding the Establishment of a Politicized Constitutional Review System

The establishment of a weak and politicized constitutional review system in Ethiopia is compatible with contemporary theories on the origins of judicial empowerment. Judicial empowerment has the effect of allowing judges, often deliberately insulated from direct political control, to constrain the powers and legal and policy choices of politicians who often dominate constitutional reform processes. Judicial empowerment seems to run against the interests of rational political power holders. It is, therefore, counter-intuitive that politicians willingly establish independent constitutional review mechanisms with the attendant effect of constraining their powers.

Conventional theories attribute the growing empowerment of courts to two main factors: federalism and the constitutionalization of fundamental rights. Auer argues that: '[f]ederalism was first in bringing the constitution to the courts, long before civil

following established procedures is considered valid regardless of its consequences or implications. Rule *of* law, on the other hand, represents a case where a government rules based on laws that comply with constitutional or other higher law standards. 'Although no canonical formula exists for the rule of law, a moral ideal lies at the core.' The rule of law requires that laws comply with certain substantive requirements in addition to the procedural requirements of making laws; see generally Brian Z Tamanaha, *On the Rule of Law: History, Politics and Theory* (Cambridge University Press 2004); Kenneth Winston, 'The Internal Morality of Chinese Legalism' (2005) 2 *Singapore Journal of Legal Studies* 313; Adriaan Bedner, 'An Elementary Approach to the Rule of Law' (2010) 2 *Hague Journal on the Rule of Law* 48.

120 'Peaceful Political Rallies: A Right Besieged by Hurdles', *The Ethiopian Reporter* (Addis Ababa, 31 January 2015) http://archiveenglish.thereporterethiopia.com/content/peaceful-political-rallies-right-besieged-hurdles (last accessed 15 April 2017).

121 This failure to challenge the constitutionality of the law and the decision of the agency in the Council and the House may raise questions regarding the exhaustion of available local remedies, which is a precondition before cases may be submitted to the African Commission on Human and Peoples' Rights and other international human rights tribunals. Indeed, in May 2016, the African Commission ruled that the case was inadmissible for failure to approach the Council of Constitutional Inquiry. See *Human Rights Council and Others v Ethiopia*, Communication No 445/13, African Commission on Human and Peoples' Rights (19 May 2016).

rights and liberties did the same'.[122] Shapiro, similarly, observes that successful constitutional review is, among others, caused by and a requisite to genuine federalism.[123] The logic is that, since federalism necessarily creates different levels of governments, each with its own legislative and executive mandates, conflict over jurisdiction is inevitable. A neutral constitutional arbiter is conceived to ensure the peaceful resolution of such disputes as they arise.

Since constitutional review has become popular not only in federal states, but also in unitary states, the division of power hypothesis does not provide a comprehensive explanation to the phenomenon of judicial empowerment. Many political scientists link the proliferation of constitutional review in recent years to the post-1945 rights awareness and to the popularity of limits on the exercise of political power.[124] The ideological commitment to human rights partly explains why countries have in modern times established constitutional review. The rights hypothesis is said to have motivated the establishment of constitutional review by several African and East European states after the fall of the Berlin Wall.[125] Constitutional review is, therefore, associated with the entrenchment of human rights and democratic values.

The Ethiopian constitution establishes a federal system of government, with a guaranteed right to secession, and enshrines internationally recognized rights.[126] According to the above hypotheses, therefore, the combination of the two features should have led to the establishment of a strong judiciary with robust constitutional review powers. Nevertheless, as indicated above, Ethiopian courts lack the power to even review the constitutionality of decisions of low level administrative agencies, let alone those of the highest political organs. The establishment of a weak and politicized constitutional review system may best be explained through the perspective of the 'insurance' theory of judicial empowerment.[127]

[122] Andreas Auer, 'The Constitutional Scheme of Federalism' (2005) 12 *Journal of European Public Policy* 419, 427.

[123] Martin Shapiro, 'The Success of Judicial Review and Democracy' in Martin Shapiro and Alec Stone Sweet, *On Law, Politics and Judicialization* (Oxford University Press 2002) 149.

[124] See Shapiro (n 123) 153.

[125] Tom Ginsburg, 'The Global Spread of Constitutional Review' in Gregory A Caldeira, R Daniel Kelemen, and Keith E Whittington (eds), *The Oxford Handbook of Law and Politics* (Oxford University Press 2008) 90.

[126] For a discussion of the Ethiopian bill of rights see Adem Abebe, 'Human Rights under the Ethiopian Constitution: A Descriptive Overview' (2011) 5 *Mizan Law Review* 41.

[127] In addition to the three theories, some theorists have linked the decision to establish judicial review in some countries to transnational legal influence and diffusion, such as when a state establishes a constitutional review system similar to its colonial master; Zachary Elkins and Beth Simmons, 'On Waves, Clusters and Diffusion? A Conceptual Framework' (2005) 598 *Annals of American Academy of Political Science* 33. This theory underrates the relevance of domestic political, cultural, and economic forces in shaping the recognition and institutional design of constitutional review and other institutional features. In the Ethiopian context, diffusion seems to have mainly influenced the substantive parts of the constitution, such as the bill of rights, which shows significant resemblance to and makes reference to the UDHR (s 13). When it comes to institutions, ideology, rather than foreign influence, appears to have triggered institutional innovation. On top of this, Ethiopia does not have a strong colonial or similar connection to any of the dominant systems. To the extent that diffusion was relevant, the attitude of the drafters towards judicialization of politics in the United States, which bred fears of potential judicial adventurism, justified the relegation of the judiciary; see Assefa (n 49) 161. In some countries, the desire to attract foreign direct investment has been identified as the main driving factor for the recognition of constitutional review. See eg Tamir Moustafa, 'Law and Resistance in Authoritarian States: The Judicialisation of Politics in Egypt' in Tom Ginsburg and Tamir Moustafa (eds), *Rule by Law: The Politics of Courts in Authoritarian Regimes* (Cambridge University Press 2008) 151. See also Tamir Moustafa, *The Struggle for Constitutional Power: Law, Politics, and Economic Development in Egypt* (Cambridge University Press 2007). Attracting foreign investment has not induced the establishment of a strong constitutional review system in Ethiopia, perhaps for two main reasons. First, stability and political dominance seemed to be the main goals at the time of adoption of the constitution. Once the country started to open up for international business, the constitutional review system did not seem to discourage international aid or foreign direct investment. In any

Unlike the federalism and rights hypotheses, the insurance theory focuses on the motivations of the dominant political forces at the time of constitution making in establishing a weak or strong judicial review mechanism. According to this theory, institutions matter and institutional choices are, therefore, not accidental. Rather, institutional choices reflect the desires and interests of the elites who design them. The insurance ('party-alternation') theory posits that constitutional review is established as a response to the problem of political uncertainty at the time of constitution-making.[128] Ginsberg observes that: '[p]arties that believe they will be out of power in the future are likely to prefer constitutional review by an independent court, because the court provides an alternative forum for challenging government action'.[129]

This theory holds that if political groups under whose auspices a constitution is being drafted are uncertain that they will continue to control power after the adoption of the constitution (a situation of electoral uncertainty), they are likely to prefer constitutional review by an independent court. Constitutional review is seen as an instrument to ameliorate the effects of potential electoral loss after the adoption of constitutional democracy. On the other hand, a dominant political group controlling the constitutional drafting process, which is confident that it will be able to govern for an extended period after the adoption of the constitution, has little motivation to establish a strong and independent constitutional review system.[130]

The insurance theory best explains the establishment of a weak constitutional review system in Ethiopia. The drafting process of the Ethiopian constitution was totally dominated by the EPRDF, a cohesive coalition of ethnic-based political parties, with very little influence by and input from competing groups.[131] There was no fear or expectation that the EPRDF would lose power after the adoption of the constitution.[132] The commitment of the EPRDF towards the rights of ethnic groups explains the empowerment of the House to exercise constitutional review. However, there was no desire to establish strong institutional constraints on the powers of the government. Consequently, the constitutional review system was designed to be part of and to work in harmony with the governing political elite, rather than as a veto point outside of the political process. Given the continued dominance of the EPRDF, there has not been, and is unlikely to be, any official talk of reforming the constitutional review system. Some opposition political parties have, nevertheless, included reform of the constitutional review system as part of their political agenda. For instance, the programme of Unity for Democracy and Justice, one of the main

case, multinational companies increasingly rely on investment agreements, which often provide for mandatory international arbitration to resolve disputes, rather than domestic judicial institutions to guarantee their rights, thereby reducing the motivation for encouraging domestic judicial reform processes.

128 See generally Tom Ginsburg, *Judicial Review in New Democracies: Constitutional Courts in Asian Cases* (Cambridge University Press 2003); Jodi S Finkel, *Judicial Reform as Political Insurance: Argentina, Peru, and Mexico in the 1990s* (University of Notre Dame Press 2008). Finkel and Ginsburg observe that political groups in transition to democracy in Latin American and Asian countries established constitutional review as political insurance against the risk of losing elections.

129 See Ginsburg (n 125) 90.

130 Mary Volcansek, 'Bargaining Constitutional Design in Italy: Judicial Review as Political Insurance' (2010) 23 *West European Politics* 280, 282.

131 See notes 12 and 13 and accompanying text.

132 This confidence in continued dominance has been vindicated. A combination of systematic narrowing of political space, cooptation, repressive laws, and the fragmentation and weakness of opposition parties has enabled the EPRDF to win every election organized since the adoption of the constitution. In fact, in the latest May 2015 elections, the EPRDF and its affiliates won every seat in the House of Peoples' Representatives.

opposition political parties, clearly provides that the 'power to interpret the constitution shall be vested in the courts'.[133]

6. Conclusion

As may be garnered from the experiences of many countries, constitutional review can play a significant role in advancing the realization of human rights. Socio-economic rights litigation in India[134] and litigation relating to sexual minorities in South Africa[135] provide evidence of the potential role of constitutional review in ensuring the realization of rights and the transformation of law and society. The existence of a reasonably expansive panoply of constitutional rights in Ethiopia provides the basic normative foundation for constitutional rights litigation as a desired critical standard against which any government action or inaction—whether legislative, executive, or judicial—may be tested.

Nevertheless, however robust and ideal the principles and standards are which a constitution embodies, including constraints on the democratic majority, they will be nonsensical unless there are independent courts and effective institutional arrangements to ensure that the constraints actually shape the behaviour of constitutionally bound actors, and that any violations are addressed and reversed. Unless given proper meaning and enforced through a 'puissant judiciary', constitutional rights will remain 'printed futility'.[136] Constitutional review mechanisms, while never sufficient, are necessary and crucial to ensure that limits on the exercise of government power are given effect to.[137]

In conferring the power of interpreting the constitution on the second house of parliament, the 1995 Constitution of Ethiopia has established a unique constitutional review system. As a consequence, challenges to the constitutionality of laws adopted by the ruling party in the House of Peoples' Representatives are to be reviewed by the House dominated by the same party. In fact, given the fact that the members of the House of Federation are appointed by the dominant party in regional legislative councils, and the lack of any rules requiring the proportional representation of all parties represented in the regional councils, the possibility that the House of Federation may be dominated exclusively by a single party is very high. In fact, even at times when opposition parties occupied a few seats in the House of Peoples' Representatives, the House of Federation was composed exclusively of members of the ruling party or its affiliates. The existence of the Council does not ameliorate the problem, as its members, other than the two judges of the Supreme Court, have been selected mainly from members or sympathizers of the ruling party or its affiliates.

133 The programme of Unity for Democracy and Justice (UDJ) party, para 3.3.3. (Hard copy on file with the author).

134 Prafullachandra Bhagwati, 'Judicial Activism and Public Interest Litigation' (1984–1985) 23 *Columbian Journal of Transnational Law* 561; Konakuppakatil Gopinathan Balakrishnan, 'Growth of Public Interest Litigation in India' (2008) (Address at the Singapore Academy of Law, Fifteenth Annual Lecture) http://journalsonline.academypublishing.org.sg/Journals/Singapore-Academy-of-Law-Journal/e-Archive/ctl/eFirstSALPDFJournalView/mid/495/ArticleId/623/Citation/JournalsOnlinePDF (last accessed 15 April 2017).

135 Iain Currie and Johan de Waal, *The Bill of Rights Handbook* (Juta 2005) 25; Stu Woolman and others (eds), *Constitutional Law of South Africa* (Juta 2007) 35–64—35–69.

136 V R Krishna Iyer, *Justice at the Crossroads* (Deep and Deep Publications 1992) 59.

137 Issachnaroff identifies two major justifications for the idea of constitutionalism and constitutional review: to protect individual and minority rights including against majoritarian will, and to ensure that: 'majorities can change, that the rules of the [democratic] game remain fair, and that those elected remain accountable to the electorate'; Samuel Issachnaroff, 'Constitutionalizing Democracy in Fractured Societies' (2003/2004) 82 *Texas Law Review* 1861, 1862–3.

Because of the political nature of the constitutional review system, the total number of constitutional cases submitted to the Council, while increasing steadily, has been insignificant. According to the Secretariat,[138] the Council received more than 852 cases in five years. Of these, the Council found the need for constitutional interpretation in only one case, the first such case in more than a decade. As a result, the impact of the constitutional review system on constitutionalism in Ethiopia has at best been minimal. Despite the adoption of a number of controversial laws that potentially contravene the constitution, none of these laws has so far been challenged as unconstitutional. Opposition parties and other usual litigators, such as civil society organizations (CSOs), raise the unconstitutionality of these laws in political, academic, and other forums. CSOs, human rights advocates, and opposition political parties will only rely on constitutional review when there is at least a slight possibility that the constitutional adjudicator may uphold their claim.[139]

The Ethiopian experience demonstrates the symbiotic relationship between constitutional adjudicators and litigation support structures. Active adjudicators attract cases, while politicized adjudicators drive litigators away. While the existence of an independent constitutional adjudicator cannot guarantee an effective constitutional review system, the absence of a formally independent adjudicator undermines the value of a constitutional review system.

More than two decades after the entry into force of the Ethiopian constitution, there have been very few 'successful' constitutional cases. The Council and the House have been reluctant to invalidate laws and executive decisions on constitutional grounds. In fact, the total number of constitutional cases submitted to the Council and House has been negligible. Almost all matters of constitutional significance are discussed only in political and academic fora. The Council and the House have not had the chance finally and authoritatively to settle some of the most pertinent questions of constitutional law. In particular, constitutional review on human rights grounds remains a rather nominal feature of the system. Regular courts have also been timid in invoking the constitution, despite dealing with cases that had a direct bearing on the constitution. Overall, constitutional adjudication in Ethiopia has been more notional than real. It has had no or very little impact on the legal, political, social, and economic evolution of the nation.

It should be emphasized that the chapter does not argue that the constitution has not had an impact on political life. Although it is difficult to gauge, the constitution does matter. Despite criticism that the constitution is not worth the paper it is written on, constitutional provisions have provided justification for different public measures. The government regularly rejects allegations of violations of constitutional requirements. The government also uses the constitution to coordinate the activities of political elites. Moreover, there have been occasions where the government revised draft laws after considering public views, including the comments of CSOs. There are, therefore, internal and external incentives and constrains on the activities of the ruling party and the legislature to comply with the constitution.

[138] See Solomon Goshu, 'Questions Concerning Constitutional Interpretation', *The Ethiopian Reporter* (Amharic Version) (Addis Ababa, 23 August 2015) (hard copy on file wih the author).

[139] It should, however, be noted that strategic litigation may be pursued even when the prospect of success is low. Even losing cases can have significant positive implications to social movements; Douglas NeJaime, 'Winning through Losing' (2010–2011) 96 *Iowa Law Review* 941. In the context of Israel, Dotan and Hofnung observe that political parties and individual politicians resort to constitutional litigation, even when the chances of winning are marginal, to gain considerable media exposure (publicity); Yoav Dotan and Menachem Hofnung, 'Legal Defeats—Political Wins: Why Do Elected Representatives Go to Court?' (2005) 38 *Comparative Political Studies* 75.

The main argument of the chapter is, rather, that the constitutional review system, or threat of resort to the system, has not had any impact on constitutionalism. Constitutional review has failed to ensure the realization of human rights and constitutionalism because of the institutional design deficit and, consequently, the reluctance of CSOs, opposition groups, and human rights advocates relentlessly to challenge the constitutionality of laws and executive decisions. The absence of an independent constitutional review system has made litigation a futile endeavour.

Bibliography

Abebe A, 'Human Rights under the Ethiopian Constitution: A Descriptive Overview' (2011) 5 *Mizan Law Review* 41

Abebe A, 'Limiting Limitations of Human Rights under the Ethiopian Constitution' (2011) 4 *Ethiopian Constitutional Law Series* 60

Abebe A, 'Rule *by* Law in Ethiopia: Rendering Constitutional Limits on Government Power Nonsensical' (April 2012) *CGHR Working Paper 1*, Cambridge: University of Cambridge Centre of Governance and Human Rights

Abebe A, 'A constitution without a guardian: Is the Ethiopian Constitution really supreme?' (2013) 5 *Ethiopian Human Rights Law Series* 9

Assefa G, 'All about Words: Discovering the Intention of the Makers of the Ethiopian Constitution on the Scope and Meaning of Constitutional Interpretation' (2010) 24 *Journal of Ethiopian Law* 139

Auer A, 'The Constitutional Scheme of Federalism' (2005) 12 *Journal of European Public Policy* 419

Balakrishnan J, 'Growth of Public Interest Litigation in India' (2008) (Address at the Singapore Academy of Law, Fifteenth Annual Lecture) http://journalsonline.academypublishing.org.sg/Journals/Singapore-Academy-of-Law-Journal/e-Archive/ctl/eFirstSALPDFJournalView/mid/495/ArticleId/623/Citation/JournalsOnlinePDF (last accessed 15 April 2017)

Bedner A, 'An Elementary Approach to the Rule of Law' (2010) 2 *Hague Journal on the Rule of Law* 48

Belai E, 'Disabling a Political Rival in the Name of Fighting Corruption in Ethiopia: The Case of Prime Minster vs Ex-defence Minister Seeye Abraha' (August 2004) http://www.aigaforum.com/TheCaseofSiye.pdf (last accessed 15 April 2017)

Besselink L, 'The Protection of Human Rights in Federal Systems: The Case of Ethiopia' in B Yimam and others (eds), *Proceedings of the 14th International Conference of Ethiopian Studies* vol 3 (Institute of Ethiopian Studies 2002) 1372

Bhagwati P, 'Judicial Activism and Public Interest Litigation' (1984–1985) 23 *Columbian Journal of Transnational Law* 561

Bulto T, 'Judicial Referral of Constitutional Disputes in Ethiopia: From Practice to Theory' (2011) 19 *African Journal of International and Comparative Law* 99

Currie I, 'Judicious Avoidance' (1999) 15 *South African Journal on Human Rights* 138

Currie I and De Waal J, *The Bill of Rights Handbook* (Juta 2005)

Donovan D, 'Levelling the Playing Field: The Judicial Duty to Protect and Enforce the Constitutional Rights of Accused Persons Unrepresented by Counsel' (2002) 1 *Ethiopian Law Review* 31

Dotan Y and Hofnung M, 'Legal Defeats—Political Wins: Why Do Elected Representatives Go to Court?' (2005) 38 *Comparative Political Studies* 75

Elkins Z and Simmons B, 'On Waves, Clusters and Diffusion? A Conceptual Framework' (2005) 598 *Annals of American Academy of Political Science* 33

Ferejohn J, Rosenbluth F, and Shipan C, 'Comparative Judicial Politics' (October 2004), observing that: 'court actions overturning the government can serve as a useful measure of judicial independence' 19 http://leitner.yale.edu/sites/default/files/files/resources/docs/comparativejudicialpolitics.pdf (last accessed 15 April 2017)

Finkel J, *Judicial Reform as Political Insurance: Argentina, Peru, and Mexico in the 1990s* (University of Notre Dame Press 2008)

Fiseha A, 'Constitutional Interpretation: The Respective Role of the Courts and the House of Federation' in A Fiseha and T Regassa (eds), *Courts and the Constitution: Proceedings of the Symposium on the Role of Courts in the Enforcement of the Constitution, June 2000* 32(3) (Institute of Development Studies 2001) 6

Fiseha A, 'Federalism and the Adjudication of Constitutional Issues: The Ethiopian Experience' (2005) 52(1) *Netherlands International Law Review* 1

Fiseha A, 'Some Reflections on the Role of the Judiciary in Ethiopia' (2011) 14 *Recht in Afrika* 1

Friedman B, 'The Birth of an Academic Obsession: The History of the Counter-majoritarian Difficulty, Part Five' (2002) 112 *Yale Law Journal* 153

Ginsburg T, *Judicial Review in New Democracies: Constitutional Courts in Asian Cases* (Cambridge University Press 2003)

Ginsburg T, 'The Global Spread of Constitutional Review' in K Whittington and others (eds), *Law and Politics* (Oxford University Press 2008) 90

Goshu, S 'Questions Concerning Constitutional Interpretation' *The Ethiopian Reporter* (Amharic Version) (Addis Ababa, 23 August 2015) (Hard copy with the author)

Haile M, 'Comparing Human Rights in Two Ethiopian Constitutions: The Emperor's and the "Republic's"—*Cucullus Non Facit Monachum*' (2005) 13 *Cardozo Journal of International and Comparative Law* 1

Idris I, 'Constitutional Adjudication under the 1994 FDRE (Federal Democratic Republic of Ethiopia) Constitution' (2002) 1 *Ethiopian Law Review* 62

Issachnaroff S, 'Constitutionalizing Democracy in Fractured Societies' (2003/2004) 82 *Texas Law Review* 1861

Iyer V, *Justice at the Crossroads* (Deep and Deep Publications 1992)

Moustafa T, *The Struggle for Constitutional Power: Law, Politics, and Economic Development in Egypt* (Cambridge University Press 2007)

Moustafa T, 'Law and Resistance in Authoritarian States: The Judicialization of Politics in Egypt' in T Ginsburg and T Moustafa (eds), *Rule by Law: The Politics of Courts in Authoritarian Regimes* (Cambridge University Press 2008)

Mulatu A, 'Who is 'the Interested Party' to Initiate a Challenge to the Constitutionality of Laws in Ethiopia (Under the 1994 FDRE Constitution)' (1999) *The Law Student Bulletin* 2

Nahom F, *A Constitution for a Nation of Nations* (Red Sea Press 1997)

NeJaime D, 'Winning through Losing' (2010–2011) 96 *Iowa Law Review* 941

Pasquino P, 'The New Constitutional Adjudication in France: The Reform of the Referral to the French Constitutional Council in Light of the Italian Model' 18 https://www.pravo.unizg.hr/_download/repository/Pasquino_New-Constitutional-adjudication-France.pdf (last accessed 18 April 2017)

Paul J, 'Ethnicity and the New Constitutional Orders of Ethiopia and Eritrea' in Y Ghai (ed), *Autonomy and Ethnicity: Negotiating Competing Claims in Multi-ethnic States* (Cambridge University Press 2000) 189

'Peaceful Political Rallies: A Right Besieged by Hurdles' *The Ethiopian Reporter* (Addis Ababa, 31 January 2015) http://archiveenglish.thereporterethiopia.com/content/peaceful-political-rallies-right-besieged-hurdles (last accessed 15 April 2017)

Programme of Unity for Democracy and Justice (UDJ) Party, para 3.3.3 (Hard copy with the author)

Regassa T, 'Courts and the Human Rights Norms in Ethiopia' in A Fiseha and T Regassa (eds), *Courts and the Constitution: Proceedings of the Symposium on the Role of Courts in the Enforcement of the Constitution, June 2000* (2001) 116

Regassa T, 'Making Legal Sense of Human Rights: The Judicial Role in Protecting Human Rights in Ethiopia' (2009) 3 *Mizan Law Review* 287

Shapiro M, 'The Success of Judicial Review and Democracy' in M Shapiro and A Stone Sweet, *On Law, Politics and Judicialization* (Oxford University Press 2002)

Tadesse, F 'One Case, Contrary Decisions' *Addis Fortune* (Addis Ababa 5 January 2015) http://addisfortune.net/articles/one-case-contrary-decisions/ (last accessed 18 October 2017)

Tadesse M, *Ye'Ethiopia Hig'ena Fitih Getsitawoch (Features of Law and Justice in Ethiopia)* (2006)

Tamanaha B, *On the Rule of Law: History, Politics and Theory* (Cambridge University Press 2004)

Vestal T, 'An Analysis of the New Constitution of Ethiopia and the Process of Adoption' (1996) 3 *Northeast African Studies* 21
Volcansek M, 'Bargaining Constitutional Design in Italy: Judicial Review as Political Insurance' (2010) 23 *West European Politics* 280
Winston K, 'The Internal Morality of Chinese Legalism' (2005) 2 *Singapore Journal of Legal Studies* 313
Woolman S and Bishop M (eds), *Constitutional Law of South Africa* (Juta 2007)
Young J, 'Regionalism and Democracy in Ethiopia' (1998) 19 *Third World Quarterly* 191

PART 3

THE IMPACT OF TRANSJUDICIALISM ON CONSTITUTIONAL ADJUDICATION

9

The Effects of International Law Norms on Constitutional Adjudication in Africa

Magnus Killander

1. Introduction

Since the first written constitutions emerged in the late eighteenth century, states have borrowed from each other in designing their constitutions. In Africa, the colonial heritage is still evident in constitutional design. African states have also borrowed liberally from each other (and from outside the continent) when revising their constitutions, something that occurs quite regularly in most African states. Nowadays, constitutional design is an industry with consultants travelling the globe and international organizations, such as the United Nations (UN) and the African Union (AU), involved in constitutional design processes, particularly in post-conflict societies.[1]

Many ideas in constitutional design have their origin in both international and foreign national laws. Some international law principles may have their origin in foreign national laws, just as some principles found in many constitutions may originally have emerged from international law. The direct influence of international law on constitutional design is most clearly evident in the area of human rights, although here foreign national laws also play a role.

This chapter deals with how international law has impacted on African constitutional law and constitutional adjudication in Africa.[2] The focus is on human rights protection, the main issue in constitutional adjudication. How has international human rights law, in theory and in practice, found its way into national constitutional human rights protection?

The chapter is divided into five parts. The first section deals with the way in which international law has influenced the text of national constitutions, and the type of international law that has particularly influenced national constitutional law in Africa. Attention is particularly focused on the influence of international human rights law, whether directly or

[1] United Nations, 'Constitution-making' https://www.un.org/ruleoflaw/thematic-areas/governance/constitution-making/ (last accessed 17 April 2017); Mugambi Laibuta, 'The African Union and Kenya's Constitution-building Process' (International IDEA 2014). See also Zaid Al-Ali, 'Constitutional Drafting and External Influence' in Tom Ginsburg and Rosalind Dixon (eds), *Comparative Constitutional Law* (Edward Elgar Publishing 2011) 77.

[2] For other aspects of internationalization of constitutional law see Charles M Fombad, 'Internationalization of Constitutional Law and Constitutionalism in Africa' (2012) 60 *American Journal of Comparative Law* 439. The focus in this chapter is on treaty law. A few states include specific references to customary international law in their constitutions (Angola art 13(1); Cape Verde art 11(1); Malawi s 211(3); Zimbabwe s 326). For constitutional provisions in this article see www.constituteproject.org (last accessed 17 April 2017). I have discussed some of the issues raised in this chapter in other works; see eg Magnus Killander, 'The Role of International Law in Human Rights Litigation in Africa' in Emmanuel K Quansah and William Binchy (eds), *The Judicial Protection of Human Rights in Botswana* (Clarus Press 2009); Magnus Killander and Horace Adjolohoun, 'International Law and Domestic Human Rights Litigation in Africa: An Introduction' in Magnus Killander (ed), *International Law and Domestic Human Rights Litigation in Africa* (Pretoria University Law Press 2010); Magnus Killander, 'How International Human Rights Law Influences Domestic Law in Africa' (2013) 17 *Law, Democracy and Development* 378.

through comparative international law. The third section deals with constitutional adjudication. This section first discusses how international law is incorporated into national law, before turning to the influence of international law on constitutional adjudication in practice. The fourth section deals with one of the critiques of the internationalization of constitutional adjudication, namely, the assertion that international law lacks democratic legitimacy. The final section contains concluding remarks.

2. International Law in African Constitutions

2.1 Influence of international law on African constitutions

The external influence on constitutional design in Africa has a long history. The Bond of 1844 between the British and the chiefs in what today is Ghana included a requirement that the chiefs should ensure 'protection of individuals and property' and abolish 'barbarous' customs in exchange for the British respecting the authority of the traditional authorities.[3] The 1847 constitution of Liberia was, as could be expected of a constitution drafted by freed American slaves and their descendants, inspired by the constitution of the United States.[4] The 1931 constitution of Ethiopia, the first modern constitution of the country, was based on the Japanese Meiji constitution.[5]

These are clear examples of the influence of foreign law on constitutional design. Before the second half of the twentieth century, one could not talk of the influence of international law. International law had no influence on how a state regulated its own affairs. This changed after the Second World War, in particular through the emergence of international human rights law.[6] The former colonial powers significantly influenced the independence constitutions of African states. This included the adoption in whole or in part of their governance structures, whether the British Westminster model or the French Fifth Republic model. However, there was also some international law influence. Former French colonies included adherence to the Universal Declaration of Human Rights (UDHR) in the preamble to their constitutions. One of the main inspirations for the bills of rights of former British colonies was the European Convention on Human Rights (ECHR).[7]

The influence of international law continued as African states amended their constitutions or adopted new constitutions. No African state has retained its independence constitution without amendments. Most have adopted completely new constitutions. In the 2000s, new constitutions have been adopted in twenty-three of fifty-five African states.[8] Some of these constitutions have already been amended, while many older constitutions have been extensively amended over the years. Constitutions are usually adopted by referendum after having been drafted by a constitutional assembly, representative of

[3] Taslim Olawale Elias, *Ghana and Sierra Leone: The Development of Their Laws and Constitutions* (Stevens 1962) 17.

[4] www.onliberia.org/con_1847.htm (last accessed 17 April 2017).

[5] Joseph Calvitt Clarke III, 'Seeking a Model for Modernization: Ethiopia's Japanizers' fch.fiu.edu/FCH-2002/Clarke-Seeking%20a%20Model%20for%20Modernization-2002.htm (last accessed 17 April 2017).

[6] Some would view comparative foreign influence also as international; see *K v K and Others* (MAHGB-000291-14) [2015] BWHC 1 [178] (2 February 2015).

[7] Christof Heyns, 'African Human Rights Law and the European Convention' (1995) 11 *South African Journal on Human Rights* 252. See also Charles Parkinson, *Bills of Rights and Decolonization* (OUP 2007).

[8] Angola (2010); Burundi (2005); Central African Republic (2013); Comoros (2001); Democratic Republic of the Congo (DRC) (2005); Congo (2001); Côte d'Ivoire (2000); Egypt (2014); Guinea (2010); Kenya (2010); Libya (2011); Madagascar (2010); Morocco (2011); Mozambique (2004); Niger (2010); Rwanda (2003); Senegal (2001); Somalia (2012); South Sudan (2011); Sudan (2005); Swaziland (2005); Tunisia (2014); and Zimbabwe (2013).

various stakeholders in society. The drafting itself is usually done by a smaller group, often assisted by international advisers. However, national drafters have often had extensive international exposure through, for example, study abroad. Even where the constitutional drafters would have had all their education in their home country, they would have had exposure to international law, in particular international human rights law. Of course, this exposure also relates to comparative foreign law.

Should international law eventually mean the convergence of constitutions? Laibuta argues that: '[t]he AU should have a model constitutional text that member states can adapt to their own contexts. Minimum standard constitutional provisions would promote uniformity in constitutionalism and rule of law provisions among its members'.[9] The AU has adopted model laws with some success in some areas, such as access to information. However, many would argue that a constitution should be home-grown, even though it may borrow from different sources. Nonetheless, the AU and other international organizations, such as the UN, provide some guidance to states on constitutional design.

While not a 'model constitutional text', the African Charter on Democracy, Elections and Governance (African Democracy Charter) provides extensive guidance to states, even though it only calls for a revision of national law and regulations and not specifically of constitutions.[10] However, the African Democracy Charter does provide that: '[s]tates parties shall ensure that the process of amendment or revision of their constitution reposes on national consensus, obtained if need be, through referendum'.[11] As of April 2017, the African Democracy Charter had been ratified by twenty-four of the fifty-five AU member states. The regional human rights system also provides that a state must ensure, through constitutional or other means, that human rights violations are addressed to avoid being held accountable by regional bodies. The same follows from UN membership and the extensive ratification by African states of UN human rights treaties.

Explicit references to international law in African constitutions are relatively rare. Most references relate to the ratification of treaties and their applicability in national law and adherence to, or incorporation of, international human rights instruments, as is discussed below. A number of African constitutions provide that the state should act in accordance with the UN Charter.[12] Mention is sometimes also made of the AU[13] and other regional organizations or simply international organizations of which the state is a member.[14] A few constitutions provide that the state may join international organizations that may limit their sovereignty.[15]

Issues on which African constitutions make reference to international law include sovereignty;[16] respect for international treaties;[17] natural resources;[18] asylum;[19] property;[20] use of force;[21] boundaries;[22] diplomatic protection of citizens abroad;[23] elections;[24] foreign

[9] See Laibuta (n 1) 19.

[10] African Charter on Democracy, Elections and Governance art 44. However, see art 15(2) (independence of public institutions). See Fombad (n 2) for an extensive discussion of AU governance instruments and the internationalization of constitutional law.

[11] Article 10(2).

[12] Algeria art 28; Angola art 12; Burundi, preamble; Cameroon, preamble; Central African Republic, preamble; Comoros, preamble; Ghana art 40; Guinea preamble; Mozambique art 17; São Tomé and Principe art 12(2).

[13] Angola art 12; Comoros, preamble (also Pact of the League of Arab States); Ghana art 40 (also the Commonwealth, ECOWAS, and other international organizations of which it is a member); Guinea, preamble (also ECOWAS); Mozambique art 17; São Tomé and Principe art 12(2).

[14] Equatorial Guinea art 8.

[15] DRC art 217; Congo art 182; Côte d'Ivoire art 122; Madagascar art 137; Senegal art 96.

[16] Angola art 3(2).

[17] ibid art 11(1).

[18] ibid art 16.

[19] ibid art 71(1); Somalia art 37.

[20] Angola art 95(1).

[21] ibid arts 203 and 210; South Africa s 200; Swaziland s 191.

[22] Ethiopia art 2; Somalia art 7.

[23] Gabon art 1(9); Morocco art 16.

[24] Morocco art 11.

policy;[25] foreigners in public functions;[26] international criminal law;[27] protection of the child;[28] extradition;[29] dumping of waste;[30] national security;[31] and wildlife protection.[32] Other provisions are clearly inspired by international law, even though not explicitly making reference to it. For example, the constitutions of Congo-Brazzaville, Ethiopia, Malawi, Rwanda, and Senegal have provisions dealing with genocide or crimes against humanity. Article 143(4) of the Kenyan constitution is directly attributable to developments in international criminal law, in particular the Rome Statute of the International Criminal Court, to which Kenya is a party.

Article 143(4) of the Kenyan constitution provides: 'The immunity of the President under this article shall not extend to a crime for which the President may be prosecuted under any treaty to which Kenya is party and which prohibits such immunity'. This provision remains in place, even though there have been calls for its amendment, in line with the Kenyan government's opposition to the indictment of President Kenyatta before the International Criminal Court.[33] Kenya encouraged the inclusion of immunity in the Protocol set to provide the African Court of Justice and Human Rights with criminal jurisdiction over international crimes, including crimes against humanity.[34] This is an example of how international law can influence a constitutional provision which is later succeeded by events that cause the state to push for a revision of the international law in a particular area.

2.2 Influence of international law on constitutional provisions relating to human rights

The incorporation of human rights provisions in African constitutions has a long history. A bill of rights was included in the 1847 constitution of Liberia. A number of human rights provisions were included in Ethiopia's 1931 constitution, including freedom of movement and the prohibition of arbitrary arrest.[35] Human rights provisions were in one way or another included in all independence constitutions (except that of South Africa), ranging from a brief mention in the preamble, such as in the 1962 Tanzanian constitution, to the mention of some rights in the constitutions of Ghana (1957),[36] Niger (1960), and Mali (1961), to extensive bills of rights.[37]

[25] Ghana arts 40, 73; Nigeria s 19; Sierra Leone s 10; South Sudan art 43; Swaziland ss 61, 236; Zimbabwe s 12(1).

[26] Guinea-Bissau art 27(2).

[27] Rwanda art 20; Somalia art 13.

[28] Rwanda art 28.

[29] Somalia art 36.

[30] ibid art 45(3).

[31] South Africa s 198.

[32] South Sudan art 157(7).

[33] Laban Wanambisi, 'MP Wants Kenya's Leaders Shielded from Any Trials' *Capital News* (19 January 2015) http://www.capitalfm.co.ke/news/2015/01/mp-wants-kenyas-leaders-shielded-from-any-trials/ (last accessed 17 April 2017).

[34] Statute of the African Court of Justice and Human Rights, adopted by the AU Assembly (July 2014) art 46A*bis*.

[35] http://www.worldstatesmen.org/Ethiopia_1931.txt (last accessed 17 April 2017).

[36] See Elias (n 3) 51.

[37] Libya (1951); Guinea (1958); Somalia (1960); Rwanda (1962); Nigeria (1963); vMalawi (1964); Senegal (1963); and Uganda (1963). For the text of the constitutions mentioned in this paragraph see Amos J Peaslee *Constitutions of Nations—Volume 1 Africa* (3rd edn, Martinus Nijhoff 1965). For the text of the 1951 Libyan Constitution see http://www.libyanconstitutionalunion.net/constitution%20of%20libya.htm (last accessed 17 April 2017).

References to human rights instruments in the preamble[38] or elsewhere in the constitution[39] are included in many constitutions. These references are most often to the Universal Declaration of Human Rights (UDHR), but references to the African Charter on Human and Peoples' Rights (ACHPR) are relatively common. The constitution of Guinea even makes reference to the Protocol to the ACHPR on the Rights of Women in Africa (Maputo Protocol) and the Protocol on Democracy and Good Governance of the Economic Community of West African States (ECOWAS). The once common reference in former French colonies to the French Declaration of the Rights of Man and the Citizen has disappeared from many constitutions after the post-1990 wave of constitutional reforms on the continent.[40] The constitution of South Sudan is an exception in that, in addition to international human rights treaties, it makes repeated reference to the Millennium Development Goals (MDGs).[41] The limitation of references to instruments such as the MDGs is based on the fact that that they have a limited temporal scope. For example, the MDGs were goals set to be achieved by 2015 and have been replaced by the Sustainable Development Goals.

The inclusion of references to international human rights treaties in constitutions in most instances does not mean that these treaties form part of the constitution. Where this is the intention, it is explicitly done, as in the case of the Benin constitution.[42] In effect, the inclusion of a human rights treaty as constitutional text causes the state in question to have two bills of rights, as illustrated by the Constitutional Court of Benin, where violations of both the human rights set out in the constitutional text and the ACHPR are often found.[43] As long as there are no conflicting norms, this should not pose a problem.

More common than actual inclusion in the constitution is the influence of human rights treaties on the formulation of national bills of rights. This influence in Africa dates back to the influence of the ECHR on the bill of rights in the constitutions of states that gained independence from Britain. On the other hand, it was the UDHR that influenced the approach of states that gained independence from France and Belgium. International

[38] Burkina Faso (UDHR, ACHPR, and 'international instruments concerning economic, political, social and cultural problems'); Burundi (UDHR, 1966 covenants, ACHPR); Cameroon (UDHR, ACHPR, and 'all duly ratified international conventions relating thereto'); Central African Republic (UDHR, 1966 covenants, ACHPR, 'all the international conventions duly ratified, in particular those relative to the prohibition of any discrimination against women and those relative to the protection of children's rights'); Chad (UN Charter, UDHR, ACHPR); Comoros (UDHR, ACHPR, and the 'international conventions, particularly those relation to children's and women's rights'); DRC (CRC and CEDAW and 'international instruments concerning the protection and promotion of human rights'); Côte d'Ivoire (UDHR, ACHPR); Egypt (UDHR); Equatorial Guinea (UDHR); Gabon (UDHR, ACHPR); Guinea (UDHR, UN treaties, ACHPR, Maputo Protocol, ECOWAS Protocol on Democracy and Good Governance); Mali (UDHR, ACHPR); Mauritania (UDHR, ACHPR, and other ratified treaties); Niger (UDHR, 1966 covenants, ACHPR); Rwanda (UN Charter, Genocide Convention, UDHR, CERD, ICCPR, ICESCR, CEDAW, CRC, ACHPR); Senegal (international instruments adopted by the UN and AU, notably UDHR, CEDAW, CRC, ACHPR); Togo (UN Charter, UDHR, 1966 covenants, ACHPR).

[39] São Tomé and Principe art 12(2) (UDHR).

[40] It is still included in the preamble of the constitutions of Gabon and Senegal.

[41] Articles 37(1), 169(4), and 193(2).

[42] Benin preamble: 'Reaffirm our attachment to the principles of democracy and human rights as they have been defined by the Charter of the United Nations of 1945 and the Universal Declaration of Human Rights of 1948, by the African Charter on Human and Peoples' Rights adopted in 1981 by the Organization of African Unity and ratified by Benin on January 20, 1986 and whose provisions make up an integral part of this present Constitution and of Beninese law and have a value superior to the internal law'. The preamble of the Constitution of Cameroon includes the following affirmation: 'Affirm our attachment to the fundamental freedoms enshrined in the Universal Declaration of Human Rights, the Charter of United Nations and the African Charter on Human and Peoples' Rights'. Article 65 of the Constitution provides that: '[t]he Preamble shall be part and parcel of this Constitution'. However, arguably this provision does not incorporate the international instruments in the same way as the Benin provision.

[43] Armand Tanoh and Horace Adjolohoun, 'International Law and Human Rights Litigation in Côte d'Ivoire and Benin' in Killander (ed), *International Law and Domestic Human Rights Litigation in Africa* (n 2) 116.

human rights law has continued to influence constitution drafters.[44] When South Africa finally emerged as a democracy, international human rights law was one of the main inspirations for the drafters of the interim and final constitutions.[45] In fact, one of the constitutional principles included in the interim constitution to guide the drafting of the final constitution provided that: '[e]veryone shall enjoy all universally-accepted fundamental rights, freedoms and civil liberties'.[46] The influence of international law has apparently been indirect, with states borrowing provisions from other states in the process of constitution drafting.[47]

It appears that the influence of African regional human rights treaties is limited. For example, Heyns and Kaguongo note that only seven constitutions recognize the rights of 'peoples', despite the prominence given to these rights in the ACHPR.[48] At the time their study was conducted, Heyns and Kaguongo noted that five rights were recognized in all fifty-three (excluding Morocco) African constitutions: non-discrimination; freedom of opinion and expression; freedom of movement; and the rights to privacy and property.[49] It is worth noting that the right to privacy is not explicitly included in the ACHPR.

3. International Law in Constitutional Adjudication: Incorporation, Application, and Interpretation

3.1 International law in the national legal order

As noted above, only a few states give specific human rights treaties constitutional status, thus creating parallel bills of rights. However, these treaties play an important role in the national legal order in most other states. This section explores the different approaches of states to the relationship between international law and national law, with a particular focus on human rights treaties.

The executive negotiates and concludes bilateral and multilateral treaties. Many states provide in their constitutions that all treaties[50] or specific categories of treaties, such as those relating to human rights,[51] 'concerning the status of persons'[52] or 'involving international organizations',[53] must be ratified by parliament. Article 114 of the Gabonese constitution is typical of that of many African civil law states, and provides as follows:

> Peace treaties, commercial treaties, treaties relative to international organizations, treaties which engage the finances of the state, and treaties concerning the status of persons can only be approved and ratified by virtue of a law.

Clearly, human rights treaties fall within the scope of a provision such as this. A number of African constitutions explicitly incorporate specific international instruments as

[44] See eg with regard to Benin, Frédéric Joël Aivo, *Le juge constitutionnel et l'état de droit en Afrique—L'exemple du modèle beninois* (L'Harmattan 2006) 73–4.

[45] John Dugard, 'International Law and the South African Constitution' (1997) 1 *European Journal of International Law* 77, 84.

[46] Constitutional Principle II, Sch 4 of the interim constitution.

[47] For a discussion of constitutional human rights provisions and how they relate to human rights see Christof Heyns and Waruguru Kaguongo, 'Constitutional Human Rights Law in Africa' (2006) 22 *South African Journal on Human Rights* 673.

[48] ibid 678.

[49] ibid 683.

[50] Congo art 178; Eritrea art 32(4); The Gambia s 79(1); Ghana art 75; Libya art 17; Zimbabwe s 327.

[51] Central African Republic art 96; Morocco art 55.

[52] Algeria art 131.

[53] Angola art 161; Chad art 219; DRC art 214, Côte d'Ivoire art 85; Djibouti art 62; Gabon art 114; Guinea art 149; Madagascar art 137; Mauritania art 78; Niger art 169; Rwanda art 189; Senegal art 96; and Tunisia art 67.

part of the constitution,[54] or make treaties superior to national law but not to constitutional norms,[55] or incorporate such norms as ordinary law.[56] Most civil law constitutions include the requirement of publication in the national gazette before a ratified treaty is applicable in the national legal order.[57] Malawi incorporates treaties ratified before the commencement of the constitution, which include many of the major human rights treaties.[58]

Section 34 of the 2013 constitution of Zimbabwe is exceptional. It provides that: '[t]he state must ensure that all international conventions, treaties and agreements to which Zimbabwe is a party are incorporated into domestic law'. Zimbabwe remains a dualist state and, therefore, requires action to be taken to transform treaties into national law. The question remains whether Zimbabwean courts will interpret section 34 as an invitation to rely on international treaties even where the state has failed to incorporate these, as it is constitutionally obliged to do. In the *Mapingure* case, decided under the new constitution, the Supreme Court held that:[59]

> In strict constitutional terms, the prescriptions of [international law] instruments cannot operate to override or modify domestic law unless and until they are internalised and transformed into rules of domestic law ... Nevertheless, it is proper and necessary for national courts, as part of the judicial process, to have regard to the country's international obligations, whether or not they have been incorporated into domestic law. By the same token, it is perfectly proper in the construction of municipal statutes to take into account the prevailing international human rights jurisprudence.

Another aspect regarding the ratification of treaties, namely, how states should ensure that existing national legislation is in conformity with new treaty obligations, is rarely dealt with in constitutional law.[60]

The constitutions of many civil law countries contain a reciprocity provision stating that the application of the treaty is dependent on the reciprocal application of the treaty by the other party.[61] This requirement, clearly, cannot apply to multilateral treaties, particularly to human rights treaties. However, only the constitution of Burundi explicitly limits the application of the rule of reciprocity to bilateral treaties.[62] Article 42 of the constitution of the Republic of Congo is particularly problematic. It states:

[54] Benin art 7 (ACHPR); Burundi art 19 (UDHR, 1966 covenants, ACHPR, CEDAW, CRC); Congo (preamble, 'the fundamental principles' in the UN Charter, UDHR, ACHPR, ratified human rights treaties); Djibouti (UDHR, ACHPR); South Sudan art 9(3); Sudan art 27(3) (ratified human rights treaties); Togo (UDHR and ratified international instruments); Tanzania art 9 (UDHR).

[55] Cape Verde art 11(4); Central African Republic art 97; Côte d'Ivoire art 87; DRC art 215; Mauritania art 80; Niger art 171; Rwanda art 190 ('more binding than organic laws'); Senegal art 98; Tunisia art 20.

[56] Ethiopia art 9(4); Mozambique art 18; Namibia art 144.

[57] Angola art 13; Burkina Faso art 151; Central African Republic art 97; DRC art 215; Egypt art 93; Gabon art 114; Guinea art 150; Madagascar art 137; Mauritania art 80; Mozambique art 18; Niger art 171; Rwanda art 190; Senegal art 98.

[58] Article 211. See also, with regard to Uganda, Henry Onoria, 'Uganda' in Dinah Shelton (ed), *International Law and Domestic Legal Systems* (OUP 2011) 594.

[59] *Mildred Mapingure v Minister of Home Affairs and Others*, Civil Appeal 406/12, Judgment SC 22/14.

[60] However, see Malawi s 135(a): 'The Law Commission shall have the powers to review and make recommendations regarding any matter pertaining to the laws of Malawi and their conformity with this Constitution and applicable international law'.

[61] Burkina Faso art 151; Congo art 184; Guinea art 151; Madagascar art 137; Mauritania art 80; Rwanda art 190; Senegal art 98.

[62] Burundi art 292.

> Foreigners benefit, on the territory of the Republic of the Congo, from the same rights and freedoms as nationals within the conditions determined by the treaties and the laws, under reserve of reciprocity.

Such a provision could be used by the state as the basis for violating the rights of foreigners in retaliation for violations of its own nationals' rights abroad.

While some constitutions, as noted above, state where a treaty stands in the legal hierarchy of norms, other constitutions that incorporate treaties as law are quiet on this issue. Article 144 of the constitution of Namibia incorporates treaties, but what transpires is only a weak monism. According to the Namibian Supreme Court:[63]

> International agreements such as the Convention [on the Rights of the Child] appear to have similar force of law as accorded to legislation, in the absence of any constitutional provision or Act of Parliament contradicting the law or agreement in question.

Article 2(6) of the Kenyan constitution provides that: '[a]ny treaty or convention ratified by Kenya shall form part of the law of Kenya under this constitution'. This does not give any indication as to whether these norms should be seen as ordinary legislation or as higher norms that are only subject to the constitution. Kenyan courts have yet to settle this issue definitively.[64]

International treaties are sometimes incorporated *verbatim* into national law. Nigeria, for example, incorporated the ACHPR into national law. However, the role of the ACHPR in the national legal order is uncertain. For example, how can the non-justiciability of socio-economic rights under the Nigerian constitution be reconciled with the inclusion of socio-economic rights in the ACHPR?[65] How does the fact that the chief justice issued international law-friendly Fundamental Rights Enforcement Procedure Rules affect constitutional litigation based on international law sources?[66]

The issue of the non-justiciability of human rights norms, recognized by the state at the international level, also exists for states that have not incorporated treaties in the national legal order. The African Commission on Human and Peoples' Rights and the African Court on Human and Peoples' Rights could view non-justiciability as an exemption from the requirement of the exhaustion of local remedies. Similarly, in West Africa, the broad jurisdiction of the ECOWAS Community Court of Justice could potentially push constitutional reform to provide for broader human rights jurisdiction of national courts, similar to what has happened in many European states in relation to the ECHR.[67]

63 *Thudinyane v Edward* (SA 17/2005) [2012] NASC 22 [18] (12 October 2012).

64 See eg *Zipporah Wangui Mathara* [2010] eKLR (Civil Procedure Act declared unconstitutional to the extent inconsistent with the ICCPR); *Diamond Trust Bank v Daniel Mwema Mulwa* [2010] eKLR (ratified treaties at the same level as Acts of Parliament); *Beatrice Wanjiku and Another v Attorney-General and Others* [2012] eKLR ('adopt the interpretation that most favours the enforcement of a right' in the bill of rights even if this means disregarding the treaty provision).

65 Stanley Ibe, 'Implementing Economic, Social and Cultural Rights in Nigeria: Challenges and Opportunities' (2010) 10 *African Human Rights Law Journal* 197.

66 See Abiola Sanni, 'Fundamental Rights Enforcement Procedure Rules, 2009, as a Tool for the Enforcement of the African Charter on Human and Peoples' Rights in Nigeria: The Need for Far-reaching Reform' (2011) 11 *African Human Rights Law Journal* 511.

67 Cf Helen Keller and Alec Stone Sweet, 'Assessing the Impact of the ECHR on National Legal Systems' in Helen Keller and Alec Stone Sweet (eds), *A Europe of Rights* (OUP 2008) 686. However, the number of repetitive cases from some states to the European Court illustrates that this system also has far to go before functioning ideally; cf Parliamentary Assembly of the Council of Europe, Committee on Legal Affairs and Human Rights, 'The Effectiveness of the European Convention on Human Rights: the Brighton Declaration and beyond' Doc 13719 (2015)

Treaties and other international obligations may also be incorporated into legislation by reference, either by including substantively similar provisions as a treaty in national legislation or by citing a treaty or other international obligation in the preamble of legislation.[68]

3.1.1 Role of international law in constitutional adjudication

National legislation is to a large extent needed in both monist and dualist states to make international treaty norms effective.[69] The monist structure of most African civil law states is, in reality, more of a fiction than anything else.[70]

Where constitutional litigation is possible, the role that international law can play varies. International law tends to play a more important role in constitutional adjudication in Anglophone states in Africa than in civil law jurisdictions. The constitutions of Ghana and Uganda provide that the human rights provisions in the bill of rights are not exhaustive.[71] Such provisions could be used to incorporate rights not mentioned in the bill of rights, but which are recognized in international instruments.

Direct application of international law is rare and usually deals with treaties that have been incorporated into national legislation. For example, in April 2015 the Supreme Court of Uganda declared that the Amnesty Act was consistent with the Geneva Conventions Act as it did not provide for blanket amnesty for all crimes.[72]

Some constitutions provide that human rights in the bill of rights or legislation should be interpreted in accordance with human rights treaties or declarations.[73] South Africa and Malawi have provisions to the effect that courts must consider international law in interpreting the bill of rights. Section 35 in the draft constitution of Zambia provided that a body (such as the Human Rights Commission or a court) in interpreting the bill of rights 'may consider international law'. Considering that Zambian judges have generally dealt very conservatively with international law, it may be useful to have such a provision to point them to this body of law as a possible consideration. However, this provision was not included in the Constitution of Zambia Act 2016.

The South African constitution provides in section 233:

> When interpreting any legislation, every court must prefer any reasonable interpretation of the legislation that is consistent with international law over any alternative interpretation that is inconsistent with international law.[74]

[68] For examples of such legislation see Killander 'How International Human Rights Law Influences Domestic Law in Africa' (n 2) 388.

[69] ibid 378. See also Babacar Kante, 'Models of Constitutional Jurisdiction in Francophone West Africa' (2008) 3 *Journal of Comparative Law* 158.

[70] See Killander and Adjolohoun (n 2).

[71] Ghana art 33(5) ('the rights, duties, declarations and guarantees relating to the fundamental human rights and freedoms specifically mentioned in this chapter shall not be regarded as excluding others not specifically mentioned which are considered to be inherent in a democracy and intended to secure the freedom and dignity of man'); Uganda art 45 ('the rights, duties, declarations and guarantees relating to the fundamental and other human rights and freedoms specifically mentioned in this Chapter shall not be regarded as excluding others not specifically mentioned').

[72] *Uganda v Thomas Kwoyelo*, Supreme Court of Uganda, Constitutional Appeal No 1 of 2012, judgment of 8 April 2015, 65.

[73] Angola art 26(2); Cape Verde art 16(3) (UDHR); Ethiopia art 13 (UDHR and ratified international instruments); Mozambique art 43; Malawi s 11(2) ('where applicable have regard to current norms of public international law ...'); Somalia art 40(2) ('may consider ... international law'); South Africa s39 ('must consider international law'); Zimbabwe s 46(1).

[74] See also Zimbabwe ss 326(2) and 327(6). These provisions reflect a common law principle of statutory interpretation; see Fombad (n 2).

The Constitutional Court noted in the *Glenister* case that there is 'no escape from the manifest constitutional injunction to integrate, in a way the constitution permits, international law obligations into our domestic law'.[75] However, as noted by the same court in the *Florence* case, this duty arises only 'when international law is not irreconcilable with our own explicit law'.[76]

Interpretation in light of international law cannot mean only reliance on the treaty text. Such an approach would clearly not be of any significance as most bills of rights would already reflect these instruments. Article 48 of the constitution of the Seychelles goes much further, providing that:

> The court shall, when interpreting the provision of this chapter, take judicial notice of:
> (a) the international instruments containing these obligations;
> (b) the reports and expression of views of bodies administering or enforcing these instruments;
> (c) the reports, decisions or opinions of international and regional institutions administering or enforcing conventions on human rights and freedoms;
> (d) the Constitutions of other democratic states or nations and decisions of the courts of the states or nations in respect of their constitutions.

Arguably, it is not only courts in the Seychelles that can go beyond the treaty text for interpretive guidance. The interpretation of treaties must be considered with adequate consideration of interpretations by authoritative bodies. What the International Court of Justice said in *Diallo*, with reference to the interpretation of the International Covenant on Civil and Political Rights (ICCPR) by the UN Human Rights Committee and the ACHPR by the African Commission, should also apply to national courts:[77]

> Although the Court is in no way obliged, in the exercise of its judicial functions, to model its own interpretation of the Covenant on that of the Committee, it believes that it should ascribe great weight to the interpretation adopted by this independent body that was established specifically to supervise the application of that treaty. The point here is to achieve the necessary clarity and the essential consistency of international law, as well as legal security, to which both the individuals with guaranteed rights and the states obliged to comply with treaty obligations are entitled.

Some national courts in African common law jurisdictions have used authoritative views by international treaty bodies to interpret constitutional provisions. Thus, the South African Constitutional Court in the *Doctors for Life* case, referring to the UN Human Rights Committee's decision in *Marshall v Canada*, said:[78]

> The precise nature and scope of the international law right to participate in the conduct of public affairs is a matter for individual states to determine through their laws and policies. Under article 25 of the ICCPR, states are to establish powers and the means by which individual citizens exercise the right to participate in the conduct of public affairs protected by article 25 in national constitutions and other laws. As the Human Rights Committee has explained, 'it is for the legal and constitutional system of the state party to provide for the modalities of such participation'.

[75] *Glenister v President of the Republic of South Africa and Others* (CCT 48/10) [2011] ZACC 6 [202].

[76] *Florence v Government of the Republic of South Africa* (CCT 127/13) [2014] ZACC 22; 2014 (6) SA 456 (CC); 2014 (10) BCLR 1137 (CC) [144] (26 August 2014).

[77] *Ahmadou Sadio Diallo (Republic of Guinea v Democratic Republic of the Congo)*, (Merits, Judgment) [2010] ICJ Rep 639 [66] http://www.icj-cij.org/docket/index.php?p1=3&p2=3&case=103&p3=4.

[78] *Doctors for Life International v Speaker of the National Assembly and Others* (CCT12/05) [2006] ZACC 11; 2006 (12) BCLR 1399 (CC); 2006 (6) SA 416 (CC) [95] (17 August 2006).

Further, the court quoted General Comment 25 of the UN Human Rights Committee:[79]

> [W]hatever form of constitution or government is in force, the [ICCPR] requires states to adopt such legislative and other measures as may be necessary to ensure that citizens have an *effective* opportunity to enjoy the rights it protects.

In a recent Kenyan case, *Eric Gitari v Non-governmental Organisations Coordination Board and Attorney-General*, the High Court quoted extensively from the jurisprudence of the African Commission on Human and Peoples' Rights in relation to freedom of association and also cited the UN Declaration on Human Rights Defenders to find that the non-registration of an NGO that promoted the rights of lesbian, gay, bisexual, transsexual, and intersex (LGBTI) persons was unconstitutional.[80]

A court does not need to follow the approach of, for example, a UN treaty-monitoring body. In the *Catholic Commission* case, the Zimbabwe Supreme Court held that detention for a prolonged period on death row constituted inhuman or degrading treatment. Justice Gubbay, writing for the Court, referred to two decisions of the Human Rights Committee against Jamaica, where the Committee held that the death row phenomenon in itself did not constitute inhumane or degrading treatment. Justice Gubbay aligned himself with the minority member on the Committee who had found it a violation.[81] By contrast, the Botswana Court of Appeal referred to both the Zimbabwean case and the Human Rights Committee decisions and followed the approach of the majority of the Committee.[82]

The relevance of international law is recognized even in states with no provisions in their constitutions explicitly referring to international law. Thus, the Court of Appeal of Lesotho has noted that: '[w]here there is uncertainty as regards the terms of domestic legislation, a treaty becomes relevant, because there is a *prima facie* presumption that the legislature does not intend to act in breach of international law, including treaty obligations'.[83] In addition to provisions of the International Covenant on Civil and Political Rights (ICCPR), the Convention on the Elimination of All Forms of Discrimination Against Women (CEDAW) and the ACHPR, the court went on to cite a General Comment of the UN Human Rights Committee and the Southern African Development Community (SADC) Declaration on Gender and Development in discussing affirmative action.

There are cases from other Anglophone jurisdictions, such as Malawi[84] and Namibia,[85] which cite recommendations and views of treaty-monitoring bodies as interpretive guidance. There are many other types of soft law, such as resolutions by international organizations, which can be used by national courts in their interpretation of the constitution and national legislation.

Cases such as those cited above remain an exception. When courts make reference to international law, it is mostly only to treaty texts, which often read the same as constitutional provisions. Courts rarely engage with the question of what constitutes relevant authority. The most important issue, however, is that the outcome of a case reflects a state's international obligations. In this respect, the use of strong authority arguably makes a judgment more persuasive.

[79] ibid [131] (original emphasis by the Constitutional Court).

[80] Petition 440 of 2013, High Court of Kenya at Nairobi, judgment of 24 April 2015.

[81] *Catholic Commission for Justice and Peace in Zimbabwe v Attorney-General and Others* (2001) AHRLR 248 (ZwSC 1993) [88]–[90].

[82] *Kobedi v The State* (Criminal Appeal No 25 of 2001) [2003] BWCA 22 (19 March 2003).

[83] *Molefi v Independent Electronical Commission and Others* (11/05 CC:135/05) [16].

[84] *Okeke v Minister of Home Affairs and Another* (Civil Cause No 73 of 1997).

[85] *Alexander v Minister of Justice and Others* (SA 32/2008) [2010] NASC 2 (9 April 2010).

In the absence of a specific constitutional mandate to consider international law, informed counsel, making use of international law arguments, is probably the main incentive for a court to invoke international law in its reasoning.[86] National judges may also feel pressure to consider international law because of alternative courts that apply international law, such as the ECOWAS Community Court of Justice in West Africa and the East African Court of Justice.[87] The 2013 constitution of Zimbabwe provides that members of the judiciary 'must keep themselves abreast of developments in domestic and international law'.[88] Such a provision, it may be argued, mandates judges to consider international law in cases before them.

The discussion in this section has dealt with African common law jurisdictions. Civil law constitutional jurisprudence in Africa, in general, cites only the legal provision applied, be it the constitution, national legislation, or a treaty.[89] Whether in common law or civil law states, the fact that something is not cited does not mean that it has not been considered. However, the extent of the influence of material that has not been cited would require empirical investigation, which is beyond the scope of this chapter.

4. Democratic Legitimacy and Effectiveness of International (Human Rights) Law

Few courts in Africa would accept the argument put forward by the presiding officer of the Customary Court of Appeal before the High Court of Botswana that: '[m]uch as one might appreciate the fact that international law is against any form of discrimination, it is not always the case that such a position will be adopted by every state that has ratified the treaty or convention embodying such'.[90] As noted above, non-discrimination is enshrined in all national bills of rights in Africa.[91] The role of international law here is the same as the role of foreign law: to help the national court in its interpretation of what constitutes prohibited discrimination. To achieve this, the judge needs to move beyond the treaty text. However, the question raised here is whether the court, in doing so, would act undemocratically.

Is international human rights law democratic? Democratic legitimacy may be seen as following from parliament's control over the ratification of international treaties in most states, and that such treaties are often explicitly referred to in constitutions that have been adopted by the people through referenda. Some constitutions even make it an obligation of the state to educate the population about international law. The Benin constitution imposes a duty to educate people about the constitution and international human rights instruments.[92] Somalia's constitution provides for training of security forces on the implementation of the international treaties to which Somalia is a party.[93] Nonetheless, international human rights law remains controversial in many states.

[86] See Killander and Adjolohoun (n 2).

[87] These courts do not require the exhaustion of local remedies and therefore function as parallel jurisdictions to the national courts.

[88] See s 165(7).

[89] Centre for Human Rights, *The Impact of the African Charter and Women's Protocol in Selected African States* (PULP 2012) 189; see Killander and Adjolohoun (n 2).

[90] *Mmusi and Others v Ramantele and The Presiding Officer, Customary Court of Appeal* (MAHLB-000836-10) [2012] BWHC 125 [53] (12 October 2012).

[91] Many independence constitutions included an exception to the non-discrimination clause in relation to customary law. Such exceptions have been removed in most post-1990 constitutions but still appear in older constitutions, such as Botswana's constitution of 1966 and Lesotho's 1993 constitution.

[92] Benin art 40. See also Guinea art 25; DRC art 45.

[93] Article 127(1). See also South Africa s 199(5).

Hall and Young note the following with regard to the 1990 Mozambican constitution:[94]

> In the wave of euphoria that has followed the collapse of the Soviet bloc, accompanied by a largely thoughtless universalization of the language of 'rights', there seems little room for scepticism about the adoption by Third World countries of some variant of the Western liberal package.

They note that both the independence constitution and the 1990 constitution rely on 'abstract concepts derived from political experience elsewhere; both are to be imposed on people by state power; both are rather remote from Mozambican realities on the ground (except perhaps establishment circles in Maputo)'.

As indicated above, international human rights law has a long history in Africa. However, the distance between the elite and the population is often significant. Rights related to the public sphere, such as freedom of expression, are often ignored, and rights related to the private sphere, such as many women's rights, often remain controversial among major sections of the population. These rights exist but in practice lack meaning.

International human rights law aims to be transformative, but at the same time cannot neglect lived realities. Patriarchy should be challenged, but change cannot be immediate and imposed by state power; it must grow gradually from within through exposure and dialogue. No culture is static, but to try to impose change from above may be counter-productive. The international human rights movement still has a streak of the civilizing mission underlying the Bond of 1844.

Mali illustrates the limitation of imposing human rights norms derived from international law from above. Mali was seen as one of West Africa's democratic success stories for two decades, until a recent military *coup* and secession attempt in the north of the country occurred.[95] The independence constitution included a provision on the prohibition of discrimination on the grounds of gender. Mali ratified CEDAW in 1985, making it one of the first African states to ratify this important treaty aimed at gender equality. Mali did not make any reservation to the treaty. It presented its first state report to the CEDAW Committee in 1986 and its second report seventeen years later, in 2003. In 2000, Mali ratified the Optional Protocol to CEDAW. In its 2003 report to the CEDAW Committee, the government asserted that there was certain national legislation in violation of CEDAW, but that it had since 1998 engaged all sectors of Malian society to achieve 'the widest possible consensus' with regard to a revised family law abolishing discrimination.

The draft new family law was said to have been finalized and awaiting enactment. In its Concluding Observations, the CEDAW Committee noted that Article 116 of the constitution of Mali provided that a ratified treaty took precedence over national legislation.[96] The Committee expressed its concern that, despite this, discriminatory legislation continued to be applied on issues such as the 'transmission of nationality, marriage and family relations and access to land'.[97] The Committee further urged the state to 'view culture as a dynamic aspect of the country's social fabric and life subject, therefore, to change' and to take measures to alter discriminatory cultural practices.[98] In January 2005, Mali ratified

[94] Margaret Hall and Tom Young, 'Recent Constitutional Developments in Mozambique' (1991) 35 *Journal of African Law* 102, 114.

[95] Zeric Kay Smith, 'Mali's Decade of Democracy' (2001) 12(3) *Journal of Democracy* 73.

[96] Concluding Observations, CEDAW/C/MLI/CO/5, [9].

[97] ibid [11].

[98] ibid [18].

the Protocol to the African Charter on the Rights of Women in Africa, which provides for even more detailed protection of women against discrimination than CEDAW.

> The revised family code was finally adopted by the Malian Parliament in 2009. However, the president, under pressure from conservative forces, refused to sign it into law. The bill was revised and the new family law adopted in 2011 is clearly discriminatory against women and girls in violation of Mali's obligations under CEDAW and the Maputo Protocol.[99] The question is whether constitutional adjudication could change the situation. Judge Dingake of the Botswana High Court noted in *Mmusi*[100] that it is axiomatic that by ratifying the above international legal instruments, states parties commit themselves to modify the social and cultural patterns of conduct that adversely affect women through appropriate legislative, institutional and other measures, with a view to achieving the elimination of harmful cultural and traditional practices and all other practices which are based on the idea of the inferiority or the superiority of either of the sexes, or on stereotyped roles for women and men.
>
> Although courts may interpret customary law in a manner that will reflect changes in social and cultural patterns, it is questionable whether litigation in itself can change discriminatory practices.

5. Conclusion

In their 2002 study, Heyns and Viljoen note:[101]

> The international system has had its greatest impact where treaty norms have been made part of domestic law more or less spontaneously (for example as part of constitutional and legislative reform), and not as a result of norm enforcement (through reporting, individual complaints or confidential inquiry procedures).

A 2012 study by the Centre for Human Rights, University of Pretoria, on the impact of the ACHPR and the Maputo Protocol in selected African states found that these two instruments were not widely known and that, while the rights recognized in these instruments are, to some extent, recognized in constitutional and legislative provisions, the interpretive guidance provided by the African Commission is very rarely referred to by courts.[102]

Most African states are quick to ratify international human rights treaties. The norms they espouse are often included in national constitutions and legislation. However, the lived reality of most Africans is very different from what is written in the constitution and national legislation. Anyone attempting to achieve change must assess what role litigation and what role international law can play in this strategy.

States do not only incorporate international human rights law through their national bills of rights or through national legislation. Some states incorporate international human rights treaties in their constitutions or incorporate a treaty into its national legislation. In some states, international treaties automatically become part of the law of the land. However, even where treaties form part of national law, courts, particularly those

99 www.fidh.org/Mali-s-new-Family-Law-women-s; www.guardian.co.uk/global-development/2012/may/01/womens-rights-mali-50-years (both last accessed 17 April 2017).

100 See *Mmusi* (n 90) [187].

101 Christof Heyns and Frans Viljoen, *The Impact of the United Nations Human Rights Treaties on the Domestic Level* (Kluwer Law International 2002) 5.

102 Centre for Human Rights (n 89).

in civil law Africa, often avoid applying these treaties, relying instead on other national legislation.

Most common law states in Africa view international treaties as separate from national law. However, in many of these states, treaties still have an important role as interpretive guidance. This also applies to soft law, whether resolutions adopted by an international organization or interpretations by treaty-monitoring bodies, for example, general comments and guidelines, and the jurisprudence of international courts and quasi-judicial bodies. Informed counsel should play an important role in pushing for an interpretation of national law in a manner consistent with international human rights law. The importance of individual judges and international networking should also not be underestimated.

While the impact of international human rights law should generally be seen in a positive light, the issue of democratic legitimacy, to which the effectiveness of such law is linked, must also be considered. In most African states parliament is involved in the ratification of international treaties and, through the process of ratification (in democratic states), gives democratic legitimacy to the treaties. However, there are many undemocratic states and, even in many of Africa's democracies, rights related to the public sphere are ignored when the interests of the elite are at stake. Rights related to the private sphere are often controversial among major sections of the population. Courts may intervene to develop customary law to be interpreted in light of international human rights law. However, litigation may often be ineffective in this context and education and other advocacy efforts may be more effective.

Bibliography

Al-Ali Z, 'Constitutional Drafting and External Influence' in T Ginsburg and R Dixon (eds), *Comparative Constitutional Law* (Edward Elgar Publishing 2011)

Aivo F J, *Le juge constitutionnel et l'état de droit en Afrique—L'exemple du modèle beninois* (L'Harmattan 2006)

Calvitt Clarke III J, 'Seeking a Model for Modernization: Ethiopia's Japanizers' fch.fiu.edu/FCH-2002/Clarke-Seeking%20a%20Model%20for%20Modernization-2002.htm (last accessed 17 April 2017)

Centre for Human Rights, *The Impact of the African Charter and Women's Protocol in Selected African States* (PULP 2012)

Dugard J, 'International Law and the South African Constitution' (1997) 1 *European Journal of International Law* 77

Elias T O, *Ghana and Sierra Leone: The Development of Their Laws and Constitutions* (Stevens 1962)

Fombad C M, 'Internationalization of Constitutional Law and Constitutionalism in Africa' (2012) 60 *American Journal of Comparative Law* 439

Hall M and Young T, 'Recent Constitutional Developments in Mozambique' (1991) 35 *Journal of African Law* 102

Heyns C, 'African Human Rights Law and the European Convention' (1995) 11 *South African Journal on Human Rights* 252

Heyns C and Kaguongo W, 'Constitutional Human Rights Law in Africa' (2006) 22 *South African Journal on Human Rights* 673

Heyns C and Viljoen F, *The Impact of the United Nations Human Rights Treaties on the Domestic Level* (Kluwer Law International 2002)

Ibe S, 'Implementing Economic, Social and Cultural Rights in Nigeria: Challenges and Opportunities' (2010) 10 *African Human Rights Law Journal* 197

Kante B, 'Models of Constitutional Jurisdiction in Francophone West Africa' (2008) 3 *Journal of Comparative Law* 158

Keller H and Stone Sweet A (eds), *A Europe of Rights* (OUP 2008)

Killander M, 'The Role of International Law in Human Rights Litigation in Africa' in E Quansah and W Binchy (eds), *The Judicial Protection of Human Rights in Botswana* (Clarus 2009)

Killander M and Adjolohoun H, 'International Law and Domestic Human Rights Litigation in Africa: An Introduction' in M Killander (ed), *International Law and Domestic Human Rights Litigation in Africa* (PULP 2010)

Killander M, 'How International Human Rights Law Influences Domestic Law in Africa' (2013) 17 *Law, Democracy and Development* 378

Laibuta M, 'The African Union and Kenya's Constitution-building Process' (International IDEA 2014)

Onoria H, 'Uganda' in D Shelton (ed), *International Law and Domestic Legal Systems* (OUP 2011)

Parkinson C, *Bills of Rights and Decolonization* (OUP 2007)

Peaslee A J, *Constitutions of Nations—Volume 1 Africa* (3rd edn, Martinus Nijhoff 1965)

Sanni A, 'Fundamental Rights Enforcement Procedure Rules, 2009 as a Tool for the Enforcement of the African Charter on Human and Peoples' Rights in Nigeria: The Need for Far-reaching Reform' (2011) 11 *African Human Rights Law Journal* 511

Smith Z K, 'Mali's Decade of Democracy' (2001) 12(3) *Journal of Democracy* 73

Tanoh A and Adjolohoun H, 'International Law and Human Rights Litigation in Côte d'Ivoire and Benin' in M Killander (ed), *International Law and Domestic Human Rights Litigation in Africa* (PULP 2010)

United Nations 'Constitution-making' https://www.un.org/ruleoflaw/thematic-areas/governance/constitution-making/ (last accessed 17 April 2017)

Wanambisi L, 'MP Wants Kenya's Leaders Shielded from Any Trials' *Capital News* (19 January 2015) http://www.capitalfm.co.ke/news/2015/01/mp-wants-kenyas-leaders-shielded-from-any-trials/ (last accessed 17 April 2017)

10

The Impact of Regional and Sub-regional Courts and Tribunals on Constitutional Adjudication in Africa

Bonolo Ramadi Dinokopila

1. Introduction

National courts have, over the years, made reference to the jurisprudence of regional and sub-regional bodies when adjudicating constitutional disputes. However, insufficient attention has been paid to the extent to which such decisions have influenced the outcome of cases at the national level. This is mainly because such an exercise is often ignored in favour of the more usual discourse on the monist and dualist international law debate. Another factor that encourages such indifference to the influence of such jurisprudence may be the fact that it is usually difficult to assess the extent to which such jurisprudence has had an impact on the outcome of a particular case. Again, it is usually not clear where this impact is or should be felt.

Over the years, Africa has seen an increase in the number of institutions and instruments containing norms that promote and protect human rights, democracy, the rule of law, and constitutionalism on the continent. The integration process in the region has resulted in the emergence of regional norms and institutions that contribute to the promotion of human rights, democracy, the rule of law, and constitutionalism. The increase in the number of institutions is not surprising. Initially, the African Commission on Human and Peoples' Rights (African Commission) was perhaps the only institution specifically mandated to promote and protect human rights on the continent. In addition to the Commission, a number of regional and sub-regional courts have been established. This has coincided with the democratization process in Africa, which process is underlined by a commitment to the respect for the rule of law and good governance by states.

Today, these institutions continue to thrive and some—such as the Southern African Development Community (SADC) Tribunal—were established, dismantled, and resuscitated. Some of these bodies have faced opposition from member states, with some opting not to ratify instruments establishing the institutions. The remarkably low involvement and ratification of instruments establishing these bodies by African governments has not been fatal to the operation of these bodies. Their tenacity is evident in the small but evidently growing jurisprudence.

The jurisprudence of these bodies has not been and cannot be ignored by national courts. Despite their initial mandate, and considering the interconnectedness of constitutional and human rights law, these regional and sub-regional courts have made pronouncements on norms that have greatly aided constitutionalism in Africa. The importance of these courts in the adjudication of disputes at the international, regional, and sub-regional levels is no longer in dispute. Their importance becomes even more pronounced when one has regard to the ever-contested issues of constitutional and human rights at the national level. Their decisions or recommendations—as the case may be—are useful to national courts in the overall exposition of the obligations of member states under the various treaties adopted at the regional and sub-regional levels. Most importantly, the jurisprudence of these fora points to a broader interaction between international and constitutional law, with the overall influence of such trans-judicialism being manifested through the use of this jurisprudence.[1]

This chapter will illustrate that the use of the jurisprudence of regional and sub-regional courts in the resolution of constitutional disputes by national courts has, over the years, gained significant momentum. The chapter argues that this widespread use of the jurisprudence of regional and sub-regional courts is important to the extent that it is able positively to affect the outcome of constitutional cases. The discussion, therefore, seeks to illustrate the extent to which the jurisprudence of regional and sub-regional courts has been positively used in the resolution of constitutional disputes by national courts in Africa. It is noted that the interplay between international and national law should not be looked at solely from the perspective of the monist and dualist paradigm. It appears that the use of the jurisprudence of regional and sub-regional courts by national courts does not necessarily conform to the monist–dualist approach by states. The use of such jurisprudence, therefore, sometimes presents a challenge to both the sovereignty of member states and the question of state consent in the application of international law.

Following the introduction, section 2 discusses regional and sub-regional courts and fora in Africa. The discussion makes reference to both judicial and quasi-judicial bodies, with particular emphasis on their potential role in the promotion of constitutionalism. Section 3 discusses the use of the jurisprudence of regional and sub-regional courts in the adjudication of constitutional disputes in some countries. The section also proffers an insight into the possible impact of such jurisprudence. Section 4 examines the basis and theoretical issues raised by invoking the jurisprudence of regional and sub-regional courts in constitutional adjudication. Section 5 draws conclusions from the discussion.

2. Regional and Sub-regional Courts and Forums in Africa

This section examines the various regional and sub-regional courts currently active in Africa. It is by no means an exhaustive discussion of the nature of these institutions, as they have elsewhere been the subject of extensive academic scrutiny.[2] To this end, it becomes necessary only to make reference to the nature of the decisions and the possible role they could play in enhancing constitutionalism in Africa. As already indicated, the integration process in Africa has been driven at both regional and sub-regional level. This has resulted in the establishment of judicial and quasi-judicial bodies at both levels. At the regional level, we have seen the establishment of the African Court on Human and Peoples' Rights (African Court) and the African Court of Justice and Human Rights (African Court of Justice) as judicial bodies. The African Court of Justice, it appears, will never come into being, having been established by African Union (AU) member states in 2003 under the Protocol Establishing an African Court of Justice. This is despite the fact

[1] Armin von Bogdandy, 'Constitutionalism in International Law: Comments on a Proposal from Germany' (2006) 47 *Harvard International Law Journal* 223, highlighting that: '[i]n Tomuschat's view, some rules of international law fulfil a constitutional function with respect to the international and municipal realms. This function is "to safeguard international peace, security and justice in relations between states, and human rights as well as the rule of law domestically inside states for the benefit of human beings, who, in substance, are the ultimate addressees of international law"'.

[2] See eg Laurence Helfer and Karen Alter, 'Legitimacy and Lawmaking: A Tale of Three International Courts' (2013) 14 *Theoretical Inquiries in Law* 479.

that it has obtained the necessary fifteen ratifications by AU member states and entered into force on 11 February 1999.[3] The AU has since taken the decision to merge the African Court on Human and Peoples' Rights and the African Court of Justice and Human Rights.[4] Pending the entry into force of the Protocol Establishing the African Court of Justice and Human Rights, the African Court on Human and Peoples' Rights remains operational. At the sub-regional level, there has been the establishment of the East African Court of Justice (EACJ), the Economic Community of West African States Community Court of Justice (ECOWAS Community Court of Justice) and the SADC Tribunal in East, West, and Southern Africa respectively.

It is important to note that these courts are specifically mandated to receive communications alleging the violation of the provisions of the various treaties they are mandated to enforce. For example, the African Commission is mandated to receive communications from state parties,[5] non-state communications, or other communications relating to the violation of the African Charter on Human and Peoples' Rights (ACHPR) and other relevant instruments.[6] Such communications may be submitted by individuals, their representatives, or non-governmental organizations (NGOs) with observer status before the Commission.[7] Before it was disbanded and re-established, the SADC Tribunal was mandated to receive individual communications dealing with the provisions of the SADC Treaty.[8]

Another common feature of these bodies is that they are all mandated to provide advisory opinions to clearly identified institutions on their respective areas of operation or mandate.[9] Advisory opinions are, by their nature, not binding but have been described as useful for the elaboration of the norms and obligations of the parties.[10] It is expected that the advisory opinions of the regional and sub-regional courts and other forums, even though not binding, will prove to be relevant to the elaboration of norms contained in the various instruments relevant to that body. The elaboration of such norms will no doubt have a positive impact on the resolution of constitutional disputes as they are likely to provide a clear exposition of the various provisions of treaties.

[3] Frans Viljoen, 'AU Assembly Should Consider Human Rights Implications before Adopting the Amending Merged Court Protocol' *Africa Law* (23 May 2012) http://africlaw.com/tag/african-court-on-human-and-peoples-rights/ (last accessed April 2017).

[4] For a detailed discussion on the merger of the African Court on Human and Peoples' Rights and the African Court of Justice see Viljoen (n 3); Chris M Peter, 'The Proposed African Court of Justice: Jurisprudential, Procedural, Enforcement Problems and Beyond' (1993) 1 *East African Journal of Peace and Human Rights* 117; Nsongurua J Udombana, 'An African Human Rights Court and an African Union Court: A Needful Duality or a Needless Duplication' (2003) 28 *Brooklyn Journal of International Law* 811. According to the list of countries that have signed, ratified/acceded to the Protocol on the Statute of the African Court of Justice and Human Rights, 44 states have signed the Protocol, but only sixteen states have ratified/acceded and deposited their instruments with the African Union Commission (AUC), namely Benin, Burkina Faso, Congo, Libya, and Mali http://au.int/en/treaties (last accessed 15 April 2017).

[5] ACHPR art 47. [6] ibid art 55.

[7] Communications other than those of state parties under art 55 of the ACHPR have been interpreted widely by the African Commission to make reference to individual communications. See generally Frans Viljoen, 'Admissibility under the African Charter' in Malcom Evans and Rachel Murray (eds), *The African Charter on Human and Peoples' Rights: The System in Practice, 1986–2000* (Cambridge University Press 2002) 75.

[8] See generally Fredrick Cowell, 'The Death of the Southern African Development Community Tribunal's Human Rights Jurisdiction' (2013) 13 *Human Rights Law Review* 153.

[9] For example, to date the African Court has received about ten requests for advisory opinions. The Court has handed down one advisory opinion; five of the requests are indicated as pending, while four of the requests have been finalized by the Court without any advisory opinion being rendered http://en.african-court.org/#advisory-opinions (last accessed 20 May 2016).

[10] Frans Viljoen, *International Human Rights Law in Africa* (OUP 2012) 446.

Another notable feature of these bodies is the nature of their findings. There are binding decisions and non-binding findings or decisions. In respect of the latter, there are the decisions or findings of the African Commission and the African Committee of Experts on the Rights and Welfare of the Child (African Children's Committee). The findings of these two bodies are not binding and are referred to as recommendations.[11] Viljoen, however, is of the view that the findings of the African Commission become 'final (and arguably "binding") once they are contained in the Commission's Activity Report and are approved by the OAU/AU Assembly or Executive Council'.[12]

The African Charter on the Rights and Welfare of the Child (African Children's Charter) does not contain any provision that makes reference to the status of the findings of the African Children's Committee. It is, therefore, safe to conclude that its findings have the same status as the findings of the African Commission. They are not binding on member states. It is perhaps apposite to point out that Article 45(2) of the African Children's Charter provides that the Children's Committee is enjoined to present its report before the Assembly of Heads of State and Government, which report should include information on any communications submitted to it. As already mentioned, Viljoen is of the view that the findings of the African Commission may become 'final' (or 'binding') once approved by the AU Assembly or Executive Council.[13] If this argument is correct, the findings of the African Children's Committee may become binding to the extent that the final decisions of the OAU/AU Assembly or Executive Council are binding.[14]

The unique position these bodies occupy should be noted. For example, the great potential of the African Children's Committee rests in the development of norms that are specific, protecting the rights of the children in Africa. It is expected that through the jurisprudence of the Committee, constitutional courts in Africa will be aware of the distinct and specific rights of children. The jurisprudence of the Committee has the potential to influence the outcome of constitutional cases dealing specifically with children's rights and those that do not, but have a bearing on the enjoyment of rights by children.

An example of the latter includes cases dealing with the rights of indigenous people and the provision of essential services, such as food and water.[15] The decisions of the rest of the bodies referred to above, being the African Court,[16] the EACJ,[17] the ECOWAS Court of Justice,[18] and the SADC Tribunal,[19] are binding on the parties to the dispute. Member states have undertaken to comply with the decisions of these bodies.[20] These decisions are final and binding and are, therefore, not subject to appeal.[21] All decisions or findings are supposed to be reasoned judgments of the Court.[22]

The significance of the decisions of these institutions to constitutional adjudication and constitutionalism in Africa flows from the point made earlier regarding the interaction between international and national law. Regional and sub-regional courts will no doubt

[11] See generally Frans Viljoen and Lirrette Louw, 'State Compliance with the Recommendations of the African Commission on Human and Peoples' Rights, 1994–2004' (2007) 101 *American Journal of International Law* 12, 13.

[12] See Viljoen (n 10) 339. [13] ibid. [14] ibid.

[15] An example of such cases is the Botswana High Court decision in *Sesana and Others v Attorney-General* [2002] 1 BLR 452 (HC).

[16] Court Protocol art 30.

[17] See generally Ally Possi, 'The East African Court of Justice: Towards Effective Protection of Human Rights in the East African Community' in Armin von Bogdandy and Rüdiger Wolfrum (eds), *Max Planck Yearbook of United Nations Law* (2013) 17.

[18] The Supplementary Protocol Amending the Protocol Relating to the Community of Justice art 6; Protocol on the Community Court of Justice art 24(1).

[19] SADC Protocol art 35(1). [20] See eg Court Protocol art 30. [21] EACJ Protocol art 35(1).

[22] ibid.

provide a clear exposition of the normative principles of AU law relevant to constitutional law in Africa. Where necessary, the courts at the respective levels will reconcile regional and sub-regional norms. This potential role is crucial within the larger framework of the AU where, over the years, we have witnessed a parallel growth of regional and sub-regional courts or bodies. As will be seen later in this chapter, the jurisprudence of the African Commission has gained prominence and has been used by some national courts in the resolution of constitutional disputes.

Most of the founding treaties of these institutions embody principles that address or are an aid to constitutionalism. The same applies to sub-regional courts, despite the fact that some of the sub-regional instruments do not contain a specific human rights mandate. For example, the African Commission and the African Court are specifically established to ensure compliance by member states with the provisions of the ACHPR. The jurisprudence of these courts reflects the aspirations of member states in so far as the principles of good governance, democracy, the rule of law, and human rights are concerned. The discussion below uses selected examples to illustrate how such jurisprudence has been used in the resolution of constitutional disputes.

3. Use of the Jurisprudence of Regional and Sub-regional Courts in Constitutional Adjudication in Africa: Selected Examples

In some countries, certain courts have freely used the jurisprudence of international, regional, and sub-regional courts in the adjudication of constitutional disputes. In this respect, South Africa has been one of the leading countries. In the widely cited case of *S v Makwanyane and Another*,[23] Chaskalson P explained the position as follows in the Constitutional Court:

> [P]ublic international law would include non-binding as well as binding law. They may both be used under the section as tools of interpretation. International agreements and customary international law accordingly provide a framework within which [the bill of rights] can be evaluated and understood, and for that purpose, decisions of tribunals dealing with comparable instruments, such as the United Nations Committee on Human Rights, the Inter-American Commission on Human Rights, the Inter-American Court of Human Rights, the European Commission on Human Rights, and the European Court of Human Rights, and, in appropriate cases, reports of specialised agencies such as the International Labour Organisation, may provide guidance as to the correct interpretation of particular provisions of [the bill of rights].

It is perhaps necessary to point out that most courts, in the adjudication of constitutional matters, refer to international instruments more often than to the jurisprudence of regional and sub-regional courts.[24] Their preference may be attributable to the fact that, in their use of international instruments, courts simply want to assert the existence of specific rights. They will proceed to interpret those provisions, read together with local laws, in accordance with their specific constitutional framework and other factors that are relevant in the determination of constitutional disputes. To this end, as rightly pointed out by Oppong, the use of the decisions of these courts 'range[s] from mere reference to

[23] 1995 (3) SA 391 (CC), 1995 (6) BCLR 665 (CC).

[24] See generally Centre for Human Rights 'Country Reports (October 2011) on the Implementation of the African Charter and the Protocol Thereto on the Rights of Women in Selected African States' (2011) http://www1.chr.up.ac.za/images/files/research/impact_african_charter/Report%20African%20Charter%20Project%20OXFAM%20final.pdf (last accessed 20 May 2016).

direct application'.[25] Oppong further indicates that in the period between 'January 2000 and August 2005 there were about fifty reported cases in which South African courts made use of the decisions from various international tribunals'.[26]

As is shown below, the jurisprudence of these courts has so far provided interpretative guidance to constitutional courts in respect of the treaties adopted by member states. The jurisprudence of sub-regional bodies is most likely to capture the correct exposition of the international human rights principles embodied in the various sub-regional treaties. This assumption flows from the fact that these fora have been specifically mandated to interpret the provisions of these treaties. In all probability, these courts and fora will be able to apply such provisions without the limitations usually imposed on national courts by domestic legislation (such as matters of personal law). However, the interpretation and application of these treaties may be subject to the margin of appreciation, the careful application of which is unlikely to erode the normative content totally.

The use of the jurisprudence of these courts, therefore, allows domestic courts to shape the domestic legal rules in line with international law.[27] This way, nationals of member states are likely to benefit from the protection provided for under regional and sub-regional treaties. As correctly pointed out by Oppong, the influence of international law at the domestic level has in some instances led to the abolition of legal principles that do not respond to the dictates of international law.[28] Just as the use of international law in general has contributed to 'reshaping and re-imagining'[29] international law, the use of the jurisprudence of these courts is likely to have the same impact at the national level.

The South African Constitutional Court in *President of the Republic of South Africa v Modderklip Boerdery (Pty) Ltd*[30] made reference to the African Commission's decisions in *Social and Economic Rights Action Centre (SERAC) and Another v Nigeria*[31] and *Commission Nationale des Droits de l'Homme et des Libertés v Chad*.[32] The eviction of squatters in the *Modderklip* case was held to be contrary to the provisions of section 25(1) of the South African constitution in that the South African government had failed in its duty to protect the applicants' right to property.[33] Citing these two decisions and the decision of the Inter-American Court of Human Rights,[34] the court confirmed the opinion of the lower court that the state had a duty under section 7(2) of the constitution to 'respect, protect, promote and fulfil the rights' in the bill of rights.[35] There was no discussion beyond this point, as there was no elaboration as to what extent the decision was used by the court. It only made reference to the decisions of the African Commission. In another South African case, *National Commissioner of Police v Southern African Human Rights Litigation Centre and Another*,[36] the court referred to the decision of the African Commission in *Huri-Laws v Nigeria*.[37] The court cited with approval the decision of the African Commission, and stated:

[25] Richard F Oppong, 'Re-imagining International Law: An Examination of Recent Trends in the Reception of International Law into National Legal Systems in Africa' (2006–2007) *Fordham International Law Journal* 318.

[26] ibid 319. [27] ibid 296. [28] ibid. [29] ibid. [30] 2004 (6) SA 40 (SCA).

[31] (2001) AHRLR 60 (ACHPR 2001). [32] (2000) AHRLR 66 (ACHPR 1995).

[33] See *Modderklip Boerdery* (n 30) 41.

[34] *Velásquez Rodriguez v Honduras* (1989) 28 ILM 291 pt XI.

[35] See *Modderklip Boerdery* (n 30) 55. [36] 2015 (1) SA 315 (CC).

[37] (2000) AHRLR 273 (ACHPR 2000).

> On a regional level both South Africa and Zimbabwe have signed and ratified the African Charter on Human and Peoples' Rights, 27 June 1981 (African Charter) and are therefore bound by it. The African Charter in art 5 protects the rights to dignity and to be free from all forms of exploitation and degradation, including torture and cruel, inhuman or degrading punishment and treatment. The African Commission on Human and Peoples' Rights (African Commission), the institution charged with ensuring compliance with the African Charter, has declared that the prohibition in art 5, which includes torture, must be interpreted to include the widest possible array of physical and mental abuse.[38]

The use of the decisions of regional and sub-regional courts may thus promote respect for international law at the domestic level. It is known that there is generally a problem as far as respect for international law by member states is concerned. The enforcement of regional and sub-regional norms is complicated by the unwillingness of member states to domesticate such norms.

The use of the jurisprudence of regional and sub-regional courts at the domestic level demonstrates the role of national courts in the reception of international law, in particular regional and sub-regional norms. This use is proof that courts play a vital role in the reception of international law at the domestic level. Such an approach obviously is outside the normal method of reception of international law, which usually is best described by the monist and dualist debate. Until recently, not enough attention was paid to the reception of international law principles through the use of the jurisprudence of regional and sub-regional courts. Perhaps this is because the jurisprudence of regional and sub-regional courts has recently gained prominence because of the increasing attention it has received. On the other hand, decisions of international tribunals, such as the International Court of Justice, the International Criminal Court, the Inter-American Court of Human Rights, and the European Court of Human Rights, have been used extensively in the adjudication of constitutional disputes.[39]

The South African Constitutional Court in *Koyabe and Others v Minister for Home Affairs and Others (Lawyers for Human Rights as* Amicus Curiae)[40] referred to and applied the decision of the African Commission relating to the exhaustion of domestic remedies. In this case, the issue was whether the failure to exhaust internal remedies, as required by the applicable Act of Parliament, meant that the applicants were barred from making an application to the High Court challenging their deportation. The High Court dismissed their application on the basis that the applicants, by having failed to request the minister to review the decision, had not exhausted internal remedies.

According to the decision of the High Court, this was as a result of there being no exceptional circumstances condoning the failure to exhaust internal remedies. In her discussion of the exhaustion of remedies under international law, Mokgoro J pointed out that the position of the African Commission was 'that the remedy must be "available, effective and sufficient" to redress the complaint'.[41] She further noted that the African Commission had held that a 'remedy is considered available if the petitioner can pursue it without impediment, it is effective if it offers a prospect of success and is sufficient if it is able to redress the harm complained of'.[42] Finally, she concluded:

> As the international jurisprudence illustrates, judicial enforcement of the duty to exhaust internal remedies, in giving content to the 'exceptional circumstances' exemption, must consider the availability, effectiveness and adequacy of the existing internal remedies.[43]

[38] *Southern African Human Rights Litigation Centre* (n 36) 330. [39] See Oppong (n 25) 318.
[40] 2010 (4) SA 327 (CC). [41] ibid 344. [42] ibid. [43] ibid 345.

As is the case in South Africa, in several cases in Nigeria reference was made to some of the instruments or treaties of the AU. The ACHPR features prominently, perhaps because of the fact that there is a specific Act of Parliament domesticating the Charter.[44] As correctly pointed out by Oppong, most often decisions used by national courts emanate from tribunals to which the state is not even a party.[45] By pointing this out, Oppong posits that it is significant that there was no 'formal state treaty-mandated relationship between these African national courts and the international courts from which they are borrowing'.[46]

This approach suggests that, if there is no problem with the use of the jurisprudence of international tribunals by national courts in Africa, there should not be any problem with the use of the jurisprudence of regional and sub-regional courts. This is because, in the case of the latter, there is a 'formal state treaty-mandated relationship', which does not exist in the case of some of the international tribunals the jurisprudence of which is used by national courts in Africa. Another perspective may be that, whether a 'formal state treaty-mandated relationship' exists or not is irrelevant considering the universal nature of human rights norms, as well as the non-binding nature of decisions of regional and sub-regional bodies.

The African Commission's jurisprudence on the right to life found favour in the Ghana High Court of Justice decision in *Asare and Three Other Individuals v Ga West District Assembly and the Attorney-General*.[47] The court held that the right to life, guaranteed by the constitution of Ghana in Article 13(1), warranted the broad interpretation adopted by the African Commission in *Aminu v Nigeria*.[48] Also in line with the jurisprudence of the African Commission, the court held that leading a life which derogated from living a full life constituted a violation of the right to life. To this end, the demolition of buildings and forceful eviction of the residents were considered to constitute a violation of the applicants' right to life.[49]

The Zimbabwean Supreme Court in *Kachingwe and Others v Minister of Home Affairs and Commissioner of Police*,[50] a case dealing with freedom from torture and cruel, inhuman, or degrading treatment, indicated that the decisions of the African Commission were persuasive authority. The Court cited a number of these decisions and indicated that the international norms established in these cases provided useful guidance for the determination of the constitutional dispute before it.[51]

The Supreme Court in The Gambia in *Sabally v Inspector General of Police and Others*[52] applied a decision of the African Commission dealing with the legality of the nullification, by way of legislation, of pending judicial proceedings.[53] The Court pointed out that the principles set out by the Commission were applicable and relevant to the determination of the dispute before them. Influenced by this, the Court held that the application of an Act

[44] See generally *Abacha and Others v Fawehinmi* (2000) 6 NWLR 228, in which case the Supreme Court was asked to determine whether or not the African Charter was applicable in Nigerian law and whether a treaty rule incorporated into domestic law prevailed over a conflicting statute; *Gumne and Others v Attorney-General of Nigeria* [2003] 1 LRC 764, ILDC 22 (NG 2002), in which case the Court had to decide whether or not a Nigerian court had jurisdiction to hear a case in which it was alleged that the Nigerian government had a duty to bring a claim for self-determination.

[45] ibid. [46] ibid. [47] Suit No AP 36/2007, ILDC 1488 (GH 2008).

[48] (2000) AHRLR 258 (ACHPR 2000). [49] ILDC 1488 (GH 2008) [30].

[50] [2004] ZWSC 145, ILDC 722 (ZW 2005).

[51] The decisions of the African Commission cited by the Zimbabwean Constitutional Court are *Civil Liberties Organisation v Nigeria* (2000) AHRLR 243 (ACHPR 1999); *Huri-Laws v Nigeria* (n 37); and *Ouko v Kenya* (2000) AHRLR 135 (ACHPR 2000).

[52] (2002) AHRLR 87 (GaSC 2001).

[53] This was in the case of *Constitutional Rights Project and Others v Nigeria* (2000) AHRLR 227 (ACHPR 1999).

of Parliament to terminate legal proceedings instituted by the plaintiff and pending at the time of the enactment was unconstitutional.[54] This was so because it would retroactively have deprived the applicant of his vested right to continue proceedings.[55] It is perhaps necessary to point out that the facts placed before the Supreme Court for adjudication were not similar to those of the *Media Rights Agenda* case on which the Court relied. The Court held that:

> Although the Commission was there concerned not with the constitutionality of the measures complained of but their compatibility with the legal obligations undertaken by Nigeria under the Charter, an instrument to which The Gambia incidentally is also a state party, the principles laid down are pertinent and relevant to the instant case.[56]

The opinion of the Supreme Court in *Sabally v Inspector General of Police and Others* seems to suggest that in applying the *Media Rights Agenda* case, the Court took into account the fact that The Gambia was a state party to the ACHPR. This is not at all surprising, considering that the decisions of the African Commission are mostly applied or taken into account by the courts of state parties to the ACHPR.

The decisions of the African Commission have also been relied on by the courts in Kenya. In the case of *Eric Gitari v Non-governmental Organisations Co-Ordination Board and Others*,[57] the High Court relied on the jurisprudence of the African Commission in deciding the dispute placed before it. The case dealt with a refusal to register a proposed non-governmental organization (NGO) which sought to address 'the violence and human rights abuses suffered by gay and lesbian people'.[58] The registration of the proposed NGO was rejected because it sought to protect the rights of gay and lesbian persons.[59] The applicant argued that the case was concerned with 'the ability and right of citizens to associate in a manner recognized by the state and to share their thoughts and opinions in a collective manner'.[60] According to the applicant, the refusal to register the proposed NGO was contrary to the provisions of the constitution relating to 'the right to equality before the law, and is a denial of the freedom of expression as well as freedom to access information irrespective of one's sexual orientation'.[61]

The court pointed out that the African Commission had recognized the right to associate freely as an effective tool that protects people from arbitrary power. It noted, in particular, that the right to freedom of association was a safeguard against the banning of political parties, the persecution of people on the basis of political opinions and convictions, and the deportation of political opponents.[62] The court, in ascertaining the content and import of the right to freedom of association, relied on the decisions of the African Commission.[63]

The Nairobi High Court in *June Seventeen Enterprises Ltd v Kenya Airport Authority and 3 Others*[64] made reference to the decision of the African Commission relating to evictions and the right to housing.[65] It relied on the Commission's decision in *Satrose Ayuma and Others v The Registered Trustees of the Kenya Railways Staff Retirement Benefits Scheme and 3 Others*,[66] a case which dealt with eviction and respect for the human rights of the people concerned.

[54] ILDC11 (GM 2001) [14]. [55] ibid. [56] ibid 13. [57] Petition No 440 of 2013.

[58] ibid 1. [59] ibid 2. [60] ibid 24. [61] ibid 29.

[62] *Eric Gitari* case (n 57) 81. The judgment wrongly mentions that the decision, *Jawara v The Gambia*, was decided by the African Court on Human and Peoples' Rights instead of the African Commission.

[63] The court referred to the following decisions of the African Commission: *Jawara v The Gambia* (2000) AHLR 107 (ACHPR 2000); *Amnesty International v Zambia* (2000) AHRLR 325 (ACHPR 1999); *Aminu v Nigeria* (n 48); *Law Office of Ghazi Suleiman v Sudan (II)* (2003) AHRLR 144 (ACHPR); *Civil Liberties Organisation (in respect of Bar Association) v Nigeria* (2000) AHRLR 186 (ACHPR 1995).

[64] Constitutional Petition No 356 of 2013. [65] *SERAC* case (n 31).

[66] Nairobi High Court Constitutional Petition No 65 of 2010.

The African Commission in this case held that there was an obligation to pay adequate compensation for damage incurred and that sufficient and immediate accommodation should be provided.[67] As a result, there is no doubt that the jurisprudence of the African Commission has been applied in many jurisdictions across Africa.[68]

The use of the jurisprudence of sub-regional courts is not as pronounced as that of regional bodies such as the African Commission. This may be attributable to several factors. One of the reasons may be that courts have not yet identified with the jurisprudence of these courts. It may also be owing to the fact that the treaties establishing some of these bodies exclude individual access. In respect of the SADC Tribunal, the North Gauteng High Court made reference to *Campbell v Zimbabwe*[69] (*Campbell* case) in its decision concerning the protection of the rights of a South African citizen in a foreign state, the foreign state in that instance being the Republic of Zimbabwe.[70] The court pointed out that South African officials should have taken advantage of the decision of the SADC Tribunal in the *Campbell* case if they wanted to protect the rights of the applicant.[71]

In particular, Prinsloo J was of the view that they could have taken the decision 'as fortification for effective diplomatic interventions on behalf of the applicant'.[72] The *Campbell* case was also cited by the Zimbabwean High Court in *Gramara (Private) Limited and Others v Government of Zimbabwe and Attorney-General of Zimbabwe*.[73] The issue here was whether a judgment of the SADC Tribunal was capable of being recognized and enforced in Zimbabwe.[74] Considering that the SADC Tribunal had been disbanded and re-established with a totally new mandate which excludes individual access, it is most likely that future decisions of the tribunal will have more relevance to the adjudication of constitutional disputes at the domestic level.

It is important to point out that the jurisprudence of regional and sub-regional courts and tribunals may also have an indirect impact on the resolution of constitutional disputes. Examples are instances where the jurisprudence of such bodies influences the outcome of political processes or systems and legislation. This usually happens where a state has been brought before an international, regional, or sub-regional court on allegations of the violation of certain treaty provisions and where a finding is made against such a state. In most instances, the state will then have to implement the judgment of that court or tribunal and, in the process, enforce international law principles at the domestic level. Examples of such cases include the African Commission's decision in *Mouvement Burkinabé des Droits de l'Homme et des Peuples v Burkina Faso*.[75] In this case, a decision which was likely to have a positive impact on the domestic court's findings on separation of powers and the independence of the judiciary was made.[76]

[67] *SERAC* case (n 31).

[68] For example, the Zambian Supreme Court made reference to the decision of the African Commission, *Amnesty International v Zambia* (2000) AHRLR 325 (ACHRPR 1999), in *Attorney-General v Clarke* 96A/2004, ILDC 1340 (ZM 2008); the Zimbabwean Constitutional Court in *Kachingwe and Others v Minister of Home Affairs and Commissioner of Police*, Decision No SC 145/04, [2004] ZWSC 145, ILDC 722 made reference to the following decisions of the African Commission: *Civil Liberties Organisation v Nigeria* (n 51); *Huri-Laws v Nigeria* (n 51); and *Ouko v Kenya* (n 51).

[69] Main decision, Case No 2 of 2007.

[70] *Von Abo v Government of the Republic of South Africa and Others* 2010 (3) SA 269 (GNP).

[71] ibid 288. [72] ibid. [73] HH 169/2009, ILDC 1746 (ZW 2010). [74] ibid 24.

[75] (2001) AHRLR 51 (ACHPR 2001).

[76] In this communication, the African Commission found that the manner in which magistrates were dismissed from their positions, under the so-called *Conseil National de la Révolution* regime, was irregular. In doing so, the Commission held that there was a violation of arts 18 and 19 of the Fundamental Principles on

Another decision with similar consequences at the domestic level was that of the African Court in *Christopher Mtikila v The United Republic of Tanzania*,[77] which dealt with the right to stand as an independent candidate for national elections in Tanzania. In this case, the applicants challenged a constitutional amendment according to which any candidate for political office was required to be a member of and be sponsored by a political party.[78] They sought an order declaring that that the said law was in violation of Articles 2 and 13(1) of the ACHPR, as well as Articles 3 and 25 of the International Covenant on Civil and Political Rights (ICCPR).[79] The Court held that the law in issue was in violation of the right to participate freely in the government of one's country,[80] the right to freedom of association,[81] the right to equal protection of the law, and right to freedom from discrimination.[82] The Court proceeded to order that the government of Tanzania should 'take constitutional, legislative and all other necessary measures within a reasonable time to remedy the violations found by the Court'.[83]

In addition to the above findings, the Court ordered the government of Tanzania, within six months of the judgment, to report to the Court on the measures it had taken to implement the decision. From this, it is clear that several pieces of legislation will have to be amended by the government of Tanzania in order to comply with this judgment.[84] Further, the government is likely to amend the constitution so as to comply with the decision of the Court. A constitutional amendment, which is subject to a referendum, was proposed on 2 October 2014, according to which independent candidates will have the right to participate in elections.

It is important to point out that the use by courts of the jurisprudence of these bodies is relevant to the question of integration at both the regional and sub-regional levels. This is so primarily because studies on the subject have indicated that the reason why integration is failing in Africa is attributable to the lack of binding norms and laws.[85] The argument is that, in the absence of binding laws and norms, it will be almost impossible for African states to achieve supranationalism of any kind.[86] The arguments made are relevant both for regional and sub-regional bodies on the continent. As a result of this and other pressures, there have over the years been attempts, both at regional and sub-regional levels, at moving towards adopting binding obligations aimed at ensuring collective decision-making and, perhaps, accountability.

The notable features of this transformation are the proliferation of attempts to strengthen both regional and sub-regional parliamentary bodies; the continued adoption of treaties; and the desire to see the implementation of these laws or norms. There is, therefore, a movement towards the acceptance of common principles relating to human rights,

the Independence of the Judiciary, adopted by the 7th United Nations Congress on Crime Prevention and the Treatment of Offenders, held from 26 August to 6 September 1985, and confirmed by the General Assembly in its Resolutions 40/32 of 29 November 1985 and 40/146 of 13 December 1985. The implementation of this communication is likely to reduce the harassment and irregularities in the promotion of some of the magistrates as well as the subordination of their profession. This will greatly enhance the independence of the judiciary in the country.

[77] Application No 0009/2011. [78] ibid 111. [79] ibid 76. [80] ibid 109. [81] ibid 114.
[82] ibid 119. [83] ibid 126(3).

[84] The pieces of legislation include the following: the Local Authorities (Elections) Act as amended by the Local Authorities (Elections) Act No 7 of 2002, Cap 292 RE 2002; the Local Government (Urban Authorities) Act 1982; Cap 288 RE 2002; the Local Government (District Authorities) Act 1982, Cap 287 RE 200; and the National Election Act 2010.

[85] Babatunde O Fagbayibo, 'A Supranational African Union? Gazing into the Crystal Ball' (2008) 3 *De Jure* 499.

[86] ibid.

international law, principles of good governance, the rule of law, and constitutionalism, which is clearly championed by the jurisprudence of regional and sub-regional bodies. One can, therefore, argue that there is consolidation of law-making and norm building in Africa, both at the regional and sub-regional levels. The significance of this development lies in the fact that the jurisprudence of regional and sub-regional courts and bodies are most likely to play a positive role in the adjudication of constitutional disputes in Africa.

However, much still depends on the role of other stakeholders in their interaction with national courts during the litigation of constitutional disputes. In particular, the use of public interest litigation in such a manner as to give prominence to the jurisprudence of these courts and bodies is most likely to result in their positive influence on the outcome of constitutional disputes on the continent. Once lawyers cite decisions of regional and sub-regional courts in cases before national courts, it is expected that, eventually, decisions of courts on constitutional matters will increasingly be in line with states' regional and sub-regional international law obligations.

Further, trans-judicialism has ensured that judges are aware of legal developments in other jurisdictions and has encouraged the use of the jurisprudence of international courts by national judges. This is positive peer pressure, as judges do not want to find themselves in a situation where their decisions are criticized for failing to keep up with contemporary standards. The role played by academia through their critique of decisions of constitutional courts is also critical to the improved use of the jurisprudence of regional and sub-regional courts. Academic writings, more often than not, indicate to justices of the constitutional courts the relevance of decisions of regional and sub-regional courts which they have failed to apply in the adjudication of a constitutional disputes.

From the above discussion it is clear that there is an increased use of the decisions of the African Commission, but little evidence of the use of the jurisprudence of other regional and sub-regional courts or bodies such as the African Court and the African Children's Committee. This is perhaps owing to the fact that Africa's supranational courts and tribunals, apart from the African Commission, are relatively young compared to their European counterparts. As a result, not many judgments have been delivered. Notwithstanding this, it is surprising that there is hardly any reference to the decisions of the ECOWAS Court by the Nigerian Supreme Court, even though the ECOWAS Court is located fairly close to the Supreme Court in the federal capital, Abuja. This scant reliance on the jurisprudence of regional and sub-regional bodies is perhaps attributable to the fact that these bodies are relatively new and their jurisprudence is yet to be referred to at the domestic level. From the experience of the African Commission, it may be concluded that it will take some time before the decisions of other bodies have an impact on the adjudication of constitutional disputes at the domestic level.

Be that as it may be, the use of international jurisprudence raises a number of practical and theoretical issues. We now turn to some of these issues.

4. The Basis and Theoretical Issues Involved in Invoking the Jurisprudence of Regional and Sub-regional Courts in Constitutional Adjudication

Bahdi notes that the reasons given by judges for relying on non-binding international law norms include concern for the rule of law; the desire to promote universal values; the desire to uncover values inherent within the domestic regime; the willingness to invoke the logic of judges in other jurisdictions; and the concern to avoid negative judgment from the international community.[87] The reasons given by Bahdi are applicable to the use by national courts of the jurisprudence of regional and sub-regional courts. Even though most of these judgments do not specifically mention these reasons, there is no doubt that the application of the jurisprudence of regional and sub-regional bodies is connected to one or more of the reasons that have been cited above.

In most cases, one finds that the use of the jurisprudence of regional and sub-regional courts is connected to the use of international law by the courts. However, usually there is not much discussion on why and the extent to which international law or the jurisprudence of regional and sub-regional courts and bodies is being applied in arriving at a particular decision. The flipside of this approach may be that this is an indication that national courts have come to accept that the jurisprudence of regional and sub-regional courts is relevant to the adjudication of constitutional disputes. The use of the jurisprudence can lead one to conclude that national courts strive to ensure that their decisions on constitutional issues are in conformity with accepted international standards.

The use of the jurisprudence of these bodies by national courts is part of the larger project of trans-judicial dialogue on human rights, the rule of law, and constitutionalism in Africa. While scholars have over the years paid attention to this 'trans-judicial global dialogue, conversation and communication',[88] courts have been at the forefront of nurturing such a dialogue. Nowadays, it is very rare to find that the resolution of constitutional disputes is done in isolation and without reference to the jurisprudence of other jurisdictions, international tribunals, and regional and sub-regional courts. In the end, courts are able to offer better protection through the adjudication of constitutional disputes as the courts continue to 'denationalise' constitutional law.[89]

As a result, there are a myriad of ways in which international law and, by necessary extension, the jurisprudence of regional and sub-regional courts and bodies, is used at the national level. The extent of such use is dependent on how international law is received in a particular country.

One way in which this occurs is where a constitution has provisions providing for the reception and use of international law at the domestic level.[90] In some other countries, the constitutions make specific reference to regional or sub-regional treaties[91] and the use of decisions or opinions of international and regional institutions dealing with human rights.[92] For example, in South Africa, international law is expressly referred to in section 39(1) of the constitution. According to this section, in the interpretation of the bill of rights, a court, tribunal, or forum 'must consider international law'. Other countries where reference is made to international law in constitutions include Malawi,[93] Kenya,[94]

[87] Reem Bahdi, 'Globalization of Judgment: Transjudicialism and the Five Faces of International Law in Domestic Courts' (2002) 34 *George Washington International Law Review* 556, 557; Anne-Marie Slaughter, 'A Typology of Trans-judicial Communication' (1994–1995) 29 *University of Richmond Law Review* 127, 128.

[88] See generally Christopher McCrudden, 'A Common Law of Human Rights? Transjudicial Conversations on Constitutional Rights' (2000) 20 *Oxford Journal of Legal Studies* 499; David S Law and Wen-Chen Chang, 'The Limits of Global Judicial Dialogue' (2011) 86 *Washington Law Review* 523; Cheryl Saunders, 'Comparative Constitutional Law in the Courts: Is There a Problem? (2006) 91 *Current Legal Problems* 91.

[89] See generally Charles M Fombad, 'Internationalization of Constitutional Law and Constitutionalism in Africa' (2012) 60 *American Journal of Comparative Law* 439.

[90] See generally Tom Ginsburg, Svitlana Chernykh, and Zachary Elkins, 'Commitment and Diffusion: How and Why National Constitutions Incorporate International Law' (2008) *University of Illinois Law Review* 208 https://illinoislawreview.org/wp-content/ilr-content/articles/2008/1/Ginsburg.pdf (last accessed 15 April 2017).

[91] Studies (see Ginsburg and others (n 90) 208) indicate that the ACHPR is referred to in constitutions of about 23 member states and has been incorporated into the constitutions of about four countries.

[92] Constitution of the Seychelles art 48.

[93] Constitution of the Republic of Malawi s 11(2).

[94] Constitution of the Republic of Kenya art 2(5).

and Namibia.[95] Most of these constitutions only make allowance for the use of international law, but do not place limitations on the nature and extent of the use of international law. In the end, the extent to which international law will be applied at the domestic level is dependent on the willingness or ability of courts to apply international law.

In some countries the use of the jurisprudence of regional and sub-regional courts is sanctioned by legislation. In many of these countries the constitution is silent on the matter. For example, the constitution of Botswana does not make any reference to the use or applicability of international law. Instead, the authority to use international law in constitutional adjudication is sanctioned by section 24(1) of the Interpretation Act, which authorizes courts, when interpreting statutes, to have regard to several sources, including treaties. However, in most states the authority of the jurisprudence of international courts and tribunals is only persuasive in nature.[96]

Under common law, courts are generally allowed to make reference to the decisions of other courts in their decision-making processes. Such use of past decisions by courts in the resolution of disputes is widely accepted in common law jurisdictions. Courts are, therefore, able to make reference to the decisions of international tribunals, forums, and regional and sub-regional courts when deciding cases. In some countries, the concept of *stare decisis* under common law is the basis upon which the jurisprudence of such bodies is used in the resolution of constitutional disputes. To the extent that such decisions will not be emanating from local courts or relevant courts, the jurisprudence of such bodies is considered as persuasive authority.

4.1 The monist–dualist paradigm and the jurisprudence of regional and sub-regional courts

The level and extent of the reception of international law at the domestic level depend on whether a country is a dualist or a monist state. It is usually assumed that international law finds greater enforcement and implementation in monist states. This is because in such states, treaties ratified by the state automatically form part of the country's domestic law. Studies have shown that this assumption is false, considering that courts in African civil law countries which are traditionally monist are generally reluctant to apply international law.[97]

In some instances, there are procedural steps that the monist state must follow in order to ensure that the treaty provisions find domestic application.[98] For example, it has been noted that the use of international case law in Côte d'Ivoire has been minimal.[99] In the case of dualist states, the opposite is usually presumed to be true. However, the reality is that common law countries, which are traditionally dualist states, have been more willing to apply international law in the adjudication of constitutional law disputes.[100]

[95] Constitution of the Republic of Namibia art 44.

[96] Magnus Killander, 'How International Human Rights Law Influences Domestic Law in Africa' (2013) 17 *Law, Democracy and Development* 378, 383.

[97] Magnus Killander and Horace Adjolohoun, 'International Law and Domestic Human Rights Litigation in Africa: An Introduction' in Magnus Killander (ed), *International Law and Domestic Human Rights Litigation in Africa* (PULP 2010) 3, 4.

[98] Armand Tanoh and Horace Adjolohoun, 'International Law and Human Rights Litigation in Côte d'Ivoire and Benin' in Killander (n 97) 109, 115.

[99] ibid 114. [100] ibid.

The monist–dualist distinction, insofar as the reception of international law is concerned, has in recent years been challenged by the treatment and application of international law by national courts. Of late, common law courts, in their application of the principles of international law, seem to ignore this strict dualist nature of their national jurisdictions. Waters calls this emerging approach to international law by courts in dualist states 'creeping monism', and describes this as follows:

> a phenomenon in which common law courts are abandoning their traditional dualist orientation and are beginning to utilize unincorporated human rights treaties in their work despite the absence of legislation giving domestic legal effect to the treaties. In so doing, these judges are entrenching their nations' international treaty obligations into domestic law, thus becoming powerful domestic enforcers of international human rights law.[101]

An example of this 'creeping monism' is the Botswana case of *Attorney-General v Dow*,[102] where the Court of Appeal applied international law in the matter even though there was no apparent ambiguity, as required by the Interpretation Act, in the constitution or the Citizenship Act.[103] In this case, the litigants challenged the provisions of the then Citizenship Act,[104] which in essence prevented a female citizen from passing citizenship to her children born to her and a non-national partner. Consequently, children born to a Motswana woman and a foreign partner were considered aliens in Botswana. However, children born to a Batswana (male citizen) and a foreign partner automatically acquired Botswana citizenship. The litigants thus sought, and were granted, an order declaring that the relevant provisions of the Citizenship Act which provided for this anomalous situation should be declared unconstitutional on the grounds that they were a violation of sections 3 and 15 of the constitution of Botswana.[105]

At the time, section 15 of the constitution did not proscribe, ex facie, discrimination on the basis of sex.[106] A literal interpretation and application of the two provisions would probably have led to a different conclusion.[107] Notwithstanding this, the Court of Appeal held that there was gender-based discrimination and cited with approval various international and regional instruments that Botswana had signed and ratified but had not

[101] Melissa A Waters, 'Creeping Monism: The Judicial Trend toward Interpretative Incorporation of Human Rights Treaties' (2007) 107 *Columbia Law Review* 633, 634.

[102] [1992] BLR 119 (CA).

[103] See generally Bugalo Maripe, 'Giving Effect to International Human Rights Law in the Domestic Context of Botswana: Dissonance and Incongruity in Judicial Interpretation' (2014) 14 *Oxford University Commonwealth Law Journal* 273.

[104] For a detailed discussion of the *Unity Dow* case see generally Bonolo Dinokopila, 'The *Unity Dow* Case and the Constitutional Protection of Women in Botswana' (2015) 3 *Africa Nazarene University Law Journal* 35.

[105] *Unity Dow* case (n 102) 122. The then ss 4 and 5 of the Citizenship Act provided as follows: '4(1) A person born in Botswana shall be a citizen of Botswana by birth and descent if, at the time of his birth—(a) his father was a citizen of Botswana; or (b) in the case of a person born out of wedlock, his mother was a citizen of Botswana. (2) A person born before the commencement of this Act shall not be a citizen by virtue of this section unless he was a citizen at the time of such commencement. 5(1) A person born outside Botswana shall be a citizen of Botswana by descent if, at the time of his birth—(a) his father was a citizen of Botswana; or (b) in the case of a person born out of wedlock, his mother was a citizen of Botswana ... (3) A person born before the commencement of this Act shall not be a citizen by virtue of this section unless he was a citizen at the time of such commencement'.

[106] The then s 15(1)(3) of the Constitution provided as follows: 'In this section, the expression 'discriminatory' means affording different treatment to different persons, attributable wholly or mainly to their respective descriptions by race, tribe, place of origin, political opinions, colour or creed whereby persons of one such description are subjected to disabilities or restrictions to which persons of another such description are not made subject or are accorded privileges or advantages which are not accorded to persons of another such description'.

[107] See Maripe (n 103) 262.

domesticated.[108] These instruments included the Convention on the Elimination of All Forms of Discrimination Against Women (CEDAW) and the ACHPR.

A similar approach was adopted by the South African Constitutional Court in *Glenister v President of the Republic of South Africa*.[109] In this case the court held that the country's ratification of international treaties, even without the domestication of such instruments, had domestic constitutional impact.[110] The court proceeded to hold that South Africa's obligations under international law were relevant to the interpretation of the state's obligations under the bill of rights.[111] The approach by the South African Constitutional Court in the *Glenister* decision and that of the Botswana Court of Appeal in the *Unity Dow* case have correctly been described as instances where, even though the 'courts cannot compel governments to domesticate these international treaties and conventions, they can at least compel them not to act in breach of them'.[112]

The use of foreign decisions, decisions of international tribunals, and regional and sub-regional courts clearly presents a challenge to the monist–dualist understanding of the reception of international law. Dualist states have as a result witnessed the application of treaties and decisions of international tribunals or regional courts despite the fact that there is no 'formal state treaty-mandated relationship between the member states and the international courts from which they are borrowing'.[113] The assault on dualism is now carried out through the application of the jurisprudence of these bodies to the resolution of constitutional disputes. Judges have accepted that the jurisprudence of these courts is relevant to the interpretation of provisions of domestic law.[114] Those who nowadays ignore these decisions do so at the risk of having their decisions considered wanting.

Proponents of the use of, or reference to, international treaties to which a state is not party strongly argue that this is an indication of the emergence of transnational law that merges national and international law.[115] Those who oppose this approach are of the view that this use of 'foreign authority' in the adjudication of constitutional disputes is not acceptable.[116] They argue that, by using unincorporated treaties, the judiciary is now engaged in the domestication of international treaties, a function which is not for the judiciary to undertake. They further argue that the use of unincorporated treaties is an affront to the principles of constitutional democracy and the separation of powers. This point is captured well by Phooko,[117] who argues that the approach by the South African Supreme Court of Appeal in *Government of the Republic of Zimbabwe v Fick and Others*[118] did not respect the 'roles reserved for other branches of government'.[119]

He is also of the view that the approach taken by the South African Supreme Court of Appeal in this case was a violation of 'the principle of separation of powers as the Court preferred common law over the Constitution'.[120] The case concerned the recognition and enforcement of the SADC Tribunal decision by South African courts, even though South

[108] ibid. [109] [2011] ZACC 6.

[110] Edwin Cameron, 'Constitutionalism, Rights, and International Law: The *Glenister* Decision' (2013) 23 *Duke Journal of Comparative and International Law* 389, 402.

[111] ibid 404.

[112] Charles M Fombad and Madeleine Fombad, 'Rethinking Anti-corruption Strategies in Africa: Constitutional Entrenchment as Basis for Credible and Effective Anti-corruption Clean-ups' in Charles C Jalloh and Olufemi Elias (eds), *Shielding Humanity: Essays in International Law and Policy in Honour of Abdul G Koroma* (Martinus Nijhoff Brill 2015).

[113] See Oppong (n 25) 318. [114] See Waters (n 101) 630. [115] ibid. [116] ibid.

[117] Moses R Phooko, 'Legal Status of International Law in South Africa's Municipal Law: *Government of the Republic of Zimbabwe v Fick and Others* (657/11) [2012] ZASCA 407' (2014) 22 *African Journal of International and Comparative Law* 399.

[118] (657/11) [2012] ZASCA 407. [119] See Phooko (n 117) 406. [120] ibid.

Africa at the time had not domesticated either the SADC Treaty or the SADC Protocol on the tribunal.[121] The Court in that case held that it had the power to recognize the decisions of the tribunal as they were in compliance with the common law grounds for the enforcement of a foreign judgment.

Generally, decisions of regional and sub-regional courts only carry persuasive authority in the domestic courts of common law countries. This approach follows that obtaining in international law, according to which the concept of judicial precedent does not apply. In fact, some constitutions grant courts the permission to 'consider' or 'consult' and not to apply international law when interpreting the relevant provisions of their respective constitutions.[122] However, and as previously indicated, courts have in some instances applied unincorporated provisions of international treaties in instances where the relevant legal provisions called for the consultation or consideration of such principles.

While the focus is usually on dualist states when the reception of international law is discussed, monist states may be faced with a similar challenge in so far as the use of the jurisprudence of regional and sub-regional courts is concerned. This is so because the decisions of these courts usually take into account other instruments or treaties which the country may not have ratified. As mentioned before, although there is no concept of judicial precedent at the regional and international levels, courts at these levels usually take into account their past decisions. While the monist state may have consented to that treaty automatically becoming part of its domestic law, it may not have consented to the other obligations emanating from a particular treaty that may have influenced the previous decision of that body.

It has been correctly pointed out that: '[c]reeping monism is a judicial response to the tension between historical common law dualism and the modern era of human rights internationalism'.[123] In the final analysis, in spite of practical and theoretical reservations, it has to be conceded that the use of the jurisprudence of regional and sub-regional courts at the domestic level enhances the protection of human rights and respect for the rule of law.

5. Conclusion

The use of the jurisprudence of international, regional, and sub-regional courts or bodies in the determination of constitutional courts has thus far escaped intense scrutiny by scholars. This is because of the fact that the reception of international law at the national level is often viewed from the perspective of the monist–dualist debate and the domestication of international law. This chapter has, however, shown that the jurisprudence of these bodies is increasingly being relied upon and is being used by national courts in the resolution of constitutional disputes. The cases discussed above attest to this. Of course, the use of or reference to regional and sub-regional treaties continues to surpass the application of the jurisprudence of these institutions.

The legal basis for the use of such jurisprudence differs from country to country and, to a large extent, is dependent on whether the country is a monist or dualist state. In some instances, specific legislation or constitutional provisions exist sanctioning the use of such jurisprudence. To this end, the use of the jurisprudence of regional and sub-regional

[121] ibid 400.
[122] Constitution of the Republic of South Africa 1996 s 39; Constitution of the Republic of Malawi s 11(2).
[123] See Waters (n 101) 634.

courts, especially those of the African Commission, is more pronounced in Anglophone countries. In spite of their dualist approach to the reception of international law, in some of these countries, for example Botswana and South Africa, the issue of domestication is sometimes not considered relevant in applying international instruments.

Even though this approach has been criticized by some, the *Dow* and *Glenister* cases are indicative of a progressive trend which, if adopted by other common law jurisdictions, will pave the way for an enhanced role by the jurisprudence of regional and sub-regional courts for constitutional adjudication in Africa. The situation in the civil law countries in Africa which follow the monist approach to the reception of international law is different, and there is little evidence of the influence of the jurisprudence of regional and sub-regional courts in constitutional adjudication in these countries.

Considering the regional integration project in Africa, the use of this jurisprudence is evidence of the emergence of the consistent and uniform application of uniform principles of international human rights law. This will ultimately aid the integration process in Africa, as it has been indicated that the process is failing owing to the lack of application of uniform laws, norms, and practices.

Of concern, however, is the fact that in the few instances where the jurisprudence has been invoked, courts are vague as to the instances where they invoke the jurisprudence of regional and sub-regional courts. Further, the extent and nature of the application of such jurisprudence are not clear. Notwithstanding this, the result of the use of such jurisprudence has been useful as it has provided important guidance to the resolution of constitutional disputes at the domestic level. It has also resulted in the improved protection of constitutional rights. Over the years, Africa has witnessed a significant improvement in the reception of principles of international human rights at the domestic level. The use of the jurisprudence of regional and sub-regional courts has, no doubt, played an important role in achieving this change.

Bibliography

Bahdi R, 'Globalization of Judgment: Transjudicialism and the Five Faces of International Law in Domestic Courts' (2002) 34 *Geo Washington International Law Review* 556, 557

Cowell F, 'The Death of the Southern African Development Community Tribunal's Human Rights Jurisdiction' (2013) 13 *Human Rights Law Review* 153

Fagbayibo B O, 'A Supranational African Union? Gazing into the Crystal Ball' (2008) 3 *De Jure* 499

Fombad C M, 'Internationalization of Constitutional Law and Constitutionalism in Africa' (2012) 60 *The American Journal of Comparative Law* 439

Ginsburg T, Chernykh S, and Elkins Z, 'Commitment and Diffusion: How and Why National Constitutions Incorporate International Law' (2008) *University of Illinois Law Review* 208 https://illinoislawreview.org/wp-content/ilr-content/articles/2008/1/Ginsburg.pdf (last accessed 15 April 2017).

Helfer L and Alter K, 'Legitimacy and Lawmaking: A Tale of Three International Courts (2013) 14 *Theoretical Inquiries in Law* 479

Law D S and Chang W, 'The Limits of Global Judicial Dialogue' (2011) 86 *Washington Law Review* 523

Maripe B, 'Giving Effect to International Human Rights Law in the Domestic Context of Botswana: Dissonance and Incongruity in Judicial Interpretation' (2014) 14 *Oxford University Commonwealth Law Journal* 273

McCrudden C, 'A Common Law of Human Rights? Transjudicial Conversations on Constitutional Rights' (2000) 20 *Oxford Journal of Legal Studies* 499

Oppong R F, 'Re-imagining International Law: An Examination of Recent Trends in the Reception of International Law into National Legal Systems in Africa' (2006–2007) 30(2) *Fordham International Law Journal* 318

Peter C M, 'The Proposed African Court of Justice: Jurisprudential, Procedural, Enforcement Problems and Beyond' (1993) 1 *East African Journal of Peace and Human Rights* 117

Possi A, 'The East African Court of Justice: Towards Effective Protection of Human Rights in the East African Community' in A von Bogdandy and R Wolfrum (eds), *Max Planck Yearbook of United Nations Law* (Martinus Nijhoff Brill 2013) 17

Saunders S, 'Comparative Constitutional Law in the Courts: Is There a Problem? (2006) 91 *Current Legal Problems* 91

Slaughter A-M, 'A Typology of Trans-judicial Communication' (1994–1995) 29 *University of Richmond Law Review* 127, 128

Udombana N J, 'An African Human Rights Court and an African Union Court: A Needful Duality or a Needless Duplication' (2003) 28 *Brooklyn Journal of International Law* 811

Viljoen F, *International Human Rights Law in Africa* (OUP 2012) 446

Viljoen F, 'Admissibility under the African Charter' in M Evans and R Murray (eds), *The African Charter on Human and Peoples' Rights: The System in Practice, 1986–2000* (Cambridge University Press 2002) 75

Viljoen F, 'AU Assembly Should Consider Human Rights Implications before Adopting the Amending Merged Court Protocol' *Africa Law* (23 May 2012) http://africlaw.com/tag/african-court-on-human-and-peoples-rights/ (last accessed 15 April 2017)

Viljoen F and Louw L, 'State Compliance with the Recommendations of the African Commission on Human and Peoples' Rights, 1994–2004' (2007) 101 *American Journal of International Law* 12, 13

Von Bogdandy A, 'Constitutionalism in International Law: Comments on a Proposal from Germany' (2006) 47 *Harvard International Law Journal* 223

Waters M A, 'Creeping Monism: The Judicial Trend toward Interpretative Incorporation of Human Rights Treaties' (2007) 107 *Columbia Law Review* 633, 634

PART 4

CONSTITUTIONAL ADJUDICATION AND PROMOTION OF CONSTITUTIONALISM

11

'Made in Courts' Democracies? Constitutional Adjudication and Politics in African Constitutionalism

Sègnonna Horace Adjolohoun

1. Introduction

Paraphrasing Alexis de Tocqueville, Hirschl holds that: '[t]here is now hardly any public policy dilemma or political disagreement in the world of "new constitutionalism" that does not sooner or later become a judicial one'.[1] Such a view probably best epitomizes a worldwide agreement on the omnipresence and activism of courts in constitutional democracies.[2] Commentators have correctly referred to the 'rise of constitutional courts', which was concomitant with the advent of new constitutionalism and the proliferation of the American model of judicial review across the globe.[3] What has attracted relatively less attention, however, is the expanding operation of constitutional courts, which is proving to evolve beyond their traditionally contemplated functions. Empirical illustrations, indeed, abound, no longer of judicial supremacy but of an emerging trend towards 'juristocracy'.[4]

Thriving constitutional adjudication in all parts of the globe provides a wide and varied set of instances pointing to the advent of an era where adjudication is exploding beyond mere judicial supremacy. Some of these include the determination by top domestic courts of the place of Germany in the European Union, the future of Quebec in the Canadian federation, the constitutionality of the West Bank barrier, or the dispute over 'who is a Jew' in Israel, the restoration of South Korean impeached President Roh Moo Hyun, or the endorsement of General Pervez Musharraf's *coup* in Pakistan on the ground of necessity. A most notable adjudicatory move of the twenty-first century, arguably, is the 26 June 2015 judgment in which the United States Supreme Court ruled that: 'the rights of same-sex couples to marry … is part of the liberty promised by the Fourteenth Amendment'.[5]

[1] Ran Hirschl, 'The New Constitutionalism and the Judicialization of Pure Politics Worldwide' (2006) 75 *Fordham Law Review* 772.

[2] Writers have singled out a diverse set of functions that courts perform in that respect from 'protecting the constitution and democracy', to 'policing the democratization process', or 'regulating policy or institutional conflicts'. See among others Aron Barak, 'The Role of a Supreme Court in a Democracy, and the Fight Against Terrorism' (2003–2004) 58 *University of Miami Law Review* 125; Tom Ginsburg, 'Courts and New Democracies: Recent Works' (June 2012) *Public Law and Legal Theory Working Paper Series* No 388; Sylvain Brouard and Christoph Hönnige, 'Constitutional Courts and Democracy, Varying Patterns of Courts' Role in Democratic Transition, Consolidation and Breakdown' (ECPR General Conference 2011) 2–6.

[3] Miguel Schor, 'An Essay on the Emergence of Constitutional Courts: The Cases of Mexico and Columbia' (2009) 16(1) *Indiana Journal of Global Legal Studies* 173–94; Samuel Issacharoff, 'Constitutional Courts and Democratic Hedging' (2011) 99 *The Georgetown Law Journal* 960; Arthur Chaskalson, 'Constitutional Courts and Supreme Courts: A Comparative Analysis with Particular Reference to the South African Experience' http://www.ecln.net/elements/conferences/book_berlin/chaskalson.pdf (last accessed 17 April 2017).

[4] See, in general, Ran Hirschl, *Towards Juristocracy: The Origins and Consequences of the New Constitutionalism* (Harvard University Press 2007).

[5] See Daniel Fisher, 'Supreme Court Rules Same-Sex Marriage is A Constitutional Rights' https://www.forbes.com/sites/danielfisher/2015/06/26/supreme-court-rules-same-sex-marriage-is-a-constitutional-right/#1614e645cdd0 (last accessed 17 April 2017).

With the advent of the so-called third wave of democratization inaugurated in the 1990s, constitutional democracy has flourished in Africa, based largely on the Western model.[6] Most constitutions adopted during this era endorsed the main features and principles of modern constitutionalism, namely, the separation of powers, the rule of law, representative democracy, a bill of rights, and a top court vested with powers to adjudicate issues arising from the operation of the constitutional order.[7] Notwithstanding some variances in the models adopted under the new constitutional orders, extensive constitutional adjudication and an increasing intervention of constitutional courts in the political arena have become a frequent occurrence in Africa.[8] Particularly, in a third term debate era, characterized by the resurgence of political crisis resulting from persistent attempts to amend constitutions and elongate presidential terms, African constitutional courts have come under popular scrutiny for their interventions, perceived as either protecting or threatening democracy.[9]

Recent judicial interventions on the continent are indicative of how constitutional adjudication is shaping political spheres, whether interventions are believed to have a negative or positive impact. To consider a few examples, in 2009, President Mamadou Tandja of Niger disbanded the Constitutional Court after the body had opposed three successive attempts to amend the constitution for a third term. In 2010, the Constitutional Court of Togo endorsed the impeachment, without prior hearing, of nine members of parliament who had recently split from their original political party in response to a unilateral leadership decision to join the ruling coalition. In Senegal, through a laconic ruling on the candidatures for the 2012 presidential election, the Constitutional Council endorsed then incumbent President Abdoulaye Wade's bid for a third term, despite months of public debate and popular protests against the project. Another now famous intervention occurred in 2015, when the Constitutional Court of Burundi approved President Pierre Nkurunziza's bid for a third term, despite prior unsuccessful attempts by parliament, express term limit provisions in the constitution, and weeks of protests by Burundians opposing the bid. Similar judicially endorsed third term moves have been observed in Rwanda and Congo.

This chapter discusses similar trends with a view to assessing the extent to which the judicialization of politics in Africa may be reconciled with the fundamental tenets of constitutionalism, such as the separation of powers, the rule of law, and representative democracy. The purpose is not necessarily to portray judicialization as a threat to constitutionalism, but merely to indicate instances where matters that are political or of a political nature are decided by courts and the consequences for constitutionalism, whether positive or negative. The chapter is divided into five sections, including this introduction. Section

[6] See Samuel P Huntington, *The Third Wave: Democratization in the Late Twentieth Century* (University of Oklahoma Press 1991); Babacar Guèye, 'La Démocratie en Afrique: Succès et Résistances' (2009) 2 *Pouvoirs* 5–26.

[7] See Ezeanyika S Ezeanyika, 'Can Western Democracy Models be Institutionalized in Africa? Reviewing Contemporary Problems and Prospects' (2011) 36 *Ufahamu Journal of African Studies* 1–21; Gérard Conac, 'Quelques réflexions sur les transitions démocratiques en Afrique' http://democratie.francophonie.org/article.php3?id_article=1314&id_rubrique=753 (last accessed 17 April 2017).

[8] See, in general, Kader Asmal, 'Constitutional Courts: A Comparative Survey' (1991) 24 *Comparative and International Law Journal of Southern Africa* 315. For the purpose of this chapter, we refer to 'constitutional courts' as the highest domestic courts vested with jurisdiction to entertain major constitutional matters, including review of laws, interpretation of the constitution, separation of powers disputes, human rights complaints, and electoral disputes. These bodies may be ordinary, lower or supreme courts vested with similar powers, depending on the structuring and organization of the judicial system in different countries.

[9] See Augustin Loada, 'La limitation du nombre de mandats présidentiels en Afrique francophone' (2003) 3 *Revue Electronique Afrilex* 139–74.

two will briefly recall the major manifestations of the judicialization of politics as experienced around the world, particularly since the 1990s, and why these trends raise some questions about the prospects of constitutionalism. Section three sketches interventions, mainly by national courts, in the political arena in selected jurisdictions across Africa. Section four examines similar trends in African supranational courts. In conclusion, section five assesses the extent to which the judicialization of politics is expanding in Africa, and points out the peculiarities in terms of the context and causes of and consequences for African constitutionalism.

2. Trend towards the Judicialization of Politics

In discussing how the world has witnessed a rapid judicialization of matters inherently belonging to politics, we consider various opposing schools. We search the motives of hyper judicialization not only in judicial deference to the political branches of government but also as a genuine defence of the constitution and democracy or pure judicial activism. In doing so, we refer to Hirschl's approach to judicialization both for its elaborate categorization and motivation. We, however, explore propositions challenging Hirschl's absolute deference approach. These alternative postulates interestingly find echoes in the African context, as discussed later.

2.1 The rise of judicialization from standard adjudication to juristocracy

Hirschl identifies three faces of the judicialization of politics: the spread of legal discourse, which was previously dealt with in non-judicial settings; the determination of public policy outcomes, including through rights jurisprudence; and the judicialization of issues that are naturally political either in their substantive, institutional, or procedural perspective.[10] With respect to the first two dimensions of the 'politicization' of adjudication, the author suggests that they are largely accepted or standard.[11] It cannot be denied that even determinations such as administrative adjudication that look procedural, inextricably come with the substantive matters brought under constitutional review.[12] Although such types of adjudication may initially be individual rights-centred, their political neutrality could be challenged in situations of politically controlled civil societies.[13] As Hirschl concludes that those sections of adjudication have become standard, he focuses on an empirical demonstration of how the third dimension is increasingly becoming problematic in the light of some core principles of constitutionalism, which he also terms 'juristocracy'.

The relevant question this type of judicialization raises is whether, and to what extent, issues so deeply within the precincts of political entities are matters for courts to determine. Borrowing again from Hirschl, three main categories of questions are involved: First,

[10] See Hirschl (n 1) 721–31.

[11] See Iain Currie and Johan de Waal, *The Bill of Rights Handbook* (Juta 2005) 8–9; *Marbury v Madison*, 5 US (1 Cranch) 137, 170 (1803); Alec Stone Sweet, 'Constitutional Courts and Parliamentary Democracy' (2002) 25 *West European Politics* 77–100; Rait Marutse, 'The Role of the Constitutional Court in a Democratic Society' (2007) 13 *Juridica International Law Review* 8–13.

[12] See Ran Hirschl, 'Juristocracy: Political, Not Juridical' (2004) 13 *The Good Society* 6–11; Jared P Cole, 'The Political Question Doctrine: Justiciability and the Separation of Powers' (Congressional Research Service 2014).

[13] See Moises Naim, 'What Is A GONGO? How Government-sponsored Groups Masquerade Civil Society' (Foreign Policy 2009) http://foreignpolicy.com/2009/10/13/what-is-a-gongo/ (last accessed 17 April 2017); Jérôme Larché, 'Corruption in the NGO World: What It Is and How to Tackle It?' (Humanitarian Practice Network 2011) http://www.odihpn.org/humanitarian-exchange-magazine/issue-52/corruption-in-the-ngo-world-what-it-is-and-how-to-tackle-it (last accessed 17 April 2017).

electoral processes as well exemplified in *Bush v Gore*;[14] second, judicialization of prerogatives of the executive or legislature—namely the tendency by courts that anything brought before them is legal because everything would otherwise be political;[15] third, regime change;[16] and fourth, adjudication that tends to define the polity such as the status of the status of Quebec in the Canadian federation; 'who is a Jew' in Israel; and the status of Shari'a rules in Egypt. In the African context, as argued later, we would put constitutional amendment, and even presidential term limits, under this category for reasons that will become obvious later in this discussion. For now, we turn to ascertaining why this trend towards juristocracy is a weary one in light of the core principles of constitutionalism.[17]

2.2 Why courts engage in the judicialization of politics

It is important to inquire into the causes of hyper-judicialization because this helps to differentiate between legally based interventions of courts in the resolution of political matters and when judges decide to abuse their constitutional prerogatives to step out of their domain, whether for their own sake or under pressure from the political branches of government.

Authorities on judicialization defend different approaches to its rationale. As indicated earlier, Hirschl argues that judicialization is inherent to the phenomenon of 'new constitutionalism' by which courts are constitutionally vested with the power of authority about almost every aspect of social life.[18] The novelty in Hirschl's empirically backed argument is that legally founded judicialization is not a reflection of a genuine move by the polity, but rather a phenomenon sponsored by threatened political or economic elites to protect their own interests.[19] As a consequence of such a proposition, Hirschl concludes that political support is a necessary prerequisite for the judicialization of pure politics. The problem with this approach is that, as several commentators have suggested, it appears somewhat limiting and promotes unwarranted generalization.

In a review of Hirschl's major contribution on juristocracy, Perju considers these views simplistic in that he 'fails to capture the dialectic relationship between empirical assumptions and normative commitments'. In other words, Perju does not accept the idea that judges are doomed to be manipulated by those who appointed them.[20] In fact, this raises another proposition by Hirschl, that judicialization is generated by the fear of a backlash from the political branches of government, particularly the executive. Randhawa points out that there is much more to judicialization than political deference and a fear of political backlash.[21]

Referring mainly to India, but also to South Africa, Randhawa illustrates how self-restraint, protection of the constitution as well as strengthening judges' own public image may lead to the judicialization of pure politics.[22] Randhawa stresses personal attitudes and policy preferences of judges in India,[23] recognition of limited expertise by courts in

[14] *Bush v Gore* 531 US 98, 104 (2000).

[15] See Barak (n 2) 125–42; and generally Hirschl (n 1).

[16] ibid. The authors cite among others, Fiji Appeal Court's move restoring the constitution and government; the reinstatement by the Constitutional Court of Korea of President Roh Moo Hyun, who had been impeached by parliament; and the endorsement by the Supreme Court of Pakistan of General Musharaf's 1999 *coup d'état*.

[17] See Hirschl (n 1) 6–11.

[18] ibid 217.

[19] ibid 218.

[20] Vlad Perju, 'Reviews' (2005) 68 *The Modern Law Review* 1039.

[21] See Jasdeep Randhawa, 'Understanding Judicialization of Mega Politics: The Basic Structure Doctrine and Minimum Core' (2011) 6 *Jus Politicum* 1.

[22] ibid 4. See also in general Alec Stone Sweet, *Governing with Judges: Constitutional Politics in Europe* (Oxford University Press 2002).

[23] See Randhawa (n 21) 4; C Neal Tate, 'Why the Expansion of Judicial Power?' in C Neal Tate and Torbjorn Vallinder (eds), *The Global Expansion of Judicial Power* (New York University Press 1995).

South Africa;[24] fragmentation of powers in political branches in India;[25] self-protection as illustrated by the 'basic structure doctrine' in India.[26] The basic structure doctrine may be compared with the *principe à valeur constitutionnelle* in the Benin Constitutional Court as discussed later.

It follows from the foregoing that any conclusion on the rationale and consequences of judicialization on constitutionalism requires case-by-case empirical demonstration. Before conducting this exercise in the African context, we first discuss why and how judicialization of politics may hamper constitutionalism.

2.3 Why and how judicialization may hamper constitutionalism

Judicial determination of matters that are purely political may have consequences that run against the very idea of constitutionalism, even where the law provides for this. We will briefly set out the ways in which the judicialization of politics may hamper not only constitutionalism as a principle in itself but also two of its major tenets, namely the separation of powers and democracy. We also allude to exacerbated presidentialism as one cause of juristocracy, which may lead to imbalances in the distribution of powers.

To begin with, juristocracy threatens constitutionalism as courts may end up grabbing more powers than they are granted by the constitution whereas the very idea of limitation applies to all branches including the judiciary.[27] Secondly, an expansive judicialization of politics may belie the separation of powers. This is because, the separation of powers, as contemplated in modern constitutionalism, is not for the sake of separation, but rather for the sake of delineation, limitation, and to avoid the abuse of power.[28] Here, one is confronted with what has extensively been discussed under modern constitutional adjudication as the political question doctrine. Given that this chapter is not devoted to the political question doctrine, we will limit ourselves to making a few observations about the substance of the doctrine.

Chief Justice Marshall set out the doctrine in the famous *Marbury v Madison*[29] judgment by holding that: '[q]uestions, in their nature political, or which are, by the constitution and laws, submitted to the executive, can never be made in this court'. There is abundant work on the political question doctrine, which discusses, among other topics, what is political and what is not; when and under which conditions the political question doctrine applies; or whether the doctrine may apply in individual rights cases. Inquiries

[24] *Soobramoney v Minister of Health* 1998 (1) SA 765; *Republic of South Africa v Grootboom* 2001 (1) SA 46; See *Minister of Health v Treatment Action Campaign (TAC)* (2002) 5 SA 721.

[25] See Randhawa (n 21) 5; John Ferejohn, 'Judicializing Politics, Politicizing Law' (2002) 65 *Law and Contemporary Problems* 41.

[26] See *Kesavananda Bharthi v Union of India* AIR 1973 SC 1461; *Gupta v Union of India* AIR 1982 SC 14; *Bommai v Union of India* AIR 1994 SC 1918.

[27] See Currie and de Waal (n 11) 8–9; Marc Chevrier, 'Trois Visions de la Constitution et du Constitutionnalisme Contemporain' (2008) 2 *Revue Québécoise de Droit Constitutionnel* 72–129; Jeremy Waldron, 'Constitutionalism: A Skeptical View' (Georgetown University Law Centre Lecture 2010) http://scholarship.law.georgetown.edu/cgi/viewcontent.cgi?article=1002&context=hartlecture (last accessed 17 April 2017); Greg Russell, 'Constitutionalism: America and Beyond' (Democracy Papers) http://www.ait.org.tw/infousa/zhtw/DOCS/Demopaper/dmpaper2.html (last accessed 17 April 2017); Murray Gleeson, 'Courts and the Rule of Law' (The Rule of Law Series 2001) http://www.hcourt.gov.au/assets/publications/speeches/former-justices/gleesoncj/cj_ruleoflaw.htm (last accessed 17 April 2017); John Baptist Kotmair Jr, 'Do Courts Have Law Making Powers' (Save A Patriot 2005) http://save-a-patriot.org/files/Do_Courts_Have_Law_Making_Powers.pdf (last accessed 17 April 2017).

[28] See in general M J C Ville, *Constitutionalism and the Separation of Powers* (Indianapolis Liberty Fund 1998); Richard Benwell and Oonagh Gay, 'The Separation of Powers' (House of Common Library 2011).

[29] *Marbury v Madison* 5 US (1 Cranch) 137, 170 (1803).

even suggest a 'secret life' of the doctrine.[30] At least one advantage of the political question doctrine debate in respect of the separation of powers is that, although the doctrine has been applied inconsistently and on a case-by-case basis, core benchmarks have emerged.

The first benchmarks were set in *Marbury*. In 1803, the US Supreme Court held that a matter is political when it falls within the discretion of the executive; but acts of the executive that breach individual rights are justiciable. However, in 1849, the same court reversed *Marbury* in part by declining to apply the political question doctrine in *Luther v Borden*,[31] which involved individual rights and matters committed to the discretion of congress, thus the legislature. To the *Marbury* benchmarks, Luther added prudential considerations, namely judicial restraint motivated by the chaos that could ensue if courts adjudicated political matters with a certain outcome.

In 1962, the court took a greater step in *Baker v Carr*,[32] where it fleshed out the doctrine, coming up with the lack of—legal—criteria by which a court could determine the political matter brought before it as yet another prudential consideration in support of judicial restraint. In fact, through *Baker*, the court set what today represents the modern articulation of the political question doctrine. The court set the following benchmarks for determining when the doctrine should apply: (i) the constitution textually commits the issue to a political department; (ii) there are no discoverable and manageable standards to resolve the matter; (iii) it is not possible to adjudicate the matter without an initial non-legal or judicial determination; (iv) it is impossible for a court to independently determine the matter without lacking respect for coordinate branches of government; (v) there is an unusual need for unquestioning adherence to a political decision already made; or (vi) there is a potential risk of embarrassment from multiple decisions by various bodies on the same question. The court held that these factors could be exclusive or cumulative.

Prior to and following *Baker*, the US Supreme Court made a number of pronouncements that dealt with specific issues relating to the separation of powers on when or how the political question doctrine should or should not apply.[33] It is worth noting that, where individual rights were involved in *Baker*, the Court declined to apply the political question doctrine.

Despite long-standing disagreement among commentators on the exact foundation of the doctrine, two major considerations arose.[34] First, under the classical version of the doctrine, constitutional considerations demand that when seized of a matter that the constitution has expressly vested with them, courts must adjudicate such and not decline for prudential reasons. A political question, thus, arises only when the constitution has vested its determination in a political branch of government. In such cases, the courts must decline jurisdiction, yet through an appropriate interpretation of the constitution.[35]

Secondly, while adjudicating matters with a political connotation, courts must apply prudential considerations. Bickel explains how courts should preserve their legitimacy as an unelected branch of government by applying these considerations through what he calls 'passive virtues'.[36] Observing these virtues would involve declining jurisdiction to

[30] See eg Louis Michael Seidman, 'The Secret Life of the Political Question Doctrine' (2004) 37 *John Marshall Law Review* 441.

[31] *Luther v Borden* 48 US 1 (1849).

[32] *Baker v Carr* 369 US 186 (1962).

[33] *Coleman v Miller* 307 US 433 (1939). *O'Brien v Brown* 409 US 1 (1972). *Japan Whaling Association v American Cetacean Society* 478 US 221, 223 (1986). *Nixon v United States* 506 US 224, 226–27 (1993). *Vieth v Jubelirer* 541 US 267, 281 (2004).

[34] For a comprehensive analysis on recent trends on the question, namely, in the US see Cole (n 12) 6.

[35] On constitutional considerations see Fritz W Scharpf, 'Judicial Review and the Political Question: A Functional Analysis' (1966) 75 *Yale Law Journal* 517, 518.

[36] See also Floyd Abrams, 'Online Alexander Bickel Symposium: On Rereading the Least Dangerous Branch', SCOTUSblog http://www.scotusblog.com/2012/08/online-alexander-bickel-symposium-on-rereading-the-least-dangerous-branch/ (last accessed 17 April 2017).

avoid losing legitimacy in the eyes of the public,[37] but also allowing the political branches to resolve issues over time.[38]

In drawing the list of instances where the PQD applies, it bears noting that human rights are nowhere to be found.[39] As I note later in this chapter, courts appear to have very little appetite for hyper-judicialization and judicial activism when it comes to human rights matters as opposed to mega-politics.[40] As discussed in the relevant sections below, South African and Indian courts make an exception to this rule.

It is necessary to complete this overview with some observations about some manifestations of the doctrine in the civil law tradition or continental legal systems. In these jurisdictions, the political question doctrine is unknown to courts, at least as such. Above all, the doctrine, as described above, is mainly an invention of common law courts. In spite of this, French courts are accustomed to dealing with issues related to the political question doctrine.[41]

The main mechanism used by the French Constitutional Council in this regard is that of the *contrôle de l'erreur manifeste d'appréciation* (review of manifest error of determination or decision) of parliament in discharging its law-making functions. The Council resorts to this review mechanism when a bill or enacted legislation is brought for its scrutiny, to vet whether parliament properly appreciated the scope of its powers or whether it acted beyond its prerogative. An analysis of the Council's case law reveals that the body has consistently avoided adjudicating the opportunity for the legislator to make law, except where the legislative error is serious. For instance, the Council held that 'it does not have powers of appreciation and decision similar to those of parliament' and 'may not determine if the objectives that parliament assigned itself could have been achieved through different means, as long as provisions of the law are not manifestly inappropriate to the objectives'.[42] In the common law understanding of the political question doctrine, this is called respect for coordinate branches of government.

Similarly, the French Constitutional Council has considered the difficulty to determine certain matters owing to their very technical nature. For instance, the Council acknowledges its technical limitations while conducting certain types of constitutional review. For example, in 2010, using the mechanism of the *question prioritaire de constitutionnalité* (referral of a constitutional issue in an ongoing trial before an ordinary court), the Council declined acknowledging its technical limitations.[43] It further declined jurisdiction over contested provisions by holding that those provisions fell within the margin of appreciation left to parliament in the determination of the means to achieve its legislative goals, which courts must respect.[44]

In the final analysis, the crux of the matter is that the separation of powers stands as a fundamental principle of constitutionalism; the political question doctrine does not

[37] Alexander M Bickel, 'The Supreme Court 1960 Term Foreword: The Passive Virtues' (1961) 75 *Harvard Law Review* 40, 48–59.

[38] See Alexander M Bickel, *The Least Dangerous Branch: The Supreme Court at the Bar of Politics* (Yale University Press 1962) 184; Gerald Gunther, 'The Subtle Vices of the Passive Virtues: A Comment on Principle and Expediency in Judicial Review' (1964) 64 *Columbia Law Review* 1, 3.

[39] See Jesse Choper, 'The Political Question Doctrine: Suggested Criteria' (2005) 54 *Duke Law Journal* 1457–523; Erwin Chemerinsky, *Constitutional Law: Principles and Policies* (Aspen Law & Business 2002) 130.

[40] The term is coined by Hirschl to refer to issues of a purely political nature. See Hirschl (n 1) 772.

[41] See Thibault Caffoz, 'Le Contrôle de l'Erreur Manifeste d'Appréciation dans la Procédure de la Question Prioritaire de Constitutionnalité' http://www.droitconstitutionnel.org/congresLyon/CommLA/A-caffoz_T2.pdf (last accessed 17 April 2017).

[42] Decision No 2010-28 QPC of 17 September 2010.

[43] Decision No 2010-29/37 QPC of 22 September 2010.

[44] Decision No 2011-180 QPC of 13 October 2011.

substitute or supersede the separation of powers as such but, rather, strengthens the principle. The letter of the constitution—not its expanded interpretation—at all times remains not only supreme but the reference point.

Another tenet of constitutionalism, which comes to mind when one discusses the expansive adjudication of political questions, is representative democracy. Democracy is known as the political proposition by which the people should have full discretion to make choices concerning their lives, directly or through their elected representative.[45] The issue with the judiciary is that it is the only branch of government that has no direct connection with the people in terms of how power to adjudicate is accrued to them. In a sense, Bickel's passive virtues suggest that, by adjudicating matters that are so political that the people themselves or their elected representatives, namely the executive and the legislature, should have addressed them, courts cannot avoid impeding representative democracy. It is true that, in many democracies, mostly of Anglo-Saxon influence, judges are elected by parliament. It is no less true that, in many other countries, political officers appoint judges. Both examples are found in Africa, as discussed later in this chapter.

It cannot be overemphasized that courts are as bound by the constitution and its principles as are the executive and the legislature. Democracy, therefore, loses much of its substance when courts begin to elect the president or rewrite the constitution under the umbrella of constitutional review, take guardianship of the constitution, and protection of the people, ostensibly as the saviours of democracy. The politicization of constitutional review becomes a threat to representative democracy when it targets the legislature.[46]

There is yet another insidious threat to constitutional democracy posed by the rise of hyper-presidentialism, or what can be referred to as the imperial presidential system.[47] Consider a situation where politicians can obtain unlimited powers through an expansive judicialization of politics. In the African context—and this is true elsewhere for any incumbent administration—the executive makes it a matter of principle and strives to control parliament. This phenomenon has developed into an obsession in presidential regimes where presidential majority almost systematically coincides with parliamentary majority.[48] With the constitutionally entrenched powers for executive appointment of judges—and exclusively so for those sitting in courts of final instance in a number of jurisdictions—an imperial executive may easily undermine democracy through an expansive judicialization of politics. This political situation is still plausible in the most optimistic hypothesis of courts appearing to rule according to the will of the majority of the people and against that of the incumbent president, because juristocracy can even deal with a parliament hostile to the executive.

[45] See Richard Bellamy, 'The Political Form of the Constitution: The Separation of Powers, Rights and Representative Democracy' (1996) 44 *Political Studies* 436–56.

[46] See Gretchen MacMillan, 'The Referendum, the Courts and Representative Democracy in Ireland' (1992) 40 *Political Studies* 67–78; Herbert J Gans, 'Fixing Representative Democracy' (2015) 14 *Logos*; Jocelyn Maclure, 'Droit et Démocratie: un Gouvernement des Juges?' http://induecourse.ca/droit-et-democratie-un-gouvernement-des-juges-partie-1/ (last accessed 17 April 2017); Sévérine Brondel, Norbert Foulquier, and Luc Heuschling, *Gouvernement des Juges et Démocratie* (Publication de la Sorbonne 2001).

[47] See H Kwasi Prempeh, 'Presidential Power in Comparative Perspective: The Puzzling Persistence of Imperial Presidency in Post-authoritarian Africa' (2008) 35 *Hastings Constitutional Law Quarterly* 761–834; Juan José Linz, 'The Perils of Presidentialism' (1990) 1 *Journal of Democracy* 51–69; Franck Moderne 'Les Avatars du Présidentialisme dans les Etats Latino Américains' (2001) 98 *Pouvoirs* 63–87; Horace S Adjolohoun, 'Between Presidentialism and a Human Rights Approach to Constitutionalism: Twenty Years of Practice and the Dilemmas of Amending the 1990 Constitution of Benin' in Morris Mbondenyi and Tom Ojienga (eds), *Constitutionalism and Democratic Governance in Africa: Contemporary Perspectives from Sub-Saharan Africa* (Pretoria University Law Press 2013).

[48] See Albert Bourgi, 'L'évolution du Constitutionnalisme en Afrique: Du Formalisme à l'Effectivité' (2004) 4 *Revue Française de Droit Constitutionnel* 721–48; Gérard Conac, 'Quelques Réflexions sur le Nouveau Constitutionnalisme Africain' (Symposium International de Bamako) http://democratie.francophonie.org/

We now examine how some of these principles have been brought to bear in constitutional adjudication following the advent of the new constitutionalism inaugurated by the 1990s democratization processes in Africa. We first look at judicial pronouncements in national constitutional or supreme courts, before turning to supranational or international courts operating on the continent. The focus, however, is on the jurisdiction and mandate of the bodies rather than on their designation. Depending on the country and system, as Fombad pointed out in Chapter 1, these bodies are referred to differently as either constitutional courts or councils or supreme courts, and extend to lower courts in systems with non-Kelsenian courts, where some lower courts in the hierarchy of courts are given the powers to entertain constitutional matters.

3. Politicized Adjudication in African Constitutional Courts

This section will focus on human rights adjudication, electoral processes, the separation of powers vis-à-vis the coordinate branches of government, and issues of 'pure politics' in certain jurisdictions that are reasonably reflective of the main constitutional traditions operating on the continent.

3.1 Human rights adjudication

3.1.1 Benin

New constitutionalism and human rights were at the core of the restoration of democracy in Benin following the national conference, which dismantled a two decade-old military regime in 1989.[49] At the apex of its unique constitutional edifice, Benin established a constitutional court with equally unique features, arguably the most Kelsenian constitutional court in the new constitutionalism in Africa.[50] Individuals may directly access the court for violations of the constitution's bill of rights, which fully incorporates the African Charter on Human and Peoples' Rights (ACHPR).[51] In twenty years of adjudication since its inception in 1991, the Court received more than 1,000 human rights cases, reaching over 100 annual petitions in 2003.[52]

IMG/pdf/bamako.297.pdf (last accessed 17 April 2017); Centre pour la Gouvernance Démocratique Burkina Faso, 'Constitutionnalisme et Révisions Constitutionnelles en Afrique de l'Ouest: Les Cas du Bénin, du Burkina Faso et du Sénégal' (2009) 10–15 http://www.maep.bf/gestdoc/uploads/56.pdf (last accessed 17 April 2017); Adama Kpodar, 'Bilan sur un Demi-Siècle de Constitutionnalisme en Afrique Noire Francophone' *Afrilex* 7–12 http://afrilex.u-bordeaux4.fr/sites/afrilex/IMG/pdf/BILAN_SUR_UN_DEMI-SIECLE_DE_CONSTITUTION NALISME_EN_ AFRIQUE_NOIRE_FRANCOPHONE.pdf (last accessed 17 April 2017).

[49] See Horace S Adjolohoun, 'Benin' in Rudiger Wolfrum and Rainer Grote (eds), *Constitutions of the Countries of the World Online* (Oxford University Press 2012); Noël Dossou-Yovo, 'The Experience of Benin' (1999) 16 *Journal on World Peace* 59; Bruce A Magnusson, 'Testing Democracy in Benin' in Richard Joseph (ed), *State, Conflict and Democracy in Africa* (Lynne Rienner Publishers 1999) 221.

[50] See Alioune B Fall, 'Le juge constitutionnel, artisan de la démocratie en Afrique' http://www.droitconstitutionnel.org/congresmtp/textes7/FALL.pdf (last accessed 17 April 2017); Gilles Badet, *Les Attributions Originelles de la Cour Constitutionnelle du Bénin* (Friedrich Ebert Stiftung 2013).

[51] Article 7 of the constitution of Benin 1990 makes all the rights and duties in the African Charter part of the constitution. The full text of the African Charter is further annexed to the text of the constitution. Constitutions of other African countries only refer to the African Charter in their preambles. Regarding direct access, while individuals or groups may directly engage in human rights litigation in several Anglophone countries, constitutions of African countries in Francophone Africa do not allow individuals to file a petition before the constitutional court directly, except in electoral disputes and in cases of constitutional referral in a matter pending before an ordinary court. The same applies in France. Direct access is filtered in Belgium, Germany, South Africa, and Spain.

[52] See Horace S Adjolohoun, *Droits de l'Homme et Justice Constitutionnelle en Afrique: Le Modèle Béninois à la Lumière de la Charte Africaine des Droits de l'Homme et des Peuples* (L'Harmattan 2011).

The Court has exclusive and final jurisdiction over human rights and constitutional matters. Direct access for individuals, standing for associations and groups, as well as *ex officio* and *proprio motu* adjudication, are some of the features borne by the Court, notably different from its counterparts in Africa and beyond.[53] Compared with similarly situated courts in South Africa and Senegal, for instance, the Benin court is clothed with the most liberal human rights adjudication mechanism.[54] While the Court has actively adjudicated a significant number of politically charged cases, against agencies of government, its approach to injunctive remedy and reparations for victims remains relatively restrictive for a body with such powers. Furthermore, compliance by political branches of government remained largely poor, leaving the Court itself merely as a moral remedy for human rights violations in the absence of specific injunctions. A few illustrations are indicative of how *Marbury* was influential in the human rights jurisprudence of the Benin Constitutional Court.

First, it took the Court ten years to recognize a right to remedy for victims of human rights violations. In many of its initial pronouncements, the Court granted victims only declaratory relief, mainly on the grounds that it lacked express powers to award damages and making injunctions would breach the separation of powers. The Court eventually assumed the right to award reparation for human rights violations in the *Fanou* case,[55] decided in 2002, where it found the police responsible for the complainant's arbitrary detention, as well as cruel, inhuman and degrading treatment. After concluding that the violation thus found 'opened up' a right to reparation, the Court failed to grant any injunctive or reparatory relief. In a number of cases, it declined to issue injunctions to the executive when the latter's agents were involved in violations of individual rights.[56] However, in other cases it issued injunctions,[57] before declining again as a general trend in human rights cases.[58]

Secondly, the Court adopted a 'no quantum' policy in over two decades of human rights adjudication. After initially recognizing the right to reparation in the *Favi* ruling,[59] the Court declined to assess the quantum of reparation and issued no injunction to that effect to the relevant political agencies. Reparation for human rights violations has remained sparse in the post-*Fanou* era, and a few complainants have struggled to obtain monetary compensation by seeking the enforcement of the Constitutional Court's decisions in ordinary lower level courts.

Finally, the vast majority of human rights cases decided by the Court involved executive agencies, including the police, the gendarmerie, members of the cabinet, and ordinary courts. Non-compliance with these decisions remained widespread. In all, the Court,

[53] For a comparative analysis to France, Germany, and Belgium see Adjolohoun (n 52) 86–7.

[54] ibid 83–94.

[55] DCC 02-052 of 31 May 2002.

[56] See eg DCC 95-024 of 6 July 1995 and DCC 95-029 of 17 August 1995. In Benin's constitutional practice, case referencing is unlike that of the South African *TAC* case (n 24) or the Botswana case of *Attorney-General v Dow* (2001) AHRLR 99 (BwCA 1992). Rather, they are numbered as DCC (for *Décision de la Cour Constitutionnelle)* followed by the two last digits of the year and the incoming number of the case in that year. Accordingly, DCC 06-074 of 8 July 2006 should be read as the 74th decision of the Constitutional Court delivered in 2006, on 8 July. In a very few instances, the incoming number of the case appears before the year, eg DCC 33-94 of 24 November 1994. DCC is replaced with EL for decisions relating to electoral matters.

[57] See eg DCC 05-067 of 12 July 2005 and DCC 06-016 of 31 January 2006, where the Court ordered the reinstatement of 30 candidates to take part in the law school examination.

[58] For instance, in DCC 03-083 of 28 May 2003, concerned with the unfair dismissal of civil servants, the Court was of the view that it could not order their reinstatement.

[59] This is illustrated by DCC 02-058 of 4 July 2002 (*Favi* case), where the victim filed a case against the state before the tribunal of first instance of Cotonou, and was eventually paid an amicably-settled compensation only three years after the Constitutional Court decision.

whose members are appointed by parliament and the president of the republic, took a restrictive approach to remedying human rights violations by executive officers in the first decade of adjudication. The Court subsequently shifted to a right of reparation without, however, specifying the type or quantum of reparation, which were left to ordinary courts to decide. This is, at least, surprising for a court, largely celebrated as a model of judicial activism, as explained later in the discussion of its determination of highly political matters, including constitutional amendments. On the face of it, the Benin Court's self-restraint regarding the right to a remedy and to monetary compensation and its no-injunction policy seems suspect for a court with unique powers and exclusive jurisdiction over human rights matters.[60] We will now turn to and compare the situation in Uganda and South Africa.

3.1.2 Uganda and South Africa

An interesting recent illustration of the judicialization of politics in Uganda is probably the *CEHURD Right to Health*[61] case decided by the Constitutional Court of Uganda on 5 June 2012. Before discussing the question of how the political question was brought to bear in this case, it is necessary to undertake an overview on the use of the doctrine in Ugandan case law.

It is worth noting that the political question doctrine in Uganda was influenced by American jurisprudence. When introducing the doctrine in the 1966 *Matovu* case,[62] the Ugandan Supreme Court referred to both the *Luther* and *Baker* judgments. In fact, in both jurisdictions the matter involved the similar and politically weighty issue of which regime was the true government of Uganda in the *Matovu* case. It all depended on the question of whether the Ugandan Supreme Court was legally empowered to make such a determination. Relying on the political question doctrine, the Court found the matter justiciable as it provided a discoverable and manageable standard for determination.

In 1997, the Ugandan Supreme Court arrived at a different result in the case of *Attorney-General v David Tinyefuza*,[63] when it declined to determine whether the executive appointment of the defendant, who had resigned from the army, had been effected properly. Here, the Court took the view that the power to bring the executive to account in these circumstances was vested in parliament and not in the temples of justice. More than a decade later, the Supreme Court held that, because the constitution expressly empowered parliament to set up committees, adjudicating the matter brought before it in *Severino Twinobusingye v Attorney-General* 'would amount to interfering with the legitimate internal workings of parliament'.[64] The discussion now turns to the human rights case of *CEHURD*, which apparently supports

[60] See Anna Rotman, 'Benin's Constitutional Court: An Institutional Model for Guaranteeing Human Rights' (2004) 17 *Harvard Human Rights Journal* 283; Célestin Monteiro, 'Le contrôle de la constitutionnalité des actes juridiques du Bénin' (2001) 17 *Bulletin de droit et d'information de la Cour Suprême* 24; Cyrille Gangnon, 'Les Droits Fondamentaux de la Personne Humaine' *Actes du Séminaire de formation des journalistes* Cotonou (2 August 2005) 1; Adjolohoun (n 52) 118–20.

[61] *Centre for Health, Human Rights and Development (CEHURD) and Three Others v Attorney-General* Constitutional Petition No 16 of 2011, in the Court of Appeals of Uganda sitting as a constitutional court in constitutional matters. On the political question doctrine in Uganda see Brian Dennison, 'The Political Question Doctrine in Uganda: A Reassessment in the Wake of the CEHURD' (2014) 18 *Law, Democracy and Development* 264–88; Timothy Amerit, 'The Doctrine of Political Question: Is its Non-Justiciability at the Brink of Erosion in the Legal Jurisprudence of Uganda?' (Legal Wheels 2014) http://timothyamerit.blogspot.hu/2014/08/the-doctrine-of-political-question-is.html (last accessed 17 April 2017).

[62] *Uganda v Commissioner of Prisons, Ex parte Matovu* (1966) EA 514.

[63] *Attorney-General v David Tinyefuza* Supreme Court Constitutional Appeal No 1 of 1997.

[64] *Severino Twinobusingye v Attorney-General* Constitutional Petition No 27 of 2011.

the argument that courts mostly do not show much interest in strong judicialization where human rights are involved.

The *CEHURD* petition was filed in 2011, jointly by representatives of the organization and individuals whose relatives had died in Ugandan hospitals owing to a lack of basic maternal health care. On the main counts, the petitioners alleged that the unacceptable numbers of maternal deaths in Uganda were attributable to the government's failure to provide basic health care packages and poor attendance of expectant mothers on the part of health care workers. Specific details were provided as to what Uganda's commitment was under both constitutional and international standards, namely, those set by the World Health Organization. The Court declined jurisdiction on the ground that the matter raised a political question, as it required it to determine 'the policies in the health sector in relation to the allocation of resources to other sectors and their implementation'. Relying heavily on American case law, the Ugandan Supreme Court opined that the political and legal responsibility to determine this matter fell on the executive.

The findings in *CEHURD* appear to be erroneous in light not only of doctrinal propositions, but also of traditional case law on whether and how the political question doctrine should apply in human rights adjudication. As indicated earlier, individual rights should always be justiciable except where the constitution expressly provides for an exclusive political determination or where there is no standard to determine the matter. In this case, neither of the two conditions was met. Furthermore, US case law, on which the Ugandan Supreme Court relied, applies the political question doctrine on a case-by-case basis. For instance, in *Nebraska Coalition for Education Equity and Adequacy v Heineman* of 2007, the Supreme Court of Nebraska rejected the leg of the claim relating to the failure to allocate necessary funds for 'adequate' and 'quality' public education, but found that access to free education was justiciable.[65]

The South Carolina Supreme Court followed the same approach in *Abbeville v State*,[66] where it went further than merely setting the minimum threshold of adequate education to define the content of the core minimum. Judicial engagement in favour of economic and social rights went even further in South African courts, namely, in the famous *Grootboom*[67] and *Treatment Action Campaign*[68] judgments. Conversely, Senegalese constitutional judges showed very little appetite for human rights activism in the *Gender Parity in Political Representation* case,[69] discussed later in this chapter.

There are widely divergent views on the finding in *CEHURD*. On the one hand, there is the view that the decision was erroneous in light of the traditional jurisprudential position of American courts that purely individual rights cases should always be justiciable.[70] On the other hand, it was suggested that entertaining the suit would have amounted to forcing the executive to address problems relating to economic and social rights with related issues of the availability of resources, which generally arise regarding the implementation of these rights. South African progressive jurisprudence is said not to be applicable to Uganda because of the difference in context.[71]

One could have agreed with the second view if the Ugandan constitution had economic and social rights exclusively under its National Objectives and Directive Principles of State Policy (DPSPs), which is not the case. The reality is that in the constitution of Uganda,

[65] *Nebraska Coalition for Education Equity and Adequacy v Heineman* 731 NW 2d 164, 1787-83 (Neb 2007).

[66] *Abbeville County School District* 515 SE 2d 535 (SC 1999).

[67] See *Grootboom* (n 24).

[68] See *TAC* case (n 24).

[69] Decision 97/2007 of 27 April 2007 Constitutional Council of Senegal.

[70] See Amerit (n 61); Jesse H Choper, 'The Political Question Doctrine: Suggested Criteria' (2005) 54 *Duke Law Journal* 1457–523.

[71] See Dennison (n 61) 9–10.

socio-economic rights fall both under the DPSPs and within the bill of rights. Notably, in section XIV(b) of the DPSPs in Uganda's constitution, 'the state endeavours to ensure that all Ugandans enjoy the right to health'.[72] As to the value and enforceability of the DPSPs in Uganda, section I(i) of the Principles provides that: 'they shall guide all organs and agencies of state in applying or interpreting the constitution'. In their petition before the Ugandan courts, the *CEHURD* litigants and victims mainly claimed the rights to life and health, which are guaranteed both under the DPSPs and the bill of rights. As a consequence, the matter at hand was properly before the Constitutional Court.

The outcome of subsequent litigation in the *CEHURD* case appears to support these views. On 30 October 2015, the Ugandan Supreme Court considered the complainants' appeal and unanimously overturned the decision of the Court of Appeal. The justices were of the view that the lower court had erred by arguing that it had no mandate to hear the health rights case. They consequently ordered the court to hear the merits of the case.[73]

There is little dispute over the fact that the Appeal Court missed a unique opportunity to not necessarily make an order for monetary compensation, but, more importantly, to flesh out the right to health according to Uganda's obligations. This would have provided guidance for future judicial determination and also avoided setting a weak precedent that courts could use to decline the adjudication of human rights cases imposing good governance standards on the executive, particularly the allocation of resources. Whatever the case may be, it appears that more than one of the *Baker* benchmarks were met, namely, they were specific standards, which the petitioners pointed out, and a finding of a violation in the specific case of the petitioners would have left purely political prerogatives safe. As it did, the Appeal Court confirmed the position that expansive judicialization resulted in courts caring less about individual rights than preserving the precincts of the political branches of government.

If addressing the specific human rights concerns of the petitioners in *CEHURD* was to affect the executive's resource allocation policies so badly, South African courts would have avoided arriving at their findings in both *State v Makwanyane*[74] (death penalty, 1995) and *Stransham-Ford v Minister of Justice and Correctional Services and Others*[75] (euthanasia, 2015). *Makwanyane* no doubt is one of the landmark judgments of the South African Constitutional Court and a progressive human rights ruling at large. Here, expansive judicialization, otherwise known as judicial activism, leant towards individual rights as opposed to the traditional approach described earlier, namely in American and Ugandan courts. Using the opportunity of only two individuals challenging the constitutionality of the death sentence imposed on them in accordance with valid criminal legislation, the court settled both the individual case and the legal inconsistency.

In light of representative democracy, one could have criticized *Makwanyane* for allowing judges to decide on behalf of the people of South Africa whether convicts involved in cold-blooded murder should be allowed to escape the harshest possible sentence provided for by law. However, there seems to be relevant legal and social reasons behind this death penalty case in the South African Constitutional Court. Notably, the South African Constitutional Court relied on the US Supreme Court finding in *West Virginia State Board*

[72] Constitution of Uganda 1995, as amended in 2005.

[73] See Asia Russell, 'Real Justice Could Finally be Delivered in Uganda by Key Ruling on Maternal Health' *The Guardian* (2 November 2015) http://www.theguardian.com/global-development/2015/nov/02/real-justice-could-finally-be-delivered-uganda-key-ruling-maternal-health (last accessed 17 April 2017).

[74] *S v Makwanyane and Another* (CCT3/94) [1995] ZACC 3, 1995 (6) BCLR 665, 1995 (3) SA 391, [1996] 2 CHRLD 164, 1995 (2) SACR 1 (6 June 1995).

[75] *Stransham-Ford v Minister of Justice and Correctional Services and Others* (27401/15) [2015] ZAGPPHC 230 (4 May 2015).

of Education v Barnette with the very purposive statement by Justice Jackson, that: '[t]he very purpose of a bill of rights was to withdraw certain subjects from the vicissitudes of political controversy, to place them beyond the reach of majorities and officials and to establish them as legal principles to be applied by the courts'.[76]

It may be argued that South Africans authorized the *Makwanyane* move by agreeing to the guarantee of unqualified rights to life and dignity in their constitution, and empowering the Constitutional Court to give life to those rights and international law duly ratified by their representatives in parliament. The same reasoning may apply to the *Stransham-Ford* case, where the North Gauteng High Court permitted euthanasia in the specific case of the applicant. Upholding the relative criminal law provisions proscribing murder and homicide, the court issued specific declarations and made it clear that its ruling was not to be read as endorsing a proposed bill on ending life, which had for two decades been advocated in South Africa.[77]

The latter case is different from the case of *Makwanyane*, as it properly applied 'passive virtues' and prudential considerations by allowing the ongoing debate on euthanasia follow its normal course in South African society. In any event, the rights of the petitioner were upheld, which the Ugandan *CEHURD* judges failed to do as a bare minimum for an adjudicatory body with express human rights jurisdiction. It cannot be said that from *Makwanyane*, *Grootboom* and *TAC* to *Stransham-Ford*, two decades of constitutional adjudication have passed, yet successive benches of the South African Constitutional Court have consistently pursued a journey of judicialization with greater and more detailed pronouncements in favour of human rights, merely because they chose to ignore the separation of powers and the boundaries of coordinate branches of government. This would have led to a political outcry in a country with an ANC-dominated executive and legislature that are socially deeply entrenched. There is also no evidence to suggest that the political branches in South Africa connived with courts to let the courts indirectly implement black economic empowerment on their behalf.[78] It remains to be seen which approach Uganda's constitutional body will follow when it hears the matter afresh.

3.2 Electoral processes

3.2.1 Côte d'Ivoire

The Constitutional Council of Côte d'Ivoire has adjudicated interesting issues relating to the representation of political parties in the Electoral Commission. Two major adjudication instances in 2001 and 2014 are compared.

At the heart of the 2001 Independence of the National Electoral Commission case[79] was a fierce challenge from former long-ruling Houphouet-Boigny's Parti Démocratique de Côte d'Ivoire (PDCI), a political party launched in the 1950s by the first President, Félix Houphouet-Boigny. The PDCI became the main opposition party after Laurent Gbagbo's Front Populaire Ivoirien (FPI) won the 2000 election. At a National Reconciliation Forum

[76] See *Makwanyane* (n 74) para 99; *West Virginia State Board of Education v Barnette* [1943] USSC 130, 319 US 624, 638 (1943).

[77] *Stransham-Ford* (n 75) para 26.

[78] See Dennison (n 61) 9–10, where he suggests that Ugandan CEHURD judges wisely declined jurisdiction because South Africa is not Uganda, where the social justice agenda is not charged with the same political urgency.

[79] Arrêt No 20-2001 du 06 août 2001 (*Independence of the National Electoral Commission* case) Cour suprême de Côte d'Ivoire—Chambre Constitutionnelle.

held in September–November 2001, political parties attempted to reach an agreement on the composition of the Commission. They agreed to 'set up an independent national electoral commission whose composition will be beyond any dispute'. However, the Forum did not finalize the actual composition of the Commission, that is, the number of members and their origin.[80]

In a petition to the Supreme Court of Côte d'Ivoire—Constitutional Chamber—the PDCI challenged the constitutionality of the Electoral Commission's bill mainly on the grounds that it was biased in favour of Gbagbo's ruling FPI and, therefore, lacked the independence required of such a body pursuant to Article 32 of the constitution of Côte d'Ivoire. The petitioner specifically contended that the proposal to have the Chairperson of the Electoral Commission and several members appointed either directly by the president of the republic or jointly with the speaker of parliament, violated the Commission's independence.

In its ruling, the Court first found that it had jurisdiction as the petition met the procedural conditions set out in the constitution. On the merits, the Court held that the provisions of the bill dealing with conditions of appointment and term limits of members of the Commission constituted sufficient guarantees for its independence. It proceeded to mention the remuneration, incompatibility with other public offices, and the partly non-permanent composition of the Commission as further guarantees of independence.[81] The ruling was a disappointment for the opposition PDCI, who probably expected the Court to take cognizance of the obvious lack of constitutional provisions dealing with membership of the Commission in terms of both numbers and origin. Indirectly, the Court asserted jurisdiction over the determination of the composition of the Commission, which was exclusively within the realm of the legislator or political parties. It is enlightening to observe how the Court handled a very similar petition more than a decade after this pronouncement.

The issue of the independence of the Electoral Commission again arose in 2014 when twenty-nine members of parliament from the opposition group filed a petition for constitutional review of a proposed bill to amend the provisions of the Commission Act dealing with its membership. As was the case in the first ruling on the independence of the Commission, political protagonists had, at the Linas Marcousis Round Table, agreed to a 'better representation of stakeholders in the Commission', without first defining its composition.[82] The petition was based on exactly the same substantive ground as in the first case, namely that the composition of the Commission was biased in favour of the ruling party.

Opposition members of parliament contended that the appointment on the Commission of representatives of the president of the republic and speaker of parliament, who were running or were qualified to run for the upcoming election, violated the principle of equality enshrined in Article 2 of the constitution vis-à-vis other candidates. They further contended that the appointment of representatives of the Ministries of Interior and Finance on the Commission was unnecessary, given the fact that the Commission Act compelled all state agencies to provide it with any information and funds upon simple request. The petition also challenged the membership of magistrates and prefects appointed by the president as an over-representation in his favour and a serious breach of

[80] See République de Côte d'Ivoire, 'Rapport Général du Forum pour la Réconciliation Nationale' (2001) 47 http://www.seydouelimanediarra.net/Docs/Tome%20II.pdf (last accessed 17 April 2017).

[81] See *Independence of the National Electoral Commission* case (n 79).

[82] See France Diplomatie, Texte de l'Accord de Linas-Marcoussis (24 January 2003) http://www.diplomatie.gouv.fr/fr/dossiers-pays/cote-d-ivoire/colonne-droite/documents-de-reference/article/accord-de-linas-marcoussis (last accessed 17 April 2017).

equality to the detriment of other candidates and, therefore, a threat to the independence of the Commission.

The then Constitutional Council, which had replaced the Supreme Court's Constitutional Chamber, dismissed the allegation of breach of equality on the grounds that the petitioner had 'failed to prove a pending application by the President and Speaker for the election'. It held that: 'the public announcement by the President of his candidature is merely political and may not therefore be considered as an actual candidature in its legal sense'. The Council further found that the president correctly made those appointments as president of the republic and not as candidate and that, as such, the petition was baseless.[83] While finding that the Act and proposed amendments were not in breach of the right to equality, it did not appear to the Council that the fact of over-representation of the executive on the Commission was a real problem. This led the body also to rule that the Act sufficiently guaranteed the independence of the Commission through the immunities and privileges conferred on its members, their swearing in before the Constitutional Council and the independent discharge of their mandate subsequent to their appointment by organs of state. It is to be noted that the Council declined to determine the composition of the Commission, which it held fell within the powers of the legislature.

While it may be considered that, in the second case, the Council made an appropriate finding in respect of the composition of the Commission; the same cannot be said regarding the issue of independence. In fact, even if it decided to decline a finding of 'actual' breach of equality for lack of evidence, the issue of the independence of the Commission was paramount in the circumstances. It remained unresolved, despite the Council having had all the necessary evidence to determine the matter.

Furthermore, in both cases, matters taken to the Court had been unsuccessfully deliberated upon in political fora, with the result that they became political issues. The constitution does not provide for the composition of the Commission to be decided by courts, but within political settings. Where issues arise as to the composition of the body, they should be referred back to the political settings for consideration and determination. In the first case, the Court decided to make such a determination arguable, in violation of the constitution. In the second case, it rejected claims of rights violations for purely technical reasons, but failed to make a proper legally backed determination of the central issue of independence of the Commission.

3.2.2 Senegal

The *Use of Presidential Attributes for Campaign* case[84] discussed here could as well have been discussed under the section on human rights adjudication. However, the context was chiefly political and electoral. The case arose in the immediate aftermath of the 2000 presidential election in which the opposition leader, Abdoulaye Wade, emerged as winner. Wade's coalition had his name and photograph printed on its list of candidates and on the ballot paper for the 2001 parliamentary election.

After the Ministry of the Interior had endorsed the list by an order, representatives of three opposition parties challenged the legality of the order in the Constitutional Council. Among other relief, they sought the annulment of the order and the invalidation of the

[83] Décision No CI-2014-138/16-06/CC/SG of 16 June 2014, Conseil constitutionnel de Côte d'Ivoire.

[84] Décision du 26 mars 2001, Conseil constitutionnel du Sénégal, Affaires No 2/E/2001, No 3/E/2001, No 4/E/2001.

list bearing the name and photograph of President Wade. The Council based its reasoning mainly on the 'constitutional principle' of equality, by virtue of which it was held that: '[a]ll political parties or coalitions of parties must enjoy the same treatment; therefore, none of them, while competing in an election during which the President of the Republic is not running, should make use of his image and constitutional attributes'. The Council ordered that the impugned decree be repealed and the attributes removed from the relevant electoral documents. This decision otherwise amounted to forbidding an incumbent head of the executive to campaign for an election in which he is not a candidate.[85]

This case is an illustration of how courts can adjudicate matters that have a political connotation without necessarily deferring to political pressure or out of fear of backlash. In this case, the court was prompted by the petitioners and acted within its mandate. Besides, no coordinate branch of government's mandate was affected by the Council's asserting jurisdiction. It may, therefore, be argued that the Council was doing nothing more than acting within its powers. It also appears that, free from political influence, the court was more concerned about asserting its own authority and upholding the right to equality. In fact, although the Constitutional Council of Senegal, unlike its Benin counterpart, has no jurisdiction to hear individual human rights complaints, it has done so through constitutional review and the adjudication of disputes, particularly in the framework of electoral events.

3.3 Separation of powers and prerogatives of coordinate branches of government

In this section, we discuss how courts in Africa have used their mandate to review legislation or interpret the constitution in a way that appears to either encroach upon the preserve of political organs of the state or to refrain from doing so. While the court in the Democratic Republic of the Congo did not expressly rule on the political question doctrine, its counterparts in Ghana and Nigeria did so. The difference with previous analyses is that the cases discussed here did not arise within the framework of electoral disputes adjudication, but as part of the judicial or constitutional review of laws and acts of political branches.

3.3.1 Democratic Republic of the Congo

In its 2006 constitution, the Democratic Republic of the Congo (DRC) established a Constitutional Court mandated, among others, to 'review laws and acts having force of law'.[86] The constitution further provided that, pending the establishment of the Constitutional Court, the Supreme Court of Justice would discharge the former's mandate.[87] The case discussed below reveals how the Supreme Court of Justice is expanding its express mandate to deal with issues that should otherwise have been resolved by the political branches of government.

As part of the constitutional jurisdiction vested in the Supreme Court of Justice, the constitution expressly enumerated issues falling within the constitutional review mandate of the Court. These issues include laws, acts having the force of law, legislative acts, internal regulations of parliamentary chambers and congress, those of the National Independent Electoral Commission, the High Media Council, and international treaties.[88]

[85] ibid para 8. See SeneWeb, 'Il Bat Campagne en Dépit des Interdits du Juge Constitutionnel: Macky Foule aux Pieds la Loi Fondamentale' 2012 http://www.seneweb.com/news/Politique/il-bat-campagne-en-depit-des-interdits-du-juge-constitutionnel-macky-foule-aux-pieds-la-loi-fondamentale_n_69746.html (last accessed 17 April 2017); All Africa, 'Sénégal: L'interdiction de l'Effigie de Wade sur les Bulletins à la Une' 2001 http://fr.allafrica.com/stories/200103300582.html (last accessed 17 April 2017).

[86] Constitution of the DRC 2006 art 160. [87] ibid art 223. [88] ibid arts 161–7, 216.

The constitution provides for review both *a priori* (preventive) and *a posteriori*, that is, once the law has been passed. The Supreme Court of Justice is also competent to deal with issues relating to the interpretation of the constitution, the resolution of separation of powers disputes between the executive and the legislature, as well as between the state and provinces.[89] Granted the specific and, thus, exhaustive list of matters falling under the material jurisdiction of the Court, all other matters not listed escape constitutional review, and necessarily fall under the mandate of a coordinate branch of government.

The case of *Trésor Kapuku Ngoy v Assemblée Provinciale du Kasaï Occidental*[90] involved the constitutionality of the vote of no confidence moved by the provincial legislature of Kasaï against Governor Trésor Kapuku Ngoy. Before the newly elected governor could be sworn in and assume office, the Provincial Assembly moved a *motion de censure* (vote of no confidence) to express their disapproval of the governor's policies and to force him to resign.[91] The governor challenged the vote in the Supreme Court of Justice, seeking a declaration that it was unconstitutional and should consequently be annulled. On the merits of the case, the Court held that the vote was premature and declared it unconstitutional for having been moved before the governor could be sworn in and have his executive programme adopted by a majority vote of the Assembly, as prescribed in Article 198 of the constitution. This pronouncement seems obvious and the case, therefore, is otherwise of interest only in how the Court assumed jurisdiction over the matter.

The constitution provides for generous standing rules, as Article 162(1) allows 'any person to file a suit with the Constitutional Court to challenge the constitutionality of any legislative or regulatory act'. To assert jurisdiction over the case, the Court held that:[92]

> [a] no-confidence vote moved by a Provincial Assembly is a legislative act in terms of article 162(2) as the term "legislative act" encompasses not only laws *stricto sensu* or texts having force of law, but also *any document or act* emanating from or taken in the discharge of legislative power as is the impugned vote of no confidence.

This is the ground on which the Court brought the vote of no confidence under constitutional review. It may be argued that such a finding was wrong because the contrary is rather evident. The Court, arguably, stretched its material jurisdiction to hear a matter that would otherwise fall within the powers of the legislature.

The first argument to support hyper-judicialization is that the scope of constitutional review thus assumed by the Court is too broad to leave any space for legislative activity. Indeed, 'any document or act of the legislature' would basically amount to any occurrences in the daily operation of the Assembly that are justiciable before the Court.[93] Worse still, the Court's interpretation of 'legislative act' would literarily prevent the legislature from performing one of its key functions of controlling the executive and would, therefore, undermine the checks and balances component of constitutionalism.[94] This interpretation of 'legislative act' in Article 162(1), cited earlier, probably evolves beyond the wildest possible imagination of material jurisdiction of constitutional review in modern

89 ibid art 161(3).

90 See Arrêt R.CONST.51/TSR (31 juillet 2007) Cour suprême de justice, Toutes Sections Réunies.

91 See La Toupie, 'Censure, Motion de Censure' http://www.toupie.org/Dictionnaire/Censure.htm (last accessed 15 April 2017).

92 Emphasis added.

93 See David Mumbere Bamlango, 'Des "Actes Législatives" et du "Pouvoir Régulateur": Quand la CSJ Donne une Portée Expansive aux Attributions de la Cour Constitutionnelle' (2008) 5 *Revue Horizons* 34.

94 See Auguste Mampuya Kanunk'a-Tshiabo, 'Congo-Kinshasa: Non, Messieurs—Une Motion de Défiance n'est pas un Acte Législatif' *All Africa* (20 November 2007) http://fr.allafrica.com/stories/200711200733.html (last accessed 17 April 2017).

constitutionalism, more especially where the Congolese Court has expressly enumerated and attributed competence.[95]

3.3.2 Ghana

The judicialization of politics in Ghana has been cast largely on the model of American jurisprudence. The initial appearance of the political question doctrine is said to have occurred as early as 1980 in the case of *Tuffour v Attorney-General*.[96] In this case, the Court of Appeal, sitting as the Supreme Court, held that: '[c]ourts cannot enquire into the legality or illegality of what happened in parliament. Insofar as parliament has acted by virtue of the powers conferred upon it by the constitution, its actions within parliament are closed book'.[97] Despite its sustained use in courts, it is the scope, rationale, and validity or applicability of the doctrine in Ghana that has been the subject of dispute.[98] A number of cases in Ghanaian jurisprudence show that the doctrine is at the least viewed as a necessary function of the principle of separation of powers. Here, we sketch and discuss the most relevant decisions.

In the *New Patriotic Party v Attorney-General* (*31 December* case),[99] decided in 1993, the plaintiff sought a declaration that the planned public holiday and celebration of the 31 December 1981 *coup d'état* in Ghana violated the constitution. The executive argued that such a matter was a non-justiciable political question. The Supreme Court held that almost every matter of interpretation or enforcement that may arise from the constitution, which is essentially a political document, is bound to be political or to have a political dimension.[100] The Court was of the view that, in exercising its constitutional duty of interpreting and enforcing the constitution, it had jurisdiction to determine controversies of a political nature. In other words, the nature of the question proposed for its adjudication was not important. Its jurisdiction is the primary concern, and everything is political. It is worth noting that the decision was reached by a five-to-four vote, with dissenting judges holding the view that the matter was purely political and should have been taken to parliament.[101]

The Court changed course in *Ghana Bar Association v Attorney-General*,[102] where the plaintiff brought a suit objecting to the appointment of the chief justice and seeking a declaration that the appointee was not a person of high moral character and proven integrity. The Ghana Bar Association asked the Court to declare both the appointment and approval by parliament unconstitutional. The defendant challenged the jurisdiction of the Supreme Court to hear a purely political matter falling within the discretion of the political branches of government. According to the petitioner, it did not matter that the issue was political, as long as the Court had the final judicial power to determine whether any authority had properly performed its constitutionally vested functions.

The Court dismissed the case, holding that the matter was political in light of the separation of powers, and that the political question doctrine was part of a constitutional design

[95] See Constitution of the DRC arts 1–62. See Marcel Wetsh'okonda Koso Senga, 'La Définition des Actes Législatifs dans l'Arrêt de la CSJ No RCONST.51/TSR du 31 Juillet 2007 à l'Epreuve de la Constitution du 18 Février 2006' (2008) 5 *Revue Horizons* 13–23; Katuala Kaba Kashala, *La Jurisprudence Electorale Congolaise Commentée* (The Carter Center 2007).

[96] *Tuffour v Attorney-General of Ghana* [1980] GLR 637.

[97] ibid 651–2.

[98] See Mtendeweka Owen Mhango, 'Separation of Powers in Ghana: The Evolution of the Political Question Doctrine' (2014) 17 *Potchefstroom Electronic Law Journal* 2704–44.

[99] *New Patriotic Party v Attorney-General* (*31 December* case) [1993–94] (2 GLR 35).

[100] ibid para 65.

[101] ibid para 153.

[102] *Ghana Bar Association v Attorney-General* (*Abban* case) [1995–96] 1 GLR 598.

that did not allow the judiciary to give content to all constitutional provisions. Judges sitting in the Ghana Bar Association case went further by criticizing and dismissing the proposition supporting the findings in the *31 December* case.[103] However, in a subsequent case the Court reverted to the *31 December* jurisprudence.

In *Mensah v Attorney-General*,[104] the Supreme Court refused to acknowledge the political nature of the appointment of cabinet ministers approved by parliament shortly before a new parliament was elected. The Court held that, unlike in the US Supreme Court, which derives its power of judicial review from jurisprudential authority, the Supreme Court of Ghana did so through express provisions of the constitution. According to the Court's understanding, any limitation on the extent and scope of constitutional review had to find express support in the constitution.[105]

As is the case in the United States, the judicialization of politics reached the lowers courts in Ghana, as illustrated in *Asare v Attorney-General*.[106] In this case, a member of parliament was arrested and detained in the United States for unlawfully importing narcotics into that country. On the basis of the presumption of innocence, parliament approved a recommendation by a committee on privileges that the leave initially sought by the Member of Parliament be extended indefinitely to enable him to defend the charges. In the case, the plaintiff, Stephen Asare, argued that the Member of Parliament's seat had become vacant, and challenged the authority of parliament to grant such leave. The High Court held that the mandate to determine the reasonableness or otherwise of explanations provided by the member of parliament in support of his application for leave belonged exclusively to parliament. In the court's view, it followed that the outcome of this test was purely political and not subject to judicial scrutiny.[107]

As the political question doctrine mainly involves the justiciability (or not) of certain issues, the case of *Ghana Lotto Operators Association and Others v National Lottery Authority* is worth noting.[108] This case involved the justiciability of provisions in Chapter 6 of the constitution of Ghana, namely, the Directive Principles of State Policy (DPSPs). There has been a protracted debate among scholars over the justiciability of the DPSPs, some of whom hold a strong view that these are not enforceable in courts, but remain mere guidelines for the political branches of the state.[109] If the political question doctrine is anything to go by, the DPSPs should normally not be justiciable in courts of law, except if otherwise expressly provided for by the constitution. The same ambiguity that has long been entertained as to the justiciability of socio-economic rights under the DPSPs in Chapter 2 of the 1999 Nigerian constitution entered into the debate on whether the DPSPs in Chapter 6 of the 1992 constitution of Ghana were enforceable. The Nigerian

103 ibid para 294.

104 *J H Mensah v Attorney-General* 1996–97 SCGLR 320.

105 ibid para 368.

106 *Prof Stephen Kwaku Asare v Attorney-General* High Court of Justice (Fast Track Division) Accra—AD 2006 Suit No AP 21/2006 (15 September 2006) unreported case http://www.ghanaweb.com/GhanaHomePage/politics/artikel.php?ID=110647 (last accessed 17 April 2017).

107 ibid.

108 *Ghana Lotto Operators Association v National Lottery Authority* 2007–2008 SCGLR 1088.

109 See Kofi Quashigah, 'Trends in the Promotion and Protection of Human Rights under the 1992 Constitution' in Kwame Boafo-Arthur (ed), *Ghana: One Decade of the Liberal State* (Codesria 2007) 25–46; Abdi Jibril Ali, 'Justiciability of Directive Principles of State Policy in Africa: The Experiences of Ethiopia and Ghana' (2013) 1 *Ethiopian Journal of Human Rights* 1; Atudiwe P Atupare, 'Reconciling Socio-economic Rights and Directive Principles with a Fundamental Law of Reason in Ghana and Nigeria' (2014) 27 *Harvard Human Rights Journal* 71–106; Onyekachi Duru, 'The Justiciability of the Fundamental Objectives and Directive Principles of State Policy under Nigerian Law' (Academia.edu) https://www.academia.edu/5185441/THE_JUSTICIABILITY_OF_THE_FUNDAMENTAL_OBJECTIVES_AND_DIRECTIVE_PRINCIPLES_OF_STATE_POLICY_UNDER_NIGERIAN_LAW_By (last accessed 17 April 2017).

situation could differ slightly, as the ambiguity could be sourced in written provisions of the constitution.[110]

The *Ghana Lotto Operators* case illustrates the way in which courts may regard the lack of clawback clauses as a leeway to justiciability. The Supreme Court in this case held that: '[a]ll provisions of the constitution are justiciable, unless there are strong indications to the contrary in the text or context of the constitution'.[111] Having economic and social rights in mind, the Ghanaian Court may be at odds with its counterpart in the *CEHURD* case.

However, precedents in Ghana have not always been as clear as in *Ghana Lotto Operators*, which seems to be the completion of the journey to construct a coherent understanding of how the political question doctrine may apply in cases involving the DPSPs. Indeed, in the *31 December* ruling, the Court took the view that the constitution, when looked at as a whole document, the DPSPs are justiciable because the judiciary could not be guided by those principles otherwise than in the process of enforcing them.[112] In response to the argument that the *travaux préparatoires* of the constitution included the DPSPs as non-justiciable, the Court responded that such a provision would have been included in the constitution if that had been the intention of the drafters.[113] In its subsequent pronouncement in *New Patriotic Party*, referred to earlier, the Ghanaian Supreme Court ruled that the DPSPs were not justiciable when: (i) they form part of self-enforceable rights; (ii) they are read in conjunction with enforceable provisions; and (iii) they can be interpreted to mean the creation of legal rights.[114]

The overall observation in the Ghanaian approach to the judicialization of politics is that it was mainly influenced by American standards. However, Ghanaian courts based their use of the political question doctrine on the provisions in the constitution prescribing a separation of powers. They wisely applied judicial restraint and passive virtues, without necessarily abdicating their powers and duties under the constitution.[115] Nigerian courts seem to have adopted similar attitudes, although in recent years a tendency towards 'all is justiciable' has been revealed.

3.3.3 Nigeria

Jurisprudential inconsistencies in the judicialization of politics in Nigeria have caused one commentator to wonder whether the end is in sight for the political question doctrine in this country.[116] The adjudication of political issues in Nigeria has been influenced mainly by American case law dealing with judicial review. Inaugurating the doctrine in the 1982 case of *Balarabe Balarabe Musa v Auta Hamzat*,[117] the Court of Appeal held that the impeachment of the Kaduna state governor according to section 170 of the 1979 Constitution was a political question and that, in addition, the constitutional provisions ousting the judicial review of impeachment bound the Court.[118] However, in the

[110] See Horace S Adjolohoun, *Giving Effect to the Human Rights Jurisprudence of the ECOWAS Court of Justice: Compliance and Influence* (LLD thesis, Pretoria, 2013) 281–5.

[111] *Ghana Lotto Operators Association* case (n 108).

[112] See *31 December* case (n 99) paras 66–7.

[113] ibid para 69.

[114] *New Patriotic Party* 745–7.

[115] See Bickel (nn 37 and 38); Gunther (n 38).

[116] See Enyinna Nwauche, 'Is the End Near for the Political Question Doctrine in Nigeria?' in Charles M Fombad and Christina Murray (eds), *Fostering Constitutionalism in Africa* (PULP 2010) 31–60.

[117] *Balarabe Musa v Auta Hamzat* (1982) 3 NCLR 229. Nigerian courts used the doctrine prior to *Balarabe* and the adoption of the 1979 Constitution without classifying it as such. See eg *Attorney-General Eastern Nigeria v Attorney-General of the Federation* (1964) All NLR 218, where the Supreme Court held that the determination of a margin of error in a census was a political question.

[118] See *Balarabe Musa v Auta Hamzat* (1982) 3 NCLR 229.

1983 *Onuoha v Okafor* case[119] the Nigerian Supreme Court laid down the benchmarks for the determination of political questions by relying on the *Baker* judgment of the US Supreme Court.

In *Onuoha*, the Supreme Court laid down two benchmarks for determining political questions: (i) the lack of a satisfactory criterion for judicial determination; and (ii) the appropriateness of attributing finality to the action of the political department and political parties under the Nigerian constitution and system of government.[120]

According to section 6(6)(b) of the 1979 Constitution, powers of judicial review extended to 'all matters between persons or between government or authority and any person in Nigeria and to all actions and proceedings relating thereto, for the determination of any question as to the civil rights and obligations of that person'. These provisions influenced two trends of constitutional review under the 1979 Constitution.

During the first trend, courts applied full judicial review. An illustration of this is the Supreme Court's rejection of the application of the political question doctrine by holding in *Attorney-General of Bendel State v Attorney-General of the Federation*[121] that it had jurisdiction to determine the way in which the legislature exercised its law-making powers. The line was clearly drawn between the procedural prescriptions of parliament under the constitution and internal proceedings of the legislature.[122] To assert full powers of constitutional review, the Supreme Court even went as far as disregarding statutory ouster clauses in the *Bendel State* case. In the subsequent *Balarabe* case, the Court held that the application of the ouster clause was subject to strict compliance with the provisions of the relevant statute.[123] *Balarabe* was valuable in that it established two principles: (i) that a constitutional commitment to a different branch of government will be respected and the statutory interpretation cannot apply; (ii) that some conflicts are political in nature and not subject to judicial determination.

In the second period, represented by *Onuoha*, courts asserted limited jurisdiction. The Supreme Court endorsed the *Balarabe* principles by classifying nominations by political parties as a political question in respect of which courts lack the judicial yardstick to determine. In the field of fundamental rights, Nigerian courts offered a mixed reaction, treating the rights issue as secondary.[124]

There was again a shift during the fourth republic under the 1999 Constitution. In Nwauche's view, this era saw the demise of the political question doctrine in Nigeria. Nwauche provides a few explanations for this approach to the judicialization of politics in the 1999 constitutional dispensation. First, the judicial avoidance of political issues in the previous era encouraged an increased breach of constitutional provisions. Secondly, with the 1984 military takeover, courts battled with endless ouster clauses. Thirdly, even under the 1999 Constitution, politicians misunderstood judicial self-restraint as a weapon to deal with their opponents.[125] These reasons, other commentators believe, led the judiciary to intervene in the activities of

[119] See *Onuoha v Okafor* (1983) NSCC 494.

[120] See the *Balarabe* case (n 117) para 503.

[121] (1982) 10 SC 1.

[122] For instance, the requisite majority stipulated in the constitution for the removal of the deputy-speaker was defined as a constitutional matter in *Ekpenkhio v Egbadon* (1993) 7 NWLR (Pt 308) 717. Conversely, in *Asogwa v Chukwu* (2004) FWLR (Pt 189) 1204, the court held that the question of whether the two-thirds majority required to remove the speaker of the House of Assembly was properly constituted is an internal affair of parliament.

[123] See the *Balarabe* case (n 117) para 245. The court here relied mainly on the principle adopted in *Anisminic v Foreign Compensation Commission* (1969) AC 149, that once a court comes to the conclusion that a body has not acted within the jurisdiction of an enabling statute, no words in that statute can oust jurisdiction for review.

[124] See Nwauche (n 116).

[125] ibid.

political parties.[126] The consequent return to constitutional supremacy is manifested in *Attorney-General of the Federation v Attorney-General of Abia State*,[127] where the Supreme Court overwhelmingly held that all is justiciable.

The approach adopted by courts during this period indicates how hyper-judicialization can lead to juristocracy. For example, in response to contentions that Nigerian courts had links with American jurisprudence on the political question doctrine, the Supreme Court reasoned in *Inakoju v Adeleke*[128] that, because provisions relating to the removal from office differed in the two constitutions, American precedents did not bind the Nigerian Supreme Court. Arguably, to carve its approach in stone, while section 188(1) of the constitution provides that the legislature shall determine what amounts to 'gross misconduct', the Supreme Court defined what in its own opinion amounted to 'gross misconduct'.[129] Moreover, the Court added professional qualifications, age, gender, and psychological features to the conditions expressly stated in the constitution that members of the panel should fulfil.[130]

In probably one of its most progressive moves, the Supreme Court held in *Ugwu v Ararume*[131] that 'in view of the contemporary occurrences in the Nigerian political scene' it is the duty of the Court to delve into intra-party democracy to protect threats to the enthronement of representative government.[132] This practically amounts to protecting democracy against itself. The difficulty with these judicial encroachments on political preserves is their inconsistency. Nwauche points out the strikingly different approach to the political question doctrine between *Onuoha* and *Ararume*, even where the Court did not succeed in demonstrating that the facts of the two cases were not distinguishable.[133] In the *Ararume* case, the Court eventually decided who the actual candidate of a party should be in the following election, in full negation of an internal decision of that party. Forced to support a candidate chosen for it by the Supreme Court, the People's Democratic Party (PDP) expelled Senator Ararume, withdrew from the race and supported another candidate.[134]

Nigerian courts seem to have adopted a wiser approach in dealing with technical issues. For instance, in *Esiaga v University of Calabar*,[135] the Supreme Court held that it was ill-equipped to handle academic matters.[136] In light of the Nigerian experience, it may be reasonably concluded that the expansive judicialization of politics proceeded earlier from the importation of the American approach to the political question doctrine before shifting to a contextualized perspective to the separation of powers in the successive constitutions of Nigeria. The post-1999 trend towards the adjudication of political issues appears to find ground in the need to curtail increasing tendencies on the part of the political branches of government to abuse self-restrained adjudication. At the same time, there is evidence that the reaction of political branches to expansive judicialization may render the judicial office vulnerable to social and political backlashes and possibly to be less respected. The next issue is what may be seen as the unacceptable or, rather, unprecedented moves towards juristocracy in African constitutionalism.

[126] See eg Benjamin Obi Nwabueze, *The Presidential Constitution of Nigeria* (Hurst & Co with Nwamife Publishers 1982) 143; Mike Ikhariale, 'Impeachment Proceedings and the Political Question Doctrine: The Nigerian Experience' (1990) 1 *LASU Law Journal* 54.

[127] *Attorney-General of the Federation v Attorney-General of Abia State* (2001) FWLR (Pt 64) para 202.

[128] *Inakoju v Adeleke* (2007) All FWLR (Pt 353).

[129] ibid paras 85–6.

[130] ibid paras 81–2.

[131] *Ugwu v Ararume* (2007) 12 NWLR (Pt 1048).

[132] ibid paras 367 and 461.

[133] See Nwauche (n 116).

[134] ibid.

[135] *Esiaga v University of Calabar* (2004) All FLWR (Pt 206) para 381. See also *Magit v University of Agriculture Makurdi* (2006) All FWLR (Pt 298).

[136] ibid para 1313.

3.4 'Pure politics': when democracies are made in courts?

The cases discussed below evolve from less 'life-changing' situations to more dramatic jurisprudential moves, concluding with amendments of constitutions and the debate about term limits.

3.4.1 Benin

One of the most empowered constitutional bodies in the new constitutionalism in Africa, at least in Francophone Africa, is arguably the Constitutional Court of Benin. I have earlier alluded to the distinctive features of the Benin Court when discussing its human rights mandate.[137] Pursuant to Article 117 of the constitution, the Court is competent to hear disputes arising from presidential and parliamentary elections. Benin has a Kelsenian Constitutional Court, which stands outside the judicial apparatus, where a supreme court is placed at the apex of the ordinary court system, with jurisdiction over criminal, administrative, and financial matters. Decisions of the Constitutional Court are binding on all authorities, including courts.[138] Article 131 of the constitution provides that decisions of the Supreme Court are binding on all branches of government and all tribunals, the Constitutional Court and the High Court of Justice being two of them that equally make final and binding pronouncements.[139]

In a bid to revise the voters' register that led to the 2011 presidential election, political actors agreed to set up the *Conseil d'Orientation et de Supervision* (COS) as a supervisory body composed of representatives of the ruling coalition and opposition groups. However, as a result of political disagreements, the COS was pulled from all sides. Launched in 2013, its operation was stalled, dragging on for over two years, with no tangible list to show a few months before the 2015 parliamentary and local elections. In the face of the foreseen impossibility for the National Independent Electoral Commission (CENA) to set a date for the local elections, a citizen filed a suit before the Constitutional Court requesting the body to set a date for the COS to produce the register.

While the complainant specifically sought 'an urgent finalisation of a reliable voters' register', the Court in its Review of the Voters' Register ruling[140] not only ordered the COS to finalize the register before a specific date, but proceeded to set the dates of both parliamentary and local elections. Pursuant to Article 305(1) of the Electoral Code, the Constitutional Court is competent to hear issues arising from voters' registration and, therefore, set a deadline for the COS to produce the list. However, the issue before the Constitutional Court was not whether the dates of the parliamentary and local elections were within the jurisdiction of the Supreme Court. The Constitutional Court did not explain how it had assumed jurisdiction to set the dates for both elections. Some commentators argue that the decision was not sound in both fact and law, even though they believed that the Court had prevented a political stalemate.[141]

[137] See Gilles Badet, *Les Attributions Originelles de la Cour Constitutionnelle du Bénin* (Friedrich Ebert Stiftung 2013); Fondation Konrad Adenauer, *Commentaire de la Constitution Béninoise du 11 Décembre 1990: Esprit, Lettre, Interprétation et Pratique de la Constitution par le Bénin et ses Institutions* (FKA 2009); see also Adjolohoun (n 52).

[138] Article 124.

[139] The *Haute Cour de Justice* is mandated to try the president of the republic and members of the cabinet for offences committed during their term in office and enumerated in the constitution. See Adjolohoun (n 49).

[140] DCC 15-001 of 9 January 2015.

[141] See Joël Aivo, 'Joël Aïvo sur la Dcc 15-001: "Dans l'impasse, c'est la seule décision à prendre"' http://www.lanouvelletribune.info/benin/politique/22449-joel-aivo-sur-la-dcc-15-001-dans-l-impasse-c-est-la-seule-decision-a-prendre (last accessed 17 April 2017); Victor Topanou, '"Cette décision risque de ne pas

The difficulty in understanding the Constitutional Court's position was palpable in a decision given a few weeks later. In DCC 15-093,[142] when the court was called upon to endorse a proposal by political stakeholders to postpone the initial dates fixed for local elections, the Constitutional Court declined jurisdiction on the ground that it was the Supreme Court that had competence over disputes relating to local elections. The Constitutional Court explained that it had arrived at its Review of Voters' Register ruling on the dates by assuming its mandate to regulate the functioning of state institutions as provided for in the constitution. Only then did it appear that the Constitutional Court had assumed jurisdiction to set the dates in a bid to avoid a new postponement of the overdue elections and to dissipate political tension in the country. The Electoral Commission reverted to political parties, who eventually agreed on a date for the local elections. The Commission, however, went back to the Court with a request for authorization to proceed with the date, which the Court endorsed through a new judgment.[143]

This case illustrates how a court can stretch its mandate to deal with a matter that actually rests with political stakeholders. Although the purported motive is to protect democracy, the ruling begs the question whether the end can justify the means. Such a position raises more suspicion, particularly in a constitutional setting where the executive appoints almost all members of a body as powerful as the Constitutional Court.

The Constitutional Court has made far-reaching rulings in the past. A landmark case, without doubt, is that of the *Majority—Minority* or *Political Representation in Parliament* case, where the court had to deal with an issue that arose in a dispute between the executive and legislature on the representation of political parties in the Bureau of Parliament and its committees. In its DCC 09-002 ruling of 8 January 2009, the court held that the political minority was entrusted with rights in parliament since the principle of 'the winner takes all' was not acceptable in a democratic society. The court defined the rights of the political minority- the party or coalition of parties with the lowest number of members in parliament—as a *principe à valeur constitutionnelle*.[144]

At the time of the ruling, members of the Constitutional Court were believed to be in favour of the presidential coalition, which had recently lost the support of the majority of members of parliament. As Fombad points out, most constitutional courts in Francophone Africa adopted an appointment mechanism whereby the president of the republic directly or indirectly appointed half, if not all, the judges.[145] In some jurisdictions, the other half are appointed by parliament, which in most cases is made up of members of the ruling party or coalition.[146]

Surprisingly, the Constitutional Court, with the same composition, overturned its precedent two years later in the same circumstances, but with the difference that the presidential coalition had now secured a majority in parliament. In DCC 11-047 of 21 July 2011

être appliquée" dixit Victor Topanou' http://www.24haubenin.info/?Cette-decision-risque-de-ne-pas (last accessed 17 April 2017).

142 Decision of 15 April 2015.

143 See Horace S Adjolohoun, 'Incertitudes Electorales au Bénin: Quand la Juristocratie prend le pas sur la Démocratie?' *Fraternité* (1 June 2015) 2, 3.

144 A constitutional principle, meaning principles not provided for in the text of the constitution but derived from particular clauses, structure of the constitution, or political theory. The Constitutional Court of Benin, however, does not provide any definition of constitutional principles.

145 See Charles M Fombad, 'Appointment of Constitutional Adjudicators in Africa: Some Perspectives on How Different Systems Yield Similar Outcomes' (2014) 46(2) *Journal of Legal Pluralism and Unofficial Law* 249–75.

146 See Adama Kpodar, 'Bilan sur un Demi-Siècle de Constitutionnalisme en Afrique Noire Francophone' http://afrilex.u-bordeaux4.fr/sites/afrilex/IMG/pdf/BILAN_SUR_UN_DEMI-SIECLE_DE_CONSTITUTIONNALISME_EN_AFRIQUE_NOIRE_FRANCOPHONE.pdf (last accessed 17 April 2017); see also Adjolohoun (n 49).

the Court ruled that proportionality regarding representation on parliamentary committees and other external positions must be determined *in casu*, and the 'majority-minority' doctrine must be 'enlightened' by the *summa divisio* 'presidential coalition versus opposition'. Such a jurisprudential move led opposition groups in parliament—the minority of the day—to blame the constitutional tribunal for devaluing the 'minority principle' to the rank of a *principe à géométrie variable*.[147] In this particular case, even if the Constitutional Court acted within its constitutional review mandate, political interference was plausible considering the appointment factor, the unchanged composition of the Court, and the shift of majority in parliament against the executive. The case reveals a trend of the executive using the Constitutional Court to overcome losses incurred in purely political processes conducted in compliance with the rules of parliament. Within that span of time, the executive adopted a consistent trend of systematically litigating every disagreement with the new majority group in parliament.[148] The trend has led critics to suggest that the Court had positioned itself as a de facto second chamber of parliament.[149]

The appointment factor is relevant in light of the fact that such trends were even more surprising from a court that had consistently defended the strict separation of powers. It had held, inter alia, that parliament had discretionary powers to decide how its internal elections should be conducted, as long as the ballot is secret and candidates are members of parliament;[150] that a presidential decree suspending the execution of court orders was in violation of the constitution as it interfered with the independence of the judiciary;[151] and that an order by the Minister of Justice to release a detainee constituted an interference with the judiciary and violated the constitution.[152] In light of the foregoing examples, the 2011 decision poses a problem for the principle of separation of powers.[153]

The cases discussed next involve the power to amend the constitution. The question that arose was whether parliament could legally amend provisions of the constitution on its own and if the adjudicatory power of the Constitutional Court superseded the right of the people to amend the constitution. As in the case of most other constitutions, Benin's constitution of 1990 may under certain conditions be amended. What the fundamental law does not say, however, is whether 'non-consensual' revision is in violation of the spirit of the constitution. The Constitutional Court of Benin responded by carving consensual revision in stone. When the issue arose in 2006 and 2007, the Court dismissed attempts to amend the constitution mainly on the grounds that the people had adopted the fundamental law through a national consensus reached at the 1990 National Conference.

The landmark decision of the Constitutional Court in this respect is DCC 06-074 of 12 January 2001, where the Court held that such national consensus had become a *principe à valeur constitutionnelle* (principle with constitutional status), which ought to apply whenever

[147] The term was used by some political stakeholders to mean 'a principle that moves according to the minority or the majority of the day'. On a critical analysis of DCC 09-002 of 8 January 2009 and the '*principes à valeur constitutionnelle*'; see Adama Kpodar, 'Décision de la Cour Constitutionnelle du Bénin DCC 09-002 Du 8 Janvier 2009 "Une bonne année à la démocratie pluraliste"' in La Constitution en Afrique http://www.la-constitution-en-afrique.org/article-28611580.htmln (last accessed 17 April 2017); Stéphane Bolle, 'Décision DCC 09-002: Le Bon Grain et l'Ivraie' in La Constitution en Afrique http://www.la-constitution-en-afrique.org/article-26613703.html (last accessed 17 April 2017).

[148] See, in general, Adjolohoun (n 49).

[149] See eg Frédéric Joël Aivo, 'Le Parlement Béninois sous le Renouveau Démocratique: Réussites et Echecs', RADC-CRDA Conférence annuelle sur 'L'internationalisation du droit constitutionnel', Rabat, Morocco (20 January 2011) 3–4.

[150] DCC 03-168 of 26 November 2003; see also DCC 01-13 of 29 January 2009.

[151] DCC 07-175 of 27 December 2007.

[152] DCC 01-018 of 9 May 2001.

[153] See Abraham Hervé Diompy, 'Les Dynamiques Récentes de la Justice Constitutionnelle en Afrique Francophone' http://afrilex.u-bordeaux4.fr/les-dynamiques-recentes-de-la.html (last accessed 17 April 2017).

any amendments to the constitution were contemplated. The case concerned an amendment effected by members of parliament to extend their term of office from four to five years. In the Court's view, the principle of 'national consensus' was established by the February 1990 National Conference, which also initiated the December 1990 constitution. As a consequence, any amendment of the constitution should follow the public and open process adopted by that conference. The Court thus declared the term extension contrary to the constitution.

Adopting a similar approach, the Constitutional Court subsequently quashed indirect attempts by the executive when it held in DCC 05-139 and DCC 05-145 that the economic arguments used to justify amendments to the constitution and to extend presidential term limits were not in conformity with the constitution.[154] The executive had in fact launched a campaign proposing an amendment to hold presidential and parliamentary elections together in order to reduce the substantial election-related expenditure. This proposal, however, raised fear among the public that it would open a Pandora's box to amend the term limit provision and allow the incumbent president to run for a third term.[155] In its next decision regarding constitutional amendments, the Court went a step further. This situation remained until the *Unamendable Constitutional Clauses*[156] case was decided in 2011.

The *Unamendable Constitutional Clauses* case is a mixture of issues bearing on the amendment of the constitution, the presidential term limit, and referendum. On 11 October 2011, the president of the republic filed a request for a review of the Organic Law on Referendum adopted by parliament in accordance with Articles 117 and 121 of the constitution. In providing for limitations to the scope of referenda, that is, matters that may not be submitted to referendum, Article 6 of the Referendum Law, not surprisingly, relied on the text of the constitution. Article 156 of the constitution provides that: '[n]o amendment procedure may commence or proceed when the integrity of the territory is under threat. The republican form and secular nature of the state may not be subject to amendment'.

In DCC 11-067 of 20 October 2011, the court found that Article 6 of the Referendum Law was inconsistent with the constitution as it did not enumerate all fundamental options of the February 1990 National Conference, which are stated in Articles 42, 44, and 54 of the constitution. These constitutional provisions prescribe a two-term limit, set the age limit for candidates (40–70 years), and the presidential type of the political regime. The court went on to redraft Article 6 of the Referendum Law as follows: '[M]ay not be subjected to referendum, the fundamental options of the February 1990 National Conference, which are ...'.[157] In a decision less than two pages in length, the court apparently displaced the original constituent power, and rewrote the constitution.

The amendment and referendum cases raise a more complex question, namely, whether the people retain the power to amend the constitution directly, through referendum or through their elected representatives. As the outcome has inevitable implications for representative democracy, it is relevant to interrogate the propriety of the Court's pronouncements. The amendment cases had political motives, as members of parliament had sought to extend their terms in office, and the executive indirectly wanted to extend the second and last term of the president. In these cases, the Court decided the matters free from political pressure. Furthermore, the reviews occurred in the context of strong public opposition to amendments believed to be opportunistic, as there was a fear that this could

[154] DCC 05-139 of 17 November 2005 and DCC 05-145 of 1 December 2005.

[155] See Gilles Badet, *Bénin, Démocratie et Participation à la Vie Politique: Une Evaluation de 20 ans de 'Renouveau Démocratique'* (OSIWA 2010) 112–15.

[156] DCC 11-067 of 20 October 2011.

[157] DCC 11-067 of 20 October 2011.

open a Pandora's box for removing the presidential two-term limit.[158] The rationale behind judicialization here is, therefore, rather to affirm the position of the Court concerning consensual amendments and to strengthen its image among a citizenry largely opposed to opportunistic constitutional amendments.

In the referendum case, supporters of the Constitutional Court mainly argue that the power of the original constituent body to alter unamendable provisions of the constitution is exercised once: at the time of the adoption of the constitution. Any power exercised thereafter must be in accordance with the constitution and its interpretation by the court.[159] The argument is based on the principle that when it acts as a constituted constituent power (secondary constituent body), the people may not effect changes to the fundamental principles of the constitution. Doing so would amount to acting as the original or primary constituent (constitution-making) body.[160] Thus, as commentators argue, even the people must abide by the pre-established rules for revision under the review supervision of the Constitutional Court.[161] This proposition should hold except that, in the case of Benin, the Court extended the expressly unamendable provisions to three more provisions of the constitution. The Court raised the amendable provisions to unamendable ones using the proceedings of the 1990 National Conference that led to the drafting and adoption of the constitution.[162]

Proponents argue that the Court may add to the unamendable provisions as long as the new provisions are found in the constitution, which it has the power to protect against encroachment. They suggest that the purposive interpretation by the Court sought to protect key pillars of the constitution, such as regime change and the national consensus that prevailed during the discussions leading to the adoption of the constitution.[163] Examples from Burkina Faso, Germany, and Turkey support the historical and evolving approach to constitutional review relating to constitutional amendments.[164]

It may be argued that the reasons put forward by the Court were more political than legal. To begin with, the constitution itself has cited issues that may not be subjected to referendum, and the Court was bound by the limited list of these issues. Expanding

[158] See Mouhamadou Moustapha Aidara, 'Le Juge Constitutionnel Africain et le Contrôle des Lois portant Révision de la Constitution: Contribution à un Débat' http://afrilex.u-bordeaux4.fr/le-juge-constitutionnel-africain.html (last accessed 17 April 2017); Lise Rakner and Ingvild Skage, 'Don't Touch My Constitution: Civil Society Resistance and Political Turnovers in Africa's Pluralist Regimes' https://projectcontentiouspolitics.files.wordpress.com/2015/02/rakner-skage-isa-workshop-feb-2015.pdf (last accessed 17 April 2017); Voice of America, 'Benin Court Rejects Longer Terms for Lawmakers' http://m.voanews.com/a/a-13-2006-07-10-voa40/320437.html (last accessed 17 April 2017).

[159] See Adama Kpodar, 'La Cour Constitutionnelle du Bénin peut-elle Soumettre, aux "Options Fondamentales de la Conférence Nationale", le Peuple dans l'Exercice de son Pouvoir de Révision?' (2013) 1 *Annuaire Béninois de Justice Constitutionnelle* 703–16.

[160] See Alain Laquièze, 'La Réception de Sieyès par la Doctrine Publiciste Française' in Pierre-Yves Quiviger, Vincent Denis, and Jean Salem (eds), *Figure de Sieyès* (Publications de la Sorbonne 2008) 114.

[161] See Richard Stacey, 'Constituent Power and Carl Schmitt's Theory of Constitution in Kenya's Constitution Making Process' (2011) 9 *International Journal of Constitutional Law* 587–614; Claude Klein, 'Le Contrôle des Lois Constitutionnelles: Introduction à une Problématique Moderne' (2010) 27 *Cahier du Conseil Constitutionnel*.

[162] See Geneviève Koubi, *Le Préambule de la Constitution de 1946: Antinomies Juridiques et Contradictions Politiques* (Presses universitaires de France 1996) 9. The author suggests that the constitution is also about its history.

[163] See Kpodar (n 159) 714–15.

[164] See eg Decision No 2012-008/CC of 26 April 2012 of the Constitutional Council of Burkina Faso (the Council assumed jurisdiction while the constitution was silent and extended the list of unamendable provisions); Decision of 23 April 1991 of the Constitutional Court of Germany Cases No 1 BvR 1170, 1174, 1175/90 (the court relied on 'fundamental principles of justice' in order assume review jurisdiction); Decision of 3 April 1971 of the Constitutional Court of Turkey Application No 1971 /37 41 (the court referred to 'necessity of contemporary civilisation' and 'coherence of the constitutional order').

the list beyond these issues amounted to rewriting the constitution.[165] Furthermore, compared to the German constitution, for instance, the Benin constitution does not include any 'fundamental options or principles'. The drafters would have included in the text all the principles that have been added by the Court had they wanted the proceedings of the National Conference to be incorporated into the constitution.[166] Commentators on both sides agree that the Court adjudicated a purely political matter by prohibiting amendments.[167]

Even most ardent defenders of judicial activism—such as Favoreu—did not go that far, that is to contemplate the constitutional judge rising above the primary constituent, namely, the people.[168] As Vedel opined, the government of judges materializes when courts move beyond applying or interpreting the constitution to completing or correcting it through its own rules, even with the best intentions.[169] The Benin Constitutional Court may have saved democracy and protected the people against opportunistic amendments to the constitution, but the question is whether it acted in compliance with fundamental principles of constitutionalism. Assuming the court acted as the guardian of the constitution, who watches the gatekeeper? This question finds an interesting echo in constitutional adjudication in Burundi, where the court also rewrote the constitution to allow the president run for a third term.

3.4.2 Burundi

The Constitutional Court of Burundi has earned worldwide fame for its pronouncement in the *Presidential Third Term* case. In the aftermath of the 21 October 1993 *coup* that ousted President Melchior Ndadaye, a civil war broke out in Burundi that led to inter-ethnic massacres. Following years of negotiation under the aegis of international and regional organizations, the warring parties signed the Arusha Peace and Reconciliation Agreement (Arusha Agreement) on 28 August 2000. Burundi incorporated the Arusha Agreement through an Act of Parliament, namely, Law No 1/017 of 1 December 2000, thus making it domestic law. Notably, Article 7(1)(a) of Protocol II of the Arusha Agreement provides that: '[s]ave for the very first presidential election, the President of the Republic shall be elected through direct suffrage'. Article 7(1)(c) states that: '[f]or the first election, to be held during the transition period, the President shall be indirectly elected—ie by parliament—as specified in Article 20 below'. Finally, Article 7(3) provides that: '[t]he President shall be elected for a term of five years, renewable only once. No one may serve more than two presidential terms'.

Two provisions of the 2005 constitution of Burundi set out conditions according to which the president shall be elected and serve his term. Article 96 prescribes that: '[t]he President shall be elected by direct universal suffrage for a five-year term renewable once'. Article 302 provides that: '[e]xceptionally, the first President of the Republic to be elected during the post-transition period will be elected by the National Assembly and the Senate in a joint Congress meeting'.

[165] See Emmanuel J Seyès, *Qu'est-ce que le Tiers Etat?* (Boucher 2002) 50.

[166] See Georges Vedel, 'Souveraineté et Supra Constitutionnalité' (1993) 67 *Pouvoirs* 79–97.

[167] See Dodzi Kokoroko, 'La Cour Constitutionnelle du Bénin peut-elle Soumettre, aux "Options Fondamentales de la Conférence Nationale", le Peuple dans l'Exercice de son Pouvoir de Révision?' (2013) 1 *Annuaire Béninois de Justice Constitutionnelle* 717–28.

[168] See Jean-Eric Schoettl, 'Le Conseil Constitutionnel peut-il Contrôler une Loi Constitutionnelle?' (2003) 70 *Les Petites Affiches* 18.

[169] See Georges Vedel, 'La Place de la Déclaration de 1789 dans le Bloc de Constitutionnalité' in Conseil Constitutionnel, *La Déclaration des Droits de l'Homme et du Citoyen et la Jurisprudence* (PUF 1898) 63.

The dispute that led to the case adjudicated by the Constitutional Court of Burundi arose when President Pierre Nkunrunziza, who had served two terms (elected in 2000 and re-elected in 2005), announced his intention to run again. On 21 March 2014, President Nkunrunziza failed to pass a bill amending the constitution through parliament.[170] He subsequently contemplated a referendum, which was eventually abandoned after civil society organizations, the Catholic Church, and prominent members of his CNDD-FDD political coalition had opposed the bid.[171] On 26 April 2015, the president nonetheless obtained a nomination by his party to run for the forthcoming presidential election that had been scheduled for 26 June 2015. According to opponents of the bid, the president's move violated the constitution and the Arusha Agreement and his governance credentials did not earn him any further term as the President of Burundi. Street protests broke out following the announcement of the nomination and led to violence and loss of lives in only a few weeks.

Against this background, on 28 April 2015, fourteen senators, members of the presidential coalition, filed a request for interpretation of Articles 96 and 302 of the constitution. In decision RCCB 303 of 5 May 2015, the Constitutional Court of Burundi endorsed the president's bid for a third term through two main arguments. First, the Court held that, on the interpretation of Article 96, '[t]he number of terms derived through direct universal suffrage is limited to only two, but article 302 creates a special term through indirect universal suffrage, which is not related to the two terms provided for in article 96'.[172] Secondly, the court concluded that: '[a]s a matter of law, the renewal one last time of the ongoing presidential term through direct universal suffrage for five years is not inconsistent with the constitution'.[173] The sky did not fall, but this could rightly be termed as a constitutional tsunami. The magnitude of the quake caused the vice-president of the court to flee the country the day before the ruling, subsequently reporting death threats against him and his colleagues who disagreed with the court's interpretation but were forced to endorse it.[174]

It suffices to stress that the Constitutional Court recognized the Arusha Agreement as the bedrock and one of the fundamental bases of the constitution. It further recalled that the agreement was part of Burundian law, and held that bypassing these fundamental principles would amount to a violation of the constitution. The court stated that the Arusha mediators had clearly intended to prevent any president from running for more than two terms. However, it held that the drafters of the constitution had misunderstood the 'recommendations' of the Arusha Agreement. The court thus concluded that, instead of an exception to the mode of election, Article 302 was an exception to Article 96 and, therefore, to the two-term limit.

This reasoning has striking similarities to that of the Constitutional Chamber of the Supreme Court of Honduras which, in a unanimous judgment dated 22 April 2015, removed the term limit provision altogether, paving the way for the incumbent

[170] Gratien Rukindikiza, 'Le Ciel est Tombé sur la tête de Nkurunziza' https://burundi24.wordpress.com/2014/03/25/le-ciel-est-tombe-sur-la-tete-de-nkurunziza/ (last accessed 17 April 2017); Agenzia Fides 'Révision constitutionnelle: Vers une Tentative de Référendum après l'échec de la Procédure Parlementaire?' http://www.fides.org/fr/news/37486-AFRIQUE_BURUNDI_Revision_constitutionnelle_vers_une_tentative_de_referendum_apres_l_echec_de_la_procedure_parlementaire#.VXTeho6Abdk (last accessed 17 April 2017).

[171] See Eric Bizimana, 'Arrêt RCCB 303: la Cour constitutionnelle du Burundi au Secours du Président Pierre Nkurunziza' (newspaper article on file with author) (2015).

[172] See Decision RCCB 303 of 5 May 2015 para 4.

[173] RCCB 303 of 5 May 2015 para 5.

[174] See Jeune Afrique, 'Burundi: Le Vice-Président de la Cour Constitutionnelle Dénonce des Pressions et s'enfuit' http://www.jeuneafrique.com/depeches/231076/politique/burundi-le-vice-president-de-la-cour-constitutionnelle-denonce-des-pressions-et-senfuit/ (last accessed 17 April 2017).

president to run. In this case the provisions were unamendable and made the promotion of presidential re-election unconstitutional, illegal, and punishable with imprisonment of five to ten years and loss of citizenship. Interestingly, the incumbent president moved the amendment.[175] Whether in Honduras or Burundi, courts of final instance ruled on behalf of and above the people. Even the fear of wrecking the constitutional edifice no longer constrains top judges' appetite for the anti-constitutional adjudication of matters that are normally the exclusive preserve of the people and their elected representatives. Senegal experienced a slightly different third presidential term situation.

3.4.3 Senegal

The first case here involved a political figure that Senegal and Africa will remember as a prolific engineer of constitutional amendments. During his term as President of Senegal from 2000 to 2012, lawyer and economist Abdoulaye Wade successfully initiated more than fifteen amendments to the 2001 Constitution. Although about twenty of these amendments occurred under his immediate predecessor, Abdou Diouf, it is not in dispute that President Wade alone engineered the highest number of changes introduced by a single president in the shortest time. From independence to 2014, the 1963 Constitution was amended thirty-four times, of which thirty-two amendments were brought about by the president of the republic and the other two by parliament.[176] According to a Senegalese commentator, the vast majority of these amendments were 'de-consolidating', that is, personalized and used as means to solving personal grievances with political opponents, and the opposition-led majority in parliament.[177]

In 2007, Wade spearheaded the adoption by his large majority in parliament of (Gender Parity) Law No 23/2007, amending the Electoral Code to introduce gender parity into the list of candidates for parliament. In response, opposition members of the National Assembly of Senegal initiated a constitutional review before the Constitutional Council. The petitioners requested the top court to declare the Gender Parity Law unconstitutional on the ground that its relevant provisions violated the preamble and Article 1 of the constitution, which provides for equality and non-discrimination in access to public office. In its *Gender Parity in Political Representation* judgment,[178] the Council found in favour of the petitioners and declared the Law in violation of the constitution for drawing a distinction between candidates on the basis of their gender.[179] The Council stressed that the right to access public office did not supersede that of equality before the law, although both were constitutional principles.[180]

[175] See David Landau and Brian Sheppard, 'The Honduran Constitutional Chamber's Decision Erasing Presidential Term Limits: Abusive Constitutionalism by Judiciary?' http://www.iconnectblog.com/2015/05/the-honduran-constitutional-chambers-decision-erasing-presidential-term-limits-abusive-constitutionalism-by-judiciary/ (last accessed 17 April 2017).

[176] See Mously Ndiaye, 'Tripatouillage de la Charte fondamentale: la Constitution du Sénégal a été révisée 37 fois en 52 ans' (Seneweb 2012) http://www.seneweb.com/news/Politique/tripatouillages-de-la-charte-fondamentale-la-constitution-du-senegal-a-ete-revisee-37-fois-en-52-ans_n_57252.html (last accessed 17 April 2017).

[177] See Ismaila Madior Fall, 'La Révision de la Constitution au Sénégal' http://afrilex.u-bordeaux4.fr/sites/afrilex/IMG/pdf/La_revision_de_la_Constitution_au_Senegal_Ismaila.pdf (last accessed 17 April 2017).

[178] Decision 97/2007 of 27 April 2007 Conseil Constitutionnel du Sénégal.

[179] ibid para 5.

[180] ibid para 4. The Council also relied on the equality clause in art 6 of the Declaration of the Rights of Man and of the Citizen.

Although the Council did not make any express mention of a political question being raised by the petitioners, it appears that it chose to settle, through the lens of human rights, and probably ordinary judicial review of legislation, a matter that was highly politically charged, for at least two reasons. First, it was brought by a head of the executive whose legislative endeavours are known to be strongly politically motivated,[181] although in favour of rights and in this particular case applauded by women's rights activists.[182] Secondly, whether political parties must file a list that includes an equal number of male and female candidates for universal suffrage-based election is certainly a matter for the people or, at the very least, their elected representatives in the executive or legislature to decide. The Council itself relied on Article 3 of the constitution, which provides that: '[n]ational sovereignty belongs to the people of Senegal who exercise it through their representatives or through referendum'.

In this case, the president of the republic and parliament, therefore, acted within the ambit of their constitutionally conferred powers. The Council should probably have construed equality in the constitution to suit the will of the people expressed through their representatives.[183] At worst, the Council would have declined jurisdiction or ruled the matter political. President Wade's response to the Council's ruling was very telling of what the political backlash to such judicial activism could have resulted in. He had his majority in parliament decide to amend the constitution to include the equality clause cast aside by the Constitutional Council.[184] The Constitutional Council of Senegal also heard a number of electoral disputes based on the equality provision in the constitution, although in most instances jointly with relevant provisions of the Electoral Code.[185]

In conclusion, regarding the *Gender Parity in Political Representation* case, it is worth noting that the Council raised and dealt with the gender equality issue not only as a human rights matter but also, indirectly, as a political question. On the first approach, the Council appropriately picked the human rights side but, surprisingly, shied away from the rather proactive and human rights activist body it revealed itself to be in the *Use of Presidential Attributes for Campaign* case. On the second approach, it certainly stepped into the spheres of both the executive and legislature by making a substantive determination on the core issue of the case. It did not, as would have been expected of a court that respects the coordinate branches and acts within 'passive virtues', to provide directions as to the proper procedure for the parity project to translate into constitutionally viable provisions. That could have been done effectively either by asserting jurisdiction and reading the law under review into the constitutional provisions, or directing the political branches to seek an amendment.

The second case almost brought Senegal to the brink of a political crisis. The *Presidential (Second–Third) Term Limit* case[186] arose in the wake of the 2012 presidential election in which the incumbent, President Wade, announced that he would run again after serving a

[181] Illustrations abound of changes made to the constitution merely to satisfy personal egos, for popularity, to remove allies who disagreed with the president or to prevent opponents from getting hold of a strategic political position. See Babacar Kanté, 'Le Sénégal: Un Exemple de Continuité et d'Instabilité Constitutionnelle' (1989) *Revue Juridique Politique et Economique du Maroc* 154; see also Fall (n 177).

[182] See Daouda Diop, 'La Parité Rejetée par le Conseil Constitutionnel du Sénégal' http://www.genreenaction.net/La-parite-rejetee-par-le-Conseil-Constitutionnel.html (last accessed 17 April 2017).

[183] One further reason for adopting this approach to adjudication was that the preamble to the constitution 'incorporates' CEDAW.

[184] See Loi Constitutionnelle No 2008-30 of 7 August 2008 modifying arts 7, 63, 68, 71, and 82 of the constitution.

[185] For an overview of decisions of the Constitutional Council of Senegal see ACCPUF, 'Le Conseil constitutionnel du Sénégal' http://www.accpuf.org/images/pdf/cm/senegal/054-jc-decisions_CC_1993-2005.pdf (last accessed 17 April 2017).

[186] Affaire No E/2012, Decision of 27 January 2012, Conseil constitutionnel du Sénégal.

seven and a later a five-year term from 2000. An appropriate background to this case originates in 2000 when the resilient political opponent, Wade, who had been arrested several times,[187] defeated President Abdou Diouf's forty-year ruling *Parti Socialiste*.[188] Wade won his first term under the political slogan of *Sopi* (change in Ouolof local dialect), as part of which he pledged to bring radical change to political governance in Senegal.[189] It was public knowledge that, in 2007, the last year of his first seven-year term, Wade publicly made an undertaking not to run for another term if he was re-elected in that year's election. Wade is said to have backed off close to the 2012 election, after he had stated in his annual address to the country: 'I made a pledge; I withdraw it'.[190]

There is, however, more to the countrywide uprising in which the judicial part of the story led Senegal. In an attempt to solve the second–third term conundrum, President Wade spearheaded several amendments. Elected in 2000 for seven years in a 'no term limit' era, he had the duration of the term reduced to five years renewable once in the year following his accession into power, that is, 2001. After having won a second—then five-year—term in 2007, he restored the seven-year term through a new constitutional amendment in 2008.[191] The term sought by Wade in the 2012 election was, therefore, to his understanding a second term as the two-term limit introduced in 2001 did not apply to his first term assumed in 2000. Opponents to his 2012 bid strongly challenged this as an attempt to seek a third term in violation of the constitution, but also of his *Sopi* governance motto and public pledge not to run for more than two terms.[192]

The subsequent nationwide debate over the constitutionality of his bid and the interpretation of relevant constitutional provisions led to fierce socio-political disputes between political leaders. Opposition leaders formed a coalition with civil society organizations and demanded that Wade should drop his bid, to no avail. Political moves by the president appeared to support suggestions that he acted maliciously, fully aware of the fact that his 2012 bid was illegal. One such move that occurred a year before the end of his second and last term in 2011 was Wade's attempt to introduce, through an amendment of the constitution, a one-round presidential election with a presidential ticket (president and vice-president elected at the same time) and a 25 per cent threshold to win. Following violent street protests in reaction to this attempt seeking to bring in his son as a running mate, he abandoned the amendment project.[193] As was foreseen, pro- and anti-Wade forces failed to reach an agreement.

[187] *Senego*, 'Ce que Abdoulaye Wade a dit à Karim Wade à Reubess' (2015) http://senego.com/2015/02/16/ce-que-abdoulaye-wade-a-dit-a-karim-wade-a-reubess_218408.html (last accessed 17 April 2017); *Jeune Afrique*, 'Karim: Sa Vie à la Prison de Rebeuss' (2013) http://www.jeuneafrique.com/135744/politique/s-n-gal-karim-wade-sa-vie-la-prison-de-rebeuss/ (last accessed 17 April 2017).

[188] The Parti Socialiste ruled Senegal for 40 years from independence to 2000, first under Presidents Leopold Sedar Senghor and Abdou Diouf. See Dakar Actu, 'Congrès du parti socialiste de 1957 à 2014: Chronique d'un rituel controversé' http://www.dakaractu.com/Congres-du-parti-socialiste-de-1957-a-2014-Chronique-d-un-rituel-controverse_a67045.html (last accessed 17 April 2017); Wikipedia, 'Socialist Party of Senegal' http://en.wikipedia.org/wiki/Socialist_Party_of_Senegal (last accessed 17 April 2017).

[189] See Momar-Coumba Diop, *Le Sénégal sous Abdoulaye Wade: le Sopi à l'Epreuve du Pouvoir* (Khartala 2013).

[190] Regards Croisés, 'Abdoulaye Wade ou l'Archétype de l'Inconstance Africaine' 2012 http://regardscroises.ivoire-blog.com/archive/2012/01/28/abdoulaye-wade-ou-l-archetype-de-l-inconsistance-africaine.html (last accessed 17 April 2017); Libération, 'Sénégal: Wade en Lice une Troisième Fois' 2012 http://www.liberation.fr/monde/2012/01/28/senegal-wade-en-lice-une-3e-fois_791866 (last accessed 17 April 2017).

[191] Stéphane Bolle, 'Quand Wade Fait Réviser sa Constitution' (La Constitution en Afrique) http://www.la-constitution-en-afrique.org/article-19524487.html (last accessed 17 April 2017);

[192] Malickou Ndiaye, 'Abdoulaye Wade: mon Troisième Mandat n'est Pas un Débat' http://koaci.com/m/senegal-abdoulaye-wade-troisieme-mandat-n'est-debat--73323-i.html (last accessed 17 April 2017); Oumar Ndiaye, 'L'impossible Troisième Mandat de Abdoulaye Wade' (Mediapart 2011) http://blogs.mediapart.fr/blog/oumar-ndiaye/270811/senegal-limpossible-3eme-mandat-de-abdoulaye-wade (last accessed 17 April 2017).

[193] On Wade's 2012 bid see Ca M'intéresse, 'Pourquoi ça Chauffe au Sénégal' http://www.caminteresse.fr/economie-societe/senegal-revolte-wade-1120855/ (last accessed 17 April 2017).

Against this background, the Constitutional Council of Senegal was called upon to approve and publish the list of candidates for the 2012 presidential election, as required under Article 29 of the constitution. As a challenge to Wade's bid would have been premature in terms of procedure, and in the absence of an advisory opinion mechanism in the Senegalese constitutional system, the Council's vetting of candidature was expected to settle the third term question as a preliminary issue. The ruling was, therefore, central to the resolution of an issue that had, for the two years preceding the election, split the people of Senegal. In one of the shortest rulings that could be expected from the highest court, and on the determination of such a divisive matter, the Constitutional Council endorsed Wade's candidature. The decision was supported with no reasoning other than taking judicial notice of the fact that the candidate properly filed his candidature, and obtained the requested nomination from his party.[194]

Considering the background provided earlier, the second–third term debate in Senegal's 2012 election was manifestly a political issue, but equally a legal issue requiring the interpretation of constitutional provisions. However, the Council not only observed no 'passive virtues', but also chose to determine the matter in the most simplistic judicial way. Even when offered an opportunity to review its ruling in the social and political environment of the day, the Council dismissed the petitions filed by seven candidates and confirmed the first finding. The street protests that followed led to grave human rights violations, including several deaths and other breaches of civil and political rights by security forces.[195] The Court's pronouncement was not for lack of strong opposition backed by legal arguments provided by many eminent and respected Senegalese constitutional lawyers and other elites in the country and abroad.[196] Nevertheless, this was ignored by a Council composed of renowned jurists and lawyers.

Drafted under the 2001 *Sopi* constitution, Article 26(1) of the constitution introduced a two-term limit that did not exist in the 1963 Constitution. As Wade had already begun a seven-year term under the 1963 Constitution in force in 2000, the drafters sought to ensure that the new five-year term provision applied only after the completion of the ongoing seven-year term.[197] That safety clause was the rationale behind the newly introduced Article 104 of the 2001 Constitution, which provided that: '[t]he incumbent assumes his on-going term in full. All other provisions of this constitution apply to him'. It follows that the special exemption, and the delayed applicability of the 2001 five-year term, applied to the duration of the term without affecting the term limit. The provision in Article 104 that '[a]ll other clauses of the constitution applied to the incumbent President' was sufficient

[194] See Affaire No E/2012, Decision of 27 January 2012, Conseil constitutionnel du Sénégal, paras 9, 25 http://www.rewmi.com/l-integralite-de-l-arret-du-conseil-constitutionnel-du-27-janvier-2012_a55819.html (last accessed 17 April 2017).

[195] See L'Expresse, 'Au Sénégal: la Candidature d'Abdoulaye Wade Confirmée' 2012 http://www.lexpress.fr/actualite/monde/afrique/au-senegal-la-candidature-d-abdoulaye-wade-confirmee_1076779.html (last accessed 17 April 2017); OBS, 'Sénégal: Candidature de Wade Validée, ses Opposants Ecartés' http://tempsreel.nouvelobs.com/monde/20120130.OBS0087/senegal-candidature-de-wade-validee-ses-oppo sants-ecartes.html (last accessed 17 April 2017).

[196] See Babacar Guèye, 'Wade a Epuisé ses Mandats' (Médiapart 2011) https://blogs.mediapart.fr/oumar-ndiaye/blog/270811/senegal-limpossible-3eme-mandat-de-abdoulaye-wade (last accessed 17 April 2017); Ismaila Madior Fall, 'Le Président Wade ne Peut Pas Briguer un Troisième Mandat' (Rewmi 2010) http://www.rewmi.com/ismaila-madior-fall-le-president-wade-ne-peut-pas-briguer-un-troisieme-mandat_a36207.html (last accessed 17 April 2017); Guy Carcassonne, 'L'inconstitutionnalité de la Candidature de Me Wade, Ne Fait à Mes Yeux, Aucun Doute' (Xalima 2010) http://xalimasn.com/guy-carcassonne-«-l'inconstitutionnalite-de-la-candidature-de-me-wade-ne-fait-a-mes-yeux-aucun-doute-»/ (last accessed 17 April 2017).

[197] See Babacar Guèye (n 196). Constitutional Law Expert, Professor Babacar Guèye, was a prominent member of the Commission that drafted the 2001 constitution.

proof that the number of terms was not affected. Term limit clauses in the Senegalese constitution share similarities with the Burundi case discussed earlier.

The Senegal case study illustrates how courts can handle, and have handled, highly disputed and sensitive issues of a social and political nature in the lightest manner, in the same way as for any other ordinary judicial review question. Through constitutional review or the interpretation of provisions of the constitution, courts end up making determinations on issues such as term limits that fall within the sovereign discretion of the people in a constitutional and representative democracy. The question is whether courts, from being guardians of the constitution and guarantors of constitutionalism and democracy, are increasingly turning into constituent bodies through hyper-judicialization.

4. Judicialization of Politics in African Regional Forums

The reason for discussing adjudication in regional bodies is that most of these bodies have a mandate to consider human rights complaints. This allows for a relevant analysis of how this subject matter could easily provide a cover for the judicialization of politics. Although regional bodies do not use national constitutions as their substantive law, the provisions of their founding instruments are meant for domestic incorporation. In addition, decisions made by them are enforced in the municipal sphere and, therefore, inevitably impact on the constitutional order of member states and their case law. In other words, some of the issues they deal with may be merely the transfer of domestic disputes to the international plane. The discussion proceeds from the continental to the sub-regional levels.

The African Commission on Human and Peoples' Rights (African Commission) is the oldest regional human rights body in Africa. Established by the African Charter on Human and Peoples' Rights (African Charter) in 1981, the African Commission began its operation in 1987. With a mandate to promote and protect human rights in Africa, the African Commission may entertain individual complaints alleging violations against state parties that are ultimately all African Union (AU) member states.[198] The African Commission also has jurisdiction to interpret the African Charter.[199] The Commission may under certain conditions receive complaints, the most frequently disputed being the exhaustion of local remedies.[200]

In nearly three decades of its operation, the African Commission has received over 500 complaints, of which more than 100 have been decided on the merits as at June 2015.[201] As the premier continental human rights body in Africa, the African Commission was called upon to solve some of the key challenges faced by African states, both during the Cold War dictatorial regimes of the 1980s and the recent democratic dispensations inaugurated in the 1990s.[202] Here two such prominent questions are discussed, which in their nature are rather political than judicial: self-determination (secession) and nationality.

Article 20(1) of the African Charter provides that all peoples 'shall have the unquestionable and inalienable right to self-determination'. In the case of *Katangese Peoples' Congress v Zaire*,[203] the president of the Katangese Peoples' Congress (KPC) filed a complaint alleging

[198] ACHPR art 55. [199] ibid art 45(3). [200] ibid art 56(5).

[201] Information obtained through on-the-record consultation. The identity of related sources is disclosed for reasons of confidentiality. It must be noted that about 100 of those complaints were found inadmissible, several cases were joined, struck out, and a substantial number of the rest are pending consideration.

[202] See Rachel Murray, *The African Commission on Human and Peoples' Rights and International Law* (OUP 2000); Mutoy Mubiala, *Le Système Régional Africain de Protection des Droits de l'Homme* (Bruylant 2005).

[203] (2000) AHRLR 72 (ACHPR 1995) para 1.

a violation of Article 20(1) of the African Charter. The complainant requested the African Commission to recognize that the KPC was entitled to support the achievement of independence for Katanga.

In its decision, the African Commission held the view that, to the understanding of the African Charter, self-determination may be exercised in any way as long as it is fully cognizant of sovereignty and territorial integrity. The Commission concluded that, in the absence of concrete evidence of violations of human rights to the extent that the territorial integrity of Zaire should be called to question, and in the absence of evidence that the people of Katanga were denied the right to participate in government, as guaranteed by Article 13(1) of the African Charter, the Commission held the view that Katanga was obliged to exercise a variant of self-determination that is compatible with the sovereignty and territorial integrity of Zaire (now Democratic Republic of the Congo (DRC)).[204] The Commission proceeded to dismiss the case for lack of merit under the African Charter.

The *Katanga* ruling by the African Commission was in line with the internationally recognized principle of *uti possidetis*, which is Latin for 'may you continue to possess such as you do possess'.[205] During its creation on 25 May 1963, the Organisation of African Unity (OAU) incorporated the principle in Article 3(3) of its Charter to carve in stone the intangibility of borders inherited from the colonial era.[206] Adopting the principle arguably avoided open border wars between newly independent African states.[207] However, the reality of diverse ethnic communities being abruptly forced into independence states' borders by the 1884–1885 Berlin conference, and the socio-economic marginalization to which dominant groups subjected their fellow citizens within the same territories, led to internal conflicts and demands for self-determination.[208]

The claims of self-determination adjudicated by the African Commission illustrate how such demands were not only political but also socio-economic, as revealed in *Media Rights Agenda and Others v Nigeria*,[209] where the Commission held that 'government by force is not compatible with the rights of peoples to freely determine their political future'; and *Front for the Liberation of the State of Cabinda v Angola*,[210] in which case the right to social and economic development was recognized under self-determination as long as the latter was compatible with the rule of *uti possidetis* applied in the *Katanga* case.

The African Commission considered issues of a similar nature in cases relating to nationality. For instance, in *Modise v Botswana*[211] and *Legal Resources Foundation v Zambia*,[212] the Commission declared the denial of citizenship in violation of the right to legal personality under Article 5 of the African Charter. The cases mainly raised the question of whether nationality should accrue only to people born within the territory of a state to parents also born in that state, or to any person who claims a connection with the state concerned.[213] The political nature of such claims is best illustrated in *Open Society Justice Initiative v Côte d'Ivoire*,[214] where the Commission held that the denial of citizenship to

[204] ibid paras 4–6.

[205] Paul R Hensel, Michael E Allison, and Ahmed Khanani, 'The Colonial Legacy and Border Stability: *Utis Possidetis* and Borders Claims in the Americas' http://www.paulhensel.org/Research/io05.pdf (last accessed 17 April 2017).

[206] Article 4(b) of the Constitutive Act of the African Union retained the principle.

[207] In 1964, the OAU passed a resolution stating that the principle would apply across Africa to settle disputes by means of a treaty and not a recourse to force. See OAU Resolution on Border Disputes, 21 July 1964, Cairo.

[208] See Bronwen Manby, *Nationality in Africa* (Open Society 2011) 17–25.

[209] (2000) AHRLR 200 (ACHPR 1998).

[210] Communication 328/06.

[211] (2000) AHRLR 30 (ACHPR 2000).

[212] (2001) AHRLR 84 (ACHPR 2001).

[213] See *Modise* (n 211) para 88 and *Legal Resources Foundation* (n 212) para 71.

[214] Communication 318/06 (decided on 25 February 2015) 17th extraordinary session.

thousands of members of the Dioula ethnic groups who lived in Côte d'Ivoire prior to independence and who had connections with no other state violated the right to legal personality.

Across Africa, and particularly in Côte d'Ivoire, the issue of nationality has remained a highly divisive one, triggering political conflicts owing to discriminatory and xenophobic legislation and policy applied by successive governments. As was the case in *Katanga*, the decades-long blunt denial of legitimate entitlement to belongingness resulted in the armed conflict that brought Côte d'Ivoire to the brink of civil war following the death of its independence president in 1993.[215] Against the background of these cases, the question arises as to whether such demands were legal or political in nature.

In all other regional human rights forums, human rights claims brought in recent years mostly carry domestic politics to the international plane. In the case of *Mtikila v Tanzania*,[216] the African Court on Human and Peoples' Rights held, in its first ever substantive judgment, that the provision of the Tanzanian constitution prescribing political party membership as a condition to stand for an election violated the right to political participation guaranteed in Article 13(1) of the African Charter.[217] The Court ordered Tanzania to amend its constitution to bring it in conformity with the Charter.[218]

The African Court also made a ruling on whether Rwanda may withdraw its declaration recognizing the jurisdiction of the Court and which conditions should govern such withdrawal. In February 2016, Rwanda withdrew the declaration it filed under Article 34(6) of the Protocol establishing the Court on the ground that, by receiving applications from Rwandan citizens allegedly involved in or denying the Tutsi genocide, the Court exceeded its mandate. As the declaration allowed individuals and NGOs direct standing, Rwanda in fact challenged the jurisdiction of the Court to proceed with the consideration of the case on the ground that its withdrawal was with immediate effect. In the *Rwanda Withdrawal Ruling*, the Court held that Rwanda is at liberty to withdraw mainly under the umbrella of state sovereignty to adhere international convention but that such withdrawal may take effect only one year after the depositary authority was notified.[219]

One last jurisprudence move that is of interest in the present discussion is when the African Court determined the independence and impartiality of national electoral commissions. In its 2016 *APDH* judgment, the Court found that the Independent Electoral Commission of Côte d'Ivoire was neither independent nor impartial as it is composed in majority of members of the ruling coalition, members of cabinet and other executive authorities. The Court relied mainly on the principles of equality and public perception.[220]

The Economic Community of West African States (ECOWAS) Court of Justice addressed similar concerns in *Ameganvi (Removal of Members of Parliament) v Togo*,[221] which concerned the unlawful removal of nine opposition members of parliament without prior

[215] See Manby (n 208).
[216] Consolidated Matter of *Tanganyika Law Society and the Legal and Human Rights Centre v Tanzania* (Application 009/2011) and *Reverend Christopher R Mitikila v Tanzania* (Application 014/2011) African Court Judgment (14 June 2013).
[217] The African Court was established in 1998, and operated from 2006. It is vested with judicial powers to complement the protection mandate of the African Commission.
[218] See *Mitikila* (n 216) paras 107.2–111.
[219] See *Ingabire Victoire Umuhoza v Rwanda* (Application 003/2014 Ruling on Jurisdiction) 5 September 2016.
[220] See *Actions pour la Protection des Droits de l'Homme v Côte d'Ivoire* (Application 001/2014 Judgment on the Merits) 18 November 2016.
[221] *Ms Manavi Isabelle Ameganvi and 8 Others v Togo* ECW/CCJ/JUD/09/11 (7 October 2011).

hearing.[222] The Constitutional Court of Togo endorsed the removal process held in parliament, which the members of parliament challenged in the ECOWAS Court. In its ruling, the regional court held that the process violated fair trial rights and ordered the defendant state to 'remedy the violation' and 'pay compensation to the complainants'.[223] Following the state's refusal to conduct the process afresh, the complainants filed a new suit in which the Court declined jurisdiction to order their reinstatement in parliament.[224] In *Ugokwe v Nigeria*,[225] the same Court held that it lacked jurisdiction over electoral issues. However, in the case of *SERAP v Nigeria*,[226] the Court asserted jurisdiction over socio-economic rights claims (the right to education) and found that the embezzlement of funds allocated to basic education in ten states of the Nigerian Federation violated these rights. The ruling dismissed arguments by the defendant state that socio-economic rights were not justiciable in Nigeria. The Nigerian constitution placed those rights under Directive Principles of State Policies and expressly excluded them from being questioned in courts of law.

The SADC Tribunal considered an even more problematic issue in the famous *Campbell v Zimbabwe* case[227] involving land redistribution in Zimbabwe.[228] The complainants alleged that the land reform programme incorporated in the constitution violated their rights to non-discrimination under the SADC Social Charter and other international instruments adopted by Zimbabwe. Finding for the complainants, the tribunal ruled that their rights had been violated and ordered that the seized lands be returned.[229] In retaliation for that ruling, Zimbabwe spearheaded a campaign that led to the demise of the tribunal. All attempts to enforce the judgment remained largely unsuccessful, both in Zimbabwe and in other SADC countries, despite existing community law permitting this.[230]

5. Conclusion

This extensive tour of recent constitutional adjudication has offered the reader adequate evidence that the judicialization of politics is a vivid reality in Africa, both domestically and in regional adjudicatory forums. However, viewed through a comparative lens, this trend towards the judicialization of matters normally or technically reserved to the political branches of government is not peculiar to African constitutionalism. As the introductory sections to this chapter show, the judicialization of politics or politicized adjudication is a global phenomenon.

Having said that, the consequences of judicialization of politics in African constitutionalism reveal critical causes that may be catalytic in addressing the root of the problem

[222] The ECOWAS Court is the judicial organ of the Economic Community of West African States (ECOWAS). Created in 1991, the Court remained barely idle until 2005 when it was granted jurisdiction to consider individual human rights complaints.

[223] *Ameganvi* (n 221). [224] Judgment of 13 March 2012.

[225] *Hon Dr Jerry Ugokwe v Nigeria* ECW/CCJ/JUD/03/05 (7 October 2005). An appeal court had dismissed the complainant's claim and confirmed the electoral tribunal's decision.

[226] *The Registered Trustees of the Socio-Economic Rights Action Project (SERAP) v Nigeria* ECW/CCJ/JUD/07/10 (30 November 2010).

[227] *William Campbell and Another v Republic of Zimbabwe* SADC (T) 3/2009.

[228] The SADC Tribunal is the judicial organ of the Southern African Development Community. It was established in 2005.

[229] See *Campbell* (n 227) operative part.

[230] See Erika de Wet, 'The Rise and Fall of the Tribunal of the Southern African Development Community: Implications for Dispute Settlement in Southern Africa' (2013) 28 *ICSID Review* 45–63; *Fick v Government of the Republic of Zimbabwe* Case No 77881/2009 (North Gauteng High Court of South Africa) 25 February 2010 in execution of *Louis Karel Fick and Others v Republic of Zimbabwe* SADC (T) 1/2010.

caused to constitutionalism. The first question in this respect is how much of the judicialization of politics came with African constitutions themselves. A simplistic answer could be that judicialization is inherent to the 'new constitutionalism' in Africa.

The difficulty with this approach is that it ignores a number of other features of constitutionalism that the very idea of constitutional adjudication is supposed to uphold. These features include the separation of powers, the rule of law, human rights, and constitutionalism itself as an independent principle. As it emerges from this discussion, the problem is mainly not with the features of constitutionalism provided in the constitution, but increasingly with the behaviour of judicial authorities and political stakeholders. In short, juristocracy is the art of courts, but politicians provide the raw material.

Conclusions made here do not in any way overlook several instances where courts have acted within their powers, advanced democracy and constitutionalism, or protected the constitution against imperial political branches of government. The African experience of judicialization of politics, however, raises peculiar issues that need to be addressed if the culture of constitutionalism should thrive on the continent. These peculiar features include hyper-presidentialism, weak institutions and mechanisms, and the inadequate organization of political activity.

First, most African post-1990 constitutional democracies initially adopted a presidential regime of government. Even traditionally rooted parliamentary democracies soon moved to presidentialism, which arguably afforded the executive greater powers and control over government. Here, we will single out the powers of the president of the republic to appoint members of the judiciary and, particularly, judges of constitutional tribunals, and the endemic tendency to control the legislature through majority-securing politics. Although the issue is more pervasive in some Francophone African countries, the deficit of judicial independence is a widespread problem.

Secondly, it seems that adjudication has increasingly become the major route for accessing and remaining in power in Africa. The systematic tendency of executives to refer to courts matters of a purely political nature that turn in the advantage of opposition groups has caused serious problems for democracy and constitutionalism. In addition, the poor quality of electoral processes has compromised the democratic project in Africa. Unfair electoral processes are compounded by the politicized adjudication of electoral outcomes mainly by judges appointed by the executive, who are dragged into politics through processes of judicial review and the adjudication of electoral disputes.

Thirdly, we equally blame the juristocracy in Africa on the weak and inadequate political structure. In many democracies around the continent, the plethora of political parties defeats the very purpose of both order and socio-economic development. Three decades after the democratic renewal, the wide majority of African democracies are still embroiled in unlimited multiparty systems, with dozens of political parties for countries with populations varying between 20 and 80 million, and a very low level of literacy. In most cases, an elite minority holds the constitution and the people to ransom. Inhibited by party patronage politics, executives sponsored by ruling heterogeneous coalitions are unable to deliver on constitutional promises as they spend the bulk of state resources on entertaining a wide network of courtesans. The ensuing hyper-presidentialism mostly results in an obsession to elongate incumbency in a bid to catch up with poor socio-economic delivery. Hence, the amendment cycles for the extension of presidential terms.

The other face of the inadequate political structure is the lack of properly functioning electoral processes and related mechanisms. In most African democracies, electoral systems are still weak, if not rudimentary, and electoral events are mostly marred by intimidation, fraud, and violence. In these circumstances election periods put increased pressure on courts. The role of courts in the elaboration of voters' registers has also increased their power in shaping the face of democracy, by virtually deciding who is allowed to stand, to vote, and, chiefly, who wins the election. Because of poorly crafted electoral laws, judges usually lack proper and fair benchmarks to use in assessing the processes.

Finally, the blame must be apportioned to the courts themselves. It appears that they belong to the elite, and have in many instances betrayed the values they ought to have upheld. As this chapter shows, African courts have, on critical occasions, failed the constitution and the people. Even where the fundamental law has afforded them strong shields against executive attempts to tamper with their independence, many judges have eagerly surrendered. In certain circumstances, constitutional courts have made legally unreasoned or politically based decisions that have brought the citizenry to the verge of chaos, and breached every watermark of constitutionalism. In instances where the moves matched the popular expectation of the day, it still blatantly tampered with key tenets of constitutionalism. As such, courts basically breached the very constitution they were supposed to protect, arguably in order to save democracy and the constitutional order.

In all, there appears to be a need to address a number of issues if constitutional adjudication is to advance constitutionalism in Africa. First, there is a need to curb hyper-presidentialism by restoring the legislature to its true function, and limiting the powers of the executive in the direct appointment and operation of the judiciary, including constitutional bodies. On the other hand, more effective organization of political parties may help release political pressure from both the executive and the courts. Smooth political mechanisms should allow appropriate consultation among stakeholders to avoid the systematic judicialization of matters that are otherwise not legal in nature. Politicians should, indeed, take responsibility for their political failures and avoid dragging courts into political adventures that threaten democracy and constitutionalism.

Similarly, incumbent executives should be relieved from perpetuating party patronage through limited multiparty democracy, which has the potential to curb the tendency towards the elongation of incumbency. Addressing the systemic failure of electoral processes is another challenge facing constitutional democracies in Africa. It could be suggested that the more open and effective electoral processes and procedures become, the less pressure there is on courts to endorse rigged and unfair elections, which trump democracy. In the same vein, courts must apply virtues, show respect for the separation of powers and abstain from expanding their sphere of review and interpretation.

Unfortunately, the current picture of constitutional adjudication in Africa has mainly resulted in courts moving counter-democracy and constitutionalism by yielding powers either to the elite or themselves. As such, courts have brought whole societies to the verge of disorder, causing civil strife and conflicts, reversing the course of history, making and unmaking democracy, rewriting the constitution, endorsing illegality, and rising above the people who designed the constitutional order of which courts are mere agents. African polities ought to address these issues if constitutional democracy is to retain its fundamentals.

Bibliography

Abrams F, 'Online Alexander Bickel Symposium: On Rereading the Least Dangerous Branch' SCOTUSblog http://www.scotusblog.com/2012/08/online-alexander-bickel-symposium-on-rereading-the-least-dangerous-branch/ (last accessed 17 April 2017)

ACCPUF, 'Le Conseil constitutionnel du Sénégal' http://www.accpuf.org/images/pdf/cm/senegal/054-jc-decisions_CC_1993-2005.pdf (last accessed 17 April 2017)

Adjolohoun H S, 'Benin' in Rudiger Wolfrum and Rainer Grote (eds), *Constitutions of the Countries of the World Online* (Oxford University Press 2012)

Adjolohoun H S, *Droits de l'Homme et Justice Constitutionnelle en Afrique: Le Modèle Béninois à la Lumière de la Charte Africaine des Droits de l'Homme et des Peuples* (L'Harmattan 2011)

Adjolohoun H S, *Giving Effect to the Human Rights Jurisprudence of the ECOWAS Court of Justice: Compliance and Influence* (Doctoral Thesis, Pretoria, 2013) 281–85

Adjolohoun H S, 'Between Presidentialism and a Human Rights Approach to Constitutionalism: Twenty Years of Practice and the Dilemmas of Amending the 1990 Constitution of Benin' in Mbondenyi M and Ojienga T (eds), *Constitutionalism and Democratic Governance in Africa: Contemporary Perspectives from Sub-Saharan Africa* (Pretoria University Law Press 2013)

Adjolohoun H S, 'Incertitudes Electorales au Bénin: Quand la Juristocratie prend le pas sur la Démocratie?' (1 juin 2015) *Fraternité* 2, 3

Afrique J, 'Burundi: Le Vice-Président de la Cour Constitutionnelle Dénonce des Pressions et s'enfuit' http://www.jeuneafrique.com/actu/20150504T203319Z20150504T203254Z/ (last accessed 17 April 2017)

Afrique J, 'Karim: Sa Vie à la Prison de Rebeuss' (2013) http://www.jeuneafrique.com/Article/JA2754p032.xml0/ (last accessed 17 April 2017)

Aidara M M, 'Le Juge Constitutionnel Africain et le Contrôle des Lois portant Révision de la Constitution: une Contribution' http://afrilex.u-bordeaux4.fr/le-juge-constitutionnel-africain.html (last accessed 17 April 2017)

Aivo J, 'Joël Aïvo sur la Dcc 15-001: "Dans l'impasse, c'est la seule décision à prendre"' http://www.lanouvelletribune.info/benin/politique/22449-joel-aivo-sur-la-dcc-15-001-dans-l-impasse-c-est-la-seule-decision-a-prendre (last accessed 17 April 2017)

Aivo F J, 'Le Parlement Béninois sous le Renouveau Démocratique: Réussites et Echecs', RADC-CRDA Conférence annuelle sur 'L'internationalisation du droit constitutionnel', Rabat, Morocco (20 January 2011) 3–4

Ali A J, 'Justiciability of Directive Principles of State Policy in Africa: The Experiences of Ethiopia and Ghana' (2013) 1 *Ethiopian Journal of Human Rights* 1–40

All Africa, 'Sénégal: L'interdiction de l'Effigie de Wade sur les Bulletins à la Une' 2001 http://fr.allafrica.com/stories/200103300582.html (last accessed 17 April 2017)

Amerit T, 'The Doctrine of Political Question: Is Its Non-justiciability at the Brink of Erosion in the Legal Jurisprudence of Uganda?' (Legal Wheels 2014) http://timothyamerit.blogspot.com/2014/08/the-doctrine-of-political-question-is.html (last accessed 17 April 2017)

Asmal K, 'Constitutional Courts—A Comparative Survey' (1991) 24 *Comparative and International Law Journal of Southern Africa* 315

Atupare A P, 'Reconciling Socio-economic Rights and Directive Principles with a Fundamental Law of Reason in Ghana and Nigeria' (2014) 27 *Harvard Human Rights Journal* 71–106

Badet G, *Bénin, Démocratie et Participation à la Vie Politique: Une Evaluation de 20 ans de "Renouveau Démocratique"* (OSIWA 2010) 112–15

Badet G, *Les Attributions Originelles de la Cour Constitutionnelle du Bénin* (Friedrich Ebert Stiftung 2013)

Bamlango D M, 'Des "Actes Législatives" et du "Pouvoir Régulateur": Quand la CSJ Donne une Portée Expansive aux Attributions de la Cour Constitutionnelle' (2008) 5 *Revue Horizons* 34

Barak A, 'The Role of a Supreme Court in a Democracy, and the Fight against Terrorism' (2003–2004) 58 *University of Miami Law Review* 125

Bellamy R, 'The Political Form of the Constitution: The Separation of Powers, Rights and Representative Democracy' (1996) XLIV *Political Studies* 436–56

Benwell R and Gay O, 'The Separation of Powers' (House of Common Library 2011)

Bickel A M, 'The Supreme Court 1960 Term Foreword: The Passive Virtues' (1961) 75 *Harvard Law Review* 40, 48–59

Bickel A M, *The Least Dangerous Branch: The Supreme Court at the Bar of Politics* (Yale University Press 1962) 184

Bizimana E, 'Arrêt RCCB 303: La Cour Constitutionnelle du Burundi au Secours du Président Pierre Nkurunziza' newspaper article on file with author (2015)

Bolle S, 'Décision DCC 09-002: Le Bon Grain et l'Ivraie' http://www.la-constitution-en-afrique.org/16-categorie-10195442.html (last accessed 17 April 2017)

Bolle S, 'Quand Wade Fait Réviser sa Constitution' (La Constitution en Afrique) http://www.google.gm/url?q=http://laconstitutionenafrique.org/article19524487.html&sa=U&ei-=kOxxVZfEDaT5yQPjq4GACw&ved=0CBUQFjAA&usg=AFQjCNExBfTpZoVKbx24WE7g69CIywRjTw (last accessed 17 April 2017)

Bourgi A, 'L'évolution du Constitutionnalisme en Afrique: Du Formalisme à l'Effectivité' (2004) 4 *Revue Française de Droit Constitutionnel* 721–48

Brondel S and others, *Gouvernement des Juges et Démocratie* (Publication de la Sorbonne 2001)

Brouard S and Hönnige C, 'Constitutional Courts and Democracy, Varying Patterns of Courts Role in Democratic Transition, Consolidation and Breakdown' (ECPR General Conference, 2011) 2–6

Caffoz T, 'Le Contrôle de l'Erreur Manifeste d'Appréciation dans la Procédure de la Question Prioritaire de Constitutionnalité' http://www.droitconstitutionnel.org/congresLyon/CommLA/A-caffoz_T2.pdf (last accessed 17 April 2017)

Ca M'intéresse, 'Pourquoi ca Chauffe au Sénégal' http://www.caminteresse.fr/economie-societe/senegal-revolte-wade-1120855/ (last accessed 17 April 2017)

Carcassonne G, 'L'inconstitutionnalité de la Candidature de Me Wade, Ne Fait à Mes Yeux, Aucun Doute' (Xalima 2010) http://xalimasn.com/guy-carcassonne-«-l'inconstitutionnalite-de-la-candidature-de-me-wade-ne-fait-a-mes-yeux-aucun-doute- (last accessed 17 April 2017)

Centre pour la Gouvernance Démocratique Burkina Faso, 'Constitutionnalisme et Révisions Constitutionnelles en Afrique de l'Ouest: Les Cas du Bénin, du Burkina Faso et du Sénégal' (2009) 10–15 http://www.maep.bf/gestdoc/uploads/56.pdf (last accessed 17 April 2017)

Chaskalson A, 'Constitutional Courts and Supreme Courts: A Comparative Analysis with Particular Reference to the South African Experience' http://www.ecln.net/elements/conferences/book_berlin/chaskalson.pdf (last accessed 17 April 2017)

Chemerinsky E, *Constitutional Law: Principles and Policies* (Aspen Law & Business 2002) 130

Chevrier M, 'Trois Visions de la Constitution et du Constitutionnalisme Contemporain' (2008) 2 *Revue Québécoise de Droit Constitutionnel* 72–129

Choper J H, 'The Political Question Doctrine: Suggested Criteria' (2005) 54 *Duke Law Journal* 1457–523

Cole J P, 'The Political Question Doctrine: Justiciability and the Separation of Powers' (Congressional Research Service 2014)

Conac G, 'Quelques Réflexions sur les Nouveau Constitutionnalisme Africain (Symposium International de Bamako) http://democratie.francophonie.org/IMG/pdf/bamako.297.pdf (last accessed 17 April 2017)

Conac G, 'Quelques réflexions sur les transitions démocratiques en Afrique' http://democratie.francophonie.org/article.php3?id_article=1314&id_rubrique=753 (last accessed 17 April 2017)

Conseil constitutionnel, *La Déclaration des Droits de l'Homme et du Citoyen et la Jurisprudence* (PUF 1898) 63

Croisés R, 'Abdoulaye Wade ou l'Archétype de l'Inconstance Africaine' 2012 http://regardscroises.ivoire-blog.com/archive/2012/01/28/abdoulaye-wade-ou-l-archetype-de-l-inconsistance-africaine.html (last accessed 17 April 2017)

Currie I and de Waal J, *The Bill of Rights Handbook* (J 2005) 8–9

Dakar Actu, 'Congrès du parti socialiste de 1957 à 2014: Chronique d'un rituel controversé' http://www.dakaractu.com/Congres-du-parti-socialiste-de-1957-a-2014-Chronique-d-un-rituel-controverse_a67045.html (last accessed 17 April 2017)

De Wet E, 'The Rise and Fall of the Tribunal of the Southern African Development Community: Implications for Dispute Settlement in Southern Africa' (2013) 28 *ICSID Review* 45–63

Dennison B, 'The Political Question Doctrine in Uganda: A Reassessment in the Wake of the CEHURD' (2014) 18 *Law, Democracy and Development* 264–88

Diompy A H, 'Les Dynamiques Récentes de la Justice Constitutionnelle en Afrique Francophone' http://afrilex.ubordeaux4.fr/sites/afrilex/IMG/pdf/JOURNEE_DE_LA_JEUNE_RECHERCHE_EN_DROIT_CONSTITUTIONNEL.pdf (last accessed 17 April 2017)

Diop D, 'La Parité Rejetée par le Conseil Constitutionnel du Sénégal' http://www.genreenaction.net/La-parite-rejetee-par-le-Conseil-Constitutionnel.html (last accessed 17 April 2017)

Diop M C, *Le Sénégal sous Abdoulaye Wade: Le Sopi à l'Epreuve du Pouvoir* (Khartala 2013)

Dossou-Yovo N, 'The Experience of Benin' (1999) 16 *Journal on World Peace* 59

Duru O, 'The Justiciability of the Fundamental Objectives and Directive Principles of State Policy under Nigerian Law' (Academia.edu) https://www.academia.edu/5185441/THE_JUSTICIABILITY_OF_THE_FUNDAMENTAL_OBJECTIVES_AND_DIRECTIVE_PRINCIPLES_OF_STATE_POLICY_UNDER_NIGERIAN_LAW_By (last accessed 17 April 2017)

Ezeanyika E S, 'Can Western Democracy Models be Institutionalized in Africa? Reviewing Contemporary Problems and Prospects' (2011) 36 *Ufahamu Journal of African Studies* 1–21

Fall A B, 'Le juge constitutionnel, artisan de la démocratie en Afrique' http://www.droitconstitutionnel.org/congresmtp/textes7/FALL.pdf (last accessed 17 April 2017)

Fall I M, 'La Révision de la Constitution au Sénégal' http://afrilex.u-bordeaux4.fr/sites/afrilex/IMG/pdf/La_revision_de_la_Constitution_au_Senegal_Ismaila.pdf (last accessed 17 April 2017)

Fall I M, 'Le Président Wade ne Peut Pas Briguer un Troisième Mandat' (Rewmi 2010) http://www.rewmi.com/ismaila-madior-fall-le-president-wade-ne-peut-pas-briguer-un-troisieme-mandat_a36207.html (last accessed 17 April 2017)

Ferejohn J, 'Judicializing Politics, Politicizing Law' (2002) 65 *Law and Contemporary Problems* 41

Fides A, 'Révision constitutionnelle: vers une tentative de référendum après l'échec de la procédure parlementaire?' http://www.fides.org/fr/news/37486-AFRIQUE_BURUNDI_Revision_constitutionnelle_vers_une_tentative_de_referendum_apres_l_echec_de_la_procedure_parlementaire#.VXTeho6Abdk (last accessed 17 April 2017)

Fisher D, 'Supreme Court Rules Same-Sex Marriage is A Constitutional Rights' https://www.forbes.com/sites/danielfisher/2015/06/26/supreme-court-rules-same-sex-marriage-is-a-constitutional-right/#1614e645cdd0 (last accessed 17 April 2017).

Fombad C M, 'Appointment of Constitutional Adjudicators in Africa: Some Perspectives on How Different Systems Yield Similar Outcomes' (2014) 46(2) *Journal of Legal Pluralism and Unofficial Law* 249–75

Fondation Konrad Adenauer, *Commentaire de la Constitution Béninoise du 11 Décembre 1990: Esprit, Lettre, Interprétation et Pratique de la Constitution par le Bénin et ses Institutions* (FKA 2009)

France Diplomatie, Texte de l'Accord de Linas-Marcoussis (24 Janvier 2003) http://www.diplomatie.gouv.fr/fr/dossiers-pays/cote-d-ivoire/colonne-droite-1347/documents-de-reference/article/accord-de-linas-marcoussis (last accessed 17 April 2017)

Gangnon C, 'Les Droits Fondamentaux de la Personne Humaine' *Actes du Séminaire de formation des journalistes* Cotonou (2 August 2005) 1

Gans H J, 'Fixing Representative Democracy' (2015) 14 *Logos* http://logosjournal.com/2014/gans/

Ginsburg T, 'Courts and New Democracies: Recent Works' (June 2012) *Public Law and Legal Theory Working Paper Series* 388

Gleeson M, 'Courts and the Rule of Law' (The Rule of Law Series 2001) http://www.hcourt.gov.au/assets/publications/speeches/former-justices/gleesoncj/cj_ruleoflaw.htm (last accessed 17 April 2017)

Guèye B, 'La Démocratie en Afrique: Succès et Résistances' (2009) 2 *Pouvoirs* 5–26.

Guèye B, 'Wade a Epuisé ses Mandats' (Socialisme République Sénégal 2011) https://blogs.mediapart.fr/oumar-ndiaye/blog/270811/senegal-limpossible-3eme-mandat-de-abdoulaye-wade (last accessed 17 April 2017)

Gunther G, 'The Subtle Vices of the Passive Virtues: A Comment on Principle and Expediency in Judicial Review' (1964) 64 *Columbia Law Review* 1, 3

Hensel P R, Allison M E, and Khanani A, 'The Colonial Legacy and Border Stability: *Utis Possidetis* and Borders Claims in the Americas' http://www.paulhensel.org/Research/io05.pdf (last accessed 17 April 2017)

Hirschl R, 'Juristocracy: Political, not Juridical' (2004) 13 *The Good Society* 6–11

Hirschl R, 'The New Constitutionalism and the Judicialization of Pure Politics Worldwide' (2006) 75 *Fordham Law Review* 772

Hirschl R, *Towards Juristocracy: The Origins and Consequences of the New Constitutionalism* (Harvard University Press 2007)

Huntington S P, *The Third Wave: Democratization in the Late Twentieth Century* (University of Oklahoma Press 1991)

Ikhariale M, 'Impeachment Proceedings and the Political Question Doctrine: The Nigerian Experience' (1990) 1 *LASU Law Journal* 54

Issacharoff S, 'Constitutional Courts and Democratic Hedging' (2011) 99 *Georgetown Law Journal* 960

Kanté B, 'Le Sénégal: un Exemple de Continuité et d'Instabilité Constitutionnelle' (1989) 22 *Revue Juridique Politique et Economique du Maroc* 150, 154

Kanunk'a-Tshiabo A M, 'Congo-Kinshasa: Non, Messieurs—Une Motion de Défiance n'est pas un Acte Législatif' (All Africa 20 November 2007) http://fr.allafrica.com/stories/200711200733.html (last accessed 17 April 2017)

Kashala K K, *La Jurisprudence Electorale Congolaise Commentée* (The Carter Centre 2007)

Klein C, 'Le Contrôle des Lois Constitutionnelles: Introduction à une Problématique Moderne' (2010) 27 *Cahier du Conseil Constitutionnel*

Kokoroko D, 'La Cour Constitutionnelle du Bénin peut-elle Soumettre, aux "Options Fondamentales de la Conférence Nationale", le Peuple dans l'Exercice de son Pouvoir de Révision?' (2013) 1 *Annuaire Béninois de Justice Constitutionnelle* 717–28

Koso Senga M W, 'La Définition des Actes Législatifs dans l'Arrêt de la CSJ No RCONST.51/TSR du 31 Juillet 2007 à l'Epreuve de la Constitution du 18 Février 2006' (2008) 5 *Revue Horizons* 13–23

Kotmair J B Jr, 'Do Courts Have Law-making Powers' (Save A Patriot 2005) http://save-a-patriot.org/files/Do_Courts_Have_Law_Making_Powers.pdf (last accessed 17 April 2017)

Koubi G, 'Le Préambule de la Constitution de 1946: Antinomies Juridiques et Contradictions Politiques' (Presses universitaires de France 1996) 9

Kpodar A, 'Bilan sur un Demi-Siècle de Constitutionnalisme en Afrique Noire Francophone' http://afrilex.u-bordeaux4.fr/sites/afrilex/IMG/pdf/BILAN_SUR_UN_DEMI-SIECLE_DE_CONSTITUTION NALISME_EN_AFRIQUE_NOIRE_FRANCOPHONE.pdf (last accessed 17 April 2017)

Kpodar A, 'Décision de la Cour Constitutionnelle du Bénin DCC 09-002 du 8 Janvier 2009 "Une bonne année à la démocratie pluraliste"' http://www.la-constitution-en-afrique.org/article-28611580.html (last accessed 17 April 2017)

Kpodar A, 'La Cour Constitutionnelle du Bénin peut-elle Soumettre, aux "Options Fondamentales de la Conférence Nationale", le Peuple dans l'Exercice de son Pouvoir de Révision?' (2013) 1 *Annuaire Béninois de Justice Constitutionnelle* 703–16

L'Expresse, 'Au Sénégal: la Candidature d'Abdoulaye Wade Confirmée' 2012 http://www.lexpress.fr/actualite/monde/afrique/au-senegal-la-candidature-d-abdoulaye-wade-confirmee_1076779.html (last accessed 17 April 2017)

La Toupie, 'Censure, Motion de Censure' http://www.toupie.org/Dictionnaire/Censure.htm (last accessed 17 April 2017)

Landau D and Sheppard B, 'The Honduran Constitutional Chamber's Decision Erasing Presidential Term Limits: Abusive Constitutionalism by Judiciary?' http://www.iconnectblog.com/2015/05/the-honduran-constitutional-chambers-decision-erasing-presidential-term-limits-abusive-constitutionalism-by-judiciary/ (last accessed 17 April 2017)

Laquièze A, 'La Réception de Sieyès par la Doctrine Publiciste Française' in Quiviger P-Y, Denis V, and Salem J (eds), *Figure de Sieyès* (Publications de la Sorbonne 2008) 114

Larché J, 'Corruption in the NGO World: What It Is and How to Tackle it?' (Humanitarian Practice Network 2011) http://www.odihpn.org/humanitarian-exchange-magazine/issue-52/corruption-in-the-ngo-world-what-it-is-and-how-to-tackle-it (last accessed 17 April 2017)

Libération, 'Sénégal: Wade en Lice une Troisième Fois' 2012 http://www.liberation.fr/monde/2012/01/28/senegal-wade-en-lice-une-3e-fois_791866 (last accessed 17 April 2017)

Linz J J, 'The Perils of Presidentialism' (1990) 1 *Journal of Democracy* 51–69

Loada A, 'La Limitation du nombre de mandats présidentiels en Afrique francophone' (2003) 3 *Revue Electronique Afrilex* 139–74
MacMillan G, 'The Referendum, the Courts and Representative Democracy in Ireland' (1992) 40 *Political Studies* 67–78
Maclure J, 'Droit et Démocratie: un Gouvernement des Juges?' http://induecourse.ca/droit-et-democratie-un-gouvernement-des-juges-partie-1/ (last accessed 17 April 2017)
Magnusson B A, 'Testing Democracy in Benin' in Joseph R (ed), *State, Conflict and Democracy in Africa* (Lynne Rienner Publishers 1999) 221
Manby B, *Nationality in Africa* (Open Society 2011) 17–25
Marutse R, 'The Role of the Constitutional Court in a Democratic Society' (2007) 13 *Juridica International Law Review* 8–13
Mhango M O, 'Separation of Powers in Ghana: The Evolution of the Political Question Doctrine' (2014) 17 *Potchefstroom Electronic Law Journal* 2704–44
Moderne F 'Les Avatars du Présidentialisme dans les Etats Latino Américains' (2001) 98 *Pouvoirs* 63–87
Monteiro C, 'Le contrôle de la constitutionnalité des actes juridiques du Bénin' (2001) 17 *Bulletin de droit et d'information de la Cour Suprême* 24
Mubiala M, *Le Système Régional Africain de Protection des Droits de l'Homme* (Bruylant 2005)
Murray R, *The African Commission on Human and Peoples' Rights and International Law* (OUP 2000)
Naim M, 'What Is A GONGO? How Government-sponsored Groups Masquerade Civil Society' (Foreign Policy 2009) http://foreignpolicy.com/2009/10/13/what-is-a-gongo/ (last accessed 17 April 2017)
Ndiaye O, 'L'impossible Troisième Mandat de Abdoulaye Wade' (Mediapart 2011) http://blogs.mediapart.fr/blog/oumar-ndiaye/270811/senegal-limpossible-3eme-mandat-de-abdoulaye-wade (last accessed 17 April 2017)
Ndiaye M, 'Abdoulaye Wade: mon Troisième Mandat n'est Pas un Débat' http://koaci.com/m/senegal-abdoulaye-wade-troisieme-mandat-n'est-debat--73323-i.html (last accessed 17 April 2017)
Ndiaye M, 'Tripatouillage de la Charte fondamentale: la Constitution du Sénégal a été révisée 37 fois en 52 ans' (Seneweb 2012) http://www.seneweb.com/news/Politique/tripatouillages-de-la-charte-fondamentale-la-constitution-du-senegal-a-ete-revisee-37-fois-en-52-ans_n_57252.html (last accessed 17 April 2017)
Nwabueze B O, *The Presidential Constitution of Nigeria* (Hurst & Co with Nwamife Publishers 1982) 143
Nwauche E, 'Is the End Near for the Political Question Doctrine in Nigeria?' in Fombad C and Murray C (eds), *Fostering Constitutionalism in Africa* (PULP 2010) 31–60
OBS, 'Sénégal: Candidature de Wade Validée, ses Opposants Ecartés' http://tempsreel.nouvelobs.com/monde/20120130.OBS0087/senegal-candidature-de-wade-validee-ses-oppo sants-ecartes.html (last accessed 17 April 2017)
Out-Law.com, 'What is Judicial Review' (2013) http://www.out-law.com/en/topics/dispute-resolution-and-litigation/judicial-review/judicial-review/ (last accessed 17 April 2017)
Perju V, 'Reviews' (2005) 68 *The Modern Law Review* 1039
Prempeh H K, 'Presidential Power in Comparative Perspective: The Puzzling Persistence of Imperial Presidency in Post-authoritarian Africa' (2008) 35 *Hastings Constitutional Law Quarterly* 761–834
Public Law Project, *An Introduction to Judicial Review* http://www.publiclawproject.org.uk/data/resources/6/PLP_Short_Guide_3_13 05.pdf (last accessed 17 April 2017)
Quashigah K, 'Trends in the Promotion and Protection of Human Rights under the 1992 Constitution' in Boafo-Arthur K (ed), *Ghana: One Decade of the Liberal State* (Codesria 2007) 25–46
Rakner L and Skage I, 'Don't Touch My Constitution! Civil Society Resistance and Political Turnovers in Africa's Pluralist Regimes' https://projectcontentiouspolitics.files.wordpress.com/2015/02/rakner-skage-isa-workshop-feb-2015.pdf (last accessed 17 April 2017)
Randhawa J, 'Understanding Judicialization of Mega Politics: The Basic Structure Doctrine and Minimum Core' (2011) 6 *Jus Politicum* 1–44

République de Côte d'Ivoire, 'Rapport Général du Forum pour la Réconciliation Nationale' (2001) 47 http://www.seydouelimanediarra.net/Docs/Tome%20II.pdf> (last accessed 17 April 2017)

Rotman A, 'Benin's Constitutional Court: An Institutional Model for Guaranteeing Human Rights' (2004) 17 *Harvard Human Rights Journal* 283

Rukindikiza G, 'Le Ciel est Tombé sur la tête de Nkurunziza' https://burundi24.wordpress.com/2014/03/25/le-ciel-est-tombe-sur-la-tete-de-nkurunziza/ (last accessed 17 April 2017)

Russell A, 'Real Justice Could Finally be Delivered in Uganda by Key Ruling on Maternal Health' *The Guardian* (2 November 2015) http://www.theguardian.com/global-development/2015/nov/02/real-justice-could-finally-be-delivered-uganda-key-ruling-maternal-health (last accessed 17 April 2017)

Russell G, 'Constitutionalism: America and Beyond' (Democracy Papers) http://www.ait.org.tw/infousa/zhtw/DOCS/Demopaper/dmpaper2.html (last accessed 17 April 2017)

Scharpf F W, 'Judicial Review and the Political Question: A Functional Analysis' (1966) 75 *Yale Law Journal* 517, 518

Schoettl J E, 'Le Conseil Constitutionnel peut-il Contrôler une Loi Constitutionnelle?' (2003) 70 *Les Petites Affiches* 18

Schor M, 'An Essay on the Emergence of Constitutional Courts: The Cases of Mexico and Columbia' (2009) 16(1) *Indiana Journal of Global Legal Studies* 173–94

Seidman L M, 'The Secret Life of the Political Question Doctrine' (2004) 37 *John Marshall Law Review* 441–80

Sene Web, 'Il Bat Campagne en Dépit des Interdits du Juge Constitutionnel: Macky Foule aux Pieds la Loi Fondamentale' 2012 http://www.seneweb.com/news/Politique/il-bat-campagne-en-depit-des-interdits-du-juge-constitutionnel-macky-foule-aux-pieds-la-loi-fondamentale_n_69746.html (last accessed 17 April 2017)

Senego, 'Ce que Abdoulaye Wade a dit à Karim Wade à Reubess' (2015) http://senego.com/2015/02/16/ce-que-abdoulaye-wade-a-dit-a-karim-wade-a-reubess_218408.html (last accessed 17 April 2017)

Seyès E J, *Qu'est-ce que le Tiers Etat?* (Boucher 2002) 50

Stacey R, 'Constituent Power and Carl Schmitt's Theory of Constitution in Kenya's Constitution-making Process' (2011) 9 *International Journal of Constitutional Law* 587–614

Stone Sweet A, 'Constitutional Courts and Parliamentary Democracy' (2002) 25 *West European Politics* 77–100

Stone Sweet A, *Governing with Judges: Constitutional Politics in Europe* (Oxford University Press 2002)

Tate C N, 'Why the Expansion of Judicial Power?' in Tate CN and Vallinder T (eds), *The Global Expansion of Judicial Power* (New York University Press 1995)

Topanou V, "Cette décision risque de ne pas être appliquée" dixit Victor Topanou' https://bj.jolome.com/news/article/cette-decision-risque-de-ne-pas-etre-appliquee-dixit-victor-topanou (last accessed 17 April 2017)

Vedel G, 'La Place de la Déclaration de 1789 dans le Bloc de Constitutionnalité' in Conseil

Vedel G, 'Souveraineté et Supra Constitutionnalité' (1993) 67 *Pouvoirs* 79–97

Ville M J C, *Constitutionalism and the Separation of Powers* (Indianapolis Liberty Fund 1998)

Voice of America, 'Benin Court Rejects Longer Terms for Lawmakers' http://m.voanews.com/a/a-13-2006-07-10-voa40/320437.html (last accessed 17 April 2017)

Waldron J, 'Constitutionalism: A Sceptical View' (Georgetown University Law Centre Lecture 2010) http://scholarship.law.georgetown.edu/cgi/viewcontent.cgi?article=1002&context=hartlecture (last accessed 17 April 2017)

Wikipedia, 'Socialist Party of Senegal' http://en.wikipedia.org/wiki/Socialist_Party_of_Senegal (last accessed 17 April 2017)

12

Exploring the Contribution of *Ubuntu* in Constitutional Adjudication—Towards the Indigenization of Constitutionalism in South Africa?

Christa Rautenbach

1. Introduction

Ubuntu may be regarded as South Africa's gift to constitutionalism,[1] and the judiciary is to thank for that, particularly the South African Constitutional Court.[2] *Ubuntu* is an age-old[3] indigenous concept, which has earned itself the appellation of 'African equity',[4] 'African value',[5] 'African dignity',[6] 'African humanism',[7] 'African

[1] In this context, constitutionalism refers to 'the principles, spirit, or system of government in accord with' the constitution (Constitution of the Republic of South Africa, 1996); see Collins Online Dictionaries 'Constitutionalism' (2015) http://www.collinsdictionary.com/dictionary/english/constitutionalism (last accessed 17 April 2017). Adjudication denotes the legal process of resolving a dispute. Thus, 'constitutional adjudication' means the legal process of resolving a dispute in terms of the constitution. In South Africa, the constitution reigns supreme (see s 2 of the constitution) and all law (public and private law) is subject to the constitution. In *Everfresh Market Virginia (Pty) Ltd v Shoprite Checkers (Pty) Ltd* 2012 (1) SA 256 (CC) 48, the Constitutional Court confirmed that a scrutiny of the constitutionality of a principle of the common law of contract raises a constitutional issue: 'The common law, like all other laws, must be viewed through the prism of the objective normative value system set by the constitution and, where it is found to fall short, must be reshaped in order to conform to our supreme law'. See also Mwiza Jo Nkhata, 'Towards Constitutionalism and Democratic Governance: *Ubuntu* and Equity as a Basis for Regulating Public Functionaries in Common Law Africa' in Frank Diedrich (ed), *Ubuntu, Good Faith and Equity: Flexible Legal Principles in Developing a Contemporary Jurisprudence* (Juta 2011) 88, 94–6 for a discussion of the meaning of constitutionalism in Africa.

[2] In general, the idea that *ubuntu* has contributed considerably to the development of constitutional law in South Africa was also explored by S F Khunou and Seth Nthai, 'The Contribution of *Ubuntu* to the Development of Constitutional Jurisprudence in a Democratic South Africa' in Diedrich (n 1) 50.

[3] Christian B N Gade, 'The Historical Development of the Written Discourses on *Ubuntu*' (2011) 30(3) *South African Journal of Philosophy* 303 demonstrates that there have been written accounts of the term *ubuntu* since at least 1846.

[4] Tom Bennett, '*Ubuntu*: An African Equity' (2011) 14(4) *Potchefstroom Electronic Law Journal* 29 //dx.doi.org/10.4314/pelj.v14i4.2 (last accessed 17 April 2017).

[5] Irma J Kroeze, 'Doing Things with Values II: The Case of *Ubuntu*' (2002) 13 *Stellenbosch Law Review* 252; Narnia Bohler-Müller, 'The Story of an African Value' (2005) 20 *SA Public Law* 266; André Mukheibir, '*Ubuntu* and the *Amende Honorable*—A Marriage between African Values and Medieval Canon Law' (2007) 28 *Obiter* 583; Chuma Himonga, Max Taylor, and Anne Pope, 'Reflections on Judicial Views of *Ubuntu*' (2013) 16(5) *Potchefstroom Electronic Law Journal* 371, 378–80http://dx.doi.org/10.4314/pelj.v16i5.8 (last accessed 17 April 2017).

[6] *Dikoko v Mokhatla* 2006 (6) SA 235 (CC) 68 (*Dikoko* case): 'In our constitutional democracy the basic constitutional value of human dignity relates closely to *ubuntu* or *botho*, an idea based on deep respect for the humanity of another'.

[7] Gardiol J van Niekerk, 'A Common Law for Southern Africa' (1998) 31 *Comparative and International Law Journal of Southern Africa* 158, 167; Richman Mqeke, 'Customary Law and Human Rights' (1996) 126 *South African Law Journal* 364; Drucilla Cornell and Karin van Marle, 'Exploring *Ubuntu*: Tentative Reflections' (2005) 5 *African Human Rights Law Journal* 206–7; Narnia Bohler-Müller, 'Beyond Legal Metanarratives: The Interrelationship between Story Telling, *Ubuntu* and Care' (2007) 18 *Stellenbosch Law Review* 133, 140.

justice',[8] 'constitutional value',[9] or 'social value',[10] and many others.[11] It is a value-laden concept with many meanings,[12] which has drawn a fair amount of both praise and criticism,[13] causing it to become a much-debated topic in legal circles. In essence, it refers to the key values of group solidarity, namely compassion, respect, human dignity, conformity to basic norms, and collectivity.[14] The spirit of *ubuntu* is captured in the belief that the well-being of the individual and that of the community are inextricably linked—the one cannot exist without the other. Furthermore, the well-being of the community is inextricably linked to a harmonious relationship with both its ancestors and with nature.[15]

Although primarily derived from African philosophy and coloured with a deep religious significance,[16] *ubuntu* was introduced into the legal landscape via the postamble of the transitional constitution,[17] which provided, amongst other things, that there is 'a need for understanding but not for vengeance, a need for reparation but not for retaliation, a need for *ubuntu* but not for victimisation'.

The text gave no explanation as to the meaning of *ubuntu*, and it was omitted from the final constitution for unknown reasons,[18] leading to some speculation that it suffered a quick death.[19] However, this fear was unfounded. Although it had a slow start, *ubuntu*, in

[8] O Oko Elechi, Sherill V C Morris, and Edward J Schauer, 'Restoring Justice (*Ubuntu*): An African Perspective' (2010) 20 *International Criminal Justice Review* 73.

[9] Thino Bekker, 'The Re-emergence of *Ubuntu*: A Critical Analysis' (2006) 21 *SA Public Law* 335–8. Bekker comes to the conclusion, however, that the concept of *ubuntu* will have to be redefined to make it useful as a workable constitutional value (at 344). See also Himonga, Taylor, and Pope (n 5) 378–80.

[10] John L B Eliastam, 'Exploring *Ubuntu* Discourse in South Africa: Loss, Liminality and Hope' (2015) 36 *Verbum et Ecclesia* http://www.ve.org.za/index.php/VE/article/view/1427 (last accessed 17 April 2017).

[11] Regarding 'African spirit' see *Port Elizabeth Municipality v Various Occupiers* 2005 (1) SA 217 (CC) [37]; van Niekerk (n 7) 168; for 'African legal theory' see Nkiruka Ahiauzu, '*Ubuntu* and the Obligation to Obey the Law' (2006) 37 *Cambrian Law Review* 17; for 'African ethics' see R Dolamo, '*Botho/uBuntu*: The Heart of African Ethics' (2013) 1 *Scriptura* 1; for 'moral theory' see Thaddeus Metz, '*Ubuntu* as a Moral Theory and Human Rights in South Africa' (2011) 11 *African Human Rights Law Journal* 532. For criticism of Metz's moral theory see Oritsegbubemi Anthony Oyowe, 'Strange Bedfellows: Rethinking *Ubuntu* and Human Rights in South Africa' (2013) 13 *African Human Rights Law Journal* 103.

[12] See Himonga, Taylor, and Pope (n 5) 376–8, who discuss the problem of defining *ubuntu* and comes to the conclusion that attempts to pin it down are misguided; it should remain open-ended to allow for development. See also Bennett (n 4) 52, who cautions against 'defining *ubuntu* and circumscribing its area of operation too soon'. It should be allowed to develop to provide a new set of principles to South African law. See also Antjie Krog, 'Research into Reconciliation and Forgiveness at the South African Truth and Reconciliation Commission and Homi Bhabha's "Architecture of the New"' (2015) 30 *Canadian Journal of Law and Society* 202, 209, who describes *ubuntu* as a 'new' philosophy, because it does not have an English equivalent. To her, *ubuntu* represents an interconnectedness to become a whole person ('wholeness'), which can only 'be reached through and with others, including ancestors and the cosmos'.

[13] For some of the criticisms against the notion of *ubuntu* see Metz (n 11) 533–4. Ilze Keevy, 'The Constitutional Court and *Ubuntu*'s "Inseparable Trinity"' (2009) 34 *Journal for Juridical Science* 61, 85 critically evaluates the Constitutional Court's definitions of *ubuntu* and comes to the conclusion that it is inseparable from African religion; and that the court's inception of *ubuntu* values into the legal realm boils down to unfair discrimination based on religion, because other religious philosophies are not treated equally. See Ilze Keevy, '*Ubuntu* versus the Core Values of the South African Constitution' (2009) 34 *Journal for Juridical Science* 19. See also the discussion in Himonga, Taylor, and Pope (n 5) 384–91.

[14] This chapter draws somewhat from Christa Rautenbach and Jan Christoffel Bekker (eds), *Introduction to Legal Pluralism in South Africa* (4th edn, LexisNexis 2014) 27–9.

[15] Gardiol J van Niekerk, 'Succession, Living Indigenous Law and *Ubuntu* in the Constitutional Court' (2005) 26 *Obiter* 474; van Niekerk (n 7) 168; L J Nyaumwe and Q Mkabela, 'Revisiting the Traditional African Cultural Framework of *Ubuntuism*: A Theoretical Perspective' (2007) 6 *Indilinga* 152–3.

[16] Ilze Keevy, '*Ubuntu*: Ethnophilosphy and Core Constitutional Values' in Diedrich (n 1) 26–36.

[17] Constitution of the Republic of South Africa 200 of 1993. The Afrikaans text was signed by the President and did not contain the word *ubuntu* but 'medemenslikheid' (directly translated as 'humanism').

[18] The reasons for the absence of *ubuntu* from the final constitution have been widely speculated on. See Stewart Motha, 'Archiving Colonial Sovereignty: From *Ubuntu* to a Jurisprudence of Sacrifice' (2009) 24 *SA Public Law* 305–6.

[19] Bernard Matolino and Wenceslaus Kwindingwi, 'The End of *Ubuntu*' (2013) 32 *South African Journal of Philosophy* 197.

all its forms and manifestations, continued to be critiqued, discussed, translated, developed, applied, and embraced by the South African judiciary, the legislature, and legal scholars worldwide. There are also an increasing number of cases from the rest of Africa that use the term *ubuntu*, supporting the perception that *ubuntu* jurisprudence is more and more being acknowledged in other parts of Africa, making it one of the most successful contributions to constitutional adjudication 'out of Africa'.[20]

Against this background, this chapter analyses the role *ubuntu* jurisprudence has so far played in constitutional adjudication, particularly in South Africa. The first part gives an overview of the seepage of *ubuntu* into the legal discourse through the decisions of the Constitutional Court, which has been instrumental to the inception of *ubuntu* into the legal landscape and for giving content to it.[21] In this part, some of the viewpoints of scholars regarding the meaning, scope, and role of *ubuntu* are dealt with. The second part explores a few examples of statutes where *ubuntu* principles have been incorporated, either directly or indirectly, into legislation.[22] In the last part, some cases in other African jurisdictions, where *ubuntu* has also received the attention of the judiciary, are discussed,[23] before a conclusion is reached on the question of whether the development of *ubuntu* can (or should) be seen as a gradual movement towards the Africanization or indigenization of South African law in general, and constitutional law in particular.[24]

Finally, it is important to acknowledge that it is not possible to address the issue of 'Africanization' or 'indigenization' and the role *ubuntu* plays in this quest to its fullest in the confines of a contribution such as this; neither is the intention to offer a comprehensive critique of the development of *ubuntu* in constitutional jurisprudence. The aim is merely to give a broad overview of how *ubuntu* arose in South African Constitutional Court cases, legislation, and in some other African countries.[25]

2. *Ubuntu* in the South African Constitutional Court

The Constitutional Court has been instrumental in the advancement of *ubuntu* in legal discourse.[26] It was mentioned for the first time in the inaugural decision of the Constitutional

[20] The expression 'out of Africa' denotes the migration of things from Africa to other parts of the world and signifies the movement of *ubuntu* from African philosophy into the legal landscape, and also into other parts of the world. It was borrowed from the memoir *Out of Africa* written by the Danish author Karen von Blixen-Finecke, first published in 1937.

[21] See the discussion in section 2. Although *ubuntu* has been embraced by the South African judiciary in general, this chapter focuses mainly on the decisions of the Constitutional Court. See also the cases discussed by Koos Malan, 'The Suitability and Unsuitability of *Ubuntu* in Constitutional Law: Inter-communal Relations Versus Public Office-bearing' (2014) 47 *De Jure* 233–40.

[22] See the discussion in section 3. [23] See the discussion in section 4. [24] See section 5.

[25] Two authors have done phenomenal work in this regard. See Mogobe B Ramose, *African Philosophy through Ubuntu* (Mond Books 1999) and Leonhard Praeg, *A Report on Ubuntu* (University of KwaZulu-Natal Press 2014).

[26] See eg *S v Makwanyane* 1995 (3) SA 391 (CC); *Azanian Peoples Organization (AZAPO) v President of the Republic of South Africa* 1996 (4) SA 672 (CC); *Christian Education South Africa v Minister of Education* 2000 (4) SA 757 (CC); *Hoffmann v South African Airways* 2001 (1) SA 1 (CC); *Bhe v Magistrate, Khayelitsha* 2005 (1) SA 580 (CC); *Port Elizabeth Municipality v Various Occupiers* 2005 (1) SA 217 (CC); *Dikoko* case (n 6); *Union of Refugee Women v Director, Private Security Industry Regulatory Authority* 2007 (4) BCLR 339 (CC); *Barkhuizen v Napier* 2007 (5) SA 323 (CC); *S v M* 2008 (3) SA 232 (CC); *Gumede v President of the Republic of South Africa* 2009 (3) SA 152 (CC); *Masetlha v President of the Republic of South Africa* 2008 (1) SA 566 (CC); *Bertie Van Zyl (Pty) Ltd v Minister for Safety and Security* 2010 (2) SA 181 (CC); *Du Toit v Minister for Safety and Security* 2010 (1) SACR 1 (CC); *Joseph v City of Johannesburg* 2010 (4) SA 55 (CC); *Koyabe v Minister for Home Affairs* 2010 (4) SA 327 (CC); *Van Vuren v Minister of Correctional Services* 2012 (1) SACR 103 (CC); *City of Johannesburg Metropolitan Municipality v Blue Moonlight Properties 39 (Pty) Ltd* 2012 (2) SA 104 (CC); *Everfresh Market Virginia (Pty) Ltd v Shoprite Checkers (Pty) Ltd* 2012 (1) SA 256 (CC); *Le Roux v Dey* 2011 (3) SA 274 (CC); *The Citizen 1978 (Pty) Ltd v McBride* 2011 (4) SA 191 (CC); *KwaZulu-Natal Joint Liaison*

Court in *S v Makwanyane*, which dealt with the constitutionality of the death sentence.[27] Six of the eleven judges referred to *ubuntu* in their separate judgments.[28] Langa J, as he then was, highlighted human dignity as 'an outstanding feature of *ubuntu* in a community sense',[29] and explained its meaning as follows:[30]

> The concept is of some relevance to the values we need to uphold. It is a culture which places some emphasis on communality and on the interdependence of the members of a community. It recognizes a person's status as a human being, entitled to unconditional respect, dignity, value and acceptance from the members of the community such person happens to be part of. It also entails the converse, however. The person has a corresponding duty to give the same respect, dignity, value and acceptance to each member of that community. More importantly, it regulates the exercize of rights by the emphasis it lays on sharing and co-responsibility and the mutual enjoyment of rights by all.

It is evident that Langa J regarded *ubuntu* as a communitarian value that elicits both rights and duties, emphasising the reciprocal responsibilities between individuals and the community. Also, Madala J highlighted these features of *ubuntu* which, according to him, 'calls for a balancing of the interests of society against those of the individual, for the maintenance of law and order, but not for dehumanizing and degrading the individual'.[31]

Mokgoro J recognized the fact that *ubuntu* was, at that time anyway, still in its infancy, but she predicted that *ubuntu* would be 'generally articulated in this country'.[32] South Africa needed something to symbolize the 'bridge between a history of gross violations of human rights and humanitarian principles, and a future of reconstruction and reconciliation'.[33] She articulated her own understanding of *ubuntu* as follows:[34]

> Generally, *ubuntu* translates as 'humaneness'. In its most fundamental sense it translates as personhood and 'morality'. Metaphorically, it expresses itself in *umuntu ngumuntu ngabantu*,[35] describing the significance of group solidarity on survival issues so central to the survival of communities. While it envelops the key values of group solidarity, compassion, respect, human dignity, conformity to basic norms and collective unity, in its fundamental sense it denotes humanity and morality. Its spirit emphasizes respect for human dignity, marking a shift from confrontation to conciliation.

Mokgoro J did not attempt to give a more exact definition of *ubuntu* because, as she admitted in a subsequent scholarly article,[36] *ubuntu* is not easily definable but is something one recognizes when one sees it.[37] Her viewpoint is based on the premise that one has

Committee v MEC Department of Education, KwaZulu-Natal 2013 (4) SA 262 (CC); *Mayelane v Ngwenyama* 2013 (4) SA 415 (CC); *South African Police Service v Solidarity obo Barnard* 2014 (6) SA 123 (CC); *Shoprite Checkers (Pty) Limited v Member of the Executive Council for Economic Development, Environmental Affairs and Tourism, Eastern Cape* 2015 (6) SA 125 (CC).

[27] 1995 (3) SA 391 (CC) (*Makwanyane* case). This was the second decision of the Constitutional Court, but was undoubtedly ground-breaking and is still widely cited. It has been referred to by Bernard E Harcourt, 'Mature Adjudication: Interpretive Choice in Recent Death Penalty Cases' (1996) 9 *Harvard Human Rights Journal* 255 as an example of 'mature adjudication'.

[28] See Chaskalson P [130–31]; Langa J [223–7]; Madala J [237–60]; Mahomed J [263]; Mokgoro J [307–13]; and Sachs J [374].

[29] See *Makwanyane* case (n 27) [225]. [30] ibid [224]. [31] ibid [250]. [32] ibid [307].

[33] Irma J Kroeze, 'Doing Things with Values: The Role of Constitutional Values in Constitutional Interpretation' (2001) 12 *Stellenbosch Law Review* 265, 273 is of the opinion that the vague terms used to define *ubuntu* do not explain sufficiently what the role of *ubuntu* as a constitutional value is.

[34] See *Makwanyane* case (n 27) [308].

[35] The phrase *umuntu ngumuntu ngabantu* is a Zulu expression, literally meaning that 'a person is a person by or through other people'.

[36] Yvonne Mokgoro, '*Ubuntu* and the Law in South Africa' (1998) 1(1) *Potchefstroom Electronic Law Journal* 14 http://www.nwu.ac.za/sites/www.nwu.ac.za/files/images/1998x1x_Mokgoro_art.pdf (last accessed 17 April 2017).

[37] ibid 16. The undefinable nature of *ubuntu* led to cynical critiques from a number of scholars, eg Kroeze (n 5) 260.

knowledge or experience of what *ubuntu* is: 'In one's own experience, *ubuntu*, it seems, is one of those things that you recognize when you see it'. Such a viewpoint is not trouble-free. It presupposes that everyone (at least in South Africa) knows what *ubuntu* means. However, during the first few years after the commencement of the transitional constitution, very few legal scholars schooled in the Western legal tradition[38] were aware of the existence of the word '*ubuntu*', let alone of the role it was to play in constitutional adjudication in the years to come. Nowadays, it is a legal as well as a populist notion, frequently used by both the legal profession and the popular media.[39]

Mokgoro also sees *ubuntu* as much more than just a constitutional value. Quoting from one of her first articles about *ubuntu*, it is evident that she regards it as a founding principle of law, with the potential to influence South African law:[40]

> *Ubuntu*(-ism), which is central to age-old African custom and tradition however, abounds with values and ideas which have the potential of shaping not only current indigenous law institutions, but South African jurisprudence as a whole.

Her prediction in 1998 that *ubuntu*[41] 'can ... become central to a new South African jurisprudence and to the revival of sustainable African values as part of the broader process of the African renaissance'[42] has proven to be completely accurate.

Although *ubuntu* took centre stage in the reasoning of the *Makwanyane* case, it appears as if it was, at that early stage of constitutional adjudication, nothing more than 'something to be desired, a commendable attribute which the [South African] nation should strive for', as explained by Langa J[43] and also by Mahomed J:[44]

> 'The need for *ubuntu*' expresses the ethos of an instinctive capacity for and enjoyment of love towards our fellow men and women; the joy and the fulfilment involved in recognizing their innate humanity; the reciprocity this generates in interaction within the collective community; the richness of the creative emotions which it engenders and the moral energies which it releases both in the givers and the society which they serve and are served by.

After the *Makwanyane* case,[45] *ubuntu* initially did not receive much attention in subsequent decisions of the Constitutional Court,[46] but academic discussions continued, and it was never completely forgotten.[47] A few prophets of doom did not believe that *ubuntu*

[38] 'Western' in this context refers to the legal systems of the United Kingdom and the Netherlands in general and more specifically the English and Roman–Dutch law, which make up the common law mix of South Africa.

[39] A general search on the internet reveals 114,000,000 hits on the term *ubuntu* on 17 April 2017).

[40] See Mokgoro (n 36) 22.

[41] She regarded *ubuntu* to be in accordance with constitutional values; see Mokgoro (n 36) 19–21.

[42] See Mokgoro (n 36) 25.

[43] See *Makwanyane* case (n 27) [227].

[44] ibid [263]. Again, the communitarian features of *ubuntu* were highlighted.

[45] Johan van der Walt, 'Vertical Sovereignty and Horizontal Plurality: Normative and Existential Reflections on the Capital Punishment Jurisprudence Articulated in *S v Makwanyane*' (2005) *SA Public Law* 256–69 regards the Court's reference to *ubuntu* as a new foundational value of the constitution as 'almost absurd' and 'rather disingenuous'. He, for one, was of the opinion that: 'the reference to *ubuntu* in *Makwanyane* does suggest that continued use of *ubuntu* in South African jurisprudence would require a good deal of critical inquiry and honest critical thinking to distil from the feudal, hierarchical, and thus vertical trappings of this concept a constitutionality that would be markedly different from the jurisprudence of sovereignty that has characterized Western jurisprudence for centuries'.

[46] One exception is *Azanian Peoples Organization (AZAPO) v President of the Republic of South Africa* 1996 (4) SA 672 (CC). To date (17 April 2017), at least 31 decisions of the Constitutional Court have referred to *ubuntu*, although in many of the cases, it was referred to only in passing with reference to the *Makwanyane* case or the postamble of the transitional constitution. See eg *Christian Education South Africa v Minister of Education* 2000 (4) SA 757 (CC) para 60.

[47] The High Court did, however, continue to refer to *ubuntu* in subsequent cases, although it was only in passing or with reference to the *Makwanyane* case. See eg *S v Williams* 1994 (4) SA 126 (C) 135; *Dulabh v*

would persevere in the legal domain. Kroeze,[48] for one, was not convinced that *ubuntu* would withstand the test of time. She suspected that it was only the 'flavour of the month' and that it would soon be surpassed by other innovative legal thinking. In addition, the indefinability of *ubuntu* was seen as a stumbling block which 'rendered [it] ineffective as a constitutional value because it did not fit within the discourse of traditional legal thinking'. In contrast to the damning picture Kroeze sketched, Cornell[49] recognized the potential of *ubuntu* and suggested that:

> *ubuntu* thinking ... is crucial to the fundamental purpose of the South African constitution, which is to develop an interpretation of the Bill of Rights that goes way beyond the limited notion of such a bill as only a defence against state intrusion and based on negative freedoms.

In 1996, in *Azanian Peoples Organization (AZAPO) v President of the Republic of South Africa*,[50] one of the few cases that brought up *ubuntu* in the five years after the *Makwanyane* case, Mahomed DP mentioned *ubuntu* in the context of the well-known 'historical bridge' metaphor,[51] but did not pay further attention to its content, except by referring with approval to the discussion of *ubuntu* in the *Makwanyane* case.[52]

In 2001, Ngcobo J considered the constitutionality of the practice of the South African Airways not to employ people who are living with HIV as cabin attendants, in *Hoffmann v South African Airways*.[53] He came to the conclusion that 'we must show *ubuntu* to them [people with HIV]',[54] and with reference to the *Makwanyane* case, explained its meaning to be 'the recognition of human worth and respect for the dignity of every person'.[55] Ever since the *Hoffmann* case, *ubuntu* has been inextricably linked to the concept of 'equality', although some authors make a strong case for the argument that *ubuntu* and dignity are—at least historically from a Western viewpoint—altogether two different things. Cornell explains that dignity is usually associated with individual human rights and *ubuntu* with communalism, although she concedes that *ubuntu* could be understood as the value—or *grundnorm*, as she calls it—that informs dignity in constitutional adjudication.[56] The need to reconcile dignity with *ubuntu* has been described as futile by Mokgoro and Woolman because, according to them, there is no need for reconciliation:[57]

> No one has suggested that we need to square *ubuntu* with equality or freedom, or reduce it entirely to community rights. We might do well to consider allowing these values to occupy their

Department of Land Affairs 1997 (4) SA 1108 (LCC) 1126; *Willamson v Schoon* 1997 (3) SA 1053 (T) 1070; *Ryland v Edros* 1997 (2) SA 690 (C) 708; *Inkatha Freedom Party v Truth and Reconciliation Commission* 2000 (3) SA 119 (C) 123.

48 See Kroeze (n 5) 260–1, 264. She argues that the 'formalism in constitutional adjudication is the reason why *ubuntu* has [or could] not been used in further arguments'.

49 Drucilla Cornell, 'A Call for a Nuanced Constitutional Jurisprudence: *Ubuntu*, Dignity, and Reconciliation' (2004) 19 *SA Public Law* 666, 675.

50 1996 (4) SA 672 (CC) (*AZAPO* case). The case dealt with the constitutionality of the amnesty provision in the Truth and Reconciliation Act 34 of 1995; see s 20(7).

51 The proverbial 'historic bridge' between the apartheid era and the new democratic era. See also *The Citizen 1978 (Pty) Ltd v McBride* 2011 (4) SA 191 (CC) (*Citizen* case) [165].

52 See *AZAPO* case (n 49) [19].

53 2001 (1) SA 1 (CC) (*Hoffmann* case).

54 ibid [31].

55 ibid [31].

56 Drucilla Cornell, 'Is There a Difference that Makes a Difference between *Ubuntu* and Dignity?' (2010) 25 *SA Public Law* 382–3. Cornell's discussion of the differences between *ubuntu* and dignity is based on the Kantian understanding of dignity. See also Cornell (n 48) 666. Freddy Mnyongani, 'De-Llinking *Ubuntu*: Towards a Unique South African Jurisprudence' (2010) 31 *Obiter* 134, 145 argues that *ubuntu* must be delinked from the Western legal paradigm to reach its full potential as a unique South African value in its own right.

57 Yvonne Mokgoro and Stu Woolman, 'Where Dignity Ends and *Ubuntu* Begins: An Amplification of, as well as an Identification of a Tension in, Drucilla Cornell's Thoughts' (2010) 25 *SA Public Law* 400, 407.

> own separate spaces—closely aligned and overlapping, but with different roles to play when we apply our minds to constitutional conflicts. ... *ubuntu* and dignity do not map directly on to one another, but they do rhyme.

Other scholars, similarly, have no problem reconciling *ubuntu* and dignity. For example, Metz regards *ubuntu* as the inspiration of dignity. He explains:[58]

> One is to develop one's humanness by communing with those who have a dignity in virtue of their capacity for communing. That is, individuals have a dignity insofar as they have a communal nature, that is, the inherent capacity to exhibit identity and solidarity with others.

After 2004, *ubuntu* came to be a regular feature in the decisions of the Constitutional Court. In *Port Elizabeth Municipality v Various Occupiers*,[59] Sachs J was of the opinion that '[t]he spirit of *ubuntu*, part of the deep cultural heritage of the majority of the population, suffuses the whole constitutional order',[60] and interpreted the Prevention of Illegal Evictions From and Unlawful Occupation of Land Act[61] with the communitarian features of *ubuntu* in mind:[62]

> PIE expressly requires the court to infuse elements of grace and compassion into the formal structures of the law. It is called upon to balance competing interests in a principled way and promote the constitutional vision of a caring society based on good neighbourliness and shared concern. The constitution and PIE confirm that we are not islands unto ourselves. The spirit of ubuntu, part of the deep cultural heritage of the majority of the population, suffuses the whole constitutional order. It combines individual rights with a communitarian philosophy. It is a unifying motif of the bill of rights, which is nothing if not a structured, institutionalised and operational declaration in our evolving new society of the need for human interdependence, respect and concern.

In 2004, the Constitutional Court in *Bhe v Magistrate, Khayelitsha*[63] dealt with the constitutionality of the customary rule of male primogeniture.[64] Two of the judges commented on *ubuntu* in their separate judgments. Langa DCJ, who delivered the majority decision, referred to *ubuntu* as a 'communitarian tradition'; a valuable aspect of the customary law.[65] Similarly, Ngcobo J, who delivered a minority decision, linked the communitarian feature of customary law with *ubuntu* by declaring:[66]

> A sense of community prevailed from which developed an elaborate system of reciprocal duties and obligations among the family members. This is manifest in the concept of *ubuntu* — *umuntu ngumuntu ngabantu* — a dominant value in African traditional culture. This concept encapsulates communality and the inter-dependence of the members of a community. As Langa DCJ put it, it is a culture which 'regulates the exercise of rights by the emphasis it lays on sharing and co-responsibility and the mutual enjoyment of rights'. It is this system of reciprocal duties and obligations that ensured that every family member had access to basic necessities of life such as food, clothing, shelter and healthcare.

[58] See Metz (n 11) 544.

[59] 2005 (1) SA 217 (CC) (*Port Elizabeth Municipality* case).

[60] ibid [37].

[61] No 19 of 1998 (PIE Act). The municipality unsuccessfully sought an eviction order against a number of people who had been occupying shacks on privately-owned land within the municipality.

[62] See *Port Elizabeth Municipality* case (n 59) [37].

[63] 2005 (1) SA 580 (CC) (*Bhe* case). Some scholars are of the opinion that the majority decision of the court does not reflect a commitment to honour the status of customary law in South Africa. See van Niekerk (n 15) 487.

[64] *Bhe* case (n 63) [45], especially n 49. Primogeniture refers to the right of the eldest son to inherit from his father to the exclusion of younger brothers and all his sisters.

[65] He cited with approval Mokgoro J's explanation of *ubuntu* in the *Makwanyane* case (n 27) [45].

[66] *Bhe* case (n 63) [163] (notes omitted). He also cited with approval the definition put forward by Mokgoro J in the *Makwanyane* case (n 27).

Since the *Bhe* case, the Constitutional Court has regularly referred to *ubuntu*.[67] It has become much more than just the flavour of the month and now it is undoubtedly deeply entrenched in the legal reasoning of the Constitutional Court. In addition, *ubuntu* jurisprudence is trickling down to other decisions of South African high courts as a result of the *stare decisis* principle followed in South African law.[68] It is impossible to analyse all the Constitutional Court cases since 2004 that mentioned *ubuntu* in their judgments within the confines of a chapter such as this, but some warrant mentioning.

In the *Dikoko* case,[69] two of the judges[70] pronounced that the almost forgotten common law remedy of *amende honorable* (honourable amends) has a place in the law of defamation and, in addition, that it is compatible with *ubuntu*.[71] Sachs J, who delivered a separate minority judgment, also explained:[72]

> Although *ubuntu-botho* and the *amende honorable* are expressed in different languages intrinsic to separate legal cultures, they share the same underlying philosophy and goal. Both are directed towards promoting face-to-face encounter between the parties, so as to facilitate resolution in public of their differences and the restoration of harmony in the community. In both legal cultures the centrepiece of the process is to create conditions to facilitate the achievement, if at all possible, of an apology honestly offered, and generously accepted.

Although the *Dikoko* case did not deal with a public law issue[73] but with the law of defamation, it is worth noting that both Mokgoro J[74] and Sachs J[75] saw the advantages of mixing common and customary law principles to reach a just outcome acceptable to both parties.[76] In the words of Sachs J:[77]

> A good beginning for achieving greater remedial suppleness might well be to seek out the points of overlap between *ubuntu-botho* and the *amende honorable*, the first providing a new spirit,

[67] The statistics are as follows: 2005 (one case); 2006 (two cases); 2007 (two cases); 2008 (two cases); 2009 (four cases); 2010 (one case); 2011 (five cases); 2012 (one case); 2013 (two cases); 2014 (one case); 2015 (one case); 2016 (three cases); and 2017 (no cases so far). The cases of the Constitutional Court can be accessed on its official website; see Constitutional Court of South Africa (2015).

[68] The Western Cape High Court in Cape Town refers to *ubuntu* in quite a number of cases. The results can be obtained from SAFLII (2015).

[69] The High Court (*Mokhatla v Dikoko* 2005 JDR 0610 (T)) awarded damages in the amount of R110,000 to the chief executive officer (Mokhatla) for defamatory remarks made by the Executive Mayor (Dikoko) of the Southern District Municipality in the North West Province. Dikoko's leave for appeal to the Supreme Court of Appeal failed and he approached the Constitutional Court for a similar order. The Constitutional Court (*Dikoko* case) reduced the quantum of the damages awarded by the High Court. See [68]–[69] for the court's detailed explanation of *ubuntu*.

[70] Mokgoro J ([68]–[69]) and Sachs J ([112]–[116]). However, their views were not shared by the majority because the issue was not raised in the trial court; see [86].

[71] The *amende honorable* existed in Roman–Dutch law and involved a public apology to repair the damage done by a defamatory statement. For a more elaborate discussion of the remedy see the *Dikoko* case (n 6) [63]–[67], and also Mukheibir (n 5) 584–5.

[72] See *Dikoko* case (n 6) [116].

[73] The Court held that the question of liability and privilege of municipal councillor and members of provincial legislatures and the regulation of their constitutional powers were indeed constitutional issues and that it was, therefore, in the interests of justice to hear the matter. See *Dikoko* case (n 6) [29]–[30].

[74] ibid [69]. [75] ibid [121].

[76] I have argued before, in the context of the customary and common law of succession, that it is time to explore the benefits of these two systems working together instead of their always being at loggerheads. See Christa Rautenbach, 'A Few Comments on the (Possible) Revival of the Customary Rule of Male Primogeniture: Can the Common Law Principle of Freedom of Testation Come to Its Rescue?' (2014) *Acta Juridica* 132, 134. See also Gardiol J van Niekerk, '*Amende Honorable* and *Ubuntu*: An Intersection of *Ars Boni et Aequi* in African and Roman–Dutch Jurisprudence' (2013) 19 *Fundamina* 397, 412, who explains the Constitutional Court's mixing of Western and African principles as follows: 'Our courts have shown that they are willing to internalise concepts of African customary law and to utilise them at practical level', which 'confirms same movement towards a functional convergence of our (essentially Roman–Dutch) common law and African customary law'.

[77] This comment was made by Sachs J; see *Dikoko* case (n 6) [121].

the second a time-honoured legal format. Whatever renovatory modalities are employed, and however significant to the outcome the facts will have to be in each particular case, the fuller the range of remedial options available the more likely will justice be done between the parties. And the greater the prospect of realising the more humane society envisaged by the constitution.

In the *Everfresh Market* case,[78] Yacoob J took the idea that *ubuntu* was a founding principle of law, to a new level within the area of the law of contract:[79]

> The values embraced by an appropriate appreciation of *ubuntu* are also relevant in the process of determining the spirit, purport and objects of the constitution. The development of our economy and contract law has thus far predominantly been shaped by colonial legal tradition represented by English law, Roman law and Roman Dutch law. The common law of contract regulates the environment within which trade and commerce take place. Its development should take cognisance of the values of the vast majority of people who are now able to take part without hindrance in trade and commerce. And it may well be that the approach of the majority of people in our country place (*sic*) a higher value on negotiating in good faith than would otherwise have been the case. Contract law cannot confine itself to colonial legal tradition alone.

The common law remedy of *amende honorable* was again linked with *ubuntu* in *Le Roux v Dey*,[80] which also dealt with a defamation claim.[81] The court remarked as follows:[82]

> We think it is time for our Roman-Dutch common law to recognise the value of this kind of restorative justice [based on *ubuntu*]. Moreover, we think it can be done in a manner which, at the same time, recognises the shared values of fairness that underlie both our common law and customary law, and which form the basis of the values and norms that our constitutional project enjoins us to strive for.

The defendants were ordered to tender an unconditional apology to the defamed teacher, in addition to having to pay a reduced monetary penalty.[83]

Possibly the most helpful contribution to understanding the core features of *ubuntu* in a jurisprudential context is found not in the jurisprudence of the Constitutional Court already discussed, but in a decision of the Equality Court, *Afriforum v Malema*,[84] which explained the core features of *ubuntu* as follows, namely that it:[85]

[78] 2012 (1) SA 256 (CC) (*Everfresh Market* case).

[79] ibid [23]. See also references to *ubuntu* at [24], [61], [71], and [72]. The judgment was delivered soon after Bennett (n 4) 44 explained that contract law has proven to be resistant to *ubuntu*.

[80] 2011 (3) SA 274 (CC) (*Le Roux* case).

[81] The majority of the court found the image depicting the deputy-principal of a school naked in a sexually suggestive position with the principal as defamatory.

[82] See the *Le Roux* case (n 80) [197]. Froneman J and Cameron J, however, cautioned against the melding of *amende honorable* and *ubuntu* into a single system of law in spite of the plausible links between them, because this would require a 'mature reflection and consideration on a future occasion'; see [200].

[83] *Le Roux* case (n 80) [10]. In the *Citizen* case (n 51) [134], McBride instituted a defamation claim against the *Citizen* newspaper for referring to him as a criminal and a murderer. The Constitutional Court dealt with the question of whether an apology would be a suitable order in the case of the media, and came to the conclusion that it would not be in this case, considering the complexities involved when a court orders a media-defendant to apologize.

[84] 2011 (6) SA 240 (EqC) [18] (*Afriforum* case). In order to determine whether the publication of pejorative words ('shoot the Boer') in a political song constituted hate speech, the Equality Court referred to the '*ubuntu*-based jurisprudence', which had been developed by the Constitutional Court, establishing *ubuntu* as an important source of law 'within the context of strained or broken relationships amongst individuals or communities and as an aid for providing remedies which contribute towards more mutually acceptable remedies for the parties in such a case'. Malan (n 21) 252, although satisfied with the outcome of the case, is of opinion that the order of the Court is unenforceable because it was made against a large number of people.

[85] Equality courts are special courts as referred to in s 166(e) of the constitution. They have been established to deal exclusively with equality cases in terms of the Promotion of Equality and the Prevention of Unfair Discrimination Act 4 of 2000.

1. is to be contrasted with [a] vengeance;
2. dictates that a high value be placed on the life of a human being;
3. is inextricably linked to the values of and which places a high premium on dignity, compassion, humaneness and respect for [the] humanity of another;
4. dictates a shift from confrontation to mediation and conciliation;
5. dictates good attitudes and shared concern;
6. favours the re-establishment of harmony in the relationship between parties and that such harmony should restore the dignity of the plaintiff without ruining the defendant;
7. favours restorative rather than retributive justice;
8. operates in a direction favouring reconciliation rather than estrangement of disputants;
9. works towards sensitising a disputant or a defendant in litigation to the hurtful impact of his actions to the other party and towards changing such conduct rather than merely punishing the disputant;
10. promotes mutual understanding rather than punishment;
11. favours face-to-face encounters of disputants with a view to facilitating differences being resolved rather than conflict and victory for the most powerful;
12. favours civility and civilised dialogue premised on mutual tolerance.

It is evident from the few cases discussed that the South African judiciary—especially the Constitutional Court—engages actively with *ubuntu* jurisprudence. This approach illustrates the court's willingness to include other (indigenous) legal norms into their reasoning—a development which was predicted by Zimmermann and Visser[86] as early as in 1996. They prophesized that the newly-acquired status of customary law's might lead to the 'Africanisation of the Roman-Dutch law in the twenty-first century'.[87]

The concept of *ubuntu* is ever-evolving. It is in the process of being shaped by the judiciary, lawmakers, and scholars.[88] It is no longer only the flavour of the month, as its seepage into South African legislation has proven.

3. *Ubuntu* in South African Legislation

The inception of *ubuntu* into South African legislation is further evidence of its legal importance.[89] A recent example is the Child Justice Act,[90] which expresses a commitment to *ubuntu* as one of its objectives. Section 2(b) stipulates that the object of the Act is to promote the spirit of *ubuntu* in the child justice system through –

(i) fostering children's sense of dignity and worth;
(ii) reinforcing children's respect for human rights and the fundamental freedoms of others by holding children accountable for their actions and safeguarding the interests of victims and the community;
(iii) supporting reconciliation by means of a restorative justice response; and

[86] Reinhard Zimmermann and Daniel P Visser, 'South African Law as a Mixed Legal System' in Reinhard Zimmermann and Daniel P Visser (eds), *Southern Cross: Civil and Common Law In South Africa* (Oxford University Press 1996) 2. See also Christa Rautenbach, 'South African Common and Customary Law of Intestate Succession: A Question of Harmonisation, Integration or Abolition' (2008) 12 *Electronic Journal of Comparative Law* http://www.ejcl.org/121/abs121-20.html (last accessed 17 April 2017).

[87] For a discussion of the legal status of customary law in South Africa see Rautenbach and Bekker (n 14) 38–41.

[88] See Bennett (n 4) 52.

[89] A detailed discussion of the relevant legislation falls outside the scope of this chapter. A few examples are discussed to illustrate the point the author wishes to make, namely, that there is an ongoing process of indigenization of South African law, in general, and constitutional law, in particular.

[90] No 75 of 2008. The Act commenced on 1 April 2008.

(iv) involving parents, families, victims and, where appropriate, other members of the community affected by the crime in procedures in terms of this Act in order to encourage the reintegration of children.

The Act does not define *ubuntu*, but Sloth-Nielsen and Gallinetti[91] convincingly argue that the text of the Act can be interpreted to give content to it. First of all, sections 2(b)(ii) and (iii) reinforce the notion that the child's well-being is dependent on his or her relationship with others, a recurring theme in *ubuntu* literature. In addition, the objective in section 2(e) calls for an integrated, holistic approach to the implementation of the Act. This provision stipulates that the object is to

> promote co-operation between government departments, and between government departments and the non-governmental sector and civil society, to ensure an integrated and holistic approach in the implementation of this Act.

Where an 'integrated and holistic' approach is required, one may expect an approach based on communitarian values—thus an approach recognizing the connection between the child and the community, in line with the spirit of *ubuntu,* with the focus on the undeniable link between the individual and the community. An approach that ignores this link will fail the child justice system. Secondly, section 2(b)(iii), which supports 'reconciliation by means of a restorative justice response', seems to be in line with the argument that *ubuntu* and restorative justice are interconnected.[92] Thirdly, the salient features of *ubuntu*, as formulated in the *Afriforum* case, are easily recognized, not only in the objectives of the Act already mentioned, but also those listed in the remaining sections, namely, sections 2(c) and (d):

(c) provide for the special treatment of children in a child justice system designed to break the cycle of crime, which will contribute to safer communities, and encourage these children to become law-abiding and productive adults;

(d) prevent children from being exposed to the adverse effects of the formal criminal justice system by using, where appropriate, processes, procedures, mechanisms, services or options more suitable to the needs of children and in accordance with the constitution, including the use of diversion.

A fourth indication is found in section 3(e), which lists one of the guiding principles in the application of the Act to be the treatment of a child 'in a manner which takes into account his or her cultural values and beliefs'.[93] These features and others not discussed here led the authors to conclude that the Child Justice Act was an Africanized statute 'based on the prominence given to restorative justice and *ubuntu*', which have to be embraced by the criminal justice system to benefit the offender, the victim, and the community.[94]

An earlier example of the influence of *ubuntu* on legislation is the Promotion of National Unity and Reconciliation Act,[95] which made provision for the establishment of the Truth and Reconciliation Commission (TRC) with the object of promoting national unity and

[91] Julia Sloth-Nielsen and Jacqui Gallinetti, '"Just Say Sorry?" *Ubuntu*, Africanisation and the Child Justice System in the Child Justice Act 75 of 2008' in Diedrich (n 1) 75–7.

[92] See Christa Rautenbach, 'Legal Reform of Traditional Courts in South Africa: Exploring the Links between *Ubuntu*, Restorative Justice and Therapeutic Jurisprudence' (2015) 2 *Journal of International and Comparative Law* 275.

[93] This provision is another indication for Sloth-Nielsen and Gallinetti (n 91) 77 of the indigenization (or Africanization, as they call it) of the child justice system.

[94] See Sloth-Nielsen and Gallinetti (n 91) 86.

[95] No 34 of 1995.

reconciliation through transitional justice mechanisms.[96] The preamble to the Act placed *ubuntu* at the heart of the transitional process by repeating the words contained in the transitional constitution, namely, 'AND SINCE the Constitution states that there is a need for understanding but not for vengeance, a need for reparation but not for retaliation, a need for *ubuntu* but not for victimization ...'. The TRC and the role played by *ubuntu* in its successes and failures have been the subject of many scholarly debates. Stuit, who commented on the flexibility and vagueness of *ubuntu*, came to the conclusion that it is 'exactly the ambiguity of *ubuntu* as a concept that provides it with the necessary dynamics and flexibility to be both criticized and reformulated in constructive ways'.[97] The potential of *ubuntu* as a transitional justice mechanism from a European perspective and its (possible) adoption by other countries in transition and international structures, such as the International Court of Justice, has also been recognized.[98]

The importance of *ubuntu* in the two statutes is evident. The relationship between children and their families is the cornerstone of the Child Justice Act. Considering that the concept of family is crucial to many African families, the presence of *ubuntu* is not surprising. The occurrence of *ubuntu* in the Promotion of National Unity and Reconciliation Act is equally obvious. The reconciliation process called for a unique situation, where the reconciliatory value, instead of vengeance and retaliation, of *ubuntu* became prominent.

Draft legislation regarding traditional courts is in the pipeline but, contrary to expectations and also to the importance attached to *ubuntu*, it has been omitted from the Traditional Courts Bill of 2012, without any obvious reasons given.[99] Instead, the bill refers to restorative justice, social cohesion, and reconciliation as values of the traditional justice system. Granted that social cohesion and reconciliation are two meanings attributed to *ubuntu*, one would have expected that the latter is nowadays so entrenched in South African law that it is no longer necessary to defend its existence by means of legal gymnastics. There are other statutes operating in the mainstream legal sphere that explicitly refer to *ubuntu*, and it does not make sense that a bill which regulates traditional courts contains no reference to *ubuntu*, while the two statutes discussed do refer to it.[100] Nevertheless, although the bill does not mention *ubuntu*, it explicitly affirms the role of traditional leaders in the 'promotion of social cohesion, co-existence and peace and harmony in traditional communities', and all of these are core elements of *ubuntu*. The bill has also been linked to *ubuntu* in the media[101] and, for now, we can assume that the bill is intended to uphold *ubuntu* values in a customary law setting.

[96] The Commission operated from 1996 to 1998 and consisted of three main structures: the Human Rights Violation Committee; the Amnesty Committee; and the Reparation and Rehabilitation Committee. The Commission's final report is accessible at SABC, 'TRC Documents' (2015) http://sabctrc.saha.org.za/documents.htm (last accessed 17 April 2017). Paras 80–88 deal with the role of *ubuntu* in promoting restorative justice.

[97] Hanneke Stuit, '*Ubuntu*, the Truth and Reconciliation Commission, and South African National Identity' (2010) 20 *Thamyris/Intersecting* 83, 98.

[98] Inga Švarca, '*Ubuntu* in the Transitional Justice Mechanisms of South Africa' in Diedrich (n 1) 115–22.

[99] The bill provides for the designation of traditional leaders as presiding officers of traditional courts with civil and criminal jurisdiction for certain areas, and is currently being debated in parliament. The bill with its memorandum is accessible at Republic of South Africa, 'Traditional Courts Bill' (2012) http://pmg-assets.s3-website-eu-west-1.amazonaws.com/bills/120125b1-12.pdf (last accessed 17 April 2017). For a discussion of the possible links between *ubuntu*, restorative justice, and therapeutic jurisprudence see Rautenbach (n 92) 275.

[100] For example, the Promotion of National Unity and Reconciliation Act 34 of 1995 contains a reference to *ubuntu* in its preamble. See also s 2 of the Child Justice Act 75 of 2008.

[101] Jan Willem Bornman, 'Challenging the Constitution for Tradition' (*Joburg Justice*, date unknown) http://journalism.co.za/indepth/joburgjustice/?page_id=881 (last accessed 17 April 2017). Although CONTRALESA supported the drafting of the bill, it does not agree with its outcome, because it imposes a Western perspective on traditional courts, which is unacceptable to African communities and leaders. See Anon, 'Traditional Courts

4. *Ubuntu* into and out of Africa

Judges involved in constitutional adjudication often engage in comparative analyses of foreign cases,[102] and *ubuntu* is no exception. I have already alluded to the fact that *ubuntu* has attracted the attention of the judiciary in Africa and elsewhere.[103] A cursory perusal reveals that some other judges in Southern Africa have from time to time also incorporated *ubuntu* reasoning in their judgments.[104] One such case is *Mokoena v Mokoena*,[105] where the High Court of Lesotho dealt with intricate questions regarding customary land rights, irrelevant to this discussion.[106] What is important is what the court said about the African idea of justice, namely:[107]

> The widow has a customary law right to expect her late husband's relatives to protect her and the property that her husband left her with ... It is contrary to Basotho culture, good conscience and a sense of what is right in the African sense—that applicant should be attempting to deprive the widow of her house and arable lands (*masimo*). *It is not botho or ubuntu to dispossess a widow.*

The court did not explain the meaning of *ubuntu*, and it is evident that, being a native Sesotho speaker,[108] he, and probably everyone else involved in the case, knew exactly what it meant from 'experience'.

In a second example, also from Lesotho, a soldier diagnosed with HIV was retired from the Lesotho defence force on medical grounds. He approached the court for an order for reinstatement and constitutional damages based on discrimination. Although the court, in *Thabo Fuma v The Commander, Lesotho Defence Force*,[109] did not refer to *ubuntu* per se, it cited from the South African *Hoffmann* case,[110] where dignity and *ubuntu* had been linked, to find that the denial of employment to an HIV-positive person constituted unfair discrimination.

The South African judiciary's liaison with *ubuntu* was commented upon in the Constitutional Court of Uganda in *Salvatori Abuki v Attorney-General*,[111] where the court had to deal with the constitutionality of the Witchcraft Act.[112] In a separate but concurring judgment, Tabaro J referred to the South African *Makwanyane* case, and declared:[113]

Bill "Inadequate"' *News24* (22 February 2012) http://www.news24.com/Archives/City-Press/Traditional-Courts-Bill-inadequate-20150430 (last accessed 17 April 2017).

[102] The phenomenon has been given many names, such as 'transjudicialism', 'transjudicial communication', 'constitutionalist dialogue', 'judicial globalization', 'constitutional cross-fertilization', 'transnational contextualization', 'globalization of judgment', 'globalization of national courts', 'constitutional borrowing', 'constitutional comparativism', and 'judicial comparativism'. See eg the edited collection of Tania Groppi and Marie-Claire Ponthoreau (eds), *The Use of Foreign Precedents by Constitutional Judges* (Hart Publishing 2013); and the article by Christa Rautenbach and Lourens du Plessis, 'In the Name of Comparative Constitutional Jurisprudence: The Consideration of German Precedents by South African Constitutional Court Judges' (2013) 14 *German Law Journal* 1539.

[103] This is not a detailed discussion, but merely an overview to illustrate the movement of *ubuntu* discourses to other parts of Africa and elsewhere.

[104] The data was obtained from the SAFLII database (SAFLII, 'Southern African Legal Information Institute Home' (2015) http://www.saflii.org (last accessed 17 April 2017).

[105] [2007] LSHC 14 (16 January 2007) (*Mokoena* case).

[106] In general, private land ownership is not possible in Lesotho. The land belongs to the Basotho people and is held in trust by the king on behalf of the people. In addition, land will be allocated to citizens of Lesotho only. In this case, the applicant claimed that the first respondent (his deceased brother's surviving spouse) was not entitled to her deceased husband's land because he became a South African citizen before he died and was, therefore, no longer entitled to the land. The court refused to grant an interdict for the removal of the first respondent, because that would be contrary to Basotho customary law; see *Mokoena* case (n 105) [3].

[107] See *Mokoena* case (n 105) [36]–[37] (emphasis added).

[108] ibid [23].

[109] [2013] LSHC 68 (10 October 2013) [46].

[110] 2001 (1) SA 1 (CC) (n 53).

[111] [1997] UGCC 5 (12 June 1997).

[112] Cap 108 Laws of Uganda.

[113] *Salvatori Abuki v Attorney-General* [1997] UGCC 5 (12 June 1997) 8–9.

> The myth of Africans requiring harsh punishment has been exploded by the judgment of the South African Supreme Court in *S v Makwanyane* an (*sic*) M MCHUNU Case No CCT/3/94 delivered on 6th June, 1995, discussing the constitutionality of the death penalty in which it is shown that African values are based on 'need for understanding but not for vengeance, and need for reparation but not retaliation, a need for *ubuntu* bat (*sic*) not for victimization'. Of course the concept of '*ubuntu*', the idea that being human entails humaneness to other people is not confined to South African or any particular ethnic group in Uganda. It is the whole mark of civilised societies. For application of the concept herein explained, see the judgment Mohamed J *Makwanyane* case, reported [1995] (5) BCLR 665. It will be recalled that the word '*ubuntu*' though linguistically peculiar to only certain groups, is a concept embraced by all the communities of Uganda. I would gladly associate myself with the view expressed by Madala J in the same case (of *Makwanyane* (ibid)) that the African concept embodies within itself humaneness, social justice and fairness, and permeates fundamental human rights. Langa J in the same case expressed the sane ideas when he concluded that the concept carries with it the idea of human dignity end (*sic*) true humanity.

So far, legal discourse on *ubuntu* has mostly been between South African scholars and published primarily in South African literature. The first comprehensive casebook on the relationship between *ubuntu* and the law was published in 2012.[114] The book focuses on South African scholarship in the main, but one of the editors is an American scholar and the publisher is also US based.[115] She admits that her contemporary thoughts on feminist theories were challenged during the time she was involved in the *ubuntu* project in South Africa:[116]

> Although the thinking of race, class, and ethnic difference clearly influenced my rethinking of the feminine within sexual difference, I was not yet, in 1991, involved with a more complex effort to think through transnational feminism, even though I had already been an anti-imperialist activist. For the last eight years, I have been involved in what is called 'the *ubuntu* project' in South Africa, and I have lived in South Africa from 2007 to 2010. During that time, I held the National Research Foundation Chair in Customary Law, Indigenous Ideals, and the Dignity Jurisprudence. There is simply no way to think about the living customary law, let alone indigenous ideals, with all the complexity that attends to the notion of the indigenous, without also having to rethink the very idea of modernity as some kind of aspirational ideal.

5. Conclusion

There are both sceptical critics and devoted followers of *ubuntu*.[117] *Ubuntu* has been criticized for being too vague and ambiguous;[118] for promoting communalism at the

[114] Drucilla Cornell and Nyoko Muvangua, Ubuntu *and the Law: African Ideals and Post-apartheid Jurisprudence* (Fordham University Press 2012).

[115] Drucilla Cornell is an American philosopher and feminist theorist. She is a professor of Political Science, Comparative Literature and Women's and Gender Studies at Rutgers University, the State University of New Jersey.

[116] Drucilla Cornell, 'Revisiting Beyond Accommodation after Twenty Years' (2011) 1(1) *feminist@law* fn 19 http://journals.kent.ac.uk/index.php/feministsatlaw/article/view/13/56#txt19 (last accessed 17 April 2017).

[117] See Bennett (n 4) 46–48, who discusses a few examples from both camps.

[118] Heinz Klug, *Constituting Democracy: Law, Globalism and South Africa's Political Reconstruction* (Cambridge University Press 2000) 164. However, Bennett (n 4) 46–47 convincingly argues that its vagueness is also its saviour. It is neither a principle nor a rule but a value that may be compared to the Hindu concept of *dharma*. An exact definition would restrict its meaning, which is still in a developmental phase.

cost of individual autonomy;[119] for being redundant;[120] for being a political tool;[121] and for being exclusive of other races and groups.[122] The cynical view of Matolino and Kwindingwi[123] of *ubuntu* is evident in the following passage:

> [B]oth the constitution and the policy frameworks of the government only pay lip service to *ubuntu*. We cannot take seriously the idea that *ubuntu* is the cornerstone of public law, governance and public life in South Africa. On the contrary, we suggest that *ubuntu* is only advanced to serve a certain Africanist agenda when it best suites (*sic*) the elite. When used by ordinary people, it amounts to nothing more than a catch phrase with soap opera soothing qualities. The reason for this is that adherents of *ubuntu* are hard to come by. Even in academia the learned defenders of *ubuntu* do so from the point of view of seeing it as a viable authentic ethic of the sub-Saharan people, if not altogether a theoretical postulation albeit with an alleged historical context.

Another author argues that *ubuntu* is merely a 'marketing device to put an African imprimatur on a set of civil liberties and freedoms forged out of Western instruments'.[124]

Not everyone is as critical of *ubuntu* as this. The general viewpoint is in favour of affording *ubuntu* a greater role in judicial decision-making—to contribute towards the development of a legal system that is home-grown and acceptable to the majority of the people for whom *ubuntu* has always been a way of life. Mokgoro J, for one, is of the opinion that it has already become a domestic justiciable principle with reference to the interpretation clause[125] in the transitional constitution:[126]

> I am of the view that our own (ideal) indigenous value systems are a premise from which we need to proceed and are not wholly unrelated to our goal of a society based on freedom and equality.

And again later in the context of the final constitution:[127]

> The flexibility of *ubuntu* has the potential to enrich our ever-evolving constitutional jurisprudence; to see this we need only to look at the various circumstances in which *ubuntu* has informed the outcome of the decisions of our courts.

[119] See Bennett (n 4) 47.

[120] The argument is that dignity (s 10 of the constitution) encompasses everything, rendering concepts such as *ubuntu* unnecessary; see Bennett (n 4) 47. I have already referred to the debate on the overlapping of *ubuntu* and dignity in section 2 of this chapter, and there is enough evidence that the one is not necessarily exclusive of the other, but that they complement each other.

[121] See Matolino and Kwindingwi (n 19) 197, who argue that the success of *ubuntu* depends on the existence of 'small and tight-knit communities that are relatively underdeveloped', where interdependence is crucial to the existence of *ubuntu* values. Without such communities, *ubuntu* is merely a political tool 'to coerce society towards the same ideology' as that of political leaders. In philosophical circles, debates around *ubuntu* seem to become intense. The authors' viewpoint that *ubuntu* has reached its end point is hotly debated by Thaddeus Metz, 'Just the Beginning for *Ubuntu*: Reply to Matolino and Kwindingwi' (2014) 33 *South African Journal of Philosophy* 65, 65. His reply was met with a response by Bernard Matolino, 'A Response to Metz's Reply on the End of *Ubuntu*' (2015) 34 *South African Journal of Philosophy* 214.

[122] Christian B N Gade, 'What is *Ubuntu*? Different Interpretations among South Africans of African Descent' (2012) 31 *South African Journal of Philosophy* 488, 494 reveals that *ubuntu* is regarded as the moral quality of a person or a phenomenon according to which persons are interconnected, provided that: 'being black, having been incorporated into personhood, or behaving in a morally acceptable manner are seen as *necessary conditions* for being a person'.

[123] See Matolino and Kwindingwi (n 19) 202.

[124] Rosalind English, '*Ubuntu*: The Quest for an Indigenous Jurisprudence' (1996) 12 *South African Journal on Human Rights* 641.

[125] Section 35, now s 39 in the new constitution.

[126] See *Makwanyane* case (n 27) [304].

[127] Yvonne Mokgoro, '*Ubuntu* as a Legal Principle in an Ever-changing World' in Diedrich (n 1) 2.

Bohler-Müller[128] is also in favour of *ubuntu* playing a greater role in adjudication: 'It is advisable that South African courts continue to explore the usefulness of the spirit of *ubuntu* in a post-apartheid landscape, where we need to rethink the role of law in our lives'. Again later, in another scholarly article:[129]

> A lot can go wrong when we 'defend ideals' such as *ubuntu*. It is a risky business and the traps are numerous, but if we dare to risk failure, if we dare to ask what good we are without others, if we dare to imagine a revitalised philosophy of *ubuntu*, if we dare to do it differently, we may have stories worth telling future generation of South Africans. Stories of hope.

The need for developing a truly South African legal system was also put forward by Keep and Midgley, who claim that there is[130]

> [a] real need in South Africa for legitimating the legal system and to develop a legal culture that expresses values originating in African societies.[131] A break from past domination of one school of thought over another needs to be emphasized and the notion of inclusivity that is inherent in *ubuntu-botho* makes it an ideal overarching vehicle for expressing shared values.

They do not foresee a problem with harmonizing common and customary law values, and come to the conclusion that it is possible 'to harmonise values that arise from diverse and essentially foreign sources' such as 'those from Roman and African legal cultures';[132] in other words, a harmonization between values embodied by Western models and those embodied by *ubuntu* to create a truly South African law with both common and customary law elements.

There is value in the view of Sachs that what is developing in South Africa should be called South African law: 'Roman Dutch law will survive in the future by infusing itself with African law, shedding its name, and becoming an integral part of a new South African law'.[133]

> The 'Africanization' or 'indigenization' of South African law is also what Khunou and Nthai had in mind when they declared:[134]
>
> The notion of *ubuntu* provides the South African courts with a constitutional value and a 'home grown flavour', intrinsically linked to a troubled past and the ongoing bridge-building process of South African society. The adoption of an African concept of *ubuntu* into constitutional jurisprudence should be encouraged.

Similarly, to quote Bennett:[135]

[128] See Bohler-Müller (n 5) 280.

[129] Narnia Bohler-Müller, 'Some Thoughts on the *Ubuntu* Jurisprudence of the Constitutional Court' (2007) 28 *Obiter* 590, 599.

[130] Helen Keep and Rob Midgley, 'The Emerging Role of *Ubuntu-Botho* in Developing a Consensual South African Legal Culture' (2007) *Recht der Werkelijkheid* 29, 48.

[131] Jacqueline Church, 'Sustainable Development and the Culture of *Ubuntu*' (2012) 45(2) *De Jure* 511, 526 points out that *ubuntu* is part of the South African legal culture and, thus, has to be taken into consideration in sustainable development debates.

[132] See Keep and Midgley (n 130) 47.

[133] Albie Sachs, *Protecting Human Rights in a New South Africa* (Oxford University Press 1990) 91. This process may be metaphorically described as a 'potjiekos' mix, which is distinctively South African. Elsewhere, I have argued that: '[b]y putting all of the different laws [in South Africa] into one big pot, letting it simmer and infusing all of the ingredients with all the different flavours, we might eventually have a wonderfully integrated "potjiekos" mix, distinctively South African, to be enjoyed by all'. See Christa Rautenbach, 'Mixing South African Common and Customary Law of Intestate Succession: "Potjiekos" in the Making' in Esin Örücü (ed), *Mixed Legal Systems at New Frontiers* (Wildy, Simmonds & Hill 2010) 222, 240.

[134] See Khunou and Nthai (n 2) 67.

[135] See Bennett (n 4) 53 (notes omitted).

> Whether embracing a different set of values or simply expressing universal values differently, *ubuntu* is being deployed to give voice to something distinctively African, and we may concur with the attempt to incorporate that quality 'into the legal system so as to form a cohesive, plural, South African legal culture'. This culture will be one characterized by such ideas as reconciliation, sharing, compassion, civility, responsibility, trust and harmony.

Hlophe JP caused a commotion in 2009, declaring that we should Africanize South African law because, according to him,[136]

> there is a huge void in our legal system ... If we do not transform the legal system we will have a problem because people will not identify with the system. We need to have the situation where people obey the law not because they fear being sent to jail, but because they feel that it is the right thing to do and something they are proud of.

As illustrated above, many share the positive sentiments. The general viewpoint is that South African law must be Africanized or indigenized.[137] The finer points on how this may be achieved currently remain vague. It is clear, however, that *ubuntu* as a legal concept goes a long way towards facilitating this process, and its role in achieving a truly South African law acceptable by all South Africans should be embraced. However, the development and use of *ubuntu* by the judiciary and the legislature are still a long way from calling South African law Africanized, although at least the legal fraternity seems determined to acknowledge the importance of indigenous concepts in contemporary South African law.

Finally, considering the fluid meaning of comparable Western concepts such as '*boni mores*' or 'public policy',[138] the flexibility of *ubuntu* should not be seen as its downfall but rather as one of its strengths. The South African society is rapidly changing and new meanings are being shaped by the judiciary and legal scholars to keep in pace with these changes. Considering that *ubuntu* is closely link to society, it is prudent that it is moulded in a way that allows for change.

Bibliography

Ahiauzu N, '*Ubuntu* and the Obligation to Obey the Law' (2006) 37 *Cambrian Law Review* 17

Anon, 'Traditional Courts Bill "Inadequate"' *News24* (22 February 2012) http://www.news24.com/Archives/City-Press/Traditional-Courts-Bill-inadequate-20150430 (last accessed 17 April 2017)

Bekker T, 'The Re-emergence of *Ubuntu*: A Critical Analysis' (2006) 21 *SA Public Law* 333

Bennett T W, '*Ubuntu*: An African Equity' (2011) 14(4) *Potchefstroom Electronic Law Journal* 29 http://dx.doi.org/10.4314/pelj.v14i4.2 (last accessed 17 April 2017)

Bohler-Müller N, 'The Story of an African Value' (2005) 20 *SA Public Law* 266

Bohler-Müller N, 'Some Thoughts on the *Ubuntu* Jurisprudence of the Constitutional Court' (2007) 28 *Obiter* 590

[136] See Sapa, 'Our Laws Must Be Africanised—Hlophe' *IOL* (9 July 2009) http://www.iol.co.za/news/south-africa/our-laws-must-be-africanised-hlophe-1.449189#.Vl2mFL9pG0I (last accessed 17 April 2017).

[137] I agree with Pierre de Vos, 'Yes, We Should "Africanise" Our Law' *Constitutionally Speaking Blog* (13 July 2009) http://constitutionallyspeaking.co.za/yes-we-should-africanise-our-law/ (last accessed 17 April 2017), that the term 'indigenisation' is to be preferred, because the term 'Africanisation' is not sufficiently delimitated. He explains that: 'given the fact that "Africanisation" is not a term that tells us with sufficient precision what is required. Africa—like Europe—is a large continent with many different legal traditions and systems and it might not be very helpful to talk of the "Africanisation" of our law because it could mean many different things'.

[138] These concepts stand for 'the general sense of justice of the community, the *boni mores*, manifested in public opinion'. See *Napier v Barkhuizen* 2006 (4) SA 1 (SCA) para 73.

Bohler-Müller N, 'Beyond Legal Metanarratives: The Interrelationship between Storytelling, *Ubuntu* and Care' (2007) 18 *Stellenbosch Law Review* 133
Bornman J W, 'Challenging the Constitution for Tradition' *Joburg Justice* (date unknown) http://journalism.co.za/indepth/joburgjustice/?page_id=881 (last accessed 17 April 2017)
Church J, 'Sustainable Development and the Culture of *Ubuntu*' (2012) 45(2) *De Jure* 511
Collins Online Dictionaries, 'Constitutionalism' (2015) http://www.collinsdictionary.com/dictionary/english/constitutionalism (last accessed 17 April 2017)
Constitutional Court of South Africa, 'Home Page' (2015) http://www.constitutionalcourt.org.za (last accessed 17 April 2017)
Cornell D, 'A Call for a Nuanced Constitutional Jurisprudence: *Ubuntu*, Dignity, and Reconciliation' (2004) 19 *SA Public Law* 666
Cornell D, 'Is There a Difference that Makes a Difference between *Ubuntu* and Dignity?' (2010) 25 *SA Public Law* 382
Cornell D, 'Revisiting Beyond Accommodation after Twenty Years' (2011) 1(1) *feminist@law* http://journals.kent.ac.uk/index.php/feministsatlaw/article/view/13/56#txt19 (last accessed 17 April 2017)
Cornell D and Muvangua N, *Ubuntu and the Law: African Ideals and Post-Apartheid Jurisprudence* (Fordham University Press 2012)
Cornell D and van Marle K, 'Exploring *Ubuntu*: Tentative Reflections' (2005) 5 *African Human Rights Law Journal* 195
De Vos P, 'Yes, We Should "Africanize" Our Law' *Constitutionally Speaking Blog* (13 July 2009) http://constitutionallyspeaking.co.za/yes-we-should-africanise-our-law/ (last accessed 17 April 2017)
Dolamo R, '*Botho/Ubuntu*: The Heart of African Ethics' (2013) 1 *Scriptura* 1
Elechi O O, Morris S V C, and Schauer E J, 'Restoring Justice (*Ubuntu*): An African Perspective' (2010) 20 *International Criminal Justice Review* 73
Eliastam J L B, 'Exploring *Ubuntu* Discourse in South Africa: Loss, Liminality and Hope' (2015) 36 *Verbum et Ecclesia* http://www.ve.org.za/index.php/VE/article/view/1427 (last accessed 17 April 2017)
English R, '*Ubuntu*: The Quest for an Indigenous Jurisprudence' (1996) 12 *South African Journal on Human Rights* 641
Gade C B N, 'The Historical Development of the Written Discourses on *Ubuntu*' (2011) 30(3) *South African Journal of Philosophy* 303
Gade C B N, 'What is *Ubuntu*? Different Interpretations among South Africans of African Descent' (2012) 31 *South African Journal of Philosophy* 484
Groppi T and Ponthoreau M-C (eds), *The Use of Foreign Precedents by Constitutional Judges* (Hart Publishing 2013)
Harcourt B E, 'Mature Adjudication: Interpretive Choice in Recent Death Penalty Cases' (1996) 9 *Harvard Human Rights Journal* 255
Himonga C, Taylor M, and Pope A, 'Reflections on Judicial Views of *Ubuntu*' (2013) 16(5) *Potchefstroom Electronic Law Journal* 371 http://dx.doi.org/10.4314/pelj.v16i5.8 (last accessed 17 April 2017)
Keep H and Midgley R, 'The Emerging Role of *Ubuntu-Botho* in Developing a Consensual South African Legal Culture' (2007) 3 *Recht der Werkelijkheid* 29
Keevy I, '*Ubuntu* versus the Core Values of the South African Constitution' (2009) 34 *Journal for Juridical Science* 19
Keevy I, 'The Constitutional Court and *Ubuntu*'s "Inseparable Trinity"' (2009) 34 *Journal for Juridical Science* 61
Keevy I, '*Ubuntu*: Ethnophilosphy and Core Constitutional Values' in F Diedrich (ed), *Ubuntu, Good Faith and Equity: Flexible Legal Principles in Developing a Contemporary Jurisprudence* (Juta 2011)
Khunou S F and Nthai S, 'The Contribution of *Ubuntu* to the Development of Constitutional Jurisprudence in a Democratic South Africa' in F Diedrich (ed), *Ubuntu, Good Faith and Equity: Flexible Legal Principles in Developing a Contemporary Jurisprudence* (Juta 2011)

Klug H, *Constituting Democracy: Law, Globalism and South Africa's Political Reconstruction* (Cambridge University Press 2000)

Kroeze I J, 'Doing Things with Values: The Role of Constitutional Values in Constitutional Interpretation' (2001) 12 *Stellenbosch Law Review* 265

Kroeze I J, 'Doing Things with Values II: The Case of *Ubuntu*' (2002) 13 *Stellenbosch Law Review* 252

Krog A, 'Research into Reconciliation and Forgiveness at the South African Truth and Reconciliation Commission and Homi Bhabha's "Architecture of the New"' (2015) 30 *Canadian Journal of Law and Society* 202

Malan K, 'The Suitability and Unsuitability of *Ubuntu* in Constitutional Law—Inter-Communal Relations versus Public Office-Bearing' (2014) 47 *De Jure* 231

Matolino B, 'A Response to Metz's Reply on the End of *Ubuntu*' (2015) 34 *South African Journal of Philosophy* 214

Matolino B and Kwindingwi W, 'The End of *Ubuntu*' (2013) 32 *South African Journal of Philosophy* 197

Metz T, '*Ubuntu* as a Moral Theory and Human Rights in South Africa' (2011) 11 *African Human Rights Law Journal* 532

Metz T, 'Just the Beginning for *Ubuntu*: Reply to Matolino and Kwindingwi' (2014) 33 *South African Journal of Philosophy* 65

Mnyongani F, 'De-linking *Ubuntu*: Towards a Unique South African Jurisprudence' (2010) 31 *Obiter* 134

Mokgoro Y, '*Ubuntu* and the Law in South Africa' (1998) 1(1) *Potchefstroom Electronic Law Journal* 14 http://www.nwu.ac.za/sites/www.nwu.ac.za/files/images/1998x1x_Mokgoro_art.pdf (last accessed 17 April 2017)

Mokgoro Y, '*Ubuntu* as a Legal Principle in an Ever-changing World' in F Diedrich (ed), *Ubuntu, Good Faith and Equity: Flexible Legal Principles in Developing a Contemporary Jurisprudence* (Juta 2011)

Mokgoro Y and Woolman S, 'Where Dignity Ends and *Ubuntu* Begins: An Amplification of, as well as an Identification of a Tension in, Drucilla Cornell's Thoughts' (2010) 25 *SA Public Law* 400

Motha S, 'Archiving Colonial Sovereignty: From *Ubuntu* to a Jurisprudence of Sacrifice' (2009) 24 *SA Public Law* 297

Mqeke R, 'Customary Law and Human Rights' (1996) 126 *South African Law Journal* 364

Mukheibir A, '*Ubuntu* and the *Amende Honorable*—A Marriage between African Values and Medieval Canon Law' (2007) 28 *Obiter* 583

Nkhata M J, 'Towards Constitutionalism and Democratic Governance: *Ubuntu* and Equity as a Basis for Regulating Public Functionaries in Common Law Africa' in F Diedrich (ed), *Ubuntu, Good Faith and Equity: Flexible Legal Principles in Developing a Contemporary Jurisprudence* (Juta 2011)

Nyaumwe L J and Mkabela Q, 'Revisiting the Traditional African Cultural Framework of *Ubuntuism*: A Theoretical Perspective' (2007) 6 *Indilinga* 152

Oyowe A O, 'Strange Bedfellows: Rethinking *Ubuntu* and Human Rights in South Africa' (2013) 13 *African Human Rights Law Journal* 103

Praeg L, *A Report on* Obuntu (University of KwaZulu-Natal Press 2014)

Ramose M B, *African Philosophy through* Ubuntu (Mond Books 1999)

Rautenbach C, 'South African Common and Customary Law of Intestate Succession: A Question of Harmonization, Integration or Abolition' (2008) 12 *Electronic Journal of Comparative Law* http://www.ejcl.org/121/abs121-20.html (last accessed 17 April 2017)

Rautenbach C, 'Mixing South African Common and Customary Law of Intestate Succession: "Potjiekos" in the Making' in Esin Örücü (ed), *Mixed Legal Systems at New Frontiers* (Wildy, Simmonds & Hill 2010) 222

Rautenbach C, 'A Few Comments on the (Possible) Revival of the Customary Rule of Male Primogeniture: Can the Common Law Principle of Freedom of Testation come to Its Rescue?' (2014) *Acta Juridica* 132

Rautenbach C, 'Legal Reform of Traditional Courts in South Africa: Exploring the Links between *Ubuntu*, Restorative Justice and Therapeutic Jurisprudence' (2015) 2 *Journal of International Comparative Law* 275

Rautenbach C and Bekker J C (eds), *Introduction to Legal Pluralism in South Africa* (4th edn, LexisNexis 2014)

Rautenbach C and du Plessis L, 'In the Name of Comparative Constitutional Jurisprudence: The Consideration of German Precedents by South African Constitutional Court Judges' (2013) 14 *German Law Journal* 1539

Republic of South Africa, 'Traditional Courts Bill' (2012) http://pmg-assets.s3-website-eu-west-1.amazonaws.com/bills/120125b1-12.pdf (last accessed 17 April 2017)

SABC, 'TRC Documents' (2015) http://sabctrc.saha.org.za/documents.htm (last accessed 17 April 2017)

Sachs A, *Protecting Human Rights in a New South Africa* (Oxford University Press 1990)

SAFLII, 'Southern African Legal Information Institute Home' (2015) http://www.saflii.org (last accessed 17 April 2017)

Sapa, 'Our Laws Must Be Africanized—Hlophe' *IOL* (9 July 2009) http://www.iol.co.za/news/south-africa/our-laws-must-be-africanised-hlophe-1.449189#.Vl2mFL9pG0I (last accessed 17 April 2017)

Sloth-Nielsen J and Gallinetti J, '"Just Say Sorry?" *Ubuntu*, Africanization and the Child Justice System in the Child Justice Act 75 of 2008' in F Diedrich (ed), *Ubuntu, Good Faith and Equity: Flexible Legal Principles in Developing a Contemporary Jurisprudence* (Juta 2011) 70

Stuit H, '*Ubuntu*, the Truth and Reconciliation Commission, and South African National Identity' (2010) 20 *Thamyris/Intersecting* 83

Švarca I, '*Ubuntu* in the Transitional Justice Mechanisms of South Africa' in F Diedrich (ed), *Ubuntu, Good Faith and Equity: Flexible Legal Principles in Developing a Contemporary Jurisprudence* (2011)

Van der Walt J, 'Vertical Sovereignty and Horizontal Plurality: Normative and Existential Reflections on the Capital Punishment Jurisprudence Articulated in *S v Makwanyane*' (2005) 20 (2) *SA Public Law* 253

Van Niekerk G J, 'A Common Law for Southern Africa' (1998) 31(2) *Comparative and International Law Journal of Southern Africa* 158

Van Niekerk G J, 'Succession, Living Indigenous Law and *Ubuntu* in the Constitutional Court' (2005) 26 *Obiter* 474

Van Niekerk G J, '*Amende Honorable* and *Ubuntu*: An Intersection of *Ars Boni et Aequi* in African and Roman-Dutch Jurisprudence' (2013) 19 *Fundamina* 397

Zimmermann R and Visser D P, 'South African Law as a Mixed Legal System' in R Zimmermann and D P Visser (eds), *Southern Cross: Civil and Common Law in South Africa* (Oxford University Press 1996)

PART 5

DECISION-MAKING AND WORKING PRACTICES

13

Handling of Petitions by the Constitutional Court of Benin

Theodore Holo

1. Introduction

The onset of the democratic transition in Benin in February 1990 started a new era of constitutional justice in which the Constitutional Court became a cornerstone of its institutional architecture and a key instrument to building a culture of constitutionalism, democracy, and respect for the rule of law. In the process, constitutional justice has been used not only as a basis for entrenching constitutionalism and regulating the powers of government but, most importantly, for protecting the fundamental human rights of the citizens. Prior to the 1990 constitutional reforms, there was hardly any form of judicial review in Benin, in spite of the provision made for a constitutional chamber within the Supreme Court in the earlier constitutions. Be that as it may, the Benin Constitutional Court became the first court amongst the Francophone African countries that inherited the French model of constitutional review that made constitutional justice accessible to ordinary citizens.

In this respect, the constitutional court model adopted by Benin in 1990 varies between the classic type and an original model. In the classic sense, the Constitutional Court controls the constitutionality of norms. Articles 117 to 123 of the constitution, and Article 19 of Law 91-009 of 31 May 2001 establishing the Organic Law on the Constitutional Court, state that: '[o]rganic laws adopted by the National Assembly are referred to the Constitutional Court by the President of the Republic for a constitutionality check'. Other powers are conferred on the Court by Article 123 of the constitution, repeated in Article 21 of the Organic Law on the Constitutional Court, which states thus:

> Prior to their implementation, internal regulations and changes to regulations adopted by the National Assembly, the High Authority for Audio-visual and Communications and the Economic and Social Council must be referred to the Constitutional Court by the president of each body concerned.

Article 121 of the constitution also provides that: '[a]t the request of the President of the Republic or any member of the National Assembly, the Constitutional Court may rule on the constitutionality of laws before they are promulgated'. It should be added that Article 22 of the Organic Law on the Constitutional Court, detailing conditions for the implementation of Article 117 of the constitution, provides:

> Similarly, laws and regulatory acts which may threaten fundamental human rights and public freedoms ... may be referred to the Constitutional Court by the President of the Republic or by any citizen, association or non-governmental human rights organization.

Finally, Article 122 of the constitution provides as follows:

> Any citizen may seise the Constitutional Court on the constitutionality of laws, either directly or by raising a plea of unconstitutionality in a court case involving him/her. The latter must

stay its judgement until the Constitutional Court rules on the matter, which it must do within thirty days.

Beyond its powers of constitutional review of laws, as well as its competence in litigation concerning national elections and referenda, the writers of the 1990 constitution conferred an original attribute to the Constitutional Court of Benin. Article 117 of the constitution provides that the Constitutional Court may decide 'in general on the violation of human rights'. Similarly, while the powers 'to regulate the functioning of institutions and the activity of government' under Article 114 of the constitution of Benin of 11 December 1990 is applied in a rather restrictive manner by several constitutional courts, the apex court of Benin has developed an innovative jurisprudence around this attribute.

As will shortly be shown, the Benin Constitutional Court is a very busy court with a heavy case load. The question does arise as to how such a busy court is able to deal with the numerous petitions that it receives. Is it not likely to be strict in applying the rules for the admissibility of petitions in an effort to reduce its workload? In this respect, an examination of the rules of procedure reveals that not only is access to the court very easy, but in addition, a series of strictly regulated steps allow this apex court to handle petitions in a professional manner right up to the delivery and publication of its decisions. One of the key features of the court is its flexible processes, to which we will now turn.

2. Flexibility in the Handling of Petitions

Access to the Constitutional Court of Benin is very simple. There are no complicated rules with which petitioners are required to comply. In fact, in many instances, the court will overlook errors made by the petitioner in filing the petition and ignore the failure to comply with certain formal filing rules.

2.1 Absence of excessive formalism

A defining characteristic of the rules governing the seising of the Constitutional Court is the absence of excessive formalism. However, a distinction is usually made between cases where the petitioner is a political authority or institution and cases where the petitioner is an ordinary citizen.

Political authorities or institutions are often involved in filing abstract petitions. The referral rules are strictly applied to them. It is assumed that, since these political authorities, such as the president and parliament, are usually involved in making laws, they are aware of procedural issues and ought to be able to comply with them with no difficulty. In dealing with this class of petitioners, the court is therefore strict in its handling of non-compliance with rules of form relating to referral. Thus, for example, rules pertaining to the status of the applicant must be followed rigorously. Only the president of the republic is competent to seise the Constitutional Court with regard to the constitutionality of organic laws before they are promulgated (Article 19 of the Organic Law on the Constitutional Court). The Constitutional Court sanctions any violation of this principle of referral, as it did in its decision DCC 95-020 of 22 March 1995. The same applies to non-compliance with rules of referral regarding the constitutionality of the rules of procedure and amendments thereto of the National Assembly, the High Authority for Audio-visual and Communication, and the Economic and Social Council. In all these cases, the president of each institution is competent to seise the court and must do so in strict compliance with the rules of procedure (Article 21 of the Organic Law on the Constitutional Court).

Although this model of constitutional review usually grants the right of abstract petition to the president of the republic and members of parliament, between the passage of the law and its promulgation, the drafters of the constitution deemed it necessary to grant, for the first time, access to ordinary citizens with respect to matters concerning the violation of their human rights and issues dealing with the respect for the constitutional order. Thus, Article 3 of the constitution of 11 December 1990, after recalling that 'national sovereignty belongs to the people' and that 'no section of the population, no community, no corporation, no political party or association, no union nor any individual may arrogate its exercise', states that 'sovereignty is exercised in accordance with the present constitution, which is the supreme law of the state', and that 'any law, statutory instrument or administrative act contrary to these provisions will be null and void. Consequently, any citizen has the right to seise the Constitutional Court with regard to any alleged unconstitutional laws, texts and acts'.

Article 122 of the same text confirms that '[a]ny citizen may seise the Constitutional Court on the constitutionality of laws', either directly or by raising a plea of 'exception to unconstitutionality' (*exception d'inconstitutionnalité*) in a court case involving him or her. Such a court must stay the proceedings until the Constitutional Court has ruled on the question of constitutionality, which it must do within 30 days'.

With regard to laws and regulatory acts in general, therefore, 'every citizen' is competent without the requirement of having an interest. The term 'citizen' initially led the High Council of the Republic, temporarily acting as Constitutional Court, to reject an appeal by Senegalese individuals because they were not citizens of Benin (in Decision 12 DC of 13 August 1992). However, the Constitutional Court subsequently declared admissible a 'complaint of human rights violation' brought by a foreigner. In Decision DCC 96-060 of 26 September 1996, Ms Angela Melo Gomez brought a case of 'violation of human rights, in particular the right to come and go as she pleases, due to the seizure of her passport'. However, it is Decision DCC 97-045 of 13 August 1997 which confirmed that, under Article 39 of the Constitution of Benin, any 'citizen' as well as any 'foreigner' may bring an action for annulment. The court made it clear that: '[o]n the territory of the Republic of Benin, foreigners enjoy the same rights and freedoms as citizens of Benin'.

Further evidence of the absence of excessive formalism is that in all the above-mentioned cases, the Constitutional Court was seised by a simple letter containing the full name, street address, and signature or fingerprint of the applicant (Article 31 of the Rules of Procedure of the Constitutional Court). In order to facilitate access for those who cannot write or sign, the fingerprint may replace the signature at the bottom of the petition. It should be noted that applicants may have the assistance of counsel before the court. It should also be added that the procedure is written and is free. Petitioners incur no filing charges or fees. As a result, litigation before the Constitutional Court has become so popular that it has given rise to an aphorism that one needs nothing more than a pen and a piece of paper to litigate before the court.

The court's caseload over the years is a reflection of how popular it has become from its establishment. In fact, from 1991 when it was established to 2008, the court had successfully delivered 2,400 judgments, of which 1,728 were review judgments. It is significant that 80 per cent of the cases that the court dealt with were based on individual petitions.[1]

[1] See Gilles Badet, *Les Attributions Originelles de la Cour Constitutionnelle du Bénin* (Friedrich Ebert Stiftung 2013) 158–63.

On the other hand, between 1993 and 2010, the court received more than 1,000 petitions from individuals and groups.[2]

Despite its heavy caseload and the backlog it faced from 2001 onwards, the court did not try to alter its flexible rules giving unfettered direct access to individuals through sieving mechanisms such as that introduced, for instance, in the German and Belgian courts.[3] Individual petitioners seeking *a posteriori* review of constitutionality of laws are not subject to their action being time barred. An example of the Constitutional Court's flexibility are the petitions challenging the 1969 Strike Act for violating fair trial rights under the African Charter on Human and Peoples' Rights, which was brought more than twenty years after the said law was adopted.[4] This is surprising as constitutional review *a priori* must be undertaken within fifteen days of the transmission of a newly adopted law to the president for promulgation.

This flexibility in applying the rules and the risk of ensuing cluttering could easily have led to the strict enforcement of the rules of form. However, the court is also lenient when it comes to the application of some of the rules dealing with issues of form. For example, the court may even go beyond the applicant's request.

2.2 Possible extension of the scope of referral or accepting inadmissible cases by the Constitutional Court assuming jurisdiction on its own initiative

Assuming jurisdiction on its own initiative (*mero metu)* appears to be a specific procedure aimed at protecting an individual's fundamental rights. Article 121(2) of the constitution, reproduced in Article 33(4) of the Organic Law on the Constitutional Court and Article 30 of the Rules of Procedure of the Court, provides that the Constitutional Court 'may decide on its own initiative on the constitutionality of laws and all other regulations that allegedly undermine the fundamental rights and public freedoms of the individual'. Over a period of ten years, from the establishment of the court in June 1993 to June 2003, 16 per cent of the court's decisions were on its own initiative, out of a total of sixty-seven petitions. In fact, the Constitutional Court may act on its own initiative when dealing with the constitutionality of a law, since Article 20(4) of the Organic Law on the Constitutional Court states that the court 'may ... examine an impugned law in its entirety even if the referral is limited to certain provisions of the law' and, as confirmed by Article 33 of its Rules of Procedure, that: '[t]he Constitutional Court rules on the entirety of a law, both in form and substance'.

Mero metu assumption of jurisdiction in certain matters has its merits as the applicant may not on his own perceive all the grounds of unconstitutionality afflicting the law submitted to the review of the court. Assuming that Constitutional Court judges are experts in the matter, their power of assuming jurisdiction on their own initiative gives them the opportunity to rid the problematic text of all its imperfections in both form and substance. The assumption of jurisdiction on its own initiative also allows the court to take notice of certain cases, even though they may be inadmissible or even where the applicant

[2] See Horace S Adjolohoun, *Droits de l'Homme et Justice Constitutionnelle en Afrique: le Modèle Béninois à la Lumière de la Charte Africaine des Droits de l'Homme et des Peuples* (L'Harmattan 2011) 183.

[3] See Badet (n 1) 206–8.

[4] See DCC 95-026 of 11 July 1995 in which the court declared unconstitutional the Ordonnance no 69-14/PR/MFPRAT of 19 June 1969 relating to the exercise of the right to go on strike. See also DCC 11-019 of 21 April 2011 declaring provisions of the Penal Code adopted during the colonial era unconstitutional.

may have withdrawn the case. This is because, once it has been seised, and given the fact that the problem relates to an alleged violation of fundamental rights, the court invokes Article 121(2) of the constitution, Article 33(4) of the Organic Law on the Constitutional Court, and Article 30 of the Rules of Procedure of the court. Each of these articles provides that the Constitutional Court 'may decide on its own initiative on the constitutionality of laws and other regulations which allegedly threaten individual fundamental rights and public freedoms'.

It is by virtue of the assumption of jurisdiction on its own initiative, for example, that the Constitutional Court ruled on the issue of discrimination, the right to be heard, and the right of defence in Decision DCC 06-099 of 11 August 2006. In this case, the applicant stated that he had been appointed on contract as a lecturer on 19 November 2001 for a period of two years, with the possibility of an extension for a further two years. At the start of the school year in October 2003, while awaiting the minister's decision on the renewal of his contract, he was surprised to receive, on 29 April 2004, an undated letter from the rector of the university informing him that his fixed-term contract had been terminated since 3 December 2003. He alleged that this decision by the rector also affected his colleague, Gérard Olodo. He stated that he had immediately challenged this decision on the basis that, since his fixed term contract had not been renewed, it had automatically become a permanent contract. He further alleged that the original contract provided in its Article 9 that, in case of a disciplinary offence, the lecturer's right to defence was guaranteed.

On this basis he alleged that he had written to the rector challenging the decision. However, he pointed out that, despite his numerous inquiries at the rector's office and the ministry, there was no formal commitment to afford him a hearing. He further alleged that, on 22 February 2005, the authorities in the rector's office invited his colleague, Gerard Olodo, who had been dismissed on the same day, to resume work. This Mr Olodo did. He alleged that his investigations revealed that political pressure had compelled the authorities in the rector's office to take this decision. The applicant, therefore, asked the court to find a violation of Articles 8(2) and 26(1) of the constitution and Article 7 of the African Charter on Human and Peoples' Rights.

The court ruled that in this case the question did not relate to the prior exercise of the right to defence guaranteed to everyone, but rather to the unilateral termination of a fixed-term contract by the employer and, therefore, a question of legality. Hence, Article 7 invoked by the applicant was inapplicable. The petition was, therefore, declared inadmissible. Nevertheless, the court, after having drawn attention to Article 26(1) of the constitution, which provides that '[t]he state guarantees everyone equality before the law without distinction of origin, race, sex, religion, political opinion or social status', and having noted that it had in the past consistently ruled that '[t]he concept of equality means as a rule that persons of the same category should be subject to the same treatment without discrimination', decided to examine the case. The court, therefore, exercised its discretion to investigate and decide the case on its own initiative as the case involved the alleged violation of fundamental rights.

The Constitutional Court's use of its *mero motu* jurisdiction when dealing with cases about the constitutionality of laws and other regulations allegedly threatening the fundamental rights of the individual and public freedoms has led it to rely on Article 121(2), even when it was not directly seised by any of the parties. In other words, the court can exercise its *mero motu* jurisdiction in cases that have been referred and are pending before administrative or judicial authorities.

This situation may be illustrated by Decision DCC 05-043 of 26 May 2005, where the court received a copy of a letter addressed to the president of the republic by the Association of Rural Development Agents. This letter had been signed on behalf of the Association by Messrs Louis Koudjrohede, Alphonse Voïtan, and Zannou Degnon. Apart from the copy of this letter to the president of the republic, the court was directly seised with a request dated 25 August 2003 signed, on behalf of the Association of Rural Development Controllers, by Messrs Alphonse Voïtan and Léon Iwa and Ms Gisele Alapini. Although it was only directly seised by a single petition, the court referred to 'petitions' that demonstrate the violation of human rights and the right to equal treatment. This was because both cases raised the issue of the discriminatory manner in which the reclassification of certain members of the Associations of Rural Development Agents was made in implementing decrees on the Individual Status of Rural Development Personnel Corps.

The court observed that the signatories of the petitions had not furnished any evidence to establish the association's capacity to be party to legal proceedings. On this basis, it declared the two petitions inadmissible. However, the court pointed out that, since the petitions alleged violations of human rights, and of the right to equal treatment under Article 121(2), it would exercise its *mero motu* discretion to decide the matter.

The Benin Constitutional Court has, therefore, developed an approach that favours the examination of each petition as soon as it finds that there is a suspected case of fundamental rights violations. The court generally considers that the importance of sanctioning violations of human rights outweighs the errors or deficiencies of the procedure adopted in seising the court. This desire to deal with each situation of violations of human rights is equally noticeable in the further processing of cases because there, too, complying with the various requirements is too technical for the ordinary citizen.

3. Processing of Cases before the Court

The petition is handled by the Constitutional Court according to a complex process that culminates in the public communication of the decision.

3.1 Internal process

When the court is seised by a citizen, the application follows several steps before reaching the applicant's objective, which is the decision of the Constitutional Court. The procedure is as onerous as it is fascinating. This involves registering the correspondence, processing it, investigating the case, registering it on the roll for a decision, holding a hearing, and rendering a decision.

The applicants send their correspondence to the president of the Constitutional Court. It is handed in at the central administrative secretariat. The mail office registers it, and assigns it a sequence number indicating the date and time of its arrival at the court. The registered mail is then forwarded to the Secretary-General, who deals with it according to its subject matter. The purpose of the petition is noted on the record. The Secretary-General examines it to ensure that it deals with a matter that may form the basis of a petition before sending it to the president of the Constitutional Court for his opinion and the appointment of a rapporteur. After the president has approved it, the mail is then returned to the mail office for registration in the appropriate register. The mail service records the name of the rapporteur in its register before transmitting the entire record of the proceedings to the Appeals Management Service for it to be given a registration number. The application is reproduced in three copies: the original copy is sent to the secretariat, one copy is sent to the rapporteur, and another to the Directorate of Legal Affairs and Appeals Management.

In order to assist the rapporteur in his work of preparing a draft decision, the court has a pool of assistants based in the Directorate of Legal Studies and Appeals Management. Once seised, the directorate assigns the case to an assistant, who is assigned to work on the matter with the rapporteur. Where appropriate, this phase allows the rapporteur to invite persons involved in the case to file their observations or other useful information. The rapporteur may even decide, at this stage, to hear the parties or any person whose testimony he deems appropriate. In the case of written observations, the rapporteur will advise the parties of the deadlines within which to file their responses. He may even order investigations. The parties may be assisted by any competent natural or legal person. The latter may submit heads of argument signed by the parties concerned. The process is essentially adversarial in nature.

After all these steps have been completed, which could last several months, depending on the procedures and the complexity of the issues, the rapporteur may, with the help of the assistant, draw up a draft report. The draft report soon becomes a draft decision. This draft decision, together with the report, will be sent to the other judges. The report and the draft decision are then submitted to the secretariat-general to be put on the roll.

Ten copies are made of the entire case file (consisting of the petition, the investigation report, the responses to the investigation, and other elements, including the report and the draft decision). The Secretary-General schedules a hearing. The hearing takes place on the basis of a summons containing the files to be examined. The central mail secretariat is responsible for distributing copies of this summons to members of the court, secretary-generals, and directors of the Appeals Management services.

At the hearing, the report is presented by the rapporteur. Following comments from the judges of the court, this report is (i) either adopted and a decision is handed down; or (ii) the matter is adjourned while supplementary information is obtained, in order for the court to make a decision.

It should be noted that, in general, consensus among the judges is what is sought. This is how decisions are arrived at, and there is hardly ever recourse to the vote. This does not, however, prevent open and serious debate.

3.2 Communication of the decision to the parties and the public

Once a decision has been taken, it is necessary before anything else to notify the applicant and all those directly affected by the implementation of the decision. The formal procedure ends with the communication of the decision to the different parties, as well as to any other person whose testimony was considered necessary during the investigation of the case.

The original case file is removed from the general secretariat and filed in the archives. This is the archiving stage. This ends the process of dealing with petitions filed before the Constitutional Court.

Next follows the phase of communication to the public. This may be done in several ways. The first, provided for by law, is to publish the decision in the official *Gazette*. This step is more a formality than anything else.

In order to publicize its decisions in a manner that will enhance understanding of the application of the rule of law, the court has developed a means for communicating with the general public. To this end, the information technology department of the Constitutional

Court ensures that all its decisions are published on its website. These decisions are classified according to the different years, by applicant, and by theme on the court's website. When the court considers a decision as being of general interest, in view of the subject matter or sensitivity of the issue, it sends the decision by email to the media. This helps to prevent rumours and gives experts the opportunity to react to decisions immediately. Different media regularly publish decisions in their entirety.

In addition to this approach, which is conditioned by the topical nature of the subject matter, another method is by publishing the court's decisions in the yearbook that contains all decisions, either in hard copy or on CD ROM.

For the time being, the practice of dissenting opinions is not allowed in the work of the Constitutional Court of Benin. Furthermore, an obligation incumbent on judges is not to speak publicly against the decisions of the court and not to reveal details of its secret deliberations. Nevertheless, academics, journalists, and the general public comment extensively on decisions of the court. When the court considers it necessary to clarify a decision that is not understood by the general public, a press release is issued by the secretary-general of the court, sent to the media, and posted on the court's website.

4. Conclusion

In the final analysis, the processing of a petition brought before the Constitutional Court illustrates a determination by the court to focus on issues of human rights violations and defence of the constitutional order without dwelling too much on errors of procedure or form committed by the parties. It certainly is a question of treating issues with objectivity because, beyond what the decision offers the applicant, it is capable of having an impact on the entire population if properly communicated. In the current phase of teaching and learning around democracy and the rule of law, this approach has helped to bring political stability, respect for the rule of law, and progressive entrenchment of a culture of constitutionalism in Benin.

Bibliography

Badet G, *Les Attributions Originelles de la Cour Constitutionnelle du Bénin* (Friedrich Ebert Stiftung 2013).

Adjolohoun H S, *Droits de l'Homme et Justice Constitutionnelle en Afrique: le Modèle Béninois à la Lumière de la Charte Africaine des Droits de l'Homme et des Peuples* (L'Harmattan 2011).

14

The Birth of the South African Constitutional Court

Richard J Goldstone

1. Introduction

The post-Second World War German constitution that came into force on 23 May 1949 established the German Constitutional Court. It began sittings in 1951 at its seat in Karlsruhe. The model was influenced by that of the United States Supreme Court and the Austrian Constitutional Court. The new German Constitutional Court, with jurisdiction over only constitutional issues, was placed above the then-existing court system.

In turn, it was the German model that influenced President Nelson Mandela's demand for a new South African Constitutional Court to be the guardian of the South African constitution, which was to be the foundation of a democracy in the post-apartheid era.[1] Mandela took into account that, during the last fifteen or so years of the apartheid era, some progressive judges were able to interpret apartheid laws in a way that these laws impacted less oppressively on the disenfranchised black majority. A substantial number of these cases were brought to the courts by the Legal Resources Centre (LRC), a public interest law firm established in 1980 with substantial input and expertise from the United States. Indeed, the LRC was basically modelled on the Legal Defense Fund of the National Association for the Advancement of Colored People (NAACP). The founding director of the LRC was Arthur Chaskalson, who led the LRC for fourteen years until his appointment by President Mandela as the first president of the new Constitutional Court of South Africa.

The LRC came to pass in consequence of the first ever human rights conference held in South Africa, which was convened in 1979 at the University of Cape Town. The establishment of the LRC was made possible with generous funding from United States foundations. It was not to be a legal aid bureau. It brought cases on issues that would affect whole communities. It chose its cases carefully and notched up an impressive record of successes. In two significant cases, the enforcement of the draconian and hated 'pass laws' was effectively ended.[2] They established the rights of families of black South Africans to join their husbands and fathers, who were permitted to live and work in urban areas. For decades, such permits had been held by lower courts not to allow such family rights. The effect of these laws was the severe dislocation of millions of South Africans. It resulted in husbands and fathers being kept away from their families for over eleven months every year. The number of single parent mothers burgeoned. The decisions beneficially affected the lives of many hundreds of thousands of South Africans.

[1] In ascribing this demand and other views to Mandela, I take into account the important input from other leaders of the African National Congress and its constitutional advisers. However, from personal discussions with Mandela during 1992 and 1993, I was left in no doubt as to his own strong views about the Constitutional Court and its establishment being a non-negotiable demand.

[2] *Komani NO v Bantu Affairs Administration Board, Peninsula Area* 1980 (4) SA 448 (A); *Oos-Randse Administrasieraad v Rikhoto* 1983 (3) SA 595 (A).

In another case brought by the LRC, the enforceability of residential segregation under the notorious Group Areas Act was effectively ended by a decision that people living in the 'wrong' group area could not be evicted unless there was proof that alternative accommodation was available to them.[3] These and other decisions were politically controversial. However, the apartheid government of the day found these decisions politically advantageous in that it could boast in the international arena that South Africa had an independent judiciary. When criticized for these developments, the government disingenuously blamed these progressive legal and social developments on the judges, thereby implicitly denying their responsibility. As will be seen below, it is significant that, while four of the justices on the new Constitutional Court were required to be sitting judges appointed during the apartheid era, President Mandela appointed six of them—a majority of the eleven-judge court.

Notwithstanding these developments, Mandela did not wish only the judges who had been appointed during the apartheid era to have the final word on the interpretation or application of the constitution. This was not surprising, having regard to the fact that, to a greater or lesser extent, the overwhelming majority of those judges supported the system of apartheid and felt no discomfort in implementing racially-oppressive laws. Mandela also wanted a court that would be representative of the people of South Africa. At the time, the superior courts were 99 per cent white and 99 per cent male. The last apartheid president, F W de Klerk, reluctantly accepted the uncompromising demand for a new Constitutional Court. However, de Klerk, in turn, demanded that four of the judges on the new court should be sitting judges. Mandela agreed on the basis that the new court would consist of a bench of eleven judges.

2. The New Constitutional Court

From its inauguration by President Mandela on 15 February 1995 until 23 August 2013, the jurisdiction of the Constitutional Court was limited to constitutional matters, and the Supreme Court of Appeal (formerly the Appellate Division of the Supreme Court) was the highest court in respect of all other matters. According to the provisions of the Superior Courts Act 10 of 2013, the Constitutional Court became the highest court with respect to all issues which it decides are in the interests of justice to be decided by it. From 1995 until 2001, the position of chief justice was held by the senior judge in the Supreme Court of Appeal. However, since 2001 that office has been held by the senior justice in the Constitutional Court.

The first eleven justices of the Constitutional Court were appointed under the interim constitution that was in operation as the basic law of South Africa from 17 April 1994 until it was superseded by the final constitution on 4 February 1997. As already mentioned, the first president (before he was appointed as chief justice) was Arthur Chaskalson. He was appointed by President Mandela under the provisions of section 97(2)(a) of the interim constitution, which provided:

> There shall be a President of the Constitutional Court, who shall … be appointed by the President in consultation with the Cabinet and after consultation with the Chief Justice.

The concurrence of the cabinet was, thus, required after good faith consultation with the then chief justice, Michael Corbett.

[3] *S v Govender* 1986 (3) SA 969 (T).

The four existing judges were appointed in terms of the provisions of section 99(3) of the interim constitution, which provided that:

> Four judges of the Constitutional Court shall be appointed from among the judges of the Supreme Court by the President in consultation with the Cabinet and with the Chief Justice.

Here the concurrence of both the cabinet and chief justice was required. The remaining six justices were appointed in terms of section 99(4) and (5) of the interim constitution. These provisions required a shortlist of ten nominees to be provided by the new Judicial Service Commission after public hearings had been held by it on the suitability of those nominated for office. President Mandela appointed the six judges with the concurrence of the cabinet and good faith consultation with President Chaskalson.

In 1994 few, if any, South African judges or legal practitioners had received formal academic training in constitutional law or human rights law, as neither were relevant to law practice during the apartheid era. South Africa had no constitution, and the fundamental human rights of the majority of South Africans were violated by the myriad of apartheid laws under which they suffered. Without a constitution, there was no power of judicial review.

3. First Meetings of the Constitutional Court Justices: Fashioning a New Court

The first time the eleven justices met together was not in South Africa, but in Karlsruhe, Germany. The then German ambassador to South Africa, Hans-Christian Ueberschaer, recognized the connection between the German and South African Constitutional Courts. He suggested to the then president of the German Constitutional Court, Jutta Limbach, that she should invite the eleven justices to join the members of her court for a five-day seminar on issues that might be useful for judges on a brand new constitutional court. This was a wonderful opportunity, and we learned much from our German colleagues. Enduring friendships were also made during that visit, and some indeed last until today.

Our first meetings were devoted to deciding how we would function in our new court. We agreed that in both appearance and procedure, our court should indicate to the people of South Africa that we were embarking on a new path under a democratic constitution. South African judges traditionally wore the robes that were inherited from English colonial times. We designed new robes that looked very different. We chose a green robe with stripes in the colours of South Africa on the sleeves, and wore French-style bibs. Importantly, the robes were unisex.

We decided that we would abandon the traditional form of addressing judges as 'My Lord' and 'My Lady', and opted for the United States practice of being called 'Justice' or, in the case of the president 'Mr President'. When the presiding justice of the Constitutional Court became the chief justice, he was addressed simply as 'Chief Justice'. It took some time for members of the bar to become accustomed to this change.

We also abandoned the system of judicial seniority. This decision was forced upon us, as some of the black members of the court would not have been eligible, in practice, for judicial appointment during the apartheid years. The existing judges were not prepared to have their seniority as judges taken into account. The president and deputy-president presided, and in each of the four terms every year, the nine other justices occupied different seats in an order chosen randomly by the president. The justices, thus, walk into and out of the courtroom in a different order each term. Judgments of the court are signed in alphabetical order. This procedure has continued to operate, with the chief justice and deputy chief justice presiding.

During the apartheid era, law clerks or researchers assisting judges were uncommon in South Africa. South African judges, following the example of the English and most other Commonwealth systems, did their own research and had no assistance in the writing of judgments. The interim constitution and, later, the final constitution, obliged South African judges, in interpreting the constitution, to have regard for international law, and invited them to have regard for foreign law. It was obvious that the new Constitutional Court judges would require considerable research assistance, and it was agreed that we would each have one law clerk in our chambers. A substantial United States foundation, Atlantic Philanthropies, generously agreed to fund a second law clerk for each of the justices, on condition that the appointment of the second law clerk was made on an affirmative action basis; that is, that he or she came from a disadvantaged background.

After about two years, the South African government agreed to pay also for the additional law clerks. Additionally, the court has every year accepted up to five foreign law clerks. These law clerks are provided with office accommodation in the chambers of the judges, but they have to secure their own funding for travel and subsistence. These clerks have come from the United States, Canada, Germany, and South Korea and, in recent years, from some African countries. The law clerks have made a substantial contribution to the work of the justices and, in turn, their experiences have given them a substantial advantage in their future careers in law. The Supreme Court of Appeal has also instituted a system of law clerks.

4. The Constitutional Court and the Media

Important new committees were established by the justices. It was decided that it was important that the decisions of the Constitutional Court should reach and be understood by as many people in the country as possible. During the apartheid era, there was no formal communication between judges and the media, and the few journalists who devoted their time to the courts had to do the best they could to inform the public of decisions of the courts. The justices of the Constitutional Court established a special media committee with a brief to make the court media-friendly. The first innovation was to attach a media summary to every written judgment of the court. This is prepared by the chambers of the justice who writes the lead judgment. It is not an official document, and the full judgment constitutes the only official version of the judgment. The media summary contains a one or two-page précis of the judgment, including any dissent, written in lay language, and designed for immediate use by journalists. Facilities were set up at the court for use by journalists, including telephone and computer facilities, to enable them to be in rapid contact with their newspapers and so to facilitate the swift reporting of important decisions.

The problems associated with television cameras broadcasting live from the courtroom took some years to be resolved. The views of the justices were split between those who saw live broadcasting as a good means of making the hearings of the court accessible to a wide audience, and those who felt strongly that it would inhibit the free flow of discussion during oral hearings. There was also the fear that short clips in news bulletins would misrepresent what had actually transpired in the courtroom. It frequently happens that propositions are put to counsel not because the judge putting the question subscribes to that view, but rather to test submissions made by counsel. A clip of such a question, so it was feared, could be embarrassing and misleading. On the other hand, so it was argued, this danger also existed in the case of written reports by journalists present during the hearing. One justice threatened that if television cameras were allowed in court, he would refrain from asking questions. This did not happen.

I had had previous experience of cameras in court: in the United Nations International Criminal Tribunals for the former Yugoslavia and Rwanda. From the outset, there was live feed to television stations around the world. It was the experience of the judges and counsel that, after a while, they were not conscious of the cameras and were able to proceed with the work of the court unaffected by the cameras.

The way forward was an incremental one. At first, the television cameras were allowed to show only the justices walking into court and taking their seats. As soon as the appeal was called, the cameras had to be switched off. This became a rather tedious spectacle and caused embarrassment when old footage was used to introduce a television report during the evening news bulletin of a hearing in which one of the judges shown on the video clip had recused himself. The next development was allowing the cameras into court for the handing down of judgments. This was always accompanied by a short oral statement by the judge who writes the lead opinion. At first, this judge was restricted to reading from the opinion. This changed when some justices decided to explain the decision in lay language.

Eventually, one of the television stations threatened to bring an application for an order allowing full television broadcasting of oral argument. The claim was that the ban on television cameras constituted a violation of the freedom of the media, protected in the bill of rights. The justices pre-empted this application by agreeing to allow cameras in court during oral argument. Once permission had been granted for cameras to be in the courtroom, the novelty soon wore off and only important cases attracted the attention of television stations.

Other courts in South Africa have followed the lead of the Constitutional Court, and in cases of public interest it is not uncommon for the presiding judge or judges to allow live television broadcasting from the courtroom. Perhaps the most widely-broadcast South African trial was the recent case of Oscar Pistorius, the Paralympic 'blade runner' who was charged with murdering his girlfriend. This trial was watched by many millions of people around the world. I have no doubt that this development has been a positive one and in the interests of allowing many South Africans to gain a better understanding of the justice system.

Another innovation introduced by the media committee was a very informal annual meeting between some justices and the editors of major newspapers and broadcasters. Both sides were able to have frank discussions on positive and negative experiences. Misunderstandings were removed, and at least one positive outcome was the improvement of facilities for journalists at the court. In the early years of the Constitutional Court, the judges hosted a one-day workshop on court reporting. Leading South African journalists were joined by Anthony Lewis, a celebrated former United States Supreme Court reporter for the *New York Times*. This was a good learning experience for the judges and journalists.

Yet another committee that was established was for the law clerks. This consisted of two or three justices and three or four South African law clerks and one foreign law clerk. The law clerks were able to bring to the attention of the judges any problems they were encountering and were able to make suggestions for improvement. This committee constantly reviewed the working conditions of the clerks.

5. New Constitutional Court Building

For the first nine years of its existence, the Constitutional Court operated from rented accommodation in Johannesburg. The first justices were consulted on the features of the accommodation. For example, it was decided that the bench should not be high above the level of counsel's tables or the public gallery. We did not wish to replicate the colonial heritage of judges sitting high above ordinary mortals. We wished to be able to converse easily with counsel and be at eye level with them. We realized that we would require an extensive constitutional law library, and sufficient space had to be allocated for it. As a consequence, the court has built up the largest constitutional law library on our continent.

In 2004, the Constitutional Court moved into new premises in Johannesburg. It was the first post-apartheid government building in South Africa. After much debate, it was decided to situate it on what was known as Johannesburg's Braamfontein ridge, now renamed Constitution Hill. It was the site of a former British fort that later became a prison complex. Many thousands of South Africans were jailed there, including Mahatma Gandhi, Albert Luthuli, and Nelson Mandela. The prison was closed in 1983 but remained a constant reminder of the dark apartheid era. It was thought to be an appropriate place both to remember the oppressive past and to look to the democratic future.

The design of the building was the result of a government-sponsored international architectural competition. The brief given to the contestants was to design a building that was at one with the South African landscape and history. The competition was widely advertised in newspapers and architectural journals around the world, and an international jury was set up to judge the entries. There were almost 200 entries, including forty from abroad. The jury was not aware of the names of the entrants or the countries from which they came. In the result, a South African firm of architects was chosen by the jury. The firm consisted of three young South African architects from Durban and Johannesburg. At the ceremony to announce the winner of the competition, former President Nelson Mandela, said:[4]

> The Constitutional Court building, indeed the entire Constitutional Hill precinct, will also stand as a beacon of light, a symbol of hope and celebration. Transforming a notorious icon of repression into its opposite, it will ease the memories of suffering inflicted in the dark corners, cells and corridors of the Old Fort Prison. Rising from the ashes of that ghastly era, it will shine forth as a pledge for all time that South Africa will never return to that abyss. It will stand as an affirmation that South Africa is indeed a better place for all.

The building is a welcoming and warm one and has several unusual features. The courtroom has one wall of old face brick that was taken from the awaiting-trial block of the former prison. Three prison buildings remain on the site and have been converted into an important and interesting museum. There is also a conference facility. The building was inaugurated by President Thabo Mbeki on South African Human Rights Day in May 2004. The proceedings took place in the presence of chief justices and appellate judges from many countries in Africa and other continents.

A hallmark of the court building is its impressive art collection. It was the result of a passion on the part of one the original eleven justices, Albie Sachs. The works are

[4] Quoted on the website of Gauging Province, 'The Constitutional Court of South Africa' http://www.gauteng.net/attractions/entry/the_constitutional_court_of_south_africa/ (last accessed 1 July 2015).

predominantly by South African artists, and all of them have some connection with the constitution and its norms and values. Some of the works were donated by the artists, and financial contributions came from foreign governments and foundations.

6. Writing of Judgments

The procedures adopted by the justices in the writing of judgments appear to differ substantially from those adopted in most other apex courts, and especially from those of the United States Supreme Court. Prior to the hearing of oral argument, the chief justice allocates one member of the court to circulate the first draft judgment. After the hearing, the judges discuss the case in conference. If there is unanimity, the judge pre-appointed will circulate a draft by email to the other chambers. After exchanges of emails, the draft will be discussed and finalized in conference. Where differences of opinion emerge in conference, the matter will be debated until there clearly is no room for reaching agreement. In difficult and contentious cases, the judges might confer repeatedly for some weeks. These debates were always a joy and privilege to attend, and in which to participate. The arguments on all sides were honed and the eventual decisions benefited enormously from this rigorous procedure. The final judgment or judgments were also considered in conference with the aim of making them, whether majority or minority, the best they could be. This procedure also helped to develop the warm atmosphere of camaraderie that marks the relationship between the justices.

While it may be time-consuming, it contributes substantially to the quality of the judgments and, fortunately, the Constitutional Court controls the size of its own docket. There is no automatic right of appeal—leave to appeal from the court is required for cases to reach the court. Whether this deliberative process will continue in the same form if and when the caseload of the court increases remains to be seen. I would suggest that it is worthwhile keeping the docket sufficiently contained to allow this invaluable procedure to continue. The procedure I have described also explains the sometimes unusual order in which some judgments of the Constitutional Court are reported. The first draft judgment circulated will, of necessity, contain the relevant background and history of the case. Even if this judgment becomes a sole dissent, it will be reported first in order that the judgments that follow are understood.

As all appellate judges will agree, heads of argument are an essential aid to the members of the bench. They influence the direction of research prior to the oral hearing and allow ideas and analysis to be considered that might not otherwise be present to the minds of the judges. In my opinion, however, there is also considerable assistance from hearing full oral argument. The United States Supreme Court deprives itself of much of the latter assistance by allowing only limited oral hearings. The practice in England is to the contrary: in some cases oral hearings on one appeal may occupy some days. In the South African Constitutional Court, no more than one appeal is heard on any day. In cases where there are long records or complex issues, the appeal may be set down for more than one day. This allows the judges sufficient time to discuss their problems, views, and approach with counsel. It was my experience that I seldom left the courtroom after oral argument with the same views that I had prior to the hearing. Even in cases where my view about the outcome of the appeal may not have changed, I seldom failed to develop a more nuanced approach to some of the arguments justifying the conclusion.

7. International and Foreign Law

For many decades South African judges frequently turned to foreign law for inspiration. The law reports during the apartheid years are replete with foreign law references with regard to commercial law—companies, intellectual property, and negotiable instruments—and criminal law and procedure. In those areas of the law, South Africa borrowed a great deal from the laws of England and other Commonwealth countries and, in later years, from those of the United States. Those foreign sources were certainly not regarded as binding on South African judges, but rather as guides to legal developments and trends in other similar jurisdictions.

The bill of rights expressly obliges judges to have regard to international law and invites judges to have regard to foreign law.[5] Section 233 of the constitution requires a court when interpreting legislation to 'prefer any reasonable interpretation of the legislation that is consistent with international law over any alternative interpretation that is inconsistent with international law'. It is further provided that customary international law is law in South Africa unless inconsistent with the constitution or an act of parliament. Section 36 of the constitution provides that the rights in the bill of rights may only be limited by a law of general application and 'only to the extent that the limitation is reasonable and justifiable in an open and democratic based on human dignity, equality and freedom'. Therefore, in interpreting the bill of rights, judges are obliged to consider the limitations of rights that have been discussed and considered in other open and democratic jurisdictions and, in interpreting legislation, judges are obliged to consider international law. It is thus not surprising that, in its earliest cases, the Constitutional Court was obliged to consider what was embraced by the references to 'international law' and 'foreign law'.

The first case in which oral argument was heard by the Constitutional Court related to the constitutionality of the death sentence. With regard to international law, the President of the Court, Arthur Chaskalson, said, with regard to the relevant provision of the interim constitution:[6]

> [P]ublic international law would include non-binding as well as binding law. They may both be used under the section as tools of interpretation. International agreements and customary international law accordingly provide a framework within which the Bill of Rights can be evaluated and understood, and for that purpose, decisions of tribunals dealing with comparable instruments, such as the United Nations Committee on Human Rights, the Inter American Commission on Human Rights, the Inter-American Court of Human Rights, the European Commission on Human Rights, and the European Court of Human Rights, and, in appropriate cases, reports of specialised agencies such as the International Labour Organisation, may provide guidance as to the correct interpretation of particular provisions of the Bill of Rights.

The use of foreign law was especially important in the absence of South African precedents relating to human rights.

8. Operating as a Single Bench

It is important for a court of final appeal to sit in bench. There are few such courts that do not do so. One exception is the Supreme Court of the United Kingdom. Its twelve judges sit

[5] The Constitution of the Republic of South Africa 1996 s 36(1).

[6] *S v Makwanyane* 1995 (3) SA 391 (CC) 413–14.

in panels of three, five, seven, or nine judges. Especially in controversial cases, where there is unanimity or near unanimity on the bench, an important message is sent to the nation. This was significant when the Constitutional Court was called upon to certify that the 'final constitution', drafted by the democratically-elected Constitutional Assembly, complied with the requirements of the interim constitution. A split court would have conveyed an unfortunate message. The fact that there was unanimity in first refusing to certify the constitution[7] and, after amendment by the Constitutional Assembly, in agreeing to certify the final constitution,[8] was crucial to the credibility of both the court and, more importantly, of the constitution itself.

9. Social and Economic Rights

A similar unanimity marked early decisions on the interpretation and implementation of the social and economic rights entrenched in the bill of rights.[9] With regard to its social and economic rights jurisprudence, the court has been criticized, mainly by academics, for having been too deferential to the executive and for failing to adopt and apply the 'minimum core' approach that has for some decades been applied by United Nations Committee on Economic, Social and Cultural Rights (ESCR Committee). In its General Comment No 3 of 1990, the Committee said:

> It is of the view that a minimum core obligation to ensure the satisfaction of, at the very least, minimum essential levels of each of the rights is incumbent upon every state party. Thus, for example, a state party in which any significant number of individuals is deprived of essential foodstuffs, of essential primary health care, of basic shelter and housing, or of the most basic forms of education is, prima facie, failing to discharge its obligations under the Covenant.

In refusing to follow this approach, the Constitutional Court said:[10]

> It is not possible to determine the minimum threshold for the progressive realisation of the right of access to adequate housing without first identifying the needs and opportunities for the enjoyment of such a right. These will vary according to factors such as income, unemployment, availability of land and poverty. The differences between city and rural communities will also determine the needs and opportunities for the enjoyment of this right. Variations ultimately depend on the economic and social history and circumstances of a country. All this illustrates the complexity of the task of determining a minimum core obligation for the progressive realisation of the right of access to adequate housing without having the requisite information on the needs and the opportunities for the enjoyment of this right.

Further, in the *Treatment Action Campaign* judgment,[11] the court added:

> Courts are ill suited to adjudicate upon issues where court orders could have multiple social and economic consequences for the community. The constitution contemplates rather a restrained and focused role for the courts, namely, to require the state to take measures to meet its constitutional obligations and to subject the reasonableness of these measures to evaluation. Such determinations of reasonableness may in fact have budgetary implications, but are not in themselves directed at rearranging budgets. In this way, the judicial, legislative and executive functions achieve appropriate constitutional balance.

[7] *Certification of the Constitution of the Republic of South Africa* 1996 (4) SA 744 (CC).

[8] *Certification of the Amended Text of the Constitution of the Republic of South Africa* 1997 (2) SA 97 (CC).

[9] *Soobramoney v Minister of Health, KwaZulu-Natal* 1998 (1) SA 765 (CC); *Government of the Republic of South Africa v Grootboom and Others* 2001 (1) SA 765 (CC); *Minister of Health and Others v Treatment Action Campaign and Others* 2002 (5) SA 721 (CC).

[10] See *Grootboom* (n 9) [32].

[11] See *Treatment Action Campaign* (n 9) [38].

The court was not able, on the facts placed before it in any of these social and economic rights cases, to fashion a minimum core. It was not for a court of final appeal to initiate a fact-finding exercise for which it is ill-equipped. As is the case with most courts of appeal, the Constitutional Court is bound by the record placed before it.

It was recently suggested that the court should appoint commissions of inquiry to gather the relevant evidence. I would suggest that the court should not embark upon this path without appropriate enabling legislation. If that is to be the path to be taken, I would suggest that it be preceded by careful research. Apparently this is the procedure in the Indian Supreme Court.[12] On my understanding, there have been long delays and inefficiencies following upon the use of such a procedure. There are so many questions that would have to be considered. These include the manner in which such commissions are to be established, who should sit on the commissions, and the liability for the considerable costs that would be incurred. Perhaps most important of all is the question of whether such a procedure, if it were to be introduced, might not be better situated at the level of trial courts, in order to avoid the huge additional burden that would be placed upon the Constitutional Court. Apart from the work load of the court, this is not, I would suggest, a function that should be performed by an apex court consisting of eleven judges who all participate in all cases coming before the court. While easier access to justice by poor and disempowered members of our society is urgent and essential, attempts should not be made to achieve this end at the expense of the efficiency and credibility of the Constitutional Court.

In general, expectations with regard to social and economic rights have been set too high, and this has resulted in an inevitable sense of disappointment and frustration for many people. At the same time, litigating social and economic rights has substantially empowered civil society and made government departments more accountable for their policies and their implementation. This process should be pursued with vigour and in full recognition that the role of courts is complementary to the other two branches of government.

10. Conclusion

All courts require the support of the state in order for their orders to be implemented. The independence of judges is crucial. In older democracies, this tends to be taken for granted. South Africa has been fortunate in that President Mandela explicitly promoted respect for the courts, and especially for the Constitutional Court. When the court ruled against the government, President Mandela promptly indicated that its decisions would be respected. This approach has been followed by his successors. In recent times, there have been some unfortunate instances in which government officials have been slow to implement some judicial decisions. At the time of writing, the government, at the highest level, appeared to be in contempt of a decision of the High Court prohibiting President Al-Bashir of Sudan departing from South Africa (where he attended a meeting of African Union heads of state) pending a decision on whether he should be arrested pursuant to a warrant issued for his arrest by the International Criminal Court.

On 13 March 2016, the Supreme Court of Appeal held that the South African government was under an obligation to cooperate with the ICC in arresting Sudanese President Omar Al-Bashir.[13] In doing so, the Court dismissed the state's appeal against a High

[12] The Commissions of Inquiry Act 1952, No 60, Acts of Parliament 1952 (India).

[13] See *The Minister of Justice and Constitutional Development and Others v The Southern Africa Litigation Centre and Others* http://www.saflii.org/za/cases/ZASCA/2016/17.pdf (last accessed 17 April 2017).

Court ruling that the government's failure to arrest Al-Bashir was inconsistent with its constitutional duties. The Court further said that the Al-Bashir's case was of substantial public importance and it had been unlawful for the government to allow him to leave the country. The South African government is presently appearing before the ICC to explain why it did not arrest Al-Bashir.[14]

The Constitutional Court has played, and continues to play, a crucial role in the development of our new democracy. The demand for such a court by President Nelson Mandela has been fully justified during the first two decades of our new democracy.

[14] See 'South Africa Grilled by the ICC over Decision not to Arrest Al-Bashir' http://www.702.co.za/articles/251616/south-africa-grilled-by-icc-over-decision-to-not-arrest-al-bashir (last accessed 17 April 2017).

15

Decision-making and Working Practices of the Supreme Court of Ghana

Samuel Kofi Date-Bah

1. Introduction

After a chequered history of civilian and military rule, since 1993 Ghana has enjoyed a stable period of constitutional democracy. This democracy has been underpinned by the work of the Supreme Court of Ghana, among other state institutions. The Supreme Court, although a Constitutional Court, combines that function with other jurisdictions which will be discussed below. This chapter provides an overview of the way in which the Supreme Court of Ghana makes decisions on cases brought before it and outlines some of the working practices that have evolved in relation to its decision-making. To facilitate an understanding of this decision-making process, the chapter starts with some background information on the Supreme Court, its composition, and jurisdictions.

2. Background to the Supreme Court of Ghana

This section provides a brief background to the functioning of the Supreme Court of Ghana as a constitutional court.[1] The origin of the current Supreme Court of Ghana, as an apex court, may be traced back to the Supreme Court established in 1960 under the constitution of the First Republic of Ghana. Prior to that, a supreme court had existed in the country, but not as an apex court. The First Republic's Supreme Court supplanted the Judicial Committee of the Privy Council of the United Kingdom of Great Britain and Northern Ireland as the final court of appeal in Ghana. Article 42(1) of the 1960 Constitution provided that the Supreme Court was the final court of appeal, with such appellate and other jurisdiction as was provided for by law. Article 42(2) conferred an original jurisdiction on the Court in respect of 'all matters where a question arises whether an enactment was made in excess of the powers conferred on parliament by or under the constitution'. If any such matter arose before the High Court or an inferior court, further hearing on the matter was to be adjourned and the matter referred for decision to the Supreme Court.

The power of judicial review of legislation conferred on the Supreme Court of the First Republic was not very significant, as the constitution of that republic did not contain an entrenched bill of rights. The legislative authority of parliament was almost that of a Westminster type sovereign parliament, although some legislative power was said to have been reserved by the constitution to the people.[2]

[1] For a more a detailed account of the operations of the Supreme Court of Ghana see Samuel Kofi Date-Bah, *Reflections on the Supreme Court of Ghana* (Wildy, Simmonds & Hill Publishing 2015).

[2] See 1960 Constitution art 20.

A supreme court that better resembles the current Supreme Court was established in 1969. That Supreme Court of the Second Republic was based on a draft constitution prepared by a Constitution Review Commission, which reported in 1968. The Commission made a clear recommendation for the express vesting of a power of judicial review of legislation in the Supreme Court. The Commission did not wish to take the chance of leaving the power to be inferred by the Court. According to the Commission:[3]

> 509 [I]n this respect we would like to refer to the views of Sir Alladi Krishnaswani Ayyar, a distinguished Indian jurist and one of the architects of the Indian Constitution, on the necessity for spelling out in the Constitution the power of judicial review in the Supreme Court of India as opposed, possibly, to leaving the existence of this power to judicial inference.
>
> 510 Sir Alladi Ayyar's view was that judicial review in the United States, although favoured by the framers of the Constitution, had been inferred from the Constitution, and that despite the decision of Chief Justice Marshall in *Marbury v Madison* aforesaid, it should not be assumed that judicial review 'is a necessary incident of a written constitution', and he referred to the Swiss Constitution in support of that view. His conclusion was that it was necessary therefore that judicial review be expressly named in the Constitution as one of the powers of the Judiciary.
>
> ...
>
> 512 *We therefore propose that the power of Judicial Review with all its ramifications be expressly vested in the Judiciary.* Ordinarily the power of judicial review is essential for the safeguarding of fundamental rights and the observance of due process, and it is our considered view that when that power is given a basis in the Constitution it acquires an additional quality that far transcends the usual operative limits of due process.

This recommendation was accepted by the Constituent Assembly that prepared the Constitution of the Second Republic, except that a part of the recommendation that proposed conferring an advisory jurisdiction on the Court was rejected. The basic concept of the Supreme Court of the Second Republic, enshrined in the 1969 Constitution, was retained in the subsequent constitutions of the Third and Fourth Republics of 1979 and 1992 respectively.

In addition to this constitutional court role of the Supreme Court of Ghana, it is a multi-function court with other jurisdictions that will be identified later in this chapter. Although, in this author's view, the current Supreme Court of the Fourth Republic is a new court,[4] it has an organic relationship to the supreme courts of the earlier republics. It thus has much tradition, history, and convention to guide it. Its practices have, however, evolved over time. Thus, currently the justices no longer wear wigs when in session, but only their black robes without headgear. However, on ceremonial occasions, they continue to wear their crimson robes with full-bottomed wigs. Thus while retaining much of the British heritage derived from the history of the Ghanaian legal system, the Court is very much a contemporary Ghanaian institution that looms large in the political and social landscape of Ghana in the perception of many ordinary Ghanaians. The current high profile of the Supreme Court is attributable to the exercise of its jurisdictions as a Constitutional Court and as an election court in relation to presidential elections.

[3] See *Memorandum on the Proposals for a Constitution for Ghana* (Constitutional Commission 1968) (emphasis added).

[4] See Date-Bah (n 1) 9 ff.

3. Composition of the Court and its Influence on Its Decision-making

The Supreme Court of Ghana consists of the chief justice and not less than nine other justices.[5] A person is qualified for appointment to be a justice of the Supreme Court only if he is of high moral character and proven integrity and of not less than fifteen years' standing as a lawyer.[6] In practice, the justices of the court have usually been appointed direct from the bar, or on promotion from justices of the Court of Appeal. Even those justices appointed to the Supreme Court on promotion from the Court of Appeal were, of course, initially appointed to the bench from the bar. Only occasionally have lawyers with an academic background been appointed directly to the Court. Such legal academics also have to satisfy the constitutional requirement of being lawyers of fifteen years' standing. Accordingly, all appointments to the Supreme Court are from the bar, either directly or indirectly. This fact of recruitment from the bar is of significance. Justice Michael Kirby, formerly of the Australian High Court, has argued[7] that practice at the common law bar gives an independence of mind which is then carried into the judiciary when members of the bar are appointed to the bench. His contention is that recruitment from the bar results typically in a judiciary that is independent and accustomed to thinking for itself.

This contention has plausibility and is a factor worth bearing in mind when analysing the behaviour of common law superior court judges. The contrast to the common law approach to judicial selection is the recruitment and training of law graduates for a career as a judge, which is the norm in the civil law tradition. Specific training for potential recruits to the judiciary has its advantages, but it does not nurture the kind of independence that may be imbibed by being a member of an independent bar and being appointed to a judiciary with constitutional protections intended to foster the judiciary's independence.

4. Jurisdictions of the Court and their Impact on its Working Practices

The Supreme Court of Ghana has several jurisdictions that exert an influence on its working practices. The final court immediately after Ghana's independence in 1957 was the Judicial Committee of the Privy Council. It had the attribute of being exclusively an appeal court. That simple situation is now long gone as the 1960 Constitution of Ghana's First Republic introduced an original jurisdiction for the Supreme Court, alongside its appellate jurisdiction. Currently, the Supreme Court of the Fourth Republic has original, appellate, supervisory, and review jurisdictions, in addition to its jurisdictions over certain miscellaneous matters and as an election court in relation to presidential elections.

The working practices of the Supreme Court can vary, depending on which jurisdiction it is exercising. For instance, by administrative practice, the chief justice empanels a bench of nine judges to hear constitutional cases. On the other hand, the review jurisdiction is required by the 1992 Constitution to be exercised by a panel of not less than seven justices.[8] For the exercise of its other jurisdictions, the Supreme Court usually sits in panels of five justices. Occasionally, a single justice may sit to dispose of interlocutory matters.[9]

[5] See 1992 Constitution art 128. [6] ibid art 128(4).

[7] See Michael Kirby, 'Judicial Dissent: Common Law and Civil Law Traditions' (2007) 123 *Law Quarterly Review* 379.

[8] 1992 Constitution art 133(2). [9] ibid art 134.

The Supreme Court of Ghana may legitimately be viewed primarily as an appellate court, which has been given additional responsibilities. Its appellate jurisdiction is the one with the most history from its predecessor courts. Its other jurisdictions may be thought of as engrafted on its primary appellate jurisdiction. Its standing and stature in Ghanaian society flow from the public perception of it as the final court. Much of its working practices flow from its position as the final or apex court. The constitutional provision that '[t]he Supreme Court shall be the final court of appeal and shall have such appellate and other jurisdiction as may be conferred on it by this constitution or by any other law'[10] reflects this perception.

A final court of appeal has to manifest sagacity and give strategic authoritative guidance to the courts below. Accordingly, its members should be among the most experienced and learned of the local legal profession. In a common law jurisdiction, it will have the opportunity of interstitial judicial law-making, which has its limits and is unlike parliamentary legislation. Nevertheless, through the opportunity presented by judicial law-making, the Supreme Court can, to a degree, adapt the law to changing circumstances.

For those who in this time and age continue to deny that judges make law, the author's favourite response is a quote from Lord Reid, who stated:[11]

> There was a time when it was thought almost indecent to suggest that judges make law—they only declare it. Those with a taste for fairy tales seem to have thought that in some Aladdin's cave there is hidden the common law in all its splendour and that on a judge's appointment there descends on him [or her] knowledge of the magic words Open Sesame. Bad decisions are given when the judge has muddled the password and the wrong door opens. But we do not believe in fairy tales any more.

The justices exercising the limited law-making function of the final court of appeal become invested with much authority because of this function. This authority is buttressed by the trappings of authority transmitted down the generations by successive final courts of the land. Accordingly, when the final court exercises an original jurisdiction, the authority of its decision-making is unlike that of a High Court or other lower court. Presumably that is why the makers of the constitutions of the Second, Third, and Fourth Republics of Ghana decided to grant the final court an exclusive original jurisdiction in all matters relating to the enforcement or interpretation of the constitution; and all matters arising as to whether an enactment was made in excess of the powers conferred on parliament or any other constitutional body.[12] Because constitutional disputes can destabilize the political system, an early and authoritative pronouncement by the highest court in the land can contribute to the stability of the state. This context for the exercise of the Supreme Court's original jurisdiction in constitutional matters has significance for its working practices. Its significance extends also to the exercise of all of its other jurisdictions.

5. Working Practices of the Supreme Court

Decision-making at the Supreme Court of Ghana for all its jurisdictions is by a majority decision of the panel of judges sitting on the particular case. The Supreme Court Rules 1996 provide that, at the conclusion of hearing of a matter before the Court, each justice is at liberty to express an opinion on the matter before the court.[13] Accordingly, a justice of

[10] ibid art 129(1).

[11] See Lord Reid 'The Judge as Law-maker' (1972) 12 *Journal of the Society Public Teachers of Law* 22.

[12] See eg art 130(1) of the 1992 constitution.

[13] See Rule 74(1) of the Supreme Court Rules 1996 (CI 16).

the Supreme Court is entitled to write an individual opinion, concur with one written by another justice, deliver a dissenting opinion, or concur with a dissenting opinion. These working practices of the Court are ways of facilitating decision- making by the justices.

Cases are assigned to panels of judges by the Chief Justice. The most senior justice on each panel has the privilege of presiding over the panel during the proceedings. The presiding justice determines whether there is a need for any meetings or consultations prior to the hearing of the case. On the whole, there tend to be no meetings to consider a case before the date of the hearing. Some presiding justices hold a meeting on the day of the hearing just before the hearing, to gauge preliminary reactions to particular cases. Generally, however, prior to the hearing of a case, deliberation on the cases is for the individual judges alone, studying the materials in the case file and reading around the issues the case raises.

5.1 Law clerks and other research support available to the Court

The law clerk system is still under development at the Ghanaian Supreme Court. After some experiments in the past, law clerks were recruited for justices of the Supreme Court under financial sponsorship of a United States of America Law School. This has been phased out, but the experiment served to establish the value of the system of law clerking. Thus, some law clerks have since been recruited under the Ghana judiciary's own budget, but not every justice has a clerk. The regularization of the recruitment of law clerks for all justices of the Supreme Court on the judiciary's budget would be a significant improvement of the working practice of the Court. In the practice of the Supreme Court of Ghana, law clerks only assist with the research needed for the proper discharge of the responsibilities of the justices, but do not draft judgments for them. The principal burden for the research needed to write judgments thus continues to rest on the justices themselves. The justices, therefore, have to stay abreast of current developments in the law.

5.2 Role of the written statement of case

The Supreme Court Rules[14] require parties to submit written statements of case in relation to the exercise by the Court of its various jurisdictions. These statements are of great assistance to the deliberations of the justices. They are intended to enunciate clearly the legal submissions of the parties. For instance, according to the rule on contents of statements of case in relation to the appellate jurisdiction:[15]

> The statement of case or in answer of each party to the appeal:
> (a) shall set out the full case and the arguments to be advanced by the party including the relevant authorities and references to the decided cases and the statute law on which the party intends to rely; and
> (b) in the case of the respondent may include a contention that the decision of the Court be varied.

On the whole, the introduction of the written statement of case in Ghana's final court constitutes a positive improvement in the Court's working practice, as compared to the old days of long oral arguments. One finds that because of the prior filing of the statement

[14] Supreme Court Rules 1996 (CI 16). [15] ibid r 15(6).

of case, counsel tend to dispense with extended oral argument, particularly in relation to appeals. The written statements of case enable better preparation by the justices prior to the hearing of the case.

5.3 Role of oral argument

Prior to the usual judgment conference where the justices take a decision on the outcome of a case, there is a hearing. Counsel for the parties are entitled to appear and to present an oral argument on the issues raised. If any party is unrepresented by counsel, the party himself or herself is entitled to appear to make an oral presentation of his or her case. The nature and scope of oral argument by counsel or by a party himself or herself depends on the particular jurisdiction of the Supreme Court that is in play. Perhaps the greatest scope for oral argument is where a party has invoked the original jurisdiction of the Supreme Court by writ. Actions to invoke the original jurisdiction are commenced by writ in the form set out in the Schedule to the Supreme Court Rules, 1996. The writ has to set out, as concisely as possible, the nature of the relief sought by the plaintiff.[16] The plaintiff has to file a statement of case either with his writ or within fourteen days of filing the writ. Fourteen days after service on the defendant of the plaintiff's statement of case, the defendant has to file a statement of case in response.

After this exchange of statements of case, the parties may agree to file a memorandum specifying the issues agreed by them to be tried at the hearing of the action.[17] Even where the parties do not so agree, the Court may order them to file such a memorandum. The Court may, after submission of the memorandum, order any of the parties to clarify or state fully in writing any further arguments of law with a list of decided cases and of statutes in support of the case, where the matter in issue has not already been dealt with in the statement of case or in the memorandum of issues.

After the statements of case have been exchanged and the memorandum of issues filed, the case is ready for hearing. The Supreme Court Rules provide that the Court may, after considering the statements of case, the memorandum of issues, and arguments of law, decide to determine the action and give judgment on a fixed date without further argument. However, this never happens. By the custom of the Court, a time is then appointed for the parties to appear before the Court for oral arguments.

No time limits have been set in the Rules for the length of these oral arguments. Thus, their length is at the discretion of the Court. Because the original jurisdiction often involves important constitutional issues, the Court tends to allow counsel a liberal amount of time to develop their arguments. Oral arguments, however, do not ordinarily extend beyond the day set aside for the hearing. Indeed, few last for more than one hour. Counsel usually highlight the main elements of their legal arguments and, in their turn, members of the judicial panel hearing the case probe counsel's arguments and seek clarification on particular points. The oral exchange between the bench and counsel may be quite helpful in the process of crystallizing the views of the bench. The judicial interrogation of the issues raised by the case through probing counsel's arguments relates to both the facts and the law.

As regards the facts, these are usually placed before the Court through affidavits, in cases invoking the original jurisdiction of the Court. However, they may also be introduced by *viva voce* testimony. The Supreme Court Rules provide a basis for the hearing of

[16] ibid r 45(2). [17] ibid r 50.

oral evidence.[18] While the rules allow for evidence to be led by oral examination in court as well as by affidavit, or by deposition taken before an examiner, the usual method is evidence by affidavit. Nevertheless, the availability of alternatives provides a further opportunity for oral advocacy by counsel before the Supreme Court. In 2011, for instance, the Supreme Court conducted a trial by oral evidence in a case about whether a member of parliament was still the holder of a British passport and, therefore, disqualified from being a Ghanaian member of parliament.[19] The trial was, however, not concluded because of the ill-health of the member of parliament.

The only election petition thus far heard by the Supreme Court was a full-scale trial, with both oral evidence and evidence by affidavit. This was the historic case of *In re Presidential Election Petition; Akufo-Addo, Bawumia and Obetsebi-Lamptey (No 4) v Mahama, Electoral Commission and National Democratic Congress (No 4)*,[20] which was the main case with which the Supreme Court was preoccupied in 2013. Because its proceedings were broadcast live, the case gripped the attention of the Ghanaian nation to an extent never seen before. It was tried by a panel of nine justices. It was obvious that decision-making by the panel, in the face of counsel's objections to evidence and other procedural issues, was awkward. Ascertaining the views of members of the panel on many issues required the court to rise often to consider its rulings. Future judicial panels may need to consider how to minimise such cumbersome decision-making. Evidence by deposition before an examiner is an avenue worth exploring in this connection. (Incidentally, counsel's performance and advocacy in this case made the individuals concerned household names in Ghana.)

There is no doubt that oral argument enlivens proceedings at the Supreme Court. Apart from its role in the exercise by the Court of its original jurisdiction, it also plays an important role in the exercise by the Court of its supervisory, review, and election jurisdictions. However, its role in the appellate jurisdiction has much diminished since the introduction of written statements of case and the convention that has evolved since then. Counsel usually state that they rely on their written statements of case and do not seek to expatiate further on the contents of these statements.

5.4 Role of the judgment conference

After the hearing of a case within the jurisdiction of the Supreme Court, unless the matter is disposed of summarily on the day of the hearing, the judgment conference is the forum for the coordination and articulation of the position of the justices on the matters in controversy. This is a meeting convened by the presiding judge to discuss the case and decide on how it is to be disposed of. The judges will at this conference indicate their opinion on the case and their reasons for their individual positions. The meeting will usually be in the chambers of the presiding judge, or sometimes in one of the meeting rooms at the Supreme Court. The latter option is more likely if it is a large panel, such as a panel for a constitutional case.

There is an emerging desirable practice by which the presiding judge ascertains the views of the judges at the conference in an order that is the reverse of seniority. In other words, the most junior judge is asked for his or her opinion first and then the other judges asked for their views in accordance with ascending seniority. This is intended to ensure

18 ibid r 53(3).

19 See *Sumaila Bielbiel v Adamu Dramani and Attorney-General* [2012] 1 SCGLR 374.

20 [2013] SCGLR (Special Edition) 73.

that more senior judges do not dominate discussions at the conference. In any case, the mischief that this desirable practice is intended to cure is, however, an unlikely prospect in relation to the Supreme Court of Ghana, since the author has not known any junior member of a panel cowed by a senior member.

Presiding judges differ with regard to their attitude to the presentation of draft judgments at judgment conferences. During the author's tenure at the Court, there was one presiding judge who thought that judges should attend judgment conferences without fixed views. They should come ready to modify their initial views. He was, accordingly, not enthused with draft judgments at the conference. Other presiding judges, however, have been more open to panel members circulating draft judgments and, indeed, some have encouraged them to submit drafts at the conference. Nevertheless, with or without draft judgments, the judgment conference is an important forum for a full discussion of the case and for determining whether the case will be determined by a unanimous decision or not. It is from discussions at the conference that it will become clear whether there will be any dissenting judgments, a lead judgment with or without concurrent judgments, and so on. The presiding judge, who chairs the conference, provides leadership in the deliberations. Depending on these deliberations, he or she may nominate a particular member of the panel to write the lead judgment, if the panel is inclined to go down that route.

The choice of that member will, of course, be influenced by his or her expression of willingness to write a judgment and the likelihood of there being consensus on the draft prepared by a particular justice. He or she will also be made aware of who is going to write a dissenting opinion. On the whole, a laissez-faire approach is adopted to the writing of dissenting opinions. No pressure is applied on dissenting justices to fall in line with the majority. Lead judgments tend to attract closer scrutiny than dissenting judgments. Dissenting judgments are regarded as the responsibility of the dissenting judge concerned, whereas a lead judgment is representative of all the judges who have consented to it. Accordingly, all those judges feel free to comment and to seek amendments to the lead judgment. In some high profile cases where the justices deem it prudent so to do, they will each write an opinion. However, this practice is now the exception rather than the rule. There is often only one judgment delivered, where there is no dissent. On some occasions, however, a concurring opinion is added by one or two justices who want to explore dimensions of the applicable law from a different angle than that embodied in the lead judgment.

What is important at the judgment conference is that an opportunity and atmosphere are created that facilitate a constructive discussion of the facts and law governing a particular case, so that a just result emerges. After the initial indication by the justices of their views on a particular case, there is a discussion and exchange of views among them. Depending on the merits of a particular case, some judges will come to the conference with more fixed views than others, while others may come with somewhat tentative views, which could change in the course of the conference. In difficult cases, more than one case conference may be necessary. In general, however, the outcome of most cases is determined after one conference.

5.5 Role of the panel system in the decision-making of the Court

Members of the Supreme Court rarely sit as single justices. A single justice of the Supreme Court may exercise a power vested in the Supreme Court only when it does not involve a decision on a cause or matter before the court.[21] Thus, decisions of the Court, other than

[21] See 1992 Constitution art 134.

occasional interlocutory ones, are made by a panel of justices. An understanding of the dynamics of the panel system is, therefore, important for a comprehension of the decision-making process of the Court.

The first feature of the panel system that needs to be highlighted is the high degree of autonomy accorded every member of the panel. Neither the presiding judge nor any other member of the bench seeks to put pressure on a panel member to decide in a particular way. When members of the panel reveal at the judgment conference their preliminary views on the issues in contention, they will often trade arguments justifying their particular viewpoints and seek to persuade other members of the panel to agree with them. However, this persuasion usually does not persist beyond the judgment conference. This feature of the Ghanaian Supreme Court may be contrasted with the picture presented in accounts of the deliberations of the United States Supreme Court in the seminal case of *Brown v Board of Education*,[22] where it is believed that Chief Justice Warren of the United States, by his persistence, managed to secure the unanimous decision from the US Supreme Court, which he considered to be the correct decision. The view of most scholars is that Chief Justice Warren's leadership and political skills are what secured the unanimous judgment of the US Supreme Court.[23]

There are advantages and disadvantages to a presiding judge applying persuasion on his panel over a period of time to ensure that the panel decides in a particular way. Excessive laissez-faire may result in the panel members not being challenged enough before reaching their decision. On the other hand, excessive persuasive efforts by other members of the panel may lead to the independence of the other judges being undermined. In the practice of the Ghanaian Supreme Court, there would not be scope for the kind of leadership exhibited by Chief Justice Warren.

Respect for autonomy, a strong feature of the Ghanaian Supreme Court, implies that dissent by members of the panel is not frowned upon. Dissent is thus alive and well in the Supreme Court of Ghana. In many cases, however, the Supreme Court delivers unanimous judgments or one lead judgment with a dissent or concurring judgment. In the early years of the Supreme Court of the Fourth Republic, it was the usual practice for all members of the panel to write their individual opinions. This practice accorded with the Supreme Court Rules, which provide in Rule 74:

> (1) At the conclusion of the hearing of any matter before the Court, each judge shall be at liberty to express his opinion on the matter before the Court.
> (2) The judgment, order or decree of the Court shall be pronounced by the presiding justice or such other justice of the Court hearing the question or matter as the presiding justice may direct.
> (3) Opinions of the justices of the Court shall be handed over to the registrar of the Court immediately after delivery for the compilation of a composite opinion of the Court and copies thereof shall upon payment of the requisite fees be given to the parties and the public after they have been duly certified by the registrar of the Court in accordance with section 99(I) of the Courts Act, 1993 (Act 459).

Despite this right of justices to deliver individual opinions, in the past decade the practice has increasingly evolved by which a single judgment of the court is delivered by one particular judge nominated at the judgment conference. The practice of a judgment by

[22] 347 US 483 (1954).
[23] See eg Michael Klarman, *From Jim Crow to Civil Rights: The Supreme Court and the Struggle for Racial Equality* (Oxford University Press 2006).

the Court avoids unnecessarily repetitive presentations of the law. However, where at the judgment conference a judge wishes to explore a dimension of the law that will not be examined adequately in the lead judgment, he or she is free to decide to write a concurring opinion.

Also, depending on the nature of the case, it may sometimes be decided at the judgment conference that individual opinions should be written by the justices. The panel sometimes decides that this should be done in particularly controversial or high-profile cases. It is sometimes deemed useful for the individual opinions of all the members of the panel to be made known in their own words. This practice is a product of Ghanaian history. As a matter of principle, a cogent counter-argument could be made that, in difficult or controversial cases, the reverse would be a preferable practice and that the Court should rather endeavour to speak with one voice in one judgment, if this is achievable. This would facilitate the authoritative and clear communication of the Court's view. The Supreme Court, of course, follows the common law tradition of judgments being signed by the judges who give them, in contrast to the civil law practice of unsigned collective judgments.[24]

5.6 Practice in relation to foreign law

The attitude of the Ghanaian Supreme Court to foreign law is summarized as follows by Justice Ocran in *Hanna Assi (No 2) v GIHOC Refrigeration and Household Products Ltd (No 2)*:[25]

> Essentially, I am more comfortable with working with local decisions and statutory law whenever they are available and relevant, while utilising foreign legal norms and practices as secondary sources of legal reasoning. This way we are able to partake of the richness of comparative law without being absorbed by foreign law. For, as Sowah CJ remarked in *Fosuhene v Pomaa* [1987-88] 2GLR 105 at 115, SC: 'Our Supreme Court is not heir to or successor of any court in any other jurisdiction.' And Adade JSC, in the same case, commented (at page 119 of the report) that the courts that were set up in 1960 under the Republican Constitution [and thereafter, I should add] 'were not offshoots of the British courts, they were courts in their own right, for an independent nation called Ghana'. What Adade JSC said of the Ghanaian courts created in 1960 should be even truer with the courts of Ghana in 2007.

This attitude of the Supreme Court, expressed by Justice Ocran, flows from the constitutional provisions on precedent embodied in the 1992 and in all the previous republican constitutions of Ghana, going as far back as the Constitution of the First Republic in 1960. The relevant current provision is Article 129 of the 1992 Constitution, which provides:

> (1) The Supreme Court shall be the final court of appeal and shall have such appellate and other jurisdiction as may be conferred on it by this constitution or by any other law.
> (2) The Supreme Court shall not be bound to follow the decisions of any other court.
> (3) The Supreme Court may, while treating its own previous decisions as normally binding, depart from a previous decision when it appears to it right to do so; and all other courts shall be bound to follow the decisions of the Supreme Court on questions of law.

The Supreme Court has interpreted this provision as affording it the liberty to develop Ghanaian law independently of any other jurisdiction in the world. No foreign decision is binding on it. Foreign decisions may only be of persuasive value. That said, it is

[24] See William D Popkin, *Evolution of the Judicial Opinion* (New York University Press 2007) 179 ff.
[25] [2007–2008] SCGLR 16 at 35.

nevertheless true that, given its history and culture, the Supreme Court is more likely to find persuasive foreign decisions that are from a common law jurisdiction. The Court has thus far not fully explored the opportunity given it by a particular constitutional provision to resort to foreign decisions relating to human rights provisions not specifically provided for in the Ghanaian constitution. The reference here is to Article 33(5) of the 1992 Constitution, which provides:

> The rights, duties, declarations and guarantees relating to the fundamental human rights and freedoms specifically mentioned in this chapter shall not be regarded as excluding others not specifically mentioned which are considered to be inherent in a democracy and intended to secure the freedom and dignity of man.

This provision, in the author's view, impliedly authorizes Ghanaian courts to borrow from courts anywhere in their development of the law relating to fundamental human rights to supplement what has been specifically provided for in the 1992 Constitution. However, the Ghanaian courts have not made much use of the provision. The Court, if it is inclined to rely on foreign law, ascertains it from the submissions made in the statements of case filed by the parties and by the independent research done by the individual justices themselves and/or through their law clerks, where available.

5.7 Role of the chief justice

The chief justice of the Republic of Ghana is a member of the Supreme Court and of all other courts in Ghana, namely, the Court of Appeal, the High Court, the circuit court and the district court. When she empanels herself, she presides over the Supreme Court. The chief justice, however, does not play a role in the determination of cases by panels of which she is not a member. Her initial function is to constitute the panel. However, after the panel has been constituted, she plays no further role in the processes leading to the determination of the merits of the dispute, unless she is a member of the panel.

The parties to a case may petition her administratively, in which case she may exercise the administrative powers she possesses. However, in terms of in-court processes, she has no further role after establishing the panel. The chief justice, however, has the authority to investigate administratively allegations of misconduct made against any judge, including justices of the Supreme Court.

The practice that has evolved is for the chief justice to appoint a superior court judge or judges to investigate allegations made against a judge. This is not to suggest that Ghanaian judges in general misconduct themselves. However, the chief justice's powers are part of the measures available to hold judges to account. If adverse findings are made by the judge or judges appointed by her, then the chief justice reports the matter to the Judicial Council, the constitutional body charged with the responsibility of advising her. The Judicial Council then refers the complaint against the judge to its Appointments and Disciplinary Committee. If this Committee reports that the judge concerned has misbehaved to a degree that merits his or her removal, the Judicial Council petitions the president, through the chief justice, to institute impeachment proceedings against the judge concerned.

This process, which has been invoked only a few times, was impugned by a High Court judge who had been put through it. One of his arguments was that the Judicial Council and the chief justice were not proper parties to petition the president, as they were interested parties. This argument was rejected in the Supreme Court case of *Justice Ansu-Gyeabour v*

The Attorney-General.[26] The case provides an insight into the accountability mechanisms of the Ghanaian judiciary, which are launched administratively by the chief justice.

The plaintiff in the case was a High Court judge. He brought the action in the High Court to restrain the defendant, a nominal defendant representing the president, from bringing impeachment proceedings against him. The facts of the case were as follows. A complaint was made to the complaints unit of the Judicial Service by a plaintiff in a case before Justice Ansu-Gyeabour. The chief justice set up a three-member committee, chaired by a justice of the Supreme Court, to investigate the allegations made against the judge. The committee found that the judge had received money from the complainant, as he had alleged. The committee recommended that the disciplinary aspect of the matter be referred to the Judicial Council.

The Judicial Council in turn referred the committee's report to its Appointments and Disciplinary Committee for consideration. Justice Ansu-Gyeabour was invited by the Committee to appear before it. He was informed of his right to attend the hearing with counsel of his choice. The judge chose to appear without counsel. After the conclusion of its deliberations on the matter, the Committee recommended to the Judicial Council that the chief justice should bring the matter to the attention of the president for the necessary impeachment action to be taken under Article 146 of the Constitution. Accordingly, the chief justice petitioned the president for the removal of Justice Ansu-Gyeabour in accordance with Article 146.

Upon receipt of the petition from the chief justice, the president referred it back to the chief justice for a determination, in accordance with Article 146(3), of whether there was a prima facie case against the judge. After satisfying herself that a prima facie case had been established against the judge, the chief justice proceeded to appoint an impeachment committee under Article 146(4) to investigate the complaint against the judge and report to her. The impeachment committee consisted of three superior court justices and two other persons who were not members of parliament nor lawyers.

When the Committee invited the judge to appear before it, he instituted action in the High Court. He contended that the chief justice's power to determine whether a prima facie case had been established against a judge to be impeached was not delegable. The chief justice was under an obligation to investigate personally an allegation made against a judge, before she could make a prima facie determination. He further contended that the use of the proceedings before the complaints unit and the Appointments and Disciplinary Committee of the Judicial Council as a basis for impeachment proceedings under Article 146 of the constitution was unconstitutional. Moreover, he argued that the Judicial Council had no constitutional mandate to forward a petition to the president for the impeachment of a superior court justice. The High Court judge considered these issues to be constitutional and, therefore, referred them to the Supreme Court for determination under its original jurisdiction.

The Supreme Court held that the chief justice did not have to interrogate the judge personally in order to make a determination as to the existence of a prima facie case. She was entitled to make the determination relying on the reports of the complaints unit of the Judicial Service and the Appointments and Disciplinary Committee of the Judicial Council. The Court also decided that the Judicial Council had the constitutional mandate to forward a petition to the president for the impeachment of a superior court justice.

[26] J6/1/2012. Judgment of the Supreme Court delivered on 31 January 2013 (to be reported in [2013] SCGLR).

This case strengthens the accountability of superior court justices. Most complaints about judges' misbehaviour tend to be made to the judicial administration. It, therefore, makes sense that the Judicial Council should have the authority to set in motion processes for the impeachment of judges whose conduct has been established by it to constitute prima facie misconduct. The fact that the effort by a serving judge to undermine the authority of the Judicial Council on this matter failed was good and in the interests of judicial accountability.

6. Rules on Access to the Supreme Court

Article 2(1) of the 1992 Constitution provides:

> A person who alleges that—
> (a) an enactment or anything contained in or done, under the authority of that or any other enactment;
> or
> (b) any act or omission of any person
> is inconsistent with or is in contravention of a provision of this constitution, may bring an action in the Supreme Court for a declaration to that effect.

This provision has been interpreted by the Supreme Court as giving very wide access to the Court in constitutional cases. Early in the life of the Fourth Republic, the Supreme Court asserted firmly that the only standing needed to bring an action under Article 2(1) of the constitution is that of citizenship. It rejected an argument that only a person whose interests had been adversely affected by a dispute or controversy concerning the interpretation of an enactment could bring an action under Article 2(1) of the 1992 Constitution. In *Sam (No 2) v Attorney-General*,[27] the Solicitor-General argued:[28]

> It is clear that all over the realms of the civilized world, courts exist to settle disputes and that it is only those whose interests have been adversely affected in one way or the other by the construction of a said enactment or a provision of that enactment, who are entitled to a declaration. The 1992 constitution, therefore, assumed this as given and did not elaborate this expressly in the Constitution.

This was roundly rejected by the Supreme Court. Justice Bamford-Addo, in the lead judgment, declared:

> The standing of the plaintiff to bring this action was raised by the defendant. The law is that any person who goes to court must have standing before the court and the standing of persons entitled to apply to the Supreme Court under its original interpretative jurisdiction is provided in articles 2(1) and 130(1) of the constitution. Under these, any person who is a citizen is entitled to bring a suit to the Supreme Court if he alleges that an enactment or anything contained in an enactment is inconsistent with or in contravention of the constitution and to obtain a declaration to that effect.

In additional clarification of her view of the law, the learned judge stated further in her judgment:[29]

[27] [2000] SCGLR 305. [28] ibid 312. [29] ibid 317.

> Clearly, therefore, it can be seen that in actions initiated under article 2(1) such as this present one, the plaintiff does not need to have a personal interest in the case before invoking the special original jurisdiction of the Supreme Court.

Justice Atuguba has also declared that: '[i]t is axiomatic that a citizen of Ghana needs no *locus standi* to defend the constitution, 1992'.[30] The argument which has been accepted by the Supreme Court is that, since the 1992 Constitution imposes an obligation on citizens to defend it,[31] this implies that all citizens have standing to go before the Supreme Court in their quest to defend the constitution.

The only qualification on this broad access by citizens to the Supreme Court in constitutional cases is that the constitution confers original jurisdiction on the High Court,[32] rather than on the Supreme Court, in relation to the enforcement of fundamental human rights. Thus, actions for the enforcement of fundamental human rights go to the High Court, although actions for the interpretation of those rights go to the Supreme Court. This was made explicitly clear in *Adjei-Ampofo (No 1) v Accra Metropolitan Assembly and Attorney-General (No 1)*,[33] where Justice Sophia Akuffo said:[34]

> Hence articles 2(1) and 33(1) are not different sides of the same coin; rather they are intended to serve two entirely different purposes. In article 2(1) the objective is to foster the enforcement of all provisions of the constitution by encouraging all Ghanaians (whether natural persons or corporate) to access the original jurisdiction of the Supreme Court in the interest of the general polity ... Whilst the outcome of an action under article 2(1) is invariably, primarily of benefit to the citizens in general, it may not necessarily inure to the direct or personal benefit of the plaintiff therein. The objective of article 2(1) is to encourage all Ghanaians to help ensure the effectiveness of the constitution, as a whole, through legal action in the Supreme Court. For that reason, therefore, every Ghanaian, natural or artificial, has *locus standi* to initiate an action in the Supreme Court to enforce any provision of the constitution.
>
> In respect of article 33(1), however, the objective is to facilitate the enforcement by any person of his or her individual fundamental human rights and freedoms under chapter 5 of the constitution, through access to the High Court, in the first instance for redress.

Under the well-established case law of the Supreme Court, the Court has exclusive original jurisdiction to interpret any vague or ambiguous provisions of the constitution.[35] Finally, on the original jurisdiction of the Court, it is evident from the discussion above that the usual rules on standing apply to non-citizens who seek to invoke the original jurisdiction of the Court.

There is, of course, access to the Supreme Court by claimants other than plaintiffs in constitutional matters. The extent of access by these other claimants tends to be more restricted than that under the original jurisdiction because of the nature of the other jurisdictions under which they resort to the Supreme Court. Appellants before the Supreme Court, for instance, come from the limited universe of those whose appeals have not succeeded in the Court of Appeal or before the National House of Chiefs. Applicants for the exercise of the review jurisdiction come from the even more limited universe of those dissatisfied with final decisions of the Supreme Court. Only seemingly defeated presidential candidates may invoke the election jurisdiction. The supervisory jurisdiction gives access

30 *New Patriotic Party v Attorney-General* [1997–98] GLR 378 at 440.

31 1992 Constitution art 3(4). 32 ibid art 33. 33 [2007–2008] SCGLR 611. 34 ibid 620.

35 See eg *Republic v Special Tribunal, Ex parte Akosa* [1980] GLR 592 and *Sam (No 2) v Attorney-General* [2000] SCGLR 305.

to those aggrieved by fundamental errors in the High Court or Court of Appeal or by unlawful administrative action.

Access by parties to the Supreme Court through its original, appellate, supervisory, review, and election jurisdictions is available through counsel or by the parties themselves through self-representation. The Supreme Court Rules 1996 define a party to include both the party and counsel of that party.[36] Thus, parties are free to be unrepresented by counsel if they so wish. Indeed, there have been some actions taken before the Supreme Court without representation by counsel, although these are very limited. Also, some non-governmental organizations (NGOs) have exercised their right of access to the Court by bringing actions before it or intervening as *amici curiae*. For instance, in one leading case, the Centre for Human Rights and Civil Liberties, an NGO, sued the Attorney-General and the Electoral Commission to compel the state to respect the right of prisoners to vote.[37]

7. Conclusion

The decision-making and working practices of the Supreme Court of Ghana are principally those of an appellate court. The Court has a relatively collegial approach while, at the same time, preserving individual autonomy for the judges. However, the chapter has also shown that the Court has important original as well as election jurisdictions, which make it a trial court over certain issues. The impression of the author is that, when exercising its original jurisdiction, the Supreme Court is more comfortable when considering evidence by affidavit than when taking *viva voce* evidence. A panel is less suited to making quick-fire decisions on procedural issues during the hearing of oral evidence.

It is, therefore, just as well that, in most of its cases, the evidence it needs to determine the matters in controversy before it is supplied to it through affidavit evidence or by evidence already on the record through oral evidence given in a lower trial court. The Ghanaian Supreme Court is clearly a hybrid court, combining its appellate functions with those of a trial court. Its working practices will need to continue evolving to adapt it to its layered functions. Because of the importance of this hybrid court to the maintenance of constitutionalism in Ghana, the judiciary and the legal profession in general owe a duty to keep the Court's working practices under constant review to ensure that they are fit for purpose and promote efficiency. This is particularly so as the Court is assuming an increasingly important political and social role in Ghanaian society.

Bibliography

Date-Bah S K, *Reflections on the Supreme Court of Ghana* (Wildy, Simmonds & Hill Publishing 2015)

Kirby M, 'Judicial Dissent: Common Law and Civil Law Traditions' (2007) 123 *Law Quarterly Review* 379

Klarman M, *From Jim Crow to Civil Rights: The Supreme Court and the Struggle for Racial Equality* (Oxford University Press 2006)

Memorandum on the Proposals for a Constitution for Ghana (Constitutional Commission, 1968)

Popkin W D, *Evolution of the Judicial Opinion* (New York University Press 2007) 179

Reid 'The Judge as Law-maker' (1972) 12 *Journal of the Society Public Teachers of Law* 22

[36] See Supreme Court Rules 1996 r 82.

[37] *Ahumah-Ocansey v Electoral Commission; Centre for Human Rights and Civil Liberties (CHURCIL) v Attorney-General and Electoral Commission (Consolidated)* [2010] SCGLR 575.

PART 6

CONCLUSION

16

Constitutional Adjudication and Constitutional Justice in Africa's Uncertain Transition

Mapping the Way Forward

Charles M Fombad

1. Introduction

Post-independence African constitutions, by design or default, facilitated the perpetuation of the harsh and repressive authoritarian colonial system in which the judiciary was an active accomplice. It was, therefore, not surprising that respect for and compliance with the dictates of the constitution was the exception rather than the rule. However, the constitutional reforms of the 1990s attempted, at least in most African countries, to entrench some of the core elements of constitutionalism, of which the main goals were to free the judiciary from the stranglehold of the other two branches. Provisions providing for judicial independence and the separation of powers, for the first time, have given African judicial institutions an opportunity to redeem their poor image and play their role as the ultimate custodians of constitutionalism and the rule of law. Nevertheless, as the various chapters in this book have shown, the historical legacy of weak judicial institutions under executive-minded judges has been difficult, if not impossible, to overcome in all jurisdictions. The different accounts in the preceding chapters reveal a variation both across countries and over time within the different countries of the way in which judges across the continent have responded within the constraints, incentives, and opportunities provided by recent reforms.

Unlike in the past, many African courts or courts exercising constitutional jurisdiction are more independent today than they have ever been, and play a more active, meaningful, and constructive role promoting democracy and constitutionalism.[1] Whilst much has been accomplished, the struggle for independent and effective judiciaries prepared to enforce the constitution without fear, favour, or prejudice, is not won simply by the constitutional entrenchment of provisions guaranteeing the independence of the judiciary or even by simply empowering courts to deal with all or some issues relating to the interpretation of the constitution.

In fact, the judicial role in constitutional adjudication is never a condition that can be established fully and is enjoyed without debate, controversy, or challenge. Whilst the history of Africa's transition to constitutional democracy based on the fundamental principles of constitutionalism is in the process of being written, the role of judicial institutions

[1] Many aspects of this chapter have previously been discussed in Charles M Fombad, 'The Expansion of Judicial Power in Africa and Democratic Consolidation: Opportunities: Challenges and Future Prospects' in Muna Ndulo and Mamoudou Gazibo (eds), *Growing Democracy in Africa: Elections, Accountable Governance and Political Economy* (James Currey Publishers 2016) 47–85.

that need to sustain this effort and the challenges faced are critical aspects that have largely been ignored. Two recent contrasting examples illustrate the growing importance of African courts in dealing with sensitive constitutional issues.

The first is decision RCCB 303 of 5 May 2015 of the Burundi Constitutional Court, discussed by Horace Adjolohoun in Chapter 11. In this case, the Burundian Constitutional Court, on rather weak and implausible legal grounds, endorsed President Pierre Nkunrunziza's bid for a third term in spite of the two-term limit in the constitution. This decision paved the way for presidential elections, which President Nkunrunziza won easily, after what most international observers agreed was a deeply flawed process. However, since his swearing-in for the third term, there have been serious civil disturbances leading to thousands of deaths and hundreds of thousands fleeing from the country. Today, the continuous violence has led to fears of another civil war and possible genocide.

The second, and more recent, example is the decision by Chief Justice Mogoeng Mogoeng of the South African Constitutional Court in *Economic Freedom Fighters v Speaker of the National Assembly and Others* and *Democratic Alliance v Speaker of the National Assembly and Others* of 31 May 2016.[2] In what may be regarded as a landmark decision, Mogoeng CJ held, inter alia, that the failure by President Jacob Zuma to comply with the remedial action taken against him by the public protector was a violation of his duty to uphold, defend, and respect the constitution, as well as his duty to assist and protect the office of the public protector to ensure its independence, impartiality, dignity, and effectiveness. This was a decision that led to a parliamentary motion for the president's impeachment, but which failed because of the large majority that the president's ruling African National Congress (ANC) has in parliament.[3] These two cases, which raised serious constitutional issues in two different jurisdictions, had two different outcomes and, in many respects, reflect the mixed and sometimes confusing trajectory of constitutional justice in Africa today.

In spite of better constitutional frameworks today, one cannot, for many reasons, be sanguine about the future prospects of constitutional adjudication, generally, and constitutional justice in Africa. Democratic progress and constitutionalism as a whole depend on the effective operation of each of the three organs of government within their constitutionally defined domain. The frequent tensions between the three branches, especially between the judiciary and the executive, as each tries to defend and protect its turf in the new democratic dispensation, is a permanent source of friction. This is likely to increase rather than to decrease. For example, as Fowkes points out in Chapter 7, in South Africa, because of several court decisions against the government, senior officials within the ruling ANC have regularly criticized the judiciary and referred to it as 'counter-revolutionaries'. President Zuma has gone further by condemning the judiciary for what he refers to as 'low-intensity "law-fare", which attempts to divert the legitimate democratic outcomes in our country'.[4]

[2] 2016 ZACC 11 (CC).

[3] Because of the ANC's 249 majority in a parliament of 400, the defeat of the motion was predictable, but the opposition's point had been made.

[4] See Matuma Letsoalo, Pontsho Pilane, and Carien du Plessis, 'The Big Talking Points from Zuma's ANC Anniversary Address' http://mg.co.za/article/2016-01-09-the-big-talking-points-from-zumas-anc-anniversary-address (last accessed 17 April 2017), where Zuma, in criticizing continuous court challenges to what he termed 'exercise of lawful executive and legislative power', said: 'The party that wins elections must be given space to govern. The ANC must be given space to govern. This is a fundamental basic principle of democracy and is practised throughout the world'.

If the judiciary in South Africa, with one of the most liberal constitutions in the world, can be put under such pressure, how much more is in store for the judiciaries in other African countries? This becomes a major challenge, because the ability of the judiciary to influence change is inherently limited as their success depends entirely on the cooperation of the other two branches of government. They remain, in the famous words of Hamilton in *The Federalist No 78*,[5] the least dangerous branch, vulnerable to manipulation. Hence, in spite of a better protective framework today, the future role of African judicial institutions in promoting democracy and constitutionalism will depend on how they can overcome the present challenges to their authority, and fully regain and sustain public confidence in their ability and willingness to discharge their sacred responsibilities as guardians of the constitution.

Commenting on some aspects of what lies ahead, two important issues will be discussed here. First are some transitional challenges and anomalies that persist and impact negatively on the ability of courts to ensure constitutional justice for all. Second are some of the issues that need to be addressed to enhance the prospects for an effective system of constitutional adjudication.

2. Transitional Challenges and Anomalies

The almost complete acceptance of the role of constitutional review in protecting the integrity of modern African constitutions has not come without its own problems. Some of these have resulted from flaws in design, others from difficulties in implementation and, in some cases, the hangover effect of the past, which continues to haunt the present. A number of these issues will now be examined briefly before considering the way forward.

The first issue worth noting is one that has surprisingly not attracted much attention. This is the distinction drawn between disputes concerning the interpretation of the constitution, that are reserved for specialized constitutional courts and operate outside the ordinary judicial system, and disputes that are unconnected to the interpretation of the constitution, that are reserved for the ordinary courts. This distinction is one of the critical features of the centralized system. The assumption must be that a clear difference can be made between disputes raising constitutional issues and those that do not. As Fowkes has convincingly shown in Chapter 7, it is a distinction that is theoretically and practically difficult to draw or even to justify. If the constitution is the source of all laws in any country, and all laws are subject to the constitution, it becomes difficult to see how any dispute can be said to be unconnected to the constitution. It is an anomalous distinction that caused much confusion in the post-apartheid South African constitutional review system introduced by the 1996 Constitution, not only in the minds of litigants but also amongst the courts.

It was, therefore, not surprising that in 2013 the constitution was amended to remove this anomaly. The separation of constitutional adjudication from other forms of adjudication remains a fundamental aspect of the civilian system operating in Francophone, Lusophone, and Hispanophone Africa. One can only speculate that a possible reason why it has survived has been not only the imaginative framing of matters to downplay the constitutional aspect, as was the case in South Africa before 2013, but also the generally

[5] See Gerald N Rosenberg, *The Hollow Hope: Can Courts Bring About Social Change?* (University of Chicago 1991) 15.

limited scope for vindicating constitutional violations, especially by private individuals in these jurisdictions. Perhaps because of the fact that it goes to the heart of this model of constitutional adjudication, it is one that will be difficult to reform satisfactorily without radically changing the entire system.

Another issue which emerges clearly and, in this respect, confirms the views of many scholars, as Fombad points out in Chapter 1, is the link between progress in the transition to democracy and the introduction of constitutional review. It is, therefore, not surprising that the two countries discussed in this volume whose constitutions provide either for limited or very ineffective constitutional review, namely Cameroon and Ethiopia, correspond with two of the countries that have since the 1990s made the least progress in transiting from autocratic one-man rule to democratic and accountable governance based on the rule of law.[6] In both countries, particularly in the case of Cameroon, the constitution has no more than symbolic value as it is only obeyed when it suits the convenience of the president and the ruling elites, and the Constitutional Council is there solely to give the government electoral legitimacy.

However, beyond cases such as Cameroon, where constitutional adjudication only has symbolic value and political elites may do as they please, there are many other situations where the scope for political interference and the politicization of the judiciary limit its ability to operate independently, objectively, and fairly. The abuse of the powers of appointment is probably one of the most insidious problems that have survived the post-1990 constitutional reforms. Where a judge is appointed not on merit, but rather on his perceived or actual loyalty to the government, he will feel beholden to the executive and will decide matters not on the basis of the law but rather in a manner that will favour those who appointed him.

Although systems of appointment have generally improved, the reality is that the scope for the executive to interfere and manipulate the appointment process in a partisan manner is considerably higher in most civilian jurisdictions than is the case in common law jurisdictions.[7] However, as Fowkes points out in Chapter 7, efforts by the ruling ANC to pack the bench has not significantly affected the willingness of South African judges to deliver independent, objective, and well-reasoned decisions. By contrast, this has not been the case in civilian jurisdictions, as Fombad in Chapter 3 and Thomashausen in Chapter 4 show.

Beyond appointments, the increased involvement of judges in the resolution of many sensitive matters of a social, political, and economic nature has brought about the risks of constant friction within the judiciary. As the accounts by Fombad (Chapters 1 and 3), Quashigah (Chapter 5) and Horace Adjolohoun (Chapter 11) indicate, this occurs most often in electoral disputes or disputes involving the abuse of powers. Where government is on the losing side, the tactics commonly used are to instigate hostile verbal attacks or criticisms of the judiciary, using either government-owned newspapers or NGOs funded

[6] One useful indicator is Freedom House's survey of the state of freedom in the world, which shows that these two countries are amongst the few in Africa which have consistently, since the 1990s, been rated as 'not free'. See further https://freedomhouse.org/sites/default/files/01152015_FIW_2015_final.pdf (last accessed 17 April 2017).

[7] Although in almost all jurisdictions, the appointments are effectively made by the president, the processes are such that in common law jurisdictions there are other stakeholders who play a meaningful role in the process as compared to the civilian jurisdiction, where the role of other stakeholders is more symbolic than real. See, further, Charles M Fombad, 'Appointment of Constitutional Adjudicators in Africa: Some Perspectives on How Different Systems Yield Similar Outcomes' (2014) 46(2) *Journal of Legal Pluralism and Unofficial Law* 249.

by them. Many of these instances have been noted, as in Fowkes' account on South Africa. Examples of these practices have also been reported in Namibia, Zambia, and Zimbabwe.[8] As noted earlier, even high-ranking government officials such as presidents have been involved in such attacks. For example, in Uganda, President Museveni accused the judiciary of 'unprofessional bias against the Movement government [the ruling party] and corruption'.[9]

Another recurring problem is that of resources. In fact, many studies on the judiciary in Africa during the last two decades have drawn attention to the problem of a lack of resources.[10] Without adequate resources the judiciary cannot operate either independently or efficiently. In some instances, the unwillingness to provide adequate resources may be a deliberate political ploy to exert pressure on the judiciary. There have been complaints in some countries that judicial budgets had been cut because of judgments given against the government.[11] It is particularly easy to use judicial appropriations to exert undue pressure on the judiciary in certain systems, such as those obtaining in Francophone and Lusophone countries, where the judicial budget is not protected by being part of the consolidated fund.

Generally, the shortage of trained judicial personnel is a common problem in most African countries. The lack of well-trained and experienced judicial officers becomes particularly problematic in civilian jurisdictions, where a single court has exclusive jurisdiction to deal with all constitutional disputes in the country. Challenges relating to staffing are exacerbated where the constitutional courts alone have jurisdiction to deal with all election-related disputes and, in most cases, have to neglect their normal responsibilities in order to deal with these. The effect is not only that these constitutional courts are often saddled with a huge backlog of cases but, as Fombad points out in Chapter 3, as in many civilian jurisdictions, the many election petitions are usually disposed of in a summary manner within unreasonable time limits in a manner that makes a mockery of justice.

Other common problems constraining the performance of judicial institutions on the continent and, therefore, impact negatively on their ability to deliver constitutional justice include poor infrastructure, a lack of adequate funds to cover running expenses, insufficient stationery and office equipment, and limited working facilities, such as courtrooms. In many countries, judges do not have access to sufficient legal information resources such as books, law reports, statute books, and gazettes. This is particularly the case in rural areas where there are no libraries or where these have over the years been neglected. This situation is often aggravated by the lack of computer skills or the lack of motivation on the part of users. In some cases, there is no access to the internet or, where there is such access, there are technical problems such as slow and erratic networks, unreliable power supplies, and poor user support and maintenance systems.

The quality of legal developments on the continent has in some countries been retarded or even reversed by the poor state of court records. This can make it very difficult for

[8] Linda van de Vijver (ed), *The Judicial Institution in Southern Africa: A Comparative Study of Common Law Jurisdictions* (Siber Ink CC 2006) 103–4; and Jennifer Widner, 'Judicial Independence in Common Law Africa' in Andreas Schedler, Larry Diamond, and Mark Plattner (eds), *The Self-Restraining State: Power and Accountability in New Democracies* (Lynne Rienner Publishers 1999).

[9] See van de Vijver (n 8) 218.

[10] See examples of this in van de Vijver (n 8); Siri Gloppen, Roberto Gargarella, and Elin Skaar (eds), *Democratization and the Judiciary: The Accountability Function of Courts in New Democracies* (Frank Cass 2004) 17–31; and Report of the Partners for Gender Justice Conference, *The Role of the Judiciary in Promoting Gender Justice in Africa* http://www.ilac.se/download/reports_documents/thematic-reports_documents/Ghana%20Report-English.pdf (last accessed 17 April 2017).

[11] See examples of this in van de Vijver (n 8) and in Gloppen, Gargarella, and Skaar(n 10).

superior courts to deal with appeals. Perhaps the most detrimental aspect of this has been the absence of a reliable and regular system of law reporting in some countries, such as Cameroon, or the fact that reporting is erratic in other countries, such as Malawi and Botswana. Without an efficient system of record keeping or reporting on court cases, the operation of the legal system, especially where it is based on the rule of *stare decisis*, cannot function properly.

In spite of advances made in the last two decades, there is not sufficient evidence to prove that African judges are alive to the new spirit of progressive constitutional rights of the 1990s or, if so, have sufficiently incorporated this in their approach to constitutional interpretation. It is also not clear whether constitutional court judges are making an effort to learn from what is occurring in neighbouring countries faced with similar issues.

Be that as it may, it is clear from preceding chapters that the apparent expansion of constitutional review powers will continue to be under constant threat. This is particularly so because of numerous ominous signs of the resurgence of authoritarianism. The frequent attempts by African leaders to expand their already exorbitant powers through the repeal of constitutional term limits provisions have been confounded by their control over the increasingly dominant parties that, as we saw in the case of South Africa's ANC, are incapable of holding the executive to account.

As more and more African presidents struggle to find loopholes in constitutions to hold onto power, the pressure on the judiciary to decide cases, especially politically sensitive cases in deference to the executive, will increase. The future of constitutional adjudication depends on the way in which African judiciaries overcome the numerous challenges they face in an increasingly volatile and polarized climate, where the new generation of leaders and the dominant parties manifest all the instincts and techniques of the pre-1990 dictators and their one-party systems. The question arises as to how constitutional courts will be able to curb these stealthy threats to Africa's second attempt at entrenching constitutionalism.

3. Mapping the Way Forward for an Effective System of Constitutional Review

The prospects for entrenching and sustaining an effective and efficient system of constitutional adjudication in Africa depends as much on the judiciary as it does on the other two branches of government. In almost all African countries, with the exception of a few Francophone countries that are saddled with the original ineffective Gaullist system of constitutional review and a few other countries, such as Ethiopia and Eritrea, the foundations for establishing an effective system of constitutional review have been laid.

Whilst it can be said that the judicial institutions on the continent are more independent today than they have ever been, their ability to promote constitutional justice is subject to them overcoming numerous challenges. We will focus on three factors that are amongst some of the important factors critical for the emergence and sustenance of an effective system of constitutional review. These are, first, the willingness of the judiciary to defend constitutionalism against its enemies; secondly, their willingness to be part of the global judicial dialogue striving to promote constitutionalism, respect for the rule of law, and good governance; and, thirdly, the need to improve the level of judicial training.

3.1 Progressive judicialism and constitutional justice

An important lesson to be learnt from the landmark decision of Chief Justice Mogoeng Mogoeng in the *Economic Freedom Fighters* case is that a passive judiciary in the face of Africa's overbearing and increasingly unruly executives will certainly take Africa back to the dark days of one-party dictatorship and destroy any hopes for constitutionalism and democracy. Judicial independence in the post-independence period was not only compromised by the intolerance of executives, but also by the 'enthusiastic abdication of judicial responsibilities by the judges'.[12] Constitutionalism and democracy in Africa today can only develop and grow with judges who are liberal, progressive, activist, or have 'bold spirits' and not the 'timorous souls'[13] of the passive judges of the past. Even in those countries where the institutional framework remains weak, there is nevertheless scope and space for what may be referred to as progressive judicialism. The imperatives and foundations for such an approach are threefold.

First, it can be argued that most modern African constitutions provide considerable scope for creative and broad purposive interpretation of their provisions, even if this is the case in some countries more than in others. This invites judges, as an imperative, to adopt a more principled and rights-sensitive approach to interpreting constitutions in a manner that takes account of the radical political, economic, and social changes of our times and the revulsion against dictatorship. In many instances it is manifestly clear that the revised or new constitutions were not only designed to eliminate dictatorship and promote democracy and good governance, but also to promote a new human rights culture particularly sensitive to issues such as hunger, poverty, unemployment, ignorance, illiteracy, disease, and governance ills such as corruption, the embezzlement of public funds, and the abuse of power that have inflicted so much hardship on a majority of the population on the continent. Attaining these goals requires a judiciary that is willing to reflect the new spirit of constitutionalism when interpreting constitutions. This is particularly the case when dealing with issues of corruption, the abuse of office and the violation of the constitution by the executive, especially a president who has sworn an oath to uphold, defend, respect, and enforce the constitution and, hence, constitutionalism. Chief Justice Mogoeng Mogoeng did not mince his words when in the very opening paragraph of his bold and robust condemnation of the violation of the constitution by President Zuma in the *Economic Freedom Fighters* case, he said the following:[14]

> One of the crucial elements of our constitutional vision is to make a decisive break from the unchecked abuse of state power and resources that was virtually institutionalised during the apartheid era. To achieve this goal, we adopted accountability, the rule of law and the supremacy of the constitution as values of our constitutional democracy. For this reason, public office-bearers ignore their constitutional obligations at their peril. This is so because constitutionalism, accountability and the rule of law constitute the sharp and mighty sword that stands ready to chop the ugly head of impunity off its stiffened neck.

...

[12] Chidi Anselm Odinkalu, 'The Judiciary and the Legal Protection of Human Rights in Common Law: Allocating Responsibility for the Failure of Post-Independence Bills of Rights' (1996) 8 *African Society of International and Comparative Law Proceedings* 136, 137.

[13] Lord Denning in *Candler v Crane, Christmas & Co* [1951] 1 All ER 426.

[14] See *Economic Freedom Fighters* case (n 2) paras 1 and 75.

> And the role of these foundational values in helping to strengthen and sustain our constitutional democracy sits at the heart of this application.
>
> ...
>
> Our foundational value of the rule of law demands of us, as a law-abiding people, to obey decisions made by those clothed with the legal authority to make them or else approach courts of law to set them aside ...

The most effective basis for promoting progressive judicialism has been provided for by the South African constitution and the Kenyan and Zimbabwean constitutions of 2010 and 2013 respectively, which have transformative constitutionalism at their core.[15] These constitutions not only make a profound attempt at laying the foundations for a new society that will reverse the injustices of the past, but are heavily laden with values, principles, and mechanisms designed to create a just, equal, and fair society, which a judge cannot ignore when interpreting the constitution.[16] It is true that transformative constitutionalism may lead to progressive judicialism of the type that may run the risks of blurring the boundaries between law and politics. Nevertheless, it is a risk that must be accepted because, with hardly any exceptions, African politicians have over the last six decades proven that, if left unconstrained by clear constitutional rules and an effective system of constitutional review, their authoritarian instincts and impulses easily take control of them.

Progressive judicialism also means that judges should go beyond their traditional role of interpreters of the constitution and should strive to do justice by giving effect to contemporary social conditions and values. This is what in many quarters has been referred to as judicial activism and which has been reasonably successful in promoting constitutionalism in South Africa and India and, it is argued, can achieve the same in many other countries.[17]

A second approach to promoting progressive judicialism, it is argued, inheres from the very nature of a constitution itself. Far from being a document containing 'time-worn adages or hollow shibboleths',[18] or resembling a 'lifeless museum piece',[19] a constitution should be regarded as a living document designed to serve present and future generations, as well as to embody and reflect the fears, hopes, aspirations, and desires of the people.[20] In other words, judges must interpret constitutions in a manner that gives the constitution life and relevance. The fact is that judges can no longer ignore the new context in which constitutional disputes should be interpreted: the rejection of dictatorship in all its forms and sensitivity to the issues of human rights.

A third perspective to progressive judicialism is what Dinokopila refers to in Chapter 9 as 'creeping monism'. Although it could be criticized as bordering on the 'judicial

[15] It is beyond the scope of this chapter to go into the details of transformative constitutionalism. However, the rich literature on the topic usually starts with the seminal paper of Karl Klare, 'Legal Culture and Transformative Constitutionalism' (1998) 4 *South African Journal on Human Rights* 146–88; Marius Pieterse, 'What Do We Mean When We Talk about Transformative Constitutionalism?'(2005) 20 *SA Public Law* 155–66; and Theunis Roux, 'Transformative Constitutionalism and the Best Interpretation of the South African Constitution: Distinction Without a Difference?' (2009) 20 *Stellenbosch Law Review* 258–85.

[16] Judge Mogoeng Mogoeng referred to these values in the South African constitution in his judgment in the *Economic Freedom Fighters* case (n 2) paras 13 and 75.

[17] This is discussed in Charles M Fombad, 'Constitutional Reforms and Constitutionalism in Africa: Reflections on Some Current Challenges and Future Prospects' (2011) 59(4) *Law Review* 1007, 1108.

[18] Earl Warren CJ in *Trop v Dulles* 356 US 86 (1958) at 103.

[19] Aguda JA in *Attorney-General v Dow* [1992] BLR 119 at 166.

[20] Some argue that the constitution is for the living and the present generation should no longer be ruled by the dead hand of their ancestors. See Michael W McConnell, 'Textualism and the Dead Hand of the Past' (1998) 60 *George Washington Law Review* 1127–8.

incorporation of treaties', it nevertheless provides African courts with a technique of strengthening good governance and constitutionalism by exerting pressure on governments not to breach their international commitments. It is a well-known fact that African governments have no difficulty in signing international treaties and conventions and sometimes ratifying these treaties, but do not necessarily proceed to domesticate them.

Whilst courts cannot compel them to domesticate the treaties, they can at least compel them not to act in breach of them. The foundation for this approach was laid down in the famous Botswana case of *Attorney-General v Dow*.[21] In this case, dealing with the position where a treaty had been signed but had not been domesticated, Amissah JP cited with approval the following passage from the judge in the court *a quo* in the same case:

> I bear in mind that signing the Convention [the OAU Convention] does not give it the power of law in Botswana but the effect of the adherence by Botswana to the Convention must show that a construction of the section which does not do violence to the language but is consistent with and in harmony with the Convention must be preferable to a 'narrow construction' which results in a finding that section 15 of the Constitution permits discrimination on the basis of sex.[22]

In doing so, the court basically followed the well-established presumption in statutory interpretation in common law jurisdictions that courts will strive to interpret legislation in such a manner that it will not conflict with international law. The judge went further to explain this, as follows:[23]

> Botswana is a member of the community of civilised states which has undertaken to abide by certain standards of conduct, and, unless it is impossible to do otherwise, it would be wrong for its courts to interpret its legislation in a manner which conflicts with the international obligations Botswana has undertaken. This principle, used as an aid to construction as is quite permissible under section 24 of the Interpretation Act.

This approach was also adopted by the South African Constitutional Court in *Glenister v President of the Republic of South Africa*.[24] The Constitutional Court declared that the amendment to Chapter 6A of the South African Police Service Act was inconsistent with the constitution and invalid to the extent that it failed to provide for an adequate degree of independence for the corruption-fighting unit it sought to establish. Although there was no specific provision in the constitution specifying that the unit must be independent, the court held that the constitutional obligation to set up an independent unit could be inferred from the duty imposed by section 7(2) of the constitution to 'respect, protect and fulfil' the rights in the bill of rights. It went further to point out that, based on section 39(1)(b) of the constitution, which required the court in interpreting the bill of rights to consider international law, and section 231, which states that all international agreements approved by parliament are binding, the establishment of a corruption-fighting unit ignoring binding international instruments that required such a unit to be independent, was not a reasonable constitutional measure.

In this indirect manner, the court declared legislation unconstitutional for violating international law, which became relevant not only because it was based on instruments that are binding on the South African government, but also because they reflect the ethos of constitutionalism. In other words, the constitutional duty to create a corruption-fighting unit was not discharged by creating one that will be ineffective because it was placed under the

[21] [1992] BLR 119. [22] ibid 154. [23] ibid. [24] 2011 ZACC 6.

control of politicians who it is required to investigate. However, this activist approach will require a more open-minded global approach to constitutional issues.

3.2 Constitutional adjudication in an era of global judicial dialogue and transjudicialism

Although we live in an era of rapidly expanding regional integration and globalization, where geographical and, to some extent, legal boundaries are broken down, many judges, especially in civilian jurisdictions, are still too imbued with the past to recognize the enormous potential for constitutional developments these changes are providing. In order to sustain the momentum towards greater constitutional justice in Africa, judges, regardless of the constitutional review model within which they operate, need to abandon the conservative inward-looking culture that was characteristic of the old judiciary, and should see themselves as members of a global legal community where knowledge and ideas are exchanged across jurisdictions.

From the two contributions by Killander (Chapter 10) and Dinokopila (Chapter 9) in this volume, it is clear that there is not much evidence of an intra-African dialogue, either in terms of cross-fertilization, borrowing, or migration of constitutional ideas from one African constitution to another, or through the use by judges of jurisprudence from other African jurisdictions, especially across the common/civil law divide. For example, although during its early years the South African Constitutional Court relied extensively on foreign jurisprudence, hardly any of this jurisprudence was from other African jurisdictions.[25] In both constitution-making and constitutional interpretation, there still is a tendency for African constitutional designers and judges to rely and copy extensively, and sometimes almost exclusively, from the former colonial power's legal system. This negative self-defeating attitude has considerably changed in Anglophone Africa, where constitutional experts look beyond England for inspiration and guidance. In Francophone Africa, constitutional draftsmen have continued to seek inspiration from and rely almost slavishly on the Gaullist Fifth Republic model, which some still consider to be the most reliable and unassailable constitutional model.[26] Four critical issues need to be noted here.

First, besides the progressive nature of the 1996 South African constitution, the high quality of judgments delivered by the South African Constitutional Court, which in certain areas of the law, such as socio-economic rights, has laid down principles that are copied the world over, suggests that it is not necessary to continue looking outside the continent for and copy Western constitutional models. In many respects, the South African constitution has not only incorporated some of the best elements of Western constitutional systems, but has adapted this to its historical, social, and cultural context to such an extent that it is now a model which even some Western countries can emulate. In this respect, it is worth citing the famous *dictum* of Judge Guido Calabresi who, noting that several post-1945 constitutions had been modelled explicitly on the US constitution, in

[25] See Nsongurua J Udombana, 'Interpreting Rights Globally: Courts and Constitutional Rights in Emerging Democracies' (2005) 5 *African Human Rights Law Journal* 61; and Andrea Lollini, 'Legal Argumentation Based on Foreign Law: An Example from Case Law of the South African Constitutional Court' (2007) 3(1) *Utrecht Law Review* 60–74.

[26] See further Charles M Fombad, 'Constitutional Reforms in France and their Implications for Constitutionalism in Francophone Africa' (2008) http://www.africafiles.org/article.asp?ID=18777 (last accessed 17 April 2017).

arguing that experience with judicial review in those systems should operate in the US, said that '[w]ise parents learn from their children'.[27]

Secondly, the universality of certain constitutional law principles and standards is no longer in doubt. For example, a court can hardly deal with a human rights dispute today without being invited by counsel to consider one or other foreign authority. More often than not, the reliance on these foreign authorities has been somewhat eclectic, with scant or, at most, superficial reference to the techniques of comparative law. Even if a constitution does not explicitly or implicitly authorize a judge to refer to or invoke international law or to rely on comparative law, it may be argued that, in today's globalized world, it would be self-defeating and a dereliction of duty for a judge completely to ignore legal developments in the rest of the world and their actual or potential implications for national law.[28] The fundamental values underpinning most constitutions, such as equality, dignity of the human person, non-discrimination, freedom of speech, and others, are now universal values recognized in almost all constitutions. There are at least certain minimum common understandings of these concepts that should apply to all, regardless of jurisdiction.

Thirdly, because of the internationalization of many constitutional law principles, judges should resist the intoxicating notion that they 'know it all', and should be prepared to keep up with the latest developments in the law.[29] They must adopt an open mind, willing to research into and consider developments abroad, particularly in other legal systems.

Fourthly, the embarrassing absence of an intra-African judicial dialogue and its importance cannot be overemphasized. The similarity of experiences of African countries from colonialism and its aftermath to the challenges of dealing with ethnic, cultural, and religious diversity means that they should learn from each other's experiences. This is not simply to copy blindly that which obtains in other jurisdictions, but rather to attempt to draw inspiration from their dynamic and rich jurisprudence. Legal systems continue to innovate, experiment, and adopt new solutions to new problems arising daily and from which others can learn.

However, the possibility of enriching national constitutional law through the process of an intra-African judicial dialogue is unlikely to influence constitutional development and, hence, constitutional justice in Francophone and, possibly, Lusophone Africa. Following the civil law tradition, courts in these countries hardly ever rely on precedents and their judgments contain little factual and legal analysis. In addition to referring to applicable laws, these judgments hardly ever articulate the factors or policies that might have influenced a particular conclusion. This is the main reason for inconsistencies in decisions taken by the Benin Constitutional Court, as pointed out by Adjolohoun.[30] Some commentators have also correctly pointed out that there was no reason for Francophone judges to adhere to an inherited French style of formulating and rendering judgments when this is detrimental to ensuring predictability, consistency, and fairness in judicial decisions.[31]

[27] See *United States v Then* 56 F 3d 464 (2d Cir 1995) (Calabresi J concurring).

[28] See Udombana (n 25) 61.

[29] See Charles M Fombad, 'Internationalization of Constitutional Law and Constitutionalism in Africa'(2012) 60(2) *American Journal of Comparative Law* 439–73.

[30] See Horace Adjolohoun, *Droit de l'Homme et Justice Constitutionnelle en Afrique: Le Modèle Béninois. À la Lumière de l'Homme et des Peuples* (L'Harmattan 2011) 121–4.

[31] ibid 121–2. See also Anna Rotman, 'Benin's Constitutional Court: An Institutional Model for Guaranteeing Human Rights'(2004) 17 *Harvard Human Rights Journal* 310; and Bernadette Codjovi, 'La Places des Conventions Internationales dans le Droit Béninois: Le Juge Béninois Devant Les Conventions Internationale' in *Actes du Séminaire: Le Bénin et Les Conventions Internationales Relatives aux Droits de l'Homme et de la Promotion de la Démocratie* (2002) Cotonou (unpublished).

The negative aftermath of the colonial heritage is sometimes so strong that it blinds some judges to innovative provisions in their constitutions. For example, the Angolan 2010 Constitution gives one of the broadest mandates to Angolan judges to refer to and rely on international law, even 'where this has not been invoked by the parties concerned'.[32] However, as Thomashausen points out in Chapter 4, only in one of the 347 judgments of the Angolan Constitutional Court that he reviewed did the court refer to an international human rights instrument. With such conservative and, one may add, apathetic courts, where judges ignore the express provisions of the constitution authorizing them to consider international law, justice is bound to suffer.

We noted earlier the challenges of access to legal information, especially to hard copies of law reports and textbooks. Access to the internet is expanding and this opens up new possibilities for promoting access to information, especially to African literature. Today, the latest and most important decisions of African national constitutional courts and regional courts are just a mouse click away.[33] As a result of rapid advances in information and communication technology in the last two decades, not only judgments but also a large amount of constitutional material from different jurisdictions are now available. The benefits of this will be completely lost if national legal experts and judges are too unbending and attached to the past to see the benefits of learning from what is occurring elsewhere on the continent. However, an important way of overcoming this artificial mental barrier could be through cross-national networking of judges from different legal traditions. Such personal contact between judges will enable them to share their experiences and see how judges occupying similar positions elsewhere often confront the same kinds of problems.

Although there are many fora where judges from different countries meet, with the exception of the Judges' Working Group in the African Network of Constitutional Lawyers (ANCL),[34] these have often been along regional lines and have provided scant opportunity for judges from different African legal traditions to actually mix.[35] One would also expect that, as the numerous regional and continental tribunals in Africa become more active,[36] the process of internationalization through cross-jurisprudential fertilization will

[32] Most important are arts 26 and 27. These provide as follows: '26(1) The fundamental rights established in this constitution shall not exclude others contained in the laws and applicable rules of international law. (2) Constitutional and legal precepts relating to fundamental rights must be interpreted and incorporated in keeping with the Universal Declaration of the Rights of Man, the African Charter on the Rights of Man and Peoples and other international treaties on the subject ratified by the Republic of Angola. (3) *In the consideration by the Angolan courts of disputes concerning fundamental rights, the international instruments referred to in the previous point shall be applied, even if not invoked by the parties concerned.* 27. The principles set out in this chapter shall apply to the rights, freedoms and guarantees and to fundamental rights of a similar nature that are established in the constitution or are enshrined in law or international conventions' (emphasis added).

[33] The Southern African Legal Information Institute (SAFLII) now provides free online access to the latest decisions from the superior courts in Angola, Botswana, Lesotho, Kenya, Madagascar, Malawi, Mauritius, Mozambique, Namibia, Seychelles, South Africa, Swaziland, Tanzania, Uganda, Zambia, and Zimbabwe. It also provides access to the decisions of the following regional courts of justice: COMESA, the East African Court of Appeal, the East African Court of Justice, and the SADC Tribunal; http://www.saflii.org/ (last accessed 1 June 2016).

[34] This mixed judicial forum consisting of constitutional court judges from Anglophone, Francophone, Lusophone, and Hispanophone Africa was formally set up during the ANCL Annual Conference that took place in Rabat, Morocco, from 2–5 February 2011.

[35] These include the East African Magistrates and Judges' Association, the East African Community Forum of Chief Justices, and the Southern African Chief Justices Forum (SACJF). The only exception is the latter, which includes the chief justices from Angola and Mozambique.

[36] Africa has an impressive number of continental and regional international tribunals. However, there is little evidence that there is any dialogue between either national courts and these tribunals or between these tribunals themselves, perhaps with the exception of the African Commission on Human and Peoples' Rights,

be intensified. This will be particularly so where national constitutional courts, whose decisions are subject to review by these tribunals, will inevitably have to take account of the jurisprudence of these tribunals in order to avoid the embarrassment of their decisions being reversed on appeal.

Ultimately, it depends on the attitude of judges. Unless judges are prepared to learn about dealing with current developments both nationally and internationally, judicial decisions will retain a rigid, positivist orientation, which is negative for the progressive development of constitutional law in Africa. Lord McCluskey, in the opening paragraph of his book *Law, Justice, and Democracy*, highlights some of the attitudinal obstacles many African judges will have to overcome, when he says the following:[37]

> If I were to be asked what temptations any new judge is exposed to, I should have to admit that they include arrogance, self-esteem and impatience. That answer must alarm all who know that the principal qualities a judge must possess are humility, modesty and tolerance. But just think of the facts. He has been elevated to a position in which he wields a royal authority. The apparatus of state lies ready to enforce his orders. The visible symbols of his office, the way he dresses, the place in which he sits, the manner in which he is addressed, the respect which he is accorded, all are designed to buttress that authority, to intimidate those who might wish to challenge or evade it.

Judges must, therefore, resist the exhilarating notion that they 'know it all', and should be prepared to stay abreast with the latest developments in the law. The present generation of African judges not only has a special and important duty to be more receptive and attentive to other African judicial voices, but they must also make a conscious effort to contribute to building and strengthening the African perspective in their judgments in order for rest of the continent, and even the world at large, to learn from their experiences. This will, amongst other things, also depend on the quality of judicial education that judges undergo.

3.3 Progressive judicialism and judicial training

The issue of judicial training raises the critically important question as to whether our judges are sufficiently equipped to deal with contemporary issues of constitutional justice. Unlike in the civil law tradition in Francophone Africa, where judges undergo a formal two-year period of training, there is no formal training for judges in Anglophone countries. Too many people in the common law world appear to have taken too seriously Lord Devlin's view that judicial training may become a means of propaganda by the executive and, thus, intrude upon the independence of judges.[38] This attitude is currently changing and in many common law jurisdictions courses are organized to train judges, especially on their first appointment to the bench. Even if there are no formal specialized institutions

which is a non-judicial body that only makes recommendations. The African Court on Justice and Human Rights and the African Court of Human and Peoples' Rights are idle, and the Southern African Development Community (SADC) Tribunal became too active for its own good. After delivering a number of judgments against the Zimbabwean government, its operations were suspended in 2007 until further notice. The most active of these tribunals has been the Economic Community for West African States (ECOWAS) Tribunal which, since its establishment in 2002, has dealt with numerous cases, whilst others, such as the East African Court of Justice and the Common Market of Eastern and Southern Africa Court of Justice, have handled only a few cases.

[37] In Baron John Herbert McCluskey, *Law, Justice and Democracy* (Sweet & Maxwell 1987) 1.

[38] Baron P Devlin, *The Judge* (OUP 1979) 36 and 47.

for training judges, the reality is that, in most of Anglophone Africa, there are specialized short courses for newly appointed judges or those who aspire to a judicial career. In spite of Date-Bah's view, in Chapter 15, that judicial appointments from the bar rather than formal training nurtures independence in outlook and thinking, some form of training is indispensable.[39]

Nevertheless, it may be argued that one of the reasons for the judicial conservatism alluded to earlier is the relatively poor quality of training of judges, creating ample opportunity for their manipulation by politicians. This is in many cases reinforced by questionable systems of promotion, especially in civil law jurisdictions, where politics rather than competence are the prime consideration. To enable judges to deal with contemporary issues of constitutional justice and good governance adequately, judicial training should no longer be taken for granted. There are at least three ways in which judicial training needs to be enhanced to equip judges to deal with contemporary constitutional cases in a progressive manner.

In the first place, it is necessary for judges to be trained in a structured and systematic manner, whether formally, as in Francophone countries, or informally, as in Anglophone countries. Judicial training should be complemented by continuous judicial education programmes carefully designed to expose judges to new ideas, recent developments, and new experiences, and to provide them with the opportunities to share their experiences.

Secondly, in the globalized judicial world of today, there is a need for the judiciary to be familiarized with the techniques and pitfalls of comparative legal research. Once it is accepted that the consideration of international and foreign law is not only unavoidable but absolutely necessary, the question arises as to what approach to adopt in assessing the relevance and applicability especially of foreign law. Too often judges have simply accepted and adopted legal principles from other common law jurisdictions without heeding Watson's warning that, in law, as in medicine, transplants carry the risk of rejection.[40] Judges, therefore, need to be formally trained in comparative law, generally, and in particular in the techniques for the proper use and application of foreign and international legal material. In borrowing from foreign sources, therefore, there are skills and techniques with which judges must become accustomed.[41]

Finally, although debates and discussions on decolonizing African university curricula are becoming increasingly polarized, they nevertheless raise important questions about the present direction and emphasis, in the context of our discussion, of legal education

[39] For example, in South Africa, a Judicial Education Institute was provided for under the Judicial Education Institute Act 2008; Pierre de Vos, 'Urgently Wanted: Judicial Training' http://constitutionallyspeaking.co.za/urgently-wanted-judicial-training/ (last accessed 17 April 2017), writing in 2010, doubted whether it had started functioning, but even in 2016, it is not clear how effective it has been. What is perhaps more significant is his comment on a judgment on an issue of constitutional law written by a senior judge, which he criticizes as 'shoddily written while the constitutional law arguments are confusing and lacking in a basic understanding of constitutional law jurisprudence', which he attributes to a lack of further training.

[40] In Alan Watson, *Legal Transplants. An Approach to Comparative Law* (University of Georgia Press 1974) 27.

[41] For instances of the misuse of foreign law see Charles M Fombad, 'Gender Equality in African Customary Law: Has the Male Ultimogeniture Rule Any Future in Botswana' (2014) 52(3) *Journal of Modern African Studies* 475–94 and, more generally, Basil Markesinis and Jörg Fedktke, *Judicial Recourse to Foreign Law. A New Source of Inspiration?* (UCL Press 2006); Cheryl Saunders, 'The Use and Misuse of Comparative Constitutional Law'(2006) 13(1) *Indiana Journal of Global Legal Studies* 37–76; Donald Kommers, 'Comparative Constitutional Law: Its Increasing Relevance' in Vicki Jackson and M Tushnet (eds), *Defining the Field of Comparative Constitutional Law* (Westport 2002) 61–70; and Luis Magno Pinto Bastos Jr, 'Limits and Possibilities of the Use of Foreign Materials by Courts in Constitutional Adjudication: Redefining the Role of Comparativism in Theories of Constitutional Interpretation' http://www.enelsyn.gr/papers/w7/Paper%20by%20Prof.%20Luiz%20Magno%20Pinto%20Bastos%20Junior.pdf (last accessed 17 April 2017).

programmes in Africa.[42] In America, Asia, and Europe, there are many indications that legal education programmes have been adjusted to prepare students for the new globalized environment.[43] In Africa, although most of the law school programmes have been adjusted,[44] they have retained a Euro- and American-centric focus,[45] which in many respects do not fully reflect the daily realities of African societies.[46] The goal of developing an emancipatory Afro-centric legal curriculum that frees African legal education from the continuous and dominant influence of Euro- and American-centric cultural values is imperative and should provide a platform for enhancing intra-African legal understanding and cooperation. Apart from this, African law, generally, and African legal systems, specifically, will hardly be able to develop when present-day students spend most of their time, especially in some courses such as comparative law, studying Western legal systems and only have limited knowledge of their own legal systems and even less knowledge about the legal systems of neighbouring countries with which they interact daily. Legal education must reflect the needs of the environment and the living experience of the people.

In order for African legal education to be relevant and meaningful, it must prepare and equip today's lawyers to operate in a global world that takes the African context into account. This must be done within the framework of balanced programmes in which students learn about African law and have some knowledge of the legal systems and traditions operating in neighbouring countries, current developments, and emerging theories and principles from African scholars. There can be no meaningful intra-African legal and judicial dialogue or cross-fertilization of ideas between the different legal traditions operating on the continent unless a conscious effort is made to study and understand these legal systems and traditions. This contextualized vision of today's reality is vital because globalization and regional integration does not necessarily mean 'uniformizing homogenisation', but rather 'increasing hybridization in locality-coloured and culture-specific forms worldwide'.[47]

4. Conclusion

The challenges of protecting and sustaining the democratic gains of the last two decades and using these as a foundation for entrenching an ethos of constitutionalism and respect

[42] See generally Charles M Fombad, 'Africanization of Legal Education Programmes: The Need for Comparative African Legal Studies' (2014) 49(4) *Journal of Asian and African Studies* 383–98.

[43] See Werner Menski, *Comparative Law in a Global Context. The Legal Systems of Asia and Africa* (Cambridge University Press 2006); and Jan M Smits, 'European Legal Education, Or: How to Prepare Students for Global Citizenship?' (2011) 45(2) *The Law Teacher* 163–80.

[44] The most 'significant' of these changes have taken place in South Africa with the recurriculization of the LLB degree in 1997 after the end of apartheid in 1994. However, South Africa still grapples with the challenges of how far it should go in Africanizing its programmes, with debates such as those on whether or not Roman Law, which is no longer taught as a course in many European universities or only offered as an elective, should be retained. See eg Caroline Nicholson, 'The Relevance of the Past in Preparing for the Future: A Case for Roman Law and Legal History' (2011) 17(2) *Fundamina* 101–14.

[45] At independence, most African countries inherited the legal systems imposed during the colonial period. The basic structure and framework of pre- but mostly post-independence legal education programmes were essentially based on the imposed foreign laws and, for the most part, have retained this characteristic up to the present.

[46] See Piet Naudé, 'Africanising Higher Education' https://www.ru.ac.za/media/rhodesuniversity/content/institutionalplanning/documents/Africanising%20higher%20education%20-%20Piet%20Naude%2023May2011.pdf (last accessed 17 April 2017), who reminds us of how Africa was once dominant in higher education, with the brilliant School of Alexandria and the excellence of Egyptian engineering and Zimbabwean building projects.

[47] See Menski (n 43) 25.

for the rule of law, and the critical role of African judicial institutions vested with powers to interpret and apply the constitution, assume an unprecedented importance and urgency in light of the serious threats faced today. In spite of considerable gains made in making judiciaries more independent and the expansion of judicial review in the majority of countries, many practical constraints remain. In fact, a critical examination of the balance of power suggests that, as judges have gained more power, even more power has been assumed by the other two branches of government. With the pervasiveness of strong presidents with imperial powers, who control the dominant parties operating more or less like the pre-1990 single parties, the scope for political interference with the judiciaries is considerable. Apart from this, as more African leaders try to prolong their stay in power, judges are often caught on the horn of a dilemma.

Be that as it may, the different chapters in this book suggest that, save for exceptional cases such as Cameroon and Ethiopia, the foundations for a judicial review system that provides reasonable prospects for a fair and credible system of constitutional justice have been laid. Nevertheless, this is relative progress and part of an uncertain transition marked by frequent changes that are not always an improvement.

Looking at the nature and evolution of the different models of judicial review in Africa today, it may be said that colonialism and its legacy is receding rather too slowly, especially in Francophone Africa. As Fombad explained in Chapter 1, there are many signs of convergence and, significantly, of cross-systemic fertilization of ideas across the different inherited colonial models of constitutional adjudication. The Constitutional Courts of Benin and South Africa, without doubt the most effective and influential courts in terms of institutional structure and jurisprudence, prove one thing: that it is not the model but rather how well it is designed that is important. Each model has its weaknesses and strengths. Whilst it may be complicated radically to change from the centralized to the decentralized system or vice versa, because of the underlying legal culture, tradition, and structures, there is much to be said for borrowing and adopting good practices from other systems, as the constitution-makers of Benin and South Africa did. The different case studies emphasize the point that there is no perfect model of constitutional review.

Whichever model is adopted, it is clear that constitutionalism and respect for the rule of law is greatly imperilled when constitutional court judges abdicate their sacred responsibility and defer to the other two branches of government. It may be argued that, in most African countries, constitutions have given judges enough power to break the backbone of authoritarianism and the abuse of power in Africa. The onus is on these judges to assert and exercise these powers in the face of regular violations of constitutions by Africa's overbearing executives. The decision of Chief Justice Mogoeng Mogoeng in the *Economic Freedom Fighters* case is a classic example of what judges need to do in order to counter the resurgence of self-serving pseudo-democrats. He leads a team of constitutional court judges who have, over a period of more than twenty years, given Africa reason to be proud of the originality and impact of its jurisprudence on developments on other continents. The question is, what about within Africa?

The role and potential benefits of cross-systemic fertilization and intra-judicial dialogue within Africa cannot be gainsaid. This will be considerably enhanced by the Africanization of legal education programmes. The ultimate goal of such an endeavour should be to provide a platform for legal research and thinking, which encourages African scholars, students, and judges to develop the ability, attitude, and confidence to examine the jurisprudence and laws of neighbouring countries for possible solutions to legal problems in their countries. In a time of rapid change, increasing globalization, and regionalization, a purely national perception of the law or legal education is no longer sustainable.

An Africanized programme that includes a course on African legal studies should aim at being contextually and globally relevant as well as being sufficiently innovative and flexible to address the urgent needs of our times.

This is certainly a project that needs to be taken over and driven ideally by the African Union and its regional economic communities. The decolonization in a constructive manner of the legal curriculum in African universities is long overdue and, if properly executed, should provide a basis not only for a fuller understanding and appreciation of Africa's diverse legal traditions, but also for serving as the platform for the sharing of good practices and the cross-systemic fertilization of ideas.

Whilst recognizing the fact that the judicial institutions in most African countries have a better chance today of doing justice and facilitating respect for the rule of law and keeping the flames of constitutionalism and democracy burning, there is no denying the fact that there are powerful counterforces opposed to change and progress and who are fighting a rear-guard battle. These counterforces are growing bolder every day and are disguising their ultimate intentions by adopting constitutional symbolisms such as an ineffective constitutional review system that obfuscates rather than promotes justice.

The chapters in this volume provide a reasonable indication of some of the issues that need to be addressed in the next series of reforms. Whilst there is no 'best model' of constitutional review, there are, nevertheless, clear indications of what an effective and credible system should be. In looking towards the future, there is a need to ensure that constitutional matters are handled by a judicial body that is easily accessible, especially to the poor and vulnerable in society, and which is capable of handling all issues concerning the interpretation and application of the constitution. Anything short of this is certain to provide only a truncated form of constitutional justice, which is a recipe for arbitrary government. Strong constitutional review institutions are absolutely crucial to building and sustaining democracy. When such institutions are strong, they will protect all; when they are weak, they will only protect the strong in the oppression of the weak. In the absence of an effective and credible system of constitutional review, there can hardly be any prospects of democratic and accountable government guided by the core elements of constitutionalism and good governance.

Bibliography

Adjolohoun H, *Droit de l'Homme et Justice Constitutionnelle en Afrique: Le Modèle Béninois. À la Lumière de l'Homme et des Peuples* (L'Harmattan 2011)

Bastos L N P Jnr, 'Limits and Possibilities of the Use of Foreign Materials by Courts, in Constitutional Adjudication: Redefining the Role of Comparativism Limits and Possibilities of the Use of Foreign Materials by Courts in Constitutional Adjudication' http://www.enelsyn.gr/papers/w7/Paper%20by%20Prof.%20Luiz%20Magno%20Pinto%20Bastos%20Junior.pdf (last accessed 17 April 2017)

Codjovi B, 'La Places des Conventions Internationales dans le Droit Béninois: Le Juge Béninois Devant Les Conventions Internationale' in *Actes du Séminaire: Le Bénin et Les Conventions Internationales Relatives aux Droits de l'Homme et de la Promotion de la Démocratie* (2002) Cotonou (unpublished)

De Vos P, 'Urgently Wanted: Judicial Training' http://constitutionallyspeaking.co.za/urgently-wanted-judicial-training/ (last accessed 17 April 2017)

Devlin B P, *The Judge* (OUP 1979)

Fombad C M, 'Constitutional Reforms in France and their Implications for Constitutionalism in Francophone Africa' (2008) http://www.africafiles.org/article.asp?ID=18777 (last 17 April 2017)

Fombad C M, 'Post-1990 Constitutional Reforms in Africa: A Preliminary Assessment of the Prospects for Constitutional Governance and Constitutionalism' in Nhema A and Zeleza P T, *The Resolution of African Conflicts* (OSSREA 2008)

Fombad C M, 'Constitutional Reforms and Constitutionalism in Africa: Reflections on Some Current Challenges and Future Prospects' (2011) 59(4) *Buffalo Law Review* 1007

Fombad C M, 'Internationalization of Constitutional Law and Constitutionalism in Africa' (2012) 60(2) *American Journal of Comparative Law* 439

Fombad C M, 'Gender Equality in African Customary Law: Has the Male Ultimogeniture Rule any Future in Botswana' (2014) 52(3) *Journal of Modern African Studies* 475

Fombad C M, 'Africanisation of Legal Education Programmes: The Need for Comparative African Legal Studies' (2014) 49(4) *Journal of Asian and African Studies* 383

Fombad C M, 'Appointment of Constitutional Adjudicators in Africa: Some Perspectives on How Different Systems Yield Similar Outcomes' (2014) 46(2) *Journal of Legal Pluralism and Unofficial Law* 249

Fombad C M, 'The Expansion of Judicial Power in Africa and Democratic Consolidation: Opportunities, Challenges and Future Prospects' in Ndulo M and Gazibo M (eds), *Growing Democracy in Africa: Elections, Accountable Governance and Political Economy* (James Currey Publishers 2016) 47

Gloppen S, Gargarella R, and Skaar E (eds), *Democratization and the Judiciary. The Accountability Function of Courts in New Democracies* (Frank Cass 2004) 17–31; and Report of the Partners for Gender Justice Conference, *The Role of the Judiciary in Promoting Gender Justice in Africa* http://www.ilac.se/download/reports_documents/thematic-reports_documents/Ghana%20Report-English.pdf (last accessed 17 April 2017)

Klare K, 'Legal Culture and Transformative Constitutionalism' (1998) 4 *South African Journal on Human Rights* 146

Kommers D, 'Comparative Constitutional Law: Its Increasing Relevance' in Jackson V and Tushnet M (eds), *Defining the Field of Comparative Constitutional Law* (Westport 2002) 61

Letsoalo M, Pilane P, and du Plessis C, 'The Big Talking Points from Zuma's ANC Anniversary Address' http://mg.co.za/article/2016-01-09-the-big-talking-points-from-zumas-anc-anniversary-address (last accessed 17 April 2017)

Lollini A, 'Legal Argumentation Based on Foreign Law: An Example from Case Law of the South African Constitutional Court' (2007) 3(1) *Utrecht Law Review* 60

Markesinis B and Fedktke J, *Judicial Recourse to Foreign Law. A New Source of Inspiration?* (UCL Press 2006)

McCluskey B J H, *Law, Justice, and Democracy* (Sweet & Maxwell 1987)

McConnell M W, 'Textualism and the Dead Hand of the Past' (1998) 60 *George Washington Law Review* 1127

Menski W, *Comparative Law in a Global Context. The Legal Systems of Asia and Africa* (2nd edn, Cambridge University Press 2006)

Naudé P, 'Africanising Higher Education' https://www.ru.ac.za/media/rhodesuniversity/content/institutionalplanning/documents/Africanising%20higher%20education%20-%20Piet%20Naude%2023May2011.pdf (last accessed 17 April 2017)

Nicholson C, 'The Relevance of the Past in Preparing for the Future: A Case for Roman Law and Legal History' (2011) 17(2) *Fundamina* (2011) 101–14

Odinkalu C A, 'The Judiciary and the Legal Protection of Human Rights in Common Law: Allocating Responsibility for the Failure of Post-Independence Bill of Rights' (1996) 8 *African Society of International and Comparative Law Proceedings* 136, 137

Pieterse M, 'What Do We Mean When We Talk about Transformative Constitutionalism?'(2005) 20 *SA Public Law* 155

Rosenberg G N, *The Hollow Hope. Can Courts Bring About Social Change?* (University of Chicago 1991)

Rotman A, 'Benin's Constitutional Court: An Institutional Model for Guaranteeing Human Rights' (2004) 17 *Harvard Human Rights Journal* 310

Roux T, 'Transformative Constitutionalism and the Interpretation of the South African Constitution: Distinction Without a Difference?'(2009) 20 *Stellenbosch Law Review* 258

Saunders C, 'The Use and Misuse of Comparative Constitutional Law'(2006) 13(1) *Indiana Journal of Global Legal Studies* 37

Smits J M, 'European Legal Education, Or: How to Prepare Students for Global Citizenship?' (2011) 45(2) *The Law Teacher* 163

Udombana N J, 'Interpreting Rights Globally: Courts and Constitutional Rights in Emerging Democracies' (2005) 5 *African Human Rights Law Journal* 61

Van de Vijver L (ed), *The Judicial Institution in Southern Africa. A Comparative Study of Common Law Jurisdictions* (Siber Ink CC 2006)

Watson A, *Legal Transplants. An Approach to Comparative Law* (University of Georgia Press 1974)

Widner J, 'Judicial Independence in Common Law Africa' in Schedler A, Diamond L, and Plattner M (eds), *The Self-Restraining State: Power and Accountability in New Democracies* (Lynne Rienner Publishers 1999)

Index